PLAYFAIR
CRICKET ANNUAL 2014
67th edition
EDITED BY IAN MARSHALL
All statistics by the Editor unless otherwise stated

FOREWORD

A year ago, I wrote the Foreword to the 2013 Annual with snow lying on my local cricket field. As the groundstaff at Worcester are all too well aware, this winter has been very different, and 2014 will see many more changes. New heroes will emerge as we have lost three of cricket's all-time greats in recent months.

The first to depart was Sachin Tendulkar, whose final and 200th Test took place in front of an adoring Mumbai crowd in November. He was unable to leave the scene with a century, but an innings of 74 was at least a satisfactory way to bow out, and it took him to an astonishing 15,921 Test runs. If there was a feeling with Tendulkar that the time was right to retire, Jacques Kallis left us believing there could still be more from him, as he brought 2013 to a close with his 45th Test century and then retired. With 292 wickets and 200 catches to add to his 13,289 Test runs, any debate about the greatest all-rounder of all time has to include him in the reckoning, though Messrs Sobers and Botham would also lay strong claim to that title. Finally, Graeme Smith announced his retirement after 109 Tests in charge of South Africa, another world record that looks set to last a long time.

Smith bowed out with a series defeat against Australia, and it was they who were responsible for a string of departures closer to home. We said goodbye to the Ashes in the most humiliating style, as England were blown away by Mitchell Johnson's pace and hostility. The fact that Australia could then go on and beat the South Africans on their own turf shows just how strong a side they have become within a year of suffering their own whitewash in India.

The fallout from the Ashes disaster was comprehensive: Jonathan Trott returned home after one Test, and all England fans will hope he can play for the national side again. More importantly, we hope that he is soon fully recovered. Graeme Swann was next to go, deciding to retire after the third Test. In an era when so many players are so well media-trained, he brought a degree of fun and spontaneity to the proceedings. With 410 international wickets, he is England's most successful spinner of all time. At the end of the series, coach Andy Flower, who had brought so much success to the England side, decided to step aside, perhaps recognising the natural lifespan of the role.

The final departure was the one that caused the most debate of all, as Kevin Pietersen was told he was no longer wanted in the team. If England's most prolific international runscorer (13,797 in all forms of the game) went quietly, his cheerleaders spoke out loudly on his behalf, and we can expect to read his side of the story later in the year. He was a stunning cricketer to watch, and always the man the opposition most wanted to see back in the pavilion. We wait to see how England's batting fares without him.

If there was one established cricketer who managed to perform ahead of expectations in Australia, it was Stuart Broad, who was the subject of relentless abuse from the Australian media and the fans. The fact that he performed so well speaks volumes for his character and his spirit, especially as we now learn he had been struggling with a knee problem. He is deservedly our cover star for this year. As we go to press, he is preparing to lead England in the ICC World T20 in Bangladesh – let us hope he can spring a surprise.

Finally, I should mention that I have succumbed to the joys of Twitter, and I will be tweeting regularly on cricket (as well as a few other things) from @IanPlayfair. Do please follow me, and I will try to make sure I provide you with the latest news on all the summer's events. I will also be writing my weekly summer blog on www.playfaircricket.co.uk, which will showcase any notable achievements during the previous week. These days, Playfair is a year-round experience!

Ian Marshall
Eastbourne, 14 March 2014   @IanPlayfair

ACKNOWLEDGEMENTS AND THANKS

As ever, this book could not have been compiled without the help of many people giving freely of their time and expertise, so I must thank the following for all they have done to help ensure this edition of *Playfair Cricket Annual* could be written:

At the counties, I would like to thank the following for their help over the last year: Derbyshire – Tom Holdcroft and John Brown; Durham – Brian Hunt; Essex – Ashley Neave and Tony Choat; Glamorgan – Andrew Hignell; Gloucestershire – Lizzie Allen and Adrian Bull; Hampshire – Tim Tremlett and Kevin Baker; Kent – Tanya Nicholls and Lorne Hart; Lancashire – Diana Lloyd and Alan West; Leicestershire – Elaine Pickering and Paul Rogers; Middlesex – Rebecca Hart, Steven Fletcher and Don Shelley; Northamptonshire – Tony Kingston; Nottinghamshire – Helen Palmer and Roger Marshall; Somerset – Spencer Bishop and Gerald Stickley; Surrey – Steve Howes and Keith Booth; Sussex – Siobhan Edgar and Mike Charman; Warwickshire – Keith Cook and Mel Smith; Worcestershire – Joan Grundy and Dawn Pugh; Yorkshire – Janet Bairstow and John Potter.

Thanks to Chris Kelly for supplying the list of domestic umpires. To Alan Fordham, thank you for the Principal and Second XI Fixtures, and Philip August for the Minor Counties. Philip Bailey once again provided the first-class and List A career records, and he continues to be a vital help in compiling the book.

At Headline, my thanks once more go to Jonathan Taylor for his support and encouragement; Louise Rothwell remained calm under intense pressure and ensured the book was printed in no time at all; Sam Habib continues to do a great job on the *Playfair* website and in helping me to navigate the world of social media. John Skermer did a brilliant job on checking the proofs, despite the huge time pressure he was under. At Letterpart, the *Playfair* typesetter since 1994, Chris Leggett, Caroline Leggett and the whole team were remarkably patient and speedy. I know I always promise that it won't be such a late rush next year . . .

Finally, as ever, I must thank my rapidly growing daughters, Kiri and Sophia, who have found me a largely invisible presence as deadline day approached; and of course my wife, Sugra, has again been a brilliant support throughout the whole year.

GUIDE TO USING PLAYFAIR

The basic layout of *Playfair* has again remained the same for this edition. The Annual is divided into five sections, as follows: Test match cricket, county cricket, international limited-overs cricket (including Twenty20), other cricket (universities, IPL and Champions League and women's international cricket), and fixtures for the coming season. Each section, where applicable begins with a preview of forthcoming events, followed by events during the previous year, then come the player records, and finally the records section.

Within the players' register, I have added each county's Twitter address, along with the number of followers they had at the start of March. Because of the ever-increasing number of competitions that have come into existence over the years – and we welcome the latest addition to the list, the Royal London One-Day Cup – I have simplified the headers for each county, so that only those competitions the counties have actually won are listed, except where there are ongoing trophies (the County Championship and the Twenty20 Cup) that a county has yet to win.

I have also rationalised the county limited-overs records in the Register, as they had become a little confused. Records denoted by '50ov' cover any limited-overs game of 50 or more overs – in the early days, each team could have as many as 65 overs per innings. The '40ov' section refers to games of 40 or 45 overs per innings.

ENGLAND v SRI LANKA

HIGHEST INNINGS TOTALS

England	in England	551-6d	Lord's	2006
	in Sri Lanka	460	Colombo (PSS)	2011-12
Sri Lanka	in England	591	The Oval	1998
	in Sri Lanka	628-8d	Colombo (SSC)	2003-04

LOWEST INNINGS TOTALS

England	in England	181	The Oval	1998
	in Sri Lanka	81	Galle	2007-08
Sri Lanka	in England	82	Cardiff	2011
	in Sri Lanka	81	Colombo (SSC)	2000-01

HIGHEST MATCH AGGREGATE 1427 for 30 wickets Lord's 2011
LOWEST MATCH AGGREGATE 645 for 36 wickets Colombo (SSC) 2000-01

HIGHEST INDIVIDUAL INNINGS

England	in England	203	I.J.L.Trott	Cardiff	2011
	in Sri Lanka	151	K.P.Pietersen	Colombo (PSS)	2011-12
Sri Lanka	in England	213	S.T.Jayasuriya	The Oval	1998
	in Sri Lanka	213*	D.P.M.D.Jayawardena	Galle	2007-08

HIGHEST AGGREGATE OF RUNS IN A SERIES

England	in England	390	(av 97.50)	A.N.Cook	2011
	in Sri Lanka	278	(av 46.33)	A.N.Cook	2007-08
Sri Lanka	in England	277	(av 55.40)	M.S.Atapattu	2002
	in Sri Lanka	474	(av 158.00)	D.P.M.D.Jayawardena	2007-08

RECORD WICKET PARTNERSHIPS – ENGLAND

1st	168	M.E.Trescothick (76)/M.P.Vaughan (115)	Lord's	2002
2nd	202	M.E.Trescothick (161)/M.A.Butcher (94)	Birmingham	2002
3rd	251	A.N.Cook (133)/I.J.L.Trott (203)	Cardiff	2011
4th	128	G.A.Hick (107)/M.R.Ramprakash (53)	The Oval	1998
5th	173	K.P.Pietersen (158)/P.D.Collingwood (57)	Lord's	2006
6th	137	I.R.Bell (119*)/E.J.G.Morgan (71)	Southampton	2011
7th	109	I.R.Bell (74)/M.J.Prior (63)	Kandy	2007-08
8th	102	A.J.Stewart (123)/A.F.Giles (45)	Manchester	2002
9th	53	M.R.Ramprakash (42)/D.Gough (15)	The Oval	1998
10th	91	G.P.Thorpe (123)/M.J.Hoggard (17*)	Birmingham	2002

RECORD WICKET PARTNERSHIPS – SRI LANKA

1st	207	N.T.Paranavitana (65)/T.M.Dilshan (193)	Lord's	2011
2nd	109	W.U.Tharanga (52)/K.C.Sangakkara (65)	Lord's	2006
3rd	262	T.T.Samaraweera (142)/ D.P.M.D.Jayawardena (134)	Colombo (SSC)	2003-04
4th	153	D.P.M.D.Jayawardena (52)/T.M.Dilshan (100)	Kandy	2003-04
5th	150	S.Wettimuny (190)/L.R.D.Mendis (111)	Lord's	1984
6th	138	S.A.R.Silva (102*)/L.R.D.Mendis (94)	Lord's	1984
7th	183	D.P.M.D.Jayawardena (213*)/W.P.J.U.C.Vaas (90)	Galle	2007-08
8th	62	D.P.M.D.Jayawardena (180)/H.M.R.K.B.Herath (5)	Galle	2011-12
9th	105	W.P.J.U.C.Vaas (50*)/M.D.N.Kulasekara (64)	Lord's	2006
10th	64	J.R.Ratnayeke (59*)/G.F.Labrooy (42)	Lord's	1988

BEST INNINGS BOWLING ANALYSIS

England	in England	7-70	P.A.J.DeFreitas	Lord's	1991
	in Sri Lanka	6-33	J.E.Emburey	Colombo (PSS)	1981-82
Sri Lanka	in England	9-65	M.Muralitharan	The Oval	1998
	in Sri Lanka	7-46	M.Muralitharan	Galle	2003-04

BEST MATCH BOWLING ANALYSIS

England	in England	8-115	P.A.J.DeFreitas	Lord's	1991
	in Sri Lanka	10-181	G.P.Swann	Colombo (PSS)	2011-12
Sri Lanka	in England	16-220	M.Muralitharan	The Oval	1998
	in Sri Lanka	12-171	H.M.R.K.B.Herath	Galle	2011-12

HIGHEST WICKET AGGREGATE IN A SERIES

England	in England	15	(av 24.60)	M.J.Hoggard	2006
		15	(av 23.40)	C.T.Tremlett	2011
	in Sri Lanka	18	(av 29.94)	A.F.Giles	2003-04
Sri Lanka	in England	24	(av 16.87)	M.Muralitharan	2006
	in Sri Lanka	26	(av 12.30)	M.Muralitharan	2003-04

RESULTS SUMMARY

ENGLAND v SRI LANKA – IN ENGLAND

	Tests	Series			Lord's			The Oval			Birmingham			Manchester			Nottingham			Cardiff			Southampton		
		E	SL	D	E	SL	D	E	SL	D	E	SL	D	E	SL	D	E	SL	D	E	SL	D	E	SL	D
1984	1	–	–	1	–	–	1	–	–	–	–	–	–	–	–	–	–	–	–	–	–	–	–	–	–
1988	1	1	–	–	1	–	–	–	–	–	–	–	–	–	–	–	–	–	–	–	–	–	–	–	–
1991	1	1	–	–	1	–	–	–	–	–	–	–	–	–	–	–	–	–	–	–	–	–	–	–	–
1998	1	–	1	–	–	–	–	–	1	–	–	–	–	–	–	–	–	–	–	–	–	–	–	–	–
2002	3	2	–	1	–	–	1	–	–	–	1	–	–	1	–	–	–	–	–	–	–	–	–	–	–
2006	3	1	1	1	–	–	1	–	–	–	1	–	–	–	–	–	–	1	–	–	–	–	–	–	–
2011	3	1	–	2	–	–	1	–	–	–	–	–	–	–	–	–	–	–	–	1	–	–	–	–	1
	13	6	2	5	2	–	4	–	1	–	2	–	–	1	–	–	–	1	–	1	–	–	–	–	1

ENGLAND v SRI LANKA – IN SRI LANKA

	Tests	Series			Colombo (PSS)			Colombo (SSC)			Galle			Kandy		
		E	SL	D	E	SL	D	E	SL	D	E	SL	D	E	SL	D
1981-82	1	1	–	–	1	–	–	–	–	–	–	–	–	–	–	–
1992-93	1	–	1	–	–	–	–	–	1	–	–	–	–	–	–	–
2000-01	3	2	1	–	–	–	–	1	–	–	–	1	–	1	–	–
2003-04	3	–	1	2	–	–	–	–	1	–	–	–	1	–	–	1
2007-08	3	–	1	2	–	–	–	–	–	1	–	–	1	–	1	–
2011-12	2	1	1	–	1	–	–	–	–	–	–	1	–	–	–	–
	13	4	5	4	2	–	–	1	2	1	–	2	2	1	1	1
Totals	26	10	7	9												

ENGLAND v INDIA

SERIES RECORDS
1932 to 2012-13

HIGHEST INNINGS TOTALS

England	in England	710-7d	Birmingham	2011
	in India	652-7d	Madras	1984-85
India	in England	664	The Oval	2007
	in India	591	Bombay	1992-93

LOWEST INNINGS TOTALS

England	in England	101	The Oval	1971
	in India	102	Bombay	1981-82
India	in England	42	Lord's	1974
	in India	83	Madras	1976-77

HIGHEST MATCH AGGREGATE   1614 for 30 wickets   Manchester   1990
LOWEST MATCH AGGREGATE   482 for 31 wickets   Lord's   1936

HIGHEST INDIVIDUAL INNINGS

England	in England	333	G.A.Gooch	Lord's	1990
	in India	207	M.W.Gatting	Madras	1984-85
India	in England	221	S.M.Gavaskar	The Oval	1979
	in India	224	V.G.Kambli	Bombay	1992-93

HIGHEST AGGREGATE OF RUNS IN A SERIES

England	in England	752	(av 125.33)	G.A.Gooch	1990
	in India	594	(av 99.00)	K.F.Barrington	1961-62
India	in England	602	(av 100.33)	R.S.Dravid	2002
	in India	586	(av 83.71)	V.L.Manjrekar	1961-62

RECORD WICKET PARTNERSHIPS – ENGLAND

1st	225	G.A.Gooch (116)/M.A.Atherton (131)	Manchester	1990
2nd	241	G.Fowler (201)/M.W.Gatting (207)	Madras	1984-85
3rd	350	I.R.Bell (235)/K.P.Pietersen (175)	The Oval	2011
4th	266	W.R.Hammond (217)/T.S.Worthington (128)	The Oval	1936
5th	254	K.W.R.Fletcher (113)/A.W.Greig (148)	Bombay	1972-73
6th	171	I.T.Botham (114)/R.W.Taylor (43)	Bombay	1979-80
7th	162*	M.J.Prior (103*)/S.C.J.Broad (74*)	Lord's	2011
8th	168	R.Illingworth (107)/P.Lever (88*)	Manchester	1971
9th	103	C.White (94*)/M.J.Hoggard (32)	Nottingham	2002
10th	70	P.J.W.Allott (41*)/R.G.D.Willis (28)	Lord's	1982

RECORD WICKET PARTNERSHIPS – INDIA

1st	213	S.M.Gavaskar (221)/C.P.S.Chauhan (80)	The Oval	1979
2nd	314	G.Gambhir (179)/R.S.Dravid (136)	Chandigarh	2008-09
3rd	316	G.R.Viswanath (222)/Yashpal Sharma (140)	Madras	1981-82
4th	249	S.R.Tendulkar (193)/S.C.Ganguly (128)	Leeds	2002
5th	214	M.Azharuddin (110)/R.J.Shastri (111)	Calcutta	1984-85
6th	130	S.M.H.Kirmani (43)/Kapil Dev (97)	The Oval	1982
7th	235	R.J.Shastri (142)/S.M.H.Kirmani (102)	Bombay	1984-85
8th	128	R.J.Shastri (93)/S.M.H.Kirmani (67)	Delhi	1981-82
	128	M.Kaif (91)/A.Kumble (58)	Nagpur	2005-06
9th	104	R.J.Shastri (93)/Madan Lal (44)	Delhi	1981-82
10th	73	A.Kumble (110*)/S.Sreesanth (35)	The Oval	2007

BEST INNINGS BOWLING ANALYSIS

England	in England	8-31	F.S.Trueman	Manchester	1952
	in India	7-46	J.K.Lever	Delhi	1976-77
India	in England	6-35	L.Amar Singh	Lord's	1936
	in India	8-55	M.H.Mankad	Madras	1951-52

BEST MATCH BOWLING ANALYSIS

England	in England	11- 93	A.V.Bedser	Manchester	1946
	in India	13-106	I.T.Botham	Bombay	1979-80
India	in England	10-188	C.Sharma	Birmingham	1986
	in India	12-108	M.H.Mankad	Madras	1951-52

HIGHEST AGGREGATE OF WICKETS IN A SERIES

England	in England	29	(av 13.31)	F.S.Trueman	1952
	in India	29	(av 17.55)	D.L.Underwood	1976-77
India	in England	18	(av 20.33)	Z.Khan	2007
	in India	35	(av 18.91)	B.S.Chandrasekhar	1972-73

RESULTS SUMMARY
ENGLAND v INDIA – IN ENGLAND

	Tests	Series			Lord's			Manchester			The Oval			Leeds			Nottingham			Birmingham		
		E	I	D	E	I	D	E	I	D	E	I	D	E	I	D	E	I	D	E	I	D
1932	1	1	–	–	1	–	–															
1936	3	2	–	1	1	–	–	–	–	1	1	–	–									
1946	3	1	–	2	1	–	–	–	–	1	–	–	1									
1952	4	3	–	1	1	–	–	1	–	–	–	–	1	1	–	–						
1959	5	5	–	–	1	–	–	1	–	–	1	–	–	1	–	–	1	–	–			
1967	3	3	–	–	1	–	–							1	–	–				1	–	–
1971	3	–	1	2	–	–	1	–	–	1	–	1	–									
1974	3	3	–	–	1	–	–	1	–	–										1	–	–
1979	4	1	–	3	–	–	1				–	–	1	–	–	1				1	–	–
1982	3	1	–	2	1	–	–	–	–	1	–	–	1									
1986	3	–	2	1	–	1	–							–	1	–				–	–	1
1990	3	1	–	2	1	–	–	–	–	1	–	–	1									
1996	3	1	–	2	–	–	1										–	–	1	1	–	–
2002	4	1	1	2	1	–	–				–	–	1	–	1	–	–	–	1			
2007	3	–	1	2	–	–	1				–	–	1				–	1	–			
2011	4	4	–	–	1	–	–				1	–	–				1	–	–	1	–	–
52	**52**	27	5	20	11	1	4	3	–	5	3	1	7	3	2	1	2	1	2	5	–	1

ENGLAND v INDIA – IN INDIA

	Tests	Series			Mumbai			Kolkata			Chennai			Delhi			Kanpur			Bangalore			Chandigarh			Ahmedabad			Nagpur		
		E	I	D	E	I	D	E	I	D	E	I	D	E	I	D	E	I	D	E	I	D	E	I	D	E	I	D	E	I	D
1933-34	3	2	–	1	1	–	–	–	–	1	1	–	–																		
1951-52	5	1	1	3	–	–	1	–	–	1	–	1	–	–	–	1	1	–	–												
1961-62	5	–	2	3	–	–	1	–	1	–	–	1	–	–	–	1	–	–	1												
1963-64	5	–	–	5	–	–	1	–	–	1	–	–	1	–	–	1	–	–	1												
1972-73	5	1	2	2	–	–	1	–	1	–	–	1	–	1	–	–	–	–	1												
1976-77	5	3	1	1	–	–	1	1	–	–	1	–	–	1	–	–				–	1	–									
1979-80	1	1	–	–	1	–	–																								
1981-82	6	–	1	5	–	1	–	–	–	1	–	–	1	–	–	1	–	–	1	–	–	1									
1984-85	5	2	1	2	–	1	–	–	–	1	1	–	–	1	–	–	–	–	1												
1992-93	3	–	3	–	–	1	–	–	1	–	–	1	–																		
2001-02	3	–	1	2																–	–	1	–	1	–	–	–	1			
2005-06	3	1	1	1	1	–	–																–	1	–				–	–	1
2008-09	2	–	1	1							–	1	–										–	–	1						
2011-12	4	2	1	1	1	–	–	1	–	–																–	1	–	–	–	1
55	**55**	13	15	27	4	3	5	2	3	5	3	5	2	3	–	4	1	–	5	–	1	2	–	2	1	–	1	1	–	–	2

Totals	107	40	20	47

TOURING TEAMS REGISTER 2014

Neither Sri Lanka nor India had selected their 2014 touring teams at the time of going to press. The following players who had represented those teams in Test matches since 9 November 2012 were still available for selection:

SRI LANKA

Full Names	Birthdate	Birthplace	Team	Type	F-C Debut
CHANDIMAL, Lokuge Dinesh	18.11.89	Balapitiya	Nondescripts	RHB/WK	2009
DILSHAN, Tillakaratne M.	14.10.76	Kalutara	Bloomfield	RHB/OB	1993-94
ERANGA, R.M.Shaminda	23.06.86	Chilaw	Tamil Union	RHB/RFM	2006-07
FERNANDO, A.Nuwan Pradeep R.	19.10.86	Negombo	Bloomfield	RHB/RFM	2007-08
HERATH, H.M.Rangana K.B.	19.03.78	Kurunegala	Tamil Union	LHB/SLA	1996-97
JAYAWARDENA, D.P.Mahela D.	27.05.77	Colombo	Sinhalese	RHB/RM	1995-96
JAYAWARDENA, H.A.Prasanna W.	09.10.79	Colombo	Colombo	RHB/WK	1997-98
KALUHALAMULLA, H.K.Suraj Randiv	30.01.85	Matara	Bloomfield	RHB/OB	2002-03
KARUNARATNE, F.Dimuth M.	21.04.88	Colombo	Sinhalese	LHB/RM	2008-09
KULASEKARA, K.M.D.Nuwan	22.07.82	Nittambuwa	Colts	RHB/RFM	2002-03
LAKMAL, R.A.Suranga	10.03.87	Matara	Tamil Union	RHB/RMF	2007-08
MATHEWS, Angelo Davis	02.06.87	Colombo	Colts	RHB/RMF	2006-07
MENDIS, B.Ajantha W.	11.03.85	Moratuwa	Sri Lanka Army	RHB/LBG	2006-07
PARANAVITANA, N.Tharanga	15.04.82	Kegalle	Sinhalese	LHB/OB	2001-02
PERERA, M.Dilruwan K.	22.07.89	Panadura	Colts	RHB/OB	2000-01
PRASAD, K.T.G.Dammika	30.05.83	Ragama	Sinhalese	RHB/RFM	2001-02
SAMARAWEERA, Thilan T.	22.09.76	Colombo	Brothers	RHB/OB	1995-96
SANGAKKARA, Kumar C.	27.10.77	Matale	Kandurata	LHB/OB	1997-98
SENANAYAKE, S.M.Sachithra M.	09.02.85	Colombo	Sinhalese	RHB/OB	2006-07
SILVA, Jayan Kaushal	27.05.86	Colombo	Sinhalese	RHB/WK	2002-03
THIRIMANNE, H.D.R.Lahiru	08.09.89	Moratuwa	Ragama	LHB/RMF	2008-09
VITHANAGE, K.S.Kithuruwan	26.02.91	Colombo	Tamil Union	LHB/LB	2010-11
WELAGEDARA, U.W.M.B.Chanaka A.	20.03.81	Matale	Tamil Union	RHB/LFM	2002-03

NB: A.N.P.R.Fernando is also known as Nuwan Pradeep; H.K.S.R.Kaluhalamulla is also known as Suraj Randiv.

INDIA

Full Names	Birthdate	Birthplace	Team	Type	F-C Debut
ASHWIN, Ravichandran	17.09.86	Madras	Tamil Nadu	RHB/OB	2006-07
CHAWLA, Piyush Pramod	24.12.88	Aligarh	Uttar Pradesh	LHB/LB	2005-06
DHAWAN, Shikhar	05.12.85	Delhi	Delhi	LHB/OB	2004-05
DHONI, Mahendra Singh	07.07.81	Ranchi	Chennai SK	RHB/WK	1999-00
GAMBHIR, Gautam	14.10.81	Delhi	Delhi	LHB/LB	1999-00
HARBHAJAN SINGH	03.07.80	Jullundur	Mumbai Indians	RHB/OB	1997-98
JADEJA, Ravindrasinh Anirudhsinh	06.12.88	Saurashtra	Saurashtra	LHB/SLA	2006-07
KHAN, Zaheer	07.10.78	Shrirampur	Mumbai	RHB/LFM	1999-00
KOHLI, Virat	05.11.88	Delhi	Delhi	RHB/RM	2006-07
KUMAR, Bhuvneshwar	05.02.90	Meerut	Uttar Pradesh	RHB/RM	2007-08
MOHAMMED SHAMI Ahmed	09.03.90	Jonagar	Bengal	RHB/RFM	2010-11
OJHA, Pragyan Prayash	05.09.86	Bhubaneswar	Hyderabad (Ind)	LHB/SLA	2004-05
PUJARA, Cheteshwar Arvind	25.01.88	Rajkot	Saurashtra	RHB/LB	2005-06
RAHANE, Ajinkya Madhukar	05.06.88	Ashwi Khurd	Mumbai	RHB/OB	2007-08
SEHWAG, Virender	20.10.78	Delhi	Delhi	RHB/OB	1997-98
SHARMA, Ishant	02.09.88	Delhi	Delhi	RHB/RFM	2006-07
SHARMA, Rohit Gurunath	30.04.87	Nagpur	Mumbai	RHB/OB	2006
VIJAY, Murali	01.04.84	Madras	Tamil Nadu	RHB/OB	2006-07
YADAV, Umesh Tilak	25.10.87	Nagpur	Vidarbha	RHB/RFM	2008-09
YUVRAJ SINGH	12.12.81	Chandigarh	Punjab	LHB/SLA	1996-97

STATISTICAL HIGHLIGHTS IN 2013 TESTS

Including Tests from No. 2068 (Australia v Sri Lanka, 3rd Test) and No. 2069 (South Africa v New Zealand, 1st Test) to No. 2105 (Australia v England, 4th Test) and No. 2111 (South Africa v India, 2nd Test).
  † = National record

TEAM HIGHLIGHTS
HIGHEST INNINGS TOTALS

638†	Bangladesh v Sri Lanka	Galle
609-9d	New Zealand v West Indies	Dunedin

HIGHEST FOURTH INNINGS TOTAL

450-7	South Africa (set 458) v India	Johannesburg

LOWEST INNINGS TOTALS

45	New Zealand v South Africa	Cape Town
49	Pakistan v South Africa	Johannesburg
68	New Zealand v England	Lord's
99	Pakistan v South Africa	Dubai

HIGHEST MATCH AGGREGATE

1613-19	Sri Lanka (570-4d & 335-4d) v Bangladesh (638 & 70-1)	Galle

BATSMEN'S MATCH (Qualification: 1200 runs, average 60 per wicket)

84.89 (1613-19)	Sri Lanka (570-4d & 335-4d) v Bangladesh (638 & 70-1)	Galle

LARGE MARGINS OF VICTORY

Inns and 193 runs	South Africa (525-8d) beat New Zealand (121 & 211)	Port Elizabeth
381 runs	Australia (295 & 401-7d) beat England (136 & 179)	Brisbane
347 runs	England (361 & 349-7d) beat Australia (128 & 235)	Lord's
335 runs	Zimbabwe (389 & 227-7d) beat Bangladesh (134 & 147)	Harare

NARROW MARGINS OF VICTORY

14 runs	England (215 & 375) beat Australia (280 & 296)	Nottingham

CLOSE FINISH

India (280 & 421) drew with South Africa (244 & 450-7)   Johannesburg

EIGHT HUNDREDS IN A MATCH

Sri Lanka (570-4d & 335-4d) v Bangladesh (638 & 70-1)   Galle

SIX FIFTIES IN AN INNINGS

Australia (570-9d) v England   Adelaide

BATTING HIGHLIGHTS
DOUBLE HUNDREDS

D.M.Bravo	218	West Indies v New Zealand	Dunedin
M.S.Dhoni	224	India v Australia	Chennai
Mushfiqur Rahim	200†	Bangladesh v Sri Lanka	Galle
C.A.Pujara	204	India v Australia	Hyderabad
G.C.Smith	234	South Africa v Pakistan	Dubai
L.R.P.L.Taylor	217*	New Zealand v West Indies	Dunedin
Younus Khan	200*	Pakistan v Zimbabwe	Harare

HUNDREDS IN THREE CONSECUTIVE INNINGS

| K.C.Sangakkara | 142 · 105 | Sri Lanka v Bangladesh | Galle |
| | 139 | Sri Lanka v Bangladesh | Colombo, RPS |

HUNDRED IN EACH INNINGS OF A MATCH

P.G.Fulton	136	110	New Zealand v England	Auckland
K.C.Sangakkara	142	105	Sri Lanka v Bangladesh	Galle
B.R.M.Taylor	171	102*	Zimbabwe v Bangladesh	Harare

FASTEST HUNDRED

| S.Dhawan (187) | 85 balls | India v Australia | Mohali |

HUNDRED RUNS SCORED IN A SESSION

| S.Dhawan (0-106*) | | India v Australia | Mohali |

200 RUNS IN A DAY

| M.S.Dhoni (0-206*) | | India v Australia | Chennai |

HUNDRED ON TEST DEBUT

S.Dhawan (187)	India v Australia	Mohali
H.D.Rutherford (171)	New Zealand v England	Dunedin
R.G.Sharma (177)	India v West Indies	Kolkata

He then scored 111* in his second innings, v WI in Mumbai, only the fifth player ever to achieve this feat.

LONG INNINGS (Qualification: 600 mins and/or 400 balls)

Mins	Balls			
572	416	D.M.Bravo (218)	West Indies v New Zealand	Dunedin
499	417	Moh'd Ashraful (190)	Bangladesh v Sri Lanka	Galle
627	388	G.C.Smith (234)	South Africa v Pakistan	Dubai
614	404	Younus Khan (200*)	Pakistan v Zimbabwe	Harare

NOTABLE PARTNERSHIPS

Qualifications: 1st-4th wkts: 250 runs; 5th-6th: 225; 7th: 200; 8th: 175; 9th: 150; 10th: 100. † = National record

First Wicket

| 289 | M.Vijay/S.Dhawan | India v Australia | Mohali |

Second Wicket

| 370† | M.Vijay/C.A.Pujara | India v Australia | Hyderabad |

Fifth Wicket

| 338† | G.C.Smith/A.B.de Villiers | South Africa v Pakistan | Dubai |
| 267† | Moh'd Ashraful/Mushfiqur Rahim | Bangladesh v Sri Lanka | Galle |

Seventh Wicket

| 280† | R.G.Sharma/R.Ashwin | India v West Indies | Kolkata |

Tenth Wicket

| 163† | P.J.Hughes/A.C.Agar | Australia v England | Nottingham |
| 127 | B.J.Watling/T.A.Boult | New Zealand v Bangladesh | Chittagong |

BOWLING HIGHLIGHTS
SEVEN WICKETS IN AN INNINGS

K.J.Abbott	7- 29	South Africa v Pakistan	Centurion
R.Ashwin	7-103	India v Australia	Chennai
S.C.J.Broad	7- 44	England v New Zealand	Lord's
R.J.Harris	7-117	Australia v England	Chester-le-Street
H.M.R.K.B.Herath	7- 89	Sri Lanka v Bangladesh	Colombo, RPS
M.G.Johnson	7- 40	Australia v England	Adelaide
N.M.Lyon	7- 94	Australia v India	Delhi
Saeed Ajmal	7- 95	Pakistan v Zimbabwe	Harare

TEN WICKETS IN A MATCH

J.M.Anderson	10-158	England v Australia	Nottingham
R.Ashwin	12-198	India v Australia	Chennai
T.A.Boult	10- 80	New Zealand v West Indies	Wellington
S.C.J.Broad	11-121	England v Australia	Chester-le-Street
H.M.R.K.B.Herath	12-157	Sri Lanka v Bangladesh	Colombo, RPS
P.P.Ojha	10- 89	India v West Indies	Mumbai
Saeed Ajmal (2)	10-147	Pakistan v South Africa	Cape Town
	11-118	Pakistan v Zimbabwe	Harare
S.Shillingford	10- 93	West Indies v Zimbabwe	Roseau

These were the second and third of five consecutive innings in which he took five or more wickets.

T.G.Southee	10-108	New Zealand v England	Lord's
D.W.Steyn	11- 60	South Africa v Pakistan	Johannesburg
G.P.Swann	10-132	England v New Zealand	Leeds

FIVE WICKETS IN AN INNINGS ON DEBUT

K.J.Abbott	7-29	South Africa v Pakistan	Centurion
Mohammed Shami	5-47	India v West Indies	Kolkata

BOWLING UNCHANGED THROUGHOUT INNINGS

J.M.Anderson (11.3-5-23-2)/ S.C.J.Broad (11-0-44-7)	England v New Zealand	Lord's

HAT-TRICKS

Sohag Gazi	Bangladesh v New Zealand	Chittagong

60 OVERS IN AN INNINGS

H.M.R.K.B.Herath 62-11-161-2	Sri Lanka v Bangladesh	Galle

200 RUNS CONCEDED IN AN INNINGS

N.M.Lyon	47-1-215-3	Australia v India	Chennai

WICKET-KEEPING HIGHLIGHTS
SIX WICKET-KEEPING DISMISSALS IN AN INNINGS

A.B.de Villiers	6ct	South Africa v Pakistan	Johannesburg

NINE OR MORE WICKET-KEEPING DISMISSALS IN A MATCH

A.B.de Villiers	11ct†	South Africa v Pakistan	Johannesburg

† This equalled the world record set by R.C.Russell in 1995-96.

FIELDING HIGHLIGHTS
FIVE CATCHES IN AN INNINGS IN THE FIELD

D.J.G.Sammy	5ct	West Indies v India	Mumbai

LEADING TEST AGGREGATES IN 2013

1000 RUNS IN 2013

	M	I	NO	HS	Runs	Avge	100	50
M.J.Clarke (A)	13	26	3	187	**1093**	47.52	4	3
I.R.Bell (E)	14	27	3	113	**1005**	41.87	3	5

RECORD CALENDAR YEAR RUNS AGGREGATE

	M	I	NO	HS	Runs	Avge	100	50
M.Yousuf (P) (2006)	11	19	1	202	**1788**	99.33	9	3

RECORD CALENDAR YEAR RUNS AVERAGE

	M	I	NO	HS	Runs	Avge	100	50
G.St A.Sobers (WI) (1958)	7	12	3	365*	**1193**	132.55	5	3

1000 RUNS IN DEBUT CALENDAR YEAR

	M	I	NO	HS	Runs	Avge	100	50
M.A.Taylor (A) (1989)	11	20	1	219	**1219**	64.15	4	5
A.N.Cook (E) (2006)	13	24	2	127	**1013**	46.04	4	3

50 WICKETS IN 2013

	M	O	R	W	Avge	Best	5wI	10wM
S.C.J.Broad (E)	14	478.1	1600	62	**25.80**	7-44	5	1
J.M.Anderson (E)	14	531.5	1655	52	**31.82**	5-47	3	1
D.W.Steyn (SA)	9	357.4	901	51	**17.66**	6-8	4	1

RECORD CALENDAR YEAR WICKETS AGGREGATE

	M	O	R	W	Avge	Best	5wI	10wM
M.Muralitharan (SL) (2006)	11	588.4	1521	90	**16.90**	8-70	9	5
S.K.Warne (A) (2005)	14	691.4	2043	90	**22.70**	6-46	6	2

50 WICKET-KEEPING DISMISSALS IN 2013

	M	Dis	Ct	St
B.J.Haddin (A)	10	52	51	1

RECORD CALENDAR YEAR DISMISSALS AGGREGATE

	M	Dis	Ct	St
I.A.Healy (A) (1993)	16	67	58	9
M.V.Boucher (SA) (1998)	13	67	65	2

20 CATCHES BY FIELDERS IN 2013

	M	Ct
L.R.P.L.Taylor (NZ)	10	20

RECORD CALENDAR YEAR FIELDER'S AGGREGATE

	M	Ct
G.C.Smith (SA) (2008)	15	30

TEST MATCH SCORES
INDIA v AUSTRALIA (1st Test)

At M.A.Chidambaram Stadium, Chennai, on 22, 23, 24, 25, 26 February 2013.
Toss: Australia. Result: **INDIA** won by eight wickets.
Debuts: India – B.Kumar; Australia – M.C.Henriques.

AUSTRALIA

E.J.M.Cowan	st Dhoni b Ashwin	29		lbw b Ashwin	32
D.A.Warner	lbw b Ashwin	59	(3)	lbw b Harbhajan	23
P.J.Hughes	b Ashwin	6	(4)	c Sehwag b Jadeja	0
S.R.Watson	lbw b Ashwin	28	(2)	c Sehwag b Ashwin	17
*M.J.Clarke	c Kumar b Jadeja	130		lbw b Ashwin	31
†M.S.Wade	lbw b Ashwin	12		b Harbhajan	8
M.C.Henriques	lbw b Ashwin	68		not out	81
M.A.Starc	b Jadeja	3	(10)	c Tendulkar b Ashwin	8
P.M.Siddle	c Sehwag b Harbhajan	19	(8)	b Jadeja	2
J.L.Pattinson	not out	15	(9)	c Sehwag b Ashwin	11
N.M.Lyon	c Kohli b Ashwin	3		c Vijay b Jadeja	11
Extras	(B 1, LB 7)	8		(B 15, LB 2)	17
Total	**(133 overs; 495 mins)**	**380**		**(93 overs; 319 mins)**	**241**

INDIA

M.Vijay	b Pattinson	10		c Henriques b Pattinson	6
V.Sehwag	b Pattinson	2		c Clarke b Lyon	19
C.A.Pujara	b Pattinson	44		not out	8
S.R.Tendulkar	b Lyon	81		not out	13
V.Kohli	c Starc b Lyon	107			
†*M.S.Dhoni	c Wade b Pattinson	224			
R.A.Jadeja	b Pattinson	16			
R.Ashwin	b Lyon	3			
Harbhajan Singh	b Henriques	11			
B.Kumar	c Clarke b Siddle	38			
I.Sharma	not out	4			
Extras	(B 14, LB 14, W 4)	32		(B 4)	4
Total	**(154.4 overs; 685 mins)**	**572**		**(2 wkts; 11.3 overs; 48 mins)**	**50**

INDIA	O	M	R	W		O	M	R	W
Kumar	13	1	52	0					
Sharma	17	3	59	0	(4)	3	1	13	1
Harbhajan Singh	25	2	87	1	(2)	27	6	55	2
Ashwin	42	12	103	7	(1)	32	6	95	5
Jadeja	36	10	71	2	(3)	31	8	72	3
AUSTRALIA									
Starc	25	3	75	0					
Pattinson	30	6	96	5	(1)	3	1	13	1
Siddle	24.3	5	66	1		3	2	4	0
Lyon	47	1	215	3	(2)	5.3	0	29	1
Henriques	17	4	48	1					
Clarke	8	2	25	0					
Warner	3	0	19	0					

FALL OF WICKETS

	A	I	A	I
Wkt	1st	1st	2nd	2nd
1st	64	11	34	16
2nd	72	12	64	36
3rd	126	105	65	–
4th	131	196	101	–
5th	153	324	121	–
6th	304	365	131	–
7th	307	372	137	–
8th	361	406	161	–
9th	364	546	175	–
10th	380	572	241	–

Umpires: H.D.P.K.Dharmasena (*Sri Lanka*) (14) and M.Erasmus (*South Africa*) (16).
Referee: B.C.Broad (*England*) (57).   **Test No. 2074/83 (I469/A750)**

INDIA v AUSTRALIA (2nd Test)

At Rajiv Gandhi International Stadium, Hyderabad, on 2, 3, 4, 5 March 2013.
Toss: Australia. Result: **INDIA** won by an innings and 135 runs.
Debut: Australia – G.J.Maxwell.

AUSTRALIA

D.A.Warner	b Kumar	6	(2)	b Ashwin	26
E.J.M.Cowan	lbw b Kumar	4	(1)	c Sehwag b Jadeja	44
P.J.Hughes	c Dhoni b Ashwin	19		b Ashwin	0
S.R.Watson	lbw b Kumar	23		c Dhoni b Sharma	9
*M.J.Clarke	b Jadeja	91		b Jadeja	16
†M.S.Wade	c Kumar b Harbhajan	62		c Sehwag b Ashwin	10
M.C.Henriques	b Jadeja	5		run out	0
G.J.Maxwell	c Dhoni b Jadeja	13		lbw b Ashwin	8
P.M.Siddle	lbw b Harbhajan	0		c Kohli b Jadeja	4
J.L.Pattinson	not out	1		lbw b Ashwin	0
X.J.Doherty	not out	0		not out	1
Extras	(B 10, LB 3)	13		(B 7, LB 6)	13
Total	(9 wkts dec; 85 overs; 344 mins)	237		(67 overs; 237 mins)	131

INDIA

M.Vijay	c Cowan b Maxwell	167
V.Sehwag	c Wade b Siddle	6
C.A.Pujara	c Doherty b Pattinson	204
S.R.Tendulkar	c Wade b Pattinson	7
V.Kohli	c Cowan b Maxwell	34
†*M.S.Dhoni	c Doherty b Maxwell	44
R.A.Jadeja	c and b Maxwell	10
R.Ashwin	c Hughes b Doherty	1
Harbhajan Singh	c Maxwell b Doherty	0
B.Kumar	st Wade b Doherty	10
I.Sharma	not out	2
Extras	(B 1, LB 13, W 4)	18
Total	(154.1 overs; 622 mins)	503

INDIA	O	M	R	W		O	M	R	W
Kumar	15	2	53	3		6	4	7	0
Sharma	17	5	45	0	(5)	5	2	5	1
Ashwin	15	6	41	1	(2)	28	12	63	5
Harbhajan Singh	22	2	52	2	(3)	10	7	10	0
Jadeja	16	4	33	3	(4)	18	8	33	3

AUSTRALIA	O	M	R	W
Pattinson	29	11	80	2
Siddle	31	6	92	1
Henriques	21	7	45	0
Doherty	46.1	15	131	3
Maxwell	26	2	127	4
Warner	1	0	14	0

FALL OF WICKETS

Wkt	A 1st	I 1st	A 2nd
1st	10	17	56
2nd	15	387	56
3rd	57	393	75
4th	63	404	108
5th	208	460	111
6th	217	484	111
7th	233	485	123
8th	236	489	130
9th	236	491	130
10th	–	503	131

Umpires: H.D.P.K.Dharmasena (*Sri Lanka*) (15) and M.Erasmus (*South Africa*) (17).
Referee: B.C.Broad (*England*) (58).   **Test No. 2075/84 (I470/A751)**

INDIA v AUSTRALIA (3rd Test)

At Punjab C.A.Stadium, Mohali, Chandigarh, on 14, 15, 16, 17, 18 March 2013.
Toss: Australia. Result: **INDIA** won by six wickets.
Debut: India – S.Dhawan.

AUSTRALIA

E.J.M.Cowan	c Kohli b Ashwin	86	(2) lbw b Kumar		8
D.A.Warner	c Dhoni b Jadeja	71	(1) c Dhoni b Kumar		2
*M.J.Clarke	st Dhoni b Jadeja	0	(6) c Pujara b Jadeja		18
P.J.Hughes	c Dhoni b Ojha	2	(3) lbw b Ashwin		69
S.P.D.Smith	st Dhoni b Ojha	92	(4) b Kumar		5
†B.J.Haddin	b Sharma	21	(7) lbw b Ashwin		30
M.C.Henriques	b Sharma	0	(8) c and b Jadeja		2
P.M.Siddle	lbw b Jadeja	0	(9) b Ojha		13
M.A.Starc	c Dhoni b Sharma	99	(10) c Ashwin b Jadeja		35
N.M.Lyon	not out	9	(5) c Dhoni b Ojha		18
X.J.Doherty	lbw b Ashwin	5	not out		18
Extras	(B 8, LB 12, NB 3)	23	(LB 3, W 1, NB 1)		5
Total	**(141.5 overs; 532 mins)**	**408**	**(89.2 overs; 310 mins)**		**223**

INDIA

M.Vijay	lbw b Starc	153	st Haddin b Doherty		26
S.Dhawan	c Cowan b Lyon	187			
C.A.Pujara	lbw b Siddle	1	(2) lbw b Lyon		28
S.R.Tendulkar	c Cowan b Smith	37	run out		21
V.Kohli	not out	67	(3) c Hughes b Siddle		34
†*M.S.Dhoni	lbw b Starc	4	(5) not out		18
R.A.Jadeja	c Haddin b Siddle	8	(6) not out		8
R.Ashwin	c Haddin b Siddle	4			
B.Kumar	c Haddin b Henriques	18			
I.Sharma	c Haddin b Siddle	0			
P.P.Ojha	b Siddle	1			
Extras	(B 5, LB 13, NB 1)	19	(W 1)		1
Total	**(132.1 overs; 547 mins)**	**499**	**(4 wkts; 33.3 overs; 161 mins)**		**136**

INDIA	O	M	R	W		O	M	R	W
Kumar	9	0	44	0		10	1	31	3
Sharma	30	8	72	3		9	1	34	0
Ashwin	43.5	9	97	2		31	9	72	2
Ojha	28	5	98	2	(5) 21	6	46	2
Jadeja	31	7	77	3	(4) 16.2	6	35	3
Tendulkar						2	0	2	0

AUSTRALIA	O	M	R	W		O	M	R	W
Starc	23	5	74	2		10.3	1	51	0
Siddle	29.1	9	71	5		11	2	34	1
Henriques	15	1	62	1					
Lyon	31	4	124	1	(3) 5	0	27	1
Doherty	24	8	87	0	(4) 7	2	24	1
Smith	10	0	63	1					

FALL OF WICKETS				
	A	I	A	I
Wkt	1st	1st	2nd	2nd
1st	139	289	2	42
2nd	139	292	35	70
3rd	151	384	55	103
4th	198	412	89	116
5th	244	416	119	–
6th	244	427	123	–
7th	251	456	126	–
8th	348	492	143	–
9th	399	493	179	–
10th	408	499	223	–

Umpires: Alim Dar (*Pakistan*) (79) and R.A.Kettleborough (*England*) (13).
Referee: R.S.Madugalle (*Sri Lanka*) (140).   **Test No. 2076/85 (I471/A752)**

INDIA v AUSTRALIA (4th Test)

At Feroz Shah Kotla, Delhi, on 22, 23, 24 March 2013.
Toss: Australia. Result: **INDIA** won by six wickets.
Debut: India – A.M.Rahane.

AUSTRALIA

E.J.M.Cowan	b Ashwin	38	(3)	lbw b Jadeja	24
D.A.Warner	c Kohli b Sharma	0	(1)	lbw b Jadeja	8
P.J.Hughes	b Sharma	45	(4)	lbw b Ashwin	6
*S.R.Watson	st Dhoni b Jadeja	17	(5)	b Ojha	5
S.P.D.Smith	c Rahane b Ashwin	46	(6)	b Jadeja	18
†M.S.Wade	c Vijay b Ashwin	2	(7)	c Dhoni b Ojha	19
G.J.Maxwell	c Sharma b Jadeja	10	(2)	b Jadeja	8
M.G.Johnson	b Ashwin	3		b Jadeja	0
P.M.Siddle	b Ashwin	51		st Dhoni b Ashwin	50
J.L.Pattinson	c Kohli b Ojha	30		b Sharma	11
N.M.Lyon	not out	8		not out	5
Extras	(B 5, LB 7)	12		(B 8, LB 2)	10
Total	**(112.1 overs; 401 mins)**	**262**		**(46.3 overs; 169 mins)**	**164**

INDIA

M.Vijay	c Wade b Siddle	57	b Maxwell	11
C.A.Pujara	b Lyon	52	not out	82
V.Kohli	lbw b Lyon	1	lbw b Lyon	41
S.R.Tendulkar	lbw b Lyon	32	lbw b Lyon	1
A.M.Rahane	c Smith b Lyon	7	c Lyon b Maxwell	1
†*M.S.Dhoni	c Watson b Pattinson	24	not out	12
R.A.Jadeja	lbw b Maxwell	43		
R.Ashwin	lbw b Lyon	12		
B.Kumar	not out	14		
I.Sharma	b Lyon	0		
P.P.Ojha	lbw b Lyon	0		
Extras	(B 12, LB 18)	30	(B 9, LB 1)	10
Total	**(70.2 overs; 346 mins)**	**272**	**(4 wkts; 31.2 overs; 123 mins)**	**158**

INDIA	O	M	R	W		O	M	R	W
Kumar	9	1	43	0		2	0	9	0
Sharma	14	3	35	2	(5) 2	0	13	1
Ashwin	34	18	57	5	(2) 15.3	2	55	2
Ojha	26.1	6	75	1	11	2	19	2
Jadeja	29	8	40	2	(3) 16	2	58	5
AUSTRALIA								
Johnson	17	3	44	0	(3) 2	0	16	0
Pattinson	14	1	54	1	(4) 3	0	7	0
Siddle	12	3	38	1				
Lyon	23.2	4	94	7	(1) 15.2	0	71	2
Maxwell	4	0	12	1	(2) 11	0	54	2

FALL OF WICKETS

Wkt	A 1st	I 1st	A 2nd	I 2nd
1st	4	108	15	19
2nd	71	114	20	123
3rd	106	148	41	127
4th	115	165	51	128
5th	117	180	53	–
6th	129	210	94	–
7th	136	254	94	–
8th	189	266	122	–
9th	243	272	157	–
10th	262	272	164	–

Umpires: Alim Dar (*Pakistan*) (80) and R.A.Kettleborough (*England*) (14).
Referee: R.S.Madugalle (*Sri Lanka*) (141).   **Test No. 2077/86 (I472/A753)**

NEW ZEALAND v ENGLAND (1st Test)

At University Oval, Dunedin, on 6 (*no play*), 7, 8, 9, 10 March 2013.
Toss: New Zealand. Result: **MATCH DRAWN**.
Debuts: New Zealand – B.P.Martin, H.D.Rutherford.

ENGLAND

*A.N.Cook	c Rutherford b Wagner	10		c Watling b Boult	116
N.R.D.Compton	b Southee	0		lbw b Wagner	117
I.J.L.Trott	c Boult b Martin	45	(4)	c and b Wagner	52
K.P.Pietersen	lbw b Wagner	0	(5)	c Watling b Wagner	12
I.R.Bell	c Rutherford b Wagner	24	(6)	not out	26
J.E.Root	c Brownlie b Boult	4	(7)	run out	0
†M.J.Prior	c Williamson b Martin	23	(8)	not out	23
S.C.J.Broad	c Brownlie b Martin	10			
S.T.Finn	c Rutherford b Wagner	20	(3)	lbw b Martin	56
J.M.Anderson	c Wagner b Martin	23			
M.S.Panesar	not out	1			
Extras	(B 4, LB 1, W 2)	7		(B 6, LB 11, W 1, NB 1)	19
Total	**(55 overs; 243 mins)**	**167**		**(6 wkts; 170 overs; 696 mins)**	**421**

NEW ZEALAND

P.G.Fulton	c Prior b Anderson	55
H.D.Rutherford	c sub (C.R.Woakes) b Anderson	171
K.S.Williamson	b Panesar	24
L.R.P.L.Taylor	c Trott b Anderson	31
D.G.Brownlie	b Anderson	27
*B.B.McCullum	c Anderson b Broad	74
†B.J.Watling	b Broad	0
T.G.Southee	b Broad	25
B.P.Martin	c Prior b Finn	41
N.Wagner	not out	4
T.A.Boult		
Extras	(LB 8)	8
Total	**(9 wkts dec; 116.4 overs; 515 mins)**	**460**

NEW ZEALAND	O	M	R	W	O	M	R	W	FALL OF WICKETS			
										E	NZ	E
Southee	15	3	45	1	36	8	94	0	*Wkt*	*1st*	*1st*	*2nd*
Boult	15	4	32	1	35	12	49	1	1st	5	158	231
Wagner	11	2	42	4	43	9	141	3	2nd	18	249	265
Martin	14	4	43	4	44	13	90	1	3rd	18	267	355
Williamson					12	3	30	0	4th	64	310	367
									5th	71	321	386
ENGLAND									6th	108	326	390
Anderson	33	2	137	4					7th	109	350	–
Finn	26.4	3	102	1					8th	119	447	–
Broad	28	3	118	3					9th	166	460	–
Panesar	22	2	83	1					10th	167	–	–
Trott	2	0	4	0								
Root	5	1	8	0								

Umpires: Asad Rauf (*Pakistan*) (47) and P.R.Reiffel (*Australia*) (3).
Referee: R.S.Mahanama (*Sri Lanka*) (41). **Test No. 2078/95 (NZ380/E931)**

NEW ZEALAND v ENGLAND (2nd Test)

At Basin Reserve, Wellington, on 14, 15, 16, 17, 18 (*no play*) March 2013.
Toss: New Zealand. Result: **MATCH DRAWN**.
Debuts: None.

ENGLAND

*A.N.Cook	c Fulton b Wagner	17	
N.R.D.Compton	c Taylor b Martin	100	
I.J.L.Trott	c Watling b Boult	121	
K.P.Pietersen	c Fulton b Martin	73	
I.R.Bell	c Fulton b Martin	11	
J.E.Root	c Watling b Martin	10	
†M.J.Prior	c Wagner b Williamson	82	
S.C.J.Broad	c Watling b Boult	6	
S.T.Finn	c McCullum b Wagner	24	
J.M.Anderson	not out	8	
M.S.Panesar	c Taylor b Williamson	0	
Extras	(LB 3, W 7, NB 3)	13	
Total	**(146.5 overs; 615 mins)**	**465**	

NEW ZEALAND

P.G.Fulton	c Cook b Anderson	1	c Cook b Anderson		45
H.D.Rutherford	c Cook b Broad	23	c Bell b Panesar		15
K.S.Williamson	c and b Broad	42	not out		55
L.R.P.L.Taylor	b Broad	0	not out		41
D.G.Brownlie	lbw b Anderson	18			
*B.B.McCullum	c Trott b Finn	69			
†B.J.Watling	c Prior b Broad	60			
T.G.Southee	c Broad b Finn	3			
B.P.Martin	not out	21			
N.Wagner	c Prior b Broad	0			
T.A.Boult	c Prior b Broad	2			
Extras	(LB 10, W 2, NB 3)	15	(LB 1, W 5)		6
Total	**(89.2 overs)**	**254**	**(2 wkts; 68 overs; 281 mins)**		**162**

NEW ZEALAND	O	M	R	W		O	M	R	W		FALL OF WICKETS		
												E	NZ	NZ

NEW ZEALAND	O	M	R	W		O	M	R	W
Southee	32	9	77	0					
Boult	30	4	117	2					
Wagner	33	5	122	2					
Martin	48	11	130	4					
Williamson	3.5	0	16	2					

ENGLAND	O	M	R	W		O	M	R	W
Anderson	25	6	68	2		12	4	27	1
Finn	20	2	72	2	(3)	11	2	36	0
Broad	17.2	2	51	6	(2)	14	6	32	0
Panesar	26	11	47	0		26	12	44	1
Root	1	0	6	0	(6)	2	0	12	0
Trott					(5)	3	0	10	0

	FALL OF WICKETS			
		E	NZ	NZ
Wkt	1st	1st	2nd	
1st	26	6	25	
2nd	236	48	81	
3rd	267	48	–	
4th	302	85	–	
5th	325	89	–	
6th	366	189	–	
7th	374	197	–	
8th	437	239	–	
9th	465	252	–	
10th	465	254	–	

Umpires: Asad Rauf (*Pakistan*) (48) and R.J.Tucker (*Australia*) (23).
Referee: R.S.Mahanama (*Sri Lanka*) (42).   Test No. 2079/96 (NZ381/E932)

NEW ZEALAND v ENGLAND (3rd Test)

At Eden Park, Auckland, on 22, 23, 24, 25, 26 March 2013.
Toss: England. Result: **MATCH DRAWN**.
Debuts: None.

NEW ZEALAND

P.G.Fulton	c Prior b Finn	136	c Root b Finn	110
H.D.Rutherford	c Cook b Finn	37	c Bell b Broad	0
K.S.Williamson	c Prior b Anderson	91	b Anderson	1
L.R.P.L.Taylor	c and b Panesar	19	lbw b Broad	3
D.G.Brownlie	c Compton b Anderson	36	c Bell b Panesar	28
*B.B.McCullum	c Prior b Trott	38	not out	67
†B.J.Watling	c Prior b Finn	21	c Compton b Panesar	18
T.G.Southee	c Prior b Finn	44		
B.P.Martin	c Trott b Finn	10		
N.Wagner	not out	2		
T.A.Boult	c Compton b Finn	0		
Extras	(B 4, LB 4, NB 1)	9	(B 4, LB 10)	14
Total	**(152.3 overs; 634 mins)**	**443**	**(6 wkts; 57.2 overs; 264 mins)**	**241**

ENGLAND

*A.N.Cook	c Watling b Boult	4	c Brownlie b Williamson	43
N.R.D.Compton	lbw b Southee	13	c Watling b Southee	2
I.J.L.Trott	lbw b Boult	27	c Watling b Wagner	37
I.R.Bell	lbw b Southee	17	c Southee b Wagner	75
J.E.Root	b Southee	45	(6) lbw b Boult	29
J.M.Bairstow	lbw b Boult	3	(7) c Taylor b Southee	6
†M.J.Prior	c Rutherford b Wagner	73	(8) not out	110
S.C.J.Broad	c Rutherford b Boult	16	(9) c Taylor b Williamson	6
S.T.Finn	c Taylor b Boult	0	(5) c Southee b Williamson	0
J.M.Anderson	c Watling b Boult	4	c Taylor b Williamson	0
M.S.Panesar	not out	2	not out	0
Extras	(W 2)	2	(LB 4, NB 1)	5
Total	**(89.2 overs; 371 mins)**	**204**	**(9 wkts; 143 overs; 606 mins)**	**315**

ENGLAND	O	M	R	W	O	M	R	W
Anderson	30	8	79	2	17	6	59	1
Broad	30	6	94	0	17	5	54	2
Finn	37.3	8	125	6	13	1	57	1
Panesar	47	17	123	1	9.2	4	53	2
Trott	6	3	9	1	1	0	4	0
Root	2	1	5	0				

NEW ZEALAND	O	M	R	W		O	M	R	W
Boult	25	9	68	6		29	13	55	1
Southee	23.2	9	44	3		30	6	77	2
Wagner	15	3	36	1	(4)	25	8	61	2
Martin	26	10	56	0	(3)	39	18	74	0
Williamson						20	8	44	4

FALL OF WICKETS

Wkt	NZ 1st	E 1st	NZ 2nd	E 2nd
1st	79	8	4	2
2nd	260	44	5	60
3rd	289	61	8	90
4th	297	65	82	90
5th	365	72	199	150
6th	373	173	241	159
7th	424	200	–	237
8th	436	200	–	304
9th	443	204	–	304
10th	443	204	–	–

Umpires: P.R.Reiffel (*Australia*) (4) and R.J.Tucker (*Australia*) (24).
Referee: R.S.Mahanama (*Sri Lanka*) (43).　　　Test No. 2080/97 (NZ382/E933)

SRI LANKA v BANGLADESH (1st Test)

At Galle International Stadium, on 8, 9, 10, 11, 12 March 2013.
Toss: Sri Lanka. Result: **MATCH DRAWN**.
Debuts: Sri Lanka – K.D.K.Vithanage; Bangladesh – Anamul Haque, Mominul Haque.

SRI LANKA

F.D.M.Karunaratne	lbw b Gazi	41	c Abul b Shahadat		3
T.M.Dilshan	c Mominul b Gazi	54	c Abul b Mahmudullah		126
K.C.Sangakkara	c Islam b Gazi	142	c Islam b Mahmudullah		105
H.D.R.L.Thirimanne	not out	155	(6) not out		2
*A.D.Mathews	c and b Hasan	27	not out		38
†L.D.Chandimal	not out	116			
K.M.D.N.Kulasekara					
K.D.K.Vithanage			(4) b Mahmudullah		59
R.M.S.Eranga					
H.M.R.K.B.Herath					
B.A.W.Mendis					
Extras	(B 8, LB 17, W 3, NB 7)	35	(NB 2)		2
Total	**(4 wkts dec; 135 overs; 569 mins)**	**570**	**(4 wkts dec; 83 overs; 337 mins)**		**335**

BANGLADESH

Jahurul Islam	c Chandimal b Eranga	20	not out		41
Anamul Haque	b Mendis	13	b Eranga		1
Mohammad Ashraful	c Mathews b Herath	190	not out		22
Mominul Haque	c Mathews b Kulasekara	55			
Mahmudullah	st Chandimal b Herath	0			
*†Mushfiqur Rahim	lbw b Kulasekara	200			
Nasir Hossain	c Karunaratne b Dilshan	100			
Sohag Gazi	c Vithanage b Mendis	21			
Abul Hasan	not out	16			
Elias Sunny	c Chandimal b Dilshan	0			
Shahadat Hossain	b Eranga	13			
Extras	(B 2, LB 1, NB 7)	10	(B 4, LB 1, NB 1)		6
Total	**(196 overs; 764 mins)**	**638**	**(1 wkt; 22 overs; 87 mins)**		**70**

BANGLADESH	O	M	R	W		O	M	R	W
Shahadat Hossain	21	2	95	0		9	1	33	1
Abul Hasan	27	4	112	1		10	0	45	0
Sohag Gazi	50	6	164	3		15	1	58	0
Elias Sunny	20	0	89	0		20	0	76	0
Mohammad Ashraful	4	0	23	0	(6)	1	0	10	0
Mahmudullah	11	1	45	0	(7)	20	1	70	3
Mominul Haque	2	0	17	0	(5)	5	0	25	0
Nasir Hossain						3	0	18	0

SRI LANKA	O	M	R	W		O	M	R	W
Kulasekara	27	3	94	2		4	1	6	0
Eranga	34	4	122	2		3	1	10	1
Herath	62	11	161	2		4	0	15	0
Mendis	36	3	152	2		7	1	23	0
Mathews	9	2	18	0					
Dilshan	26	5	75	2	(5)	4	0	11	0
Thirimanne	2	0	13	0					

FALL OF WICKETS				
	SL	B	SL	B
Wkt	1st	1st	2nd	2nd
1st	114	23	17	2
2nd	181	65	230	–
3rd	305	170	249	–
4th	367	177	320	–
5th	–	444	–	–
6th	–	550	–	–
7th	–	581	–	–
8th	–	618	–	–
9th	–	618	–	–
10th	–	638	–	–

Umpires: R.K.Illingworth (*England*) (3) and N.J.Llong (*England*) (17).
Referee: D.C.Boon (*Australia*) (15).   **Test No. 2081/13 (SL221/B76)**
F.D.M.Karunaratne retired hurt at 46-0 and resumed at 114-1.

SRI LANKA v BANGLADESH (2nd Test)

At R.Premadasa Stadium, Colombo, on 16, 17, 18, 19 March 2013.
Toss: Sri Lanka. Result: **SRI LANKA** won by seven wickets.
Debuts: None.

BANGLADESH

Tamim Iqbal	lbw b Kulasekara	10	b Eranga		59
Jahurul Islam	c Chandimal b Eranga	33	st Chandimal b Herath		48
Mohammad Ashraful	run out	16	b Herath		4
Mominul Haque	c Chandimal b Herath	64	c Karunaratne b Herath		37
Mahmudullah	c Mathews b Herath	8	b Herath		0
*†Mushfiqur Rahim	b Herath	7	c Mathews b Herath		40
Nasir Hossain	lbw b Herath	48	b Herath		0
Sohag Gazi	st Chandimal b Herath	32	c Lakmal b Herath		26
Abul Hasan	c Karunaratne b Kulasekara	4	not out		25
Rubel Hossain	c Herath b Kulasekara	0	b Dilshan		7
Robiul Islam	not out	1	b Eranga		10
Extras	(LB 8, W 7, NB 2)	17	(B 1, LB 4, NB 4)		9
Total	**(83.3 overs; 353 mins)**	**240**	**(100.4 overs; 404 mins)**		**265**

SRI LANKA

F.D.M.Karunaratne	c Rahim b Hasan	17	lbw b Robiul	16
T.M.Dilshan	c Rahim b Robiul	0	b Robiul	57
K.C.Sangakkara	c Rahim b Hasan	139	b Gazi	55
H.D.R.L.Thirimanne	c Rahim b Robiul	0	not out	13
*A.D.Mathews	c Mahmudullah b Gazi	16	not out	13
†L.D.Chandimal	b Rubel	102		
K.D.K.Vithanage	c Mominul b Rubel	12		
K.M.D.N.Kulasekara	c Rahim b Gazi	22		
H.M.R.K.B.Herath	b Gazi	3		
R.M.S.Eranga	c Ashraful b Mahmudullah	15		
R.A.S.Lakmal	not out	0		
Extras	(B 2, LB 2, W 6, NB 10)	20	(B 2, LB 1, NB 3)	6
Total	**(111.3 overs; 493 mins)**	**346**	**(3 wkts dec; 41.4 overs; 182 mins)**	**160**

SRI LANKA	O	M	R	W		O	M	R	W		FALL OF WICKETS				
Kulasekara	18	3	54	3		12	0	36	0			B	SL	B	SL
Lakmal	16	4	44	0		9	1	26	0		*Wkt*	*1st*	*1st*	*2nd*	*2nd*
Mathews	3	1	7	0	(6)	3	2	8	0		1st	16	7	91	31
Eranga	14	2	40	1	(5)	15.4	3	39	2		2nd	51	39	96	125
Herath	28.3	6	68	5	(3)	36	9	89	7		3rd	100	43	143	135
Dilshan	4	0	19	0	(4)	25	4	62	1		4th	128	69	143	—
											5th	152	264	160	—
BANGLADESH											6th	163	280	171	—
Robiul Islam	15	1	52	2		11	0	42	2		7th	222	316	202	—
Sohag Gazi	39	4	111	3	(3)	13	1	47	1		8th	232	323	228	—
Abul Hasan	23	4	80	2	(2)	4	0	21	0		9th	232	346	239	—
Rubel Hossain	17	5	45	2		3	0	16	0		10th	240	346	265	—
Mahmudullah	11.3	1	37	1	(6)	3	0	12	0						
Mominul Haque	2	0	6	0											
Mohammad Ashraful	2	0	9	0		3.4	0	8	0						
Nasir Hossain	2	0	2	0	(5)	4	0	11	0						

Umpires: R.K.Illingworth (*England*) (4) and N.J.Llong (*England*) (18).
Referee: D.C.Boon (*Australia*) (16). **Test No. 2082/14 (SL222/B77)**
F.D.M.Karunaratne retired hurt at 46-0 and resumed at 114-1.

WEST INDIES v ZIMBABWE (1st Test)

At Kensington Oval, Bridgetown, Barbados, on 12, 13, 14 March 2013.
Toss: Zimbabwe. Result: **WEST INDIES** won by nine wickets.
Debut: Zimbabwe – T.L.Chatara.

ZIMBABWE

T.M.K.Mawoyo	c Powell b Shillingford	50	c Sammy b Gabriel	9
V.Sibanda	b Roach	12	c and b Shillingford	15
H.Masakadza	c Samuels b Roach	17	c Sammy b Shillingford	1
*B.R.M.Taylor	b Gabriel	26	(5) c Powell b Shillingford	6
C.R.Ervine	b Samuels	29	(6) not out	23
M.N.Waller	lbw b Shillingford	9	(7) c Powell b Shillingford	5
†R.W.Chakabva	c Powell b Shillingford	15	(8) b Shillingford	6
A.G.Cremer	c Bravo b Samuels	25	(9) c Ramdin b Shillingford	14
R.W.Price	not out	12	(4) b Roach	7
K.M.Jarvis	c Powell b Samuels	0	c Ramdin b Gabriel	0
T.L.Chatara	c Roach b Samuels	2	b Gabriel	0
Extras	(B 4, LB 10)	14	(B 8, LB 2, W 1, NB 1)	12
Total	**(76.4 overs)**	**211**	**(41.4 overs)**	**107**

WEST INDIES

C.H.Gayle	c Taylor b Chatara	40	not out	4
K.O.A.Powell	lbw b Jarvis	5	c Cremer b Chatara	6
K.A.J.Roach	lbw b Jarvis	0		
D.M.Bravo	c Chakabva b Jarvis	11	(3) not out	1
M.N.Samuels	c Chakabva b Masakadza	51		
S.Chanderpaul	c Chakabva b Jarvis	26		
†D.Ramdin	c Sibanda b Chatara	62		
*D.J.G.Sammy	b Masakadza	73		
S.Shillingford	c Jarvis b Price	1		
T.L.Best	c Cremer b Jarvis	24		
S.T.Gabriel	not out	0		
Extras	(B 9, LB 3, W 1, NB 1)	14	(B 1)	1
Total	**(84.2 overs)**	**307**	**(1 wkt; 5 overs; 21 mins)**	**12**

WEST INDIES	O	M	R	W		O	M	R	W
Roach	13	3	31	2		10	7	12	1
Best	12	3	33	0		8	2	26	0
Gabriel	14	5	45	1		7.4	3	10	3
Sammy	9	5	17	0					
Shillingford	22	4	58	3	(4)	16	4	49	6
Samuels	6.4	1	13	4					
ZIMBABWE									
Jarvis	17.2	4	54	5		3	1	10	0
Chatara	19	6	66	2		2	1	1	1
Cremer	20	0	103	0					
Masakadza	10	2	25	2					
Price	18	2	47	1					

FALL OF WICKETS				
	Z	WI	Z	WI
Wkt	1st	1st	2nd	2nd
1st	17	8	25	8
2nd	59	8	26	–
3rd	100	43	39	–
4th	110	81	47	–
5th	135	144	47	–
6th	158	151	58	–
7th	196	257	77	–
8th	196	268	97	–
9th	197	301	107	–
10th	211	307	107	–

Umpires: R.E.J.Martinesz (*Sri Lanka*) (1) and B.N.J.Oxenford (*Australia*) (13).
Referee: J.J.Crowe (*New Zealand*) (61).   **Test No. 2083/7 (WI489/Z88)**

WEST INDIES v ZIMBABWE (2nd Test)

At Windsor Park, Roseau, Dominica, on 20, 21, 22 March 2013.
Toss: West Indies. Result: **WEST INDIES** won by an innings and 65 runs.
Debut: Zimbabwe – S.C.Williams.

ZIMBABWE

T.M.K.Mawoyo	b Gabriel	8	(7)	c Sammy b Shillingford		0
V.Sibanda	c Roach b Gabriel	32	(1)	lbw b Sammy		35
H.Masakadza	b Shillingford	14	(2)	c Ramdin b Best		17
*†B.R.M.Taylor	b Shillingford	33	(3)	c Powell b Shillingford		7
C.R.Ervine	lbw b Samuels	18	(4)	c Gayle b Shillingford		8
S.C.Williams	c Powell b Samuels	31	(5)	c Chanderpaul b Shillingford		6
M.N.Waller	c Best b Shillingford	9	(6)	c Sammy b Samuels		20
A.G.Cremer	c Powell b Samuels	0		c Samuels b Shillingford		20
P.Utseya	lbw b Shillingford	9		not out		10
K.M.Jarvis	not out	1		c Sammy b Samuels		1
T.L.Chatara	lbw b Shillingford	4		c Gabriel b Samuels		0
Extras	(B 10, LB 4, W 1, NB 1)	16		(B 8, LB 9)		17
Total	**(60.5 overs)**	**175**		**(42.2 overs)**		**141**

WEST INDIES

C.H.Gayle	c Jarvis b Utseya	101
K.O.A.Powell	b Jarvis	24
D.M.Bravo	c Taylor b Jarvis	0
M.N.Samuels	b Chatara	26
S.Chanderpaul	c Williams b Utseya	108
†D.Ramdin	lbw b Cremer	86
*D.J.G.Sammy	c Masakadza b Cremer	9
S.Shillingford	not out	4
K.A.J.Roach	b Utseya	0
T.L.Best	not out	11
S.T.Gabriel		
Extras	(B 4, LB 7, W 1)	12
Total	**(8 wkts dec; 117 overs)**	**381**

WEST INDIES	O	M	R	W		O	M	R	W
Roach	7	0	30	0	(2)	3	0	12	0
Best	10	0	32	0	(1)	7	2	11	1
Gabriel	8	6	10	2		3	0	19	0
Sammy	5	1	15	0	(5)	5	1	13	1
Shillingford	21.5	4	59	5	(4)	15	4	34	5
Samuels	9	3	15	3		9.2	0	35	3

ZIMBABWE	O	M	R	W
Jarvis	21	3	82	2
Chatara	22	2	69	1
Masakadza	17	6	48	0
Cremer	34	6	102	2
Utseya	22	6	60	3
Williams	1	0	9	0

FALL OF WICKETS

	Z	WI	Z
Wkt	1st	1st	2nd
1st	42	35	37
2nd	43	35	64
3rd	64	114	64
4th	105	181	73
5th	141	354	92
6th	158	366	96
7th	158	370	114
8th	161	370	138
9th	171	–	141
10th	175	–	141

Umpires: A.L.Hill (*New Zealand*) (36) and R.E.J.Martinesz (*Sri Lanka*) (2).
Referee: J.J.Crowe (*New Zealand*) (62).   **Test No. 2084/8 (WI490/Z89)**

ZIMBABWE v BANGLADESH (1st Test)

At Harare Sports Club, on 17, 18, 19, 20 April 2013.
Toss: Bangladesh. Result: **ZIMBABWE** won by 335 runs.
Debuts: Zimbabwe – T.Maruma, K.O.Meth, R.Mutumbami.

ZIMBABWE

T.Maruma	lbw b Robiul	10	lbw b Robiul	10
V.Sibanda	b Robiul	5	b Robiul	4
H.Masakadza	c Mahmudullah b Haque	25	c and b Robiul	0
*B.R.M.Taylor	c Rahim b Haque	171	not out	102
M.N.Waller	b Rubel	55	c Nasir b Robiul	4
E.Chigumbura	c and b Rubel	12	c Jahurul b Robiul	27
†R.Mutumbami	c Rahim b Robiul	11	lbw b Robiul	0
A.G.Cremer	c Mahmudullah b Gazi	42	run out	43
K.O.Meth	c Nasir b Haque	21	not out	31
S.W.Masakadza	c Jahurul b Gazi	21		
K.M.Jarvis	not out	3		
Extras	(B 1, LB 5, W 2, NB 5)	13	(LB 2, W 2, NB 2)	6
Total	**(152.3 overs; 625 mins)**	**389**	**(7 wkts dec; 64 overs; 278 mins)**	**227**

BANGLADESH

Jahurul Islam	lbw b Meth	43	c Mutumbami b S.W.Masakadza	22
Shahriar Nafees	c Maruma b Jarvis	29	b Jarvis	11
Mohammad Ashraful	c Waller b S.W.Masakadza	38	run out	40
Mahmudullah	b Meth	3	c sub (S.C.Williams) b Jarvis	21
Shakib Al Hasan	c Sibanda b S.W.Masakadza	4	c Sibanda b Jarvis	4
*†Mushfiqur Rahim	lbw b S.W.Masakadza	3	c Taylor b Chigumbura	3
Nasir Hossain	c Mutumbami b Jarvis	7	b Cremer	23
Sohag Gazi	c Waller b S.W.Masakadza	0	st Mutumbami b Cremer	4
Enamul Haque II	b Jarvis	0	not out	4
Rubel Hossain	b Jarvis	0	c S.W.Masakadza b Cremer	6
Robiul Islam	not out	0	c Jarvis b Cremer	4
Extras	(B 4, LB 1, W 1)	6	(B 8, NB 1)	9
Total	**(54.1 overs; 249 mins)**	**134**	**(49.2 overs; 229 mins)**	**147**

BANGLADESH	O	M	R	W		O	M	R	W	FALL OF WICKETS				
Robiul Islam	38	11	84	3		19	1	71	6		Z	B	Z	B
Rubel Hossain	30	6	87	2		10	0	44	0	*Wkt*	*1st*	*1st*	*2nd*	*2nd*
Nasir Hossain	5	2	3	0						1st	10	53	7	21
Enamul Haque II	47	5	133	3		13	2	45	0	2nd	22	102	9	41
Sohag Gazi	22.3	1	55	2		9	0	24	0	3rd	65	112	16	77
Mahmudullah	3	0	7	0		4	2	19	0	4th	192	123	27	81
Shakib Al Hasan	7	3	14	0	(3)	9	2	22	0	5th	223	124	84	85
										6th	238	134	84	132
ZIMBABWE										7th	344	134	163	136
Jarvis	16	8	40	4		17	1	75	3	8th	344	134	–	139
Meth	20	6	41	2		12	5	16	0	9th	381	134	–	147
S.W.Masakadza	14.1	4	32	4		10	4	26	1	10th	389	134	–	147
Chigumbura	3	0	16	0		5	0	18	1					
Cremer						5.2	1	4	4					

Umpires: B.F.Bowden (*New Zealand*) (75) and A.L.Hill (*New Zealand*) (37).
Referee: B.C.Broad (*England*) (59). **Test No. 2085/10 (Z90/B78)**

ZIMBABWE v BANGLADESH (2nd Test)

At Harare Sports Club, on 25, 26, 27, 28, 29 April 2013.
Toss: Zimbabwe. Result: **BANGLADESH** won by 143 runs.
Debut: Bangladesh – Ziaur Rahman.

BANGLADESH

Batsman	1st innings		2nd innings	
Tamim Iqbal	run out	49	c Mutumbami b S.W.Masakadza	7
Jahurul Islam	c Waller b Meth	24	c Mutumbami b S.W.Masakadza	2
Mohammad Ashraful	c Cremer b S.W.Masakadza	4	lbw b Jarvis	4
Mominul Haque	c S.W.Masakadza b Chigumbura	23	c H.Masakadza b S.W.Masakadza	29
Shakib Al Hasan	c Mutumbami b Chigumbura	81	c Mutumbami b H.Masakadza	59
*†Mushfiqur Rahim	lbw b Jarvis	60	c Sibanda b H.Masakadza	93
Nasir Hossain	b Cremer	77	not out	67
Ziaur Rahman	lbw b Meth	14	st Mutumbami b Cremer	0
Sohag Gazi	c Chigumbura b Cremer	21	c Sibanda b H.Masakadza	11
Sajedul Islam	c Mutumbami b Chigumbura	0	c Mutumbami b S.W.Masakadza	4
Robiul Islam	not out	24	not out	4
Extras	(B 2, LB 7, W 1, NB 4)	14	(LB 5, W 2, NB 4)	11
Total	**(113.2 overs; 501 mins)**	**391**	**(9 wkts dec; 88 overs; 402 mins)**	**291**

ZIMBABWE

Batsman	1st innings		2nd innings	
V.Sibanda	c Rahim b Robiul	10	c Gazi b Shakib	32
R.W.Chakabva	c Rahim b Robiul	12	b Shakib	22
H.Masakadza	b Shakib	14	not out	111
*B.R.M.Taylor	c Shakib b Gazi	36	lbw b Rahman	10
M.N.Waller	c Shakib b Gazi	32	b Rahman	15
E.Chigumbura	b Robiul	86	(7) c Robiul b Gazi	2
†R.Mutumbami	lbw b Robiul	42	(8) b Rahman	12
A.G.Cremer	not out	11	(9) c Hossain b Rahman	3
K.O.Meth	c Rahim b Gazi	16	(10) lbw b Robiul	4
S.W.Masakadza	c Rahim b Robiul	5	(6) lbw b Ashraful	24
K.M.Jarvis	b Gazi	0	lbw b Shakib	7
Extras	(B 5, LB 11, W 1, NB 1)	18	(B 4, LB 7, NB 4)	15
Total	**(96 overs; 424 mins)**	**282**	**(95.3 overs; 411 mins)**	**257**

ZIMBABWE	O	M	R	W	O	M	R	W
Jarvis	25	4	105	1	22	3	80	1
Meth	22	7	41	2				
S.W.Masakadza	17	2	52	1	(2) 24	5	58	4
Chigumbura	24.2	7	75	3	14	0	54	0
Cremer	25	3	109	2	(3) 17	1	70	1
H.Masakadza					(5) 11	1	24	3

BANGLADESH	O	M	R	W	O	M	R	W
Robiul Islam	33	11	85	5	20	5	53	1
Sajedul Islam	16	5	48	0	3	1	9	0
Ziaur Rahman	7	3	80	0	(5) 23	8	63	4
Shakib Al Hasan	19	4	66	1	(3) 11.3	0	52	3
Sohag Gazi	19	1	59	4	(4) 31	11	56	1
Mohammad Ashraful	2	2	0	0	7	1	13	1

FALL OF WICKETS				
	B	Z	B	Z
Wkt	1st	1st	2nd	2nd
1st	44	23	7	36
2nd	58	26	12	66
3rd	102	45	18	96
4th	125	97	65	118
5th	248	163	149	164
6th	280	248	233	169
7th	313	257	234	200
8th	364	274	255	214
9th	367	281	279	219
10th	391	282	–	257

Umpires: I.J.Gould (*England*) (34) and A.L.Hill (*New Zealand*) (38).
Referee: B.C.Broad (*England*) (60).   **Test No. 2086/11 (Z91/B79)**

ENGLAND v NEW ZEALAND (1st Test)

At Lord's, London, on 16, 17, 18, 19 May 2013.
Toss: England. Result: **ENGLAND** won by 170 runs.
Debuts: None.

ENGLAND

*A.N.Cook	c Watling b Boult	32		c Brownlie b Boult	21
N.R.D.Compton	c Southee b Martin	16		b Wagner	15
I.J.L.Trott	c Brownlie b Boult	39		b Williamson	56
I.R.Bell	c Watling b Wagner	31	(8)	c Brownlie b Southee	6
J.E.Root	c Watling b Southee	40	(4)	b Southee	71
J.M.Bairstow	c and b Southee	41	(5)	b Southee	5
†M.J.Prior	lbw b Southee	0	(6)	c sub (M.J.Guptill) b Southee	0
S.C.J.Broad	lbw b Wagner	0	(9)	not out	26
G.P.Swann	c Watling b Wagner	5	(10)	c McCullum b Southee	1
S.T.Finn	lbw b Southee	4	(7)	c sub (M.J.Guptill) b Southee	6
J.M.Anderson	not out	7		c Southee b Williamson	0
Extras	(B 1, LB 9, W 2, NB 5)	17		(B 3, W 1, NB 2)	6
Total	**(112.2 overs; 486 mins)**	**232**		**(68.3 overs; 329 mins)**	**213**

NEW ZEALAND

P.G.Fulton	c Swann b Anderson	2		c Prior b Broad	1
H.D.Rutherford	c Cook b Anderson	4		b Broad	9
K.S.Williamson	c Prior b Anderson	60		c Finn b Broad	6
L.R.P.L.Taylor	lbw b Anderson	66		c Cook b Broad	0
D.G.Brownlie	lbw b Finn	23		c Cook b Anderson	5
*B.B.McCullum	c Prior b Broad	2		lbw b Broad	8
†B.J.Watling	c Prior b Finn	17		c Trott b Anderson	13
T.G.Southee	c Root b Finn	12		c Root b Broad	7
B.P.Martin	b Anderson	0	(10)	b Broad	1
N.Wagner	not out	6	(9)	run out	17
T.A.Boult	c Anderson b Finn	0		not out	0
Extras	(B 4, LB 8, NB 3)	15		(LB 1)	1
Total	**(69 overs; 333 mins)**	**207**		**(22.3 overs; 112 mins)**	**68**

NEW ZEALAND	O	M	R	W	O	M	R	W
Boult	27	10	48	2	15	3	56	1
Southee	28.2	8	58	4	19	4	50	6
Wagner	28	8	70	3	13	2	44	1
Martin	26	12	38	1	13	2	40	0
Williamson	3	1	8	0	8.3	2	20	2

ENGLAND	O	M	R	W	O	M	R	W
Anderson	24	11	47	5	11.3	5	23	2
Broad	21	4	64	1	11	0	44	7
Finn	15	3	63	4				
Swann	8	0	19	0				
Trott	1	0	2	0				

FALL OF WICKETS

	E	NZ	E	NZ
Wkt	1st	1st	2nd	2nd
1st	43	5	36	1
2nd	67	7	36	16
3rd	112	100	159	16
4th	157	147	167	21
5th	192	155	171	25
6th	192	177	171	29
7th	195	194	183	41
8th	201	195	200	54
9th	221	207	210	67
10th	232	207	213	68

Umpires: Alim Dar (*Pakistan*) (81) and S.J.Davis (*Australia*) (45).
Referee: D.C.Boon (*Australia*) (17). **Test No. 2087/98 (E934/NZ383)**

ENGLAND v NEW ZEALAND (2nd Test)

At Headingley, Leeds, on 24 (*no play*), 25, 26, 27, 28 May 2013.
Toss: England. Result: **ENGLAND** won by 247 runs.
Debuts: None.

ENGLAND

*A.N.Cook	c Brownlie b Bracewell	34	c Southee b Williamson	130
N.R.D.Compton	c Brownlie b Southee	1	c Rutherford b Williamson	7
I.J.L.Trott	c McCullum b Wagner	28	c McCullum b Wagner	76
I.R.Bell	c McCullum b Williamson	30	c Guptill b Williamson	6
J.E.Root	c McCullum b Boult	104	c Guptill b Wagner	28
J.M.Bairstow	c McCullum b Boult	64	not out	26
†M.J.Prior	c Taylor b Southee	39	not out	4
S.C.J.Broad	c McCullum b Boult	0		
G.P.Swann	not out	26		
S.T.Finn	b Boult	6		
J.M.Anderson	c and b Boult	0		
Extras	(B 9, LB 7, W 5, NB 1)	22	(B 8, LB 1, W 1)	10
Total	**(99 overs; 447 mins)**	**354**	**(5 wkts dec; 76 overs; 319 mins)**	**287**

NEW ZEALAND

P.G.Fulton	c and b Finn	28	c Bell b Broad	5
H.D.Rutherford	c Bell b Finn	27	c Root b Swann	42
K.S.Williamson	lbw b Swann	13	lbw b Swann	3
L.R.P.L.Taylor	b Finn	6	b Swann	70
D.G.Brownlie	b Swann	2	c Bell b Finn	25
M.J.Guptill	b Swann	1	c Trott b Swann	3
*†B.B.McCullum	c Prior b Broad	20	c and b Broad	1
T.G.Southee	lbw b Broad	19	c Trott b Swann	38
D.A.J.Bracewell	c Bell b Swann	1	c Bell b Swann	19
N.Wagner	b Anderson	27	not out	0
T.A.Boult	not out	24	c Prior b Anderson	0
Extras	(LB 5, W 1)	6	(B 2, LB 11, W 1)	14
Total	**(43.4 overs; 211 mins)**	**174**	**(76.3 overs; 328 mins)**	**220**

NEW ZEALAND	O	M	R	W		O	M	R	W
Boult	22	4	57	5		2	1	2	0
Southee	26	6	76	2		15	4	51	0
Wagner	23	4	73	1		17	3	67	2
Bracewell	19	3	83	1	(5)	13	3	49	0
Williamson	9	0	49	1	(4)	24	4	68	3
Guptill						5	0	41	0

ENGLAND	O	M	R	W		O	M	R	W
Anderson	7.4	2	34	1		11.3	4	28	1
Broad	15	2	57	2		11	3	26	2
Finn	12	3	36	3	(4)	19	5	62	1
Swann	9	1	42	4	(3)	32	12	90	6
Root						3	2	1	0

FALL OF WICKETS

	E	NZ	E	NZ
Wkt	1st	1st	2nd	2nd
1st	11	55	72	21
2nd	67	62	206	40
3rd	67	72	214	65
4th	146	79	249	144
5th	270	81	268	153
6th	279	82	–	154
7th	286	119	–	162
8th	345	122	–	218
9th	354	122	–	220
10th	354	174	–	220

Umpires: S.J.Davis (*Australia*) (46) and M.Erasmus (*South Africa*) (18).
Referee: D.C.Boon (*Australia*) (18).

Test No. 2088/99 (E935/NZ384)

ENGLAND v AUSTRALIA (1st Test)

At Trent Bridge, Nottingham, on 10, 11, 12, 13, 14 July 2013.
Toss: England. Result: **ENGLAND** won by 14 runs.
Debut: Australia – A.C.Agar.

ENGLAND

*A.N.Cook	c Haddin b Pattinson	13	c Clarke b Agar		50
J.E.Root	b Siddle	30	c Haddin b Starc		5
I.J.L.Trott	b Siddle	48	lbw b Starc		0
K.P.Pietersen	c Clarke b Siddle	14	b Pattinson		64
I.R.Bell	c Watson b Siddle	25	c Haddin b Starc		109
J.M.Bairstow	b Starc	37	c Haddin b Agar		15
†M.J.Prior	c Hughes b Siddle	1	c Cowan b Siddle		31
S.C.J.Broad	c and b Pattinson	24	c Haddin b Pattinson		65
G.P.Swann	c Hughes b Pattinson	1	c Clarke b Siddle		9
S.T.Finn	c Haddin b Starc	0	not out		2
J.M.Anderson	not out	1	c Hughes b Siddle		0
Extras	(B 6, LB 5, W 8, NB 2)	21	(B 2, LB 13, W 1, NB 9)		25
Total	**(59 overs; 281 mins)**	**215**	**(149.5 overs; 660 mins)**		**375**

AUSTRALIA

S.R.Watson	c Root b Finn	13	lbw b Broad		46
C.J.L.Rogers	lbw b Anderson	16	c Bell b Anderson		52
E.J.M.Cowan	c Swann b Finn	0	c Trott b Root		14
*M.J.Clarke	b Anderson	0	c Prior b Broad		23
S.P.D.Smith	c Prior b Anderson	53	lbw b Swann		17
P.J.Hughes	not out	81	lbw b Swann		0
†B.J.Haddin	b Swann	1	c Prior b Anderson		71
P.M.Siddle	c Prior b Anderson	1	(10) c Cook b Anderson		11
M.A.Starc	c Prior b Anderson	0	c Cook b Anderson		1
J.L.Pattinson	lbw b Swann	2	(11) not out		25
A.C.Agar	c Swann b Broad	98	(8) c Cook b Anderson		14
Extras	(LB 15)	15	(B 11, LB 10, NB 1)		22
Total	**(64.5 overs; 294 mins)**	**280**	**(110.5 overs; 467 mins)**		**296**

AUSTRALIA	O	M	R	W		O	M	R	W
Pattinson	17	2	69	3		34	8	101	2
Starc	17	5	54	2		32	7	81	3
Siddle	14	4	50	5	(4)	33.5	12	85	3
Agar	7	1	24	0	(3)	35	9	82	2
Watson	4	2	7	0		15	11	11	0

ENGLAND	O	M	R	W		O	M	R	W
Anderson	24	2	85	5		31.5	11	73	5
Finn	15	0	80	2	(4)	10	3	37	0
Swann	19	4	60	2		44	10	105	2
Broad	6.5	0	40	1	(2)	23	7	54	2
Root						2	0	6	1

FALL OF WICKETS

	E	A	E	A
Wkt	1st	1st	2nd	2nd
1st	27	19	11	84
2nd	78	19	11	111
3rd	102	22	121	124
4th	124	53	131	161
5th	178	108	174	161
6th	180	113	218	164
7th	213	114	356	207
8th	213	114	371	211
9th	213	117	375	231
10th	215	280	375	296

Umpires: Alim Dar (*Pakistan*) (82) and H.D.P.K.Dharmasena (*Sri Lanka*) (16).
Referee: R.S.Madugalle (*Sri Lanka*) (142).   **Test No. 2089/327 (E936/A754)**

ENGLAND v AUSTRALIA (2nd Test)

At Lord's, London, on 18, 19, 20, 21 July 2013.
Toss: England. Result: **ENGLAND** won by 347 runs.
Debuts: None.

ENGLAND

*A.N.Cook	lbw b Watson	12		b Siddle	8
J.E.Root	lbw b Harris	6		c Smith b Harris	180
I.J.L.Trott	c Khawaja b Harris	58		b Siddle	0
K.P.Pietersen	c Haddin b Harris	2		c Rogers b Siddle	5
I.R.Bell	c Clarke b Smith	109	(6)	c Rogers b Smith	74
J.M.Bairstow	c and b Smith	67	(7)	c Haddin b Harris	20
†M.J.Prior	c Haddin b Smith	6	(8)	not out	1
T.T.Bresnan	c Haddin b Harris	7	(5)	c Rogers b Pattinson	38
J.M.Anderson	c Haddin b Harris	12			
S.C.J.Broad	c Haddin b Pattinson	33			
G.P.Swann	not out	28			
Extras	(LB 11, W 4, NB 6)	21		(B 15, LB 8)	23
Total	**(100.1 overs; 448 mins)**	**361**		**(7 wkts dec; 114.1 overs; 464 mins)**	**349**

AUSTRALIA

S.R.Watson	lbw b Bresnan	30		lbw b Anderson	20
C.J.L.Rogers	lbw b Swann	15		b Swann	6
U.T.Khawaja	c Pietersen b Swann	14		c Anderson b Root	54
P.J.Hughes	c Prior b Bresnan	1		lbw b Swann	1
*M.J.Clarke	lbw b Broad	28		c Cook b Root	51
S.P.D.Smith	c Bell b Swann	2		c Prior b Bresnan	1
†B.J.Haddin	c Trott b Swann	7		lbw b Swann	7
A.C.Agar	run out	2		c Prior b Bresnan	16
P.M.Siddle	c Swann b Anderson	2		b Anderson	18
J.L.Pattinson	not out	10		lbw b Swann	35
R.J.Harris	c Pietersen b Swann	10		not out	16
Extras	(B 4, LB 1, W 2)	7		(B 4, LB 5, W 1)	10
Total	**(53.3 overs; 226 mins)**	**128**		**(90.3 overs; 375 mins)**	**235**

AUSTRALIA	O	M	R	W		O	M	R	W
Pattinson	20.1	3	95	1	(4)	20	8	42	1
Harris	26	6	72	5	(1)	18.1	4	31	2
Watson	13	4	45	1	(2)	12	5	25	0
Siddle	22	6	76	0	(3)	21	6	65	3
Agar	13	2	44	0	(6)	29	5	98	0
Smith	6	1	18	3	(5)	14	0	65	1

ENGLAND	O	M	R	W		O	M	R	W
Anderson	14	8	25	1		18	2	55	2
Broad	11	3	26	1		21	4	54	0
Bresnan	7	1	28	2	(4)	14	8	30	2
Swann	21.3	5	44	5	(3)	30.3	5	78	4
Root						7	3	9	2

FALL OF WICKETS

	E	A	E	A
Wkt	1st	1st	2nd	2nd
1st	18	42	12	24
2nd	26	50	22	32
3rd	28	53	30	36
4th	127	69	129	134
5th	271	86	282	135
6th	274	91	344	136
7th	283	96	349	154
8th	289	104	–	162
9th	313	104	–	192
10th	361	128	–	235

Umpires: H.D.P.K.Dharmasena (*Sri Lanka*) (17) and M.Erasmus (*South Africa*) (19).
Referee: R.S.Madugalle (*Sri Lanka*) (143). **Test No. 2090/328 (E937/A755)**

ENGLAND v AUSTRALIA (3rd Test)

At Old Trafford, Manchester, on 1, 2, 3, 4, 5 August 2013.
Toss: Australia. Result: **MATCH DRAWN**.
Debuts: None.

AUSTRALIA

S.R.Watson	c Cook b Bresnan	19	(4) c Pietersen b Bresnan		18
C.J.L.Rogers	lbw b Swann	84	(1) c Prior b Broad		12
U.T.Khawaja	c Prior b Swann	1	b Swann		24
*M.J.Clarke	b Broad	187	(5) not out		30
S.P.D.Smith	c Bairstow b Swann	89	(6) run out		19
D.A.Warner	c Trott b Swann	5	(2) c Root b Bresnan		41
†B.J.Haddin	not out	65	c Broad b Anderson		8
P.M.Siddle	b Swann	1			
M.A.Starc	not out	66	(8) c Swann b Anderson		11
R.J.Harris			(9) not out		0
N.M.Lyon					
Extras	(LB 6, W 2, NB 2)	10	(B 4, LB 2, W 3)		9
Total	**(7 wkts dec; 146 overs; 649 mins)**	**527**	**(7 wkts dec; 36 overs; 176 mins)**		**172**

ENGLAND

*A.N.Cook	c Haddin b Starc	62	lbw b Harris		0
J.E.Root	c Haddin b Siddle	8	not out		13
T.T.Bresnan	c Haddin b Siddle	1			
I.J.L.Trott	c Clarke b Harris	5	(3) c Haddin b Harris		11
K.P.Pietersen	lbw b Starc	113	(4) c Haddin b Siddle		8
I.R.Bell	b Harris	60	(5) not out		4
J.M.Bairstow	c Watson b Starc	22			
†M.J.Prior	c Warner b Siddle	30			
S.C.J.Broad	c Haddin b Lyon	32			
G.P.Swann	c Haddin b Siddle	11			
J.M.Anderson	not out	3			
Extras	(B 3, LB 17, NB 1)	21	(W 1)		1
Total	**(139.3 overs; 598 mins)**	**368**	**(3 wkts; 20.3 overs; 95 mins)**		**37**

ENGLAND	O	M	R	W		O	M	R	W
Anderson	33	6	116	0		8	0	37	0
Broad	33	6	108	1		7	2	30	1
Bresnan	32	6	114	1	(4)	6	0	25	2
Swann	43	2	159	5	(3)	15	0	74	1
Root	4	0	18	0					
Trott	1	0	6	0					

FALL OF WICKETS

	A	E	A	E
Wkt	1st	1st	2nd	2nd
1st	76	47	23	0
2nd	82	49	74	15
3rd	129	64	99	27
4th	343	110	103	–
5th	365	225	133	–
6th	427	277	152	–
7th	430	280	172	–
8th	–	338	–	–
9th	–	353	–	–
10th	–	368	–	–

AUSTRALIA	O	M	R	W		O	M	R	W
Harris	31	9	82	2		7	3	13	2
Starc	27	5	76	3		4	2	6	0
Lyon	35	12	95	1	(4)	3	0	8	0
Watson	15	7	26	0	(3)	2	2	0	0
Siddle	29.3	7	63	4		3.3	0	8	1
Smith	2	0	6	0					
Clarke					(6)	1	0	2	0

Umpires: M.Erasmus (*South Africa*) (20) and A.L.Hill (*New Zealand*) (39).
Referee: R.S.Madugalle (*Sri Lanka*) (144). **Test No. 2091/329 (E938/A756)**

ENGLAND v AUSTRALIA (4th Test)

At Riverside Ground, Chester-le-Street, on 9, 10, 11, 12 August 2013.
Toss: England. Result: **ENGLAND** won by 74 runs.
Debuts: None.

ENGLAND

*A.N.Cook	lbw b Bird	51		c Haddin b Harris	22
J.E.Root	c Haddin b Watson	16		b Harris	2
I.J.L.Trott	c Khawaja b Lyon	49		c Haddin b Harris	23
K.P.Pietersen	c Haddin b Lyon	26		c Rogers b Lyon	44
I.R.Bell	c Harris b Lyon	6		b Harris	113
J.M.Bairstow	lbw b Lyon	14		c Haddin b Lyon	28
†M.J.Prior	lbw b Siddle	17	(8)	b Harris	0
T.T.Bresnan	not out	12	(7)	c and b Harris	45
S.C.J.Broad	c Warner b Harris	3		c Smith b Harris	13
G.P.Swann	c Lyon b Harris	13		not out	30
J.M.Anderson	b Bird	16		c Haddin b Lyon	0
Extras	(B 5, LB 1, W 3, NB 6)	15		(B 4, LB 5, W 1)	10
Total	**(92 overs; 399 mins)**	**238**		**(95.1 overs; 405 mins)**	**330**

AUSTRALIA

C.J.L.Rogers	c Prior b Swann	110	c Trott b Swann	49
D.A.Warner	b Broad	3	c Prior b Bresnan	71
U.T.Khawaja	c Prior b Broad	0	lbw b Swann	21
*M.J.Clarke	c Cook b Broad	6	b Broad	21
S.P.D.Smith	c Prior b Bresnan	17	b Broad	2
S.R.Watson	c Prior b Broad	68	lbw b Bresnan	2
†B.J.Haddin	lbw b Swann	13	lbw b Broad	4
P.M.Siddle	c Cook b Anderson	5	c Anderson b Broad	23
R.J.Harris	lbw b Broad	28	lbw b Broad	11
N.M.Lyon	lbw b Anderson	4	b Broad	8
J.M.Bird	not out	0	not out	1
Extras	(B 2, LB 11, W 1, NB 2)	16	(B 6, LB 5)	11
Total	**(89.3 overs; 410 mins)**	**270**	**(68.3 overs; 293 mins)**	**224**

AUSTRALIA	O	M	R	W	O	M	R	W
Harris	19	3	70	2	28	2	117	7
Bird	22	9	58	2	20.3	6	67	0
Watson	13	6	21	1	6.3	1	22	0
Siddle	18	6	41	1	17	4	59	0
Lyon	20	7	42	4	22.1	3	55	3
Smith					1	0	1	0

ENGLAND	O	M	R	W	O	M	R	W
Anderson	25	8	65	2	16	1	73	0
Broad	24.3	7	71	5	18.3	3	50	6
Bresnan	19	3	63	1	13	2	36	2
Swann	18	5	48	2	18	6	53	2
Trott	3	0	10	0				
Root					(5) 3	2	1	0

FALL OF WICKETS

	E	A	E	A
Wkt	1st	1st	2nd	2nd
1st	34	12	17	109
2nd	107	12	42	147
3rd	149	49	49	168
4th	153	76	155	174
5th	155	205	221	175
6th	189	224	251	179
7th	193	233	251	181
8th	198	245	275	199
9th	214	258	317	211
10th	238	270	330	224

Umpires: Alim Dar (*Pakistan*) (83) and A.L.Hill (*New Zealand*) (40).
Referee: R.S.Mahanama (*Sri Lanka*) (44).   **Test No. 2092/330 (E939/A757)**

ENGLAND v AUSTRALIA (5th Test)

At The Oval, London, on 21, 22, 23, 24 (*no play*), 25 August 2013.
Toss: Australia. Result: **MATCH DRAWN**.
Debuts: England – S.C.Kerrigan, C.R.Woakes; Australia – J.P.Faulkner.

AUSTRALIA

C.J.L.Rogers	c Trott b Swann	23	(1) c and b Anderson		12
D.A.Warner	c Prior b Anderson	6	(2) c Pietersen b Swann		26
S.R.Watson	c Pietersen b Broad	176	(5) not out		28
*M.J.Clarke	b Anderson	7	(6) c Swann b Broad		7
S.P.D.Smith	not out	138			
P.M.Siddle	b Anderson	23			
†B.J.Haddin	b Trott	30	(4) c Prior b Broad		0
J.P.Faulkner	c Trott b Woakes	23	(3) c Prior b Broad		22
M.A.Starc	b Swann	13	(8) not out		13
R.J.Harris	c and b Anderson	33	(7) b Broad		1
N.M.Lyon	not out	0			
Extras	(B 1, LB 12, W 2, NB 5)	20	(LB 2)		2
Total	**(9 wkts dec; 128.5 overs; 567 mins)**	**492**	**(6 wkts dec; 23 overs; 106 mins)**		**111**

ENGLAND

*A.N.Cook	c Haddin b Harris	25	lbw b Faulkner		34
J.E.Root	c Watson b Lyon	68	c Haddin b Harris		11
I.J.L.Trott	lbw b Starc	40	lbw b Faulkner		59
K.P.Pietersen	c Watson b Starc	50	c Warner b Harris		62
I.R.Bell	c Haddin b Faulkner	45	run out		17
C.R.Woakes	c Clarke b Harris	25	not out		17
†M.J.Prior	c Starc b Faulkner	47	not out		0
S.C.J.Broad	b Starc	9			
G.P.Swann	b Faulkner	34			
J.M.Anderson	c Haddin b Faulkner	4			
S.C.Kerrigan	not out	1			
Extras	(B 11, LB 10, W 5, NB 3)	29	(LB 4, NB 2)		6
Total	**(144.4 overs; 609 mins)**	**377**	**(5 wkts; 40 overs; 184 mins)**		**206**

ENGLAND	O	M	R	W		O	M	R	W
Anderson	29.5	4	95	4		6	1	27	1
Broad	31	4	128	1		10	2	43	4
Swann	33	4	95	2		7	0	39	1
Woakes	24	7	96	1					
Kerrigan	8	0	53	0					
Trott	3	0	12	1					

AUSTRALIA	O	M	R	W			O	M	R	W
Starc	33	5	92	3	(2)	7	0	48	0
Harris	28	10	64	2	(1)	5	0	21	0
Faulkner	19.4	3	51	4	(6)	8	1	47	2
Siddle	28	7	74	0	(3)	3	0	16	0
Lyon	28	8	59	1	(4)	10	0	44	0
Smith	8	3	16	0					
Clarke					(5)	2	0	4	0
Watson					(7)	5	0	22	0

FALL OF WICKETS

	A	E	A	E
Wkt	1st	1st	2nd	2nd
1st	11	68	34	22
2nd	118	118	44	86
3rd	144	176	50	163
4th	289	217	67	170
5th	320	269	83	206
6th	385	299	85	–
7th	422	315	–	–
8th	446	363	–	–
9th	491	368	–	–
10th	–	377	–	–

Umpires: Alim Dar (*Pakistan*) (84) and H.D.P.K.Dharmasena (*Sri Lanka*) (18).
Referee: R.S.Mahanama (*Sri Lanka*) (45). **Test No. 2093/331 (E940/A758)**

ENGLAND v AUSTRALIA 2013

ENGLAND – BATTING AND FIELDING

	M	I	NO	HS	Runs	Avge	100	50	Ct/St
I.R.Bell	5	10	1	113	562	62.44	3	2	2
K.P.Pietersen	5	10	–	113	388	38.80	1	3	5
J.E.Root	5	10	1	180	339	37.66	1	1	2
I.J.L.Trott	5	10	–	59	293	29.30	–	2	6
J.M.Bairstow	4	7	–	67	203	29.00	–	1	1
A.N.Cook	5	10	–	62	277	27.70	–	3	7
T.T.Bresnan	3	5	1	45	103	25.75	–	–	–
S.C.J.Broad	5	7	–	65	179	25.57	–	1	1
G.P.Swann	5	7	2	34	126	25.20	–	–	5
M.J.Prior	5	9	2	47	133	19.00	–	–	18
J.M.Anderson	5	7	2	16	36	7.20	–	–	4

Also batted (one Test each): S.T.Finn 0, 2*; S.C.Kerrigan 1*; C.R.Woakes 25, 17*.

ENGLAND – BOWLING

	O	M	R	W	Avge	Best	5wI	10wM
S.C.J.Broad	185.5	38	604	22	27.45	6-50	2	1
G.P.Swann	249	41	755	26	29.03	5-44	2	–
J.M.Anderson	205.4	43	651	22	29.59	5-73	2	1
T.T.Bresnan	91	20	296	10	29.60	2-25	–	–

Also bowled: S.T.Finn 25-3-117-2; S.C.Kerrigan 8-0-53-0; J.E.Root 16-5-34-3; I.J.L.Trott 7-0-28-1; C.R.Woakes 24-7-96-1.

AUSTRALIA – BATTING AND FIELDING

	M	I	NO	HS	Runs	Avge	100	50	Ct/St
M.J.Clarke	5	10	2	187	381	47.62	1	1	6
S.R.Watson	5	10	–	176	418	41.80	1	1	4
C.J.L.Rogers	5	9	–	110	367	40.77	1	2	4
S.P.D.Smith	5	10	1	138*	345	38.33	1	2	3
J.L.Pattinson	2	4	2	35	72	36.00	–	–	1
A.C.Agar	2	4	–	98	130	32.50	–	1	–
P.J.Hughes	2	4	1	81*	83	27.66	–	1	3
M.A.Starc	3	6	2	66*	104	26.00	–	1	–
D.A.Warner	3	6	–	71	138	23.00	–	1	3
B.J.Haddin	5	10	1	71	206	22.88	–	2	29
R.J.Harris	4	7	2	33	99	19.80	–	–	2
U.T.Khawaja	3	6	–	54	114	19.00	–	1	2
P.M.Siddle	5	8	–	23	84	10.50	–	–	–
N.M.Lyon	3	3	1	8	12	6.00	–	–	1

Also batted (one Test each): J.M.Bird 0*, 1*; E.J.M.Cowan 0, 14 (1 ct); J.P.Faulkner 23, 22.

AUSTRALIA – BOWLING

	O	M	R	W	Avge	Best	5wI	10wM
J.P.Faulkner	27.4	4	98	6	16.33	4- 51	–	–
R.J.Harris	162.1	37	470	24	19.58	7-117	2	–
P.M.Siddle	189.5	52	537	17	31.58	5- 50	1	–
M.A.Starc	120	24	357	11	32.45	3- 76	–	–
N.M.Lyon	118.1	30	303	9	33.66	4- 42	–	–
J.L.Pattinson	91.1	21	307	7	43.85	3- 69	–	–

Also bowled: A.C.Agar 84-17-248-2; J.M.Bird 42.3-15-125-2; M.C.Clarke 3-0-6-0; S.P.D.Smith 31-4-106-4; S.R.Watson 85.3-38-179-2.

ZIMBABWE v PAKISTAN (1st Test)

At Harare Sports Club, on 3, 4, 5, 6, 7 September 2013.
Toss: Zimbabwe. Result: **PAKISTAN** won by 221 runs.
Debut: Zimbabwe – Sikandar Raza.

PAKISTAN

Batsman	1st innings	R	2nd innings	R
Khurram Manzoor	lbw b Panyangara	11	lbw b Panyangara	5
Mohammad Hafeez	c Sibanda b Chatara	5	c Mawoyo b Chatara	16
Azhar Ali	c Sibanda b S.W.Masakadza	78	lbw b Panyangara	0
Younus Khan	b Panyangara	3	not out	200
*Misbah-ul-Haq	c Sibanda b Utseya	53	c Sibanda b S.W.Masakadza	52
Asad Shafiq	c Mawoyo b Utseya	4	b Chatara	15
†Adnan Akmal	b Chatara	18	run out	64
Abdur Rehman	lbw b S.W.Masakadza	7	lbw b Utseya	9
Saeed Ajmal	b Chatara	49	lbw b Utseya	1
Junaid Khan	c Mutumbami b Panyangara	17	b Utseya	8
Rahat Ali	not out	0	not out	35
Extras	(LB 3, W 1)		(B 11, LB 1, W 2)	14
Total	(90.1 overs; 377 mins)	249	(9 wkts dec; 149.3 overs; 647 mins)	419

ZIMBABWE

Batsman	1st innings	R	2nd innings	R
T.M.K.Mawoyo	c Akmal b Junaid	13	lbw b Ajmal	2
V.Sibanda	c Akmal b Junaid	31	lbw b Junaid	6
*H.Masakadza	b Ajmal	19	c Azhar b Junaid	1
Sikandar Raza	c Misbah b Ajmal	60	c Azhar b Rehman	24
M.N.Waller	c Hafeez b Ajmal	70	c Rahat b Rehman	17
E.Chigumbura	c Azhar b Ajmal	69	c Hafeez b Rehman	28
†R.Mutumbami	lbw b Ajmal	13	not out	16
P.Utseya	b Rahat	16	b Ajmal	0
S.W.Masakadza	lbw b Ajmal	14	lbw b Ajmal	0
T.Panyangara	not out	4	lbw b Rehman	6
T.L.Chatara	c Younus b Ajmal	0	lbw b Ajmal	13
Extras	(B 5, LB 11, W 2)	18	(B 1, LB 5, NB 1)	7
Total	(103.3 overs; 440 mins)	327	(46.4 overs; 184 mins)	120

ZIMBABWE	O	M	R	W		O	M	R	W
Chatara	22.1	6	64	3		33	7	99	2
Panyangara	20	2	71	3		30	14	42	2
S.W.Masakadza	22	8	40	2	(4)	34	4	100	1
Chigumbura	2	0	15	0					
Utseya	23	1	55	2	(3)	37.3	5	137	3
H.Masakadza	1	0	1	0	(5)	15	5	29	0

PAKISTAN	O	M	R	W		O	M	R	W
Junaid Khan	25	8	71	2		10	3	20	2
Rahat Ali	23	3	70	1		7	1	35	0
Abdur Rehman	19	5	56	0	(4)	13	5	36	4
Saeed Ajmal	32.3	4	95	7	(3)	16.4	5	23	4
Younus Khan	4	1	19	0					

FALL OF WICKETS

	P	Z	P	Z
Wkt	1st	1st	2nd	2nd
1st	13	25	17	13
2nd	21	68	21	14
3rd	27	68	23	19
4th	120	195	139	49
5th	132	212	169	58
6th	157	235	287	89
7th	173	278	309	90
8th	182	310	313	90
9th	249	327	331	101
10th	249	327	–	120

Umpires: S.J.Davis (*Australia*) (47) and R.E.J.Martinesz (*Sri Lanka*) (3).
Referee: J.Srinath (*India*) (25).   Test No. 2094/16 (Z92/P374)

ZIMBABWE v PAKISTAN (2nd Test)

At Harare Sports Club, on 10, 11, 12, 13, 14 September 2013.
Toss: Zimbabwe. Result: **ZIMBABWE** won by 24 runs.
Debuts: None.

ZIMBABWE

Batsman	1st innings		2nd innings	
T.M.K.Mawoyo	c Akmal b Junaid	0	lbw b Rehman	58
V.Sibanda	b Rahat	14	(6) c Akmal b Rahat	10
H.Masakadza	c Hafeez b Ajmal	75	lbw b Rahat	44
*B.R.M.Taylor	lbw b Rehman	51	(5) c Azhar b Rahat	27
M.N.Waller	c Akmal b Junaid	23	(7) c Manzoor b Ajmal	3
E.Chigumbura	b Rehman	15	(8) c Akmal b Junaid	3
†R.Mutumbami	c Akmal b Junaid	8	(9) c Rehman b Ajmal	29
P.Utseya	c Rahat b Junaid	22	(2) c Shafiq b Rahat	5
T.Panyangara	b Rahat	24	(4) c Azhar b Rehman	0
T.L.Chatara	lbw b Rehman	21	c Akmal b Rahat	1
B.V.Vitori	not out	19	not out	0
Extras	(B 7, LB 14, W 1)	22	(B 3, LB 11, W 5)	19
Total	(109.5 overs; 454 mins)	294	(89.5 overs; 370 mins)	199

PAKISTAN

Batsman	1st innings		2nd innings	
Khurram Manzoor	run out	51	c Waller b Utseya	54
Mohammad Hafeez	c Masakadza b Vitori	22	c Vitori b Chatara	16
Azhar Ali	lbw b Panyangara	7	b Chatara	0
Younus Khan	c Mawoyo b Panyangara	77	b Vitori	29
*Misbah-ul-Haq	c Masakadza b Vitori	33	not out	79
Asad Shafiq	b Chatara	10	c Mutumbami b Utseya	14
†Adnan Akmal	c Taylor b Vitori	6	lbw b Chatara	20
Abdur Rehman	lbw b Panyangara	0	c Mutumbami b Panyangara	16
Saeed Ajmal	c Mutumbami b Vitori	7	lbw b Chatara	2
Junaid Khan	b Vitori	3	c Waller b Chatara	1
Rahat Ali	not out	1	run out	1
Extras	(B 4, LB 6, W 2, NB 1)	13	(LB 2, W 4, NB 1)	7
Total	(104.5 overs; 442 mins)	230	(81 overs; 361 mins)	239

PAKISTAN	O	M	R	W		O	M	R	W
Junaid Khan	33	11	67	4		19	6	37	1
Rahat Ali	19	7	48	2		24.5	5	52	5
Younus Khan	3	0	7	0					
Saeed Ajmal	27	6	92	1	(3)	2	7	56	2
Abdur Rehman	23.5	6	47	3	(4)	24	5	40	2
Mohammad Hafeez	4	0	12	0					

ZIMBABWE	O	M	R	W		O	M	R	W
Panyangara	22	9	43	3		16	3	43	1
Vitori	26.5	8	61	5		22	5	69	1
Chatara	27	10	45	1		23	2	61	5
Masakadza	12	5	24	0	(5)	1	0	2	0
Utseya	12	0	41	0	(4)	19	2	62	2
Chigumbura	5	2	6	0					

FALL OF WICKETS

	Z	P	Z	P
Wkt	1st	1st	2nd	2nd
1st	0	29	13	30
2nd	31	62	117	46
3rd	141	96	121	90
4th	172	182	121	100
5th	176	211	136	133
6th	187	212	149	163
7th	203	212	156	197
8th	234	224	177	214
9th	248	229	199	238
10th	294	230	199	239

Umpires: S.J.Davis (*Australia*) (48) and R.E.J.Martinesz (*Sri Lanka*) (4).
Referee: J.Srinath (*India*) (26). **Test No. 2095/17 (Z93/P375)**

BANGLADESH v NEW ZEALAND (1st Test)

At Zahur Ahmed Chowdhury Stadium, Chittagong, on 9, 10, 11, 12, 13 October 2013.
Toss: New Zealand. Result: **MATCH DRAWN**.
Debuts: Bangladesh – Marshall Ayub; New Zealand – C.J.Anderson, I.S.Sodhi.

NEW ZEALAND

P.G.Fulton	c Mominul b Nasir	73	lbw b Gazi		59
H.D.Rutherford	c Razzak b Gazi	34	lbw b Nasir		32
K.S.Williamson	lbw b Shakib	114	c Anamul b Gazi		74
L.R.P.L.Taylor	c sub (Naeem Islam) b Razzak	28	not out		54
*B.B.McCullum	lbw b Razzak	21	b Gazi		22
B.P.Martin	c Rahim b Rubel	1			
C.J.Anderson	c Nasir b Razzak	1	(6) lbw b Gazi		8
†B.J.Watling	st Rahim b Mominul	103	(7) c Rahim b Gazi		0
D.A.J.Bracewell	b Gazi	29	(8) c Shakib b Gazi		0
I.S.Sodhi	lbw b Shakib	1	(9) not out		22
T.A.Boult	not out	52			
Extras	(B 4, LB 6, NB 2)	12	(B 11, LB 4, NB 1)		16
Total	**(157.1 overs; 611 mins)**	**469**	**(7 wkts dec; 90 overs; 355 mins)**		**287**

BANGLADESH

Tamim Iqbal	c Williamson b Boult	0	c Williamson b Martin		46
Anamul Haque	lbw b Bracewell	3	c Anderson b Martin		18
Marshall Ayub	c Watling b Anderson	25	lbw b Sodhi		31
Mominul Haque	lbw b Anderson	181	not out		22
Shakib Al Hasan	c Watling b Williamson	19	not out		50
*†Mushfiqur Rahim	c Taylor b Bracewell	67			
Nasir Hossain	c Williamson b Sodhi	46			
Sohag Gazi	not out	101			
Abdur Razzak	lbw b Boult	7			
Robiul Islam	c Taylor b Bracewell	33			
Rubel Hossain	c Taylor b Sodhi	4			
Extras	(B 5, LB 8, W 1, NB 1)	15	(B 2, NB 4)		6
Total	**(148.5 overs; 637 mins)**	**501**	**(3 wkts; 48.2 overs; 177 mins)**		**173**

BANGLADESH	O	M	R	W		O	M	R	W
Robiul Islam	13	3	23	0	(6)	4	1	9	0
Rubel Hossain	20	2	77	1		6	0	21	0
Abdur Razzak	55	10	147	3	(1)	32	5	116	0
Sohag Gazi	32	6	79	2	(3)	26	4	77	6
Shakib Al Hasan	24	5	89	2	(4)	9	1	19	0
Marshall Ayub	2	0	15	0					
Nasir Hossain	5	1	19	1	(5)	9	4	20	1
Mominul Haque	6.1	0	10	1	(7)	4	0	10	0

NEW ZEALAND	O	M	R	W		O	M	R	W
Boult	24	9	50	2		4	1	9	0
Bracewell	25	2	96	3		5	0	14	0
Martin	27	3	113	0	(5)	16	4	62	2
Sodhi	28.5	3	112	2	(6)	10.2	1	57	1
Anderson	17	4	34	2	(3)	2	2	0	0
Williamson	27	4	83	1	(4)	10	3	24	0
Taylor						1	0	5	0

FALL OF WICKETS

	NZ	B	NZ	B
Wkt	1st	1st	2nd	2nd
1st	57	1	48	39
2nd	183	8	149	99
3rd	244	134	200	101
4th	276	180	250	–
5th	280	301	260	–
6th	282	301	260	–
7th	282	371	260	–
8th	339	387	–	–
9th	342	492	–	–
10th	469	501	–	–

Umpires: B.N.J.Oxenford (*Australia*) (14) and S.Ravi (*India*) (1).
Referee: J.Srinath (*India*) (27). **Test No. 2096/10 (B80/NZ385)**

BANGLADESH v NEW ZEALAND (2nd Test)

At Shere Bangla National Stadium, Mirpur, on 21, 22, 23, 24, 25 (*no play*) October 2013.
Toss: Bangladesh. Result: **MATCH DRAWN**.
Debut: Bangladesh – Al-Amin Hossain.

BANGLADESH

Tamim Iqbal	c Williamson b Wagner	95	c Taylor b Williamson		70
Anamul Haque	c Williamson b Boult	7	c Fulton b Wagner		22
Marshall Ayub	b Wagner	41	c Taylor b Wagner		9
Mominul Haque	c Watling b Anderson	47	not out		126
Shakib Al Hasan	lbw b Sodhi	20	not out		32
*†Mushfiqur Rahim	c Fulton b Wagner	18			
Nasir Hossain	c Taylor b Sodhi	19			
Sohag Gazi	c Williamson b Wagner	14			
Abdur Razzak	b Sodhi	13			
Rubel Hossain	c Watling b Wagner	4			
Al-Amin Hossain	not out	0			
Extras	(B 2, LB 1, W 1)	4	(B 8, LB 1, NB 1)		10
Total	**(74.5 overs; 323 mins)**	**282**	**(3 wkts; 89 overs; 380 mins)**		**269**

NEW ZEALAND

P.G.Fulton	lbw b Shakib	14
H.D.Rutherford	c Mominul b Shakib	13
K.S.Williamson	c Iqbal b Razzak	62
L.R.P.L.Taylor	c Nasir b Shakib	53
*B.B.McCullum	c Rubel b Shakib	11
C.J.Anderson	c Gazi b Al-Amin	116
†B.J.Watling	not out	70
D.A.J.Bracewell	c Rahim b Shakib	17
N.Wagner	c Ayub b Nasir	8
I.S.Sodhi	run out	58
T.A.Boult	lbw b Razzak	4
Extras	(B 4, LB 4, W 2, NB 1)	11
Total	**(140 overs; 559 mins)**	**437**

NEW ZEALAND	O	M	R	W		O	M	R	W
Boult	16	2	55	1		16	2	62	0
Bracewell	14	1	57	0		14	2	47	0
Wagner	19	5	64	5		18	4	52	2
Sodhi	18.5	3	59	3		14	2	37	0
Williamson	4	0	30	0	(6)	18	4	44	1
Anderson	3	0	14	1	(5)	9	2	18	0

BANGLADESH	O	M	R	W
Al-Amin Hossain	16	3	58	1
Sohag Gazi	34	8	77	0
Shakib Al Hasan	43	13	103	5
Abdur Razzak	23	1	96	2
Rubel Hossain	18	1	81	0
Nasir Hossain	3	1	7	1
Mominul Haque	3	0	7	0

FALL OF WICKETS			
	B	NZ	B
Wkt	1st	1st	2nd
1st	23	31	39
2nd	90	32	55
3rd	166	101	212
4th	208	127	–
5th	228	267	–
6th	246	287	–
7th	252	318	–
8th	266	335	–
9th	274	428	–
10th	282	437	–

Umpires: R.K.Illingworth (*England*) (5) and B.N.J.Oxenford (*Australia*) (15).
Referee: J.Srinath (*India*) (28). **Test No. 2097/11 (B81/NZ386)**
K.S.Williamson retired hurt at 76-2 and resumed at 101-3.

PAKISTAN v SOUTH AFRICA (1st Test)

At Sheikh Zayed Stadium, Abu Dhabi, on 14, 15, 16, 17 October 2013.
Toss: South Africa. Result: **PAKISTAN** won by seven wickets.
Debuts: Pakistan – Shan Masood, Zulfiqar Babar.

SOUTH AFRICA

A.N.Petersen	c Masood b Irfan	3	(2) c Akmal b Irfan		17
*G.C.Smith	c Akmal b Irfan	15	(1) st Akmal b Ajmal		32
H.M.Amla	c Younus b Irfan	118	c Akmal b Babar		10
J.H.Kallis	c Akmal b Junaid	5	lbw b Junaid		0
†A.B.de Villiers	run out	19	c Masood b Junaid		90
J.P.Duminy	c Shafiq b Babar	57	(7) lbw b Junaid		0
F.du Plessis	c Shafiq b Babar	1	(8) c and b Ajmal		9
R.J.Peterson	b Babar	5	(9) not out		47
V.D.Philander	lbw b Ajmal	3	(10) c Akmal b Ajmal		10
D.W.Steyn	st Akmal b Ajmal	15	(6) b Babar		7
M.Morkel	not out	2	c and b Ajmal		0
Extras	(B 1, LB 4, NB 1)	6	(B 4, LB 4, NB 2)		10
Total	**(93.1 overs)**	**249**	**(82.4 overs)**		**232**

PAKISTAN

Khurram Manzoor	c Kallis b Philander	146	c de Villiers b Philander		4
Shan Masood	lbw b Duminy	75	c de Villiers b Philander		0
Azhar Ali	c de Villiers b Philander	11	c Kallis b Steyn		3
Younus Khan	c Petersen b Morkel	1	not out		9
*Misbah-ul-Haq	lbw b Steyn	100	not out		28
Asad Shafiq	c Petersen b Duminy	54			
†Adnan Akmal	b Steyn	32			
Saeed Ajmal	c de Villiers b Philander	13			
Zulfiqar Babar	run out	2			
Junaid Khan	c Morkel b Steyn	3			
Mohammad Irfan	not out	0			
Extras	(LB 4, NB 1)	5	(LB 1)		1
Total	**(138.4 overs)**	**442**	**(3 wkts; 13.5 overs)**		**45**

PAKISTAN	O	M	R	W	O	M	R	W	FALL OF WICKETS				
										SA	P	SA	P
Mohammad Irfan	18.2	4	44	3	13	1	42	1	Wkt	1st	1st	2nd	2nd
Junaid Khan	18.4	2	52	1	18	1	57	3	1st	6	135	38	4
Zulfiqar Babar	27	2	89	3	(4) 19	6	51	2	2nd	19	173	57	4
Saeed Ajmal	29.1	6	59	2	(3) 32.4	7	74	4	3rd	43	178	58	7
									4th	104	290	72	–
SOUTH AFRICA									5th	199	372	104	–
Steyn	28.4	5	88	3	5	3	7	1	6th	205	394	109	–
Philander	26	5	84	3	5	1	11	2	7th	217	423	133	–
Morkel	23	6	35	1	2	0	12	0	8th	222	429	190	–
Kallis	13	2	44	0					9th	245	437	232	–
Peterson	27	2	111	0	(4) 1.5	0	14	0	10th	249	442	232	–
Duminy	19	1	68	2									
Du Plessis	2	0	8	0									

Umpires: P.R.Reiffel (*Australia*) (5) and R.J.Tucker (*Australia*) (26).
Referee: D.C.Boon (*Australia*) (19).   Test No. 2098/22 (P376/SA378)

PAKISTAN v SOUTH AFRICA (2nd Test)

At Dubai International Cricket Stadium, on 23, 24, 25, 26 October 2013.
Toss: Pakistan. Result: **SOUTH AFRICA** won by an innings and 92 runs.
Debuts: None.

PAKISTAN

Khurram Manzoor	c du Plessis b Steyn	0	(2)	c Kallis b Philander		0
Shan Masood	b Tahir	21	(1)	lbw b Steyn		0
Azhar Ali	lbw b Morkel	19		lbw b Duminy		19
Younus Khan	c de Villiers b Steyn	10		b Tahir		36
*Misbah-ul-Haq	lbw b Tahir	2		c Kallis b Elgar		88
Asad Shafiq	b Tahir	10		st de Villiers b Duminy		130
†Adnan Akmal	b Tahir	0		lbw b Tahir		5
Saeed Ajmal	run out	0		lbw b Tahir		9
Zulfiqar Babar	not out	25		absent hurt		–
Mohammad Irfan	b Tahir	0	(9)	b Duminy		14
Junaid Khan	b Steyn	4	(10)	not out		2
Extras	(B 5, LB 3)	8		(B 10, LB 5, W 1, NB 2, Pen 5)		23
Total	**(36.4 overs)**	**99**		**(135.1 overs)**		**326**

SOUTH AFRICA

A.N.Petersen	lbw b Babar	26
*G.C.Smith	c Younus b Ajmal	234
D.Elgar	c Ali b Ajmal	23
J.H.Kallis	lbw b Ajmal	7
D.W.Steyn	b Irfan	7
†A.B.de Villiers	c Akmal b Irfan	164
J.P.Duminy	b Irfan	7
F.du Plessis	not out	17
V.D.Philander	b Ajmal	8
M.Morkel	c Younus b Ajmal	7
Imran Tahir	c Misbah b Ajmal	2
Extras	(B 5, LB 8, W 2)	15
Total	**(163.1 overs)**	**517**

SOUTH AFRICA	O	M	R	W	O	M	R	W
Steyn	13.4	2	38	3	22	9	48	1
Philander	5	2	9	0	19	7	34	1
Morkel	5	1	12	1	22	7	47	0
Imran Tahir	13	3	32	5	42	14	98	3
Kallis					7	3	9	0
Duminy					21.1	3	67	3
Elgar					2	0	3	1

PAKISTAN	O	M	R	W
Mohammad Irfan	34.3	5	102	3
Junaid Khan	31.3	2	105	0
Saeed Ajmal	55.5	8	151	6
Zulfiqar Babar	36.2	2	124	1
Azhar Ali	5	0	22	0

FALL OF WICKETS

		P	SA	P
Wkt	1st	1st	2nd	
1st	0	37	0	
2nd	38	91	2	
3rd	52	119	48	
4th	60	134	70	
5th	60	472	267	
6th	60	478	278	
7th	64	486	301	
8th	76	505	323	
9th	76	515	326	
10th	99	517	–	

Umpires: I.J.Gould (*England*) (35) and R.J.Tucker (*Australia*) (27).
Referee: D.C.Boon (*Australia*) (20).   Test No. 2099/23 (P377/SA379)

INDIA v WEST INDIES (1st Test)

At Eden Gardens, Kolkata, on 6, 7, 8 November 2013.
Toss: West Indies. Result: **INDIA** won by an innings and 51 runs.
Debuts: India – Mohammed Shami, R.G.Sharma; West Indies – S.S.Cottrell.

WEST INDIES

C.H.Gayle	c Vijay b Kumar	18	c Kohli b Kumar	33
K.O.A.Powell	c Kumar b Shami	28	lbw b Ashwin	36
D.M.Bravo	run out	23	c Sharma b Ashwin	37
M.N.Samuels	b Shami	65	lbw b Shami	4
S.Chanderpaul	b Ashwin	36	not out	31
†D.Ramdin	b Shami	4	c Vijay b Shami	1
*D.J.G.Sammy	c Kumar b Ojha	16	b Shami	8
S.Shillingford	lbw b Tendulkar	5	b Shami	0
V.Permaul	c and b Ashwin	14	run out	0
T.L.Best	not out	14	c Ojha b Ashwin	3
S.S.Cottrell	b Shami	0	b Shami	5
Extras	(B 4, LB 7)	11	(LB 10)	10
Total	**(78 overs; 296 mins)**	**234**	**(54.1 overs; 225 mins)**	**168**

INDIA

S.Dhawan	b Shillingford	23
M.Vijay	st Ramdin b Shillingford	26
C.A.Pujara	c Ramdin b Cottrell	17
S.R.Tendulkar	lbw b Shillingford	10
V.Kohli	c Powell b Shillingford	3
R.G.Sharma	lbw b Permaul	177
*†M.S.Dhoni	c Ramdin b Best	42
R.Ashwin	b Shillingford	124
B.Kumar	c Gayle b Shillingford	12
Mohammed Shami	st Ramdin b Permaul	1
P.P.Ojha	not out	2
Extras	(B 4, LB 8, W 1, NB 3)	16
Total	**(129.4 overs; 533 mins)**	**453**

INDIA	O	M	R	W	O	M	R	W
Kumar	14	6	33	1	6	1	20	1
Mohammed Shami	17	2	71	4	13.1	0	47	5
Ashwin	21	9	52	2	19	2	46	3
Ojha	24	6	62	1	13	3	27	0
Tendulkar	2	1	5	1	3	0	18	0

WEST INDIES	O	M	R	W
Best	17	0	71	1
Cottrell	18	3	72	1
Shillingford	55	9	167	6
Permaul	23.4	2	67	2
Sammy	12	1	52	0
Samuels	4	0	12	0

FALL OF WICKETS

	WI	I	WI
Wkt	1st	1st	2nd
1st	34	42	33
2nd	47	57	101
3rd	138	79	110
4th	138	82	120
5th	143	83	215
6th	172	156	152
7th	192	436	152
8th	211	444	152
9th	233	451	159
10th	234	453	168

Umpires: R.A.Kettleborough (*England*) (15) and N.J.Llong (*England*) (19).
Referee: A.J.Pycroft (*Zimbabwe*) (23).   **Test No. 2100/89 (I473/WI491)**

INDIA v WEST INDIES (2nd Test)

At Wankhede Stadium, Mumbai, on 14, 15, 16 November 2013.
Toss: India. Result: **INDIA** won by an innings and 126 runs.
Debuts: None.

WEST INDIES

Batsman	First innings	Runs	Second innings	Runs
C.H.Gayle	c Sharma b Shami	11	c Dhoni b Ojha	35
K.O.A.Powell	c Dhawan b Ojha	48	c Shami b Ashwin	9
D.M.Bravo	c Dhoni b Ashwin	29	(4) c Vijay b Ashwin	11
M.N.Samuels	c Vijay b Ojha	19	(5) st Dhoni b Ojha	11
S.Chanderpaul	c Ashwin b Kumar	25	(6) lbw b Ashwin	41
N.Deonarine	c Vijay b Ashwin	21	(7) c and b Ojha	0
†D.Ramdin	not out	12	(8) not out	53
*D.J.G.Sammy	c Sharma b Ashwin	0	(9) lbw b Ojha	1
S.Shillingford	lbw b Ojha	0	(10) lbw b Ashwin	8
T.L.Best	c Dhoni b Ojha	0	(3) lbw b Ojha	9
S.T.Gabriel	c Dhoni b Ojha	1	b Shami	0
Extras	(B 8, LB 8)	16	(B 4, LB 5)	9
Total	**(55.2 overs; 232 mins)**	**182**	**(47 overs; 186 mins)**	**187**

INDIA

Batsman	Dismissal	Runs
M.Vijay	c Sammy b Shillingford	43
S.Dhawan	c Chanderpaul b Shillingford	33
C.A.Pujara	c and b Shillingford	113
S.R.Tendulkar	c Sammy b Deonarine	74
V.Kohli	c Sammy b Shillingford	57
R.G.Sharma	not out	111
*†M.S.Dhoni	c Sammy b Best	4
R.Ashwin	c and b Gabriel	30
B.Kumar	c Sammy b Shillingford	4
P.P.Ojha	run out	0
Mohammed Shami	c Best b Deonarine	11
Extras	(B 8, LB 2, W 2, NB 3)	15
Total	**(108 overs; 483 mins)**	**495**

INDIA	O	M	R	W	O	M	R	W
Kumar	17	2	45	1	3	0	4	0
Mohammed Shami	12	2	36	1	7	0	28	1
Ashwin	15	2	45	3	17	4	89	4
Ojha	11.2	2	40	5	18	6	49	5
Tendulkar					2	0	8	0

WEST INDIES	O	M	R	W
Sammy	9	1	41	0
Gabriel	16	0	85	1
Shillingford	43	6	179	5
Best	18	0	93	1
Samuels	11	0	42	0
Deonarine	11	0	45	2

FALL OF WICKETS

	WI	I	WI
Wkt	1st	1st	2nd
1st	25	77	15
2nd	86	77	28
3rd	97	221	43
4th	140	315	74
5th	148	354	87
6th	162	365	89
7th	162	409	157
8th	162	414	162
9th	172	415	185
10th	182	495	187

Umpires: R.A.Kettleborough (*England*) (16) and N.J.Llong (*England*) (20).
Referee: A.J.Pycroft (*Zimbabwe*) (24). Test No. 2101/90 (I474/WI492)

AUSTRALIA v ENGLAND (1st Test)

At Woolloongabba, Brisbane, on 21, 22, 23, 24 November 2013.
Toss: Australia. Result: **AUSTRALIA** won by 381 runs.
Debut: Australia – G.J.Bailey.

AUSTRALIA

C.J.L.Rogers	c Bell b Broad	1	c Carberry b Broad		16
D.A.Warner	c Pietersen b Broad	49	c Prior b Broad		124
S.R.Watson	c Swann b Broad	22	c Broad b Tremlett		6
*M.J.Clarke	c Bell b Broad	1	b Swann		113
S.P.D.Smith	c Cook b Tremlett	31	c Prior b Tremlett		0
G.J.Bailey	c Cook b Anderson	3	b Swann		34
†B.J.Haddin	run out	94	c Anderson b Tremlett		53
M.G.Johnson	b Broad	64	not out		39
P.M.Siddle	c Cook b Anderson	7	not out		4
R.J.Harris	c Prior b Broad	9			
N.M.Lyon	not out	1			
Extras	(LB 11, W 1, NB 1)	13	(B 4, LB 8)		12
Total	**(97.1 overs; 416 mins)**	**295**	**(7 wkts dec; 94 overs; 420 mins)**		**401**

ENGLAND

*A.N.Cook	c Haddin b Harris	13	c Haddin b Lyon		65
M.A.Carberry	c Watson b Johnson	40	b Harris		0
I.J.L.Trott	c Haddin b Johnson	10	c Lyon b Johnson		9
K.P.Pietersen	c Bailey b Harris	18	c sub (C.J.M.Sabburg) b Johnson		26
I.R.Bell	c Smith b Lyon	5	c Haddin b Siddle		32
J.E.Root	c Smith b Johnson	2	not out		26
†M.J.Prior	c Smith b Lyon	0	c Warner b Lyon		4
S.C.J.Broad	c Rogers b Siddle	32	c Haddin b Johnson		4
G.P.Swann	c Bailey b Johnson	0	c Smith b Johnson		0
C.T.Tremlett	c Lyon b Harris	8	c Bailey b Harris		7
J.M.Anderson	not out	2	c and b Johnson		2
Extras	(B 4, LB 2)	6	(LB 2, W 1, NB 1)		4
Total	**(52.4 overs; 246 mins)**	**136**	**(81.1 overs; 326 mins)**		**179**

ENGLAND	O	M	R	W	O	M	R	W	FALL OF WICKETS				
										A	E	A	E
Anderson	25.1	5	67	2	19	2	73	0	Wkt	1st	1st	2nd	2nd
Broad	24	3	81	6	16	4	55	2	1st	12	28	67	1
Tremlett	19	3	51	1	17	2	69	3	2nd	71	55	75	10
Swann	26	4	80	0	27	2	135	2	3rd	73	82	233	72
Root	3	1	5	0	15	2	57	0	4th	83	87	242	130
									5th	100	87	294	142
AUSTRALIA									6th	132	87	305	146
Harris	15	5	28	3	19	4	49	2	7th	246	89	395	151
Johnson	17	2	61	4	21.1	7	42	5	8th	265	91	–	151
Siddle	11.4	3	24	1	15	3	25	1	9th	282	110	–	172
Lyon	9	4	17	2	20	6	46	2	10th	295	136	–	179
Smith					4	1	15	0					
Watson					2	2	0	0					

Umpires: Alim Dar (*Pakistan*) (85) and H.D.P.K.Dharmasena (*Sri Lanka*) (19).
Referee: J.J.Crowe (*New Zealand*) (63).   Test No. 2102/332 (A759/E941)

AUSTRALIA v ENGLAND (2nd Test)

At Adelaide Oval, on 5, 6, 7, 8, 9 December 2013.
Toss: Australia. Result: **AUSTRALIA** won by 218 runs.
Debut: England – B.A.Stokes.

AUSTRALIA

C.J.L.Rogers	c Prior b Swann	72	c Prior b Anderson	2
D.A.Warner	c Carberry b Broad	29	not out	83
S.R.Watson	c and b Anderson	51	c Carberry b Anderson	0
*M.J.Clarke	c Anderson b Stokes	148	b Panesar	22
S.P.D.Smith	b Panesar	6	not out	23
G.J.Bailey	c Swann b Broad	53		
†B.J.Haddin	c Prior b Broad	118		
M.G.Johnson	c Broad b Swann	5		
P.M.Siddle	c Prior b Stokes	2		
R.J.Harris	not out	55		
N.M.Lyon	not out	17		
Extras	(B 8, LB 1, W 1, NB 4)	14	(B 1, LB 1)	2
Total	**(9 wkts dec; 158 overs; 634 mins)**	**570**	**(3 wkts dec; 39 overs; 163 mins)**	**132**

ENGLAND

*A.N.Cook	b Johnson	3	c Harris b Johnson	1
M.A.Carberry	c Warner b Watson	60	c Lyon b Siddle	14
J.E.Root	c Rogers b Lyon	15	c Haddin b Lyon	87
K.P.Pietersen	c Bailey b Siddle	4	b Siddle	53
I.R.Bell	not out	72	c Johnson b Smith	6
B.A.Stokes	lbw b Johnson	1	c Clarke b Harris	28
†M.J.Prior	c Haddin b Johnson	0	c Harris b Siddle	69
S.C.J.Broad	b Johnson	0	c Lyon b Siddle	29
G.P.Swann	c Clarke b Johnson	7	c Clarke b Harris	6
J.M.Anderson	b Johnson	0	not out	13
M.S.Panesar	b Johnson	2	c Rogers b Harris	0
Extras	(LB 3, W 2, NB 3)	8	(LB 1, W 4, NB 1)	6
Total	**(68.2 overs; 308 mins)**	**172**	**(101.4 overs; 439 mins)**	**312**

ENGLAND	O	M	R	W		O	M	R	W
Anderson	30	10	85	1		7	1	19	2
Broad	30	3	98	3		6	0	19	0
Swann	36	4	151	2		9	3	31	0
Panesar	44	7	157	1	(5) 10	0	41	1
Stokes	18	2	70	2	(4) 7	3	20	0

AUSTRALIA	O	M	R	W		O	M	R	W
Johnson	17.2	8	40	7	(2) 24	8	73	1
Harris	14	8	31	0	(1) 19.4	3	54	3
Lyon	20	5	64	1	(4) 26	7	78	1
Siddle	14	4	34	1	(3) 19	4	57	4
Watson	3	3	0	1		6	3	6	0
Smith						7	0	43	1

FALL OF WICKETS

	A	E	A	E
Wkt	1st	1st	2nd	2nd
1st	34	9	4	1
2nd	155	57	4	20
3rd	155	66	65	131
4th	174	111	–	143
5th	257	117	–	171
6th	457	117	–	210
7th	474	117	–	255
8th	483	135	–	293
9th	529	135	–	301
10th	–	172	–	312

Umpires: H.D.P.K.Dharmasena (*Sri Lanka*) (20) and M.Erasmus (*South Africa*) (21).
Referee: J.J.Crowe (*New Zealand*) (64).   **Test No. 2103/333 (A760/E942)**

AUSTRALIA v ENGLAND (3rd Test)

At W.A.C.A. Ground, Perth, on 13, 14, 15, 16, 17 December 2013.
Toss: Australia. Result: **AUSTRALIA** won by 150 runs.
Debuts: None.

AUSTRALIA

C.J.L.Rogers	run out	11	c Carberry b Bresnan	54
D.A.Warner	c Carberry b Swann	60	c Stokes b Swann	112
S.R.Watson	c Swann b Broad	18	run out	103
*M.J.Clarke	c Cook b Swann	24	b Stokes	23
S.P.D.Smith	c Prior b Anderson	111	c sub (J.M.Bairstow) b Stokes	15
G.J.Bailey	c Pietersen b Broad	7	not out	39
†B.J.Haddin	c Anderson b Stokes	55	c Swann b Bresnan	5
M.G.Johnson	c Prior b Broad	39	not out	0
P.M.Siddle	c Prior b Bresnan	21		
R.J.Harris	c Root b Anderson	12		
N.M.Lyon	not out	17		
Extras	(LB 6, W 3, NB 1)	10	(B 8, LB 5, W 5)	18
Total	**(103.3 overs; 469 mins)**	**385**	**(6 wkts dec; 87 overs; 347 mins)**	**369**

ENGLAND

*A.N.Cook	c Warner b Lyon	72	b Harris	0
M.A.Carberry	b Harris	43	lbw b Watson	31
J.E.Root	c Haddin b Watson	4	c Haddin b Johnson	19
K.P.Pietersen	c Johnson b Siddle	19	c Harris b Lyon	45
I.R.Bell	lbw b Harris	15	c Haddin b Siddle	60
B.A.Stokes	c Haddin b Johnson	18	c Haddin b Lyon	120
†M.J.Prior	c Haddin b Siddle	8	c Haddin b Johnson	26
T.T.Bresnan	c Haddin b Harris	21	c Rogers b Johnson	12
S.C.J.Broad	lbw b Johnson	5	(10) not out	2
G.P.Swann	not out	19	(9) c Smith b Lyon	4
J.M.Anderson	c Bailey b Siddle	2	c Bailey b Johnson	2
Extras	(B 11, LB 7, W 5, NB 2)	25	(B 13, LB 13, W 6)	32
Total	**(88 overs; 394 mins)**	**251**	**(103.2 overs; 452 mins)**	**353**

ENGLAND	O	M	R	W	O	M	R	W		FALL OF WICKETS				
Anderson	23	5	60	2	19	5	105	2			A	E	A	E
Broad	22	2	100	3						Wkt	1st	1st	2nd	2nd
Bresnan	23.3	4	81	1	(2) 14	3	53	2		1st	13	85	157	0
Stokes	17	1	63	1	(3) 18	1	82	2		2nd	52	90	183	62
Swann	17	0	71	2	(4) 27	8	92	1		3rd	106	136	223	76
Root	1	0	4	0	(5) 9	1	24	0		4th	129	146	301	121
										5th	143	190	331	220
AUSTRALIA										6th	267	198	340	296
Harris	22	10	48	3	19	2	73	1		7th	326	207	–	336
Johnson	22	7	62	2	25.2	6	78	4		8th	338	229	–	347
Watson	12	3	48	1	(5) 11	1	39	1		9th	354	233	–	349
Siddle	16	5	36	3	26	11	67	1		10th	385	251	–	353
Lyon	16	6	39	1	(3) 22	5	70	3						

Umpires: B.F.Bowden (*New Zealand*) (76) and M.Erasmus (*South Africa*) (22).
Referee: J.J.Crowe (*New Zealand*) (65).   **Test No. 2104/334 (A761/E943)**

44

AUSTRALIA v ENGLAND (4th Test)

At Melbourne Cricket Ground, on 26, 27, 28, 29 December 2013.
Toss: Australia. Result: **AUSTRALIA** won by eight wickets.
Debuts: None.

ENGLAND

*A.N.Cook	c Clarke b Siddle	27	lbw b Johnson		51
M.A.Carberry	b Watson	38	lbw b Siddle		12
J.E.Root	c Haddin b Harris	24	run out		15
K.P.Pietersen	b Johnson	71	c Harris b Lyon		49
I.R.Bell	c Haddin b Harris	27	c Johnson b Lyon		0
B.A.Stokes	c Watson b Johnson	14	c Smith b Lyon		19
†J.M.Bairstow	b Johnson	10	c Haddin b Johnson		21
T.T.Bresnan	c Bailey b Johnson	1	b Lyon		0
S.C.J.Broad	lbw b Johnson	11	c Clarke b Lyon		0
J.M.Anderson	not out	11	not out		1
M.S.Panesar	b Lyon	2	lbw b Johnson		0
Extras	(B 10, LB 7, W 1, NB 1)		(B 5, LB 6)		11
Total	**(100 overs; 435 mins)**	**255**	**(61 overs; 284 mins)**		**179**

AUSTRALIA

C.J.L.Rogers	c Pietersen b Bresnan	61	c Bairstow b Panesar		116
D.A.Warner	c Bairstow b Anderson	9	c Bairstow b Stokes		25
S.R.Watson	c Bairstow b Stokes	10	not out		83
*M.J.Clarke	b Anderson	10	not out		6
S.P.D.Smith	c Bell b Broad	19			
G.J.Bailey	c Bairstow b Anderson	0			
†B.J.Haddin	c Bairstow b Anderson	65			
M.G.Johnson	c Anderson b Bresnan	2			
R.J.Harris	c Root b Broad	6			
P.M.Siddle	c Bresnan b Broad	0			
N.M.Lyon	not out	18			
Extras	(LB 4)	4	(NB 1)		1
Total	**(82.2 overs; 360 mins)**	**204**	**(2 wkts; 51.5 overs; 232 mins)**		**231**

AUSTRALIA	O	M	R	W		O	M	R	W		FALL OF WICKETS				
Harris	24	8	47	2		10	1	34	0			E	A	E	A
Johnson	24	4	63	5		15	5	25	3		Wkt	1st	1st	2nd	2nd
Siddle	23	7	50	1	(4) 15	6	46	1		1st	48	19	65	64
Lyon	22.2	3	67	1	(3) 17	3	50	5		2nd	96	36	86	200
Watson	6.4	2	11	1		4	2	13	0		3rd	106	62	86	–
											4th	173	110	87	–
ENGLAND											5th	202	112	131	–
Anderson	20.2	4	67	4		11	2	26	0		6th	216	122	173	–
Broad	20	6	45	3		10	0	58	0		7th	230	151	174	–
Stokes	15	4	46	1	(4) 12	0	50	1		8th	231	162	174	–
Bresnan	18	6	24	2	(6) 7	1	48	0		9th	242	164	179	–
Panesar	9	2	18	0	(3) 7.5	0	41	1		10th	255	204	179	–
Root					(5) 4	1	8	0						

Umpires: Alim Dar (*Pakistan*) (86) and H.D.P.K.Dharmasena (*Sri Lanka*) (21).
Referee: R.S.Madugalle (*Sri Lanka*) (145).   **Test No. 2105/335 (A762/E944)**

AUSTRALIA v ENGLAND (5th Test)

At Sydney Cricket Ground, on 3, 4, 5 January 2014.
Toss: England. Result: **AUSTRALIA** won by 281 runs.
Debuts: England – G.S.Ballance, S.G.Borthwick, W.B.Rankin.

AUSTRALIA

C.J.L.Rogers	b Stokes	11	c and b Borthwick		119
D.A.Warner	b Broad	16	lbw b Anderson		16
S.R.Watson	lbw b Anderson	43	c Bairstow b Anderson		9
*M.J.Clarke	c Bell b Stokes	10	c Bairstow b Broad		6
S.P.D.Smith	c sub (J.E.Root) b Stokes	115	c Cook b Stokes		7
G.J.Bailey	c Cook b Broad	1	c Borthwick b Broad		46
†B.J.Haddin	c Cook b Stokes	75	b Borthwick		28
M.G.Johnson	c sub (J.E.Root) b Borthwick	12	b Stokes		4
R.J.Harris	c Anderson b Stokes	22	c Carberry b Borthwick		13
P.M.Siddle	c Bairstow b Stokes	0	c Bairstow b Rankin		4
N.M.Lyon	not out	1	not out		6
Extras	(B 10, LB 2, W 2, NB 6)	20	(LB 14, W 2, NB 2)		18
Total	**(76 overs)**	**326**	**(61.3 overs)**		**276**

ENGLAND

*A.N.Cook	lbw b Harris	7	c Haddin b Johnson		7
M.A.Carberry	c Lyon b Johnson	0	c Haddin b Johnson		43
J.M.Anderson	c Clarke b Johnson	4	(10) not out		1
I.R.Bell	c Haddin b Siddle	2	(3) c Warner b Harris		16
K.P.Pietersen	c Watson b Harris	3	(4) c Bailey b Harris		6
G.S.Ballance	c Haddin b Lyon	18	(5) lbw b Johnson		7
B.A.Stokes	b Siddle	47	(6) b Harris		32
†J.M.Bairstow	c Bailey b Siddle	18	(7) c Bailey b Lyon		0
S.G.Borthwick	c Smith b Harris	4	(8) c Clarke b Lyon		4
S.C.J.Broad	not out	30	(9) b Harris		42
W.B.Rankin	b Johnson	13	c Clarke b Harris		0
Extras	(LB 1, W 5, NB 3)	9	(B 5, LB 2, NB 1)		8
Total	**(58.5 overs)**	**155**	**(31.4 overs)**		**166**

ENGLAND	O	M	R	W		O	M	R	W
Anderson	21	3	67	1		15	6	46	2
Broad	19.5	5	65	2		14	1	57	2
Stokes	19.5	1	99	6	(4)	10	0	62	2
Rankin	8.2	0	34	0	(3)	12.3	0	47	1
Borthwick	7	0	49	1		6	0	33	3
Pietersen						4	1	17	0

AUSTRALIA	O	M	R	W		O	M	R	W
Harris	14	5	36	3		9.4	4	25	5
Johnson	13.5	3	33	3		9	1	40	3
Siddle	13	4	23	3		4	1	24	0
Watson	3	1	5	0					
Lyon	15	3	57	1	(4)	9	0	70	2

FALL OF WICKETS

	A	E	A	E
Wkt	1st	1st	2nd	2nd
1st	22	6	27	7
2nd	51	8	47	37
3rd	78	14	72	57
4th	94	17	91	87
5th	97	23	200	90
6th	225	62	239	91
7th	269	111	244	95
8th	325	112	255	139
9th	325	125	266	166
10th	326	155	276	166

Umpires: Alim Dar (*Pakistan*) (87) and M.Erasmus (*South Africa*) (23).
Referee: R.S.Madugalle (*Sri Lanka*) (146).   **Test No. 2106/336 (A763/E945)**

AUSTRALIA v ENGLAND 2013-14

AUSTRALIA – BATTING AND FIELDING

	M	I	NO	HS	Runs	Avge	100	50	Ct/St
B.J.Haddin	5	8	–	118	493	61.62	1	5	22
D.A.Warner	5	10	1	124	523	58.11	2	2	4
C.J.L.Rogers	5	10	–	119	463	46.30	2	3	4
S.P.D.Smith	5	9	1	115	327	40.87	2	–	7
M.J.Clarke	5	10	1	148	363	40.33	2	–	8
S.R.Watson	5	10	1	103	345	38.33	1	2	3
M.G.Johnson	5	8	2	64	165	27.50	–	1	4
G.J.Bailey	5	8	1	53	183	26.14	–	1	10
R.J.Harris	5	6	1	55*	117	23.40	–	1	4
P.M.Siddle	5	7	1	21	38	6.33	–	–	–
N.M.Lyon	5	6	6	18*	60	–	–	–	5

AUSTRALIA – BOWLING

	O	M	R	W	Avge	Best	5wI	10wM
M.G.Johnson	188.4	51	517	37	13.97	7-40	3	–
R.J.Harris	166.2	50	425	22	19.31	5-25	1	–
P.M.Siddle	156.4	48	386	16	24.12	4-57	–	–
N.M.Lyon	176.2	42	558	19	29.36	5-50	1	–

Also bowled: S.P.D.Smith 11-1-58-1; S.R.Watson 47.4-17-122-4.

ENGLAND – BATTING AND FIELDING

	M	I	NO	HS	Runs	Avge	100	50	Ct/St
B.A.Stokes	4	8	–	120	279	34.87	1	–	1
K.P.Pietersen	5	10	–	71	294	29.40	–	2	3
M.A.Carberry	5	10	–	60	281	28.10	–	1	6
J.E.Root	4	8	1	87	192	27.42	–	1	2
I.R.Bell	5	10	1	72*	235	26.11	–	2	4
A.N.Cook	5	10	–	72	246	24.60	–	3	7
S.C.J.Broad	5	10	2	42	155	19.37	–	–	2
M.J.Prior	3	6	–	69	107	17.83	–	1	10
J.M.Bairstow	2	4	–	21	49	12.25	–	–	10
T.T.Bresnan	2	4	–	21	34	8.50	–	–	1
J.M.Anderson	5	10	5	13*	41	8.20	–	–	6
G.P.Swann	3	6	1	19*	36	7.20	–	–	4
M.S.Panesar	2	4	–	2	4	1.00	–	–	–

Also batted (one Test each): G.S.Ballance 18, 7; S.G.Borthwick 1, 4 (2 ct); W.B.Rankin 13, 0; C.T.Tremlett 8, 7; I.J.L.Trott 10, 9.

ENGLAND – BOWLING

	O	M	R	W	Avge	Best	5wI	10wM
S.C.J.Broad	161.5	24	578	21	27.52	6-81	1	–
B.A.Stokes	116.5	14	492	15	32.80	6-99	1	–
T.T.Bresnan	62.3	14	206	5	41.20	2-24	–	–
J.M.Anderson	190.3	43	615	14	43.92	4-67	–	–
G.P.Swann	142	21	560	7	80.00	2-71	–	–

Also bowled: S.G.Borthwick 13-0-82-4; M.S.Panesar 70.5-9-207-3; K.P.Pietersen 4-1-17-0; W.B.Rankin 20.5-0-81-1; J.E.Root 32-5-98-0; C.T.Tremlett 36-5-120-4.

NEW ZEALAND v WEST INDIES (1st Test)

At University Oval, Dunedin, on 3, 4, 5, 6, 7 December 2013.
Toss: West Indies. Result: **MATCH DRAWN**.
Debuts: None.

NEW ZEALAND

P.G.Fulton	c Edwards b Sammy	61	c Ramdin b Shillingford		3
H.D.Rutherford	c Deonarine b Shillingford	62	c Gabriel b Shillingford		20
A.J.Redmond	c Samuels b Best	20	c Deonarine b Shillingford		6
L.R.P.L.Taylor	not out	217	not out		16
*B.B.McCullum	b Sammy	113	c Ramdin b Shillingford		9
C.J.Anderson	c Ramdin b Best	0	not out		20
†B.J.Watling	c Edwards b Best	41			
T.G.Southee	c Bravo b Deonarine	2			
I.S.Sodhi	c and b Deonarine	35			
N.Wagner	run out	37			
T.A.Boult					
Extras	(B 10, LB 10, NB 1)	21	(B 1, LB 3, W 1)		5
Total	(9 wkts dec; 153.1 overs)	609	(4 wkts; 30 overs; 127 mins)		79

WEST INDIES

K.A.Edwards	c Fulton b Boult	0	lbw b Sodhi		59
K.O.A.Powell	c Watling b Southee	7	c Southee b Boult		14
D.M.Bravo	c McCullum b Southee	40	b Boult		218
M.N.Samuels	c Taylor b Southee	14	c and b Southee		23
S.Chanderpaul	lbw b Boult	76	lbw b Wagner		1
N.Deonarine	c Taylor b Southee	15	c Watling b Anderson		52
†D.Ramdin	c Watling b Boult	12	b Sodhi		24
*D.J.G.Sammy	not out	27	c Sodhi b Southee		80
S.Shillingford	b Sodhi	9	c Taylor b Wagner		15
T.L.Best	run out	0	c Taylor b Wagner		3
S.T.Gabriel	lbw b Sodhi	0	not out		0
Extras	(LB 11, W 1, NB 1)	13	(B 4, LB 7, W 5, NB 2)		18
Total	(62.1 overs)	213	(162.1 overs; 681 mins)		507

WEST INDIES	O	M	R	W	O	M	R	W
Best	34.1	5	148	3	8	1	26	0
Gabriel	27.5	4	148	0	(3) 5	1	16	0
Sammy	23.1	4	79	2				
Shillingford	46	7	138	1	(2) 15	5	26	4
Deonarine	22	0	76	2	(4) 2	0	7	0
NEW ZEALAND								
Boult	18	5	40	3	(2) 35	11	81	2
Southee	16	1	52	4	(1) 29.1	4	112	2
Wagner	13	2	47	0	30	3	112	3
Sodhi	15.1	2	63	4	(5) 49	7	155	2
Anderson					(4) 14	2	29	1
Redmond					5	1	18	0

FALL OF WICKETS				
	NZ	WI	WI	NZ
Wkt	1st	1st	2nd	2nd
1st	95	4	18	3
2nd	117	24	135	15
3rd	185	70	178	31
4th	380	73	185	44
5th	385	106	307	–
6th	469	174	363	–
7th	472	183	453	–
8th	548	202	491	–
9th	609	205	507	–
10th	–	213	507	–

Umpires: N.J.Llong (*England*) (21) and P.R.Reiffel (*Australia*) (6).
Referee: R.S.Mahanama (*Sri Lanka*) (46).   **Test No. 2107/40 (NZ387/WI493)**

NEW ZEALAND v WEST INDIES (2nd Test)

At Basin Reserve, Wellington, on 11, 12, 13 December 2013.
Toss: West Indies. Result: **NEW ZEALAND** won by an innings and 73 runs.
Debuts: None.

NEW ZEALAND

P.G.Fulton	c Ramdin b Sammy	6
H.D.Rutherford	c Ramdin b Best	11
K.S.Williamson	c Sammy b Best	45
L.R.P.L.Taylor	c Shillingford b Gabriel	129
*B.B.McCullum	c Edwards b Deonarine	37
C.J.Anderson	c Powell b Shillingford	38
†B.J.Watling	b Gabriel	65
T.G.Southee	c Bravo b Sammy	21
I.S.Sodhi	c Ramdin b Best	27
N.Wagner	c Sammy b Best	0
T.A.Boult	not out	38
Extras	(B 16, LB 6, NB 2)	24
Total	**(115.1 overs; 494 mins)**	**441**

WEST INDIES

K.A.Edwards	c Rutherford b Anderson	55	c Williamson b Southee		35
K.O.A.Powell	lbw b Southee	21	b Southee		36
D.M.Bravo	c Fulton b Anderson	4	c Watling b Wagner		0
M.N.Samuels	c Watling b Boult	60	c Anderson b Southee		12
S.Chanderpaul	c Anderson b Boult	6	not out		31
N.Deonarine	c Taylor b Boult	22	b Boult		12
†D.Ramdin	not out	12	c Boult b Anderson		19
*D.J.G.Sammy	b Boult	0	lbw b Boult		0
S.Shillingford	b Boult	0	c Taylor b Wagner		1
T.L.Best	b Boult	0	c Fulton b Boult		21
S.T.Gabriel	b Southee	0	b Boult		0
Extras	(LB 8, W 1, NB 4)	13	(LB 6, W 1, NB 1)		8
Total	**(49.5 overs; 228 mins)**	**193**	**(54.5 overs; 253 mins)**		**175**

WEST INDIES	O	M	R	W		O	M	R	W
Best	21	1	110	4					
Gabriel	25.1	5	86	2					
Sammy	25	3	92	2					
Shillingford	28	4	92	1					
Deonarine	16	2	39	1					

NEW ZEALAND	O	M	R	W		O	M	R	W
Boult	15	5	40	6		12.5	2	40	4
Southee	15.5	2	58	2		11	2	24	3
Wagner	7	1	37	0		17	2	67	2
Anderson	7	1	20	2		11	1	29	1
Sodhi	3	1	18	0					
Williamson	2	0	12	0	(5)	3	1	9	0

FALL OF WICKETS

	NZ	WI	WI
Wkt	1st	1st	2nd
1st	14	46	74
2nd	24	67	75
3rd	112	103	85
4th	189	119	94
5th	257	175	117
6th	296	182	146
7th	334	182	147
8th	383	188	148
9th	383	188	175
10th	441	193	175

Umpires: I.J.Gould (*England*) (36) and P.R.Reiffel (*Australia*) (7).
Referee: R.S.Mahanama (*Sri Lanka*) (47).   **Test No. 2108/41 (NZ388/WI494)**

NEW ZEALAND v WEST INDIES (3rd Test)

At Seddon Park, Hamilton, on 19, 20, 21, 22 December 2013.
Toss: New Zealand. Result: **NEW ZEALAND** won by eight wickets.
Debuts: None.

WEST INDIES

Batsman	1st innings		2nd innings	
K.C.Brathwaite	c Williamson b Southee	45	b Boult	7
K.O.A.Powell	c Watling b Wagner	26	(3) c Southee b Boult	0
K.A.Edwards	c Watling b Southee	6	(2) c Watling b Boult	1
M.N.Samuels	c Williamson b Anderson	0	c Watling b Anderson	8
S.Chanderpaul	not out	122	c Williamson b Wagner	20
N.Deonarine	lbw b Anderson	2	c Taylor b Wagner	13
†D.Ramdin	c Watling b Anderson	107	lbw b Boult	18
*D.J.G.Sammy	c Watling b Southee	3	c Watling b Southee	24
S.P.Narine	b Boult	2	not out	0
V.Permaul	c Fulton b Southee	20	lbw b Southee	0
T.L.Best	c Watling b Sodhi	25	lbw b Southee	0
Extras	(B 2, LB 6, W 1)	9	(LB 12)	12
Total	**(116.2 overs; 504 mins)**	**367**	**(31.5 overs; 156 mins)**	**103**

NEW ZEALAND

Batsman	1st innings		2nd innings	
P.G.Fulton	c Sammy b Narine	11	c and b Sammy	10
H.D.Rutherford	c and b Sammy	10	not out	48
K.S.Williamson	lbw b Narine	58	b Permaul	56
L.R.P.L.Taylor	c Samuels b Best	131	not out	2
*B.B.McCullum	c Sammy b Narine	12		
C.J.Anderson	c Deonarine b Permaul	39		
†B.J.Watling	c Ramdin b Sammy	20		
T.G.Southee	lbw b Narine	18		
I.S.Sodhi	b Narine	9		
N.Wagner	c Edwards b Narine	22		
T.A.Boult	not out	1		
Extras	(B 6, LB 8, NB 4)	18	(B 7, NB 1)	8
Total	**(117.3 overs; 456 mins)**	**349**	**(2 wkts; 40.4 overs; 164 mins)**	**124**

NEW ZEALAND	O	M	R	W		O	M	R	W
Boult	26	2	84	1		10	4	23	4
Southee	28	3	79	4		8.5	5	12	3
Wagner	21	4	67	1	(4)	7	1	34	2
Anderson	19	3	47	3	(3)	6	0	22	1
Williamson	5	0	17	0					
Sodhi	17.2	0	65	1					

WEST INDIES	O	M	R	W		O	M	R	W
Best	14	1	63	1		7	3	22	0
Sammy	23	8	69	2	(3)	9	3	21	1
Permaul	35	6	103	1	(4)	7	1	29	1
Narine	42.3	17	91	6	(2)	16	6	39	0
Deonarine	3	0	9	0		1.4	0	6	0

FALL OF WICKETS

Wkt	WI 1st	NZ 1st	WI 2nd	NZ 2nd
1st	41	18	12	33
2nd	77	43	12	116
3rd	78	138	13	–
4th	82	174	40	–
5th	86	224	46	–
6th	286	269	75	–
7th	296	306	91	–
8th	307	317	103	–
9th	332	332	103	–
10th	367	349	103	–

Umpires: I.J.Gould (*England*) (37) and N.J.Llong (*England*) (22).
Referee: R.S.Mahanama (*Sri Lanka*) (48).   Test No. 2109/42 (NZ389/WI495)

SOUTH AFRICA v INDIA (1st Test)

At New Wanderers Stadium, Johannesburg, on 18, 19, 20, 21, 22 December 2013.
Toss: India. Result: **MATCH DRAWN**.
Debuts: None.

INDIA

M.Vijay	c de Villiers b Morkel	6	(2) c de Villiers b Kallis		39
S.Dhawan	c Tahir b Steyn	13	(1) c Kallis b Philander		15
C.A.Pujara	run out	25	c de Villiers b Kallis		153
V.Kohli	c Duminy b Kallis	119	c de Villiers b Duminy		96
R.G.Sharma	c de Villiers b Philander	14	b Kallis		6
A.M.Rahane	c de Villiers b Philander	47	c Smith b Duminy		15
*†M.S.Dhoni	c de Villiers b Morkel	19	c sub (D.Elgar) b Philander		29
R.Ashwin	not out	11	c du Plessis b Philander		7
Z.Khan	lbw b Philander	0	not out		29
I.Sharma	b Philander	0	lbw b Tahir		4
Mohammed Shami	b Morkel	0	b Tahir		4
Extras	(B 4, LB 6, W 14, NB 2)	26	(B 9, LB 7, W 8)		24
Total	**(103 overs; 454 mins)**	**280**	**(120.4 overs; 506 mins)**		**421**

SOUTH AFRICA

*G.C.Smith	lbw b Khan	68	(2) run out		44
A.N.Petersen	lbw b I.Sharma	21	(1) b Shami		76
H.M.Amla	b I.Sharma	36	b Shami		4
J.H.Kallis	lbw b I.Sharma	0	(5) lbw b Khan		34
†A.B.de Villiers	lbw b Shami	13	(6) b I.Sharma		103
J.P.Duminy	c Vijay b Shami	2	(7) b Shami		5
F.du Plessis	c Dhoni b Khan	20	(4) run out		134
V.D.Philander	c Ashwin b Khan	59	not out		25
D.W.Steyn	c R.G.Sharma b I.Sharma	10	not out		6
M.Morkel	b Khan	7			
Imran Tahir	not out	0			
Extras	(LB 4, W 1, NB 3)	8	(B 2, LB 7, W 8, NB 2)		19
Total	**(75.3 overs; 361 mins)**	**244**	**(7 wkts; 136 overs; 563 mins)**		**450**

SOUTH AFRICA	O	M	R	W		O	M	R	W
Steyn	26	7	61	1		30	5	104	1
Philander	27	6	61	4		28	10	68	3
Morkel	23	12	34	3		2	1	4	0
Kallis	14	4	37	1		20	5	68	3
Imran Tahir	8	0	47	0		15.4	1	69	2
Duminy	5	0	30	0	(7)	24	0	87	2
De Villiers					(6)	1	0	5	0

INDIA	O	M	R	W		O	M	R	W
Khan	26.3	6	88	4		34	1	135	1
Mohammed Shami	18	3	48	2	(3)	28	5	107	3
I.Sharma	25	5	79	4	(2)	29	4	91	1
Ashwin	6	0	25	0		36	5	83	0
Vijay						1	0	3	0
Dhoni						2	0	4	0
Kohli						6	0	18	0

FALL OF WICKETS				
	I	SA	I	SA
Wkt	1st	1st	2nd	2nd
1st	17	37	23	108
2nd	24	130	93	118
3rd	113	130	315	143
4th	151	130	325	197
5th	219	145	327	402
6th	264	146	358	407
7th	264	226	369	442
8th	264	237	384	–
9th	278	239	405	–
10th	280	244	421	–

Umpires: S.J.Davis (*Australia*) (49) and R.J.Tucker (*Australia*) (28).
Referee: A.J.Pycroft (*Zimbabwe*) (25).　　　　Test No. 2110/28 (SA380/I475)

SOUTH AFRICA v INDIA (2nd Test)

At Kingsmead, Durban, on 26, 27, 28, 29, 30 December 2013.
Toss: India. Result: **SOUTH AFRICA** won by ten wickets.
Debuts: None.

INDIA

S.Dhawan	c Petersen b Morkel	29	c du Plessis b Peterson		19
M.Vijay	c de Villiers b Steyn	97	c Smith b Philander		6
C.A.Pujara	c de Villiers b Steyn	70	b Steyn		32
V.Kohli	c de Villiers b Morkel	46	c de Villiers b Steyn		11
R.G.Sharma	b Steyn	0	lbw b Philander		25
A.M.Rahane	not out	51	b Philander		96
*†M.S.Dhoni	c Smith b Steyn	24	c Petersen b Peterson		15
R.A.Jadeja	c Kallis b Duminy	0	c Morkel b Peterson		8
Z.Khan	c de Villiers b Steyn	0	lbw b Peterson		3
I.Sharma	c de Villiers b Steyn	4	c de Villiers b Steyn		1
Mohammed Shami	c Smith b Morkel	1	not out		1
Extras	(LB 7, W 4, NB 1)	12	(B 4, W 2)		6
Total	**(111.3 overs; 502 mins)**	**334**	**(86 overs; 381 mins)**		**223**

SOUTH AFRICA

*G.C.Smith	c Dhawan b Jadeja	47	(2) not out		27
A.N.Petersen	c Vijay b Jadeja	62	(1) not out		31
H.M.Amla	b Shami	3			
J.H.Kallis	c Dhoni b Jadeja	115			
†A.B.de Villiers	c Kohli b Jadeja	74			
J.P.Duminy	lbw b Jadeja	28			
D.W.Steyn	c Dhoni b Khan	44			
F.du Plessis	run out	43			
R.J.Peterson	c Vijay b Khan	61			
V.D.Philander	not out	0			
M.Morkel	c and b Jadeja	0			
Extras	(B 3, LB 15, W 2, NB 3)	23	(W 1)		1
Total	**(155.2 overs)**	**500**	**(0 wkts; 11.4 overs; 48 mins)**		**59**

SOUTH AFRICA	O	M	R	W		O	M	R	W		FALL OF WICKETS				
												I	SA	I	SA
Steyn	30	9	100	6		21	8	47	3		Wkt	1st	1st	2nd	2nd
Philander	21	6	56	0		16	4	43	3		1st	41	103	8	–
Morkel	23.3	6	50	3		16	6	34	0		2nd	198	113	95	–
Kallis	11	1	36	0							3rd	199	113	68	–
Peterson	22	2	75	0	(4)	24	3	74	4		4th	199	240	71	–
Duminy	4	0	10	1	(5)	8	2	20	0		5th	265	298	104	–
Du Plessis					(6)	1	0	1	0		6th	320	384	146	–
INDIA											7th	321	387	154	–
Khan	28	4	97	2							8th	322	497	189	–
Mohammed Shami	27	2	104	1	(1)	2	1	4	0		9th	330	500	206	–
I.Sharma	31	7	114	0	(2)	5	1	29	0		10th	334	500	223	–
Jadeja	58.2	15	138	6	(3)	4	0	16	0						
R.G.Sharma	11	1	29	0	(4)	0.4	0	10	0						

Umpires: S.J.Davis (*Australia*) (50) and R.J.Tucker (*Australia*) (29).
Referee: A.J.Pycroft (*Zimbabwe*) (26).   **Test No. 2111/29 (SA381/I476)**

PAKISTAN v SRI LANKA (1st Test)

At Sheikh Zayed Stadium, Abu Dhabi, on 31 December 2013, 1, 2, 3, 4 January 2014.
Toss: Pakistan. Result: **MATCH DRAWN**.
Debuts: Pakistan – Ahmed Shehzad, Bilawal Bhatti; Sri Lanka – S.M.S.M.Senanayake.

SRI LANKA

F.D.M.Karunaratne	c Shafiq b Junaid	38	b Junaid		24
J.K.Silva	c Hafeez b Bhatti	20	c Akmal b Junaid		81
K.C.Sangakkara	c Shehzad b Junaid	16	c Younus b Bhatti		55
D.P.M.D.Jayawardena	c Akmal b Bhatti	5	c Shafiq b Bhatti		0
L.D.Chandimal	c Hafeez b Bhatti	0	c Ali b Junaid		89
*A.D.Mathews	st Akmal b Ajmal	91	not out		157
†H.A.P.W.Jayawardena	c Akmal b Junaid	5	not out		63
S.M.S.M.Senanayake	c Akmal b Junaid	5			
H.M.R.K.B.Herath	b Junaid	0			
R.M.S.Eranga	c Akmal b Ajmal	14			
R.A.S.Lakmal	not out	1			
Extras	(B 4, LB 4, NB 1)	9	(B 4, LB 7)		11
Total	**(65 overs)**	**204**	**(5 wkts dec; 168.3 overs)**		**480**

PAKISTAN

Khurram Manzoor	run out	21	c H.A.P.W.Jayawardena b Lakmal		8
Ahmed Shehzad	c Karunaratne b Eranga	38	lbw b Herath		55
Mohammad Hafeez	c Silva b Lakmal	11	not out		80
Younus Khan	b Eranga	136	not out		13
*Misbah-ul-Haq	c Sangakkara b Herath	135			
Asad Shafiq	c Silva b Lakmal	13			
†Adnan Akmal	c Senanayake b Eranga	6			
Bilawal Bhatti	c H.A.P.W.Jayawardena b Mathews	14			
Saeed Ajmal	lbw b Herath	0			
Rahat Ali	b Herath	0			
Junaid Khan	not out	4			
Extras	(LB 2, W 1, NB 2)	5	(LB 1, NB 1)		2
Total	**(129.1 overs)**	**383**	**(2 wkts; 52 overs)**		**158**

PAKISTAN	O	M	R	W	O	M	R	W
Junaid Khan	20	4	58	5	36	3	93	3
Rahat Ali	16	3	41	0	38.3	9	92	0
Bilawal Bhatti	15	1	65	3	36	8	146	2
Saeed Ajmal	14	3	32	2	49	10	115	0
Mohammad Hafeez					9	1	23	0

SRI LANKA	O	M	R	W		O	M	R	W
Lakmal	33	9	99	2		13	1	43	1
Mathews	13	1	43	1	(4)	2	0	9	0
Eranga	30	6	80	3	(2)	11	0	38	0
Herath	35.1	9	93	3	(3)	21	8	37	1
Senanayake	18	2	66	0		5	0	30	0

FALL OF WICKETS

	SL	P	SL	P
Wkt	*1st*	*1st*	*2nd*	*2nd*
1st	57	46	47	24
2nd	67	59	146	125
3rd	76	83	150	–
4th	76	301	186	–
5th	82	329	324	–
6th	104	342	–	–
7th	124	369	–	–
8th	124	378	–	–
9th	185	378	–	–
10th	204	383	–	–

Umpires: R.A.Kettleborough (*England*) (17) and B.N.J.Oxenford (*Australia*) (16).
Referee: J.Srinath (*India*) (29). **Test No. 2112/44 (P378/SL223)**

PAKISTAN v SRI LANKA (2nd Test)

At Dubai International Cricket Stadium, on 8, 9, 10, 11, 12 January 2014.
Toss: Sri Lanka. Result: **SRI LANKA** won by nine wickets.
Debuts: None.

PAKISTAN

Khurram Manzoor	c H.A.P.W.Jayawardena b Lakmal	73	c H.A.P.W.Jayawardena b Fernando	6
Ahmed Shehzad	lbw b Fernando	3	c H.A.P.W.Jayawardena b Herath	9
Mohammad Hafeez	b Fernando	21	c H.A.P.W.Jayawardena b Fernando	1
Younus Khan	c H.A.P.W.Jayawardena b Eranga	13	c H.A.P.W.Jayawardena b Lakmal	77
*Misbah-ul-Haq	c H.A.P.W.Jayawardena b Eranga	1	b Herath	97
Asad Shafiq	c Silva b Lakmal	6	c Karunaratne b Eranga	23
†Sarfraz Ahmed	c H.A.P.W.Jayawardena b Fernando	7	b Lakmal	74
Bilawal Bhatti	not out	24	b Eranga	32
Saeed Ajmal	c Silva b Herath	8	b Lakmal	21
Rahat Ali	lbw b Herath	0	c H.A.P.W.Jayawardena b Lakmal	8
Junaid Khan	lbw b Herath	2	not out	2
Extras	(LB 7)	7	(B 1, LB 8)	9
Total	**(63.5 overs)**	**165**	**(137.3 overs)**	**359**

SRI LANKA

F.D.M.Karunaratne	lbw b Junaid	32	not out	62
J.K.Silva	lbw b Hafeez	95	lbw b Ajmal	58
K.C.Sangakkara	lbw b Ali	26	not out	9
L.D.Chandimal	c Ali b Junaid	12		
D.P.M.D.Jayawardena	b Ajmal	129		
*A.D.Mathews	c Ahmed b Ali	42		
†H.A.P.W.Jayawardena	b Junaid	9		
H.M.R.K.B.Herath	run out	6		
R.M.S.Eranga	b Bhatti	14		
R.A.S.Lakmal	not out	10		
A.N.P.R.Fernando	lbw b Ajmal	3		
Extras	(B 1, LB 7, W 1, NB 1)	10	(B 3, LB 4, NB 1)	8
Total	**(134 overs)**	**388**	**(1 wkt; 46.2 overs; 190 mins)**	**137**

SRI LANKA	O	M	R	W		O	M	R	W
Lakmal	21	6	45	2		28.3	4	78	4
Eranga	14	4	25	2	(4)	36	9	74	2
Fernando	18	2	62	3	(2)	19	3	50	2
Herath	10.5	3	26	3	(3)	48	10	132	2
Mathews						5	1	9	0
Sangakkara						1	0	7	0
PAKISTAN									
Junaid Khan	36	7	102	3	(2)	10	2	34	0
Rahat Ali	36	6	131	4	(3)	11	1	29	0
Saeed Ajmal	34	11	56	2	(4)	17.2	5	45	1
Bilawal Bhatti	22	3	80	1					
Mohammad Hafeez	6	1	11	1	(1)	8	3	22	0

FALL OF WICKETS				
	P	SL	P	SL
Wkt	1st	1st	2nd	2nd
1st	28	40	11	124
2nd	78	75	12	–
3rd	107	88	19	–
4th	109	227	148	–
5th	118	320	200	–
6th	127	341	245	–
7th	129	348	312	–
8th	151	365	334	–
9th	151	377	354	–
10th	165	388	359	–

Umpires: B.N.J.Oxenford (*Australia*) (17) and S.Ravi (*India*) (2).
Referee: J.Srinath (*India*) (30). **Test No. 2113/45 (P379/SL224)**

PAKISTAN v SRI LANKA (3rd Test)

At Sharjah Cricket Stadium, on 16, 17, 18, 19, 20 January 2014.
Toss: Sri Lanka. Result: **PAKISTAN** won by five wickets.
Debut: Sri Lanka – M.D.K.Perera.

SRI LANKA

Batsman	1st innings		2nd innings	
F.D.M.Karunaratne	c Younus b Rehman	34	b Talha	8
J.K.Silva	c Ahmed b Talha	17	b Rehman	36
K.C.Sangakkara	c Manzoor b Junaid	52	c Manzoor b Rehman	8
D.P.M.D.Jayawardena	c Ali b Ajmal	47	c Ali b Ajmal	46
L.D.Chandimal	c Shafiq b Ajmal	11	b Talha	13
*A.D.Mathews	c Shehzad b Junaid	91	c Manzoor b Talha	31
†H.A.P.W.Jayawardena	c Junaid b Talha	35	c Ali b Ajmal	49
M.D.K.Perera	c Junaid b Talha	95	c Ali b Rehman	8
H.M.R.K.B.Herath	lbw b Junaid	0	c Younus b Rehman	0
R.M.S.Eranga	not out	25	c Rehman b Ajmal	3
R.A.S.Lakmal	not out	3	not out	2
Extras	(B 5, LB 11, NB 2)	18	(B 2, LB 4, W 2, NB 2)	10
Total	**(9 wkts dec; 172 overs)**	**428**	**(101.4 overs)**	**214**

PAKISTAN

Batsman	1st innings		2nd innings	
Khurram Manzoor	c H.A.P.W.Jayawardena b Eranga	52	c H.A.P.W.Jayawardena b Lakmal	21
Ahmed Shehzad	b Herath	147	c Karunaratne b Lakmal	21
Azhar Ali	c Mathews b Perera	8	c H.A.P.W.Jayawardena b Lakmal	103
Younus Khan	c H.A.P.W.Jayawardena b Herath	17	c Sangakkara b Mathews	29
*Misbah-ul-Haq	c Chandimal b Herath	63	(6) not out	68
Asad Shafiq	lbw b Eranga	18	(7) not out	1
†Sarfraz Ahmed	c H.A.P.W.Jayawardena b Herath	5	(5) c H.A.P.W.Jayawardena b Eranga	48
Abdur Rehman	c H.A.P.W.Jayawardena b Eranga	2		
Mohammad Talha	lbw b Eranga	2		
Saeed Ajmal	not out	0		
Junaid Khan	c Chandimal b Herath	16		
Extras	(B 3, LB 6, W 1, NB 1)	11	(B 6, LB 1, W 3, NB 1)	11
Total	**(109.1 overs)**	**341**	**(5 wkts; 57.3 overs)**	**302**

PAKISTAN	O	M	R	W		O	M	R	W
Junaid Khan	32	5	81	3		20	6	34	0
Mohammad Talha	32	3	99	3		23	2	65	3
Saeed Ajmal	55	16	120	2	(4)	25.4	7	53	3
Abdur Rehman	50	14	101	1	(3)	33	10	56	4
Azhar Ali	3	0	11	0					

SRI LANKA	O	M	R	W		O	M	R	W
Herath	38.1	8	125	5	(3)	19	0	100	0
Lakmal	23	4	61	0	(1)	12	0	79	3
Rahat Ali	17	1	71	1					
Eranga	24	5	60	4	(2)	15.3	0	68	1
Mathews	7	3	15	0	(4)	11	0	48	1

FALL OF WICKETS				
	SL	P	SL	P
Wkt	1st	1st	2nd	2nd
1st	31	114	13	35
2nd	65	149	37	48
3rd	125	189	66	97
4th	159	245	89	186
5th	166	274	127	295
6th	239	291	189	–
7th	351	294	203	–
8th	351	300	203	–
9th	423	325	209	–
10th	–	341	214	–

Umpires: R.A.Kettleborough (*England*) (18) and S.Ravi (*India*) (3).
Referee: J.Srinath (*India*) (31). **Test No. 2114/46 (P380/SL225)**

BANGLADESH v SRI LANKA (1st Test)

At Shere Bangla National Stadium, Mirpur, on 27, 28, 29, 30 January 2014.
Toss: Sri Lanka. Result: **SRI LANKA** won by an innings and 248 runs.
Debut: Bangladesh – Shamsur Rahman.

BANGLADESH

Batsman	Dismissal (1st)	R	Dismissal (2nd)	R
Tamim Iqbal	c Lakmal b Eranga	6	c Perera b Herath	11
Shamsur Rahman	c Perera b Eranga	33	c Chandimal b Eranga	9
Marshall Ayub	lbw b Mathews	1	c Silva b Lakmal	18
Mominul Haque	c Vithanage b Lakmal	8	lbw b Perera	50
Shakib Al Hasan	lbw b Herath	55	lbw b Perera	25
*†Mushfiqur Rahim	lbw b Lakmal	61	b Perera	14
Nasir Hossain	c Chandimal b Eranga	4	c Herath b Perera	29
Sohag Gazi	c Eranga b Lakmal	42	lbw b Lakmal	23
Robiul Islam	c Perera b Eranga	5	lbw b Lakmal	1
Rubel Hossain	b Herath	2	c Silva b Perera	17
Al-Amin Hossain	not out	6	not out	32
Extras	(LB 4, NB 5)	9	(B 9, LB 10, NB 2)	21
Total	**(63.5 overs; 292 mins)**	**232**	**(51.5 overs; 220 mins)**	**250**

SRI LANKA

Batsman	Dismissal	R
F.D.M.Karunaratne	c Islam b Shakib	53
J.K.Silva	lbw b Shakib	139
K.C.Sangakkara	c Nasir b Al-Amin	75
D.P.M.D.Jayawardena	not out	203
†L.D.Chandimal	b Shakib	40
R.A.S.Lakmal	c Nasir b Gazi	0
*A.D.Mathews	c Ayub b Gazi	86
K.D.K.Vithanage	not out	103
M.D.K.Perera		
R.M.S.Eranga		
H.M.R.K.B.Herath		
Extras	(B 12, W 12, NB 7)	31
Total	**(6 wkts dec; 187.5 overs; 790 mins)**	**730**

SRI LANKA	O	M	R	W		O	M	R	W
Lakmal	18.1	3	66	3		14	4	39	3
Eranga	17.4	2	49	4		6	1	26	1
Mathews	6	3	18	1	(5)	3	0	10	0
Perera	11	2	45	0		19.5	0	109	5
Herath	11	1	50	2	(3)	9	3	47	1

BANGLADESH	O	M	R	W
Robiul Islam	29	2	109	0
Al-Amin Hossain	32	3	118	1
Rubel Hossain	20	0	84	0
Sohag Gazi	39	5	130	2
Shakib Al Hasan	43	6	159	3
Mominul Haque	6	0	20	0
Nasir Hossain	10.5	0	60	0
Marshall Ayub	8	0	38	0

FALL OF WICKETS

Wkt	B 1st	SL 1st	B 2nd
1st	35	118	15
2nd	40	273	35
3rd	40	302	50
4th	59	374	102
5th	145	375	133
6th	150	554	150
7th	203	–	183
8th	219	–	197
9th	222	–	197
10th	232	–	250

Umpires: N.J.Llong (*England*) (23) and P.R.Reiffel (*Australia*) (8).
Referee: J.Srinath (*India*) (32). **Test No. 2115/15 (B82/SL226)**

BANGLADESH v SRI LANKA (2nd Test)

At Zahur Ahmed Chowdhury Stadium, Chittagong, on 4, 5, 6, 7, 8 February 2014.
Toss: Sri Lanka. Result: **MATCH DRAWN**.
Debuts: None.

SRI LANKA

F.D.M.Karunaratne	c Mahmudullah b Al-Amin	31	c Nasir b Mahmudullah		15
J.K.Silva	lbw b Gazi	11	lbw b Mahmudullah		29
K.C.Sangakkara	c Gazi b Nasir	319	b Gazi		105
D.P.M.D.Jayawardena	lbw b Mahmudullah	72	lbw b Shakib		11
†L.D.Chandimal	c Kayes b Shakib	27	not out		100
*A.D.Mathews	b Shakib	5	not out		43
K.D.K.Vithanage	lbw b Nasir	35			
M.D.K.Perera	lbw b Shakib	1			
B.A.W.Mendis	lbw b Shakib	47			
R.A.S.Lakmal	lbw b Shakib	0			
A.N.P.R.Fernando	not out	4			
Extras	(B 21, LB 6, W 2, NB 1, Pen 5)	35	(LB 2)		2
Total	**(156.4 overs)**	**587**	**(4 wkts dec; 75.5 overs)**		**305**

BANGLADESH

Tamim Iqbal	b Lakmal	0	b Vithanage		31
Shamsur Rahman	b Mendis	106	b Perera		45
Imrul Kayes	b Mendis	115	lbw b Perera		25
Mominul Haque	b Perera	13	not out		100
Shakib Al Hasan	c Karunaratne b Perera	50	not out		43
*†Mushfiqur Rahim	c Silva b Perera	20			
Nasir Hossain	c Chandimal b Mendis	42			
Mahmudullah	c Silva b Mendis	30			
Sohag Gazi	lbw b Mendis	0			
Al-Amin Hossain	b Mendis	9			
Abdur Razzak	not out	11			
Extras	(B 8, LB 1, NB 21)	30	(B 12, LB 2, NB 13)		27
Total	**(119.5 overs)**	**426**	**(3 wkts; 84.4 overs)**		**271**

BANGLADESH

	O	M	R	W	O	M	R	W
Al-Amin Hossain	25	5	81	1	7	1	31	0
Sohag Gazi	48	4	181	1	18.5	1	87	1
Abdur Razzak	4	1	6	0				
Shakib Al Hasan	34	3	148	5	(3) 22	2	80	1
Mahmudullah	34	2	110	1	(4) 18	4	46	2
Nasir Hossain	6.4	0	16	2	3	0	13	0
Shamsur Rahman	1	0	5	0				
Mominul Haque	4	0	8	0	(5) 7	0	46	0

SRI LANKA

	O	M	R	W	O	M	R	W
Lakmal	25	6	70	1	13	5	30	0
Fernando	15	2	96	0	(4) 9.4	1	33	0
Mendis	29.5	3	99	6	16	0	61	0
Perera	39	4	119	3	(2) 28	7	55	2
Mathews	11	1	33	0				
Vithanage					(5) 16	0	73	1
Karunaratne					(6) 2	0	5	0

FALL OF WICKETS

	SL	B	SL	B
Wkt	1st	1st	2nd	2nd
1st	39	0	36	71
2nd	49	232	49	81
3rd	227	252	78	151
4th	294	259	223	–
5th	312	319	–	–
6th	402	350	–	–
7th	405	396	–	–
8th	505	396	–	–
9th	533	409	–	–
10th	587	426	–	–

Umpires: N.J.Llong (*England*) (24) and P.R.Reiffel (*Australia*) (9).
Referee: D.C.Boon (*Australia*) (21). Test No. 2116/16 (B83/SL227)

NEW ZEALAND v INDIA (1st Test)

At Eden Park, Auckland, on 6, 7, 8, 9 February 2014.
Toss: India. Result: **NEW ZEALAND** won by 40 runs.
Debuts: None.

NEW ZEALAND

Batsman	1st innings		2nd innings	
P.G.Fulton	lbw b Khan	13	c Jadeja b Shami	5
H.D.Rutherford	c Rahane b I.Sharma	6	lbw b Shami	0
K.S.Williamson	c Dhoni b Khan	113	c Jadeja b Khan	3
L.R.P.L.Taylor	c Jadeja b I.Sharma	3	c Rahane b Khan	41
*B.B.McCullum	c Jadeja b I.Sharma	224	run out	1
C.J.Anderson	lbw b I.Sharma	77	b Shami	2
†B.J.Watling	c Dhawan b I.Sharma	1	b I.Sharma	11
T.G.Southee	b Shami	28	c Pujara b Jadeja	14
I.S.Sodhi	c R.G.Sharma b I.Sharma	23	c R.G.Sharma b I.Sharma	0
N.Wagner	c Kohli b Jadeja	0	c Jadeja b I.Sharma	14
T.A.Boult	not out	1	not out	7
Extras	(B 1, LB 5, W 5, NB 3)	14	(B 4, W 1, NB 2)	7
Total	**(121.4 overs; 541 mins)**	**503**	**(41.2 overs; 183 mins)**	**105**

INDIA

Batsman	1st innings		2nd innings	
S.Dhawan	c Williamson b Boult	0	(2) c Watling b Wagner	115
M.Vijay	b Wagner	26	(1) c Watling b Southee	13
C.A.Pujara	c Watling b Boult	1	c Watling b Southee	23
V.Kohli	c Fulton b Southee	4	c Watling b Wagner	67
R.G.Sharma	b Boult	72	c Watling b Southee	19
A.M.Rahane	c Taylor b Southee	26	lbw b Boult	18
*†M.S.Dhoni	c Watling b Wagner	10	b Wagner	39
R.A.Jadeja	not out	30	c Sodhi b Boult	26
Z.Khan	c Watling b Wagner	14	c Taylor b Wagner	17
I.Sharma	c Boult b Southee	0	c Watling b Boult	4
Mohammed Shami	c Fulton b Wagner	2	not out	0
Extras	(B 5, LB 6, W 3, NB 3)	17	(B 12, LB 7, W 2, NB 4)	25
Total	**(60 overs; 266 mins)**	**202**	**(96.3 overs; 430 mins)**	**366**

INDIA	O	M	R	W		O	M	R	W
Mohammed Shami	28	6	95	1		12	1	37	3
Khan	30	2	132	2		9	2	23	2
I.Sharma	33.4	4	134	6		10.2	3	28	3
Jadeja	26	1	120	1		9	4	10	1
Kohli	1	0	4	0					
R.G.Sharma	3	0	12	0	(5)	1	0	3	0

NEW ZEALAND	O	M	R	W		O	M	R	W
Boult	17	2	38	3		23.3	2	86	3
Southee	19	6	38	3		23	4	81	3
Anderson	5	0	29	0	(4)	7	1	22	0
Wagner	11	0	64	4	(3)	25	8	62	4
Sodhi	6	0	13	0		15	2	78	0
Williamson	2	0	9	0		3	0	78	0

FALL OF WICKETS

	NZ	I	NZ	I
Wkt	1st	1st	2nd	2nd
1st	19	1	1	36
2nd	23	3	9	96
3rd	30	10	11	222
4th	251	51	15	248
5th	384	138	25	268
6th	398	138	63	270
7th	434	167	78	324
8th	490	188	78	349
9th	495	189	80	362
10th	503	202	105	366

Umpires: S.J.Davis (*Australia*) (51) and R.A.Kettleborough (*England*) (19).
Referee: R.S.Madugalle (*Sri Lanka*) (147).   **Test No. 2117/53 (NZ390/I477)**

NEW ZEALAND v INDIA (2nd Test)

At Basin Reserve, Wellington, on 14, 15, 16, 17, 18 February 2014.
Toss: India. Result: **MATCH DRAWN**.
Debuts: New Zealand – T.W.M.Latham, J.D.S.Neesham.

NEW ZEALAND

P.G.Fulton	lbw b I.Sharma	13	lbw b Khan		1
H.D.Rutherford	c Vijay b I.Sharma	12	c Dhoni b Khan		35
K.S.Williamson	c R.G.Sharma b Shami	47	c Dhoni b Khan		7
T.W.M.Latham	c Dhoni b I.Sharma	0	c Dhoni b Shami		29
*B.B.McCullum	c Jadeja b Shami	8	c Dhoni b Khan		302
C.J.Anderson	c Kohli b I.Sharma	24	c and b Jadeja		2
†B.J.Watling	c R.G.Sharma b I.Sharma	0	lbw b Shami		124
J.D.S.Neesham	c Dhoni b Shami	33	not out		137
T.G.Southee	c Vijay b I.Sharma	32	c Pujara b Khan		11
N.Wagner	not out	5	not out		2
T.A.Boult	c Pujara b Shami	2			
Extras	(LB 2, W 8, NB 6)	16	(B 9, LB 12, W 2, NB 7)		30
Total	**(52.5 overs; 258 mins)**	**192**	**(8 wkts dec; 210 overs; 904 mins)**		**680**

INDIA

S.Dhawan	c Watling b Southee	98	(2) lbw b Boult		2
M.Vijay	c Watling b Southee	2	(1) c Anderson b Southee		7
C.A.Pujara	lbw b Boult	19	c Watling b Southee		17
I.Sharma	c Watling b Boult	26			
V.Kohli	c Rutherford b Wagner	38	(4) not out		105
R.G.Sharma	b Neesham	0	(5) not out		31
A.M.Rahane	c Boult b Southee	118			
*†M.S.Dhoni	c Watling b Boult	68			
R.A.Jadeja	c Fulton b Wagner	26			
Z.Khan	c Watling b Wagner	22			
Mohammed Shami	not out	0			
Extras	(B 8, LB 4, W 7, NB 2)	21	(W 2, NB 2)		4
Total	**(102.4 overs; 468 mins)**	**438**	**(3 wkts; 52 overs; 217 mins)**		**166**

INDIA	O	M	R	W		O	M	R	W		FALL OF WICKETS			
Khan	17	3	57	0	(2)	51	13	170	5			NZ	I	NZ	I
Mohammed Shami	16.5	4	70	4	(3)	43	6	149	2		Wkt	1st	1st	2nd	2nd
I.Sharma	17	3	51	6	(1)	45	4	164	0		1st	23	2	1	10
Jadeja	2	1	12	0		52	11	115	1		2nd	26	89	27	10
R.G.Sharma						11	0	40	0		3rd	26	141	52	54
Kohli						6	1	13	0		4th	45	162	87	–
Dhoni						1	0	5	0		5th	84	165	94	–
Dhawan						1	0	3	0		6th	86	228	446	–
											7th	133	348	625	–
NEW ZEALAND											8th	165	385	639	–
Boult	26	7	99	3		16	5	47	1		9th	184	423	–	–
Southee	20	0	93	3		16	3	50	2		10th	192	438	–	–
Wagner	22.4	3	106	3		11	3	38	0						
Anderson	16	2	66	0	(5)	4	1	6	0						
Neesham	18	2	62	1	(4)	5	0	25	0						

Umpires: S.J.Davis (*Australia*) (52) and R.A.Kettleborough (*England*) (20).
Referee: R.S.Madugalle (*Sri Lanka*) (148).   **Test No. 2118/54 (NZ391/I478)**

SOUTH AFRICA v AUSTRALIA (1st Test)

At SuperSport Park, Centurion, on 12, 13, 14, 15 February 2014.
Toss: South Africa. Result: **AUSTRALIA** won by 281 runs.
Debut: Australia – A.J.Doolan.

AUSTRALIA

C.J.L.Rogers	c Duminy b Morkel	4	b Steyn		1
D.A.Warner	b Steyn	12	c Smith b Peterson		115
A.J.Doolan	c Peterson b McLaren	27	c de Villiers b Duminy		89
S.E.Marsh	c Smith b Philander	148	c de Villiers b Steyn		44
*M.J.Clarke	c Philander b Steyn	23	not out		17
S.P.D.Smith	c Petersen b McLaren	100			
†B.J.Haddin	lbw b Peterson	0			
M.G.Johnson	b Peterson	33			
R.J.Harris	b Steyn	19			
P.M.Siddle	b Steyn	2			
N.M.Lyon	not out	4			
Extras	(B 4, LB 8, W 11, NB 2)	25	(B 3, LB 14, W 7)		24
Total	**(122 overs; 527 mins)**	**397**	**(4 wkts dec; 72.2 overs; 315 mins)**		**290**

SOUTH AFRICA

*G.C.Smith	c Marsh b Johnson	10	(2)	c Doolan b Johnson	4
A.N.Petersen	c Haddin b Johnson	2	(1)	c Haddin b Johnson	1
H.M.Amla	lbw b Siddle	17		c Marsh b Harris	35
F.du Plessis	c Clarke b Warner	3		lbw b Siddle	18
†A.B.de Villiers	c Warner b Johnson	91		c Smith b Johnson	48
J.P.Duminy	c Johnson b Lyon	25		c Doolan b Johnson	10
R.McLaren	b Johnson	8		c Haddin b Johnson	6
R.J.Peterson	c Clarke b Johnson	10		b Siddle	21
V.D.Philander	lbw b Lyon	15		not out	26
D.W.Steyn	not out	7		c Clarke b Harris	3
M.Morkel	c Haddin b Johnson	0		run out	1
Extras	(B 14, LB 2, W 1, NB 1)	18		(B 10, LB 5, W 11, NB 1)	27
Total	**(61.1 overs; 281 mins)**	**206**		**(59.4 overs; 271 mins)**	**200**

SOUTH AFRICA	O	M	R	W		O	M	R	W
Steyn	29	6	78	4	(2)	14.2	2	61	4
Philander	24	5	69	1	(1)	11	2	28	0
Morkel	22	5	73	1	(4)	13	4	38	0
McLaren	20	4	72	2	(3)	11	0	47	0
Peterson	15	0	49	2		19	0	87	1
Duminy	12	1	44	0		4	0	12	1
AUSTRALIA									
Harris	17	3	51	0		12.4	5	35	2
Johnson	17.1	1	68	7		16	3	59	5
Siddle	13	1	33	1		16	6	55	2
Lyon	14	0	38	2	(5)	13	1	33	0
Warner					(4)	2	0	3	0

FALL OF WICKETS				
	A	SA	A	SA
Wkt	1st	1st	2nd	2nd
1st	15	11	1	6
2nd	24	15	206	12
3rd	72	23	243	49
4th	98	43	290	97
5th	331	110	–	128
6th	332	126	–	140
7th	348	140	–	151
8th	391	189	–	165
9th	391	202	–	178
10th	397	206	–	200

Umpires: Alim Dar (*Pakistan*) (88) and R.K.Illingworth (*England*) (6).
Referee: R.S.Mahanama (*Sri Lanka*) (49).   Test No. 2119/89 (SA382/A764)

SOUTH AFRICA v AUSTRALIA (2nd Test)

At St George's Park, Port Elizabeth, on 20, 21, 22, 23 February 2014.
Toss: South Africa. Result: **SOUTH AFRICA** won by 231 runs.
Debut: South Africa – Q.de Kock.

SOUTH AFRICA

Batsman	1st innings		2nd innings	
*G.C.Smith	lbw b Harris	9	b Johnson	14
D.Elgar	c Harris b Lyon	83	c Haddin b Siddle	16
H.M.Amla	lbw b Johnson	0	not out	127
F.du Plessis	c Smith b Lyon	55	c Haddin b Siddle	24
†A.B.de Villiers	c and b Lyon	116	c Haddin b Johnson	29
Q.de Kock	c sub (M.C.Henriques) b Smith	7	c Clarke b Lyon	34
J.P.Duminy	lbw b Lyon	123	not out	18
V.D.Philander	c and b Clarke	6		
W.D.Parnell	c Haddin b Lyon	10		
D.W.Steyn	not out	4		
M.Morkel	run out	1		
Extras	(B 4, LB 4, W 1)	9	(B 2, LB 6)	8
Total	**(150.5 overs; 617 mins)**	**423**	**(5 wkts dec; 64 overs; 298 mins)**	**270**

AUSTRALIA

Batsman	1st innings		2nd innings	
C.J.L.Rogers	lbw b Philander	5	run out	107
D.A.Warner	c Smith b Philander	70	lbw b Duminy	66
A.J.Doolan	c de Villiers b Parnell	8	c Smith b Morkel	5
S.E.Marsh	c de Villiers b Parnell	0	lbw b Philander	0
*M.J.Clarke	c Elgar b Philander	19	c du Plessis b Steyn	1
N.M.Lyon	b Morkel	15	(11) lbw b Elgar	0
S.P.D.Smith	c de Villiers b Morkel	49	(6) lbw b Steyn	0
†B.J.Haddin	b Steyn	9	(7) b Steyn	1
M.G.Johnson	b Duminy	27	(8) lbw b Philander	6
R.J.Harris	c du Plessis b Morkel	26	(9) lbw b Steyn	6
P.M.Siddle	not out	11	(10) not out	3
Extras	(B 4, W 2, NB 1)	7	(B 2, LB 17, W 2)	21
Total	**(57 overs; 281 mins)**	**246**	**(73.4 overs; 337 mins)**	**216**

AUSTRALIA	O	M	R	W		O	M	R	W
Harris	27	6	63	1	(2)	13	1	74	
Johnson	25	5	70	1	(1)	15	1	51	2
Siddle	34	9	96	0	(4)	19	2	89	2
Lyon	46	7	130	5	(3)	17	2	48	1
Warner	3	0	10	0					
Smith	8	0	30	1					
Clarke	7.5	2	16	1					

SOUTH AFRICA	O	M	R	W		O	M	R	W
Steyn	13	3	55	1		20	5	55	4
Philander	13	0	68	3		17	3	39	2
Morkel	17	0	63	3		15	6	46	1
Parnell	8.3	2	31	2					
Elgar	0.3	0	1	0		7.4	0	24	1
Duminy	5	0	24	1	(4)	14	3	33	1

FALL OF WICKETS

	SA	A	SA	A
Wkt	1st	1st	2nd	2nd
1st	10	7	20	126
2nd	11	41	42	152
3rd	123	41	112	153
4th	181	81	167	156
5th	200	120	231	156
6th	349	128	–	166
7th	378	168	–	197
8th	413	205	–	209
9th	420	209	–	214
10th	423	246	–	216

Umpires: H.D.P.K.Dharmasena (*Sri Lanka*) (22) and R.K.Illingworth (*England*) (7).
Referee: R.S.Mahanama (*Sri Lanka*) (50). **Test No. 2120/90 (SA383/A765)**

SOUTH AFRICA v AUSTRALIA (3rd Test)

At Newlands, Cape Town, on 1, 2, 3, 4, 5 March 2014.
Toss: Australia. Result: **AUSTRALIA** won by 245 runs.
Debuts: None.

AUSTRALIA

C.J.L.Rogers	c Smith b Steyn	25		run out		39
D.A.Warner	c de Villiers b Duminy	135		c de Villiers b Abbott		145
A.J.Doolan	c Steyn b Philander	20		c Abbott b Morkel		37
*M.J.Clarke	not out	161	(5)	c sub (Q.de Kock) b Abbott		0
S.P.D.Smith	b Elgar	84	(6)	not out		36
S.R.Watson	c Amla b Duminy	40	(4)	c Duminy b Abbott		25
†B.J.Haddin	c Amla b Duminy	13		not out		3
M.G.Johnson	c de Villiers b Duminy	0				
R.J.Harris	not out	4				
J.L.Pattinson						
N.M.Lyon						
Extras	(W 6, NB 6)	12		(B 3, LB 12, NB 3)		18
Total	**(7 wkts dec; 127.4 overs; 572 mins)**	**494**		**(5 wkts dec; 58 overs; 252 mins)**		**303**

SOUTH AFRICA

*G.C.Smith	c Haddin b Harris	5	(2)	c Doolan b Johnson		3
A.N.Petersen	c Haddin b Johnson	53	(1)	lbw b Harris		9
D.Elgar	c Haddin b Pattinson	11		b Johnson		0
H.M.Amla	b Harris	38		lbw b Pattinson		41
†A.B.de Villiers	c Clarke b Johnson	14		c Haddin b Harris		43
F.du Plessis	c Warner b Johnson	67	(7)	lbw b Smith		47
J.P.Duminy	c Haddin b Harris	4	(8)	c Lyon b Harris		43
V.D.Philander	not out	37	(9)	not out		51
K.J.Abbott	b Johnson	3	(6)	b Pattinson		7
D.W.Steyn	c Watson b Johnson	28		b Harris		1
M.Morkel	c Watson b Pattinson	7		b Harris		0
Extras	(B 8, LB 3, W 6, NB 3)	20		(B 8, LB 5, W 2, NB 5)		20
Total	**(82.5 overs; 389 mins)**	**287**		**(134.3 overs; 591 mins)**		**265**

SOUTH AFRICA	O	M	R	W		O	M	R	W
Steyn	10.1	0	44	1	(5)	3	0	24	0
Philander	26.4	2	116	1	(3)	6	0	42	0
Morkel	23.5	2	94	0	(1)	13	1	67	1
Duminy	17	0	73	4		19	3	76	0
Abbott	28	11	68	0	(2)	14	2	61	3
Elgar	22	0	99	1		13	0	18	0

AUSTRALIA	O	M	R	W		O	M	R	W
Harris	22	9	63	3		24.3	15	32	4
Johnson	19	5	42	4		34	11	92	3
Pattinson	18.5	4	77	2		27	10	62	2
Watson	9	1	34	1	(5)	9	6	6	0
Lyon	12	1	53	0	(4)	22	17	10	0
Smith	2	0	7	0		13	3	43	1
Clarke						5	2	7	0

FALL OF WICKETS				
	A	SA	A	SA
Wkt	1st	1st	2nd	2nd
1st	65	7	123	12
2nd	138	42	188	12
3rd	217	95	245	15
4th	401	121	257	68
5th	456	133	290	95
6th	489	146	–	136
7th	489	241	–	173
8th	–	249	–	246
9th	–	279	–	265
10th	–	287	–	265

Umpires: Alim Dar (*Pakistan*) (89) and H.D.P.K.Dharmasena (*Sri Lanka*) (23).
Referee: R.S.Mahanama (*Sri Lanka*) (51). **Test No. 2121/91 (SA384/A766)**

INTERNATIONAL UMPIRES AND REFEREES 2014

ELITE PANEL OF UMPIRES 2014

The Elite Panel of ICC Umpires and Referees was introduced in April 2002 to raise standards and guarantee impartial adjudication. Two umpires from this panel stand in Test matches while one officiates with a home umpire from the Supplementary International Panel in limited-overs internationals.

Full Names	Birthdate	Birthplace	Tests	Debut	LOI	Debut
ALIM Sarwar DAR	06.06.68	Jhang, Pakistan	89	2003-04	159	1999-00
DAVIS, Stephen James	09.04.52	London, England	52	1997-98	122	1992-93
DHARMASENA, H.D.P.Kumar	24.04.71	Colombo, Sri Lanka	23	2010-11	51	2008-09
ERASMUS, Marais	27.02.64	George, South Africa	23	2009-10	50	2007-08
GOULD, Ian James	19.08.57	Taplow, England	37	2008-09	87	2006
ILLINGWORTH, Richard Keith	23.08.63	Bradford, England	7	2012-13	27	2010
KETTLEBOROUGH, Richard Allan	15.03.73	Sheffield, England	20	2010-11	41	2009
LLONG, Nigel James	11.02.69	Ashford, England	24	2007-08	78	2006
OXENFORD, Bruce Nicholas James	05.03.60	Southport, Australia	17	2010-11	57	2007-08
REIFFEL, Paul Ronald	19.04.66	Box Hill, Australia	9	2012	33	2008-09
TUCKER, Rodney James	28.08.64	Sydney, Australia	29	2009-10	45	2008-09

ELITE PANEL OF REFEREES 2014

Full Names	Birthdate	Birthplace	Tests	Debut	LOI	Debut
BOON, David Clarence	29.12.60	Launceston, Australia	21	2011	47	2011
BROAD, Brian Christopher	29.09.57	Bristol, England	60	2003-04	244	2003-04
CROWE, Jeffrey John	14.09.58	Auckland, New Zealand	65	2004-05	192	2003-04
MADUGALLE, Ranjan Senerath	22.04.59	Kandy, Sri Lanka	148	1993-94	279	1993-94
MAHANAMA, Roshan Siriwardena	31.05.66	Colombo, Sri Lanka	51	2004	193	2004
PYCROFT, Andrew John	06.06.56	Harare, Zimbabwe	26	2009	102	2009
SRINATH, Javagal	31.08.69	Mysore, India	32	2006	132	2006-07

INTERNATIONAL UMPIRES PANEL 2014

Nominated by their respective cricket boards, members from this panel officiate in home LOIs and supplement the Elite panel for Test matches. Specialist third umpires have been selected to undertake adjudication involving television replays. The number of Test matches/LOI in which they have stood is shown in brackets.

			Third Umpire
Australia	S.D.Fry (-/10)		J.D.Ward (-/2)
Bangladesh	Enamul Haque (1/47)	Sharfuddoula (-/8)	Anisur Rahman (-/1)
England	R.J.Bailey (-/8)	M.A.Gough (-/3)	R.T.Robinson (-/2)
India	S.Ravi (3/12)	V.A.Kulkarni (-/9)	C.Shamshuddin (-/1)
			A.Chaudhary (-/-)
New Zealand	B.F.Bowden (76/189)	C.B.Gaffaney (-/20)	D.J.Walker (-/1)
			G.A.V.Baxter (-/38)
Pakistan	Shozab Raza (-/7)	Ahsan Raza (-/13)	Zamir Haider (-/15)
South Africa	J.D.Cloete (-/37)	S.George (-/10)	A.T.Holdstock (-/3)
Sri Lanka	R.E.S.Martinesz (-/4)	R.S.A.Palliyaguruge (-/17)	R.R.Wimalasiri (-/2)
West Indies	P.J.Nero (-/22)	J.S.Wilson (-/13)	G.O.Brathwaite (-/12)
			N.Duguid (-/-)
Zimbabwe	R.B.Tiffin (44/130)	O.Chirombe (-/12)	T.J.Matibiri (-/3)

Test Match and LOI statistics to 5 April 2014.

TEST MATCH CAREER RECORDS

These records, complete to 5 April 2014, contain all players registered for county cricket in 2014 at the time of going to press, plus those who have played Test cricket since 9 November 2012 (Test No. 2055). Records are for performances for the country shown, and do not include figures for multi-national teams.

ENGLAND – BATTING AND FIELDING

	M	I	NO	HS	Runs	Avge	100	50	Ct/St
K.Ali	1	2	–	9	10	5.00	–	–	–
T.R.Ambrose	11	16	1	102	447	29.80	1	3	31
J.M.Anderson	92	127	47	34	828	10.35	–	–	55
J.M.Bairstow	14	24	2	95	593	26.95	–	4	16
G.S.Ballance	1	2	–	18	25	12.50	–	–	–
G.J.Batty	7	8	1	38	144	20.57	–	–	3
I.R.Bell	98	170	22	235	6722	45.41	20	39	78
R.S.Bopara	13	19	1	143	575	31.94	3	–	6
S.G.Borthwick	1	2	–	4	5	2.50	–	–	2
T.T.Bresnan	23	26	4	91	575	26.13	–	3	8
S.C.J.Broad	67	95	12	169	2010	24.21	1	10	20
M.A.Carberry	6	12	–	60	345	28.75	–	1	7
R.Clarke	2	3	–	55	96	32.00	–	1	1
P.D.Collingwood	68	115	10	206	4259	40.56	10	20	96
N.R.D.Compton	9	17	2	117	479	31.93	2	1	4
A.N.Cook	102	183	10	294	8047	46.51	25	35	96
S.T.Finn	23	29	14	56	169	11.26	–	1	6
J.S.Foster	7	12	3	48	226	25.11	–	–	17/1
G.O.Jones	34	53	4	100	1172	23.91	1	6	128/5
S.C.Kerrigan	1	1	1	1*	1	–	–	–	–
R.W.T.Key	15	26	1	221	775	31.00	1	3	11
J.Lewis	1	2	–	20	27	13.50	–	–	–
S.I.Mahmood	8	11	1	34	81	8.10	–	–	–
E.J.G.Morgan	16	24	1	130	700	30.43	2	3	11
G.Onions	9	10	7	17*	30	10.00	–	–	–
M.S.Panesar	50	68	23	26	220	4.88	–	–	10
S.R.Patel	5	7	–	33	109	15.57	–	–	2
K.P.Pietersen	104	181	8	227	8181	47.28	23	35	62
L.E.Plunkett	9	13	2	44*	126	11.45	–	–	3
M.J.Prior	75	116	20	131*	3920	40.83	7	27	217/13
W.B.Rankin	1	2	–	13	13	6.50	–	–	–
C.M.W.Read	15	23	4	55	360	18.94	–	1	48/6
J.E.Root	15	29	3	180	955	36.73	2	4	8
A.Shahzad	1	1	–	5	5	5.00	–	–	2
R.J.Sidebottom	22	31	11	31	313	15.65	–	–	5
B.A.Stokes	4	8	–	120	279	34.87	1	–	1
G.P.Swann	60	76	14	85	1370	22.09	–	5	54
J.W.A.Taylor	2	3	–	34	48	16.00	–	–	2
J.C.Tredwell	1	1	–	37	37	37.00	–	–	1
C.T.Tremlett	12	15	4	25*	113	10.27	–	–	4
M.E.Trescothick	76	143	10	219	5825	43.79	14	29	95
I.J.L.Trott	49	87	6	226	3763	46.45	9	18	29
C.R.Woakes	1	2	–	25	42	42.00	–	–	–

TEST   **ENGLAND – BOWLING**

	O	M	R	W	Avge	Best	5wI	10wM
K.Ali	36	5	136	5	27.20	3- 80	–	–
J.M.Anderson	3391.4	788	10522	343	30.67	7- 43	15	2
G.J.Batty	232.2	34	733	11	66.63	3- 55	–	–
I.R.Bell	18	3	76	1	76.00	1- 33	–	–
R.S.Bopara	72.2	10	290	1	290.00	1- 39	–	–
S.G.Borthwick	13	0	82	4	20.50	3- 33	–	–
T.T.Bresnan	779	185	2357	72	32.73	5- 48	1	–
S.C.J.Broad	2316	477	7215	238	30.31	7- 44	11	2
R.Clarke	29	11	60	4	15.00	2- 7	–	–
P.D.Collingwood	317.3	51	1018	17	59.88	3- 23	–	–
A.N.Cook	1	0	1	0	–	–	–	–
S.T.Finn	724.4	135	2646	90	29.40	6-125	4	–
S.C.Kerrigan	8	0	53	0	–	–	–	–
J.Lewis	41	9	122	3	40.66	3- 68	–	–
S.I.Mahmood	188.2	25	762	20	38.10	4- 22	–	–
G.Onions	267.4	50	957	32	29.90	5- 38	1	–
M.S.Panesar	2079.1	469	5797	167	34.71	6- 37	12	2
S.R.Patel	101	19	257	4	64.25	2- 27	–	–
K.P.Pietersen	218.3	15	886	10	88.60	3- 52	–	–
L.E.Plunkett	256.2	40	916	23	39.82	3- 17	–	–
W.B.Rankin	20.5	0	81	1	81.00	1- 47	–	–
J.E.Root	62	14	169	3	56.33	2- 9	–	–
A.Shahzad	17	4	63	4	15.75	3- 45	–	–
R.J.Sidebottom	802	188	2231	79	28.24	7- 47	5	1
B.A.Stokes	116.5	14	492	15	32.80	6- 99	1	–
G.P.Swann	2558.1	493	7642	255	29.96	6- 65	17	3
J.C.Tredwell	65	13	181	6	30.16	4- 82	–	–
C.T.Tremlett	483.4	114	1431	53	27.00	6- 48	2	–
M.E.Trescothick	50	6	155	1	155.00	1- 34	–	–
I.J.L.Trott	117	11	398	5	79.60	1- 5	–	–
C.R.Woakes	24	7	96	1	96.00	1- 96	–	–

TEST

AUSTRALIA – BATTING AND FIELDING

	M	I	NO	HS	Runs	Avge	100	50	Ct/St
A.C.Agar	2	4	–	98	130	32.50	–	1	–
G.J.Bailey	5	8	1	53	183	26.14	–	1	10
J.M.Bird	3	4	3	6*	7	7.00	–	–	1
D.E.Bollinger	12	14	7	21	54	7.71	–	–	2
M.J.Clarke	105	180	20	329*	8240	51.50	27	27	125
E.J.M.Cowan	18	32	–	136	1001	31.28	1	6	24
X.J.Doherty	4	7	3	18*	51	12.75	–	–	2
A.J.Doolan	3	6	–	89	186	31.00	–	1	3
J.P.Faulkner	1	2	–	23	45	22.50	–	–	–
B.J.Haddin	57	96	10	169	3033	35.26	5	17	228/5
R.J.Harris	24	35	10	68*	483	19.32	–	2	11
J.W.Hastings	1	2	–	32	52	26.00	–	–	1
M.C.Henriques	3	6	1	81*	156	31.20	–	2	1
B.W.Hilfenhaus	27	38	12	56*	355	13.65	–	1	7
P.J.Hughes	26	49	2	160	1535	32.65	3	7	15
M.E.K.Hussey	79	137	16	195	6235	51.52	19	29	85
P.A.Jaques	11	19	–	150	902	47.47	3	6	7
M.G.Johnson	59	88	14	123*	1637	22.12	1	8	22
S.M.Katich	56	99	6	157	4188	45.03	10	25	39
U.T.Khawaja	9	17	2	65	377	25.13	–	2	5
N.M.Lyon	33	41	21	40*	323	16.15	–	–	14
S.E.Marsh	9	15	–	148	493	32.86	2	1	6
G.J.Maxwell	2	4	–	13	39	9.75	–	–	2
J.L.Pattinson	13	18	7	42	331	30.09	–	–	1
R.T.Ponting	168	287	29	257	13378	51.85	41	62	196
R.J.Quiney	2	3	–	9	9	3.00	–	–	5
C.J.L.Rogers	14	27	–	119	1030	38.14	4	5	9
P.M.Siddle	53	76	11	51	926	14.24	–	2	16
S.P.D.Smith	20	38	4	138*	1361	40.02	4	6	16
M.A.Starc	12	20	6	99	431	30.78	–	3	4
M.S.Wade	12	22	4	106	623	34.61	2	3	33/3
D.A.Warner	30	56	3	180	2467	46.54	8	12	24
S.R.Watson	52	97	3	176	3408	36.25	4	22	35

AUSTRALIA – BOWLING

	O	M	R	W	Avge	Best	5wI	10wM
A.C.Agar	84	17	248	2	124.00	2- 82	–	–
J.M.Bird	105.3	36	303	13	23.30	4- 41	–	–
D.E.Bollinger	400.1	78	1296	50	25.92	5- 28	2	–
M.J.Clarke	397.5	62	1152	31	37.16	6- 9	2	–
X.J.Doherty	153	36	548	7	78.28	3-131	–	–
J.P.Faulkner	27.4	4	98	6	16.33	4- 51	–	–
R.J.Harris	830	221	2324	103	22.56	7-117	5	–
J.W.Hastings	39	3	153	1	153.00	1- 51	–	–
M.C.Henriques	53	12	155	2	77.50	1- 48	–	–
B.W.Hilfenhaus	1013	258	2822	99	28.50	5- 75	2	–
M.E.K.Hussey	98	11	306	7	43.71	1- 0	–	–
M.G.Johnson	2204.3	411	7240	264	27.42	8- 61	12	3
S.M.Katich	173.1	21	635	21	30.23	6- 65	1	–
N.M.Lyon	1225.1	260	3695	112	32.99	7- 94	5	–
G.J.Maxwell	41	2	193	7	27.57	4-127	–	–
J.L.Pattinson	425	96	1381	51	27.07	5- 27	3	–
R.T.Ponting	97.5	24	276	5	55.20	1- 0	–	–
R.J.Quiney	25	12	29	0	–	–	–	–
P.M.Siddle	1870.3	486	5522	188	29.37	6- 54	8	–
S.P.D.Smith	137	18	527	11	47.90	3- 18	–	–
M.A.Starc	408.2	74	1378	41	33.60	6-154	2	–
M.S.Wade	1	1	0	0	–	–	–	–
D.A.Warner	49	1	218	4	54.50	2- 45	–	–
S.R.Watson	802.1	211	2205	69	31.95	6- 33	3	–

TEST

SOUTH AFRICA – BATTING AND FIELDING

	M	I	NO	HS	Runs	Avge	100	50	Ct/St
K.J.Abbott	2	3	–	13	23	7.66	–	–	1
H.M.Amla	76	132	11	311*	6214	51.35	21	27	60
Q.de Kock	1	2	–	34	41	20.50	–	–	–
A.B.de Villiers	92	154	16	278*	7168	51.94	19	35	169/3
F.du Plessis	14	22	3	137	996	52.42	3	4	9
J.P.Duminy	24	38	6	166	1111	34.71	3	5	17
D.Elgar	9	13	2	103*	325	29.54	1	1	7
A.J.Hall	21	33	4	163	760	26.20	1	3	16
Imran Tahir	13	14	6	29*	90	11.25	–	–	5
J.H.Kallis	165	278	39	224	13206	55.25	45	58	196
R.K.Kleinveldt	4	5	2	17*	27	9.00	–	–	2
R.McLaren	2	3	1	33*	47	23.50	–	–	–
M.Morkel	56	67	10	40	682	11.96	–	–	14
W.D.Parnell	4	3	–	22	44	14.66	–	–	1
A.N.Petersen	30	54	3	182	1890	37.05	5	8	24
R.J.Peterson	15	20	3	84	464	27.29	–	3	9
V.D.Philander	23	30	8	74	604	27.45	–	4	6
A.G.Prince	66	104	16	162*	3665	41.64	11	11	47
J.A.Rudolph	48	83	9	222*	2622	35.43	6	11	29
G.C.Smith	116	203	13	277	9253	48.70	27	38	166
D.W.Steyn	72	91	21	76	998	14.25	–	1	19

SOUTH AFRICA – BOWLING

	O	M	R	W	Avge	Best	5wI	10wM
K.J.Abbott	70.4	24	197	12	16.41	7- 29	1	–
H.M.Amla	9	0	37	0	–	–	–	–
A.B.de Villiers	34	6	104	2	52.00	2- 49	–	–
F.du Plessis	13	0	69	0	–	–	–	–
J.P.Duminy	298	28	1054	27	39.03	4- 73	–	–
D.Elgar	38.1	0	163	3	54.33	1- 3	–	–
A.J.Hall	500.1	95	1617	45	35.93	3- 1	–	–
Imran Tahir	437.1	59	1551	36	43.08	5- 32	1	–
J.H.Kallis	3372	848	9535	292	32.65	6- 54	5	–
R.K.Kleinveldt	111.1	21	422	10	42.20	3- 65	–	–
R.McLaren	44	8	162	3	54.00	2- 72	–	–
M.Morkel	1828	380	5855	189	30.97	6- 23	6	–
W.D.Parnell	59.3	7	258	7	36.85	2- 17	–	–
A.N.Petersen	19	1	62	1	62.00	1- 2	–	–
R.J.Peterson	419.1	85	1416	38	37.26	5- 33	1	–
V.D.Philander	791.1	185	2253	112	20.11	6- 44	9	2
A.G.Prince	16	1	47	1	47.00	1- 2	–	–
J.A.Rudolph	110.4	13	432	4	108.00	1- 1	–	–
G.C.Smith	236.2	28	885	8	110.62	2-145	–	–
D.W.Steyn	2543.3	536	8333	362	23.01	7- 51	22	5

TEST   **WEST INDIES – BATTING AND FIELDING**

	M	I	NO	HS	Runs	Avge	100	50	Ct/St
T.L.Best	25	38	6	95	401	12.53	–	1	6
K.C.Brathwaite	10	19	–	68	415	21.84	–	4	5
D.M.Bravo	27	49	4	218	2011	44.68	5	8	19
G.R.Breese	1	2	–	5	5	2.50	–	–	1
S.Chanderpaul	153	261	45	203*	11219	51.93	29	62	64
S.S.Cottrell	1	2	–	5	5	2.50	–	–	–
N.Deonarine	18	30	2	82	725	25.89	–	5	16
F.H.Edwards	55	88	28	30	394	6.56	–	–	10
K.A.Edwards	12	24	1	121	821	35.69	2	6	11
S.T.Gabriel	6	9	2	13	14	2.00	–	–	3
C.H.Gayle	99	174	9	333	6933	42.01	15	34	90
S.P.Narine	6	7	2	22*	40	8.00	–	–	2
B.P.Nash	21	33	–	114	1103	33.42	2	8	6
V.Permaul	4	6	–	20	57	9.50	–	–	1
K.O.A.Powell	20	38	1	134	1044	28.21	3	2	18
D.Ramdin	56	95	13	166	2235	27.25	4	11	156/5
R.Rampaul	18	31	8	40*	335	14.56	–	–	3
K.A.J.Roach	23	37	7	41	291	9.70	–	–	8
D.J.G.Sammy	38	63	2	106	1323	21.68	1	5	65
M.N.Samuels	51	90	6	260	2983	35.51	5	20	23
R.R.Sarwan	87	154	8	291	5842	40.01	15	31	53
S.Shillingford	14	22	3	31*	159	8.36	–	–	7

WEST INDIES – BOWLING

	O	M	R	W	Avge	Best	5wI	10wM
T.L.Best	619.2	80	2291	57	40.19	6- 40	2	–
K.C.Brathwaite	7.4	0	50	1	50.00	1- 43	–	–
G.R.Breese	31.2	3	135	2	67.50	2-108	–	–
S.Chanderpaul	290	50	883	9	98.11	1- 2	–	–
S.S.Cottrell	18	3	72	1	72.00	1- 72	–	–
N.Deonarine	250.3	49	713	24	29.70	4- 37	–	–
F.H.Edwards	1600.2	183	6249	165	37.87	7- 87	12	–
K.A.Edwards	4	0	19	0	–	–	–	–
S.T.Gabriel	133.1	27	505	13	38.84	3- 10	–	–
C.H.Gayle	1149.5	224	3024	72	42.00	5- 34	2	–
S.P.Narine	275	60	851	21	40.52	6- 91	2	–
B.P.Nash	82	13	247	2	123.50	1- 21	–	–
V.Permaul	141.4	20	452	12	37.66	3- 32	–	–
R.Rampaul	573.2	111	1705	49	34.79	4- 48	–	–
K.A.J.Roach	730.1	143	2356	85	27.71	6- 48	5	1
D.J.G.Sammy	1035.5	216	3007	84	35.79	7- 66	4	–
M.N.Samuels	530.3	59	1773	34	52.14	4- 13	–	–
R.R.Sarwan	337	33	1163	23	50.56	4- 37	–	–
S.Shillingford	691.5	113	2101	65	32.32	6- 49	6	2

TEST

NEW ZEALAND – BATTING AND FIELDING

	M	I	NO	HS	Runs	Avge	100	50	Ct/St
A.R.Adams	1	2	–	11	18	9.00	–	–	1
C.A.Anderson	7	11	1	116	327	32.70	1	1	4
T.D.Astle	1	2	–	35	38	19.00	–	–	–
T.A.Boult	22	31	17	52*	264	18.85	–	1	8
D.A.J.Bracewell	18	33	2	43	337	10.87	–	–	5
D.G.Brownlie	14	25	1	109	711	29.62	1	4	17
D.R.Flynn	24	45	5	95	1038	25.95	–	6	10
J.E.C.Franklin	31	46	7	122*	808	20.71	1	2	12
P.G.Fulton	22	37	1	136	966	26.83	2	5	24
M.J.Guptill	31	59	1	189	1718	29.62	2	12	33
T.W.M.Latham	1	2	–	29	29	14.50	–	–	–
B.B.McCullum	84	145	8	302	5219	38.09	9	28	183/11
H.J.H.Marshall	13	19	2	160	652	38.35	2	2	1
B.P.Martin	5	6	1	41	74	14.80	–	–	–
C.S.Martin	71	104	52	12*	123	2.36	–	–	14
C.Munro	1	2	–	15	15	7.50	–	–	–
J.D.S.Neesham	1	2	1	137*	170	170.00	1	–	–
J.S.Patel	19	30	7	27*	276	12.00	–	–	12
A.J.Redmond	8	16	1	83	325	21.66	–	2	5
H.D.Rutherford	12	21	1	171	611	30.55	1	1	8
I.S.Sodhi	6	8	1	58	175	25.00	–	1	2
T.G.Southee	31	50	5	77*	855	19.00	–	2	17
L.R.P.L.Taylor	54	98	9	217*	4178	46.94	11	21	90
C.F.K.van Wyk	9	17	1	71	341	21.31	–	1	23/1
N.Wagner	14	21	6	37	194	12.93	–	–	4
B.J.Watling	21	35	4	124	1092	35.22	3	6	64
K.S.Williamson	31	56	2	135	1964	36.37	5	12	28

NEW ZEALAND – BOWLING

	O	M	R	W	Avge	Best	5wI	10wM
A.R.Adams	31.4	5	105	6	17.50	3- 44	–	–
C.A.Anderson	120	22	336	11	30.54	3- 47	–	–
T.D.Astle	31	6	97	1	97.00	1- 56	–	–
T.A.Boult	744.2	172	2181	82	26.58	6- 40	3	1
D.A.J.Bracewell	530.4	90	1813	50	36.26	6- 40	2	–
D.G.Brownlie	11	0	52	1	52.00	1- 13	–	–
D.R.Flynn	1	1	0	0	–	–	–	–
J.E.C.Franklin	794.3	143	2786	82	33.97	6-119	3	–
M.J.Guptill	55.2	3	258	5	51.60	3- 37	–	–
B.B.McCullum	6	1	18	0	–	–	–	–
H.J.H.Marshall	1	0	4	0	–	–	–	–
B.P.Martin	253	77	646	12	53.83	4- 43	–	–
C.S.Martin	2337.4	486	7878	233	33.81	6- 26	10	1
C.Munro	18	4	40	2	20.00	2- 40	–	–
J.D.S.Neesham	23	2	87	1	87.00	1- 62	–	–
J.S.Patel	787.1	164	2520	52	48.46	5-110	1	–
A.J.Redmond	17.3	3	80	3	26.66	2- 47	–	–
I.S.Sodhi	177.3	21	657	11	59.72	3- 59	–	–
T.G.Southee	1087.5	221	3438	112	30.69	7- 64	4	1
L.R.P.L.Taylor	16	3	48	2	24.00	2- 4	–	–
N.Wagner	502.4	98	1750	50	35.00	5- 64	1	–
K.S.Williamson	269.1	40	905	22	41.13	4- 44	–	–

TEST

INDIA – BATTING AND FIELDING

	M	I	NO	HS	Runs	Avge	100	50	Ct/St
R.Ashwin	19	26	6	124	788	39.40	2	3	6
P.P.Chawla	3	3	–	4	6	2.00	–	–	1
S.Dhawan	7	11	–	187	534	48.54	2	1	3
M.S.Dhoni	83	130	15	224	4459	38.77	6	29	226/37
G.Gambhir	54	96	5	206	4021	44.18	9	21	38
Harbhajan Singh	101	142	22	115	2202	18.35	2	9	42
R.A.Jadeja	8	11	2	43	187	20.77	–	–	9
Z.Khan	92	127	24	75	1231	11.95	–	3	19
V.Kohli	24	41	4	119	1721	46.51	6	9	27
B.Kumar	6	6	1	38	96	19.20	–	–	4
Mohammed Shami	6	9	3	11	20	3.33	–	–	1
P.P.Ojha	24	27	17	18*	89	8.90	–	–	10
C.A.Pujara	19	32	4	206*	1650	58.92	6	4	13
A.M.Rahane	5	9	1	118	379	47.37	1	2	3
V.Sehwag	103	178	6	319	8503	49.34	23	31	90
I.Sharma	55	81	28	31*	489	9.22	–	–	12
R.G.Sharma	6	10	2	177	455	56.87	2	1	8
S.R.Tendulkar	200	329	33	248*	15921	53.78	51	68	115
M.Vijay	22	37	–	167	1304	35.24	3	4	2
U.T.Yadav	9	11	5	21	36	6.00	–	–	2
Yuvraj Singh	40	62	6	169	1900	33.92	3	11	31

INDIA – BOWLING

	O	M	R	W	Avge	Best	5wI	10wM
R.Ashwin	1019.3	206	2965	104	28.50	7-103	9	2
P.P.Chawla	82	13	270	7	38.57	4- 69	–	–
S.Dhawan	1	0	3	0	–	–	–	–
M.S.Dhoni	16	1	67	0	–	–	–	–
G.Gambhir	2	0	4	0	–	–	–	–
Harbhajan Singh	4715.3	866	13372	413	32.37	8- 84	25	5
R.A.Jadeja	414.4	119	947	36	26.30	6-138	2	–
Z.Khan	3130.5	624	10247	311	32.94	7- 87	11	1
V.Kohli	24	1	70	0	–	–	–	–
B.Kumar	104	18	341	9	37.88	3- 31	–	–
Mohammed Shami	224	32	796	27	29.48	5- 47	1	–
P.P.Ojha	1272.1	298	3420	113	30.26	6- 47	7	1
V.Sehwag	621.5	74	1894	40	47.35	5-104	1	–
I.Sharma	1837.3	341	6161	164	37.56	6- 51	5	1
R.G.Sharma	26.4	1	94	0	–	–	–	–
S.R.Tendulkar	706.4	83	2492	46	54.17	3- 10	–	–
M.Vijay	1	0	3	0	–	–	–	–
U.T.Yadav	247.3	27	1040	32	32.50	5- 93	1	–
Yuvraj Singh	155.1	14	547	9	60.77	2- 9	–	–

TEST　　　　　　　　　　PAKISTAN – BATTING AND FIELDING

	M	I	NO	HS	Runs	Avge	100	50	Ct/St
Abdur Rehman	20	27	3	60	323	13.45	–	1	8
Adnan Akmal	21	29	5	64	591	24.62	–	3	66/11
Ahmed Shehzad	3	6	–	147	273	45.50	1	1	2
Asad Shafiq	26	42	4	130	1391	36.60	4	8	22
Azhar Ali	32	60	4	157	2192	39.14	5	15	27
Bilawal Bhatti	2	3	1	32	70	35.00	–	–	–
Ehsan Adil	1	2	–	12	21	10.50	–	–	–
Imran Farhat	40	77	2	128	2400	32.00	3	14	40
Junaid Khan	16	21	7	17	98	7.00	–	–	3
Khurram Manzoor	14	26	1	146	778	31.12	1	7	7
Misbah-ul-Haq	46	80	14	161*	3218	48.75	5	25	37
Mohammad Hafeez	36	70	6	196	2174	33.96	5	9	26
Mohammad Irfan	4	7	2	14	28	5.60	–	–	–
Mohammad Talha	2	1	–	2	2	2.00	–	–	–
Nasir Jamshed	2	4	–	46	51	12.75	–	–	1
Rahat Ali	6	11	5	35*	70	11.66	–	–	4
Saeed Ajmal	33	49	11	50	428	11.26	–	1	11
Sarfraz Ahmed	6	12	–	74	223	18.58	–	1	14
Shan Masood	2	4	–	75	96	24.00	–	1	2
Shoaib Malik	32	54	6	148*	1606	33.45	2	8	16
Tanvir Ahmed	5	7	2	57	170	34.00	–	1	1
Umar Gul	47	67	9	65*	577	9.94	–	1	11
Yasir Arafat	3	3	1	50*	94	47.00	–	1	–
Younus Khan	89	158	14	313	7399	51.38	23	28	98
Zulfiqar Babar	2	2	1	25*	27	27.00	–	–	–

PAKISTAN – BOWLING

	O	M	R	W	Avge	Best	5wI	10wM
Abdur Rehman	1055.1	247	2637	95	27.75	6- 25	2	–
Azhar Ali	25	2	100	1	100.00	1- 4	–	–
Bilawal Bhatti	73	12	291	6	48.50	3- 65	–	–
Ehsan Adil	12.1	2	54	2	27.00	2- 54	–	–
Imran Farhat	71.1	4	284	3	94.66	2- 69	–	–
Junaid Khan	589.4	121	1628	56	29.07	5- 38	4	–
Mohammad Hafeez	471.5	86	1190	35	34.00	4- 16	–	–
Mohammad Irfan	118.4	15	389	10	38.90	3- 44	–	–
Mohammad Talha	72	5	252	7	36.00	3- 65	–	–
Rahat Ali	227.4	37	725	16	45.31	6-127	2	–
Saeed Ajmal	1787.5	363	4642	169	27.46	7- 55	9	4
Shahid Afridi	532.2	69	1709	48	35.60	5- 52	1	–
Shoaib Malik	374.1	47	1291	21	61.47	4- 12	–	–
Tanvir Ahmed	117.5	20	453	17	26.64	6-120	1	–
Umar Gul	1599.5	256	5553	163	34.06	6-135	4	–
Yasir Arafat	104.3	12	438	9	48.66	5-161	1	–
Younus Khan	134	18	491	9	54.55	2- 23	–	–
Zulfiqar Babar	82.2	10	264	6	44.00	3- 89	–	–

TEST **SRI LANKA – BATTING AND FIELDING**

	M	I	NO	HS	Runs	Avge	100	50	Ct/St
L.D.Chandimal	12	20	3	116*	875	51.47	3	5	15/4
T.M.Dilshan	87	145	11	193	5492	40.98	16	23	88
R.M.S.Eranga	11	13	4	25*	105	11.66	–	–	4
A.N.P.R.Fernando	6	8	2	17*	35	5.83	–	–	–
H.M.R.K.B.Herath	51	70	15	80*	713	12.96	–	1	12
D.P.M.D.Jayawardena	143	240	15	374	11319	50.30	33	46	194
H.A.P.W.Jayawardena	55	77	11	154*	2061	31.22	4	5	115/32
H.K.S.R.Kaluhalamulla	12	17	1	39	147	9.18	–	–	1
F.D.M.Karunaratne	11	21	2	85	574	30.21	–	4	9
K.M.D.N.Kulasekara	20	26	1	64	381	15.24	–	1	8
R.A.S.Lakmal	19	25	11	18	93	6.64	–	–	4
A.D.Mathews	38	62	12	157*	2308	46.16	2	14	20
B.A.W.Mendis	18	18	6	78	211	17.58	–	1	2
N.T.Paranavitana	32	60	5	111	1792	32.58	2	11	27
M.D.K.Perera	3	3	–	95	104	34.66	–	1	3
K.T.G.D.Prasad	12	16	1	47	275	18.33	–	–	5
T.T.Samaraweera	81	132	20	231	5462	48.76	14	30	45
K.C.Sangakkara	122	209	17	319	11151	58.07	35	45	171/20
S.M.S.M.Senanayake	1	1	–	5	5	5.00	–	–	1
J.K.Silva	8	15	–	139	570	38.00	1	3	13/1
H.D.R.L.Thirimanne	10	20	4	155*	526	32.87	1	2	4
K.D.K.Vithanage	4	4	1	103*	209	69.66	1	1	2
U.W.M.B.C.A.Welagedara	20	28	5	48	191	8.30	–	–	4

SRI LANKA – BOWLING

	O	M	R	W	Avge	Best	5wI	10wM
T.M.Dilshan	564.1	83	1711	39	43.87	4- 10	–	–
R.M.S.Eranga	378.1	60	1201	38	31.60	4- 49	–	–
A.N.P.R.Fernando	167.4	19	714	8	89.25	3- 62	–	–
H.M.R.K.B.Herath	2322.1	431	6514	217	30.01	7- 89	17	3
D.P.M.D.Jayawardena	92.1	18	297	6	49.50	2- 32	–	–
H.K.S.R.Kaluhalamulla	524.2	70	1613	43	37.51	5- 82	1	–
F.D.M.Karunaratne	2	0	5	0	–	–	–	–
K.M.D.N.Kulasekara	557.3	115	1656	46	35.78	4- 21	–	–
R.A.S.Lakmal	561.3	101	1925	39	49.35	4- 78	–	–
A.D.Mathews	322	58	993	14	70.92	2- 60	–	–
B.A.W.Mendis	754.2	109	2349	70	33.55	6- 99	4	1
N.T.Paranavitana	17	0	86	1	86.00	1- 26	–	–
M.D.K.Perera	114.5	14	399	11	36.27	5-109	1	–
K.T.G.D.Prasad	303.2	26	1298	22	59.00	3- 82	–	–
T.T.Samaraweera	221.1	36	689	15	45.93	4- 49	–	–
K.C.Sangakkara	14	0	49	0	–	–	–	–
S.M.S.M.Senanayake	23	2	96	0	–	–	–	–
H.D.R.L.Thirimanne	3	0	20	0	–	–	–	–
K.D.K.Vithanage	16	0	73	1	73.00	1- 73	–	–
U.W.M.B.C.A.Welagedara	606.1	108	2186	54	40.48	5- 52	–	–

A.N.P.R.Fernando is also known as N.Pradeep; H.K.S.R.Kaluhalamulla is also known as S.Randiv.

TEST　　　　**ZIMBABWE – BATTING AND FIELDING**

	M	I	NO	HS	Runs	Avge	100	50	Ct/St
R.W.Chakabva	4	8	–	63	163	20.37	–	1	5
T.L.Chatara	4	8	–	21	41	5.12	–	–	–
E.Chigumbura	11	21	–	86	434	20.66	–	3	3
A.G.Cremer	11	22	2	43	216	10.80	–	–	6
C.R.Ervine	4	8	2	49	174	29.00	–	–	3
S.M.Ervine	5	8	–	86	261	32.62	–	3	7
M.W.Goodwin	19	37	4	166*	1414	42.84	3	8	10
K.M.Jarvis	8	14	6	25*	58	7.25	–	–	3
T.Maruma	1	2	–	10	20	10.00	–	–	1
H.Masakadza	25	50	2	119	1292	26.91	3	4	12
S.W.Masakadza	4	7	1	24	88	14.66	–	–	2
T.M.K.Mawoyo	8	16	1	163*	454	30.26	1	3	6
K.O.Meth	2	4	1	31*	72	24.00	–	–	–
R.Mutumbami	4	8	1	42	131	18.71	–	–	12/2
T.Panyangara	5	10	3	40*	162	23.14	–	–	–
R.W.Price	22	38	8	36	261	8.70	–	–	4
V.Sibanda	12	24	–	93	526	21.91	–	2	13
Sikandar Raza	1	2	–	60	84	42.00	–	1	–
B.R.M.Taylor	19	38	2	171	1260	35.00	4	6	18
P.Utseya	4	8	1	45	107	15.28	–	–	2
B.V.Vitori	4	7	2	19*	52	10.40	–	–	2
M.N.Waller	8	16	1	72*	386	25.73	–	3	6
S.C.Williams	1	2	–	31	37	18.50	–	–	1

ZIMBABWE – BOWLING

	O	M	R	W	Avge	Best	5wI	10wM
T.L.Chatara	148.1	34	405	15	27.00	5- 61	1	–
E.Chigumbura	225.3	38	779	16	48.68	5- 54	1	–
A.G.Cremer	269.2	30	1095	24	45.62	4- 4	–	–
S.M.Ervine	95	18	388	9	43.11	4-116	–	–
M.W.Goodwin	19.5	3	69	0	–	–	–	–
K.M.Jarvis	261.3	47	952	30	31.73	5- 54	2	–
H.Masakadza	127	35	270	10	27.00	3- 24	–	–
S.W.Masakadza	144.1	29	410	14	29.28	4- 32	–	–
K.O.Meth	54	18	98	4	24.50	2- 41	–	–
T.Panyangara	177.1	49	485	17	28.52	3- 28	–	–
R.W.Price	1022.3	242	2885	80	36.06	6- 73	5	1
B.R.M.Taylor	7	0	38	0	–	–	–	–
P.Utseya	125.3	16	410	10	41.00	3- 60	–	–
B.V.Vitori	138.5	25	464	12	38.66	5- 61	1	–
M.N.Waller	3	0	8	0	–	–	–	–
S.C.Williams	1	0	9	0	–	–	–	–

TEST **BANGLADESH – BATTING AND FIELDING**

	M	I	NO	HS	Runs	Avge	100	50	Ct/St
Abdur Razzak	12	20	6	43	245	17.50	–	–	4
Abul Hasan	3	5	3	113	165	82.50	1	–	3
Al-Amin Hossain	3	4	3	32*	47	47.00	–	–	–
Anamul Haque	3	6	–	22	64	10.66	–	–	1
Elias Sunny	4	6	1	20*	38	7.60	–	–	1
Enamul Haque II	15	26	16	13	59	5.90	–	–	3
Imrul Kayes	17	34	–	115	689	20.26	1	1	17
Jahurul Islam	7	14	1	48	347	26.69	–	–	7
Junaid Siddique	19	37	–	106	969	26.18	1	7	11
Mahmudullah	18	34	2	115	895	27.96	1	6	16
Marshall Ayub	3	6	–	41	125	20.83	–	–	2
Mohammad Ashraful	61	119	5	190	2737	24.00	6	8	25
Mominul Haque	7	13	3	181	755	75.50	3	3	4
Mushfiqur Rahim	38	71	4	200	2173	32.43	2	13	60/10
Naeem Islam	8	15	2	108	416	32.00	1	1	2
Nasir Hossain	14	23	1	100	934	42.45	1	6	10
Nazimuddin	3	6	–	78	125	20.83	–	1	1
Robiul Islam	8	15	6	33	99	11.00	–	–	5
Rubel Hossain	19	33	14	17	141	7.42	–	–	8
Sajedul Islam	3	6	–	6	18	3.00	–	–	–
Shahadat Hossain	35	65	17	40	489	10.18	–	–	8
Shahriar Nafees	24	48	–	138	1267	26.39	1	7	19
Shakib Al Hasan	34	65	5	144	2278	37.96	2	16	14
Shamsur Rahman	2	4	–	106	193	48.25	1	–	–
Sohag Gazi	10	16	1	101*	325	21.66	1	–	5
Tamim Iqbal	32	62	–	151	2269	36.59	4	14	9
Ziaur Rahman	1	2	–	14	14	7.00	–	–	–

BANGLADESH – BOWLING

	O	M	R	W	Avge	Best	5wI	10wM
Abdur Razzak	469.3	65	1550	23	67.39	3- 93	–	–
Abul Hasan	88	8	371	3	123.66	2- 80	–	–
Al-Amin Hossain	80	12	288	3	96.00	1- 58	–	–
Elias Sunny	143.5	11	518	12	43.16	6- 94	1	–
Enamul Haque II	591.3	101	1787	44	40.61	7- 95	3	1
Imrul Kayes	2	0	8	0	–	–	–	–
Junaid Siddique	3	0	11	0	–	–	–	–
Mahmudullah	418.2	44	1418	31	45.74	5- 51	1	–
Marshall Ayub	10	0	53	0	–	–	–	–
Mohammad Ashraful	288.5	14	1271	21	60.52	2- 42	–	–
Mominul Haque	39.1	0	149	1	149.00	1- 10	–	–
Naeem Islam	95.4	8	303	1	303.00	1- 11	–	–
Nasir Hossain	137.3	21	402	8	50.25	3- 52	–	–
Robiul Islam	272	45	887	23	38.56	6- 71	2	–
Rubel Hossain	531	49	2112	26	81.23	5-166	1	–
Sajedul Islam	55	10	232	3	77.33	2- 71	–	–
Shahadat Hossain	863.2	87	3633	70	51.90	6- 27	4	–
Shakib Al Hasan	1382	268	4074	122	33.39	7- 36	11	–
Shamsur Rahman	1	0	5	0	–	–	–	–
Sohag Gazi	525.1	66	1599	38	42.07	6- 74	2	–
Tamim Iqbal	5	0	20	0	–	–	–	–
Ziaur Rahman	30	11	71	4	17.75	4- 63	–	–

INTERNATIONAL TEST MATCH RESULTS

Complete to 5 April 2014.

	Opponents	Tests	Won by										Tied	Drawn
			E	A	SA	WI	NZ	I	P	SL	Z	B		
England	Australia	336	105	138	–	–	–	–	–	–	–	–	–	93
	South Africa	141	56	–	31	–	–	–	–	–	–	–	–	54
	West Indies	148	45	–	–	53	–	–	–	–	–	–	–	50
	New Zealand	99	47	–	–	–	8	–	–	–	–	–	–	44
	India	107	40	–	–	–	–	20	–	–	–	–	–	47
	Pakistan	74	22	–	–	–	–	–	16	–	–	–	–	36
	Sri Lanka	26	10	–	–	–	–	–	–	7	–	–	–	9
	Zimbabwe	6	3	–	–	–	–	–	–	–	0	–	–	3
	Bangladesh	8	8	–	–	–	–	–	–	–	–	0	–	0
Australia	South Africa	91	–	50	21	–	–	–	–	–	–	–	–	20
	West Indies	111	–	54	–	32	–	–	–	–	–	–	1	24
	New Zealand	52	–	27	–	–	8	–	–	–	–	–	–	17
	India	86	–	38	–	–	–	24	–	–	–	–	1	23
	Pakistan	57	–	28	–	–	–	–	12	–	–	–	–	17
	Sri Lanka	26	–	17	–	–	–	–	–	1	–	–	–	8
	Zimbabwe	3	–	3	–	–	–	–	–	–	0	–	–	0
	Bangladesh	4	–	4	–	–	–	–	–	–	–	0	–	0
South Africa	West Indies	25	–	–	16	3	–	–	–	–	–	–	–	6
	New Zealand	40	–	–	23	–	4	–	–	–	–	–	–	13
	India	29	–	–	13	–	–	7	–	–	–	–	–	9
	Pakistan	23	–	–	12	–	–	–	4	–	–	–	–	7
	Sri Lanka	20	–	–	10	–	–	–	–	5	–	–	–	5
	Zimbabwe	7	–	–	6	–	–	–	–	–	0	–	–	1
	Bangladesh	8	–	–	8	–	–	–	–	–	–	0	–	0
West Indies	New Zealand	42	–	–	–	12	11	–	–	–	–	–	–	19
	India	90	–	–	–	30	–	16	–	–	–	–	–	44
	Pakistan	46	–	–	–	15	–	–	16	–	–	–	–	15
	Sri Lanka	15	–	–	–	3	–	–	–	6	–	–	–	6
	Zimbabwe	8	–	–	–	6	–	–	–	–	0	–	–	2
	Bangladesh	10	–	–	–	6	–	–	–	–	–	2	–	2
New Zealand	India	54	–	–	–	–	10	18	–	–	–	–	–	26
	Pakistan	50	–	–	–	–	7	–	23	–	–	–	–	20
	Sri Lanka	28	–	–	–	–	10	–	–	8	–	–	–	10
	Zimbabwe	15	–	–	–	–	9	–	–	–	0	–	–	6
	Bangladesh	11	–	–	–	–	8	–	–	–	–	0	–	3
India	Pakistan	59	–	–	–	–	–	9	12	–	–	–	–	38
	Sri Lanka	35	–	–	–	–	–	14	–	6	–	–	–	15
	Zimbabwe	11	–	–	–	–	–	7	–	–	2	–	–	2
	Bangladesh	7	–	–	–	–	–	6	–	–	–	0	–	1
Pakistan	Sri Lanka	46	–	–	–	–	–	–	17	11	–	–	–	18
	Zimbabwe	17	–	–	–	–	–	–	10	–	3	–	–	4
	Bangladesh	8	–	–	–	–	–	–	8	–	–	0	–	0
Sri Lanka	Zimbabwe	15	–	–	–	–	–	–	–	10	0	–	–	5
	Bangladesh	16	–	–	–	–	–	–	–	14	–	0	–	2
Zimbabwe	Bangladesh	11	–	–	–	–	–	–	–	–	6	2	–	3
		2121	336	359	140	160	75	121	118	68	11	4	2	727

	Tests	Won	Lost	Drawn	Tied	Toss Won
England	945	336	273	336	–	455
Australia	767†	360†	203	202	2	388
South Africa	384	140	129	115	–	186
West Indies	495	160	166	168	1	259
New Zealand	391	75	158	158	–	197
India	478	121	151	205	1	242
Pakistan	380	118	107	155	–	176
Sri Lanka	227	68	81	78	–	124
Zimbabwe	93	11	56	26	–	53
Bangladesh	83	4	68	11	–	42

† total includes Australia's victory against the ICC World XI.

INTERNATIONAL TEST CRICKET RECORDS

(To 5 April 2014)

TEAM RECORDS

HIGHEST INNINGS TOTALS

952-6d	Sri Lanka v India	Colombo (RPS)	1997-98
903-7d	England v Australia	The Oval	1938
849	England v West Indies	Kingston	1929-30
790-3d	West Indies v Pakistan	Kingston	1957-58
765-6d	Pakistan v Sri Lanka	Karachi	2008-09
760-7d	Sri Lanka v India	Ahmedabad	2009-10
758-8d	Australia v West Indies	Kingston	1954-55
756-5d	Sri Lanka v South Africa	Colombo (SSC)	2006
751-5d	West Indies v England	St John's	2003-04
749-9d	West Indies v England	Bridgetown	2008-09
747	West Indies v South Africa	St John's	2004-05
735-6d	Australia v Zimbabwe	Perth	2003-04
730-6d	Sri Lanka v Bangladesh	Dhaka	2013-14
729-6d	Australia v England	Lord's	1930
726-9d	India v Sri Lanka	Mumbai	2009-10
713-3d	Sri Lanka v Zimbabwe	Bulawayo	2003-04
710-7d	England v India	Birmingham	2011
708	Pakistan v England	The Oval	1987
707	India v Sri Lanka	Colombo (SSC)	2010
705-7d	India v Australia	Sydney	2003-04
701	Australia v England	The Oval	1934
699-5	Pakistan v India	Lahore	1989-90
695	Australia v England	The Oval	1930
692-8d	West Indies v England	The Oval	1995
687-8d	West Indies v England	The Oval	1976
682-6d	South Africa v England	Lord's	2003
681-8d	West Indies v England	Port-of-Spain	1953-54
680-8d	New Zealand v India	Wellington	2013-14
679-7d	Pakistan v India	Lahore	2005-06
676-7	India v Sri Lanka	Kanpur	1986-87
675-5d	India v Pakistan	Multan	2003-04
674	Australia v India	Adelaide	1947-48

674-6	Pakistan v India	Faisalabad	1984-85
674-6d	Australia v England	Cardiff	2009
671-4	New Zealand v Sri Lanka	Wellington	1990-91
668	Australia v West Indies	Bridgetown	1954-55
664	India v England	The Oval	2007
660-5d	West Indies v New Zealand	Wellington	1994-95
659-8d	Australia v England	Sydney	1946-47
659-4d	Australia v India	Sydney	2011-12
658-8d	England v Australia	Nottingham	1938
658-9d	South Africa v West Indies	Durban	2003-04
657-8d	Pakistan v West Indies	Bridgetown	1957-58
657-7d	India v Australia	Calcutta	2000-01
656-8d	Australia v England	Manchester	1964
654-5	England v South Africa	Durban	1938-39
653-4d	England v India	Lord's	1990
653-4d	Australia v India	Leeds	1993
652-8d	West Indies v England	Lord's	1973
652	Pakistan v India	Faisalabad	1982-83
652-7d	England v India	Madras	1984-85
652-7d	Australia v South Africa	Johannesburg	2001-02
651	South Africa v Australia	Cape Town	2008-09
650-6d	Australia v West Indies	Bridgetown	1964-65

The highest for Zimbabwe is 563-9d (v WI, Harare, 2001), and for Bangladesh 638 (v SL, Galle, 2012-13).

LOWEST INNINGS TOTALS

† One batsman absent

26	New Zealand v England	Auckland	1954-55
30	South Africa v England	Port Elizabeth	1895-96
30	South Africa v England	Birmingham	1924
35	South Africa v England	Cape Town	1898-99
36	Australia v England	Birmingham	1902
36	South Africa v Australia	Melbourne	1931-32
42	Australia v England	Sydney	1887-88
42	New Zealand v Australia	Wellington	1945-46
42†	India v England	Lord's	1974
43	South Africa v England	Cape Town	1888-89
44	Australia v England	The Oval	1896
45	England v Australia	Sydney	1886-87
45	South Africa v Australia	Melbourne	1931-32
45	New Zealand v South Africa	Cape Town	2012-13
46	England v West Indies	Port-of-Spain	1993-94
47	South Africa v England	Cape Town	1888-89
47	New Zealand v England	Lord's	1958
47	West Indies v England	Kingston	2003-04
47	Australia v South Africa	Cape Town	2011-12
49	Pakistan v South Africa	Johannesburg	2012-13

The lowest for Sri Lanka is 71 (v P, Kandy, 1994-95), for Zimbabwe 51 (v NZ, Napier, 2011-12), and for Bangladesh 62 (v SL, Colombo PPS, 2006-07).

BATTING RECORDS
5000 RUNS IN TESTS

Runs			M	I	NO	HS	Avge	100	50
15921	S.R.Tendulkar	I	200	329	33	248*	53.78	51	68
13378	R.T.Ponting	A	168	287	29	257	51.85	41	62
13289	J.H.Kallis	SA/ICC	166	280	40	224	55.37	45	58
13288	R.S.Dravid	I/ICC	164	286	32	270	52.31	36	63
11953	B.C.Lara	WI/ICC	131	232	6	400*	52.88	34	48
11319	D.P.M.D.Jayawardena	SL	143	240	15	374	50.30	33	46
11219	S.Chanderpaul	WI	153	261	45	203*	51.93	29	62
11174	A.R.Border	A	156	265	44	205	50.56	27	63
11151	K.C.Sangakkara	SL	122	209	17	319	58.07	35	45
10927	S.R.Waugh	A	168	260	46	200	51.06	32	50
10122	S.M.Gavaskar	I	125	214	16	236*	51.12	34	45
9265	G.C.Smith	SA/ICC	117	205	13	277	48.25	27	38
8900	G.A.Gooch	E	118	215	6	333	42.58	20	46
8832	Javed Miandad	P	124	189	21	280*	52.57	23	43
8830	Inzamam-ul-Haq	P/ICC	120	200	22	329	49.60	25	46
8781	V.V.S.Laxman	I	134	225	34	281	45.97	17	56
8625	M.L.Hayden	A	103	184	14	380	50.73	30	29
8586	V.Sehwag	I/ICC	104	180	6	319	49.34	23	32
8540	I.V.A.Richards	WI	121	182	12	291	50.23	24	45
8463	A.J.Stewart	E	133	235	21	190	39.54	15	45
8240	M.J.Clarke	A	105	180	20	329*	51.50	27	27
8231	D.I.Gower	E	117	204	18	215	44.25	18	39
8181	K.P.Pietersen	E	104	181	8	227	47.28	23	35
8114	G.Boycott	E	108	193	23	246*	47.72	22	42
8047	A.N.Cook	E	102	193	10	294	46.51	25	35
8032	G.St A.Sobers	WI	93	160	21	365*	57.78	26	30
8029	M.E.Waugh	A	128	209	17	153*	41.81	20	47
7728	M.A.Atherton	E	115	212	7	185*	37.70	16	46
7696	J.L.Langer	A	105	182	12	250	45.27	23	30
7624	M.C.Cowdrey	E	114	188	15	182	44.06	22	38
7558	C.G.Greenidge	WI	108	185	16	226	44.72	19	34
7530	Mohammad Yousuf	P	90	156	12	223	52.29	24	33
7525	M.A.Taylor	A	104	186	13	334*	43.49	19	40
7515	C.H.Lloyd	WI	110	175	14	242*	46.67	19	39
7487	D.L.Haynes	WI	116	202	25	184	42.29	18	39
7422	D.C.Boon	A	107	190	20	200	43.65	21	32
7399	Younus Khan	P	89	158	14	313	51.38	23	28
7289	G.Kirsten	SA	101	176	15	275	45.27	21	34
7249	W.R.Hammond	E	85	140	16	336*	58.45	22	24
7212	S.C.Ganguly	I	113	188	17	239	42.17	16	35
7172	S.P.Fleming	NZ	111	189	10	274*	40.06	9	46
7168	A.B.de Villiers	SA	92	154	16	278*	51.94	19	35
7110	G.S.Chappell	A	87	151	19	247*	53.86	24	31
7037	A.J.Strauss	E	100	178	6	177	40.91	21	27
6996	D.G.Bradman	A	52	80	10	334	99.94	29	13
6973	S.T.Jayasuriya	SL	110	188	14	340	40.07	14	31
6971	L.Hutton	E	79	138	15	364	56.67	19	33
6933	C.H.Gayle	WI	99	174	9	333	42.01	15	34
6868	D.B.Vengsarkar	I	116	185	22	166	42.13	17	35
6806	K.F.Barrington	E	82	131	15	256	58.67	20	35
6744	G.P.Thorpe	E	100	179	28	200*	44.66	16	39
6722	I.R.Bell	E	98	170	22	235	45.41	20	39
6361	P.A.de Silva	SL	93	159	11	267	42.97	20	22

Runs			M	I	NO	HS	Avge	100	50
6235	M.E.K.Hussey	A	79	137	16	195	51.52	19	29
6227	R.B.Kanhai	WI	79	137	6	256	47.53	15	28
6215	M.Azharuddin	I	99	147	9	199	45.03	22	21
6214	H.M.Amla	SA	76	132	11	311*	51.35	21	27
6167	H.H.Gibbs	SA	90	154	7	228	41.95	14	26
6149	R.N.Harvey	A	79	137	10	205	48.41	21	24
6080	G.R.Viswanath	I	91	155	10	222	41.93	14	35
5949	R.B.Richardson	WI	86	146	12	194	44.39	16	27
5842	R.R.Sarwan	WI	87	154	8	291	40.01	15	31
5825	M.E.Trescothick	E	76	143	10	219	43.79	14	29
5807	D.C.S.Compton	E	78	131	15	278	50.06	17	28
5768	Salim Malik	P	103	154	22	237	43.69	15	29
5764	N.Hussain	E	96	171	16	207	37.19	14	33
5762	C.L.Hooper	WI	102	173	15	233	36.46	13	27
5719	M.P.Vaughan	E	82	147	9	197	41.44	18	18
5570	A.C.Gilchrist	A	96	137	20	204*	47.60	17	26
5515	M.V.Boucher	SA/ICC	147	206	24	125	30.30	5	35
5502	M.S.Atapattu	SL	90	156	15	249	39.02	16	17
5492	T.M.Dilshan	SL	87	145	11	193	40.98	16	23
5462	T.T.Samaraweera	SL	81	132	20	231	48.76	14	30
5444	M.D.Crowe	NZ	77	131	11	299	45.36	17	18
5410	J.B.Hobbs	E	61	102	7	211	56.94	15	28
5357	K.D.Walters	A	74	125	14	250	48.26	15	33
5345	I.M.Chappell	A	75	136	10	196	42.42	14	26
5334	J.G.Wright	NZ	82	148	7	185	37.82	12	23
5312	M.J.Slater	A	74	131	7	219	42.84	14	21
5248	Kapil Dev	I	131	184	15	163	31.05	8	27
5234	W.M.Lawry	A	67	123	12	210	47.15	13	27
5219	B.B.McCullum	NZ	84	145	8	302	38.09	9	28
5200	I.T.Botham	E	102	161	6	208	33.54	14	22
5138	J.H.Edrich	E	77	127	9	310*	43.54	12	24
5105	A.Ranatunga	SL	93	155	12	135*	35.69	4	38
5062	Zaheer Abbas	P	78	124	11	274	44.79	12	20

The most for Zimbabwe is 4794 (112 innings) by A.Flower, and for Bangladesh 3026 by Habibul Bashar (99 innings).

750 RUNS IN A SERIES

Runs			Series	M	I	NO	HS	Avge	100	50
974	D.G.Bradman	A v E	1930	5	7	–	334	139.14	4	–
905	W.R.Hammond	E v A	1928-29	5	9	1	251	113.12	4	–
839	M.A.Taylor	A v E	1989	6	11	1	219	83.90	2	5
834	R.N.Harvey	A v SA	1952-53	5	9	–	205	92.66	4	3
829	I.V.A.Richards	WI v E	1976	4	7	–	291	118.42	3	2
827	C.L.Walcott	WI v A	1954-55	5	10	–	155	82.70	5	2
824	G.St A.Sobers	WI v P	1957-58	5	8	2	365*	137.33	3	3
810	D.G.Bradman	A v E	1936-37	5	9	–	270	90.00	3	1
806	D.G.Bradman	A v SA	1931-32	5	5	1	299*	201.50	4	–
798	B.C.Lara	WI v E	1993-94	5	8	–	375	99.75	2	2
779	E.de C.Weekes	WI v I	1948-49	5	7	–	194	111.28	4	2
774	S.M.Gavaskar	I v WI	1970-71	4	8	3	220	154.80	4	3
766	A.N.Cook	E v A	2010-11	5	7	1	235*	127.66	3	2
765	B.C.Lara	WI v E	1995	6	10	1	179	85.00	3	3
761	Mudassar Nazar	P v I	1982-83	6	8	2	231	126.83	4	1
758	D.G.Bradman	A v E	1934	5	8	–	304	94.75	2	1
753	D.C.S.Compton	E v SA	1947	5	8	–	208	94.12	4	2
752	G.A.Gooch	E v I	1990	3	6	–	333	125.33	3	2

HIGHEST INDIVIDUAL INNINGS

400*	B.C.Lara	WI v E	St John's	2003-04
380	M.L.Hayden	A v Z	Perth	2003-04
375	B.C.Lara	WI v E	St John's	1993-94
374	D.P.M.D.Jayawardena	SL v SA	Colombo (SSC)	2006
365*	G.St A.Sobers	WI v P	Kingston	1957-58
364	L.Hutton	E v A	The Oval	1938
340	S.T.Jayasuriya	SL v I	Colombo (RPS)	1997-98
337	Hanif Mohammed	P v WI	Bridgetown	1957-58
336*	W.R.Hammond	E v NZ	Auckland	1932-33
334*	M.A.Taylor	A v P	Peshawar	1998-99
334	D.G.Bradman	A v E	Leeds	1930
333	G.A.Gooch	E v I	Lord's	1990
333	C.H.Gayle	WI v SL	Galle	2010-11
329*	M.J.Clarke	A v I	Sydney	2011-12
329	Inzamam-ul-Haq	P v NZ	Lahore	2001-02
325	A.Sandham	E v WI	Kingston	1929-30
319	V.Sehwag	I v SA	Chennai	2007-08
319	K.C.Sangakkara	SL v B	Chittagong	2013-14
317	C.H.Gayle	WI v SA	St John's	2004-05
313	Younus Khan	P v SL	Karachi	2008-09
311*	H.M.Amla	SA v E	The Oval	2012
311	R.B.Simpson	A v E	Manchester	1964
310*	J.H.Edrich	E v NZ	Leeds	1965
309	V.Sehwag	I v P	Multan	2003-04
307	R.M.Cowper	A v E	Melbourne	1965-66
304	D.G.Bradman	A v E	Leeds	1934
302	L.G.Rowe	WI v E	Bridgetown	1973-74
302	B.B.McCullum	NZ v I	Wellington	2013-14
299*	D.G.Bradman	A v SA	Adelaide	1931-32
299	M.D.Crowe	NZ v SL	Wellington	1990-91
294	A.N.Cook	E v I	Birmingham	2011
293	V.Sehwag	I v SL	Mumbai	2009-10
291	I.V.A.Richards	WI v E	The Oval	1976
291	R.R.Sarwan	WI v E	Bridgetown	2008-09
287	R.E.Foster	E v A	Sydney	1903-04
287	K.C.Sangakkara	SL v SA	Colombo (SSC)	2006
285*	P.B.H.May	E v WI	Birmingham	1957
281	V.V.S.Laxman	I v A	Calcutta	2000-01
280*	Javed Miandad	P v I	Hyderabad	1982-83
278*	A.B.de Villiers	SA v P	Abu Dhabi	2010-11
278	D.C.S.Compton	E v P	Nottingham	1954
277	B.C.Lara	WI v A	Sydney	1992-93
277	G.C.Smith	SA v E	Birmingham	2003
275*	D.J.Cullinan	SA v NZ	Auckland	1998-99
275	G.Kirsten	SA v E	Durban	1999-00
275	D.P.M.D.Jayawardena	SL v I	Ahmedabad	2009-10
274*	S.P.Fleming	NZ v SL	Colombo (SSC)	2002-03
274	R.G.Pollock	SA v A	Durban	1969-70
274	Zaheer Abbas	P v E	Birmingham	1971
271	Javed Miandad	P v NZ	Auckland	1988-89
270*	G.A.Headley	WI v E	Kingston	1934-35
270	D.G.Bradman	A v E	Melbourne	1936-37
270	R.S.Dravid	I v P	Rawalpindi	2003-04
270	K.C.Sangakkara	SL v Z	Bulawayo	2003-04
268	G.N.Yallop	A v P	Melbourne	1983-84

267*	B.A.Young	NZ v SL	Dunedin	1996-97
267	P.A.de Silva	SL v NZ	Wellington	1990-91
267	Younus Khan	P v I	Bangalore	2004-05
266	W.H.Ponsford	A v E	The Oval	1934
266	D.L.Houghton	Z v SL	Bulawayo	1994-95
262*	D.L.Amiss	E v WI	Kingston	1973-74
262	S.P.Fleming	NZ v SA	Cape Town	2005-06
261*	R.R.Sarwan	WI v B	Kingston	2004
261	F.M.M.Worrell	WI v E	Nottingham	1950
260	C.C.Hunte	WI v P	Kingston	1957-58
260	Javed Miandad	P v E	The Oval	1987
260	M.N.Samuels	WI v B	Khulna	2012-13
259*	M.J.Clarke	A v SA	Brisbane	2012-13
259	G.M.Turner	NZ v WI	Georgetown	1971-72
259	G.C.Smith	SA v E	Lord's	2003
258	T.W.Graveney	E v WI	Nottingham	1957
258	S.M.Nurse	WI v NZ	Christchurch	1968-69
257*	Wasim Akram	P v Z	Sheikhupura	1996-97
257	R.T.Ponting	A v I	Melbourne	2003-04
256	R.B.Kanhai	WI v I	Calcutta	1958-59
256	K.F.Barrington	E v A	Manchester	1964
255*	D.J.McGlew	SA v NZ	Wellington	1952-53
254	D.G.Bradman	A v E	Lord's	1930
254	V.Sehwag	I v P	Lahore	2005-06
253*	H.M.Amla	SA v I	Nagpur	2009-10
253	S.T.Jayasuriya	SL v P	Faisalabad	2004-05
251	W.R.Hammond	E v A	Sydney	1928-29
250	K.D.Walters	A v NZ	Christchurch	1976-77
250	S.F.A.F.Bacchus	WI v I	Kanpur	1978-79
250	J.L.Langer	A v E	Melbourne	2002-03

The highest for Bangladesh is 200 by Mushfiqur Rahim (v SL, Galle, 2012-13).

20 HUNDREDS

			200	Inn	Opponents									
					E	A	SA	WI	NZ	I	P	SL	Z	B
51	S.R.Tendulkar	I	6	329	7	11	7	3	4	–	2	9	3	5
45	J.H.Kallis	SA	2	280	8	5	–	8	6	7	6	1	3	1
41	R.T.Ponting	A	6	287	8	–	8	7	2	8	5	1	1	1
36	R.S.Dravid	I	5	286	7	2	2	5	6	–	5	3	3	3
35	K.C.Sangakkara	SL	9	209	2	1	3	3	3	5	9	–	2	7
34	S.M.Gavaskar	I	4	214	4	8	–	13	2	–	5	2	–	–
34	B.C.Lara	WI	9	232	7	9	4	–	1	2	4	5	1	1
33	D.P.M.D.Jayawardena	SL	7	240	8	2	5	1	3	6	2	–	1	5
32	S.R.Waugh	A	1	260	10	–	2	7	2	2	3	3	1	2
30	M.L.Hayden †	A	2	184	5	–	5	1	6	1	3	2	–	
29	D.G.Bradman	A	12	80	19	–	4	2	–	4	–	–	–	–
29	S.Chanderpaul	WI	2	261	5	5	5	–	2	7	1	–	1	3
27	M.J.Clarke	A	4	180	7	–	5	1	4	6	1	3	–	–
27	G.C.Smith	SA	5	205	7	3	–	7	2	–	4	–	1	3
27	A.R.Border	A	2	265	8	–	3	5	4	6	1	–	–	
26	G.St A.Sobers	WI	2	160	10	4	–	–	1	8	3	–	–	–
25	A.N.Cook	E	2	183	–	4	2	4	2	5	3	3	–	2
25	Inzamam-ul-Haq	P	2	200	5	1	–	4	3	3	–	5	2	2
24	G.S.Chappell	A	4	151	9	–	–	5	3	1	6	–	–	–
24	Mohammad Yousuf	P	4	156	6	1	–	7	1	4	–	1	2	2
24	I.V.A.Richards	WI	3	182	8	5	–	–	1	8	2	–	–	–

		200	Inn	E	A	SA	WI	NZ	I	P	SL	Z	B
23	Younus Khan	P	4	158	2	–	4	2	1	5	–	6	1	2
23	V.Sehwag	I	6	180	2	3	5	2	2	1	–	4	5	–
23	K.P.Pietersen	E	3	181	–	4	3	3	2	6	2	3	–	–
23	J.L.Langer	A	3	182	5	–	2	3	4	3	4	2	–	–
23	Javed Miandad	P	6	189	2	6	–	2	7	5	–	1	–	–
22	W.R.Hammond	E	7	140	–	9	6	1	4	2	–	–	–	–
22	M.Azharuddin	I	–	147	6	2	4	–	2	–	3	5	–	–
22	M.C.Cowdrey	E	–	188	–	5	3	6	2	3	3	–	–	–
22	G.Boycott	E	1	193	–	7	1	5	2	4	3	–	–	–
21	H.M.Amla	SA	2	132	4	5	–	–	4	5	2	–	–	1
21	R.N.Harvey	A	2	137	6	–	8	3	–	4	–	–	–	–
21	G.Kirsten	SA	3	176	5	2	–	3	2	3	2	1	1	2
21	A.J.Strauss	E	–	178	–	4	3	6	3	3	2	–	–	–
21	D.C.Boon	A	1	190	7	–	–	3	3	6	1	1	–	–
20	K.F.Barrington	E	1	131	–	5	2	3	3	4	–	–	–	–
20	P.A.de Silva	SL	2	159	2	1	–	–	2	5	8	–	1	1
20	I.R.Bell	E	1	170	–	4	2	1	1	3	4	2	–	3
20	M.E.Waugh	A	–	209	6	–	4	4	1	1	3	1	–	–
20	G.A.Gooch	E	2	215	–	4	–	5	4	5	1	1	–	–

† Includes century scored for Australia v ICC in 2005-06.

The most for New Zealand is 17 by M.D.Crowe (131 innings), for Zimbabwe 12 by A.Flower (112), and for Bangladesh 6 by Mohammad Ashraful (119 innings).

The most double hundreds by batsmen not included above are 6 by M.S.Atapattu (16 hundreds for Sri Lanka), 4 by L.Hutton (19 for England), 4 by C.G.Greenidge (19 for West Indies), and 4 by Zaheer Abbas (12 for Pakistan).

HIGHEST PARTNERSHIP FOR EACH WICKET

1st	415	N.D.McKenzie/G.C.Smith	SA v B	Chittagong	2007-08
2nd	576	S.T.Jayasuriya/R.S.Mahanama	SL v I	Colombo (RPS)	1997-98
3rd	624	K.C.Sangakkara/D.P.M.D.Jayawardena	SL v SA	Colombo (SSC)	2006
4th	437	D.P.M.D.Jayawardena/T.T.Samaraweera	SL v P	Karachi	2008-09
5th	405	S.G.Barnes/D.G.Bradman	A v E	Sydney	1946-47
6th	352	B.B.McCullum/B.J.Watling	NZ v I	Wellington	2013-14
7th	347	D.St E.Atkinson/C.C.Depeiza	WI v A	Bridgetown	1954-55
8th	332	I.J.L.Trott/S.C.J.Broad	E v P	Lord's	2010
9th	195	M.V.Boucher/P.L.Symcox	SA v P	Johannesburg	1997-98
10th	163	P.J.Hughes/A.C.Agar	A v E	Nottingham	2013

BOWLING RECORDS

200 WICKETS IN TESTS

Wkts			M	Balls	Runs	Avge	5 wI	10 wM
800	M.Muralitharan	SL/ICC	133	44039	18180	22.72	67	22
708	S.K.Warne	A	145	40705	17995	25.41	37	10
619	A.Kumble	I	132	40850	18355	29.65	35	8
563	G.D.McGrath	A	124	29248	12186	21.64	29	3
519	C.A.Walsh	WI	132	30019	12688	24.44	22	3
434	Kapil Dev	I	131	27740	12867	29.64	23	2
431	R.J.Hadlee	NZ	86	21918	9612	22.30	36	9
421	S.M.Pollock	SA	108	24453	9733	23.11	16	1
414	Wasim Akram	P	104	22627	9779	23.62	25	5
413	Harbhajan Singh	I	101	28293	13372	32.37	25	5
405	C.E.L.Ambrose	WI	98	22104	8500	20.98	22	3
390	M.Ntini	SA	101	20834	11242	28.82	18	4
383	I.T.Botham	E	102	21815	10878	28.40	27	4
376	M.D.Marshall	WI	81	17584	7876	20.94	22	4

Wkts			M	Balls	Runs	Avge	5 wI	10 wM
373	Waqar Younis	P	87	16224	8788	23.56	22	5
362	Imran Khan	P	88	19458	8258	22.81	23	6
362	D.W.Steyn	SA	72	15261	8333	23.01	22	5
360	D.L.Vettori	NZ/ICC	112	28670	12392	34.42	20	3
355	D.K.Lillee	A	70	18467	8493	23.92	23	7
355	W.P.J.U.C.Vaas	SL	111	23438	10501	29.58	12	2
343	J.M.Anderson	E	92	20350	10522	30.67	15	2
330	A.A.Donald	SA	72	15519	7344	22.25	20	3
325	R.G.D.Willis	E	90	17357	8190	25.20	16	–
311	Z.Khan	I	92	18785	10247	32.94	11	1
310	B.Lee	A	76	16531	9554	30.81	10	–
309	L.R.Gibbs	WI	79	27115	8989	29.09	18	2
307	F.S.Trueman	E	67	15178	6625	21.57	17	3
297	D.L.Underwood	E	86	21862	7674	25.83	17	6
292	J.H.Kallis	SA/ICC	166	20232	9535	32.65	5	–
291	C.J.McDermott	A	71	16586	8332	28.63	14	2
266	B.S.Bedi	I	67	21364	7637	28.71	14	1
264	M.G.Johnson	A	59	13227	7240	27.42	12	3
261	Danish Kaneria	P	61	17697	9082	34.79	15	2
259	J.Garner	WI	58	13169	5433	20.97	7	–
259	J.N.Gillespie	A	71	14234	6770	26.13	8	–
255	G.P.Swann	E	60	15349	7642	29.96	17	3
252	J.B.Statham	E	70	16056	6261	24.84	9	1
249	M.A.Holding	WI	60	12680	5898	23.68	13	2
248	R.Benaud	A	63	19108	6704	27.03	16	1
248	M.J.Hoggard	E	67	13909	7564	30.50	7	1
246	G.D.McKenzie	A	60	17681	7328	29.78	16	3
242	B.S.Chandrasekhar	I	58	15963	7199	29.74	16	2
238	S.C.J.Broad	E	67	13896	7215	30.31	11	2
236	A.V.Bedser	E	51	15918	5876	24.89	15	5
236	J.Srinath	I	67	15104	7196	30.49	10	1
236	Abdul Qadir	P	67	17126	7742	32.80	15	5
235	G.St A.Sobers	WI	93	21599	7999	34.03	6	–
234	A.R.Caddick	E	62	13558	6999	29.91	13	1
233	C.S.Martin	NZ	71	14026	7878	33.81	10	1
229	D.Gough	E	58	11821	6503	28.39	9	–
228	R.R.Lindwall	A	61	13650	5251	23.03	12	–
226	S.J.Harmison	E/ICC	63	13375	7192	31.82	8	1
226	A.Flintoff	E/ICC	79	14951	7410	32.78	3	–
218	C.L.Cairns	NZ	62	11698	6410	29.40	13	1
217	H.M.R.K.B.Herath	SL	51	13933	6514	30.01	17	3
216	C.V.Grimmett	A	37	14513	5231	24.21	21	7
216	H.H.Streak	Z	65	13559	6079	28.14	7	–
212	M.G.Hughes	A	53	12285	6017	28.38	7	1
208	S.C.G.MacGill	A	44	11237	6038	29.02	12	2
208	Saqlain Mushtaq	P	49	14070	6206	29.83	13	3
202	A.M.E.Roberts	WI	47	11136	5174	25.61	11	2
202	J.A.Snow	E	49	12021	5387	26.66	8	1
200	J.R.Thomson	A	51	10535	5601	28.00	8	–

The most for Bangladesh is 122 in 34 Tests by Shakib Al Hasan.

35 OR MORE WICKETS IN A SERIES

Wkts			Series	M	Balls	Runs	Avge	5 wI	10 wM
49	S.F.Barnes	E v SA	1913-14	4	1356	536	10.93	7	3
46	J.C.Laker	E v A	1956	5	1703	442	9.60	4	2
44	C.V.Grimmett	A v SA	1935-36	5	2077	642	14.59	5	3
42	T.M.Alderman	A v E	1981	6	1950	893	21.26	4	–
41	R.M.Hogg	A v E	1978-79	6	1740	527	12.85	5	2

Wkts			Series	M	Balls	Runs	Avge	5 wI	10 wM
41	T.M.Alderman	A v E	1989	6	1616	712	17.36	6	1
40	Imran Khan	P v I	1982-83	6	1339	558	13.95	4	2
40	S.K.Warne	A v E	2005	5	1517	797	19.92	3	2
39	A.V.Bedser	E v A	1953	5	1591	682	17.48	5	1
39	D.K.Lillee	A v E	1981	6	1870	870	22.30	2	1
38	M.W.Tate	E v A	1924-25	5	2528	881	23.18	5	1
37	W.J.Whitty	A v SA	1910-11	5	1395	632	17.08	2	–
37	H.J.Tayfield	SA v E	1956-57	5	2280	636	17.18	4	1
37	M.G.Johnson	A v E	2013-14	5	1132	517	13.97	3	–
36	A.E.E.Vogler	SA v E	1909-10	5	1349	783	21.75	4	1
36	A.A.Mailey	A v E	1920-21	5	1465	946	26.27	4	2
36	G.D.McGrath	A v E	1997	6	1499	701	19.47	2	–
35	G.A.Lohmann	E v SA	1895-96	3	520	203	5.80	4	2
35	B.S.Chandrasekhar	I v E	1972-73	5	1747	662	18.91	4	–
35	M.D.Marshall	WI v E	1988	5	1219	443	12.65	3	1

The most for New Zealand is 33 by R.J.Hadlee (3 Tests v A, 1985-86), for Sri Lanka 30 by M.Muralitharan (3 Tests v Z, 2001-02), for Zimbabwe 22 by H.H.Streak (3 Tests v P, 1994-95), and for Bangladesh 18 by Enamul Haque II (2 Tests v Z, 2004-05).

15 OR MORE WICKETS IN A TEST († On debut)

19- 90	J.C.Laker	E v A	Manchester	1956
17- 159	S.F.Barnes	E v SA	Johannesburg	1913-14
16-136†	N.D.Hirwani	I v WI	Madras	1987-88
16-137†	R.A.L.Massie	A v E	Lord's	1972
16- 220	M.Muralitharan	SL v E	The Oval	1998
15- 28	J.Briggs	E v SA	Cape Town	1888-89
15- 45	G.A.Lohmann	E v SA	Port Elizabeth	1895-96
15- 99	C.Blythe	E v SA	Leeds	1907
15- 104	H.Verity	E v A	Lord's	1934
15- 123	R.J.Hadlee	NZ v A	Brisbane	1985-86
15- 124	W.Rhodes	E v A	Melbourne	1903-04
15- 217	Harbhajan Singh	I v A	Madras	2000-01

The best analysis for South Africa is 13-132 by M.Ntini (v WI, Port-of-Spain, 2004-05), for West Indies 14-149 by M.A.Holding (v E, The Oval, 1976), for Pakistan 14-116 by Imran Khan (v SL, Lahore, 1981-82), for Zimbabwe 11-257 by A.G.Huckle (v NZ, Bulawayo, 1997-98), and for Bangladesh 12-200 by Enamul Haque II (v Z, Dhaka, 2004-05).

NINE OR MORE WICKETS IN AN INNINGS

10- 53	J.C.Laker	E v A	Manchester	1956
10- 74	A.Kumble	I v P	Delhi	1998-99
9- 28	G.A.Lohmann	E v SA	Johannesburg	1895-96
9- 37	J.C.Laker	E v A	Manchester	1956
9- 51	M.Muralitharan	SL v Z	Kandy	2001-02
9- 52	R.J.Hadlee	NZ v A	Brisbane	1985-86
9- 56	Abdul Qadir	P v E	Lahore	1987-88
9- 57	D.E.Malcolm	E v SA	The Oval	1994
9- 65	M.Muralitharan	SL v E	The Oval	1998
9- 69	J.M.Patel	I v A	Kanpur	1959-60
9- 83	Kapil Dev	I v WI	Ahmedabad	1983-84
9- 86	Sarfraz Nawaz	P v A	Melbourne	1978-79
9- 95	J.M.Noreiga	WI v I	Port-of-Spain	1970-71
9-102	S.P.Gupte	I v WI	Kanpur	1958-59
9-103	S.F.Barnes	E v SA	Johannesburg	1913-14

| 9-113 | H.J.Tayfield | SA v E | Johannesburg | 1956-57 |
| 9-121 | A.A.Mailey | A v E | Melbourne | 1920-21 |

The best analysis for Zimbabwe is 8-109 by P.A.Strang (v NZ, Bulawayo, 2000-01), and for Bangladesh 7-36 by Shakib Al Hasan (v NZ, Chittagong, 2008-09).

HAT-TRICKS

F.R.Spofforth	Australia v England	Melbourne	1878-79
W.Bates	England v Australia	Melbourne	1882-83
J.Briggs[7]	England v Australia	Sydney	1891-92
G.A.Lohmann	England v South Africa	Port Elizabeth	1895-96
J.T.Hearne	England v Australia	Leeds	1899
H.Trumble	Australia v England	Melbourne	1901-02
H.Trumble	Australia v England	Melbourne	1903-04
T.J.Matthews (2)[2]	Australia v South Africa	Manchester	1912
M.J.C.Allom[1]	England v New Zealand	Christchurch	1929-30
T.W.J.Goddard	England v South Africa	Johannesburg	1938-39
P.J.Loader	England v West Indies	Leeds	1957
L.F.Kline	Australia v South Africa	Cape Town	1957-58
W.W.Hall	West Indies v Pakistan	Lahore	1958-59
G.M.Griffin[7]	South Africa v England	Lord's	1960
L.R.Gibbs	West Indies v Australia	Adelaide	1960-61
P.J.Petherick[1/7]	New Zealand v Pakistan	Lahore	1976-77
C.A.Walsh[3]	West Indies v Australia	Brisbane	1988-89
M.G.Hughes[3/7]	Australia v West Indies	Perth	1988-89
D.W.Fleming[1]	Australia v Pakistan	Rawalpindi	1994-95
S.K.Warne	Australia v England	Melbourne	1994-95
D.G.Cork	England v West Indies	Manchester	1995
D.Gough[7]	England v Australia	Sydney	1998-99
Wasim Akram[4]	Pakistan v Sri Lanka	Lahore	1998-99
Wasim Akram[4]	Pakistan v Sri Lanka	Dhaka	1998-99
D.N.T.Zoysa[3]	Sri Lanka v Zimbabwe	Harare	1999-00
Abdul Razzaq	Pakistan v Sri Lanka	Galle	2000-01
G.D.McGrath	Australia v West Indies	Perth	2000-01
Harbhajan Singh	India v Australia	Calcutta	2000-01
Mohammad Sami[7]	Pakistan v Sri Lanka	Lahore	2001-02
J.J.C.Lawson[7]	West Indies v Australia	Bridgetown	2002-03
Alok Kapali[7]	Bangladesh v Pakistan	Peshawar	2003
A.M.Blignaut	Zimbabwe v Bangladesh	Harare	2003-04
M.J.Hoggard	England v West Indies	Bridgetown	2003-04
J.E.C.Franklin	New Zealand v Bangladesh	Dhaka	2004-05
I.K.Pathan[6/7]	India v Pakistan	Karachi	2005-06
R.J.Sidebottom[7]	England v New Zealand	Hamilton	2007-08
P.M.Siddle	Australia v England	Brisbane	2010-11
S.C.J.Broad	England v India	Nottingham	2011
Sohag Gazi	Bangladesh v New Zealand	Chittagong	2013-14

[1] *On debut.* [2] *Hat-trick in each innings.* [3] *Involving both innings.* [4] *In successive Tests.* [5] *His first 3 balls (second over of the match).* [6] *The fourth, fifth and sixth balls of the match.* [7] *On losing side.*

WICKET-KEEPING RECORDS
100 DISMISSALS IN TESTS†

Total			Tests	Ct	St
555	M.V.Boucher	South Africa/ICC	147	532	23
416	A.C.Gilchrist	Australia	96	379	37
395	I.A.Healy	Australia	119	366	29

Total			Tests	Ct	St
355	R.W.Marsh	Australia	96	343	12
270†	P.J.L.Dujon	West Indies	79	265	5
269	A.P.E.Knott	England	95	250	19
263	M.S.Dhoni	India	83	226	37
241†	A.J.Stewart	England	82	227	14
233	B.J.Haddin	Australia	57	228	5
230	M.J.Prior	England	75	213	13
228	Wasim Bari	Pakistan	81	201	27
219	R.D.Jacobs	West Indies	65	207	12
219	T.G.Evans	England	91	173	46
206	Kamran Akmal	Pakistan	53	184	22
201†	A.C.Parore	New Zealand	67	194	7
198	S.M.H.Kirmani	India	88	160	38
189	D.L.Murray	West Indies	62	181	8
187	A.T.W.Grout	Australia	51	163	24
178†	B.B.McCullum	New Zealand	52	167	11
176	I.D.S.Smith	New Zealand	63	168	8
174	R.W.Taylor	England	57	167	7
165	R.C.Russell	England	54	153	12
161	D.Ramdin	West Indies	56	156	5
152	D.J.Richardson	South Africa	42	150	2
151†	K.C.Sangakkara	Sri Lanka	48	131	20
151†	A.Flower	Zimbabwe	55	142	9
147	H.A.P.W.Jayawardena	Sri Lanka	55	115	32
147†	Moin Khan	Pakistan	66	127	20
141	J.H.B.Waite	South Africa	49	124	17
133	G.O.Jones	England	34	128	5
130	Rashid Latif	Pakistan	37	119	11
130	K.S.More	India	49	110	20
130	W.A.S.Oldfield	Australia	54	78	52
119	R.S.Kaluwitharana	Sri Lanka	49	93	26
112†	J.M.Parks	England	43	101	11
107	N.R.Mongia	India	44	99	8
104	Salim Yousuf	Pakistan	32	91	13
101†	J.R.Murray	West Indies	31	98	3

The most for Bangladesh is 87 (78 ct, 9 st) by Khaled Masud in 44 Tests.

† *Excluding catches taken in the field*

25 OR MORE DISMISSALS IN A SERIES

29	B.J.Haddin	Australia v England	2013
28	R.W.Marsh	Australia v England	1982-83
27 (inc 2st)	R.C.Russell	England v South Africa	1995-96
27 (inc 2st)	I.A.Healy	Australia v England (6 Tests)	1997
26 (inc 3st)	J.H.B.Waite	South Africa v New Zealand	1961-62
26	R.W.Marsh	Australia v West Indies (6 Tests)	1975-76
26 (inc 5st)	I.A.Healy	Australia v England (6 Tests)	1993
26 (inc 1st)	M.V.Boucher	South Africa v England	1998
26 (inc 2st)	A.C.Gilchrist	Australia v England	2001
26 (inc 2st)	A.C.Gilchrist	Australia v England	2006-07
25 (inc 2st)	I.A.Healy	Australia v England	1994-95
25 (inc 2st)	A.C.Gilchrist	Australia v England	2002-03
25	A.C.Gilchrist	Australia v India	2007-08

TEN OR MORE DISMISSALS IN A TEST

11	R.C.Russell	England v South Africa	Johannesburg	1995-96
11	A.B.de Villiers	South Africa v Pakistan	Johannesburg	2012-13
10	R.W.Taylor	England v India	Bombay	1979-80
10	A.C.Gilchrist	Australia v New Zealand	Hamilton	1999-00

SEVEN DISMISSALS IN AN INNINGS

7	Wasim Bari	Pakistan v New Zealand	Auckland	1978-79
7	R.W.Taylor	England v India	Bombay	1979-80
7	I.D.S.Smith	New Zealand v Sri Lanka	Hamilton	1990-91
7	R.D.Jacobs	West Indies v Australia	Melbourne	2000-01

FIVE STUMPINGS IN AN INNINGS

5	K.S.More	India v West Indies	Madras	1987-88

FIELDING RECORDS
100 CATCHES IN TESTS

Total			Tests	Total			Tests
210	R.S.Dravid	India/ICC	164	122	I.V.A.Richards	West Indies	121
200	J.H.Kallis	South Africa/ICC	166	121	A.J.Strauss	England	100
196	R.T.Ponting	Australia	168	120	I.T.Botham	England	102
194	D.P.M.D.Jayawardena	Sri Lanka	143	120	M.C.Cowdrey	England	114
181	M.E.Waugh	Australia	128	115	C.L.Hooper	West Indies	102
171	S.P.Fleming	New Zealand	111	115	S.R.Tendulkar	India	200
169	G.C.Smith	South Africa/ICC	117	112	S.R.Waugh	Australia	168
164	B.C.Lara	West Indies/ICC	131	110	R.B.Simpson	Australia	62
157	M.A.Taylor	Australia	104	110	W.R.Hammond	England	85
156	A.R.Border	Australia	156	109	G.St A.Sobers	West Indies	93
135	V.V.S.Laxman	India	134	108	S.M.Gavaskar	India	125
128	M.L.Hayden	Australia	103	105	I.M.Chappell	Australia	75
125	M.J.Clarke	Australia	105	105	M.Azharuddin	India	99
125	S.K.Warne	Australia	145	105	G.P.Thorpe	England	100
122	G.S.Chappell	Australia	87	103	G.A.Gooch	England	118

The most for Pakistan is 93 by Javed Miandad (124), for Zimbabwe 60 by A.D.R.Campbell (60) and for Bangladesh 25 by Mohammad Ashraful (61).

15 CATCHES IN A SERIES

15	J.M.Gregory	Australia v England		1920-21

SEVEN CATCHES IN A TEST

7	G.S.Chappell	Australia v England	Perth	1974-75
7	Yajurvindra Singh	India v England	Bangalore	1976-77
7	H.P.Tillekeratne	Sri Lanka v New Zealand	Colombo (SSC)	1992-93
7	S.P.Fleming	New Zealand v Zimbabwe	Harare	1997-98
7	M.L.Hayden	Australia v Sri Lanka	Galle	2003-04

FIVE CATCHES IN AN INNINGS

5	V.Y.Richardson	Australia v South Africa	Durban	1935-36
5	Yajurvindra Singh	India v England	Bangalore	1976-77
5	M.Azharuddin	India v Pakistan	Karachi	1989-90
5	K.Srikkanth	India v Australia	Perth	1991-92
5	S.P.Fleming	New Zealand v Zimbabwe	Harare	1997-98
5	G.C.Smith	South Africa v Australia	Perth	2012-13
5	D.J.G.Sammy	West Indies v India	Mumbai	2013-14

Opponents

			E	A	SA	WI	NZ	I	P	SL	Z	B
200	S.R.Tendulkar	India	32	39	25	21	24	–	18	25	9	7
168	S.R.Waugh	Australia	46	–	16	32	23	18	20	8	3	2
168†	R.T.Ponting	Australia	35	–	26	24	17	29	15	14	3	4
166†	J.H.Kallis	South Africa/ICC	31	28	–	24	18	18	19	15	6	6
164†	R.S.Dravid	India/ICC	21	32	21	23	15	–	15	20	9	7
156	A.R.Border	Australia	47	–	6	31	23	20	22	7	–	–
153	S.Chanderpaul	West Indies	32	20	21	–	18	25	14	7	8	8
147†	M.V.Boucher	South Africa/ICC	25	20	–	24	17	14	15	17	6	8
145†	S.K.Warne	Australia	36	–	24	19	20	14	15	13	1	2
143	D.P.M.D.Jayawardena	Sri Lanka	21	16	16	11	13	18	27	–	8	13
134	V.V.S.Laxman	India	17	29	19	22	10	–	15	13	6	3
133	A.J.Stewart	England	–	33	23	24	16	9	13	9	6	–
133†	M.Muralitharan	Sri Lanka/ICC	16	12	15	12	14	22	16	–	14	11
132	A.Kumble	India	19	20	21	17	11	–	15	18	7	4
132	C.A.Walsh	West Indies	36	38	10	–	10	15	18	3	2	–
131	Kapil Dev	India	27	20	4	25	10	–	29	14	2	–
131†	B.C.Lara	West Indies/ICC	30	30	18	–	11	17	12	8	2	2
128	M.E.Waugh	Australia	29	–	18	28	14	14	15	9	1	–
125	S.M.Gavaskar	India	38	20	–	27	9	–	24	7	–	–
124†	G.D.McGrath	Australia	30	–	17	23	14	11	17	8	1	2
124	Javed Miandad	Pakistan	22	24	–	17	18	28	–	12	3	–
122	K.C.Sangakkara	Sri Lanka	20	11	15	12	10	15	19	–	5	15
121	I.V.A.Richards	West Indies	36	34	–	–	7	28	16	–	–	–
120†	Inzamam-ul-Haq	Pakistan/ICC	19	13	13	15	12	10	–	20	11	6
119	I.A.Healy	Australia	33	–	12	28	11	9	14	11	1	–
118	G.A.Gooch	England	–	42	3	26	15	19	10	3	–	–
117	D.I.Gower	England	–	42	–	19	13	24	17	2	–	–
117†	G.C.Smith	South Africa/ICC	21	21	–	14	13	15	16	7	2	8
116	D.L.Haynes	West Indies	36	33	1	–	10	19	16	1	–	–
116	D.B.Vengsarkar	India	26	24	–	25	11	–	22	8	–	–
115	M.A.Atherton	England	–	33	18	27	11	7	11	4	4	–
114	M.C.Cowdrey	England	–	43	14	21	18	8	10	–	–	–
113	S.C.Ganguly	India	12	24	17	12	8	–	12	14	9	5
112†	D.L.Vettori	New Zealand/ICC	17	18	14	10	–	15	8	11	9	9
111	S.P.Fleming	New Zealand	19	14	15	11	–	13	9	13	11	6
111	W.P.J.U.C.Vaas	Sri Lanka	15	12	11	9	10	14	18	–	15	7
110	S.T.Jayasuriya	Sri Lanka	14	13	15	10	13	10	17	–	13	5
110	C.H.Lloyd	West Indies	34	29	–	–	8	28	11	–	–	–
108	G.Boycott	England	–	38	7	29	15	13	6	–	–	–
108	C.G.Greenidge	West Indies	29	32	–	–	10	23	14	–	–	–
108	S.M.Pollock	South Africa	23	13	–	16	11	12	12	13	5	3
107	D.C.Boon	Australia	31	–	6	22	17	11	11	9	–	–
105†	M.J.Clarke	Australia	30	–	14	10	11	21	8	8	–	2
105†	J.L.Langer	Australia	21	–	11	18	14	14	13	8	3	2
104	K.P.Pietersen	England	–	27	10	14	8	16	14	11	–	4
104†	V.Sehwag	India/ICC	17	23	15	10	12	–	9	11	3	4
104	M.A.Taylor	Australia	33	–	11	20	11	9	12	8	–	–
104	Wasim Akram	Pakistan	18	13	4	17	9	12	–	19	10	2
103†	M.L.Hayden	Australia	20	–	19	15	11	18	6	7	2	4
103	Salim Malik	Pakistan	19	15	1	7	18	22	–	15	6	–
102	I.T.Botham	England	–	36	–	20	15	14	14	3	–	–
102	A.N.Cook	England	–	25	11	14	11	15	11	11	–	4

			E	A	SA	WI	NZ	I	P	SL	Z	B
102	C.L.Hooper	West Indies	24	25	10	–	2	19	14	6	2	–
101	Harbhajan Singh	India	14	18	11	11	13	–	9	15	7	3
101	G.Kirsten	South Africa	22	18	–	13	13	10	11	9	3	2
101	M.Ntini	South Africa	18	15	–	15	11	10	9	12	3	8
100	G.P.Thorpe	England	–	16	16	27	13	5	8	9	2	4
100	A.J.Strauss	England	–	20	16	18	9	12	13	8	–	4

† Includes appearance in the Australia v ICC 'Test' in 2005-06. The most for Zimbabwe is 67 by G.W.Flower, and for Bangladesh 61 by Mohammad Ashraful.

100 CONSECUTIVE TEST APPEARANCES

153	A.R.Border	Australia	March 1979 to March 1994
107	M.E.Waugh	Australia	June 1993 to October 2002
106	S.M.Gavaskar	India	January 1975 to February 1987
100	A.N.Cook	England	May 2006 to January 2014

50 TESTS AS CAPTAIN

			Won	*Lost*	*Drawn*	*Tied*
109	G.C.Smith	South Africa	53	29	27	–
93	A.R.Border	Australia	32	22	38	1
80	S.P.Fleming	New Zealand	28	27	25	–
77	R.T.Ponting	Australia	48	16	13	–
74	C.H.Lloyd	West Indies	36	12	26	–
57	S.R.Waugh	Australia	41	9	7	–
56	A.Ranatunga	Sri Lanka	12	19	25	–
54	M.A.Atherton	England	13	21	20	–
53	W.J.Cronje	South Africa	27	11	15	–
53	M.S.Dhoni	India	26	14	13	–
51	M.P.Vaughan	England	26	11	14	–
50	I.V.A.Richards	West Indies	27	8	15	–
50	M.A.Taylor	Australia	26	13	11	–
50	A.J.Strauss	England	24	11	15	–

The most for Pakistan 48 by Imran Khan, for Zimbabwe 21 by A.D.R.Campbell and H.H.Streak, and for Bangladesh 18 by Habibul Bashar.

50 TEST UMPIRING APPEARANCES

128	S.A.Bucknor	(West Indies)	28.04.1989 to 22.03.2009
108	R.E.Koertzen	(South Africa)	26.12.1992 to 24.07.2010
95	D.J.Harper	(Australia)	28.11.1998 to 23.06.2011
92	D.R.Shepherd	(England)	01.08.1985 to 07.06.2005
89	Alim Dar	(Pakistan)	21.10.2003 to 05.03.2014
78	D.B.Hair	(Australia)	25.01.1992 to 08.06.2008
76	B.F.Bowden	(New Zealand)	11.03.2000 to 17.12.2013
74	S.J.A.Taufel	(Australia)	26.12.2000 to 20.08.2012
73	S.Venkataraghavan	(India)	29.01.1993 to 20.01.2004
66	H.D.Bird	(England)	05.07.1973 to 24.06.1996
52	S.J.Davis	(Australia)	27.11.1997 to 18.02.2014

THE FIRST-CLASS COUNTIES
REGISTER, RECORDS AND 2013 AVERAGES

All statistics are to 8 March 2014.

ABBREVIATIONS – General

*	not out/unbroken partnership	IT20	International Twenty20
b	born	l-o	limited-overs
BB	Best innings bowling analysis	LOI	Limited-Overs Internationals
Cap	Awarded 1st XI County Cap	Tests	International Test Matches
f-c	first-class	F-c Tours	Overseas tours involving first-class
HS	Highest Score		appearances

Awards

PCA 2013	Professional Cricketers' Association Player of 2013
Wisden 2012	One of *Wisden Cricketers' Almanack*'s Five Cricketers of 2012
YC 2013	Cricket Writers' Club Young Cricketer of 2013

ECB Competitions

BHC	Benson & Hedges Cup (1972-2002)
CB40	Clydesdale Bank 40 (2010-12)
CC	LV= County Championship
CGT	Cheltenham & Gloucester Trophy (2001-06)
FPT	Friends Provident Trophy (2007-09)
NL	National League (1999-2005)
NWT	NatWest Trophy (1981-2000)
P40	NatWest PRO 40 League (2006-09)
SL	Sunday League (1969-98)
T20	Twenty20 Competition
Y40	Yorkshire Bank 40 (2013)

Education

Ac	Academy
BHS	Boys' High School
C	College
CFE	College of Further Education
CHE	College of Higher Education
CS	Comprehensive School
GS	Grammar School
HS	High School
I	Institute
IHE	Institute of Higher Education
RGS	Royal Grammar School
S	School
SFC	Sixth Form College
SM	Secondary Modern School
SS	Secondary School
TC	Technical College
T(H)S	Technical (High) School
U	University
UWIC	University of Wales Institute, Cardiff

Playing Categories

LBG	Bowls right-arm leg-breaks and googlies
LF	Bowls left-arm fast
LFM	Bowls left-arm fast-medium
LHB	Bats left-handed
LM	Bowls left-arm medium pace
LMF	Bowls left-arm medium fast
OB	Bowls right-arm off-breaks
RF	Bowls right-arm fast
RFM	Bowls right-arm fast-medium
RHB	Bats right-handed
RM	Bowls right-arm medium pace
RMF	Bowls right-arm medium-fast
RSM	Bowls right-arm slow-medium

SLA	Bowls left-arm leg-breaks
SLC	Bowls left-arm 'Chinamen'
WK	Wicket-keeper
Teams (see also p 225)	
ACT	Australian Capital Territory
ADBP	Agricultural Development Bank of Pakistan
BS	Basnahira South
CC&C	Combined Campuses & Colleges
CD	Central Districts
EL	England Lions
EP	Eastern Province
FS	Free State
GW	Griqualand West
HB	Habib Bank Limited
SJD	Sheikh Jamal Dhanmondi
KKC	Kalabagan Krira Chakra
KRL	Khan Research Laboratories
KZN	KwaZulu-Natal Inland
ME	Mashonaland Eagles
MT	Matabeleland Tuskers
MWR	Mid West Rhinos
NBP	National Bank of Pakistan
ND	Northern Districts
NSW	New South Wales
NT	Northern Transvaal
NW	North West
(O)FS	(Orange) Free State
PDSC	Prime Doleshwar Sporting Club
PIA	Pakistan International Airlines
PNSC	Pakistan National Shipping Corporation
PTC	Pakistan Telecommunication Co
Q	Queensland
REDCO	Really Efficient Development Co
SAU	South African Universities
SNGPL	Sui Northern Gas Pipelines Limited
SR	Southern Rocks
SSGC	Sui Southern Gas Corporation
Tas	Tasmania
T&T	Trinidad & Tobago
Uni	Unicorns
UP	Uttar Pradesh
Vic	Victoria
WA	Western Australia
WAPDA	Water & Power Development Authority.
WP	Western Province
ZTB	Zarai Taraqiati Bank Limited

DERBYSHIRE

Formation of Present Club: 4 November 1870
Inaugural First-Class Match: 1871
Colours: Chocolate, Amber and Pale Blue
Badge: Rose and Crown
County Champions: (1) 1936
NatWest Trophy Winners: (1) 1981
Benson and Hedges Cup Winners: (1) 1993
Sunday League Winners: (1) 1990

Twenty20 Cup Winners: (0) best – Quarter-Finalist 2005

Chief Executive: Simon Storey, Derbyshire County Cricket Club, Grandstand Road, Derby DE21 6AF • Tel: 01332 388101 • Fax: 0844 500 8322 • Email: info@derbyshireccc.com • Web: www. derbyshireccc.com • Twitter: @DerbyshireCCC (10,065 followers)

Elite Performance Director: Graeme Welch. **Captain**: W.L.Madsen. **Vice-Captain**: None. **Overseas Player**: S.Chanderpaul. **2014 Beneficiary**: None. **Head Groundsman**: Neil Godrich. **Scorer**: John M.Brown. ‡ New registration. ᴺᑫNot qualified for England.

BORRINGTON, Paul Michael (Repton S; Chellarton S; Loughborough U), b Nottingham 24 May 1988. Son of A.J.Borrington (Derbyshire 1971-80). 5'10''. RHB, OB. Debut (Derbyshire) 2005. Loughborough UCCE 2008-09. HS 105 LU v Hants (Southampton) 2009. De HS 98 v Northants (Derby) 2012. BB –. LO HS 72 v Surrey (Oval) 2013 (Y40).

BURGOYNE, Peter Ian (St John Houghton S, Ilkeston; Derby SFC), b Nottingham 11 Nov 1993. 6'2''. RHB, OB. Debut (Southern Rocks) 2012-13. Derbyshire debut 2013. Derbyshire 2nd XI debut 2011. HS 104 and BB 3-27 SR v MWR (Kwekwe) 2012-13. De HS 62* v Sussex (Hove) 2013. De BB 3-66 v Middx (Derby) 2013. LO HS 43 SR v MWR (Masvingo) 2012-13. LO BB 3-31 v Northants (Derby) 2012 (CB40). T20 HS 38. T20 BB 2-13.

ᴺᑫ**CHANDERPAUL, Shivnarine** (Cove and John SS, Unity Village), b Unity Village, Demerara, Guyana 16 Aug 1974. 5'6''. LHB, LB. Guyana 1991-92 to date. Durham 2007-09. Lancashire 2010; cap 2010. Warwickshire 2011. Derbyshire debut 2013. *Wisden* 2007. **Tests** (WI): 153 (1993-94 to 2013-14, 14 as captain); HS 203* v SA (Georgetown) 2004-05; BB 1-2 v A (Adelaide) 1996-97. **LOI** (WI): 268 (1994-95 to 2010-11, 16 as captain); HS 150 v SA (E London) 1998-99; BB 3-18 v I (Sharjah) 1997-98. **IT20** (WI): 22 (2005-06 to 2010); HS 41 v E (Oval) 2007. F-c Tours (WI) (C=Captain): E 1995, 2000, 2004, 2007, 2009, 2012; A 1995-96, 1996-97, 2000-01, 2005-06C, 2009-10; SA 1998-99, 2003-04, 2007-08; NZ 1994-95, 1999-00, 2005-06C, 2008-09, 2013-14; I 1994-95, 2002-03, 2011-12, 2013-14; P 1997-98, 2001-02 (Sharjah), 2006-07; SL 2005C, 2010-11; Z 2001, 2003-04; B 1999-00, 2002-03, 2011-12, 2012-13; K 2001. 1000 runs (1+1); most – 1107 (2004-05). HS 303* Guyana v Jamaica (Kingston) 1995-96. CC HS 201* Du v Worcs (Worcester) 2009. De HS 129 v Surrey (Derby) 2013. BB 4-48 Guyana v Leeward Is (Basseterre) 1992-93. De BB 2-32 v Somerset (Taunton) 2013. LO HS 150 (*see LOI*). LO BB 4-22 Guyana v Trinidad (Hampton Court) 1995-96. T20 HS 87*.

CLARE, Jonathan Luke (St Theodore's HS), b Burnley, Lancs 14 Jun 1986. 6'4''. RHB, RMF. Debut (Derbyshire) 2007, taking 5-90 v Notts (Chesterfield); cap 2012. HS 130 v Glamorgan (Derby) 2011. BB 7-74 v Northants (Northampton) 2008. LO HS 57 v Warwks (Derby) 2012 (CB40). LO BB 3-39 v Scotland (Derby) 2008 (FPT). T20 HS 35*. T20 BB 2-20.

CORK, Gregory Teodor Gerald (Denstone C), b Derby 29 Sep 1994. Son of D.G.Cork (Derbyshire, Lancashire, Hampshire and England 1990-2011). RHB, LMF. Derbyshire 2nd XI debut 2011. Awaiting 1st XI debut.

COTTON, Benjamin David (Clayton Hall C; Stoke-on-Trent SFC), b Stoke-on-Trent, Staffs 13 Sep 1993. Derbyshire 2nd XI debut 2011. Awaiting 1st XI debut.

DURSTON, Wesley John (Millfield S; University C, Worcester), b Taunton, Somerset 6 Oct 1980. 5'10". RHB, OB. Somerset 2002-09. Derbyshire debut 2010; cap 2012. Unicorns 2010 (l-o only). 1000 runs (1): 1138 (2011). HS 151 v Glos (Derby) 2011. BB 5-34 v Yorks (Leeds) 2012. LO HS 120* v Unicorns (Wormsley) 2012 (CB40). LO BB 3-7 v Worcs (Derby) 2011 (CB40). T20 HS 111 v Notts (Nottingham) 2010 – De record. T20 BB 3-25.

ELSTONE, Scott Liam (Friary Grange C), b Burton-on-Trent, Staffs 10 Jun 1990. 5'8". RHB, OB. Awaiting f-c debut. Nottinghamshire 2nd XI debut 2006, aged 16y 81d. Unicorns (l-o only) 2013. Derbyshire (l-o only) 2013. LO HS 75* Uni v Somerset (Taunton) 2013 (Y40). LO BB 1-22 Nt v Scotland (Nottingham) 2010 (CB40). T20 HS 21*.

FOOTITT, Mark Harold Alan (Carlton le Willows S; West Notts C), b Nottingham 25 Nov 1985. 6'2". RHB, LFM. Nottinghamshire 2005-09. MCC 2006. No f-c appearances in 2008. Derbyshire debut 2010. HS 30 v Surrey (Oval) 2010. BB 6-53 v Durham (Chester-le-St) 2013. LO HS 4 v Middx (Chesterfield) 2011 (CB40). LO BB 5-28 v Scotland (Edinburgh) 2013 (Y40). T20 HS 2*. T20 BB 3-22.

GODLEMAN, Billy Ashley (Islington Green S), b Islington, London 11 Feb 1989. 6'3". LHB, LB. Middlesex 2005-09. Essex 2010-12. Derbyshire debut 2013. HS 130 Ex v Leics (Leicester) 2011 and 130 Ex v Glos (Cheltenham) 2012. De HS 55 v Middx (Lord's) 2013. BB –. LO HS 82 M v Scotland (Lord's) 2009 (FPT). T20 HS 69.

GROENEWALD, Timothy Duncan (Maritzburg C; South Africa U), b Pietermaritzburg, South Africa 10 Jan 1984. 6'0". RHB, RFM. Debut Cambridge UCCE 2006. Warwickshire 2006-08. Derbyshire debut 2009; cap 2011. HS 78 Wa v Bangladesh A (Birmingham) 2008. CC HS 76 Wa v Durham (Chester-le-St) 2006. De HS 60* v Leics (Derby) 2011. BB 6-50 v Surrey (Croydon) 2009. LO HS 36 Wa v Lancs (Manchester) 2007 (FPT). LO BB 4-22 v Worcs (Worcester) 2011 (CB40). T20 HS 41. T20 BB 4-21.

HIGGINBOTTOM, Matthew (New Mills SFC; Leeds Met U), b Stockport, Cheshire 20 Oct 1990. 6'2". LHB, RMF. Debut (Leeds/Bradford MCCU) 2012. Derbyshire debut 2013. Bradford/Leeds MCCU 2009-12. Derbyshire 2nd XI debut 2009. HS 31* LBU v Yorks (Leeds) 2012. De HS 9 (twice) (2013). BB 3-59 v Middx (Derby) 2013. LO HS and LO BB –.

HUGHES, Alex Lloyd (Ounsdale HS, Wolverhampton), b Wordsley, Staffs 29 Sep 1991. 5'10". RHB, RM. Debut (Derbyshire) 2013. Derbyshire 2nd XI debut 2009. HS 33 v Middx (Derby) 2013 and v Somerset (Taunton) 2013. BB 3-49 v Sussex (Hove) 2013 – on debut. LO HS 59* and LO BB 3-56 v Essex (Leek) 2013 (Y40). T20 HS 11*. T20 BB 3-32.

NQHUGHES, Chesney Francis (Albena Lake Hodge CS, Anguilla), b Anguilla 20 January 1991. 6'2". LHB, SLA. British passport. Debut (Derbyshire) 2010. Derbyshire 2nd XI debut 2009. Leeward Is 2009-10 to 2011-12 (l-o only). HS 270* v Yorks (Leeds) 2013. BB 2-9 v Middx (Derby) 2011. LO HS 81 Leeward Is v Windward Is (Kingston) 2010-11. LO BB 5-29 v Unicorns (Wormsley) 2012 (CB40). T20 HS 65. T20 BB 4-23.

JOHNSON, Richard Matthew, b Solihull, Warwicks 1 Sep 1988. RHB, WK. Warwickshire 2008-12. Derbyshire debut 2012. Herefordshire 2006. HS 72 Wa v Cambridge UCCE (Cambridge) 2008 (on debut) and 72 v Surrey (Derby) 2013. LO HS 79 v Yorks (Chesterfield) 2012 (CB40). T20 HS 14.

KNIGHT, Thomas Craig ('**Tom**') (Eckington C), b Sheffield, Yorks 28 Jun 1993. 6'0½". RHB, SLA. Debut (Derbyshire) 2011. No f-c appearances in 2012 and 2013. HS 14 v Surrey (Oval) 2011. BB 2-32 v Glamorgan (Cardiff) 2011. LO HS 10 v Hants (Derby) 2013 (Y40). LO BB 3-36 v Durham (Derby) 2013 (Y40). T20 HS 2*. T20 BB 3-16.

^{NQ}**MADSEN, Wayne** Lee (Kearsney C, Durban; U of South Africa), b Durban, South Africa 2 Jan 1984. Nephew of M.B.Madsen (Natal 1967-68 to 1978-79), T.R.Madsen (Natal 1976-77 to 1989-90) and H.R.Fotheringham (Natal, Transvaal 1971-72 to 1989-90) and cousin of G.S.Fotheringham (KwaZulu-Natal 2008-09 to 2009-10). 5'11". RHB, OB. KwaZulu-Natal 2003-04 to 2007-08. Dolphins 2006-07 to 2007-08. Derbyshire debut 2009, scoring 170 v Glos (Cheltenham); cap 2011; captain 2012 to date. 1000 runs (1): 1239 (2013). HS 231* v Northants (Northampton) 2012. BB 3-45 KZN v EP (Pt Elizabeth) 2007-08. De BB 2-9 v Sussex (Hove) 2013. LO HS 78 v Lancs (Manchester) 2013 (Y40). LO BB 3-27 v Durham (Derby) 2013 (Y40). T20 HS 61*.

MARSDEN, Jonathan (King's S, Macclesfield; St Hilda's C, Oxford), b Pembury, Kent 7 Apr 1993. RHB, RFM. Debut (Oxford U) 2013 – blue 2013. Derbyshire 2nd XI debut 2011. Awaiting 1st XI debut. HS – and BB 3-32 OU v Cambridge U (Cambridge) 2013.

‡**MOORE, Stephen** Colin (St Stithian's C, Johannesburg; Exeter U), b Johannesburg, South Africa 4 Nov 1980. 6'1". RHB, RM. Worcestershire 2003-09. Lancashire 2010-13; cap 2011. MCC 2009, 2011. F-c Tour (Eng A): NZ 2008-09. 1000 runs (4); most – 1451 (2008). HS 246 Wo v Derbys (Worcester) 2005. BB 1-13 Wo v Lancs (Worcester) 2004. LO HS 118 La v Surrey (Croydon) 2010 (CB40). LO BB 1-1 Wo v Scotland (Worcester) 2004 (NL). T20 HS 83*.

PALLADINO, Antonio Paul (Cardinal Pole SS; Anglia Polytechnic U), b Tower Hamlets, London 29 Jun 1983. 6'0". RHB, RMF. Cambridge UCCE 2003-05. Essex 2003-10. Namibia 2009-10. Derbyshire debut 2011; cap 2012. HS 106 v Australia A (Derby) 2012. CC HS 68 v Warwks (Birmingham) 2013. 50 wkts (2); most – 56 (2012). BB 7-53 v Kent (Derby) 2012. Hat-trick v Leics (Leicester) 2012. LO HS 31 Namibia v Boland (Windhoek) 2009-10. LO BB 4-32 v Kent (Canterbury) 2011 (CB40). T20 HS 8*. T20 BB 4-21.

POYNTON, Thomas (John Taylor HS, Barton-under-Needwood; Repton S), b Burton upon Trent, Staffs 25 Nov 1989. 5'10". RHB, WK. Debut (Derbyshire) 2007. No f-c appearances in 2009 and 2011. HS 106 v Northants (Northampton) 2012. BB 2-96 v Glamorgan (Cardiff) 2010. LO HS 40 v Middx (Chesterfield) 2011 (CB40). T20 HS 19.

SLATER, Benjamin Thomas (Netherthorpe S; Leeds Met U), b Chesterfield 26 Aug 1991. 5'10". LHB, LB. Debut (Leeds/Bradford MCCU) 2012. Southern Rocks 2012-13. Derbyshire 2nd XI debut 2009. HS 89 SR v ME (Harare) 2012-13. De HS 66* v Sussex (Hove) 2013. BB –. LO HS 46 SR v MWR (Masvingo) 2012-13. T20 HS 57.

TAYLOR, Thomas Alex Ian (Trentham HS, Stoke-on-Trent), b Stoke-on-Trent, Staffs 21 Dec 1994. RHB, RMF. Derbyshire 2nd XI debut 2011. Awaiting 1st XI debut.

TURNER, Mark Leif (Thornhill CS), b Sunderland, Co Durham 23 Oct 1984. 5'11". RHB, RMF. Durham 2005-06. Somerset 2007-09, no f-c appearances in 2010. Derbyshire debut 2011. HS 57 Sm v Derbys (Taunton) 2007. De HS 27* v Glamorgan (Derby) 2011. BB 5-32 v Northants (Northampton) 2011. LO HS 15* Sm v Essex (Taunton) 2009 (P40). LO BB 4-36 Sm v Worcs (Bath) 2010 (CB40). T20 HS 11*. T20 BB 4-35.

WAINWRIGHT, David John (Hemsworth HS and SFC; Loughborough U); b Pontefract, Yorks 21 Mar 1985. 5'9". LHB, SLA. Yorkshire 2004-11; cap 2010. Derbyshire debut/cap 2012. Loughborough UCCE 2005-06. British U 2006. Police Sports Club 2011-12. HS 104* (batting at No 10) Y v Sussex (Hove) 2008. De HS 54* v Surrey (Oval) 2013. 50 wkts (1): 50 (2012). BB 6-33 v Northants (Derby) 2012. LO HS 40 v Lancs (Manchester) 2013 (Y40). LO BB 4-11 v Durham (Derby) 2013 (Y40). T20 HS 15*. T20 BB 3-6.

RELEASED/RETIRED

(Having made a County First-Class or List A appearance in 2013)

EVANS, Alasdair Campbell (George Watson's C, Edinburgh; Loughborough U), b Pembury, Kent 12 Jan 1989. 6'5". RHB, RMF. Debut Loughborough UCCE 2009. Loughborough UCCE 2009. Scotland 2009-11. **LOI** (Scot): 3 (2009 to 2012); HS –; BB 1-13 v Canada (Ayr) 2012. HS 14* Scot v Ireland (Dublin) 2013. De HS 6* v Sussex (Derby) 2013. BB 6-30 Scot v Kenya (Aberdeen) 2013. De BB 1-30 v New Zealanders (Derby) 2013. LO HS 2* Scot v Somerset (Uddingston) 2012 (CB40). BB 2-34 v Northants (Derby) 2012 (CB40).

REDFERN, Daniel James (Adam's GS, Newport, Shropshire), b Shrewsbury, Shropshire 18 Apr 1990. 5'9". LHB, OB. Derbyshire 2007-13; cap 2012. HS 133 v Hants (Southampton) 2012. BB 3-33 v Durham (Chester-le-St) 2013. LO HS 57* v Yorks (Derby) 2007 (P40). LO BB 2-10 v Kent (Chesterfield) 2009 (P40). T20 HS 43. T20 BB 2-17.

WHITELEY, R.A. – see *WORCESTERSHIRE*.

C.M.Durham left the staff without making a County First-Class or List A appearance for Derbyshire in 2013.

DERBYSHIRE 2013

RESULTS SUMMARY

	Place	Won	Lost	Tied	Drew	NR
LV= County Championship (1st Division)	8th	3	10		3	
All First-Class Matches		3	11		3	
Yorkshire Bank 40 (Group B)	6th	3	6			3
Friends Life t20 (North Group)	5th	4	6			

LV= COUNTY CHAMPIONSHIP AVERAGES
BATTING AND FIELDING

Cap		M	I	NO	HS	Runs	Avge	100	50	Ct/St
2011	W.L.Madsen	16	30	2	152	1221	43.60	3	8	11
	S.Chanderpaul	15	27	4	129	884	38.43	1	7	8
	C.F.Hughes	11	20	1	270*	612	32.21	1	2	7
	R.M.Johnson	12	21	1	72	526	26.30	–	4	9
	P.M.Borrington	4	8	–	75	209	26.12	–	1	2
	T.Poynton	12	22	2	63*	443	22.15	–	3	27/3
	P.I.Burgoyne	4	7	1	62*	132	22.00	–	1	2
2012	D.J.Wainwright	9	16	4	54*	241	20.08	–	1	–
	M.L.Turner	5	7	3	23*	79	19.75	–	–	–
	B.T.Slater	10	18	1	66*	335	19.70	–	3	3
2012	A.P.Palladino	8	14	1	68	233	17.92	–	1	1
	B.A.Godleman	8	14	–	55	236	16.85	–	1	3
2012	W.J.Durston	9	16	1	50	245	16.33	–	1	8
2012	D.J.Redfern	7	13	–	61	184	14.15	–	1	6
	A.L.Hughes	6	11	–	33	136	12.36	–	–	3
2012	J.L.Clare	6	12	1	49	130	11.81	–	–	8
2011	T.D.Groenewald	15	26	5	49	231	11.00	–	–	7
	M.H.A.Footitt	12	20	5	24	131	8.73	–	–	3
	R.A.Whiteley	3	5	–	12	25	5.20	–	–	3
	M.Higginbottom	3	5	1	9	18	4.50	–	–	–

Also batted: A.C.Evans (1 match) 0, 6*.

BOWLING

	O	M	R	W	Avge	Best	5wI	10wM
A.P.Palladino	214.5	43	644	23	28.00	6-90	2	–
T.D.Groenewald	437.5	86	1404	45	31.20	5-30	3	–
J.L.Clare	124	7	554	17	32.58	5-29	1	–
M.H.A.Footitt	352.5	54	1293	36	35.91	6-53	2	–
W.J.Durston	166	21	538	10	53.80	2-29	–	–
D.J.Wainwright	296	42	924	17	54.34	3-46	–	–
Also bowled:								
M.Higginbottom	77.5	19	283	9	31.44	3-59	–	–
A.L.Hughes	71	12	230	6	38.33	3-49	–	–
M.L.Turner	91.4	9	407	6	67.83	3-51	–	–
P.I.Burgoyne	138.1	25	388	5	77.60	3-66	–	–

S.Chanderpaul 18.4-4-40-3; A.C.Evans 15-1-92-0; C.F.Hughes 5-1-19-1; W.L.Madsen 43-10-121-3; D.J.Redfern 32.1-2-119-4; R.A.Whiteley 15-1-71-1.

The First-Class Averages (pp 225–241) give the records of Derbyshire players in all first-class county matches (Derbyshire's other opponents being the New Zealanders), with the exception of:
R.A.Whiteley 4-7-0-12-273.85-0-0-3ct. 32-1-147-1-147.00-1/43-0-0.

DERBYSHIRE RECORDS

FIRST-CLASS CRICKET

Highest Total	For 801-8d		v	Somerset	Taunton	2007
	V 677-7d		by	Yorkshire	Leeds	2013
Lowest Total	For 16		v	Notts	Nottingham	1879
	V 23		by	Hampshire	Burton upon T	1958
Highest Innings	For 274	G.A.Davidson	v	Lancashire	Manchester	1896
	V 343*	P.A.Perrin	for	Essex	Chesterfield	1904

Highest Partnership for each Wicket

1st	322	H.Storer/J.Bowden	v	Essex	Derby	1929
2nd	417	K.J.Barnett/T.A.Tweats	v	Yorkshire	Derby	1997
3rd	316*	A.S.Rollins/K.J.Barnett	v	Leics	Leicester	1997
4th	328	P.Vaulkhard/D.Smith	v	Notts	Nottingham	1946
5th	302*†	J.E.Morris/D.G.Cork	v	Glos	Cheltenham	1993
6th	212	G.M.Lee/T.S.Worthington	v	Essex	Chesterfield	1932
7th	258	M.P.Dowman/D.G.Cork	v	Durham	Derby	2000
8th	198	K.M.Krikken/D.G.Cork	v	Lancashire	Manchester	1996
9th	283	A.Warren/J.Chapman	v	Warwicks	Blackwell	1910
10th	132	A.Hill/M.Jean-Jacques	v	Yorkshire	Sheffield	1986

† 346 runs were added for this wicket in two separate partnerships

Best Bowling	For 10- 40	W.Bestwick	v	Glamorgan	Cardiff	1921
(Innings)	V 10- 45	R.L.Johnson	for	Middlesex	Derby	1994
Best Bowling	For 17-103	W.Mycroft	v	Hampshire	Southampton	1876
(Match)	V 16-101	G.Giffen	for	Australians	Derby	1886

Most Runs – Season	2165	D.B.Carr	(av 48.11)	1959
Most Runs – Career	23854	K.J.Barnett	(av 41.12)	1979-98
Most 100s – Season	8	P.N.Kirsten		1982
Most 100s – Career	53	K.J.Barnett		1979-98
Most Wkts – Season	168	T.B.Mitchell	(av 19.55)	1935
Most Wkts – Career	1670	H.L.Jackson	(av 17.11)	1947-63
Most Career W-K Dismissals	1304	R.W.Taylor	(1157 ct; 147 st)	1961-84
Most Career Catches in the Field	563	D.C.Morgan		1950-69

LIMITED-OVERS CRICKET

Highest Total	50ov	366-4		v	Comb Univs	Oxford	1991
	40ov	321-5		v	Essex	Leek	2013
	T20	222-5		v	Yorkshire	Leeds	2010
Lowest Total	50ov	73		v	Lancashire	Derby	1993
	40ov	60		v	Kent	Canterbury	2008
	T20	72		v	Leics	Derby	2013
Highest Innings	50ov	173*	M.J.Di Venuto	v	Derbys CB	Derby	2000
	40ov	141*	C.J.Adams	v	Kent	Chesterfield	1992
	T20	111	W.J.Durston	v	Notts	Nottingham	2010
Best Bowling	50ov	8-21	M.A.Holding	v	Sussex	Hove	1988
	40ov	6- 7	M.Hendrick	v	Notts	Nottingham	1972
	T20	5-27	T.Lungley	v	Leics	Leicester	2009

DURHAM

Formation of Present Club: 23 May 1882
Inaugural First-Class Match: 1992
Colours: Navy Blue, Yellow and Maroon
Badge: Coat of Arms of the County of Durham
County Champions: (3) 2008, 2009, 2013
Friends Provident Trophy Winners: (1) 2007
Twenty20 Cup Winners: (0); best – Semi-Finalist 2008

Chief Executive: David Harker, Emirates Durham International Cricket Ground, Chester-le-Street, Co Durham DH3 3QR • Tel: 0191 387 1717 • Fax: 0191 387 1616 • Email: marketing@durhamccc.co.uk • Web: www.durhamccc.co.uk • Twitter: @DurhamCricket (15,709 followers)

Director of Cricket: Geoff Cook. **Head Coach**: Jon Lewis. **Assistant Coach**: A.Walker. **Captain**: P.D.Collingwood. **Vice-Captain**: None. **Overseas Player**: None. **2014 Beneficiaries**: G.R.Breese and G.J.Muchall. **Head Groundsman**: David Measor. **Scorer**: Brian Hunt. ‡ New registration. ^NQNot qualified for England.

Durham initially awarded caps immediately after their players joined the staff but revised this policy in 1998, again capping players on merit, past 'awards' having been nullified. Durham abolished both their capping and 'awards' systems after the 2005 season.

ARSHAD, Usman (Beckfoot GS, Bingley), b Bradford, Yorkshire 9 Jan 1993. RHB, RMF. Debut (Durham) 2013. Northumberland 2011. HS 83 v Sussex (Hove) 2013. BB 3-16 v Sussex (Chester-le-St) 2013. LO HS and BB –.

BORTHWICK, Scott George (Farringdon Community Sports C, Sunderland), b Sunderland 19 Apr 1990. 5'9". LHB, LBG. Debut (Durham) 2009. England U19 2008-09 to 2009. **Tests**: 1 (2013-14); HS 4 and BB 3-33 v A (Sydney) 2013-14. **LOI**: 2 (2011 to 2011-12); HS 15 v Ireland (Dublin) 2011; BB –. **IT20**: 1 (2011); HS 14 and BB 1-15 v WI (Oval) 2011. F-c Tours: A 2013-14; SL 2013-14 (EL). 1000 runs (1): 1121 (2013). HS 135 v Surrey (Chester-le-St) 2013. BB 6-70 v Surrey (Oval) 2013. LO HS 80 v Hants (Chester-le-St) 2013 (Y40). LO BB 4-51 v Hants (Southampton) 2012 (CB40). T20 HS 62. T20 BB 3-19.

BREESE, Gareth Rohan (Wolmer's BHS, Kingston; Kingston U of Technology, Jamaica), b Montego Bay, Jamaica 9 Jan 1976. 5'7". RHB, OB. Jamaica 1995-96 to 2005-06; captain/overseas player 2003-04 to 2005-06. British passport (Welsh father). Durham debut 2004; cap 2005; benefit 2014. **Tests** (WI): 1 (2002-03); HS 5 and BB 2-108 v I (Madras) 2002-03. F-c Tours (WI): E 2002 (WI A); I 2002-03. HS 165* v Somerset (Taunton) 2004. BB 7-60 Jamaica v Barbados (Bridgetown) 2000-01. Du BB 5-41 (10-151 match) v Yorks (Scarborough) 2004 – scored 35 and 68 to complete match double. LO HS 68* v Notts (Chester-le-St) 2007 (FPT). LO BB 5-41 v Derbys (Chester-le-St) 2008 (FPT). T20 HS 37. T20 BB 4-14.

BUCKLEY, Ryan Sean (Hummersknott Ac, Darlington; Darlington Queen Elizabeth SFC), b Darlington 2 Apr 1994. RHB, OB. Debut (Durham) 2013, taking 5-86 v Surrey (Oval). Durham 2nd XI debut 2011. HS 6 and BB 5-68 v Surrey (Oval) 2013.

CLARK, Graham (St Benedict's CHS, Whitehaven), b Whitehaven, Cumbria 16 Mar 1993. Brother of J.Clark (*see LANCASHIRE*). RHB, LB. Durham 2nd XI debut 2011. MCC YC 2013. Awaiting 1st XI debut.

COLLINGWOOD, Paul David (Blackfyne CS; Derwentside C), b Shotley Bridge 26 May 1976. 5'11". RHB, RM. Debut (Durham) 1996 v Northants (Chester-le-St) taking wicket of D.J.Capel with his first ball before scoring 91 and 16; cap 1998; benefit 2007; captain 2012 (*part*) to date. MBE 2005. *Wisden* 2007. Joined the England coaching staff for the ICC World T20 tournament in Bangladesh. **Tests**: 68 (2003-04 to 2010-11); HS 206 v A (Adelaide) 2006-07; BB 3-23 v NZ (Wellington) 2007-08. **LOI**: 197 (2001 to 2010-11, 25 as captain); HS 120* v A (Melbourne) 2006-07; BB 6-31 v B (Nottingham) 2005 – record analysis for E, and first to score a hundred (112*) and take six wickets in same LOI. **IT20**: 35 (2005 to 2010-11, 30 as captain); HS 79 v WI (Oval) 2007; BB 4-22 v SL (Southampton) 2006. F-c Tours: A 2006-07, 2010-11; SA 2009-10; WI 2003-04, 2008-09; NZ 2007-08; I 2005-06, 2008-09; P 2005-06; SL 2003-04, 2007-08; B 2009-10. 1000 runs (2); most – 1120 (2005), inc six hundreds (Du record). HS 206 (*see Tests*). Du HS 190 v SL (Chester-le-St) 2002 and 190 v Derbys (Derby) 2005, sharing Du record 4th wkt partnership of 250 with D.M.Benkenstein. BB 5-52 v Somerset (Stockton) 2005. LO HS 120* (*see LOI*). LO BB 6-31 (*see LOI*). T20 HS 79. T20 BB 5-6 v Northants (Chester-le-St) 2011 – Du record.

COUGHLIN, Paul (St Robert of Newminster Catholic CS, Washington), b Sunderland 23 Oct 1992. RHB, RM. Debut (Durham) 2012. Northumberland 2011. No 1st XI appearances in 2013. HS 29* and BB 1-26 v Australia A (Chester-le-St) 2012 – only f-c appearance. LO HS and BB –.

HARRISON, Jamie (Sedburgh S), b Whiston, Lancs 19 Nov 1990. 6'0". RHB, LMF. Debut (Durham) 2012. Durham 2nd XI debut 2009. Gloucestershire 2nd XI 2008. HS 35 v Yorks (Scarborough) 2013. BB 5-31 v Surrey (Chester-le-St) 2013. LO HS 7* and LO BB 2-51 v Somerset (Chester-le-St) 2012 (CB40).

JENNINGS, Keaton Karl (King Edward VII S, Johannesburg), b Johannesburg, South Africa 19 Jun 1992. Son of R.V.Jennings (Transvaal 1973-74 to 1992-93), brother of D.Jennings (Gauteng and Easterns 1999 to 2003-04), nephew of K.E.Jennings (Northern Transvaal 1981-82 to 1982-83). LHB, RMF. Debut (Gauteng) 2011-12. Durham debut 2012. HS 127 v Sussex (Hove) 2013. BB 2-8 Gauteng v WP (Cape Town) 2011-12. Du BB 1-5 v Yorks (Chester-le-St) 2013. LO HS 71* Gauteng v KZN (Johannesburg) 2011-12. LO BB –.

‡MacLEOD, Calum Scott (Hillpark S, Glasgow), b Glasgow, Scotland 15 Nov 1988. 6'1". RHB, RMF. Scotland 2013. Awaiting CC debut. Warwickshire 2008-09. Awaiting f-c debut. **LOI**: 19 (2008 to 2013-14); HS 175 v Canada (Christchurch) 2013-14; BB 2-26 v Kenya (Aberdeen) 2013. **IT20** (Scot): 15 (2009 to 2013-14); HS 57 v Netherlands (Dubai) 2011-12; BB 2-17 v Kenya (Aberdeen) 2013. F-c Tours (Scot): UAE 2011-12, 2012-13; Namibia 2011-12. HS 67 Sc v Kenya (Aberdeen) 2013. BB 4-66 Sc v Canada (Aberdeen) 2009. LO HS 175 (*see LOI*). LO BB 3-37 Sc v UAE (Queenstown) 2013-14. T20 HS 104*. T20 BB 2-17.

MORLEY, Max Gary (Holmfirth HS; New C, Huddersfield), b Huddersfield, Yorks 24 Jan 1993. LHB, SLA. Durham 2nd XI debut 2012. Awaiting f-c and l-o debut. T20 HS –. T20 BB –.

MUCHALL, Gordon James (Durham S), b Newcastle upon Tyne, Northumb 2 Nov 1982. 6'0". RHB, RM. Northumberland 1999. Older brother of P.B.Muchall (Gloucestershire 2012). Debut (Durham) 2002; cap 2005; benefit 2014. No f-c appearances in 2013. F-c Tour: SL 2002-03 (ECB Acad). HS 219 v Kent (Canterbury) 2006, sharing Du record 6th wkt partnership of 249 with P.Mustard (*see below*). BB 3-26 v Yorks (Leeds) 2003. LO HS 101* v Yorks (Leeds) 2005 (NL). LO BB 1-15 v Sussex (Hove) 2003 (NL). T20 HS 66*. T20 BB 1-8.

MUSTARD, Philip (Usworth CS), b Sunderland 8 Oct 1982. Cousin of C.Rushworth (*see below*). 5'11". LHB, WK. Debut (Durham) 2002; captain 2010 (*part*) to 2012 (*part*). Mountaineers 2011-12. Auckland 2012-13. **LOI:** 10 (2007-08); HS 83 v NZ (Napier) 2007-08. **IT20:** 2 (2007-08); HS 40 v NZ (Christchurch) 2007-08. HS 130 v Kent (Canterbury) 2006. LO HS 143 v Surrey (Chester-le-St) 2012 (CB40). T20 HS 97*.

ONIONS, Graham (St Thomas More RC S, Blaydon), b Gateshead 9 Sep 1982. 6'1". RHB, RFM. Debut (Durham) 2004. Dolphins 2013-14. MCC 2007-08. *Wisden* 2009. Missed entire 2010 season through back injury. **Tests:** 9 (2009 to 2012); HS 17* v A (Lord's) 2009; BB 5-38 v WI (Lord's) 2009 – on debut. **LOI:** 4 (2009 to 2009-10); HS 1 v A (Centurion) 2009-10; BB 2-58 v SL (Johannesburg) 2009-10. F-c Tours: SA 2009-10; NZ 2012-13; I 2007-08 (EL), 2012-13; SL 2013-14; B 2006-07 (Eng A); UAE 2011-12 (*part*). HS 41 v Yorks (Leeds) 2013. 50 wkts (5); most – 73 (2013). BB 9-67 v Notts (Nottingham) 2012. LO HS 19 v Derbys (Derby) 2008 (FPT). LO BB 4-45 v Lancs (Chester-le-St) 2013 (Y40). T20 HS 31. T20 BB 3-25.

‡**POYNTER, Stuart** William (Teddington S), b Hammersmith, London 18 Oct 1990. Younger brother of A.D.Poynter (Middlesex and Ireland 2005 to date). RHB, WK. Middlesex 2010. Ireland 2011 to date. Warwickshire 2013. Middlesex 2nd XI debut 2007. HS 63 Ire v Australia A (Belfast) 2013. CC HS 0. LO HS 0*.

PRINGLE, Ryan David (Durham SFC), b Sunderland 17 Apr 1992. RHB, OB. Awaiting f-c debut. Durham 2nd XI debut 2009. Northumberland 2011-12. LO HS 26 v Hants (Southampton) 2013 (Y40). LO BB 1-12 v Derbys (Derby) 2013 (Y40). T20 HS 14. T20 BB 2-13.

RAMANPREET SINGH (Gosforth HS), b Newcastle upon Tyne 19 Feb 1993. 5'11". RHB, OB. Debut (Durham) 2012. Durham 2nd XI debut 2009, aged 16y 181d. Northumberland 2009. No 1st XI appearances in 2013. HS 22 v Australia A (Chester-le-St) 2012 – only f-c game.

RICHARDSON, Michael John (Rondebosch HS; Stonyhurst C, Nottingham U), b Pt Elizabeth, South Africa 4 Oct 1986. Son of D.J.Richardson (South Africa, EP and NT 1977-78 to 1997-98), grandson of J.H.Richardson (NE Transvaal and Transvaal B 1952-53 to 1960-61), nephew of R.P.Richardson (WP 1984-85 to 1988-89). 5'10". RHB, WK. Debut (Durham) 2010. MCC YC 2008-09. HS 129 v Sussex (Hove) 2013. LO HS 45 v Glamorgan (Colwyn Bay) 2012 (CB40). T20 HS 8*.

RUSHWORTH, Christopher (Castle View CS, Sunderland), b Sunderland 11 Jul 1986. Cousin of P.Mustard (*see above*). 6'2". RHB, RMF. Debut (Durham) 2010. MCC 2013. Northumberland 2004-05. HS 28 v Yorks (Chester-le-St) 2010. 50 wkts (1): 55 (2013). BB 6-58 v Somerset (Chester-le-St) 2013. LO HS 12* v Northants (Chester-le-St) 2011 (CB40). LO BB 5-31 v Notts (Chester-le-St) 2010 (CB40). T20 HS 2. T20 BB 3-19.

STOKES, Benjamin Andrew (Cockermouth S), b Christchurch, Canterbury, New Zealand 4 Jun 1991. 6'1". LHB, RFM. Debut (Durham) 2010. Durham 2nd XI debut 2007 aged 16y 99d. England U19s 2009 to 2009-10. YC 2013. **Tests:** 4 (2013-14); HS 120 v A (Perth) 2013-14; BB 6-99 v A (Sydney) 2013-14. **LOI:** 18 (2011 to 2013-14); HS 70 v A (Perth) 2013-14; BB 5-61 v A (Southampton) 2013. **IT20:** 5 (2011 to 2013-14); HS 31 v WI (Oval) 2011; BB –. F-c Tours: A 2013-14; WI 2010-11 (EL). HS 185 v Lancs (Chester-le-St) 2011. BB 6-68 v Hants (Southampton) 2011. LO HS 150* v Warwks (Chester-le-St) 2011 (CB40) – Du record. LO BB 5-61 (*see LOI*). T20 HS 72*. T20 BB 2-14.

STONEMAN, Mark Daniel (Whickham CS), b Newcastle upon Tyne, Northumb 26 Jun 1987. 5'11". LHB, RM. Debut (Durham) 2007. 1000 runs (1): 1068 (2013). HS 128 v Sussex (Hove) 2011. LO HS 136* v Scotland (Chester-le-St) 2012 (CB40). T20 HS 51.

WOOD, Mark Andrew (Ashington HS; Newcastle C), b Ashington 11 Jan 1990. 5'11". RHB, RMF. Debut (Durham) 2011. Durham 2nd XI debut 2009. Northumberland 2008-10. F-c Tour (EL): SL 2013-14. HS 58* v Notts (Nottingham) 2013. BB 5-32 EL v Sri Lanka A (Colombo, RPS) 2013-14. Du BB 5-44 v Surrey (Chester-le-St) 2013. LO HS 15* v Lancs (Chester-le-St) 2013 (Y40). LO BB 3-23 v Scotland (Chester-le-St) 2013 (Y40). T20 HS 2. T20 BB 1-20.

RELEASED/RETIRED

(Having made a County First-Class or List A appearance in 2013)

BENKENSTEIN, Dale Martin (Durban HS; Michaelhouse HS), b Salisbury, Rhodesia 9 Jun 1974. Son of M.M.Benkenstein (Rhodesia, Natal B 1970-71 to 1980-81), brother of twins B.R. (Natal B 1993-94) and B.N. Benkenstein (Natal B, GW 1994-95 to 1996-97). 5'9". RHB, RM/OB. Natal/KwaZulu-Natal 1993-94 to 2003-04. Dolphins 2004-05 to 2007-08. British passport. Durham 2005-13; cap 2005; captain 2006-08, 1-o captain 2011-13. MCC 2004, 2013. *Wisden* 2008. **LOI** (SA): 23 (1998-99 to 2002-03); HS 69 v WI (Cape Town) 1998-99; BB 3-5 v Kenya (Colombo) 2002-03. F-c Tours (SA A): WI 2000; NZ 1998-99 (SA); SL 1995 (SA U-24), 1998. 1000 runs (5); most – 1500 (2006). HS 259 KZN v Northerns (Durban) 2001-02. Du HS 181 v Somerset (Taunton) 2009. BB 4-16 Dolphins v Warriors (Durban) 2005-06. Du BB 4-29 v Northants (Northampton) 2005. LO HS 107* Natal v North West (Fochville) 1997-98. LO BB 4-16 v Surrey (Chester-le-St) 2005 (NL). T20 HS 60. T20 BB 3-10.

BRATHWAITE, R.M.R. – *see HAMPSHIRE*.

CLAYDON, M.E. – *see KENT*.

SMITH, W.R. – *see HAMPSHIRE*.

THORP, Callum David (Servite C, Tuart Hill, Perth), b Mount Lawley, Perth, Australia 11 Feb 1975. 6'3". British passport (English parents). RHB, RMF. W Australia 2002-03 to 2003-04. Durham 2005-13. HS 79* v MCC (Abu Dhabi) 2010. CC HS 75 v Hants (Southampton) 2006. 50 wkts (1): 50 (2008). BB 7-88 v Kent (Canterbury) 2008. LO HS 52 v Bangladeshis (Chester-le-St) 2005. LO BB 6-17 v Scotland (Edinburgh) 2006 (CGT). T20 HS 13. T20 BB 2-32.

S.J.Harmison left the staff without making a County First-Class or List A appearance in 2013.

DURHAM 2013

	Place	Won	Lost	Tied	Drew	NR
LV= County Championship (1st Division)	1st	10	4		2	
All First-Class Matches		10	4		3	
Yorkshire Bank 40 (Group B)	4th	7	4			1
Friends Life t20 (North Group)	QF	6	5			

LV= COUNTY CHAMPIONSHIP AVERAGES

BATTING AND FIELDING

Cap		M	I	NO	HS	Runs	Avge	100	50	Ct/St
	S.G.Borthwick	16	28	2	135	1022	39.30	3	5	29
	M.D.Stoneman	16	30	1	122	1011	34.86	3	6	6
	P.Mustard	16	26	4	77	763	34.68	–	6	64/1
	M.J.Richardson	10	15	–	129	501	33.40	2	2	13
	W.R.Smith	16	28	2	153	786	30.23	1	2	13
1998	P.D.Collingwood	15	25	3	88*	646	29.36	–	5	20
2005	D.M.Benkenstein	5	10	2	74*	233	29.12	–	2	5
	U.Arshad	5	6	–	83	170	28.33	–	1	1
	K.K.Jennings	14	26	1	127	707	28.28	2	1	7
	B.A.Stokes	13	24	2	127	615	27.95	1	3	10
	G.R.Breese	3	6	2	44	110	27.50	–	–	7
	M.A.Wood	8	10	2	58*	153	19.12	–	1	1
	C.D.Thorp	7	11	2	27	147	16.33	–	–	1
	J.Harrison	4	4	–	35	60	15.00	–	–	–
	G.Onions	12	17	5	27	148	12.33	–	–	2
	C.Rushworth	14	20	8	18*	107	8.91	–	–	4

Also batted: R.S.Buckley (2 matches) 6, 4 (1 ct); M.E.Claydon (1) 18*, 12* (1 ct).

BOWLING

	O	M	R	W	Avge	Best	5wI	10wM
U.Arshad	73.1	16	249	16	15.56	3-16	–	–
G.Onions	419.1	87	1292	70	18.45	7-62	5	–
C.Rushworth	402.2	99	1202	54	22.25	6-58	3	1
C.D.Thorp	169.5	59	341	15	22.73	3-29	–	–
J.Harrison	96.1	20	336	14	24.00	5-31	1	–
M.A.Wood	209.4	38	650	27	24.07	5-44	1	–
B.A.Stokes	327.4	50	1116	42	26.57	4-49	–	–
R.S.Buckley	114.2	21	344	10	34.40	5-86	1	–
S.G.Borthwick	266.4	35	1064	28	38.00	6-70	1	–

Also bowled:
M.E.Claydon 18.5 2 56 6 9.33 3-25 – –
D.M.Benkenstein 1-0-1-0; G.R.Breese 53-18-117-4; P.D.Collingwood 35.4-14-73-1; K.K.Jennings 11.2-0-48-2; P.Mustard 1.1-0-9-1; W.R.Smith 34.2-5-137-4.

The First-Class Averages (pp 225–241) give the records of Durham players in all first-class county matches (Durham's other opponents being Durham MCCU), with the exception of M.E.Claydon, whose first-class figures for Durham are as above, and: G.Onions 13-18-6-27-169-14.08-0-0-3ct. 437.1-92-1336-71-18.81-7/62-5-0.

DURHAM RECORDS

FIRST-CLASS CRICKET

Highest Total	For 648-5d		v	Notts	Chester-le-St[2]	2009
	V 810-4d		by	Warwicks	Birmingham	1994
Lowest Total	For 67		v	Middlesex	Lord's	1996
	V 18		by	Durham MCCU	Chester-le-St[2]	2012
Highest Innings	For 273	M.L.Love	v	Hampshire	Chester-le-St[2]	2003
	V 501*	B.C.Lara	for	Warwicks	Birmingham	1994

Highest Partnership for each Wicket

1st	334*	S.Hutton/M.A.Roseberry	v	Oxford U	Oxford	1996
2nd	258	J.J.B.Lewis/M.L.Love	v	Notts	Chester-le-St[2]	2001
3rd	212	M.J.Di Venuto/D.M.Benkenstein	v	Essex	Chester-le-St[2]	2010
4th	331	B.A.Stokes/D.M.Benkenstein	v	Lancashire	Chester-le-St[2]	2011
5th	247	G.J.Muchall/I.D.Blackwell	v	Worcs	Worcester	2011
6th	249	G.J.Muchall/P.Mustard	v	Kent	Canterbury	2006
7th	315	D.M.Benkenstein/O.D.Gibson	v	Yorkshire	Leeds	2006
8th	147	P.Mustard/L.E.Plunkett	v	Yorkshire	Leeds	2009
9th	127	D.G.C.Ligertwood/S.J.E.Brown	v	Surrey	Stockton	1996
10th	103	M.M.Betts/D.M.Cox	v	Sussex	Hove	1996

Best Bowling	For 10- 47	O.D.Gibson	v	Hampshire	Chester-le-St[2]	2007
(Innings)	V 9- 36	M.S.Kasprowicz	for	Glamorgan	Cardiff	2003
Best Bowling	For 14-177	A.Walker	v	Essex	Chelmsford	1995
(Match)	V 13-110	M.S.Kasprowicz	for	Glamorgan	Chester-le-St[2]	2003

Most Runs – Season	1654	M.J.Di Venuto	(av 78.76)	2009
Most Runs – Career	8788	D.M.Benkenstein	(av 46.74)	2005-12
Most 100s – Season	6	P.D.Collingwood		2005
	6	M.J.Di Venuto		2009
Most 100s – Career	21	D.M.Benkenstein		2005-11
Most Wkts – Season	80	O.D.Gibson	(av 20.75)	2007
Most Wkts – Career	518	S.J.E.Brown	(av 28.30)	1992-2002
Most Career W-K Dismissals	568	P.Mustard	(550 ct; 18 st)	2002-13
Most Career Catches in the Field	166	P.D.Collingwood		1996-2013

LIMITED-OVERS CRICKET

Highest Total	50ov	332-4		v	Worcs	Chester-le-St[2]	2007
	40ov	325-9		v	Surrey	The Oval	2011
	T20	225-2		v	Leics	Chester-le-St[2]	2010
Lowest Total	50ov	82		v	Worcs	Chester-le-St[1]	1968
	40ov	72		v	Warwicks	Birmingham	2002
	T20	93		v	Kent	Canterbury	2009
Highest Innings	50ov	145	J.E.Morris	v	Leics	Leicester	1996
	40ov	150*	B.A.Stokes	v	Warwicks	Birmingham	2011
	T20	91	P.Mustard	v	Yorkshire	Chester-le-St[2]	2013
Best Bowling	50ov	7-32	S.P.Davis	v	Lancashire	Chester-le-St[1]	1983
	40ov	6-31	N.Killeen	v	Derbyshire	Derby	2000
	T20	5- 6	P.D.Collingwood	v	Northants	Chester-le-St[2]	2011

[1] Chester-le-Street CC (Ropery Lane) [2] Emirates Durham International Cricket Ground

Waterstones

86 Merseyway
Stockport
SK1 1QN
0161 474 1455

SALE TRANSACTION

Z PLAYFAIR CRICKET AN   £8.99
9781472212177

No. items 1
Balance to Pay   £8.99

Cash   £10
CHANGE

Refunds & exch...

We are happy to refund or...
goods within 30 days of pur...
goods must be returned with p...
of purchase, unopened in origin...
packaging and in resalable conditi...

In the event that you have a faulty
Kindle we will replace the device in the
shop when returned within 30 days.

If your Kindle is returned after 30
days, but within the manufacturer'...
warranty period, we will gladly a...
a replacement from the man...

All refun...are proce...
...er's...scretic...

DURHAM 2013

RESULTS SUMMARY

	Place	Won	Lost	Tied	Drew	NR
LV= County Championship (1st Division)	1st	10	4		2	
All First-Class Matches		10	4		3	
Yorkshire Bank 40 (Group B)	4th	7	4			1
Friends Life t20 (North Group)	QF	6	5			

LV= COUNTY CHAMPIONSHIP AVERAGES

BATTING AND FIELDING

Cap		M	I	NO	HS	Runs	Avge	100	50	Ct/St
	S.G.Borthwick	16	28	2	135	1022	39.30	3	5	29
	M.D.Stoneman	16	30	1	122	1011	34.86	3	6	6
	P.Mustard	16	26	4	77	763	34.68	–	6	64/1
	M.J.Richardson	10	15	–	129	501	33.40	2	2	13
	W.R.Smith	16	28	2	153	786	30.23	1	2	13
1998	P.D.Collingwood	15	25	3	88*	646	29.36	–	5	20
2005	D.M.Benkenstein	5	10	2	74*	233	29.12	–	2	5
	U.Arshad	5	6	–	83	170	28.33	–	1	1
	K.K.Jennings	14	26	1	127	707	28.28	2	1	7
	B.A.Stokes	13	24	2	127	615	27.95	1	3	10
	G.R.Breese	3	6	2	44	110	27.50	–	–	7
	M.A.Wood	8	10	2	58*	153	19.12	–	1	1
	C.D.Thorp	7	11	2	27	147	16.33	–	–	1
	J.Harrison	4	4	–	35	60	15.00	–	–	–
	G.Onions	12	17	5	27	148	12.33	–	–	2
	C.Rushworth	14	20	8	18*	107	8.91	–	–	4

Also batted: R.S.Buckley (2 matches) 6, 4 (1 ct); M.E.Claydon (1) 18*, 12* (1 ct).

BOWLING

	O	M	R	W	Avge	Best	5wI	10wM
U.Arshad	73.1	16	249	16	15.56	3-16	–	–
G.Onions	419.1	87	1292	70	18.45	7-62	5	–
C.Rushworth	402.2	99	1202	54	22.25	6-58	3	1
C.D.Thorp	169.5	59	341	15	22.73	3-29	–	–
J.Harrison	96.1	20	336	14	24.00	5-31	1	–
M.A.Wood	209.4	38	650	27	24.07	5-44	1	–
B.A.Stokes	327.4	50	1116	42	26.57	4-49	–	–
R.S.Buckley	114.2	21	344	10	34.40	5-86	1	–
S.G.Borthwick	266.4	35	1064	28	38.00	6-70	1	–

Also bowled:
M.E.Claydon   18.5   2   56   6   9.33   3-25
D.M.Benkenstein 1-0-1-0; G.R.Breese 53-18-117-4; P.D.Collingwood 35.4-14-73-1;
K.K.Jennings 11.2-0-48-2; P.Mustard 1.1-0-9-1; W.R.Smith 34.2-5-137-4.

The First-Class Averages (pp 225–241) give the records of Durham players in all first-class
county matches (Durham's other opponents being Durham MCCU), with the exception of
M.E.Claydon, whose first-class figures for Durham are as above, and:
G.Onions 13-18-6-27-169-14.08-0-0-3ct. 437.1-92-1336-71-18.81-7/62-5-0.

DURHAM RECORDS

FIRST-CLASS CRICKET

Highest Total	For 648-5d		v	Notts	Chester-le-St[2]	2009
	V 810-4d		by	Warwicks	Birmingham	1994
Lowest Total	For 67		v	Middlesex	Lord's	1996
	V 18		by	Durham MCCU	Chester-le-St[2]	2012
Highest Innings	For 273	M.L.Love	v	Hampshire	Chester-le-St[2]	2003
	V 501*	B.C.Lara	for	Warwicks	Birmingham	1994

Highest Partnership for each Wicket
1st	334*	S.Hutton/M.A.Roseberry	v	Oxford U	Oxford	1996
2nd	258	J.J.B.Lewis/M.L.Love	v	Notts	Chester-le-St[2]	2001
3rd	212	M.J.Di Venuto/D.M.Benkenstein	v	Essex	Chester-le-St[2]	2010
4th	331	B.A.Stokes/D.M.Benkenstein	v	Lancashire	Chester-le-St[2]	2011
5th	247	G.J.Muchall/I.D.Blackwell	v	Worcs	Worcester	2011
6th	249	G.J.Muchall/P.Mustard	v	Kent	Canterbury	2006
7th	315	D.M.Benkenstein/O.D.Gibson	v	Yorkshire	Leeds	2006
8th	147	P.Mustard/L.E.Plunkett	v	Yorkshire	Leeds	2009
9th	127	D.G.C.Ligertwood/S.J.E.Brown	v	Surrey	Stockton	1996
10th	103	M.M.Betts/D.M.Cox	v	Sussex	Hove	1996

Best Bowling	For 10- 47	O.D.Gibson	v	Hampshire	Chester-le-St[2]	2007
(Innings)	V 9- 36	M.S.Kasprowicz	for	Glamorgan	Cardiff	2003
Best Bowling	For 14-177	A.Walker	v	Essex	Chelmsford	1995
(Match)	V 13-110	M.S.Kasprowicz	for	Glamorgan	Chester-le-St[2]	2003

Most Runs – Season	1654	M.J.Di Venuto	(av 78.76)	2009
Most Runs – Career	8788	D.M.Benkenstein	(av 46.74)	2005-12
Most 100s – Season	6	P.D.Collingwood		2005
	6	M.J.Di Venuto		2009
Most 100s – Career	21	D.M.Benkenstein		2005-11
Most Wkts – Season	80	O.D.Gibson	(av 20.75)	2007
Most Wkts – Career	518	S.J.E.Brown	(av 28.30)	1992-2002
Most Career W-K Dismissals	568	P.Mustard	(550 ct; 18 st)	2002-13
Most Career Catches in the Field	166	P.D.Collingwood		1996-2013

LIMITED-OVERS CRICKET

Highest Total	50ov	332-4		v	Worcs	Chester-le-St[2]	2007
	40ov	325-9		v	Surrey	The Oval	2011
	T20	225-2		v	Leics	Chester-le-St[2]	2010
Lowest Total	50ov	82		v	Worcs	Chester-le-St[1]	1968
	40ov	72		v	Warwicks	Birmingham	2002
	T20	93		v	Kent	Canterbury	2009
Highest Innings	50ov	145	J.E.Morris	v	Leics	Leicester	1996
	40ov	150*	B.A.Stokes	v	Warwicks	Birmingham	2011
	T20	91	P.Mustard	v	Yorkshire	Chester-le-St[2]	2013
Best Bowling	50ov	7-32	S.P.Davis	v	Lancashire	Chester-le-St[1]	1983
	40ov	6-31	N.Killeen	v	Derbyshire	Derby	2000
	T20	5- 6	P.D.Collingwood	v	Northants	Chester-le-St[2]	2011

[1] Chester-le-Street CC (Ropery Lane) [2] Emirates Durham International Cricket Ground

ESSEX

Formation of Present Club: 14 January 1876
Inaugural First-Class Match: 1894
Colours: Blue, Gold and Red
Badge: Three Seaxes above Scroll bearing 'Essex'
County Champions: (6) 1979, 1983, 1984, 1986, 1991, 1992
NatWest/Friends Prov Trophy Winners: (3) 1985, 1997, 2008
Benson and Hedges Cup Winners: (2) 1979, 1998
Pro 40/National League (Div 1) Winners: (2) 2005, 2006
Sunday League Winners: (3) 1981, 1984, 1985
Twenty20 Cup Winners: (0); best – Semi-Finalist 2006, 2008, 2010

Chief Executive: Derek Bowden, The Ford County Ground, New Writtle Street, Chelmsford CM2 0PG • Tel: 01245 252420 • Fax: 01245 254030 • Email: administration@essexcricket.org.uk • Web: www.essexcricket.org.uk • Twitter: @EssexCricket (19,926 followers)

First Team Coach: Paul Grayson. **Assistant Head Coach**: Chris Silverwood. **Captain**: J.S.Foster (f-c) and R.N.ten Doeschate (l-o). **Vice-Captain**: R.S.Bopara. **Overseas Player**: None. **2014 Beneficiary**: A.N.Cook. **Head Groundsman**: Stuart Kerrison. **Scorer**: A.E. (Tony) Choat. ‡ New registration. NQ Not qualified for England.

BOPARA, Ravinder Singh (Brampton Manor S; Barking Abbey Sports C), b Newham, London 4 May 1985. 5'8". RHB, RM. Debut (Essex) 2002; cap 2005. Auckland 2009-10. Dolphins 2010-11. MCC 2006, 2008. YC 2008. **Tests**: 13 (2007-08 to 2012); HS 143 v WI (Lord's) 2009; BB 1-39 v SL (Galle) 2007-08. **LOI**: 102 (2006-07 to 2013-14); HS 101* v Ireland (Dublin) 2013; BB 4-38 v B (Birmingham) 2010. **IT20**: 29 (2008 to 2013-14); HS 65* v A (Hobart) 2013-14; BB 4-10 v WI (Oval) 2011 – England record. F-c Tours: WI 2008-09, 2010-11 (EL); SL 2007-08, 2011-12. 1000 runs (1): 1256 (2008). HS 229 v Northants (Chelmsford) 2007. BB 5-75 v Surrey (Chelmsford) 2006. LO HS 201* v Leics (Leicester) 2008 (FPT) – Ex l-o record. LO BB 5-63 Dolphins v Warriors (Pietermaritzburg) 2010-11. T20 HS 105*. T20 BB 4-10.

BROWNE, Nicholas Lawrence Joseph (Trinity Catholic HS, Woodford Green), b Leytonstone 24 Mar 1991. LHB, LB. Debut (Essex) 2013. Essex 2nd XI debut 2007. HS 22* v Worcs (Chelmsford) 2013. BB –.

COOK, Alastair Nathan (Bedford S), b Gloucester 25 Dec 1984. 6'3". LHB, OB. Debut (Essex) 2003; cap 2005; benefit 2014. MCC 2004-07. England U19 captain 2003-04. YC 2005. *Wisden* 2011. **ECB central contract 2013-14**. **Tests**: 102 (2005-06 to 2013-14, 21 as captain); HS 294 v I (Birmingham) 2011. Scored 60 and 104* v I (Nagpur) 2005-06 on debut. Third, after D.G.Bradman and S.R.Tendulkar, to score seven Test hundreds before his 23rd birthday. Second, after M.A.Taylor, to score 1000 runs in the calendar year of his debut. BB –. **LOI**: 77 (2006 to 2013-14, 54 as captain); HS 137 v P (Abu Dhabi) 2011-12. **IT20**: 4 (2007 to 2009-10); HS 26 v SA (Centurion) 2009-10. F-c Tours (C=Captain): A 2006-07, 2010-11, 2013-14C; SA 2009-10; WI 2005-06 (Eng A), 2008-09; NZ 2007-08, 2012-13C; I 2005-06, 2008-09, 2012-13C; SL 2004-05 (Eng A), 2007-08, 2011-12; B 2009-10C; UAE 2011-12 (v P). 1000 runs (5+1); most – 1466 (2005). HS 294 (*see Tests*). CC HS 195 v Northants (Northampton) 2005. BB 3-13 v Northants (Chelmsford) 2005. LO HS 137 (*see LOI*). BB –. T20 HS 100*.

CRADDOCK, Thomas Richard (Holmfirth HS; Huddersfield New C; Leeds Met U), b Huddersfield, Yorks 13 Jul 1989. 5'10". RHB, LB. Debut (Essex) 2011. Leeds/Bradford MCCU (not f-c) 2010-11. Northamptonshire 2nd XI 2010. Gloucestershire 2nd XI 2011. HS 21 v Leics (Southend) 2011. BB 5-96 v Derbys (Chelmsford) 2012. LO HS 5* and LO BB 2-38 v Somerset (Taunton) 2011 (CB40). T20 HS –. T20 BB –.

FOAKES, Benjamin Thomas (Tendring TC), b Colchester 15 Feb 1993. 6'1". RHB, WK. Debut (Essex) 2011. Essex 2nd XI debut 2008, aged 15y 172d. England U19s 2010-11. F-c Tour (EL): SL 2013-14. HS 120 v Leics (Chelmsford) 2013. LO HS 56 EL v Australia A (Hobart) 2012-13.

FOSTER, James Savin (Forest S, Snaresbrook; Collingwood C, Durham U), b Whipps Cross 15 Apr 1980. 6'0". RHB, WK. British U 2000-01. Essex debut 2000; cap 2001; captain 2010 (*part*) to date; benefit 2011. Durham UCCE 2001. MCC 2004, 2008-10. **Tests**: 7 (2001-02 to 2002-03); HS 48 v I (Bangalore) 2001-02. **LOI**: 11 (2001-02); HS 13 v I (Bombay) 2001-02. **IT20**: 5 (2009); HS 14* v P (Oval) 2009. F-c Tours: A 2002-03; WI 2000-01 (Eng A); NZ 2001-02; I 2001-02, 2007-08 (Eng A). 1000 runs (1): 1037 (2004). HS 212 v Leics (Chelmsford) 2004. BB 1-122 v Northants (Northampton) 2008 – in contrived circumstances. LO HS 83* v Durham, inc 5 sixes in 5 balls off S.G.Borthwick (Chester-le-St) 2009 (P40). T20 HS 65*.

LAWRENCE, Daniel William (Trinity Catholic HS, Woodford Green), b Whipps Cross 12 Jul 1997. RHB, LB. Essex 2nd XI debut 2013, aged 15y 321d. Awaiting 1st XI debut.

MAHMOOD, Sajid Iqbal (North C, Bolton), b Bolton, Lancs 21 Dec 1981. 6'4". RHB, RFM. Lancashire 2002-12; cap 2007. Somerset 2012 (on loan). Essex debut 2013. MCC 2005, 2009. **Tests**: 8 (2006 to 2006-07); HS 34 and BB 4-22 v P (Leeds) 2006. **LOI**: 26 (2004 to 2009-10); HS 22* v P (Birmingham) 2006. BB 4-50 v SL (North Shore, Antigua) 2006-07. **IT20**: 4 (2006 to 2009-10); HS 1* v SA (Centurion) 2009-10; BB 1-31 v SA (Johannesburg) 2009-10. F-c Tours (Eng A): A 2006-07 (Eng); WI 2005-06; NZ 2008-09; I 2003-04; SL 2004-05. HS 94 La v Sussex (Manchester) 2004. Ex HS 54 v Worcs (Worcester) 2013. BB 6-30 La v Durham (Chester-le-St) 2009. Ex BB 2-112 v Hants (Southampton) 2013. LO HS 29 La v Staffs (Stone) 2004 (CGT). LO BB 5-16 La v Sri Lanka A (Liverpool) 2007. T20 HS 34. T20 BB 4-21.

MASTERS, David Daniel (Fort Luton HS; Mid Kent CHE), b Chatham, Kent 22 Apr 1978. Son of K.D.Masters (Kent 1983-84), elder brother of D.Masters (Leicestershire 2009-10). 6'4". RHB, RMF. Kent 2000-02. Leicestershire 2003-07; cap 2007. Essex debut/cap 2008; benefit 2013. HS 119 Le v Sussex (Hove) 2003. Ex HS 67 v Leics (Chelmsford) 2009. 50 wkts (4); most – 93 (2011). BB 8-10 v Leics (Southend) 2011. LO HS 39 Le v Glos (Cheltenham) 2006 (P40). LO BB 5-17 v Surrey (Oval) 2008 (FPT). T20 HS 14. T20 BB 3-7.

MICKLEBURGH, Jaik Charles (Bungay HS), b Norwich, Norfolk 30 Mar 1990. 5'10". RHB, RM. Debut (Essex) 2008; cap 2013. Mid West Rhinos 2012-13. Essex 2nd XI debut 2007, aged 16y 160d. Norfolk 2007. England U19s 2009. HS 243 v Leics (Chelmsford) 2013. HB –. LO HS 73 MWR v ME (Kwekwe) 2012-13. T20 HS 47*.

MILLS, Tymal Solomon (Mildenhall C of T), b Dewsbury, Yorks 12 Aug 1992. 6'1". RHB, LFM. Debut (Essex) 2011. Essex 2nd XI debut 2010. England U19s 2010-11. F-c Tour (EL): SL 2013-14. HS 31* EL v Sri Lanka A (Colombo, RPS) 2013-14. Ex HS 20* v Yorks (Chelmsford) 2012. BB 4-25 v Glamorgan (Cardiff) 2012. LO HS 2* v Australians (Chelmsford) 2012. LO BB 3-23 v Durham (Chelmsford) 2013 (Y40). T20 HS 8*. T20 BB –.

NAPIER, Graham Richard (The Gilberd S, Colchester), b Colchester 6 Jan 1980. 5'9½". RHB, RM. Debut (Essex) 1997; cap 2003; benefit 2012. Wellington 2008-09. MCC 2004. F-c Tour (Eng A): I 2003-04. HS 196 v Surrey (Croydon) 2011, hitting a world record-equalling 16 sixes and being dismissed just 28 balls after reaching his century. Won 2008 Walter Lawrence Trophy with 44-ball hundred v Sussex (Chelmsford). Won 2012 Walter Lawrence Trophy with 48-ball hundred v Cambridge MCCU (Cambridge). 50 wkts (1): 51 (2013). BB 7-90 v Leics (Leicester) 2013. LO HS 79 Essex CB v Lancs CB (Chelmsford) 2000 (NWT). LO BB 7-32 v Surrey (Chelmsford) 2013 (Y40). T20 HS 152* v Sussex (Chelmsford) 2008 – record T20 Cup score (58b, 10 fours, 16 sixes); 4th highest score in all T20. T20 BB 4-10.

PANESAR, Mudhsuden Singh ('Monty') (Stopsley HS; Bedford Modern S; Loughborough U), b Luton, Beds 25 Apr 1982. 6'0". LHB, SLA. Northamptonshire 2001-09; cap 2006. British U 2002-05. Loughborough UCCE 2004. Lions 2009-10. Sussex debut/cap 2010. Essex debut 2013 (on loan). MCC 2006. Bedfordshire 1998-99. *Wisden* 2007. **Tests**: 50 (2005-06 to 2013-14); HS 26 v SL (Nottingham) 2006; BB 6-37 v NZ (Manchester) 2008. **LOI**: 26 (2006-07 to 2007-08); HS 13 v WI (Nottingham) 2007; BB 3-25 v B (Bridgetown) 2006-07. **IT20**: 1 (2006-07); HS 1 and BB 2-40 v A (Sydney) 2006-07. F-c Tours: A 2006-07, 2010-11, 2013-14; WI 2008-09; NZ 2007-08, 2012-13; I 2005-06, 2008-09, 2012-13; SL 2002-03 (ECB Acad), 2007-08, 2011-12; UAE 2011-12 (v P). HS 46* Sx v Middx (Hove) 2010. Ex HS 22 v Essex (Bristol) 2013. 50 wkts (6); most – 71 (2006). BB 7-60 (13-137 match) Sx v Somerset (Taunton) 2012. Ex BB 4-49 v Kent (Canterbury) 2013. LO HS 17* Nh v Leics (Northampton) 2008 (FPT). LO BB 5-20 ECB Acad v SL Acad XI (Colombo) 2002-03. T20 HS 3*. T20 BB 3-14.

PETTINI, Mark Lewis (Comberton Village C; Hills Road SFC, Cambridge; Cardiff U), b Brighton, Sussex 7 Aug 1983. 5'10". RHB, RM. Debut (Essex) 2001; cap 2006; captain 2007 (*part*) to 2010 (*part*). Mountaineers 2011-12 to date. MCC 2005. 1000 runs (1): 1218 (2006). HS 209 Mountaineers v MT (Bulawayo) 2013-14. Ex HS 208* v Derbys (Chelmsford) 2006. BB 1-72 v Leics (Leicester) 2012 – in contrived circumstances. LO HS 144 v Surrey (Oval) 2007 (FPT). T20 HS 87.

PHILLIPS, Timothy James (Felsted S; St Hild & St Bede C, Durham U), b Cambridge 13 Mar 1981. 6'1". LHB, SLA. Debut (Essex) 1999; cap 2006. Durham UCCE 2001-02. HS 89 v Worcs (Worcester) 2005. BB 5-41 v Derbys (Chelmsford) 2006. LO HS 58* v Glos (Cheltenham) 2011 (CB40). LO BB 5-28 v Unicorns (Bury St Edmunds) 2011 (CB40). T20 HS 57*. T20 BB 4-22.

RAMSDEN, Henry Douglas ('**Harry**') (Oundle S), b Wandsworth, Surrey 11 Nov 1992. 6'4". LHB, OB. Essex 2nd XI debut 2012. Hertfordshire 2011-13. Awaiting 1st XI debut.

^NO**SMITH, Gregory** Marc (St Stithins C), b Johannesburg, South Africa 20 Apr 1983. 5'9". RHB, RM/OB. Debut (SA Academy) 2003-04. Griqualand West 2003-04. Derbyshire 2006-11 (Kolpak registration); cap 2009; captain 2010 (*part*). Mountaineers 2010-11. Essex debut 2012. HS 177 v Glos (Bristol) 2013. BB 5-42 v Leics (Chelmsford) 2013. LO HS 89 Abahani v KKC (Savar) 2013-14. LO BB 4-53 De v Lancs (Derby) 2009 (P40). T20 HS 100*. T20 BB 5-17.

^NQ**Ten DOESCHATE, Ryan** Neil (Fairbairn C; Cape Town U), b Port Elizabeth, South Africa 30 Jun 1980. 5'10½". RHB, RMF. Debut (Essex) 2003; cap 2006; captain (l-o) 2014. EU passport – Dutch ancestry. Netherlands 2005 to date. Otago 2012-13 to date. **LOI** (Ne): 33 (2006 to 2010-11); HS 119 v E (Nagpur) 2010-11; BB 4-31 v Canada (Nairobi) 2006-07. **IT20** (Ne): 9 (2008 to 2009-10); HS 56 v Kenya (Belfast) 2008; BB 3-23 v Scotland (Belfast) 2008. F-c Tours (Ne): SA 2006-07, 2007-08; K 2005-06, 2009-10; Ireland 2005. HS 259* and BB 6-20 (9-112 match) Netherlands v Canada (Pretoria) 2006. Ex HS 164 v Sri Lankans (Chelmsford) 2011. CC HS 159* v Surrey (Guildford) 2009. Ex BB 6-57 v NZ (Chelmsford) 2008. CC BB 5-13 v Hants (Chelmsford) 2010. LO HS 180 v Scotland (Chelmsford) 2013 (Y40) – Ex 40-over record, inc 15 sixes. LO BB 5-50 v Glos (Bristol) 2007 (FPT). T20 HS 121*. T20 BB 4-24.

TOPLEY, Reece James William (Royal Hospital S, Ipswich), b Ipswich, Suffolk 21 February 1994. Son of T.D.Topley (Surrey, Essex, GW 1985-94) and nephew of P.A.Topley (Kent 1972-75). 6'7". RHB, LMF. Debut (Essex) 2011; cap 2013. Took 5-46 on CC debut. Essex 2nd XI debut 2010, aged 16y 156d. England U19s 2012-13. F-c Tour (EL): SL 2013-14. HS 9 v Derbys (Chelmsford) 2011. BB 6-29 (11-85 match) v Worcs (Chelmsford) 2013. LO HS 19 v Somerset (Taunton) 2011 (CB40). LO BB 4-26 v Derbys (Colchester) 2013 (Y40). T20 HS 4*. T20 BB 4-26.

VELANI, Kishen Shailesh (Brentwood S), b Newham, London 2 Sep 1994. 5'10". RHB, RM. Debut (Essex) 2013. Essex 2nd XI debut 2012. England U19s 2012-13. HS 13 and BB-v Hants (Southampton) 2013 – only 1st XI appearance.

WESTLEY, Thomas (Linton Village C; Hills Road SFC), b Cambridge 13 March 1989. 6'2". RHB, OB. Debut (Essex) 2007; cap 2013. MCC 2007, 2009. Durham MCCU 2010-11. Essex 2nd XI debut 2004, aged 15y 88d. Cambridgeshire 2005. HS 185 v Glamorgan (Colchester) 2012. BB 4-55 DU v Durham (Durham) 2010. CC BB 3-5 v Kent (Chelmsford) 2012. LO HS 82 v Glos (Chelmsford) 2012 (CB40). LO BB 1-9 v Worcs (Worcester) 2012 (CB40). T20 HS 13. T20 BB 1-7.

RELEASED/RETIRED

(Having made a County First-Class or List A appearance in 2013)

CHAMBERS, M.A. – *see NORTHAMPTONSHIRE.*

NO**GAMBHIR, Gautam**, b Delhi, India 14 Oct 1981. LHB, LB. Delhi 1999-00 to date. Essex 2013. **Tests** (I): 54 (2004-05 to 2012-13); HS 206 v A (Delhi) 2008-09; BB –. **LOI** (I): 147 (2002-03 to 2012-13); HS 150* v SL (Kolkata) 2009-10; BB –. **IT20** (I): 37 (2007 to 2012-13); HS 75 v P (Johannesburg) 2007-08. F-c Tours (I): E 2003 (Ind A), 2007, 2011; A 2006 (Ind A), 2011-12; SA 2001-02 (Ind A), 2010-11; WI 2002-03 (Ind A); NZ 2008-09; SL 2002 (Ind A), 2008, 2010; Z/Ken 2004 (Ind A), 2005-06; B 2004-05, 2009-10. HS 233* Delhi v Railways (Delhi) 2002-03. Ex HS 106 v Glos (Bristol) 2013. BB 3-12 India A v England (Jaipur) 2001-02. LO HS 147 (*see LOI*). LO BB 1-7. T20 HS 93.

NO**QUINEY, Robert** John, b Brighton, Victoria, Australia 20 Aug 1982. 6'4". LHB, RM. Victoria 2006-07 to date. Essex 2013. **Tests** (A): 2 (2012-13); HS 9 v SA (Brisbane) 2012-13; BB –. HS 153 Vic v Tas (Hobart) 2009-10. Ex HS 112 v Cambridge MCCU (Cambridge) 2013. CC HS 56 v Northants (Northampton) 2013. BB 2-22 Vic v WA (Melbourne) 2007-08. LO HS 122 Vic v EL (Melbourne) 2012-13. LO BB –. T20 HS 97. T20 BB –.

SHAH, Owais Alam (Isleworth & Syon S), b Karachi, Pakistan 22 Oct 1978. 6'0". RHB, OB. Middlesex 1996-2010; cap 2000; captain 2004 (*part*); benefit 2008. Cape Cobras 2010-11. Essex 2011-13; cap 2013. MCC 2002-08. YC 2001. **Tests**: 6 (2005-06 to 2008-09); HS 88 v I (Bombay) 2005-06; BB –. **LOI**: 71 (2001 to 2009-10); HS 107* v I (Oval) 2007; BB 3-15 v Ire (Belfast) 2009. **IT20**: 17 (2007 to 2009); HS 55* v WI (Oval) 2007. F-c Tours (Eng A): A 1996-97; WI 2005-06 (*part*), 2008-09 (Eng); SL 2005-06 (Eng – *part*); SL 1997-98, 2004-05, 2007-08 (Eng). 1000 runs (8); most – 1728 (2005). HS 203 M v Derbys (Southgate) 2001. Ex HS 161 v Hants (Southampton) 2012. BB 3-33 M v Glos (Bristol) 1999. Ex BB – v Kent 134 M v Sussex (Arundel) 1999 (NL). LO BB 4-11 M v Leics (Lord's) 2009 (P40). T20 HS 84. T20 BB 2-26.

R.Hassan and S.W.Tait left the staff without making a County First-Class or List A appearance in 2013.

ESSEX 2013

RESULTS SUMMARY

	Place	Won	Lost	Tied	Drew	NR
LV= County Championship (2nd Division)	3rd	5	4		7	
All First-Class Matches		5	4		8	
Yorkshire Bank 40 (Group B)	2nd	8	4			
Friends Life t20 (South Group)	3rd	5	4			1

LV= COUNTY CHAMPIONSHIP AVERAGES
BATTING AND FIELDING

Cap		M	I	NO	HS	Runs	Avge	100	50	Ct/St
2003	G.R.Napier	16	22	6	102*	796	49.75	1	7	5
2013	J.C.Mickleburgh	13	21	1	243	829	41.45	2	4	3
2005	A.N.Cook	2	4	–	60	157	39.25	–	2	2
	G.M.Smith	10	15	2	177	498	38.30	1	1	2
2001	J.S.Foster	16	24	3	143	762	36.28	1	4	48/1
2005	R.S.Bopara	7	11	–	145	397	36.09	1	2	5
2006	R.N.ten Doeschate	9	13	2	103	391	35.54	1	1	3
	G.Gambhir	5	7	–	106	239	34.14	1	–	4
	T.Westley	10	18	–	163	583	32.38	1	2	5
2013	O.A.Shah	7	11	1	120	307	30.70	1	1	10
	B.T.Foakes	14	18	1	120	500	29.41	1	3	11
2006	M.L.Pettini	8	14	3	72	319	29.00	–	1	7
	R.J.Quiney	4	7	–	56	150	21.42	–	1	5
	S.I.Mahmood	4	6	–	54	112	18.66	–	1	3
	T.S.Mills	5	6	3	17	53	17.66	–	–	1
2008	D.D.Masters	13	12	3	37*	95	10.55	–	–	3
	M.S.Panesar	6	6	–	22	55	9.16	–	–	–
	N.L.J.Browne	3	5	1	22*	26	6.50	–	–	1
2013	R.J.W.Topley	13	14	7	8*	12	1.71	–	–	6

Also batted: M.A.Chambers (2 matches) 1, 3 (1 ct); T.R.Craddock (3) 3, 1, 20; T.J.Phillips (3) 40*, 7, 0 (1 ct); H.D.Rutherford (2) 5, 0, 24 (1 ct); K.S.Velani (1) 13, 9.

BOWLING

	O	M	R	W	Avge	Best	5wI	10wM
D.D.Masters	467.4	122	1163	51	22.80	6-41	4	–
G.M.Smith	112.5	21	365	15	24.33	5-42	1	–
R.S.Bopara	129.5	24	378	14	27.00	3-41	–	–
R.J.W.Topley	411.4	78	1364	48	28.41	6-29	3	1
G.R.Napier	459.1	80	1516	48	31.58	7-90	3	–
M.S.Panesar	189.4	50	504	14	36.00	4-49	–	–

Also bowled:

	O	M	R	W	Avge	Best	5wI	10wM
T.J.Phillips	39.4	10	98	6	16.33	3-20	–	–
R.N.ten Doeschate	77	9	267	8	33.37	4-28	–	–
T.S.Mills	102.4	18	398	6	66.33	2-24	–	–

N.L.J.Browne 16.5-4-59-0; M.A.Chambers 32-2-151-1; T.R.Craddock 43-9-132-3; S.I.Mahmood 66-4-329-3; O.A.Shah 2-0-12-0; K.S.Velani 2-0-8-0; T.Westley 41-4-142-1.

The First-Class Averages (pp 225–241) give the records of Essex players in all first-class county matches (Essex's other opponents being Cambridge MCCU), with the exception of A.N.Cook, M.S.Panesar and H.D.Rutherford, whose first-class figures for Essex are as above, and:
R.S.Bopara 8-13-0-145-401-30.84-1-2-6ct. 139-26-398-15-26.53-3/41-0-0.
M.A.Chambers 3-2-0-3-4-2.00-0-0-1ct. 54-9-198-4-49.50-2/19-0-0.

ESSEX RECORDS

FIRST-CLASS CRICKET

Highest Total	For 761-6d		v	Leics	Chelmsford	1990
	V 803-4d		by	Kent	Brentwood	1934
Lowest Total	For 20		v	Lancashire	Chelmsford	2013
	V 14		by	Surrey	Chelmsford	1983
Highest Innings	For 343*	P.A.Perrin	v	Derbyshire	Chesterfield	1904
	V 332	W.H.Ashdown	for	Kent	Brentwood	1934

Highest Partnership for each Wicket

1st	316	G.A.Gooch/P.J.Prichard	v	Kent	Chelmsford	1994
2nd	403	G.A.Gooch/P.J.Prichard	v	Leics	Chelmsford	1990
3rd	347*	M.E.Waugh/N.Hussain	v	Lancashire	Ilford	1992
4th	314	Salim Malik/N.Hussain	v	Surrey	The Oval	1991
5th	339	J.C.Mickleburgh/J.S.Foster	v	Durham	Chester-le-St[2]	2010
6th	253	A.J.Wheater/J.S.Foster	v	Northants	Chelmsford	2011
7th	261	J.W.H.T.Douglas/J.Freeman	v	Lancashire	Leyton	1914
8th	263	D.R.Wilcox/R.M.Taylor	v	Warwicks	Southend	1946
9th	251	J.W.H.T.Douglas/S.N.Hare	v	Derbyshire	Leyton	1921
10th	218	F.H.Vigar/T.P.B.Smith	v	Derbyshire	Chesterfield	1947

Best Bowling	For	10- 32	H.Pickett	v	Leics	Leyton	1895
(Innings)	V	10- 40	E.G.Dennett	for	Glos	Bristol	1906
Best Bowling	For	17-119	W.Mead	v	Hampshire	Southampton	1895
(Match)	V	17- 56	C.W.L.Parker	for	Glos	Gloucester	1925

Most Runs – Season	2559	G.A.Gooch	(av 67.34)	1984
Most Runs – Career	30701	G.A.Gooch	(av 51.77)	1973-97
Most 100s – Season	9	J.O'Connor		1929, 1934
	9	D.J.Insole		1955
Most 100s – Career	94	G.A.Gooch		1973-97
Most Wkts – Season	172	T.P.B Smith	(av 27.13)	1947
Most Wkts – Career	1610	T.P.B.Smith	(av 26.68)	1929-51
Most Career W-K Dismissals	1231	B.Taylor	(1040 ct; 191 st)	1949-73
Most Career Catches in the Field	519	K.W.R.Fletcher		1962-88

LIMITED-OVERS CRICKET

Highest Total	50ov	391-5		v	Surrey	The Oval	2008
	40ov	368-7		v	Scotland	Chelmsford	2013
	T20	242-3		v	Sussex	Chelmsford	2008
Lowest Total	50ov	57		v	Lancashire	Lord's	1996
	40ov	69		v	Derbyshire	Chesterfield	1974
	T20	82		v	Somerset	Chelmsford	2011
Highest Innings	50ov	201*	R.S.Bopara	v	Leics	Leicester	2008
	40ov	180	R.N.ten Doeschate	v	Scotland	Chelmsford	2013
	T20	152*	G.R.Napier	v	Sussex	Chelmsford	2008
Best Bowling	50ov	5- 8	J.K.Lever	v	Middlesex	Westcliff	1972
		5- 8	G.A.Gooch	v	Cheshire	Chester	1995
	40ov	8-26	K.D.Boyce	v	Lancashire	Manchester	1971
	T20	6-16	T.G.Southee	v	Glamorgan	Chelmsford	2011

GLAMORGAN

Formation of Present Club: 6 July 1888
Inaugural First-Class Match: 1921
Colours: Blue and Gold
Badge: Gold Daffodil
County Champions: (3) 1948, 1969, 1997
Pro 40/National League (Div 1) Winners: (2) 2002, 2004
Sunday League Winners: (1) 1993
Twenty20 Cup Winners: (0); best – Semi-Finalist 2004

GLAMORGAN

Chief Executive: Hugh Morris, SWALEC Stadium, Cardiff, CF11 9XR • Tel: 02920 409380 • Fax: 02920 419389 • email: info@glamorgancricket.co.uk • Web: www.glamorgancricket.com • Twitter: @GlamCricket (10,532 followers)

Head Coach: Toby Radford. **Bowling Coach:** Steve Watkin. **Player Development Manager:** Richard Almond. **Captain:** M.A.Wallace (f-c) and J.Allenby (T20). **Vice-Captain:** None. **Overseas Player:** J.A.Rudolph. **2014 Beneficiary:** None. **Head Groundsman:** Keith Exton. **Scorer:** Andrew K.Hignell. ‡ New registration. ^{NQ}Not qualified for England.

ALLENBY, James (Christ Church GS, Perth), b Perth, W Australia 12 Sep 1982. 6'0". RHB, RM. Leicestershire 2006-09. Glamorgan debut 2009; cap 2010; captain (T20) 2014. 1000 runs (1): 1202 (2013). HS 138* Le v Bangladesh A (Leicester) 2008 and 138* v Leics (Leicester) 2013. BB 5-44 v Derbys (Cardiff) 2011. LO HS 91* Le v Middx (Lord's) 2007 (P40). LO BB 5-43 Le v Derbys (Leicester) 2007 (FPT). T20 HS 110. T20 BB 5-21 Le v Lancs (Manchester) 2008, inc 4 wkts in 4 balls.

BRAGG, William David (Rougemont S, Newport; UWIC), b Newport, Monmouthshire 24 Oct 1986. 5'9". LHB, RM. Debut (Glamorgan) 2007. No f-c appearances in 2008. Wales MC 2004-09. 1000 runs (1): 1033 (2011). HS 110 v Leics (Colwyn Bay) 2011. BB 2-10 v Worcs (Cardiff) 2013. LO HS 78 v Leics (Leicester) 2009 (P40). BB 1-11 v Glos (Cardiff) 2013 (Y40). T20 HS 16.

BULL, Kieran Andrew (Q Elizabeth HS, Haverfordwest), b Haverfordwest 5 Apr 1995. 6'2". RHB, OB. Wales MC 2012-13. Awaiting 1st XI debut.

COOKE, Christopher Barry (Bishops S, Cape Town; U of Cape Town), b Johannesburg, South Africa 30 May 1986. 5'11". RHB, WK. W Province 2009-10. Glamorgan debut 2013. Glamorgan 2nd XI debut 2010. HS 92 v Hants (Southampton) 2013. LO HS 137* v Somerset (Taunton) 2012 (CB40). T20 HS 57.

COSKER, Dean Andrew (Millfield S), b Weymouth, Dorset 7 Jan 1978. 5'11". RHB, SLA. Debut (Glamorgan) 1996; cap 2000; benefit 2010. MCC 2010. F-c Tours (Eng A): SA 1998-99; SL 1997-98; Z 1998-99; K 1997-98. HS 52 v Glos (Bristol) 2005. 50 wkts (1): 51 (2010). BB 6-91 (11-126 match) v Essex (Cardiff) 2009. LO HS 50* v Northants (Northampton) 2009 (FPT). LO BB 5-54 v Essex (Chelmsford) 2003 (NL). T20 HS 21*. T20 BB 3-11.

DONALD, Aneurin Henry Thomas (Pontarddulais CS), b Swansea 20 Dec 1996. RHB, OB. Glamorgan 2nd XI debut 2012, aged 15y 189d. Wales MC 2012. Awaiting 1st XI debut.

GLOVER, John Charles (Llantarnam CS; St Aidan's C, Durham), b Cardiff 29 Aug 1989. 6'4". RHB, RMF. Durham MCCU 2008-10. Glamorgan debut 2011. Glamorgan 2nd XI debut 2009. Wales MC 2008-11. HS 55 v Kent (Cardiff) 2012. BB 5-38 DU v Durham (Durham) 2009. Gm BB 4-49 v Kent (Canterbury) 2011. LO HS 10 v Hants (Cardiff) 2012 (CB40). LO BB 3-34 v Scotland (Cardiff) 2012 (CB40).

^{NQ}**GOODWIN, Murray** William (Newton Moore HS, Bunbury, WA), b Salisbury, Rhodesia 11 Dec 1972. Younger brother of D.G.Goodwin (Zimbabwe 1986-87 to 1989-90). Migrated to Australia in Nov 1986 and gained Australian citizenship in Sep 1997. Kolpak registration 2005 to date. 5'9". RHB, LB. WA 1994-95 to 1996-97, 2000-01 to 2005-06. Mashonaland 1997-98 to 1998-99. Sussex 2001-12; cap 2001. Warriors 2006-07. Glamorgan debut 2013. Netherlands 1997. **Tests** (Z): 19 (1997-98 to 2000); HS 166* v P (Bulawayo) 1997-98. **LOI** (Z): 71 (1997-98 to 2000); HS 112* v WI (Chester-le-St) 2000; BB 1-12 v SL (Sharjah) 1998-99. F-c Tours (Z): E 2000, SA 1999-00; WI 1999-00; NZ 1997-98; P 1998-99; SL 1997-98. 1000 runs (10+1); most – 1654 (2001). HS 344* Sx v Somerset (Taunton) 2009 (Sx record), sharing record Sx 4th wkt partnership of 363 with C.D.Hopkinson. Gm HS 194 v Lancs (Manchester) 2013. BB 2-23 Z v Lahore City (Lahore) 1998-99. UK BB –. LO HS 167 WA v NSW (Perth) 2000-01. LO BB 1-9 Mashonaland v Eng A (Harare) 1998-99. T20 HS 102*.

HOGAN, Michael Garry, b Newcastle, New South Wales, Australia 31 May 1981. British passport. 6'5". RHB, RFM. W Australia 2009-10 to date. Glamorgan debut/cap 2013. HS 51 and BB 7-92 v Glos (Bristol) 2013. 50 wkts (1): 67 (2013). LO HS 27 WA v Vic (Melbourne) 2011-12. LO BB 5-44 WA v Vic (Melbourne) 2010-11. T20 HS 5*. T20 BB 4-26.

LLOYD, David Liam (Darland HS; Shrewsbury S), b St Asaph, Denbighs 15 May 1992. 5'9". RHB, OB. Debut (Glamorgan) 2012. Glamorgan 2nd XI debut 2008. Wales MC 2010-11. HS 16 v Glos (Cardiff) 2013.

MURPHY, Jack Roger (Greenhill S, Tenby), b Haverfordwest 15 Jul 1995. LHB, LFM. Glamorgan 2nd XI debut 2011. Wales MC 2011-13. Awaiting 1st XI debut.

OWEN, William Thomas (Prestatyn HS; UWIC), b St Asaph, Flintshire 2 Sep 1988. 6'0". RHB, RMF. Debut (Glamorgan) 2007. Wales MC 2007-10. HS 69 v Derbys (Derby) 2011. BB 5-124 v Middx (Cardiff) 2011. LO HS 13* v Leics (Leicester) 2013 (Y40). LO BB 5-49 v Unicorns (Bournemouth) 2010 (CB40). T20 HS 8. T20 BB 3-21.

REED, Michael Thomas (De Lisle S, Leicester; Cardiff U), b Leicester 10 Sep 1988. RHB, RFM. Debut (Glamorgan) 2012. Glamorgan 2nd XI debut 2009. Wales MC 2009-10. Cardiff MCCU 2010-11 (not f-c). HS 27 v Kent (Canterbury) 2013. BB 6-34 v Cardiff MCCU (Cardiff) 2013. CC BB 5-27 v Worcs (Cardiff) 2013. LO HS and LO BB –.

REES, Gareth Peter (Coedcae CS; Bath U), b Swansea 8 Apr 1985. 6'1". LHB, OB. Wales MC 2003-05. Debut (Glamorgan) 2006; cap 2009. MCC 2012. 1000 runs (2); most – 1088 (2008). HS 154 v Surrey (Oval) 2008. BB –. LO HS 123* v Essex (Chelmsford) 2009 (FPT). T20 HS 38.

‡^{NQ}**RUDOLPH, Jacobus** Andries ('**Jacques**') (Afrikaanse Hoer Seunskool), b Springs, Transvaal, South Africa 4 May 1981. Elder brother of G.J.Rudolph (Limpopo and Namibia 2006-07 to date). 5'11". LHB, LBG. Northerns 1997-98 to 2003-04. Titans 2004-05, 2008-09 to date. Eagles 2005-06 to 2007-08. Yorkshire 2007-11 (Kolpak registration); scored 122 v Surrey (Oval) on debut; cap 2007. Surrey 2012. **Tests** (SA): 48 (2003 to 2012-13); HS 122* v B (Chittagong) 2003 – on debut; BB 1-1 v E (Leeds) 2003. **LOI** (SA): 45 (2003 to 2005-06); HS 81 v B (Dhaka) 2003. **IT20** (SA): 1 (2005-06); HS 6* v A (Brisbane) 2005-06. F-c Tours (SA): E 2003, 2012; A 2001-02, 2005-06, 2012-13; WI 2004-05; NZ 2003-04, 2011-12; I 2004-05; SL 2004, 2005-06, 2006; B 2003. 1000 runs (4+1); most – 1375 (2010). HS 228* Y v Durham (Leeds) 2010. BB 5-80 Eagles v Cape Cobras (Cape Town) 2007-08. CC BB 1-13 Y v Somerset (Scarborough) 2008. LO HS 134* SA A v Kenya (Laudium) 2001-02. LO BB 4-41 SA A v New Zealand A (Colombo) 2005-06. T20 HS 83*. T20 BB 3-16.

SALTER, Andrew Graham (Milford Haven SFC; UWIC), b Haverfordwest 1 Jun 1993. 5'9''. RHB, OB. Cardiff MCCU 2012-13. Glamorgan debut 2013. Glamorgan 2nd XI debut 2010. Wales MC 2010-11. HS 21 CfU v Warwks (Birmingham) 2012. Gm HS 16 and BB 3-66 v Leics (Swansea) 2013. LO HS 3 v Durham (Chester-le-St) 2012 (CB40). LO BB 2-41 v Notts (Nottingham) 2012 (CB40) and 2-41 v Notts (Lord's) 2013 (Y40).

SMITH, Ruaidhri Alexander James (Llandaff Cathedral S; Shrewsbury S), b Glasgow, Scotland 5 Aug 1994. 6'1''. RHB, RM. Debut (Glamorgan) 2013. Wales MC 2010-11. Glamorgan 2nd XI debut 2011. Scotland (l-o only) 2013. HS 39 and BB 3-50 v Glos (Cardiff) 2013. LO HS 7 Scot v Hants (Glasgow) 2013 (Y40). LO BB 3-48 Scot v Surrey (Oval) 2013 (Y40).

WAGG, Graham Grant (Ashlawn S, Rugby), b Rugby, Warwks 28 Apr 1983. 6'0''. RHB, LM. Warwickshire 2002-04. Derbyshire 2006-10; cap 2007. Glamorgan debut 2011, cap 2013. F-c Tour (Eng A): I 2003-04. HS 108 De v Northants (Northampton) 2008. Gm HS 70 v Glos (Bristol) 2011. 50 wkts (2); most – 59 (2008). BB 6-35 De v Surrey (Derby) 2009. Gm BB 6-44 v Derbys (Cardiff) 2012. LO HS 54 v Glos (Cardiff) 2013 (Y40). LO BB 4-35 De v Durham (Derby) 2008 (FPT). T20 HS 62. T20 BB 5-14 v Worcs (Worcester) 2013 – Gm record.

WALLACE, Mark Alexander (Crickhowell HS), b Abergavenny, Monmouthshire 19 Nov 1981. 5'9''. LHB, WK. Debut (Glamorgan) 1999; cap 2003; captain 2012 to date; benefit 2013. F-c Tour (ECB Acad): SL 2002-03. 1000 runs (1): 1020 (2011). HS 139 v Surrey (Oval) 2009. LO HS 118* v Glos (Cardiff) 2013 (Y40). T20 HS 69*.

[NO]**WALTERS, Stewart** Jonathan (Guildford GS, Perth, WA), b Mornington, Victoria, Australia 25 Jun 1983. 6'1''. RHB, RM. Surrey 2006-10. Glamorgan debut 2011. HS 188 Sy v Leics (Oval) 2009. Gm HS 159 v Essex (Colchester) 2012. BB 1-4 Sy v Durham (Chester-le-St) 2007. LO HS 91 Sy v Northants (Oval) 2008 (P40). LO BB 1-12 Sy v Yorks (Scarborough) 2007 (P40). T20 HS 53*. T20 BB 1-9.

WATERS, Huw Thomas (Llantaram CS; Monmouth S), b Cardiff 26 Sep 1986. 6'2''. RHB, RMF. Debut (Glamorgan) 2005; cap 2012. No f-c appearances in 2009. Wales MC 2004-07. HS 54 v Surrey (Cardiff) 2011. BB 7-53 v Hants (Cardiff) 2012. LO HS 8 v Hants (Swansea) 2007 (FPT). LO BB 3-47 v Durham (Chester-le-St) 2007 (P40). T20 HS 11*. T20 BB 3-30.

WRIGHT, Ben James (Cowbridge CS), b Preston, Lancs 5 Dec 1987. 5'9''. RHB, RM. Debut (Glamorgan) 2006; cap 2011. No f-c appearances in 2008. HS 172 v Glos (Cardiff) 2010. BB 1-14 v Essex (Chelmsford) 2007. LO HS 79 v Lancs (Colwyn Bay) 2010 (CB40). LO BB 1-19 v Derbys (Derby) 2009 (FPT). T20 HS 55*. T20 BB 1-16.

RELEASED/RETIRED

(Having made a County First-Class or List A appearance in 2013)

JONES, Alexander John (Cowbridge CS), b Bridgend 10 Nov 1988. RHB, LMF. Glamorgan 2011-13. Wales MC 2007-10. Cardiff MCCU 2009-10. HS 26 v Northants (Northampton) 2011. BB 1-50 v Surrey (Oval) 2011. LO HS 5 v Somerset (Taunton) 2010 (CB40). LO BB 1-26 v Leics (Leicester) 2013 (Y40). T20 HS 4*. T20 BB 3-16.

JONES, Simon Philip (Coedcae CS; Millfield S), b Morriston, Swansea 25 Dec 1978. Son of I.J.Jones (Glamorgan and England 1960-68). 6'3½''. LHB, RFM. Glamorgan 1998-2007, 2012; cap 2002. Worcestershire 2008 (no 1st XI appearances in 2009). Hampshire 2010-11. MCC 2002-04. MBE 2005. *Wisden* 2005. **Tests**: 18 (2002 to 2005); HS 44 v I (Lord's) 2002 – on debut; BB 6-53 v A (Manchester) 2005. **LOI**: 8 (2004-05 to 2005); HS 1; BB 2-43 v Z (Bulawayo) 2004-05 – on debut. F-c Tours: A 2002-03 (*part*); SA 2004-05; WI 2003-04; I 2003-04 (Eng A – *part*). HS 46 v Yorks (Scarborough) 2001. BB 6-45 v Derbys (Cardiff) 2002. LO HS 26 v Hants (Swansea) 2007 (FPT). LO BB 5-32 Wo v Hants (Worcester) 2008 (FPT). T20 HS 11*. T20 BB 4-10.

NQMcCULLUM, Nathan Leslie, b Dunedin, NZ 1 Sep 1980. Older brother of B.B.McCullum (Otago, Canterbury, Glamorgan and NZ 1999-00 to date), son of S.J.McCullum (Otago 1976-77 to 1990-91). Otago 1999-00 to date. Glamorgan 2013. **LOI** (NZ): 67 (2009 to 2013-14); HS 65 v P (Auckland) 2010-11; BB 3-24 v SA (Dhaka) 2010-11. **IT20** (NZ): 51 (2007 to 2013-14); HS 36* v SL (Lauderhill) 2010; BB 4-16 v P (Hamilton) 2010-11. F-c Tour: I 2008-09 (NZ A). HS 106* Otago v ND (Hamilton) 2007-08. BB 6-90 NZ A v India A (Chennai) 2008-09. Gm HS 35* and Gm BB 5-191 v Lancs (Manchester) 2013. LO HS 90 Otago v ND (Hamilton) 2011-12. LO BB 5-39 Otago v CD (Palmerston N) 2010-11. T20 HS 76*. T20 BB 4-16.

NQNORTH, Marcus James (Kent Street Sr HS), b Pakenham, Melbourne, Australia 28 Jul 1979. 6'1". LHB, OB. Debut (Aus Academy in Zim) 1998-99. W Australia 1999-00 to date. Durham 2004. Lancashire 2005. Derbyshire 2006. Gloucestershire 2007-08; cap 2007. Hampshire 2009 (one match only). Glamorgan 2012-13; l-o captain in 2013. **Tests** (A): 21 (2008-09 to 2010-11); scored 117 v SA (Johannesburg) 2008-09 – on debut; HS 128 v I (Bangalore) 2010-11; BB 6-55 v P (Lord's) 2010. **LOI** (A): 2 (2009); HS 5 v P (Abu Dhabi) 2009; BB –. **IT20** (A): 1 (2009); HS 20 v P (Dubai) 2009. F-c Tours (Aus): E 2009, 2010 (v P); SA 2008-09; NZ 2009-10; I 2010-11; P 2005-06 (Aus A); Z 1998-99 (Aus Acad). 1000 runs (0+1): 1074 (2003-04). HS 239* WA v Vic (Perth) 2006-07. HS 191 v Hants (Cardiff) 2013. LO HS 137* v Middx (Lord's) 2013 (Y40). LO BB 4-26 Durham CB v Bucks (Beaconsfield) 2001 (CGT). T20 HS 70. T20 BB 2-19.

N.A.James left the staff without making a County First-Class or List A appearance for Glamorgan in 2013.

BENEFITS AWARDED IN 2014

Derbyshire	–
Durham	G.R.Breese, G.J.Muchall
Essex	A.N.Cook
Glamorgan	–
Gloucestershire	–
Hampshire	Hampshire Cricket in the Community
Kent	–
Lancashire	–
Leicestershire	–
Middlesex	–
Northamptonshire	S.D.Peters
Nottinghamshire	–
Somerset	–
Surrey	–
Sussex	M.H.Yardy
Warwickshire	I.J.L.Trott
Worcestershire	–
Yorkshire	T.T.Bresnan

GLAMORGAN 2013

RESULTS SUMMARY

	Place	Won	Lost	Tied	Drew	NR
LV= County Championship (2nd Division)	8th	3	6		7	
All First-Class Matches		3	6		8	
Yorkshire Bank 40 (Group C)	Finalist	9	4			1
Friends Life t20 (Mid/Wales/West Group)	3rd	5	5			

LV= COUNTY CHAMPIONSHIP AVERAGES

BATTING AND FIELDING

Cap		M	I	NO	HS	Runs	Avge	100	50	Ct/St
2010	J.Allenby	15	23	4	138*	1116	58.73	2	8	27
	M.W.Goodwin	16	26	4	194	1263	57.40	4	7	7
2009	G.P.Rees	8	14	1	112	524	40.30	2	3	5
	C.B.Cooke	7	11	1	92	394	39.40	–	3	2
	R.A.J.Smith	3	4	1	39	100	33.33	–	–	–
2013	G.G.Wagg	10	12	1	58	308	28.00	–	2	1
2003	M.A.Wallace	16	23	–	101	631	27.43	1	2	40/3
	W.D.Bragg	14	24	2	71*	535	24.31	–	2	3
2011	B.J.Wright	13	23	2	63	499	23.76	–	2	10
	M.J.North	10	16	1	68	354	23.60	–	1	5
	S.J.Walters	9	15	–	98	343	22.86	–	2	13
2013	M.G.Hogan	14	18	3	51	297	19.80	–	1	5
2000	D.A.Cosker	15	21	6	44*	281	18.73	–	–	7
	J.C.Glover	7	9	2	51*	127	18.14	–	1	1
	M.T.Reed	11	15	7	27	71	8.87	–	–	2
	A.G.Salter	3	4	–	16	29	7.25	–	–	1

Also batted: Alex J.Jones (1 match) 5* (1 ct); D.L.Lloyd (1) 16; N.L.McCullum (1) 14, 35*; W.T.Owen (2) 5, 40, 0 (2 ct).

BOWLING

	O	M	R	W	Avge	Best	5wI	10wM
M.G.Hogan	512	133	1376	67	20.53	7- 92	4	–
R.A.J.Smith	61	6	274	10	27.40	3- 50	–	–
D.A.Cosker	429.2	82	1261	37	34.08	5-120	1	–
M.T.Reed	309.5	58	1074	31	34.64	5- 27	1	–
J.Allenby	371.5	103	909	26	34.96	4- 16	–	–
J.C.Glover	147.1	26	498	13	38.30	4- 51	–	–
G.G.Wagg	295.2	63	971	18	53.94	3- 78	–	–

Also bowled:

M.J.North	48.2	6	143	7	20.42	5- 30	1	–
A.G.Salter	55	14	182	7	26.00	3- 66	–	–
N.L.McCullum	47.4	6	191	5	38.20	5-191	1	–

W.D.Bragg 22-2-111-2; Alex J.Jones 12-0-53-0; W.T.Owen 47-8-170-1; G.P.Rees 1-0-2-0; B.J.Wright 1-0-7-0.

The First-Class Averages (pp 225–241) give the records of Glamorgan players in all first-class county matches (Glamorgan's other opponents being Cardiff MCCU), with the exception of A.G.Salter, whose first-class figures for Glamorgan are as above.

GLAMORGAN RECORDS

FIRST-CLASS CRICKET

Highest Total	For 718-3d		v	Sussex	Colwyn Bay	2000
	V 712		by	Northants	Northampton	1998
Lowest Total	For 22		v	Lancashire	Liverpool	1924
	V 33		by	Leics	Ebbw Vale	1965
Highest Innings	For 309*	S.P.James	v	Sussex	Colwyn Bay	2000
	V 322*	M.B.Loye	for	Northants	Northampton	1998

Highest Partnership for each Wicket

1st	374	M.T.G.Elliott/S.P.James	v	Sussex	Colwyn Bay	2000
2nd	252	M.P.Maynard/D.L.Hemp	v	Northants	Cardiff	2002
3rd	313	D.E.Davies/W.E.Jones	v	Essex	Brentwood	1948
4th	425*	A.Dale/I.V.A.Richards	v	Middlesex	Cardiff	1993
5th	264	M.Robinson/S.W.Montgomery	v	Hampshire	Bournemouth	1949
6th	240	J.Allenby/M.A.Wallace	v	Surrey	The Oval	2009
7th	211	P.A.Cottey/O.D.Gibson	v	Leics	Swansea	1996
8th	202	D.Davies/J.J.Hills	v	Sussex	Eastbourne	1928
9th	203*	J.J.Hills/J.C.Clay	v	Worcs	Swansea	1929
10th	143	T.Davies/S.A.B.Daniels	v	Glos	Swansea	1982

Best Bowling	For 10- 51	J.Mercer	v	Worcs	Worcester	1936
(Innings)	V 10- 18	G.Geary	for	Leics	Pontypridd	1929
Best Bowling	For 17-212	J.C.Clay	v	Worcs	Swansea	1937
(Match)	V 16- 96	G.Geary	for	Leics	Pontypridd	1929

Most Runs – Season	2276	H.Morris	(av 55.51)	1990
Most Runs – Career	34056	A.Jones	(av 33.03)	1957-83
Most 100s – Season	10	H.Morris		1990
Most 100s – Career	54	M.P.Maynard		1985-2005
Most Wkts – Season	176	J.C.Clay	(av 17.34)	1937
Most Wkts – Career	2174	D.J.Shepherd	(av 20.95)	1950-72
Most Career W-K Dismissals	933	E.W.Jones	(840 ct; 93 st)	1961-83
Most Career Catches in the Field	656	P.M.Walker		1956-72

LIMITED-OVERS CRICKET

Highest Total	50ov	429	v	Surrey	The Oval	2002
	40ov	328-4	v	Lancashire	Colwyn Bay	2011
	T20	206-6	v	Somerset	Taunton	2006
Lowest Total	50ov	68	v	Lancashire	Manchester	1973
	40ov	42	v	Derbyshire	Swansea	1979
	T20	94-9	v	Essex	Cardiff	2010
Highest Innings	50ov	162*	I.V.A.Richards	v	Oxfordshire	Swansea	1993
	40ov	155*	J.H.Kallis	v	Surrey	Pontypridd	1999
	T20	116*	I.J.Thomas	v	Somerset	Taunton	2004
Best Bowling	50ov	6-20	S.D.Thomas	v	Comb Univs	Cardiff	1995
	40ov	7-16	S.D.Thomas	v	Surrey	Swansea	1998
	T20	5-14	G.G.Wagg	v	Worcs	Worcester	2013

GLOUCESTERSHIRE

Formation of Present Club: 1871
Inaugural First-Class Match: 1870
Colours: Blue, Gold, Brown, Silver, Green and Red
Badge: Coat of Arms of the City and County of Bristol
County Champions (since 1890): (0); best – 2nd 1930, 1931,
1947, 1959, 1969, 1986
Gillette/NatWest/C&G Trophy Winners: (5) 1973, 1999,
2000, 2003, 2004
Benson and Hedges Cup Winners: (3) 1977, 1999, 2000
Pro 40/National League (Div 1) Winners: (1) 2000
Twenty20 Cup Winners: (0); best – Finalist 2007

Chief Executive: Will Brown, County Ground, Nevil Road, Bristol BS7 9EJ • Tel: 0117 910
8000 • Fax: 0117 924 1193 • Email: info@glosccc.co.uk • Web: www.glosccc.co.uk •
Twitter: @Gloscricket (8,018 followers)

Director of Cricket: John Bracewell. **Bowling Coach**: Mark Thorburn. **Captain**:
M.Klinger. **Vice-Captain**: H.J.H.Marshall. **Overseas Player**: M.Klinger. **2014 Beneficiary**:
None. **Head Groundsman**: Sean Williams. **Scorer**: Adrian J.Bull. ‡ New registration. ᴺᑫ
Not qualified for England.

*Gloucestershire revised their capping policy in 2004 and now award players with their
County Caps when they make their first-class debut.*

BEARD, Michael Adam (Lord Williams's S, Thame), b Oxford 24 Oct 1992. 6'5". LHB,
LM. Gloucestershire 2nd XI debut 2008, aged 15y 216d. Oxfordshire 2011-13. Awaiting 1st
XI debut.

COCKBAIN, Ian Andrew (Maghull HS), b Bootle, Liverpool 17 Feb 1987. Son of
I.Cockbain (Lancs and Minor Cos 1979-94). 6'0". RHB, RM. Debut (Gloucestershire)
2011; cap 2011. MCC YC 2008-10. HS 127 v Middx (Uxbridge) 2011. LO HS 79 v Notts
(Cheltenham) 2011 (CB40). T20 HS 78.

DENT, Christopher David James (Backwell CS; Alton C), b Bristol 20 Jan 1991. 5'9".
LHB, WK, occ SLA. Debut (Gloucestershire) 2010; cap 2010. Gloucestershire 2nd XI debut
2007, aged 16y 80d. England U19s 2009-10. 1000 runs (1): 1128 (2013). HS 153 v Kent
(Cheltenham) 2012. BB 1-12 v Hants (Bristol) 2013. LO HS 151* v Glamorgan (Cardiff)
2013 (Y40). LO BB 4-43 v Leics (Bristol) 2012 (CB40). T20 HS 63*. T20 BB 1-16.

ᴺᑫ**FULLER, James** Kerr (Otago U, NZ), b Cape Town, South Africa 24 Jan 1990. British
passport. 6'3". RHB, RFM. Otago debut/cap 2011. HS 57
v Leics (Cheltenham) 2012. BB 6-24 (10-79 match) Otago v Wellington (Dunedin) 2012-13.
Gs BB 5-29 v Northants (Bristol) 2012. Hat-trick v Worcs (Cheltenham) 2013. LO HS 43 v
Lancs (Bristol) 2012 (CB40). LO BB 6-35 v Netherlands (Amstelveen) 2012 (CB40). T20
HS 36. T20 BB 4-24.

GIDMAN, Alex Peter Richard (Wycliffe C), b High Wycombe, Bucks 22 Jun 1981. Elder
brother of W.R.S.Gidman (*see below*). 6'3". RHB, RM. Debut (Gloucestershire) 2002; cap
2004; captain 2009-12; benefit 2012. Otago 2007-08. MCC YC 2001. MCC 2004, 2007,
2010. F-c Tour (Eng A): SL 2004-05. Appointed captain of Eng A tour to India 2003-04 but
withdrew because of hand injury. 1000 runs (5); most – 1244 (2006). HS 211 v Kent
(Cheltenham) 2013. BB 4-47 v Glamorgan (Cardiff) 2005. LO HS 116 v Sussex (Hove) 2009
(FPT). LO BB 5-42 Eng A v Bangladesh A (Mirpur) 2006-07. T20 HS 64. T20 BB 2-24.

GIDMAN, William Robert Simon (Wycliffe C; Berkshire C of Agriculture), b High Wycombe, Bucks 14 Feb 1985. Younger brother of A.P.R.Gidman (*see above*). 6'2". LHB, RM. Durham 2007. No f-c appearances in 2008-10. Gloucesterhire debut/cap 2011, becoming first player for Gs to score 1000 runs and take 50 wkts in debut season. MCC YC 2004-06. 1000 runs (1): 1006 (2011). HS 143 and BB 6-15 (10-43 match) v Leics (Bristol) 2013 – only the fifth Gs player to score a century and take ten wkts in a match. 50 wkts (2); most – 55 (2013). LO HS 76 v Worcs (Worcester) 2012 (CB40). LO BB 4-36 Du v Hants (Chester-le-St) 2010 (CB40). T20 HS 40*. T20 BB 1-18.

HAMMOND, Miles Arthur Halhead (St Edward's S, Oxford), b Cheltenham 11 Jan 1996. LHB, OB. Debut (Gloucestershire) 2013; cap 2013. England U19s 2012-13. Gloucestershire 2nd XI debut 2010, aged 14y 120d. HS 4 v Worcs (Cheltenham) 2013. BB 1-96 v Glamorgan (Bristol) 2013. LO HS –. LO BB 2-29 v Yorks (Bristol) 2013 (Y40). T20 HS and BB –.

HERRING, Cameron Lee (Tredegar CS), b Abergavenny, Monmouthshire 15 July 1994. 5'6". RHB, WK. Debut (Gloucestershire) 2013; cap 2013. Gloucestershire 2nd XI debut 2011. HS 43 v Northants (Bristol) 2013.

HOUSEGO, Daniel Mark (Oratory S, Reading), b Windsor, Berkshire 12 Oct 1988. 5'8". RHB, LB. Middlesex 2008-11. Glamorgan debut/cap 2012. Mountaineers 2013-14. Berkshire 2006. HS 217* and BB 1-5 Mt v SR (Masvingo) 2013-14. Gs HS 150 v Essex (Chelmsford) 2013. Gs BB –. LO HS 132 v S Africans (Bristol) 2012. LO BB 1-16 Mt v SR (Masvingo) 2013-14. T20 HS 59*.

HOWELL, Benny Alexander Cameron (The Oratory S), b Bordeaux, France 5 Oct 1988. Son of J.B.Howell (Warwickshire 2nd XI 1978). 5'11". RHB, RM. Hampshire 2011. Gloucestershire debut/cap 2012. Berkshire 2007. HS 83* v Yorks (Scarborough) 2012. BB 5-57 v Leics (Leicester) 2013. LO HS 122 v Surrey (Croydon) 2011 (CB40). LO BB 2-26 v Leics (Leicester) 2012 (CB40). T20 HS 55*. T20 BB 2-14.

^NQ**KLINGER, Michael**, b Kew, Melbourne, Australia 4 Jul 1980. 5'10½". RHB. Victoria 1999-00 to 2007-08. S Australia 2008-09 to date. Worcestershire 2012; cap 2012. Gloucestershire debut/cap 2013; captain 2013 to date. 1000 runs (1+1); most – 1203 (2008-09). HS 255 S Aus v WA (Adelaide) 2008-09. UK HS 163 v Hants (Bristol) 2013. HS 140* S Aus v Tas (Sydney) 2013-14. T20 HS 108*.

McCARTER, Graeme John (Foyle and Londonderry C), b Londonderry, N.Ireland 10 Oct 1992. 6'2". RHB, RFM. Ireland 2011 to date. Gloucestershire debut/cap 2012. Gloucestershire 2nd XI debut 2008, aged 15y 292d. HS 29* v Yorks (Bristol) 2012. BB 4-95 v Lancs (Liverpool) 2013. LO HS 18* v Leics (Leicester) 2013 (Y40). LO BB 3-15 v Leics (Bristol) 2012 (CB40).

^NQ**MARSHALL, Hamish** John Hamilton (Mahurangi C, Warkworth; King C, Auckland), b Warkworth, New Zealand 15 Feb 1979. Twin brother of J.A.H.Marshall (ND and NZ 1997-98 to 2011-12). Irish passport, qualified to play in April 2011. 5'9". RHB, RM. N Districts 1998-99 to 2012-13. Gloucestershire debut 2006 (scoring 102 v Worcs on UK debut); cap 2006; Kolpak registration 2008-11. MCC 2012. Buckinghamshire 2003. **Tests** (NZ): 13 (2000-01 to 2005-06); HS 160 v SL (Napier) 2004-05. **LOI** (NZ): 66 (2003-04 to 2006-07); HS 101* v P (Faisalabad) 2003-04. **IT20** (NZ): 3 (2004-05 to 2005-06); HS 8 v A (Auckland) 2004-05. F-c Tours (NZ): A 2004-05; SA 2000-01, 2005-06; Z 2005; B 2004-05. 1000 runs (2); most – 1218 (2006). HS 170 ND v Canterbury (Rangiora) 2009-10. Gs HS 168 v Leics (Cheltenham) 2006. BB 4-24 v Leics (Leicester) 2009. LO HS 122 v Sussex (Hove) 2007 (P40). LO BB 2-21 v Hants (Southampton) 2009 (P40). T20 HS 102.

MILES, Craig Neil (Bradon Forest S, Swindon; Filton C, Bristol), b Swindon, Wilts 20 July 1994. Brother of A.J.Miles (Cardiff MCCU 2012). 6'4". RHB, RMF. Debut (Gloucestershire) 2011; cap 2011. Gloucestershire 2nd XI debut 2009, aged 14y 318d. HS 50* v Essex (Bristol) 2013. BB 6-88 v Lancs (Liverpool) 2013. LO HS 0*. LO BB 2-32 v Essex (Cheltenham) 2011 (CB40). T20 HS 2. T20 BB –.

NORWELL, Liam Connor (Redruth SS), b Bournemouth, Dorset 27 Dec 1991. 6'3". RHB, RMF. Debut (Gloucestershire) 2011; cap 2011. Gloucestershire 2nd XI debut 2009. HS 26 v Middx (Bristol) 2011. BB 6-46 v Derbys (Bristol) 2011 – on debut. LO HS 1* v Middx (Cheltenham) 2012 (CB40). LO BB 6-52 v Leics (Leicester) 2012 (CB40). T20 HS 1*. T20 BB 2-41.

PAYNE, David Alan (Lytchett Minster S), b Poole, Dorset, 15 Feb 1991. 6'2". RHB, LMF. Debut (Gloucestershire) 2011; cap 2011. Gloucestershire 2nd XI debut 2008. Dorset 2009. England U19s 2010. HS 62 v Glamorgan (Bristol) 2011. BB 6-26 v Leics (Bristol) 2011. LO HS 18 v Leics (Leicester) 2013 (Y40). LO BB 7-29 v Essex (Chelmsford) 2010 (CB40), inc 4 wkts in 4 balls and 6 wkts in 9 balls – Gs l-o record. T20 HS 10. T20 BB 3-20.

NQRODERICK, Gareth Hugh (Maritzburg C), b Durban, South Africa 29 Aug 1991. 6'0". RHB, WK. KwaZulu-Natal 2010-11 to 2011-12. Gloucestershire debut/cap 2013. Gloucestershire 2nd XI debut 2012. Northamptonshire 2nd XI 2011. British passport. HS 152* v Kent (Canterbury) 2013. LO HS 63 v Yorks (Leeds) 2013 (Y40). T20 HS 32.

SAXELBY, Ian David (Oakham S), b Nottingham 22 May 1989. Nephew of K.Saxelby (Nottinghamshire 1978-90) and M.Saxelby (Notts, Durham and Derbys 1989-2000). 6'2". RHB, RMF. Debut (Gloucestershire) 2008; cap 2008. No 1st XI appearances in 2010 and in 2013 due to injuries. Nottinghamshire 2nd XI debut 2006. England U19s 2008. HS 60* v Northants (Northampton) 2009. BB 6-48 v Leics (Cheltenham) 2012. LO HS 7* and BB 4-31 v Surrey (Bristol) 2009 (FPT). T20 HS 7*. T20 BB 4-16 v Northants (Bristol) 2012 – joint Gs record.

SHREWSBURY, Thomas Weldon (Wadebridge S), b Southampton, Hants 18 Jan 1995. RHB, OB. Debut (Gloucestershire) 2013; cap 2013. Gloucestershire 2nd XI debut 2012. HS 2* and BB 1-94 v Northants (Northampton) 2013 – only f-c game. T20 HS –. T20 BB –.

SMITH, Thomas Michael John (Seaford Head Community C; Sussex Downs C), b Eastbourne, Sussex 29 Aug 1987. 5'9". RHB, SLA. Sussex 2007-09. No f-c appearances in 2008. Surrey 2009 (l-o only). Middlesex 2010-13. Gloucestershire debut/cap 2013. HS 50 v Leics (Bristol) 2013. BB 4-91 v Worcs (Cheltenham) 2013. LO HS 65 Sy v Leics (Leicester) 2009 (P40). LO BB 3-26 M v Derbys (Lord's) 2010 (CB40). T20 HS 36*. T20 BB 5-24.

TAVARÉ, William Andrew (Bristol GS; Loughborough U), b Bristol 1 Jan 1990. Nephew of C.J.Tavaré (Kent, Somerset & England 1974-93). RHB, RM. Loughborough MCCU 2010-12. Gloucestershire 2nd XI debut 2006. Awaiting Gloucestershire 1st XI debut. HS 61 LU v Hants (Southampton) 2012.

TAYLOR, Jack Martin Robert (Chipping Norton S), b Banbury, Oxfordshire 12 Nov 1991. Elder brother of M.D.Taylor (*see below*). 5'11". RHB, OB. Debut (Gloucestershire) 2010; cap 2010. Gloucestershire 2nd XI debut 2007, aged 15y 191d. Oxfordshire 2009-11. HS 63 and 2-28 v Glamorgan (Swansea) 2012. LO HS 22* v Essex (Chelmsford) 2012 (CB40). LO BB 3-37 v Unicorns (Exmouth) 2011 (CB40). T20 HS 38. T20 BB 4-16 v Somerset (Bristol) 2011 – joint Gs record.

TAYLOR, Matthew David (Chipping Norton S), b Banbury, Oxfordshire 8 Jul 1994. Younger brother of J.M.R.Taylor (*see above*). 6'0". RHB, LM. Debut (Gloucestershire) 2013; cap 2013. Gloucestershire 2nd XI debut 2011. Oxfordshire 2011-12. HS 26* v Lancs (Bristol) 2013. BB 3-108 v Glamorgan (Cardiff) 2013. LO HS 7* and LO BB 2-43 v Notts (Cheltenham) 2011 (CB40).

RELEASED/RETIRED

(Having made a County First-Class or List A appearance in 2013)

NQ**CHRISTIAN, Daniel** Trevor, b Camperdown, NSW, Australia 4 May 1983. RHB, RFM. S Australia 2007-08 to 2012-13. Hampshire 2010. Gloucestershire 2013; cap 2013. Victoria 2013-14. **LOI** (A): 19 (2011-12 to 2013-14); HS 39 v I (Adelaide) 2011-12; BB 5-31 v SL (Melbourne) 2011-12. **IT20** (A): 13 (2009-10 to 2013-14); HS 6* v E (Hobart) 2013-14; BB 3-27 v WI (Gros Islet) 2011-12. HS 131* S Aus v NSW (Adelaide) 2011-12. CC HS 36 and CC BB 2-115 H v Somerset (Taunton) 2010. Gs HS 46 v Australia A (Bristol) 2013. BB 5-24 (9-87 match) S Aus v WA (Perth) (2009-10). LO HS 117 Vic v NSW (Sydney) 2013-14. LO BB 6-48 S Aus v Vic (Geelong) 2010-11. T20 HS 75. T20 BB 5-26.

YOUNG, Edward George Christopher (Wellington C; Oxford Brookes U), b Chertsey, Surrey 21 May 1989. 6'1". RHB, SLA. Younger brother of P.J.W.Young (Oxford UCCE 2006-08). Oxford MCCU 2009-11. Gloucestershire 2010-13; cap 2010. HS 133 OU v Lancs (Oxford) 2011. Gs HS 55* and BB 2-23 v Kent (Canterbury) 2012. LO HS 50 v Notts (Nottingham) 2011 (CB40). LO BB 3-25 v Lancs (Bristol) 2012 (CB40). T20 HS 28. T20 BB 3-21.

R.G.Coughtrie left the staff without making a County First-Class or List A appearance for Gloucestershire in 2013.

GLOUCESTERSHIRE 2013

RESULTS SUMMARY

	Place	Won	Lost	Tied	Drew	NR
LV= County Championship (2nd Division)	6th	4	4		8	
All First-Class Matches		4	5		8	
Yorkshire Bank 40 (Group C)	4th	7	4			1
Friends Life t20 (Mid/Wales/West Group)	6th	3	7			

LV= COUNTY CHAMPIONSHIP AVERAGES

BATTING AND FIELDING

Cap†		M	I	NO	HS	Runs	Avge	100	50	Ct/St
2013	M.Klinger	15	24	3	163	1105	52.61	4	4	16
2004	A.P.R.Gidman	16	22	–	211	1125	51.13	3	5	12
2006	H.J.H.Marshall	16	21	1	149	1007	50.35	4	2	5
2013	G.H.Roderick	12	17	4	152*	625	48.07	2	2	41
2010	C.D.J.Dent	15	25	2	153	1049	45.60	2	6	19
2010	J.M.R.Taylor	4	5	1	61*	178	44.50	–	1	4
2012	D.M.Housego	9	14	2	150	443	36.91	1	3	5
2011	W.R.S.Gidman	13	15	4	143	401	36.45	1	1	3
2012	B.A.C.Howell	16	22	4	60	561	31.16	–	4	7
2013	T.M.J.Smith	8	9	2	50	181	25.85	–	1	1
2013	C.L.Herring	5	5	–	43	105	21.00	–	–	12
2011	J.K.Fuller	7	6	–	42	84	14.00	–	–	2
2011	C.N.Miles	13	13	1	50*	161	13.41	–	1	1
2012	G.J.McCarter	4	6	1	20	51	10.20	–	–	–
2011	D.A.Payne	10	9	2	16	42	6.00	–	–	2
2011	L.C.Norwell	5	7	5	8*	9	4.50	–	–	1

Also batted: I.A.Cockbain (1 match – cap 2011) 0, 2 (1 ct); M.A.H.Hammond (2 – cap 2013) 0, 4 (1 ct); T.W.Shrewsbury (1 – cap 2013) 2*; M.D.Taylor (3 – cap 2013) 26*, 5, 0*; E.G.C.Young (1 – cap 2010) 0*, 2*.

BOWLING

	O	M	R	W	Avge	Best	5wI	10wM
W.R.S.Gidman	384.1	85	1127	50	22.54	6-15	2	1
C.N.Miles	358	69	1315	43	30.58	6-88	3	–
B.A.C.Howell	347	83	992	28	35.42	5-57	1	–
L.C.Norwell	119	16	491	13	37.76	3-80	–	–
J.K.Fuller	211.4	44	699	15	46.60	5-43	1	–
T.M.J.Smith	229.5	37	731	15	48.73	4-91	–	–
D.A.Payne	275.4	59	917	18	50.94	3-75	–	–

Also bowled:

	O	M	R	W	Avge	Best	5wI	10wM
J.M.R.Taylor	89.1	17	247	6	41.16	2-39	–	–
G.J.McCarter	110	19	431	9	47.88	4-95	–	–

C.D.J.Dent 19.1-5-60-1; A.P.R.Gidman 28.3-6-93-1; M.A.H.Hammond 49-3-196-1; D.M.Housego 3-0-15-0; T.W.Shrewsbury 23-0-94-1; M.D.Taylor 75-19-246-4; E.G.C.Young 5-0-25-0.

The First-Class Averages (pp 225–241) give the records of Gloucestershire players in all first-class county matches (Gloucestershire's other opponents being Australia A), with the exception of:
T.M.J.Smith 9-11-3-50-198-24.75-0-1-2ct. 241.5-38-769-16-48.06-4/91-0-0.

† Gloucestershire revised their capping policy in 2004 and now award players with their County Caps when they make their first-class debut.

GLOUCESTERSHIRE RECORDS

FIRST-CLASS CRICKET

Highest Total	For 695-9d		v	Middlesex	Gloucester	2004
	V 774-7d		by	Australians	Bristol	1948
Lowest Total	For 17		v	Australians	Cheltenham	1896
	V 12		by	Northants	Gloucester	1907
Highest Innings	For 341	C.M.Spearman	v	Middlesex	Gloucester	2004
	V 319	C.J.L.Rogers	for	Northants	Northampton	2006

Highest Partnership for each Wicket

1st	395	D.M.Young/R.B.Nicholls	v	Oxford U	Oxford	1962
2nd	256	C.T.M.Pugh/T.W.Graveney	v	Derbyshire	Chesterfield	1960
3rd	336	W.R.Hammond/B.H.Lyon	v	Leics	Leicester	1933
4th	321	W.R.Hammond/W.L.Neale	v	Leics	Gloucester	1937
5th	261	W.G.Grace/W.O.Moberley	v	Yorkshire	Cheltenham	1876
6th	320	G.L.Jessop/J.H.Board	v	Sussex	Hove	1903
7th	248	W.G.Grace/E.L.Thomas	v	Sussex	Hove	1896
8th	239	W.R.Hammond/A.E.Wilson	v	Lancashire	Bristol	1938
9th	193	W.G.Grace/S.A.P.Kitcat	v	Sussex	Bristol	1896
10th	131	W.R.Gouldsworthy/J.G.Bessant	v	Somerset	Bristol	1923

Best Bowling	For	10-40	E.G.Dennett	v	Essex	Bristol	1906
(Innings)	V	10-66	A.A.Mailey	for	Australians	Cheltenham	1921
		10-66	K.Smales	for	Notts	Stroud	1956
Best Bowling	For	17-56	C.W.L.Parker	v	Essex	Gloucester	1925
(Match)	V	15-87	A.J.Conway	for	Worcs	Moreton-in-M	1914

Most Runs – Season	2860	W.R.Hammond	(av 69.75)		1933
Most Runs – Career	33664	W.R.Hammond	(av 57.05)		1920-51
Most 100s – Season	13	W.R.Hammond			1938
Most 100s – Career	113	W.R.Hammond			1920-51
Most Wkts – Season	222	T.W.J.Goddard	(av 16.80)		1937
	222	T.W.J.Goddard	(av 16.37)		1947
Most Wkts – Career	3170	C.W.L.Parker	(av 19.43)		1903-35
Most Career W-K Dismissals	1054	R.C.Russell	(950 ct; 104 st)	1981-2004
Most Career Catches in the Field	719	C.A.Milton			1948-74

LIMITED-OVERS CRICKET

Highest Total	50ov	401-7		v	Bucks	Wing	2003
	40ov	344-6		v	Northants	Cheltenham	2001
	T20	254-3		v	Middlesex	Uxbridge	2011
Lowest Total	50ov	82		v	Notts	Bristol	1987
	40ov	49		v	Middlesex	Bristol	1978
	T20	68		v	Hampshire	Bristol	2010
Highest Innings	50ov	177	A.J.Wright	v	Scotland	Bristol	1997
	40ov	153	C.M.Spearman	v	Warwicks	Gloucester	2003
	T20	119	K.J.O'Brien	v	Middlesex	Uxbridge	2011
Best Bowling	50ov	6-13	M.J.Proctor	v	Hampshire	Southampton	1977
	40ov	7-29	D.A.Payne	v	Essex	Chelmsford	2010
	T20	4-16	J.M.R.Taylor	v	Somerset	Bristol	2011
		4-16	I.D.Saxelby	v	Northants	Bristol	2012

HAMPSHIRE

Formation of Present Club: 12 August 1863
Inaugural First-Class Match: 1864
Colours: Blue, Gold and White
Badge: Tudor Rose and Crown
County Champions: (2) 1961, 1973
NatWest/C&G/FP Trophy Winners: (3) 1991, 2005, 2009
Benson and Hedges Cup Winners: (2) 1988, 1992
Sunday League Winners: (3) 1975, 1978, 1986
Clydesdale Bank Winners: (1) 2012
Twenty20 Cup Winners: (2) 2010, 2012

HAMPSHIRE
CRICKET

Chairman: Rod Bransgrove, The Ageas Bowl, Botley Road, West End, Southampton SO30 3XH • Tel: 023 8047 2002 • Fax: 023 8047 2122 • Email: enquiries@ageasbowl.com • Web: www.ageasbowl.com Twitter: @hantscricket (15,668 followers)

CEO: David Mann. **Cricket Secretary**: Tim Tremlett. **Director of Cricket**: Giles White. **1st XI Coach**: Dale Benkenstein. **County Coach**: Tony Middleton. **Captain**: J.H.K.Adams. **Vice-Captain**: J.M.Vince. **Overseas Players**: K.J.Abbott and G.J.Maxwell (T20 only). **2014 Beneficiary**: Hampshire Cricket in the Community. **Head Groundsman**: Nigel Gray. **Scorer**: Kevin Baker. ‡ New registration. ^NQ Not qualified for England.

‡ ^NQ**ABBOTT, Kyle** John, b Empangeni, South Africa 18 Jun 1987. RHB, RFM. KwaZulu-Natal 2008-09 to 2009-10. Dolphins 2008-09 to date. **Tests** (SA): 2 (2012-13 to 2013-14); HS 13 and BB 7-29 v P (Centurion) 2012-13. **LOI** (SA): 2 (2012-13); HS 5 v P (Centurion) 2012-13; BB 1-35 v P (Bloemfontein) 2012-13. **IT20** (SA): 1 (2012-13); HS 2 and BB 1-41 v P (Centurion) 2012-13. HS 80 Dolphins v Titans (Benoni) 2010-11. BB 8-45 (12-96 match) Dolphins v Cobras (Cape Town) 2012-13. LO HS 45* Dolphins v Titans (Durban) 2013-14. LO BB 4-36 Dolphins v Warriors (Pietermaritzburg) 2010-11. T20 HS 15*. T20 BB 3-13.

ADAMS, James Henry Kenneth (Sherborne S; University C, London; Loughborough U), b Winchester 23 Sep 1980. 6'2". LHB, LM. British U 2002-04. Hampshire debut 2002; cap 2006; captain 2012 to date. Loughborough UCCE 2003-04 – scoring 107 v Somerset (Taunton) on debut. MCC 2013. Dorset 1998. F-c Tour (EL): WI 2010-11. 1000 runs (4); most – 1351 (2009). HS 262* v Notts (Nottingham) 2006. BB 2-16 v Durham (Chester-le-St) 2004. LO HS 131 v Warwks (Birmingham) 2010 (CB40). LO BB 1-34 v Essex (Chelmsford) 2007 (FPT). T20 HS 101*. T20 BB –.

BALCOMBE, David John (St John's S, Leatherhead; St Hild & St Bede C, Durham), b City of London 24 Dec 1984. 6'4". RHB, RFM. Durham UCCE 2005-07. British U 2006. Hampshire debut 2007; cap 2013. Kent 2011 (on loan). HS 73 DU v Leics (Leicester) 2005 and 73 v Leics (Leicester) 2012. BB 8-71 (11-119 match) v Glos (Southampton) 2012. LO HS 6 K v Netherlands (Rotterdam) 2011 (CB40). LO BB 4-38 v Worcs (Worcester) 2011 (CB40). T20 HS 3. T20 BB 1-23.

BARBER, Tom Edward (Bournemouth GS), b Poole, Dorset 8 Aug 1995. 6'3". RHB, LFM. Hampshire 2nd XI debut 2013. Awaiting 1st XI debut.

BATES, Michael David (Lord Wandsworth C, Hook), b Frimley, Surrey 10 Oct 1990. 5'10". RHB, WK. Debut (Hampshire) 2010. Hampshire 2nd XI debut 2007. Berkshire 2009. England U19s 2009-10. HS 103 v Yorks (Leeds) 2012. LO HS 24* v Warwks (Birmingham) 2011 (CB40). T20 HS 10.

BRATHWAITE, Ruel Marlon Ricardo (Queen's C, Barbados; Dulwich C; Loughborough U; Queens' C, Cambridge), b Bridgetown, Barbados 6 Sep 1985. 6'2". RHB, RFM. British passport. Loughborough UCCE 2006-08. British U 2006. MCC 2007. Cambridge U 2009 (blue). Durham 2010-12. Hampshire debut (on loan) 2013. HS 76* LU v Worcs (Worcester) 2007. H HS 17 v Essex (Southampton) 2013. BB 5-54 CU v Oxford U (Cambridge) 2009. CC BB 5-56 Du v Sussex (Chester-le-St) 2011. H BB 3-112 v Northants (Southampton) 2013. LO HS –. LO BB 1-19 WI v Eng Lions (Worcester) 2007. T20 HS 0. T20 BB 1-33.

BRIGGS, Danny Richard (Isle of Wight C), b Newport, IoW, 30 Apr 1991. 6'2". RHB, SLA. Debut (Hampshire) 2009; cap 2012. Hampshire 2nd XI debut 2007, aged 16y 120d. **LOI**: 1 (2011-12); HS – ; BB 2-39 v P (Dubai) 2011-12. **IT20**: 7 (2012 to 2013-14); HS 0*; BB 2-25 v A (Chester-le-St) 2013. F-c Tour (EL): WI 2010-11. HS 54 v Glos (Bristol) 2013. BB 6-45 EL v Windward Is (Roseau) 2010-11. CC BB 6-65 v Notts (Southampton) 2011. LO HS 25 and LO BB 4-32 v Glamorgan (Cardiff) 2012 (CB40). T20 HS 10. T20 BB 5-19.

CARBERRY, Michael Alexander (St John Rigby Catholic C), b Croydon, Surrey 29 Sep 1980. 6'0". LHB, OB. Surrey 2001-02. Kent 2003-05. Hampshire debut/cap 2006. MCC 2008. **Tests**: 6 (2009-10 to 2013-14); HS 60 v A (Adelaide) 2013-14. **LOI**: 3 (2013); HS 63 v A (Cardiff) 2013. F-c Tours: A 2013-14; B 2006-07 (Eng A), 2009-10. 1000 runs (3); most – 1251 (2009). HS 300* v Yorks (Southampton) 2011, sharing in UK 3rd highest and UK record 3rd-wkt partnership of 523 with N.D.McKenzie. BB 2-85 v Durham (Chester-le-St) 2006. LO HS 150* v Lancs (Southampton) 2013 (Y40). LO BB 3-37 v Derbys (Derby) 2013 (Y40). T20 HS 100*. T20 BB 1-16.

COLES, Matthew Thomas (Maplesden Noakes S; Mid-Kent C), b Maidstone 26 May 1990. 6'3". LHB, RMF. Kent 2009-13; cap 2012. Hampshire debut 2013 (on loan). Kent 2nd XI debut 2007. HS 103* K v Yorks (Leeds) 2012. H HS 68 v Lancs (Southport) 2013. 50 wkts (1): 59 (2012). BB 6-51 K v Northants (Northampton) 2012. H BB 6-71 (10-154 match) v Essex (Southampton) 2013. LO HS 47 K v Yorks (Leeds) 2011 (CB40). LO BB 6-32 K v Yorks (Leeds) 2012 (CB40). T20 HS 40. T20 BB 3-14.

DAWSON, Liam Andrew (John Bentley S, Calne), b Swindon, Wilts 1 Mar 1990. 5'8". RHB, SLA. Debut (Hampshire) 2007; cap 2013. Mountaineers 2011-12. England U19s 2007 to 2008. Wiltshire 2006-07. HS 169 v Somerset (Southampton) 2011. BB 7-51 Mountaineers v ME (Mutare) 2011-12 (also scored 110* in same match). BB 5-29 v Leics (Southampton) 2012. LO HS 97 v Bangladesh A (Southampton) 2013. LO BB 4-45 v Middx (Lord's) 2008 (P40). T20 HS 30. T20 BB 4-19.

ERVINE, Sean Michael (Lomagundi C, Chinhoyi), b Harare, Zimbabwe 6 Dec 1982. Elder brother of C.R.Ervine (Midlands, SR 2003-04 to date); son of R.M.Ervine (Rhodesia 1977-78); grandson of M.A.Den (Rhodesia 1935-36); nephew of N.B.Ervine (Rhodesia 1977-78) and G.M.Den (Rhodesia and Eastern Province 1963-64 to 1969-70). 6'2". LHB, RM. CFX Academy 2000-01 to 2001. Midlands 2001-02 to 2003-04. Hampshire debut/cap 2005; qualified for England in 2013 season. W Australia 2006-07 to 2007-08. Southern Rocks 2009-10. Matabeleland Tuskers 2011-12 to 2012-13. **Tests** (Z): 5 (2003 to 2003-04); HS 86 v B (Harare) 2003-04; BB 4-146 v A (Perth) 2003-04. **LOI** (Z): 42 (2001-02 to 2003-04); HS 100 v I (Adelaide) 2003-04; BB 3-29 v P (Sharjah) 2001-02. F-c Tours (Z): E 2003; A 2003-04. HS 237* v Somerset (Southampton) 2010. BB 6-82 Midlands v Mashonaland (Kwekwe) 2002-03. H BB 5-60 v Glamorgan (Cardiff) 2005. LO HS 167* v Ireland (Southampton) 2009 (FPT). LO BB 5-50 v Glamorgan (Cardiff) 2005 (CGT). T20 HS 82. T20 BB 4-12.

‡GATTING, Joe Stephen (Cardinal Newman C; Brighton C), b Brighton 25 Nov 1987. Son of S.P.Gatting (Middlesex 2nd XI, football for Arsenal, Brighton & Hove Albion, Charlton Athletic), nephew of M.W.Gatting (Middlesex and England 1975-95). 6'0". RHB, OB. Sussex 2009-13, scoring 152 v Cambridge UCCE (Cambridge) on debut. HS 152 (*see above*). CC HS 116* Sx v Worcs (Worcester) 2011. BB 1-8 Sx v Notts (Nottingham) 2011. LO HS 122 Sx v Worcs (Horsham) 2011 (CB40). LO BB –. T20 HS 45*. LO BB 1-12.

McMANUS, Lewis David (Clayesmore S, Bournemouth), b Poole, Dorset 9 Oct 1994. 5'10". RHB, WK. Hampshire 2nd XI debut 2011. Dorset 2011-13. Awaiting 1st XI debut.

NQMAXWELL, Glenn James, b Kew, Melbourne, Australia 14 Oct 1988. RHB, OB. Victoria 2010-11 to date. Returning to Hampshire for T20 only. **Tests** (A): 2 (2012-13); HS 13 and BB 4-127 v I (Hyderabad) 2012-13. **LOI** (A): 24 (2012 to 2013-14); HS 92 v I (Ranchi) 2013-14; BB 4-63 v WI (Perth) 2012-13. **IT20** (A): 15 (2012 to 2013-14); HS 27 (three times) v P, E, I; BB 2-15 v SL (Sydney) 2012-13. F-c Tours (A): I 2012-13; SA/Z 2013 (Aus A). HS 155* Aus A v South Africa A (Pretoria) 2013. BB 4-42 Vic v S Aus (Melbourne) 2012-13. LO HS 145* Aus A v India A (Pretoria) 2013. LO BB 4-63 *(see LOI)*. T20 HS 82. T20 BB 3-26.

‡SMITH, William Rew (Bedford S; Collingwood C, Durham U), b Luton, Beds 28 Sep 1982. 5'9". RHB, OB. Nottinghamshire 2002-06. Durham UCCE 2003-05; captain 2004-05. British U 2004-05. Durham 2007-13; captain 2009-10 *(part)*. Bedfordshire 1999-2002. HS 201* Du v Surrey (Guildford) 2008. BB 3-34 DU v Leics (Leicester) 2005. CC BB 1-5 Du v Lancs (Chester-le-St) 2007. LO HS 120* Du v Surrey (Chester-le-St) 2013 (Y40). LO BB 2-19 Du v Derbys (Derby) 2013 (Y40). T20 HS 55. T20 BB 2-20.

TAYLOR, Bradley Jacob, b Winchester 14 Mar 1997. RHB, OB. Debut (Hampshire) 2013. Hampshire 2nd XI debut 2013. HS 20 and BB 4-64 v Lancs (Southport) 2013. LO HS 2* and LO BB 2-23 v Bangladesh A (Southampton) 2013.

TERRY, Sean Paul (Aquinas C, Perth; Notre Dame U, Perth, Australia), b Southampton 1 Aug 1991. Son of V.P.Terry (Hampshire and England 1978-96). RHB, OB. Debut (Hampshire) 2012. Hampshire 2nd XI debut 2011. HS 59* v Loughborough MCCU (Southampton) 2012 – on debut. CC HS 58 v Worcs (Worcester) 2013. LO HS 33 v Lancs (Manchester) 2013 (Y40).

TOMLINSON, James Andrew (Harrow Way S, Andover; Cardiff U), b Winchester 12 Jun 1982. 6'1". RHB, LMF. British U 2002-03. Hampshire debut 2002; cap 2008. Wiltshire 2001. HS 42 v Somerset (Southampton) 2010. 50 wkts (2); most – 67 (2008). BB 8-46 (10-194 match) v Somerset (Taunton) 2008. LO HS 14 v Durham (Chester-le-St) 2010 (CB40). LO BB 4-47 v Glamorgan (Southampton) 2006 (CGT). T20 HS 5. T20 BB 1-20.

VINCE, James Michael (Warminster S), b Cuckfield, Sussex 14 Mar 1991. 6'2". RHB, RM. Debut (Hampshire) 2009; cap 2013. Hampshire 2nd XI debut 2006. Wiltshire 2007-08. F-c Tour (EL): SL 2013-14. 1000 runs (1): 1215 (2013). HS 180 v Yorks (Scarborough) 2010. BB 5-41 v Loughborough MCCU (Southampton) 2013. CC BB 2-2 v Lancs (Southport) 2013. LO HS 131 v Scotland (Southampton) 2011 (CB40). LO BB 1-18 EL v Australia A (Sydney) 2012-13. T20 HS 85*. T20 BB 1-5.

WHEATER, Adam Jack Aubrey (Millfield S), b Whipps Cross, Essex 13 Feb 1990. 5'6". RHB, WK. Essex 2008-12. Cambridge MCCU 2010. Matabeleland Tuskers 2010-11 to 2012-13. Badureliya Sports Club 2011-12. Northern Districts 2012-13. Hampshire debut 2013. Essex 2nd XI debut, aged 16y 190d. HS 164 Ex v Northants (Chelmsford) 2011. H HS 140 v Lancs (Southport) 2013. BB 1-86 Ex v Leics (Leicester) 2012 – in contrived circumstances. LO HS 70 v Derbys (Southampton) 2013 (Y40). T20 HS 29.

WOOD, Christopher Philip (Alton C), b Basingstoke 27 June 1990. 6'2". RHB, LM. Debut (Hampshire) 2010. Hampshire 2nd XI debut 2007. England U19s 2009. HS 105* v Leics (Leicester) 2012. BB 5-41 v Loughborough MCCU (Southampton) 2012. CC BB 4-35 v Worcs (Southampton) 2011. LO HS 41 v Essex (Southampton) 2013 (Y40). LO BB 5-22 v Glamorgan (Cardiff) 2012 (CB40). T20 HS 18. T20 BB 3-26.

(Having made a County First-Class or List A appearance in 2013)

^{NQ}**BAILEY, George** John, b Launceston, Tasmania, Australia 7 Sep 1982. 5'10". RHB, RM. Tasmania 2004-05 to date. Hampshire 2013. **Tests** (A): 5 (2013-14); HS 53 v E (Adelaide) 2013-14. **LOI** (A): 39 (2011-12 to 2013-14); HS 156 v I (Nagpur) 2013-14. **IT20** (A): 22 (2011-12 to 2013-14); HS 63 v WI (Colombo, RPS) 2012-13. F-c Tours (Aus A): E 2012; I 2008-09. HS 160* Tas v Vic (Hobart) 2010-11. H HS 93 v Leics (Southampton) 2013. BB –. LO HS 156 (*see LOI*). LO BB 1-19 Tas v Vic (Melbourne) 2004-05. T20 HS 63. T20 BB –.

GRIFFITHS, D.A. – *see KENT*.

^{NQ}**McKENZIE, Neil** Douglas (King Edward VII HS; Rand Afrikaans U), b Johannesburg, South Africa 24 Nov 1975. 5'9½". Son of K.A.McKenzie (N-E Transvaal and Transvaal 1966-67 to 1986-87). RHB, RM. Transvaal/Gauteng 1994-95 to 1998-99. Northerns 1999-00 to 2003-04. Lions 2004-05 to date; cap 2004-05 to 2009-10 (*part*). Somerset 2007. Durham 2008 (*part*). Hampshire 2010-13; cap 2010 (Kolpak registration). *Wisden* 2008. **Tests** (SA): 58 (2000 to 2008-09); HS 226 v B (Chittagong) 2007-08, sharing Test record 1st wkt partnership of 415 with G.C.Smith; BB –. **LOI** (SA): 64 (1999-00 to 2008-09); HS 131* v Kenya (Cape Town) 2001-02; BB –. **IT20** (SA): 2 (2005-06 to 2008-09); HS 7* v A (Brisbane) 2008-09. F-c Tours (SA): E 2003, 2008; A 2001-02, 2008-09; WI 2000-01; NZ 2003-04; I 2007-08; P 2003-04; SL 2000; Z 2001-02, 2004 (SA A); B 2003, 2007-08. 1000 runs (1): 1120 (2011). HS 237 v Yorks (Southampton) 2011, sharing in UK 3rd highest and UK record 3rd-wkt partnership of 523 with M.A.Carberry. BB 2-13 Lions v Eagles (Kimberley) 2007-08. H BB 2-30 v Lancs (Liverpool) 2010. LO HS 131* (*see LOI*). LO BB 2-19 Gauteng v GW (Kimberley) 1997-98. T20 HS 89*. T20 BB 1-4.

MASCARENHAS, Adrian Dimitri (Trinity C, Perth, Australia), b Hammersmith, London 30 Oct 1977. 6'2". Resident in Australia 1979-96. RHB, RMF. Hampshire 1996-2013, taking 6-88 v Glamorgan (Southampton) on debut; took 16 wickets in first two CC matches; cap 1998; benefit 2007; captain 2008-10. No f-c or l-o appearances in 2010 after Achilles injury. Dorset 1996. **LOI**: 20 (2007 to 2009); HS 52 v I (Bristol) 2007; hit sixes off five successive balls from Yuvraj Singh v I (Oval) 2007; BB 3-23 v I (Lord's) 2007. **IT20**: 14 (2007 to 2009); HS 31 v NZ (Auckland) 2007-08; BB 3-18 v Z (Cape Town) 2007-08. HS 131 v Kent (Canterbury) 2006. 50 wkts (1): 56 (2004). BB 6-25 v Derbys (Southampton) 2004. LO HS 79 v Worcs (Southampton) 1999 (NL) and 79 v Kent (Canterbury) 2004 (NL). LO BB 5-27 v Glos (Southampton) 2002 (NL). T20 HS 57*. T20 BB 5-14 v Sussex (Hove) 2004 – H record.

RIAZUDDIN, Hamza (Bradfield C), b Chelsea, London 19 Dec 1989. 5'11". RHB, RMF. Hampshire 2008-13. England U19s 2009. Berkshire 2008. HS 55* v Loughborough MCCU (Southampton) 2012. CC HS 28 v Glos (Southampton) 2012. BB 5-61 v Glamorgan (Cardiff) 2012. LO HS 23* v Durham (Chester-le-St) 2010 (CB40). LO BB 3-37 v Scotland (Southampton) 2011 (CB40). T20 HS 13*. T20 BB 4-15.

ROBERTS, Michael David Tudor (Oratory S, Reading; Bath U), b Oxford 13 Mar 1989. 5'11". RHB, OB. Hampshire 2013. Middlesex 2nd XI 2007-11. Hampshire 2nd XI debut 2011. Berkshire 2006-12. HS 44 v Glos (Bristol) 2013. BB –. LO HS 35 v Bangladesh A (Southampton) 2013.

ROUSE, Adam Paul (Perrins Community Sports C; Peter Symonds C, Winchester), b Harare, Zimbabwe 30 Jun 1992. 5'8". RHB, WK. Hampshire 2013. Hampshire 2nd XI debut 2008, aged 15y 331d. England U19s 2010. HS 9 v Kent (Canterbury) 2013. LO HS 7 v Bangladesh A (Southampton) 2013.

SHEPPARD, Jack David (Q Elizabeth GS, Wimborne), b Salisbury, Wilts 29 Dec 1992. 6'2". RHB, RMF. Hampshire 2nd XI debut 2010. Awaiting f-c debut. LO HS 0 and LO BB 2-49 v Bangladesh A (Southampton) 2013 – only 1st XI appearance.

SOHAIL TANVIR, b Rawalpindi, Pakistan 12 Dec 1984. LHB, LMF. Rawalpindi 2004-05 to date. KRL 2007-08 to 2008-09. Federal Areas 2007-08 to 2011-12. ZTB 2009-10 to date. Hampshire 2013. **Tests** (P): 2 (2007-08); HS 13 and BB 3-83 v I (Delhi) 2007-08. **LOI** (P): 58 (2007-08 to 2013-14); HS 59 v Hong Kong (Karachi) 2008; BB 5-48 v SL (Karachi) 2008. **IT20** (P): 38 (2007 to 2013-14); HS 41 v SL (Dubai) 2013-14; BB 3-12 v SL (Hambantota) 2012. F-c Tour (P): I 2007-08. HS 132 Fed Areas v Baluchistan (Karachi) 2007-08. H HS 38 and H BB 3-62 v Glamorgan (Cardiff) 2013. BB 8-54 (15-174 match) KRL v PIA (Mirpur) 2008-09. LO HS 93 KRL v SSGC (Rawalpindi) 2008-09. LO BB 7-34 KRL v WAPDA (Lahore) 2007-08. T20 HS 60*. T20 BB 6-14.

J.George left the staff, without making a County First-Class or List A appearance in 2013.

COUNTY CAPS AWARDED IN 2013

Derbyshire	–
Durham	–
Essex	J.C.Mickleburgh, O.A.Shah, R.J.W.Topley
Glamorgan	M.G.Hogan, G.G.Wagg
Gloucestershire	D.T.Christian, M.A.H.Hammond, C.L.Herring, M.Klinger, G.H.Roderick, T.W.Shrewsbury, T.M.J.Smith, M.D.Taylor
Hampshire	D.J.Balcombe, L.A.Dawson, J.M.Vince
Kent	B.P.Nash
Lancashire	S.M.Katich, S.C.Kerrigan
Leicestershire	M.A.G.Boyce, E.J.H.Eckersley, J.K.Naik
Middlesex	S.D.Robson
Northamptonshire	K.J.Coetzer, S.P.Crook, L.M.Daggett, D.J.Willey
Nottinghamshire	E.J.M.Cowan, S.J.Mullaney
Somerset	J.C.Buttler, A.N.Petersen
Surrey	W.H.Gordon (ex-groundsman), R.T.Ponting, G.C.Smith
Sussex	S.J.Magoffin
Warwickshire	K.H.D.Barker, W.B.Rankin, C.J.C.Wright
Worcestershire (colours)	G.Cessford, T.C.Fell, M.A.Johnson, T.T.Samaraweera, R.A.Whiteley
Yorkshire	J.A.Brooks, L.E.Plunkett

Durham abolished their capping system after 2005. Gloucestershire award caps on first-class debut. Worcestershire award club colours on Championship debut. Glamorgan's capping system is now based on a player's number of appearances and not on his performances.

HAMPSHIRE 2013

RESULTS SUMMARY

	Place	Won	Lost	Tied	Drew	NR
LV= County Championship (2nd Division)	4th	4	3		9	
All First-Class Matches		5	3		9	
Yorkshire Bank 40 (Group B)	SF	9	4			
Friends Life t20 (South Group)	SF	9	2			1

LV= COUNTY CHAMPIONSHIP AVERAGES

BATTING AND FIELDING

Cap		M	I	NO	HS	Runs	Avge	100	50	Ct/St
2013	J.M.Vince	15	22	4	148	1101	61.16	4	6	16
2013	L.A.Dawson	16	24	3	136*	1031	49.09	1	8	23
2010	N.D.McKenzie	6	10	1	146	433	48.11	1	2	1
2006	M.A.Carberry	11	16	–	154	687	42.93	1	5	3
2006	J.H.K.Adams	16	24	3	219*	833	39.66	3	1	7
	G.J.Bailey	5	7	–	93	263	37.57	–	2	3
	A.J.A.Wheater	15	18	2	140	585	36.56	2	1	19/2
	M.T.Coles	5	5	1	68	118	29.50	–	2	1
	M.D.Bates	5	4	–	71	117	29.25	–	1	16
2012	D.R.Briggs	12	12	3	54	244	27.11	–	1	6
	Sohail Tanvir	4	5	–	38	133	26.60	–	–	–
2005	S.M.Ervine	15	19	1	86	458	25.44	–	4	20
	C.P.Wood	9	12	1	69	256	23.27	–	2	6
	M.D.T.Roberts	5	8	–	44	143	17.87	–	–	2
2008	J.A.Tomlinson	15	15	8	30*	72	10.28	–	–	1
2013	D.J.Balcombe	12	13	2	30*	106	9.63	–	–	1

Also batted: R.M.R.Brathwaite (3 matches) 9, 17 (1 ct); D.A.Griffiths (2) 14, 1; A.D.Mascarenhas (1 – cap 1998) 41; A.P.Rouse (1) 9; B.J.Taylor (1) 0, 20* (1 ct); S.P.Terry (2) 58, 57 (2 ct).

BOWLING

	O	M	R	W	Avge	Best	5wI	10wM
M.T.Coles	127	27	504	21	24.00	6- 71	2	1
J.A.Tomlinson	454.5	126	1281	53	24.16	5- 44	1	–
S.M.Ervine	179.1	39	577	17	33.94	2- 17	–	–
Sohail Tanvir	107.2	19	348	10	34.80	3- 62	–	–
D.R.Briggs	270	59	798	22	36.27	3- 33	–	–
C.P.Wood	231.3	65	659	15	43.93	3- 30	–	–
D.J.Balcombe	349	80	1101	22	50.04	5-104	1	–

Also bowled:

R.M.R.Brathwaite	58	13	222	6	37.00	3-112	–	–
J.M.Vince	102.4	11	396	9	44.00	2- 2	–	–
D.A.Griffiths	53.3	7	237	5	47.40	2- 70	–	–
L.A.Dawson	196.5	49	602	9	66.88	2- 77	–	–

J.H.K.Adams 14-1-52-1; M.A.Carberry 19.3-2-87-1; N.D.McKenzie 10-4-17-1; A.D.Mascarenhas 25-7-61-4; M.D.T.Roberts 3.5-1-19-0; B.J.Taylor 22-3-106-4.

The First-Class Averages (pp 225–241) give the records of Hampshire players in all first-class county matches (Hampshire's other opponents being Loughborough MCCU), with the exception of M.T.Coles, whose first-class figures for Hampshire are as above, and: M.A.Carberry 12-18-0-154-812-45.11-2-5-5ct. 23.3-2-100-2-50.00-1/13-0-0.

HAMPSHIRE RECORDS

FIRST-CLASS CRICKET

Highest Total	For 714-5d		v	Notts	Southampton	2005
	V 742		by	Surrey	The Oval	1909
Lowest Total	For 15		v	Warwicks	Birmingham	1922
	V 23		by	Yorkshire	Middlesbrough	1965
Highest Innings	For 316	R.H.Moore	v	Warwicks	Bournemouth	1937
	V 303*	G.A.Hick	for	Worcs	Southampton	1997

Highest Partnership for each Wicket

1st	347	V.P.Terry/C.L.Smith	v	Warwicks	Birmingham	1987
2nd	373	J.H.K.Adams/M.A.Carberry	v	Somerset	Taunton	2011
3rd	523	M.A.Carberry/N.D.McKenzie	v	Yorkshire	Southampton	2011
4th	278	J.H.K.Adams/J.M.Vince	v	Yorkshire	Scarborough	2010
5th	235	G.Hill/D.F.Walker	v	Sussex	Portsmouth	1937
6th	411	R.M.Poore/E.G.Wynyard	v	Somerset	Taunton	1899
7th	325	G.Brown/C.H.Abercrombie	v	Essex	Leyton	1913
8th	257	N.Pothas/A.J.Bichel	v	Glos	Cheltenham	2005
9th	230	D.A.Livingstone/A.T.Castell	v	Surrey	Southampton	1962
10th	192	H.A.W.Bowell/W.H.Livsey	v	Worcs	Bournemouth	1921

Best Bowling	For 9- 25	R.M.H.Cottam	v	Lancashire	Manchester	1965
(Innings)	V 10- 46	W.Hickton	for	Lancashire	Manchester	1870
Best Bowling	For 16- 88	J.A.Newman	v	Somerset	Weston-s-Mare	1927
(Match)	V 17-103	W.Mycroft	for	Derbyshire	Southampton	1876

Most Runs – Season	2854	C.P.Mead	(av 79.27)	1928
Most Runs – Career	48892	C.P.Mead	(av 48.84)	1905-36
Most 100s – Season	12	C.P.Mead		1928
Most 100s – Career	138	C.P.Mead		1905-36
Most Wkts – Season	190	A.S.Kennedy	(av 15.61)	1922
Most Wkts – Career	2669	D.Shackleton	(av 18.23)	1948-69
Most Career W-K Dismissals	700	R.J.Parks	(630 ct; 70 st)	1980-92
Most Career Catches in the Field	629	C.P.Mead		1905-36

LIMITED-OVERS CRICKET

Highest Total	50ov	371-4	v	Glamorgan	Southampton	1975
	40ov	353-8	v	Middlesex	Lord's	2005
	T20	225-2	v	Middlesex	Southampton	2006
Lowest Total	50ov	50	v	Yorkshire	Leeds	1991
	40ov	43	v	Essex	Basingstoke	1972
	T20	85	v	Sussex	Southampton	2008
Highest Innings	50ov	177	C.G.Greenidge	v	Glamorgan	Southampton	1975
	40ov	172	C.G.Greenidge	v	Surrey	Southampton	1987
	T20	124*	M.J.Lumb	v	Essex	Southampton	2009
Best Bowling	50ov	7-30	P.J.Sainsbury	v	Norfolk	Southampton	1965
	40ov	6-20	T.E.Jesty	v	Glamorgan	Cardiff	1975
	T20	5-14	A.D.Mascarenhas	v	Sussex	Hove	2004

KENT

Formation of Present Club: 1 March 1859
Substantial Reorganisation: 6 December 1870
Inaugural First-Class Match: 1864
Colours: Maroon and White
Badge: White Horse on a Red Ground
County Champions: (6) 1906, 1909, 1910, 1913, 1970, 1978
Joint Champions: (1) 1977
Gillette Cup Winners: (2) 1967, 1974
Benson and Hedges Cup Winners: (3) 1973, 1976, 1978
Pro 40/National League (Div 1) Winners: (1) 2001
Sunday League Winners: (4) 1972, 1973, 1976, 1995
Twenty20 Cup Winners: (1) 2007

Cricket Chief Executive: Jamie Clifford, The Spitfire Ground, Old Dover Road, Canterbury, CT1 3NZ • Tel: 01227 456886 • Fax: 01227 762168 • Email: kent@ecb.co.uk • Web: www.kentcricket.co.uk • Twitter: @kentcricket (14,220 followers)

Head Coach: Jimmy Adams. **High Performance Director**: Simon Willis. **Assistant Coach**: Matt Walker. **Captain**: R.W.T.Key. **Vice-Captain**: S.A.Northeast. **Overseas Players**: D.E.Bollinger and B.P.Nash. **2014 Beneficiary**: None. **Head Groundsman**: Simon Williamson. **Scorer**: Lorne Hart. ‡ New registration. NQ Not qualified for England.

BALL, Adam James (Beths GS, Bexley) b Greenwich, London 1 March 1993. 6'1". RHB, LFM. Debut (Kent) 2011. No f-c appearances in 2012. Kent 2nd XI debut 2009, aged 16y 117d. England U19s 2010 to 2010-11. HS 69 v Lancs (Canterbury) 2013. BB 3-36 v Leics (Leicester) 2011. LO HS 28 v Warwks (Birmingham) 2013 (Y40). LO BB 3-36 v Sussex (Horsham) 2013 (Y40). T20 HS 18. T20 BB 2-18.

BELL-DRUMMOND, Daniel James (Millfield S), b Lewisham, London 4 Aug 1993. 6'0". RHB, RMF. Debut (Kent) 2011. Kent 2nd XI debut 2009, aged 16y 21d. England U19s 2010 to 2010-11. HS 102* v Cardiff MCCU (Canterbury) 2013. CC HS 79 v Hants (Canterbury) 2013. LO HS 42 v Worcs (Worcester) 2011 (CB40). T20 HS 31.

BILLINGS, Samuel William (Haileybury S; Loughborough U), b Pembury 15 Jun 1991. 5'11". RHB, WK. Loughborough MCCU 2011, scoring 131 v Northants (Loughborough) on f-c debut. Kent debut 2011. Kent 2nd XI debut 2007, aged 15y 349d. HS 131 (*see above*). K HS 24 v Lancs (Canterbury) 2013. LO HS 143 v Derbys (Canterbury) 2012 (CB40). T20 HS 59.

BLAKE, Alexander James (Hayes SS; Leeds Met U), b Farnborough 25 Jan 1989. 6'1". LHB, RMF. Debut (Kent) 2008. Leeds/Bradford UCCE 2009-11 (not f-c). HS 105* v Yorks (Leeds) 2010. BB 2-9 v Pakistanis (Canterbury) 2010. CC BB 1-60 v Hants (Southampton) 2010. LO HS 81* v Scotland (Canterbury) 2010 (CB40). LO BB 2-13 v Yorks (Leeds) 2011 (CB40). T20 HS 37*.

NQ‡**BOLLINGER, Douglas** Erwin (Newman C, WA; Greystanes, NSW), b Baulkham Hills, Sydney, Australia 24 July 1981. 6'4" LHB, LFM. NSW 2002-03 to date. Worcestershire 2007; cap 2007. **Tests** (A): 12 (2008-09 to 2010-11); HS 21 v P (Lord's) 2010; BB 5-28 v NZ (Wellington) 2009-10. **LOI** (A): 39 (2009 to 2011-12); HS 30 v E (Hobart) 2010-11; BB 5-35 v P (Abu Dhabi) 2009 and v I (Guwahati) 2009-10. **IT20** (A): 2 (2011-12) HS – ; BB v SA (Cape Town) 2011-12. F-c Tours (A): E 2010; SA 2008-09; NZ 2009-10; I 2008-09 (Aus A), 2010-11; P 2007-08 (Aus A). HS 31* NSW v Q (Brisbane) 2006-07. CC HS 21 Wo v Durham (Worcester) 2007. BB 6-47 NSW v S Aus (Sydney) 2008-09. CC BB 4-82 v Yorks (Kidderminster) 2007. LO HS 30 (*see LOI*). LO BB 5-35 (*see LOI*). T20 HS 17. T20 BB 4-13.

CLAYDON, Mitchell Eric (Westfield Sports HS, Sydney), b Fairfield, NSW, Australia 25 Nov 1982. 6'4''. LHB, RFM. Yorkshire 2005-06. Durham 2007-13. Canterbury 2010-11. Kent debut 2013 (on loan). HS 55 v Notts (Chester-le-St) 2012. K HS 40 and K BB 3-85 v Glamorgan (Canterbury) 2013. BB 6-104 Du v Somerset (Taunton) 2011. LO HS 19 Du v Glos (Bristol) 2009 (FPT). LO BB 4-39 Cant v Otago (Timaru) 2010-11. T20 HS 19. T20 BB 5-26.

COWDREY, Fabian Kruuse (Tonbridge S), b Canterbury 30 Jan 1993. Son of C.S.Cowdrey (Kent, Glamorgan, England 1977-92), grandson of M.C.Cowdrey (Kent, Oxford U, England 1950-76), nephew of G.R.Cowdrey (Kent 1984-97). 6'0''. RHB, SLA. Debut Cardiff MCCU 2013. Kent 2nd XI debut 2009, aged 16y 207d. Awaiting Kent f-c debut. HS 62 CfU v Glamorgan (Cardiff) 2013. BB –. LO HS 52* v Worcs (Worcester) 2013 (Y40). LO BB –. T20 HS 50. T20 BB 1-30.

DAVIES, Mark (Northfield CS, Billingham; Stockton SFC), b Stockton-on-Tees, Co Durham 4 Oct 1980. 6'3''. RHB, RMF. Durham 2002-10; cap 2005; no f-c appearances in 2011. Nottinghamshire 2007 (on loan). Kent debut 2012. F-c Tour (Eng A): NZ 2008-09. HS 62 Du v Somerset (Stockton) 2005. K HS 58 v Yorks (Leeds) 2012. 50 wkts (1): 50 (2004). BB 8-24 (11-75 match) Du v Hants (Basingstoke) 2008. K BB 5-27 v Derbys (Canterbury) 2012. LO HS 31* Du v Warwks (Chester-le-St) 2002 (NL). LO BB 4-13 Du v Sussex (Chester-le-St) 2001 (NL). T20 HS 13. T20 BB 2-14.

‡**GRIFFITHS, David** Andrew (Sandown HS, IoW), b Newport, IoW 10 Sep 1985. 6'1''. LHB, RFM. Hampshire 2006-13. HS 31* H v Surrey (Southampton) 2007. BB 6-85 H v Notts (Nottingham) 2011. LO HS 7 H v Durham (Southampton) 2011 (CB40). LO BB 4-29 H v Glos (Southampton) 2009 (P40). T20 HS 4*. T20 BB 3-13.

HAGGETT, Calum John (Millfield S), b Taunton, Somerset 30 Oct 1990. 6'3''. LHB, RMF. Debut (Kent) 2013. Somerset 2nd XI 2009-11. Kent 2nd XI debut 2012. England U19s 2009-10. HS 44* v Glos (Canterbury) 2013. BB 4-94 v Glamorgan (Canterbury) 2013. LO HS 2 v Northants (Tunbridge W) 2013 (Y40). LO BB 2-97 v Sussex (Canterbury) 2013 (Y40). T20 HS 2. T20 BB 1-15.

HARMISON, Ben William (Ashington HS), b Ashington, Northumb 9 Jan 1986. Younger brother of S.J.Harmison (Durham, Hampshire and England 1996-2012). 6'5''. LHB, RMF. Durham 2006-10, scoring 110 v Oxford U (Oxford) on debut. Scored 105 in his second match (v West Indies A) to emulate A.Fairbairn (Middlesex 1947) in scoring hundreds in first two f-c matches, those matches being in England. Kent debut 2012. HS 110 (*see above*). K HS 106 v Glos (Canterbury) 2013. BB 4-27 Du v Surrey (Guildford) 2008. K BB 1-21 v Northants (Northampton) 2013. LO HS 67 Du v Notts (Chester-le-St) 2009 (P40). LO BB 3-43 Du v Scotland (Chester-le-St) 2008 (FPT). T20 HS 24. T20 BB 3-20.

HARTLEY, Charles Frederick (Millfield S), b Redditch, Worcs 4 Jan 1994. 6'2''. RHB, RMF. Kent 2nd XI debut 2013. Awaiting 1st XI debut.

HUNN, Matthew David (St Joseph's C, Ipswich), b Colchester, Essex 22 Mar 1994. 6'5''. RHB, RMF. Debut (Kent) 2013. Essex 2nd XI 2012. Kent 2nd XI debut 2013. Suffolk 2011-13. HS 69 and BB 2-51 v Lancs (Canterbury) 2013 – only f-c game.

JONES, Geraint Owen (Harristown State HS, Toowoomba and MacGregor State HS, Brisbane, Australia), b Kundiawa, Papua New Guinea 14 Jul 1976. Welsh parents. 5'10''. RHB, WK. Debut (Kent) 2001; cap 2003; benefit 2012. MBE 2005. Papua New Guinea (l-o and T20). **Tests**: 34 (2003-04 to 2006-07); HS 100 v NZ (Leeds) 2004. **LOI**: 49 (2004 to 2006); HS 80 v Z (Bulawayo) 2004-05. **IT20**: 2 (2006); HS 19 v A (Southampton) 2005. F-c Tours: A 2006-07; SA 2004-05; WI 2003-04; I 2005-06; P 2005-06; SL 2003-04. 1000 runs (2); most – 1345 (2009). HS 178 v Somerset (Canterbury) 2010. LO HS 86 v Surrey (Oval) 2008 (FPT). T20 HS 56.

KEY, Robert William Trevor (Colfe's S), b East Dulwich, London 12 May 1979. 6'1''. RHB, RM/OB. Debut (Kent) 1998; cap 2001; captain 2006-12, 2014; benefit 2011. MCC 2002-04, 2009. *Wisden* 2004. **Tests**: 15 (2002 to 2004-05); HS 221 v WI (Lord's) 2004. **LOI**: 5 (2003 to 2004); HS 19 v WI (Lord's) 2004. **IT20**: 1 (2009); HS 10* v Netherlands (Lord's) 2009. F-c Tours: A 2002-03; SA 1998-99 (Eng A), 2004-05; NZ 2008-09 (EL – captain); SL 2002-03 (ECB Acad); Z 1998-99 (Eng A). 1000 runs (7); most – 1896 (2004). HS 270* v Glamorgan (Cardiff) 2009. BB 2-31 v Somerset (Canterbury) 2010. LO HS 144* v Netherlands (Tunbridge W) 2013 (Y40). T20 HS 98*.

^{NQ}**NASH, Brendan** Paul, b Attadale, Western Australia 14 Dec 1977. 5'8''. LHB, LM. Queensland 2000-01 to 2006-07. Jamaica 2007-08 to 2011-12. Kent debut 2012; cap 2013. **Tests** (WI): 21 (2008-09 to 2011); HS 114 v SA (Basseterre) 2010; BB 1-21 v SL (Galle) 2010-11. **LOI** (WI): 9 (2008 to 2008-09); HS 39* and BB 3-56 v Canada (King City) 2008. F-c Tours (WI): E 2009; A 2009-10; NZ 2008-09; SL 2010-11; B 2010 (WI A). 1000 runs (1): 1110 (2013). HS 207 Jamaica v T&T (St Augustine) 2010-11. K HS 199* v Glos (Cheltenham) 2013. BB 2-7 Jamaica v CC&C (Kingston) 2007-08. K BB 1-2 v Glamorgan (Canterbury) 2012. LO HS 98* v Warwks (Birmingham) 2013 (Y40). LO BB 4-20 Jamaica v Guyana (Bridgetown) 2007-08. T20 HS 26. T20 BB 1-32.

NORTHEAST, Sam Alexander (Harrow S), b Ashford 16 Oct 1989. 5'11''. RHB, OB. Debut (Kent) 2007; cap 2012. MCC 2013. England U19s 2009. HS 176 v Loughborough MCCU (Canterbury) 2011. CC HS 165 v Derbys (Canterbury) 2012. BB 1-60 v Glos (Cheltenham) 2013. LO HS 115 v Sussex (Canterbury) 2013 (Y40). T20 HS 61.

RILEY, Adam Edward Nicholas (Beths GS, Bexley; Loughborough U), b Sidcup 23 Mar 1992. 6'2''. RHB, OB. Debut (Kent) 2011. Loughborough MCCU 2012-13. Kent 2nd XI debut 2010. HS 21* and BB 7-150 v Hants (Southampton) 2013. LO HS 3* and LO BB 2-32 v Sussex (Hove) 2011 (CB40). T20 HS 5*. T20 BB 2-15.

STEVENS, Darren Ian (Hinckley C), b Leicester 30 Apr 1976. 5'11''. RHB, RM. Leicestershire 1997-2004; cap 2002. MCC 2002. Kent debut/cap 2005. F-c Tour (ECB Acad): SL 2002-03. 1000 runs (3); most – 1304 (2013). HS 208 v Glamorgan (Canterbury) 2005 and v Middx (Uxbridge) 2009. BB 7-21 (11-70 match) v Surrey (Canterbury) 2011. LO HS 133 Le v Northumb (Jesmond) 2000 (NWT). LO BB 5-32 v Scotland (Edinburgh) 2005 (NL). T20 HS 77. T20 BB 4-14.

THOMAS, Ivan Alfred Astley (John Roan S, Blackheath; Leeds U), b Greenwich, London 25 Sep 1991. 6'4''. RHB, RMF. Leeds/Bradford MCCU 2012-13. Kent debut 2012. Kent 2nd XI debut 2011. Missed most of 2013 through injury. HS 11 and BB 2-24 LBU v Yorks (Leeds) 2012. K HS 0* and K BB 2-29 v Essex (Chelmsford) 2012.

TREDWELL, James Cullum (Southlands Community CS, New Romney), b Ashford 27 Feb 1982. 6'0''. LHB, OB. Debut (Kent) 2001; cap 2007; captain 2013. MCC 2004, 2008. **Tests**: 1 (2009-10); HS 37 and BB 4-82 v B (Dhaka) 2009-10. **LOI**: 30 (2009-10 to 2013-14); HS 16 v A (Hobart) 2010-11; BB 4-44 v I (Rajkot) 2012-13. **IT20**: 8 (2012-13 to 2013-14); HS 22 and BB 1-20 v NZ (Hamilton) 2012-13. F-c Tours: NZ 2012-13 (*part*); I 2003-04 (Eng A, captain); B 2009-10. HS 123* v New Zealanders (Canterbury) 2008. CC HS 116* v Yorks (Tunbridge W) 2007. 50 wkts (1): 69 (2009). BB 8-66 (11-120 match) v Glamorgan (Canterbury) 2009. LO HS 88 v Surrey (Oval) 2007 (FPT). LO BB 6-27 v Middx (Southgate) 2009 (FPT). T20 HS 34*. T20 BB 4-21.

(Having made a County First-Class or List A appearance in 2013)

COLES, M.T. – *see HAMPSHIRE*.

NQ**PHILANDER, Vernon** Darryl, b Bellville, Cape Province, South Africa 24 Jun 1985. RHB, RMF. Western Province 2003-04 to 2009-10. WP Boland 2004-05. Cape Cobras 2005-06 to date. Middlesex 2008. Somerset 2012. Kent 2013. Devon 2004. **Tests** (SA): 23 (2011-12 to 2013-14); HS 74 v P (Centurion) 2012-13; BB 6-44 (10-114 match) v NZ (Hamilton) 2011-12. **LOI** (SA): 13 (2007 to 2013-14); HS 23 v E (Leeds) 2008; BB 4-12 v Ireland (Belfast) 2007 – on debut. **IT20** (SA): 7 (2007-08); HS 6 v E (Cape Town) 2007-08; BB 2-23 v B (Cape Town) 2007-08. F-c Tours (SA): E 2012; A 2012-13; NZ 2011-12; SL 2010 (SA A); B 2010 (SA A); UAE (v P) 2012-13. HS 168 WP v GW (Kimberley) 2004-05. UK HS 61 and UK BB 5-30 SA v E (Lord's) 2012. CC HS 38 Sm v Warwks (Birmingham) 2012. K HS 23 v Hants (Canterbury) 2013. 50 wkts (0+2); most – 59 (2009-10). BB 7-61 Cape Cobras v Knights (Cape Town) 2011-12. CC BB 5-43 Sm v Middx (Taunton) 2012. K BB –. LO HS 79* SA A v Bangladesh A (East London) 2010-11. LO BB 4-12 (*see LOI*). T20 HS 56*. T20 BB 5-17.

POWELL, Michael John (Crickhowell SS; Pontypool CFE), b Abergavenny, Monmouthshire 3 Feb 1977. 6'1". RHB, OB, occ WK. Glamorgan 1997-2011, scoring 200* v Oxford U (Oxford) on debut; cap 2000; benefit 2011. Kent 2012-13. MCC 2005. 1000 runs (5); most – 1327 (2006). HS 299 Gm v Glos (Cheltenham) 2006 – record score for Glamorgan in England. K HS 134 v Leics (Canterbury) 2012. BB 2-39 Gm v Oxford U (Oxford) 1999. CC BB –. LO HS 114* Gm v Hants (Cardiff) 2008 (FPT). LO BB 1-26 Gm v Lincs (Lincoln) 2004 (CGT). T20 HS 68*.

SHRECK, C.E. – *see LEICESTERSHIRE*.

B.W.Kemp and S.A.Shaw left the staff without making a County First-Class or List A appearance in 2013.

KENT 2013

RESULTS SUMMARY

	Place	Won	Lost	Tied	Drew	NR
LV= County Championship (2nd Division)	7th	3	2		11	
All First-Class Matches		3	2		12	
Yorkshire Bank 40 (Group A)	4th	6	6			
Friends Life t20 (South Group)	5th	3	7			

LV= COUNTY CHAMPIONSHIP AVERAGES
BATTING AND FIELDING

Cap		M	I	NO	HS	Runs	Avge	100	50	Ct/St
2005	D.I.Stevens	15	21	1	205*	1268	63.40	4	7	13
2001	R.W.T.Key	16	27	3	180	1168	48.66	5	3	3
2013	B.P.Nash	16	26	4	199*	1064	48.36	5	5	4
	B.W.Harmison	13	19	3	106	712	44.50	2	5	8
	C.J.Haggett	11	13	7	44*	249	41.50	–	–	3
	M.J.Powell	6	9	3	70	203	33.83	–	2	–
2012	S.A.Northeast	15	26	1	94	650	26.00	–	6	11
2003	G.O.Jones	14	19	2	67	403	23.70	–	2	40/1
	D.J.Bell-Drummond	13	20	–	79	466	23.30	–	4	7
	M.E.Claydon	3	4	–	40	93	23.25	–	–	1
2012	M.T.Coles	7	9	1	59	136	17.00	–	1	6
2007	J.C.Tredwell	11	14	1	48	197	15.15	–	–	9
	A.E.N.Riley	5	6	2	21*	60	15.00	–	–	2
	M.Davies	10	14	3	41	158	14.36	–	–	–
	C.E.Shreck	14	15	8	19*	82	11.71	–	–	1

Also batted: A.J.Ball (2 matches) 32, 7, 69; S.W.Billings (2) 8, 13, 24 (4 ct, 1 st); M.D.Hunn (1) 0 (1 ct); V.D.Philander (2) 2, 23.

BOWLING

	O	M	R	W	Avge	Best	5wI	10wM
M.Davies	266.3	74	629	25	25.16	4- 36	–	–
A.E.N.Riley	102.3	11	361	14	25.78	7-150	1	–
D.I.Stevens	403.4	111	1051	32	32.84	5- 39	1	–
C.J.Haggett	298	72	907	26	34.88	4- 94	–	–
C.E.Shreck	429.2	98	1294	33	39.21	4- 65	–	–
M.T.Coles	162	28	549	13	42.23	5- 31	1	–
J.C.Tredwell	331.3	67	965	17	56.76	5- 51	1	–

Also bowled: A.J.Ball 37-4-170-3; D.J.Bell-Drummond 6.5-0-54-0; M.E.Claydon 64.4-12-226-4; B.W.Harmison 37-1-161-1; H.D.Hunn 31.4-6-118-3; R.W.T.Key 9.2-0-86-0; B.P.Nash 9-0-43-1; S.A.Northeast 20-0-131-1; V.D.Philander 64-9-170-0.

The First-Class Averages (pp 225–241) give the records of Kent players in all first-class county matches (Kent's other opponents being Cardiff MCCU), with the exception of M.E.Claydon, M.T.Coles and A.E.N.Riley, whose first-class figures for Kent are as above.

KENT RECORDS

FIRST-CLASS CRICKET

Highest Total	For 803-4d		v	Essex	Brentwood	1934
	V 676		by	Australians	Canterbury	1921
Lowest Total	For 18		v	Sussex	Gravesend	1867
	V 16		by	Warwicks	Tonbridge	1913
Highest Innings	For 332	W.H.Ashdown	v	Essex	Brentwood	1934
	V 344	W.G.Grace	for	MCC	Canterbury	1876

Highest Partnership for each Wicket

1st	300	N.R.Taylor/M.R.Benson	v	Derbyshire	Canterbury	1991
2nd	366	S.G.Hinks/N.R.Taylor	v	Middlesex	Canterbury	1990
3rd	323	R.W.T.Key/M.van Jaarsveld	v	Surrey	Tunbridge Wells	2005
4th	368	P.A.de Silva/G.R.Cowdrey	v	Derbyshire	Maidstone	1995
5th	277	F.E.Woolley/L.E.G.Ames	v	N Zealanders	Canterbury	1931
6th	315	P.A.de Silva/M.A.Ealham	v	Notts	Nottingham	1995
7th	248	A.P.Day/E.Humphreys	v	Somerset	Taunton	1908
8th	177	G.O.Jones/Yasir Arafat	v	Warwicks	Canterbury	2007
9th	171	M.A.Ealham/P.A.Strang	v	Notts	Nottingham	1997
10th	235	F.E.Woolley/A.Fielder	v	Worcs	Stourbridge	1909

Best Bowling	For 10- 30	C.Blythe	v	Northants	Northampton	1907
(Innings)	V 10- 48	C.H.G.Bland	for	Sussex	Tonbridge	1899
Best Bowling	For 17- 48	C.Blythe	v	Northants	Northampton	1907
(Match)	V 17-106	T.W.J.Goddard	for	Glos	Bristol	1939

Most Runs – Season	2894	F.E.Woolley	(av 59.06)	1928
Most Runs – Career	47868	F.E.Woolley	(av 41.77)	1906-38
Most 100s – Season	10	F.E.Woolley		1928, 1934
Most 100s – Career	122	F.E.Woolley		1906-38
Most Wkts – Season	262	A.P.Freeman	(av 14.74)	1933
Most Wkts – Career	3340	A.P.Freeman	(av 17.64)	1914-36
Most Career W-K Dismissals	1253	F.H.Huish	(901 ct; 352 st)	1895-1914
Most Career Catches in the Field	773	F.E.Woolley		1906-38

LIMITED-OVERS CRICKET

Highest Total	50ov	384-6		v	Berkshire	Finchampstead	1994
	40ov	337-7		v	Sussex	Canterbury	2013
	T20	217		v	Glos	Gloucester	2010
Lowest Total	50ov	60		v	Somerset	Taunton	1979
	40ov	83		v	Middlesex	Lord's	1984
	T20	72		v	Hampshire	Southampton	2011
Highest Innings	50ov	143	C.J.Tavaré	v	Somerset	Taunton	1985
	40ov	146	A.Symonds	v	Lancashire	Tunbridge Wells	2004
	T20	112	A.Symonds	v	Middlesex	Maidstone	2004
Best Bowling	50ov	8-31	D.L.Underwood	v	Scotland	Edinburgh	1987
	40ov	6- 9	R.A.Woolmer	v	Derbyshire	Chesterfield	1979
	T20	5-17	Wahab Riaz	v	Glos	Beckenham	2011

LANCASHIRE

Formation of Present Club: 12 January 1864
Inaugural First-Class Match: 1865
Colours: Red, Green and Blue
Badge: Red Rose
County Champions (since 1890): (8) 1897, 1904, 1926, 1927, 1928, 1930, 1934, 2011
Joint Champions: (1) 1950
Gillette/NatWest Trophy Winners: (7) 1970, 1971, 1972, 1975, 1990, 1996, 1998
Benson and Hedges Cup Winners: (4) 1984, 1990, 1995, 1996
Pro 40/National League (Div 1) Winners: (1) 1999.
Sunday League Winners: (4) 1969, 1970, 1989, 1998
Twenty20 Cup Winners: (0); best – Finalist 2005

Chief Executive: Daniel Gidney, Emirates Old Trafford, Talbot Road, Manchester M16 0PX • Tel: 0161 282 4000 • Fax: 0161 282 4100 • Email: enquiries@lccc.co.uk • Web: www.lccc.co.uk • Twitter: @LancsCCC (23,683 followers)

Director of Cricket: Mike Watkinson. **Head Coach**: Peter Moores. **Assistant Coach**: Gary Yates. **Captain**: G.Chapple. **Vice-Captain**: none. **Overseas Player**: A.G.Prince. **2014 Beneficiary**: None. **Head Groundsman**: Matthew Merchant. **Scorer**: Alan West. ‡ New registration. NQ Not qualified for England.

AGATHANGELOU, Andrea Peter (Fields C, Rustenburg), b Rustenburg, South Africa 16 Nov 1989. 6'3". RHB, LB. North West 2007-08 to 2010-11. Lions 2008-09. Lancashire debut 2011. HS 158 NW v KZN (Potchefstroom) 2009-10. La HS 121 v Hants (Southampton) 2013. BB 2-18 v Glos (Liverpool) 2013. LO HS 94 NW v EP (Port Elizabeth) 2010-11. LO BB –.

‡ALI, Kabir (Moseley CS and SFC), b Moseley, Birmingham, Warwks 24 Nov 1980. 6'0". Cousin of A.K.Ali (Worcs, Glos 2000-10) and M.M.Ali (see WORCESTERSHIRE). RHB, RMF. Worcestershire 1999-2009. Rajasthan 2006-07. Hampshire 2010-12. Joined Lancashire in 2013, but still awaiting La f-c debut. Tests: 1 (2003); HS 9 and BB 3-80 v SA (Leeds) 2003. LOI: 14 (2003 to 2006); HS 39* v P (Rawalpindi) 2005-06; BB 4-45 v I (Delhi) 2005-06. F-c Tours: WI 2005-06 (Eng A); SL 2002-03 (ECB Acad). HS 84* Wo v Durham (Stockton) 2003. 50 wkts (5); most – 71 (2002). BB 8-50 Wo v Lancs (Manchester) 2007. Took 8-53 before lunch first day Wo v Yorks (Scarborough) 2003. LO HS 92 Wo v Essex (Worcester) 2003 (NL). LO BB 5-36 Wo v Yorks (Leeds) 2002 (NL). T20 HS 50. T20 BB 4-44.

ANDERSON, James Michael (St Theodore RC HS and SFC, Burnley), b Burnley 30 Jul 1982. 6'2". LHB, RFM. Debut (Lancashire) 2002; cap 2003; benefit 2012. YC 2003. Wisden 2008. **ECB central contract 2013-14. Tests:** 92 (2003 to 2013-14); HS 34 v SA (Leeds) 2008; BB 7-43 v NZ (Nottingham) 2008. **LOI:** 174 (2002-03 to 2013); HS 28 v NZ (Southampton) 2013; BB 5-23 v SA (Port Elizabeth) 2009-10. Hat-trick v P (Oval) 2003 – 1st for E in 373 LOI. **IT20:** 19 (2006-07 to 2009-10); HS 1* v A (Sydney) 2006-07; BB 3-23 v Netherlands (Lord's) 2009. F-c Tours: A 2006-07, 2010-11, 2013-14; SA 2004-05, 2009-10; WI 2003-04, 2005-06 (Eng A) (part), 2008-09; NZ 2007-08, 2012-13; I 2005-06 (part), 2008-09, 2012-13; SL 2003-04, 2007-08, 2011-12; UAE 2011-12 (v P). HS 37* v Durham (Manchester) 2006. 50 wkts (2); most – 60 (2005). BB 7-43 (see Tests). La BB 6-23 v Hants (Southampton) 2002. Hat-trick v Essex (Manchester) 2003. LO HS 28 (see LOI). LO BB 5-23 (see LOI). T20 HS 16. T20 BB 3-23.

134

BROWN, Karl Robert (Hesketh Fletcher HS, Atherton), b Bolton 17 May 1988. 5'10". RHB, RMF. Debut (Lancashire) 2006. Moors Sports Club 2011-12. HS 114 v Sussex (Liverpool) 2011. BB 2-30 v Notts (Nottingham) 2009. LO HS 101* v Essex (Manchester) 2011 (CB40). T20 HS 62.

‡**BUTTLER, Jos**eph Charles (King's C, Taunton), b Taunton, Somerset 8 Sep 1990. 6'0". RHB, WK. Somerset 2009-13; cap 2013. Somerset 2nd XI debut 2006. **LOI:** 27 (2011-12 to 2013-14); HS 99 v WI (North Sound) 2013-14. **IT20:** 28 (2011 to 2013-14); HS 54 v NZ (Hamilton) 2012-13. HS 144 Sm v Hants (Southampton) 2010. BB –. LO HS 119 EL v Sri Lanka A (Kurunegala) 2011-12. T20 HS 72*.

CHAPPLE, Glen (West Craven HS; Nelson & Colne C), b Skipton, Yorks 23 Jan 1974. 6'1". RHB, RMF. Debut (Lancashire) 1992; cap 1994; benefit 2004; captain 2009 to date. *Wisden* 2011. **LOI:** 1 (2006); HS 14 and BB – v Ireland (Belfast) 2006. F-c Tours (Eng A): A 1996-97; WI 1995-96 (La); I 1994-95. HS 155 v Somerset (Manchester) 2001. Scored 100 off 27 balls in contrived circumstances v Glamorgan (Manchester) 1993. 50 wkts (7); most – 57 (2011). BB 7-53 v Durham (Blackpool) 2007. LO HS 81* v Derbys (Manchester) 2002 (CGT). LO BB 6-18 v Essex (Lord's) 1996 (NWT) – La record. T20 HS 55*. T20 BB 3-36.

CLARK, Jordan (Sedbergh S), b Whitehaven, Cumbria 14 Oct 1990. 6'4". RHB, RM, occ WK. Awaiting f-c debut. Lancashire 2nd XI debut 2008. Cumberland 2007-08. LO HS 72 v Durham (Chester-le-St) 2013 (Y40). LO BB 2-45 v Surrey (Guildford) 2013 (Y40). T20 HS 38. T20 BB –.

CROFT, Steven John (Highfield HS, Blackpool; Myerscough C), b Blackpool 11 Oct 1984. 5'10". RHB, RMF. Debut (Lancashire) 2005; cap 2010. Auckland 2008-09. HS 154* v Surrey (Guildford) 2012. BB 6-41 v Worcs (Manchester) 2012. LO HS 107 v Somerset (Taunton) 2011 (CB40). LO BB 4-24 v Scotland (Manchester) 2008 (FPT). T20 HS 88. T20 BB 3-6.

DAVIES, Alexander Luke (Queen Elizabeth GS, Blackburn), b Darwen 23 Aug 1994. 5'7". RHB, WK. Debut (Lancashire) 2012, without batting or bowling. Lancashire 2nd XI debut 2011. HS 30* v Leics (Manchester) 2013. LO HS 13 v Bangladesh A (Manchester) 2013.

GRIFFITHS, Gavin Timothy (St Mary's C, Crosby), b Ormskirk 19 Nov 1993. 6'2". RHB, RFM. Lancashire 2nd XI debut 2011. Awaiting 1st XI debut. England U19s 2012-13.

HOGG, Kyle William (Saddleworth HS), b Birmingham, Warwks 2 Jul 1983. Son of W.Hogg (Lancashire, Warwickshire 1976-83); grandson of S.Ramadhin (Trinidad, Lancashire and West Indies 1949-50 to 1965). 6'4". LHB, RFM. Debut (Lancashire) 2001; cap 2010. Otago 2006-07. Worcestershire 2007 (on loan). Nottinghamshire 2007 (on loan). F-c Tour (ECB Acad): SL 2002-03. HS 88 v Yorks (Manchester) 2010. 50 wkts (2); most – 60 (2013). BB 7-27 v Northants (Manchester) 2013. LO HS 66* v Scotland (Manchester) 2008 (FPT). LO BB 4-20 v Hants (Southampton) 2002 (NL). T20 HS 44. T20 BB 2-10.

HORTON, Paul James (St Margaret's HS, Liverpool), b Sydney, Australia 20 Sep 1982. 5'10". RHB, RM. UK resident since 1997. Debut (Lancashire) 2003; cap 2007. Matabeleland Tuskers 2010-11 to 2011-12. 1000 runs (3); most – 1116 (2007). HS 209 MT v SR (Masvingo) 2010-11. La HS 173 v Somerset (Taunton) 2009. LO HS 111* v Derbys (Manchester) 2009 (FPT). T20 HS 71.

NQJARVIS, Kyle Malcolm (St John's C, Harare), b Harare, Zimbabwe 16 Feb 1989. Son of M.P.Jarvis (Zimbabwe 1979-80 to 1994-95). 6'4". RHB, RFM. Mashonaland Eagles 2009-10 to 2012-13. C Districts 2011-12 to 2012-13. Lancashire debut 2013 (one game). **Tests** (Z): 8 (2011 to 2013); HS 25* v P (Bulawayo) 2011; BB 5-54 v WI (Bridgetown) 2012-13. **LOI** (Z): 24 (2009-10 to 2013); HS 13 v SA (Centurion) 2009-10; BB 3-36 v Kenya (Harare) 2009-10. **IT20** (Z): 9 (2011 to 2012-13); HS 9* v SA (Hambantota) 2012-13; BB 3-15 v P (Harare) 2011. F-c Tour (Z): WI 2012-13. HS 48 ME v MWR (Harare) 2012-13. La HS 3* and La BB 3-72 v Kent (Canterbury) 2013. BB 7-35 ME v MT (Bulawayo) 2012-13. LO HS 13 (*see LOI*). LO BB 4-35 ME v Mountaineers (Mutare) 2011-12. T20 HS 10. T20 BB 3-15.

KERRIGAN, Simon Christopher (Corpus Christi RC HS, Preston), b Preston 10 May 1989. 5'9". RHB, SLA. Debut (Lancashire) 2010; cap 2013. MCC 2013. **Tests**: 1 (2013); HS 1* and BB – v A (Oval) 2013. F-c Tour (EL): SL 2013-14. HS 62* v Hants (Southport) 2013. 50 wkts (2); most – 58 (2013). BB 9-51 (12-192 match) v Hants (Liverpool) 2011. LO HS 10 v Middx (Lord's) 2012 (CB40). LO BB 3-21 EL v Sri Lanka A (Northampton) 2011. T20 HS 4*. T20 BB 3-17.

LILLEY, Arron Mark (Mossley Hollins HS; Ashton SFC), b Tameside 1 Apr 1991. 6'1". RHB, OB. Debut (Lancashire) 2013. Lancashire 2nd XI debut 2010. HS 35* v Glamorgan (Manchester) 2013. BB 1-41 v Worcs (Worcester) 2013. LO HS 10 v Hants (Manchester) 2013 (Y40). LO BB 4-30 v Derbys (Manchester) 2013 (Y40). T20 HS 18. T20 BB 1-21.

LIVINGSTONE, Liam Stephen (Chetwynde S, Barrow-in-Furness), b Barrow-in-Furness, Cumberland 4 Aug 1993. RHB, LB. Lancashire 2nd XI debut 2012. Cumberland 2011. Awaiting 1st XI debut.

NEWBY, Oliver James (Ribblesdale HS; Myerscough C), b Blackburn 26 Aug 1984. 6'5". RHB, RMF. Debut (Lancashire) 2003. Nottinghamshire 2005 (on loan). Gloucestershire (on loan) 2008; cap 2008. No f-c appearances in 2010. HS 38* Nt v Kent (Nottingham) 2005 – on Notts debut. La HS 29* v Oxford MCCU (Oxford) 2011. BB 5-69 Gs v Northants (Bristol) 2008. La BB 4-21 v Durham MCCU (Durham) 2009. LO HS 36* v Glos (Bristol) 2012 (CB40). LO BB 5-35 v Essex (Chelmsford) 2012 (CB40). T20 HS 6*. T20 BB 2-34.

PARRY, Stephen David (Audenshaw HS), b Manchester 12 Jan 1986. 5'11". RHB, SLA. Debut (Lancashire) 2007, taking 5-23 v Durham U (Durham). No 1st XI appearances in 2008. Cumberland 2005-06. **LOI**: 2 (2013-14); HS – ; BB 3-32 v WI (North Sound) 2013-14. HS 20 and CC BB 3-51 v Kent (Canterbury) 2013. BB 5-23 (*see above*). LO HS 31 v Essex (Chelmsford) 2009 (FPT). LO BB 5-17 v Surrey (Manchester) 2013 (Y40). T20 HS 11. T20 BB 4-23.

NQPRINCE, Ashwell Gavin (St Thomas Senior SS, UPE), b Port Elizabeth, South Africa, 28 May 1977. LHB, OB. E Province 1995-96 to 1997-98. W Province 1997-98 to 2003-04. W Province-Boland 2004-05. Cape Cobras 2005-06 to 2007-08. Nottinghamshire 2008. Warriors 2008-09 to date. Lancashire debut 2009; cap 2010. **Tests** (SA): 66 (2001-02 to 2011-12, 2 as captain); HS 162* v B (Centurion) 2008-09; BB 1-2 v NZ (Cape Town) 2006. **LOI** (SA): 52 (2002-03 to 2007); HS 89* v WI (Port of Spain) 2005; BB – . **IT20** (SA): 1 (2005-06); HS 5 v NZ (Johannesburg) 2005. F-c Tours (SA): E 2008; A 2005-06; WI 2000 (SA A), 2005, 2010; I 2007-08, 2009-10; P 2007-08; SL 2006; Z 2007 (SA A); B 2007-08; UAE 2010-11 (v P). 1000 runs (2+1): 1180 (2008-09). HS 254 Warriors v Titans (Centurion) 2008-09. La HS 144 v Middx (Liverpool) 2012. BB 2-11 SA v Middx (Uxbridge) 2008. CC BB –. LO HS 128 Warriors v Dolphins (East London) 2009-10. LO BB –. T20 HS 74. T20 BB –.

PROCTER, Luke Anthony (Counthill S, Oldham), b Oldham 24 June 1988. 5'11". LHB, RM. Debut (Lancashire) 2010. Cumberland 2007. HS 106 v Glos (Bristol) 2013. BB 7-71 v Surrey (Liverpool) 2012. LO HS 97 v West Indies A (Manchester) 2010. LO BB 3-29 v Unicorns (Colwyn Bay) 2010 (CB40). T20 HS 25*. T20 BB 3-22.

REECE, Luis Michael (St Michael's HS, Chorley; Leeds Met U), b Taunton, Somerset 4 Aug 1990. 6'1". LHB, LM. Leeds/Bradford MCCU 2012-13. Lancashire debut 2013. Lancashire 2nd XI debut 2008. Unicorns 2011-12. HS 114* and BB 4-28 LBU v Leics (Leicester) 2013. La HS 97 v Glos (Bristol) 2013. La BB 1-20 v Hants (Southport) 2013. LO HS 59 Unicorns v Derbys (Chesterfield) 2012 (CB40). LO BB 4-35 Unicorns v Glos (Exmouth) 2011 (CB40).

SMITH, Thomas Christopher (Parkland HS, Chorley; Runshaw C, Leyland), b Liverpool 26 Dec 1985. 6'3". LHB, RMF. Debut (Lancashire) 2005; cap 2010. Leicestershire (on loan) 2008. F-c Tour (Eng A): B 2006-07. HS 128 v Hants (Southampton) 2010. BB 6-46 v Yorks (Manchester) 2009. LO HS 117 and LO BB 4-48 v Notts (Nottingham) 2011 (CB40). T20 HS 92*. T20 BB 3-12.

WHITE, Wayne Andrew (John Port S, Etwall; Nottingham Trent U), b Derby 22 Apr 1985. 6'2". RHB, RMF. Derbyshire 2005-08. Leicestershire 2009-12; cap 2012. Lancashire debut 2013. HS 101* Le v Derbys (Derby) 2010. Scored 50* in 12 balls in contrived circumstances for Le v Essex (Leicester) 2012. La HS 61 v Glos (Liverpool) 2013. La BB 5-54 Le v Derbys (Derby) 2012. La BB 2-69 v Worcs (Manchester) 2013. LO HS 46* Le v Glamorgan (Leicester) 2009 (P40). LO BB 6-29 Le v Notts (Leics) 2010 (CB40). T20 HS 26. T20 BB 3-27.

RELEASED/RETIRED

(Having made a County First-Class or List A appearance in 2013)

CROSS, Gareth David (Moorside S; Eccles C), b Bury 20 Jun 1984. 5'9". RHB, WK, occ RMF. Lancashire 2005-13. No f-c appearances in 2009. HS 125 v Sussex (Hove) 2011. LO HS 76 v Warwks (Birmingham) 2007 (P40). LO BB 2-26 v Durham (Chester-le-St) 2008 (FPT). T20 HS 65*.

NQ**KATICH, Simon** Mathew (Trinity C, WA; U of WA), b Middle Swan, Midland, W Australia 21 Aug 1975. 6'0". LHB, SLC. W Australia 1996-97 to 2001-02. Durham 2000; cap 2000. Yorkshire (1 match) 2002. NSW 2002-03 to 2011-12. Hampshire 2003-05, 2012; cap 2003. Derbyshire 2007; cap/captain 2007. Lancashire 2010, 2013; cap 2013. **Tests** (A): 56 (2001 to 2010-11); HS 157 v WI (Bridgetown) 2008; BB 6-65 v Z (Sydney) 2003-04. **LOI** (A): 45 (2000-01 to 2006-07); HS 107* v SL (Brisbane) 2005-06. **IT20** (A): 3 (2004-05 to 2005-06); HS 39 v SA (Johannesburg) 2005-06. F-c Tours (A): E 2001, 2005, 2009, 2010 (v P); SA 2008-09; WI 2008; NZ 2004-05, 2009-10; I 2004-05, 2008-09 (Aus A), 2008-09, 2010-11; SL 1999-00, 2003-04. 1000 runs (4+4); most – 1506 (2007-08). HS 306 NSW v Q (Sydney) 2007-08. UK HS 221 De v Somerset (Taunton) 2007. La HS 200 v Northants (Northampton) 2013. BB 7-130 NSW v Vic (Melbourne) 2002-03. UK BB 4-21 H v Northants (Southampton) 2003. LO HS 136* NSW v Vic (Bowral) 2003-04. LO BB 3-21 Aus A v SA (Adelaide) 2001-02. T20 HS 75.

MOORE, S.C. – *see DERBYSHIRE*.

M.J.McClenaghan left the staff, without making a County First-Class or List A appearance in 2013.

LANCASHIRE 2013

RESULTS SUMMARY

	Place	Won	Lost	Tied	Drew	NR
LV= County Championship (2nd Division)	1st	8	1		7	
All First-Class Matches		8	1		7	
Yorkshire Bank 40 (Group B)	3rd	7	4			1
Friends Life t20 (North Group)	QF	5	4	2		

LV= COUNTY CHAMPIONSHIP AVERAGES

BATTING AND FIELDING

Cap		M	I	NO	HS	Runs	Avge	100	50	Ct/St
2013	S.M.Katich	12	16	1	200	1097	73.13	4	6	7
	L.M.Reece	10	16	3	97	722	55.53	–	8	8
2010	A.G.Prince	16	26	2	134	1169	48.70	3	7	16
2010	T.C.Smith	7	8	2	88	289	48.16	–	2	9
2007	P.J.Horton	10	16	–	156	645	40.31	3	3	1
2010	S.J.Croft	8	13	3	101*	379	37.90	1	2	4
	A.P.Agathangelou	11	16	2	121	497	35.50	1	2	24
	L.A.Procter	15	21	–	106	718	34.19	1	7	5
	K.R.Brown	10	16	–	87	428	26.75	–	3	8
2013	S.C.Kerrigan	13	11	5	62*	146	24.33	–	1	3
	G.D.Cross	13	17	–	100	409	24.05	1	2	35/2
1994	G.Chapple	14	16	3	63	308	23.69	–	3	9
	W.A.White	6	9	3	61	133	22.16	–	1	2
2010	K.W.Hogg	15	16	5	58	241	21.90	–	1	2
2011	S.C.Moore	2	4	–	34	81	20.25	–	–	–

Also batted: J.M.Anderson (2 matches – cap 2003) 26, 11*, 0 (1 ct); A.L.Davies (3) 30*, 12, 16 (3 ct); K.M.Jarvis (1) 3* (1 ct); A.M.Lilley (2) 35*, 4*; O.J.Newby (3) 9*, 1; S.D.Parry (3) 5*, 12, 20.

BOWLING

	O	M	R	W	Avge	Best	5wI	10wM
K.W.Hogg	436	105	1105	60	18.41	7-27	3	–
G.Chapple	430.4	110	1099	53	20.73	5- 9	2	–
S.C.Kerrigan	461.2	108	1191	57	20.89	7-63	5	1
O.J.Newby	68.2	12	264	12	22.00	4-71	–	–
T.C.Smith	150.5	35	498	22	22.63	4-49	–	–
L.A.Procter	194	31	633	15	42.20	4-39	–	–
Also bowled:								
J.M.Anderson	72.1	20	180	8	22.50	4-57	–	–
S.D.Parry	65.3	5	197	5	39.40	3-51	–	–
W.A.White	131	16	452	8	56.50	2-69	–	–

A.P.Agathangelou 43-12-125-3; S.J.Croft 41-6-132-1; K.M.Jarvis 34-1-179-4; A.M.Lilley 69-9-212-2; L.M.Reece 22-2-89-2.

Lancashire played no first-class fixtures outside the County Championship in 2013. The First-Class Averages (pp 225–241) give the records of their players in all first-class county matches, with the exception of J.M.Anderson, S.C.Kerrigan and L.M.Reece, whose first-class figures for Lancashire are as above.

LANCASHIRE RECORDS

FIRST-CLASS CRICKET

Highest Total	For 863		v	Surrey	The Oval	1990
	V 707-9d		by	Surrey	The Oval	1990
Lowest Total	For 25		v	Derbyshire	Manchester	1871
	V 20		by	Essex	Chelmsford	2013
Highest Innings	For 424	A.C.MacLaren	v	Somerset	Taunton	1895
	V 315*	T.W.Hayward	for	Surrey	The Oval	1898

Highest Partnership for each Wicket

1st	368	A.C.MacLaren/R.H.Spooner	v	Glos	Liverpool	1903
2nd	371	F.B.Watson/G.E.Tyldesley	v	Surrey	Manchester	1928
3rd	364	M.A.Atherton/N.H.Fairbrother	v	Surrey	The Oval	1990
4th	358	S.P.Titchard/G.D.Lloyd	v	Essex	Chelmsford	1996
5th	360	S.G.Law/C.L.Hooper	v	Warwicks	Birmingham	2003
6th	278	J.Iddon/H.R.W.Butterworth	v	Sussex	Manchester	1932
7th	248	G.D.Lloyd/I.D.Austin	v	Yorkshire	Leeds	1997
8th	158	J.Lyon/R.M.Ratcliffe	v	Warwicks	Manchester	1979
9th	142	L.O.S.Poidevin/A.Kermode	v	Sussex	Eastbourne	1907
10th	173	J.Briggs/R.Pilling	v	Surrey	Liverpool	1885

Best Bowling	For 10-46	W.Hickton	v	Hampshire	Manchester	1870
(Innings)	V 10-40	G.O.B.Allen	for	Middlesex	Lord's	1929
Best Bowling	For 17-91	H.Dean	v	Yorkshire	Liverpool	1913
(Match)	V 16-65	G.Giffen	for	Australians	Manchester	1886

Most Runs – Season	2633	J.T.Tyldesley	(av 56.02)		1901
Most Runs – Career	34222	G.E.Tyldesley	(av 45.20)		1909-36
Most 100s – Season	11	C.Hallows			1928
Most 100s – Career	90	G.E.Tyldesley			1909-36
Most Wkts – Season	198	E.A.McDonald	(av 18.55)		1925
Most Wkts – Career	1816	J.B.Statham	(av 15.12)		1950-68
Most Career W-K Dismissals	925	G.Duckworth	(635 ct; 290 st)		1923-38
Most Career Catches in the Field	556	K.J.Grieves			1949-64

LIMITED-OVERS CRICKET

Highest Total	50ov	381-3	v	Herts	Radlett	1999
	40ov	324-4	v	Worcs	Worcester	2012
	T20	220-5	v	Derbyshire	Derby	2009
Lowest Total	50ov	59	v	Worcs	Worcester	1963
	40ov	68	v	Yorkshire	Leeds	2000
		68	v	Surrey	The Oval	2002
	T20	91	v	Derbyshire	Manchester	2003
Highest Innings	50ov	162* A.R.Crook	v	Bucks	Wormsley	2005
	40ov	143 A.Flintoff	v	Essex	Chelmsford	1999
	T20	102* L.Vincent	v	Derbyshire	Manchester	2008
Best Bowling	50ov	6-10 C.E.H.Croft	v	Scotland	Manchester	1982
	40ov	6-25 G.Chapple	v	Yorkshire	Leeds	1998
	T20	5-29 M.J.McClenaghan	v	Notts	Manchester	2013

LEICESTERSHIRE

Formation of Present Club: 25 March 1879
Inaugural First-Class Match: 1894
Colours: Dark Green and Scarlet
Badge: Gold Running Fox on Green Ground
County Champions: (3) 1975, 1996, 1998
Benson and Hedges Cup Winners: (3) 1972, 1975, 1985
Sunday League Champions: (2) 1974, 1977
Twenty20 Cup Winners: (3) 2004, 2006, 2011

Chief Executive: Mike Siddall, County Ground, Grace Road, Leicester LE2 8AD • Tel: 0871 282 1879 • Fax: 0871 282 1873 • Email: enquiries@leicestershireccc.co.uk • Web: www.leicestershireccc.co.uk • Twitter: @leicsccc (8,559 followers)

Director of Cricket: Phil Whitticase. **1st XI Coach**: Ben Smith. **Captain**: R.R.Sarwan (f-c) and J.J.Cobb (l-o). **Vice-Captain**: None. **Overseas Player**: R.R.Sarwan. **2014 Beneficiary**: None. **Head Groundsman**: Andrew Ward. **Scorer**: Paul J.Rogers. ‡ New registration. ^{NQ} Not qualified for England.

BOYCE, Matthew Andrew Golding (Oakham S; Nottingham U), b Cheltenham, Glos 13 Aug 1985. 5'9". LHB, RM. Debut (Leicestershire) 2006; cap 2013. HS 135 v Kent (Leicester) 2013. BB –. LO HS 80 v Hants (Leicester) 2009 (FPT). T20 HS 63*.

BUCK, Nathan Liam (Newbridge HS; Ashby S), b Leicester 26 Apr 1991. 6'2" RHB, RMF. Debut (Leicestershire) 2009; cap 2011. Leicestershire 2nd XI debut 2008. England U19s 2009 to 2009-10. F-c Tour (EL): WI 2010-11. HS 27 v Kent (Canterbury) 2012. BB 5-99 v Glos (Bristol) 2011. LO HS 21 v Glamorgan (Leicester) 2009 (P40). LO BB 4-39 EL v Sri Lanka A (Dambulla) 2011-12. T20 HS 8*. T20 BB 3-16.

COBB, Joshua James (Oakham S), b Leicester 17 Aug 1990. Son of R.A.Cobb (Leics and N Transvaal 1980-89). 5'11½". RHB, LB. Debut (Leicestershire) 2007; l-o captain 2014. Leicestershire 2nd XI debut 2006, aged 16y 5d. England U19s 2008. HS 148* v Middx (Lord's) 2008. BB 2-11 v Glos (Leicester) 2008. LO HS 137 v Lancs (Manchester) 2012 (CB40). LO BB 3-34 v Glos (Leicester) 2013 (Y40). T20 HS 67*. T20 BB 4-22.

ECKERSLEY, Edmund John Holden ('Ned') (St Benedict's GS, Ealing), b Oxford 9 Aug 1989. 6'0". RHB, WK, occ OB. Debut (Leicestershire) 2011; cap 2013. Mountaineers 2011-12. MCC 2013. Middlesex 2nd XI 2008. Northamptonshire 2nd XI 2010. 1000 runs (1): 1302 (2013). HS 147 v Essex (Chelmsford) 2013. BB 2-29 v Lancs (Manchester) 2013. LO HS 108 v Yorks (Leicester) 2013 (Y40). T20 HS 42.

FRECKINGHAM, Oliver Henry (K Edward S, Melton Mowbray), b Oakham, Rutland 12 Nov 1988. RHB, RMF. Debut (Leicestershire) 2013. Leicestershire 2nd XI debut 2010. HS 30 v Glos (Bristol) 2013. BB 6-125 v Northants (Northampton) 2013.

^{NQ}**IRELAND, Anthony** John (Plumtree HS), b Masvingo, Zimbabwe 30 Aug 1984. 6'2". RHB, RM. Midlands 2002-03 to 2004-05. Gloucestershire 2007-10, 2012; cap 2007. Middlesex 2011. Leicestershire debut 2013. Kolpak registration. **LOI** (Z): 26 (2005-06 to 2006-07); HS 8* v K (Bulawayo) 2005-06; BB 3-41 v B (Harare) (twice) – 2006 and 2006-07. **IT20** (Z): 1 (2006-07); HS 2* and BB 1-33 v B (Khulna) 2006-07. HS 29 M v Essex (Chelmsford) 2011. Le HS 15* and Le BB 1-83 v Glamorgan (Leicester) 2013. BB 7-36 Zimbabwe A v Bangladesh A (Mirpur) 2006-07. CC BB 6-31 Gs v Leics (Bristol) 2009. LO HS 27 v Somerset (Taunton) 2013 (Y40). LO BB 4-16 Zimbabwe A v Kenya (Harare) 2005-06. T20 HS 23. T20 BB 4-11.

NAIK, Jigar Kumar Hakumatrai (Rushey Mead SS; Gateway SFC; Nottingham Trent U; Loughborough U), b Leicester 10 Aug 1984. 6'2". RHB, OB. Debut (Leicestershire) 2006; cap 2013. Loughborough UCCE 2007. Colombo CC 2010-11. HS 109* v Derbys (Leicester) 2009. BB 7-96 v Surrey (Oval) 2010. LO HS 22* v Yorks (Scarborough) 2013 (Y40). LO BB 3-21 v Lancs (Leicester) 2009 (P40). T20 HS 7*. T20 BB 3-3.

O'BRIEN, Niall John (Marian C, Dublin), b Dublin, Ireland 8 Nov 1981. Son of B.A.O'Brien (Ireland 1966-81); elder brother of K.J.O'Brien (Nottinghamshire and Ireland 2006-07 to date). 5'6". LHB, WK. Kent 2004-06. Ireland 2005-06 to date. Northamptonshire 2007-12; cap 2011. Leicestershire debut 2013. MCC 2012. **LOI** (Ire): 59 (2006 to 2013-14); HS 72 v P (Kingston) 2006-07 and 72 v Scotland (Belfast) 2007. **IT20** (Ire): 21 (2008 to 2013-14); HS 50 v Canada (Colombo, SSC) 2009-10. HS 182 Nh v Glamorgan (Cardiff) 2012. Le HS 67 v Essex (Leicester) 2013. BB 1-4 K v Cambridge UCCE (Cambridge) 2006. LO HS 121 Nh v Hants (Southampton) 2011 (CB40). T20 HS 84.

RAINE, Benjamin Alexander (St Aidan's RC SS, Sunderland) b Sunderland, Co Durham 14 Sep 1991. 6'0". LHB, RM. Durham 2011. Leicestershire debut 2013. Durham 2nd XI debut 2010. HS 72 v Lancs (Manchester) 2013. BB 4-98 v Glamorgan (Swansea) 2013. LO HS 7 v Middx (Lord's) 2013 (Y40). LO BB 2-59 v Glamorgan (Swansea) 2013 (Y40).

REDFERN, Daniel James (Adam's GS, Newport, Shropshire), b Shrewsbury, Shropshire 18 Apr 1990. 5'9". LHB, OB. Derbyshire 2007-13; cap 2012. HS 133 De v Hants (Southampton) 2008. BB 3-33 De v Durham (Chester-le-St) 2013. LO HS 57* De v Yorks (Derby) 2007 (P40). LO BB 2-10 De v Kent (Chesterfield) 2009 (P40). T20 HS 43. T20 BB 2-17.

ROBSON, Angus James (Marcellin C, Randwick; Australian C of PE), b Darlinghurst, Sydney, Australia 19 Feb 1992. Younger brother of S.D.Robson (*see MIDDLESEX*). 5'9". RHB, LB. Debut (Leicestershire) 2013. Leicestershire 2nd XI debut 2012. HS 49 v Glos (Bristol) 2013. BB –.

[NQ]**SARWAN, Ramnaresh** Ronnie (North Gromuel S), b Wakenaam Island, Essequibo, Guyana 23 Jun 1980. 5'7½". RHB, LB. Guyana 1995-96 to date (youngest to play f-c cricket in WI). Gloucestershire 2005; cap 2005. Leicestershire debut 2012; captain 2013 to date. **Tests** (WI): 87 (2000 to 2011); HS 291 v E (Bridgetown) 2008-09; BB 4-37 v B (St Lucia) 2004. **LOI** (WI): 181 (2000 to 2013); HS 120* v Z (St George's) 2012-13; BB 3-31 v NZ (Lord's) 2004. **IT20** (WI): 18 (2007 to 2010); HS 59 v E (Port of Spain) 2008-09; BB 2-10 v B (Johannesburg) 2007. F-c Tours (WI): E 2000, 2004, 2007, 2009; A 2000-01, 2005-06, 2009-10; SA 2003-04; NZ 2005-06, 2008-09; I 2002-03; P 2006-07; SL 2001-02; Z 2001, 2003-04; B 2002-03. HS 291 (*see Tests*). CC HS 117 Gs v Sussex (Hove) 2005 and 117 v Essex (Leicester) 2012. BB 6-62 Guyana v Leeward Is (Antigua) 2000-01. CC BB 2-38 Gs v Glamorgan (Bristol) 2005. Le BB –. LO HS 120* (*see LOI*). LO BB 5-10 Guyana v Bermuda (Hampton Court) 1998-99. T20 HS 70. T20 BB 2-10.

SAYER, Robert John, b Huntingdon, Cambridgeshire 25 Jan 1995. RHB, OB. Leicestershire 2nd XI debut 2013. Cambridgeshire 2013. Summer contract for 2014, awaiting 1st XI debut.

‡**SHRECK, Charles** Edward (Truro S), b Truro, Cornwall 6 Jan 1978. 6'7". RHB, RFM. Nottinghamshire 2003-11; cap 2006. Wellington 2005-06 to 2007-08. Kent 2012-13. MCC 2008. Cornwall 1997-2002. HS 19* K v Glamorgan (Canterbury) 2013. 50 wkts (3); most – 61 (2006, 2008). BB 8-31 (12-129 match) Nt v Middx (Nottingham) 2006. Hat-trick Nt v Middx (Lord's) 2006. LO HS 9* Wellington v CD (Palmerston N) 2005-06. LO BB 5-19 Cornwall v Worcs (Truro) 2002 (CGT). T20 HS 6*. T20 BB 4-22.

SMITH, Gregory Philip (Oundle S; St Hild & St Bede C, Durham U), b Leicester 16 Nov 1988. 6'0". RHB, LBG. Debut (Leicestershire) 2008. Durham MCCU 2009-11. Badureliya 2013-14. HS 158* v Glos (Leicester) 2010. BB 1-64 v Glos (Leicester) 2008. LO HS 135* v Somerset (Leicester) 2013 (Y40). T20 HS 84.

SYKES, James Stuart (St Ives S, Huntingdon), b Hinchingbrooke, Cambs 26 Apr 1992. 6'2". LHB, SLA. Debut (Leicestershire) 2013. Leicestershire 2nd XI debut 2009. Cambridgeshire 2010. HS 34 v Lancs (Manchester) 2013. BB 4-176 v Essex (Chelmsford) 2013 – on debut. LO HS 15 v Glos (Bristol) 2013 (Y40). LO BB 3-39 v Netherlands (Amstelveen) 2012 (CB40). T20 HS 2*. T20 BB 2-24.

TAYLOR, Robert Meadows Lombe (Harrow S; Loughborough U), b Northampton 21 Dec 1989. 6'3". LHB, LMF. Loughborough MCCU 2010-12. Leicestershire debut 2011. Leicestershire 2nd XI debut 2008. Northamptonshire 2nd XI 2010. LOI (Scot): 8 (2012-13 to 2013-14); HS 46* v Kenya (Christchurch) 2013-14; BB 3-39 v Kenya (Aberdeen) 2013. IT20 (Scot): 4 (2013-14); HS 41* and BB 1-16 v Netherlands (Dubai) 2013-14. HS 101* LU v Leics (Leicester) 2011. Le HS 70 v Surrey (Leicester) 2011. BB 5-91 v Kent (Leicester) 2012. LO HS 48* v Yorks (Scarborough) 2013 (Y40). LO BB 3-39 (see LOI). T20 HS 41*. T20 BB 4-11.

THAKOR, Shivsinh Jaysinh (Loughborough GS; Uppingham S), b Leicester 22 Oct 1993. 6'1". RHB, RM. Debut (Leicestershire) 2011. Leicestershire 2nd XI debut 2008, aged 14y 218d. England U19s 2010-11. HS 134 v Loughborough MCCU (Leicester) 2011 – on debut. CC HS 114 v Kent (Leicester) 2013. BB 3-57 v Surrey (Leicester) 2011. LO HS 83* v Lancs (Leicester) 2012 (CB40). LO BB 3-39 v Yorks (Scarborough) 2013 (Y40). T20 HS 42. T20 BB 3-30.

THORNELY, Michael Alistair (Brighton C), b Camden, London 19 Oct 1987. 6'1". RHB, RM. Sussex 2007-10. Mashonaland Eagles 2011-12. Leicestershire debut 2012, scoring 97 and 131 v Glamorgan (Cardiff). HS 131 (see above). BB 2-14 v Worcs (Hove) 2010. Le BB 2-29 v Glos (Cheltenham) 2012. LO HS 105* Unicorns v Somerset (Taunton) 2011 (CB40). LO BB 1-20 v Australians (Leicester) 2012. T20 HS 20. T20 BB –.

WELLS, Thomas Joshua (Gartree HS; Beauchamp C, Leicester), b Grantham, Lincs 15 Mar 1993. Father, John Wells, played rugby for Leicester. 6'2". RHB, RMF. Debut (Leicestershire) 2013. Leicestershire 2nd XI debut 2010. HS 82 v Hants (Leicester) 2013. BB 1-36 v Lancs (Leicester) 2013. LO HS 32* v Glamorgan (Swansea) 2013 (Y40). T20 HS 4.

WYATT, Alexander Charles Frederick (Oakham S), b Roehampton 23 Jul 1990. 6'7". RHB, RMF. Debut (Leicestershire) 2009. Leicestershire 2nd XI debut 2007. HS 28 v Glamorgan (Swansea) 2013. BB 3-35 v Hants (Leicester) 2012 and v Essex (Leicester) 2013. LO HS 9* v Netherlands (Leicester) 2012 (CB40). LO BB 2-36 v Durham (Leicester) 2011 (CB40). T20 HS 0*. T20 BB –.

RELEASED/RETIRED

(Having made a County First-Class or List A appearance in 2013)

[NQ]**BURNS, Joseph** Antony, b Herston, Brisbane, Australia 6 Sep 1989. RHB, RM. Queensland 2010-11 to date. Leicestershire 2013. F-c Tour (Aus A): E 2012. HS 140* Q v S Australia (Adelaide) 2010-11 – on debut. Le HS 77 v Northants (Leicester) 2013. LO HS 114 Aus A v EL (Hobart) 2012-13. T20 HS 81*.

142

HENDERSON, Claude William (Worcester HS), b Worcester, Cape Province, South Africa 14 Jun 1972. Elder brother of J.M.Henderson (Boland, Transvaal, North West, Free State and Eagles 1994-95 to 2005-06. 6'1½". RHB, SLA. Boland 1990-91 to 1997-98. W Province 1998-99 to 2003-04. Leicestershire 2004-13; cap 2004 (the first Kolpak registration); benefit 2011. Lions 2006-07 to 2007-08. Cape Cobras 2008-09 to 2010-11. **Tests** (SA): 7 (2001-02 to 2002-03); HS 30 and BB 4-116 v A (Adelaide) 2001-02. **LOI** (SA): 4 (2001-02); HS – ; BB 4-17 v Z (Harare) 2001-02. F-c Tours (SA): A 2001-02; SL 1998 (SA A); Z 2001-02. HS 81 v Glos (Leicester) 2007. 50 wkts (1): 56 (2010). BB 7-57 Boland v EP (Paarl) 1994-95. Le BB 7-74 v Durham (Leicester) 2004. LO HS 45 Lions v Eagles (Johannesburg) 2006-07. LO BB 6-29 Boland v Easterns (Paarl) 1997-98. T20 HS 32. T20 BB 3-23.

HOGGARD, Matthew James (Grangefield S, Pudsey), b Leeds, Yorks 31 Dec 1976. 6'2". RHB, RMF. Yorkshire 1996-2009; benefit 2008. Free State 1998-99 to 1999-00. Leicestershire 2010-13; cap 2010; captain 2010-12. MCC 2004-07. MBE 2005. *Wisden* 2005. **Tests**: 67 (2000 to 2007-08); HS 38 v WI (Oval) 2004; BB 7-61 (12-205 match) v SA (Johannesburg) 2004-05; hat-trick v WI (Bridgetown) 2003-04. **LOI**: 26 (2001-02 to 2005-06); HS 7 v I (Cochin) 2005-06; BB 5-49 v Z (Harare) 2001-02. F-c Tours: A 2002-03, 2006-07; SA 2004-05; WI 2003-04; NZ 2001-02, 2007-08; I 2001-02, 2005-06; P 2000-01, 2005-06; SL 2000-01, 2003-04, 2007-08; B 2003-04. HS 89* Y v Glamorgan (Leeds) 2004. Le HS 28 v Essex (Chelmsford) 2012. 50 wkts (3); most – 50 (2000, 2005, 2010). BB 7-49 Y v Somerset (Leeds) 2003. Le BB 6-63 v Middx (Lord's) 2010. Hat-tricks (3): (*see Tests*) and Y v Sussex (Hove) 2009; v Glamorgan (Leicester) 2011. LO HS 23 v Surrey (Oval) 2011 (CB40). LO BB 5-28 Y v Leics (Leicester) 2000 (NL). T20 HS 18. T20 BB 3-19.

WILLIAMS, Robert Edward Morgan (Marlborough C; St Mary's C, Durham U), b Pembury, Kent 19 Jan 1987. 6'0". RHB, RMF. Durham UCCE 2007-09. Middlesex 2007. Leicestershire 2013. MCC 2007. HS 31 DU v Lancs (Durham) 2009. Le HS 13* v Leeds/Bradford MCCU (Leicester) 2013. CC HS 15 and CC BB 5-112 M v Essex (Chelmsford) 2007. BB 5-70 DU v Lancs (Durham) 2007. Le BB 4-69 v Glos (Leicester) 2013. LO HS 5 v Glos (Bristol) 2013 (Y40). LO BB 3-34 v Glos (Leicester) 2013 (Y40). T20 HS 0. T20 BB 1-32.

LEICESTERSHIRE 2013

RESULTS SUMMARY

	Place	Won	Lost	Tied	Drew	NR
LV= County Championship (2nd Division)	9th		8		8	
All First-Class Matches			9		8	
Yorkshire Bank 40 (Group C)	5th	5	7			
Friends Life t20 (North Group)	4th	4	5	1		

LV= COUNTY CHAMPIONSHIP AVERAGES

BATTING AND FIELDING

Cap		M	I	NO	HS	Runs	Avge	100	50	Ct/St
2013	E.J.H.Eckersley	16	27	3	147	1275	53.12	4	4	4
	R.R.Sarwan	5	8	1	79	255	36.42	–	2	4
2013	M.A.G.Boyce	14	21	1	135	633	31.65	1	2	7
	S.J.Thakor	14	22	3	114	583	30.68	1	4	4
	J.A.Burns	5	8	1	77	214	30.57	–	1	4
	N.J.O'Brien	14	23	–	67	695	30.21	–	6	25/3
	B.A.Raine	5	8	1	72	190	27.14	–	1	–
	G.P.Smith	12	21	1	70	487	24.35	–	4	12
	T.J.Wells	5	8	–	82	177	22.12	–	1	2
	M.A.Thornely	10	15	–	53	269	17.93	–	1	8
	A.J.Robson	3	4	–	49	59	14.75	–	–	–
	J.J.Cobb	11	18	2	46*	234	14.62	–	–	3
	J.S.Sykes	7	12	2	34	139	13.90	–	–	3
2013	J.K.H.Naik	9	11	2	47*	123	13.66	–	–	7
	A.C.F.Wyatt	10	15	6	28	107	11.88	–	–	1
	O.H.Freckingham	15	21	2	30	204	10.73	–	–	4
2010	M.J.Hoggard	7	11	3	24	75	9.37	–	–	1
	R.E.M.Williams	5	5	1	12	18	4.50	–	–	1

Also batted: N.L.Buck (4 matches – cap 2011) 6, 16*, 15*; C.W.Henderson (1 – cap 2004) 33, 5*; A.J.Ireland (2) 15*, 0, 13; R.M.L.Taylor (2) 12, 0.

BOWLING

	O	M	R	W	Avge	Best	5wI	10wM
M.J.Hoggard	171	35	545	16	34.06	6- 66	1	–
J.K.H.Naik	286.3	53	844	21	40.19	5- 98	1	–
O.H.Freckingham	399	61	1584	36	44.00	6-125	1	–
A.C.F.Wyatt	287.4	65	904	20	45.20	3- 35	–	–
J.S.Sykes	199.3	30	733	12	61.08	4-176	–	–
Also bowled:								
B.A.Raine	98.3	17	349	9	38.77	4- 98	–	–
R.E.M.Williams	122.1	20	436	8	54.50	4- 69	–	–
N.L.Buck	94.3	19	365	6	60.83	3- 83	–	–
S.J.Thakor	133.1	21	537	7	76.71	2- 24	–	–

J.J.Cobb 58.1-5-202-0; E.J.H.Eckersley 8.1-1-42-2; C.W.Henderson 30-5-93-1; A.J.Ireland 54-7-192-2; A.J.Robson 1-0-11-0; R.R.Sarwan 2-0-11-0; R.M.L.Taylor 48.1-11-156-2; M.A.Thornely 63.2-13-262-3; T.J.Wells 37-5-129-1.

The First-Class Averages (pp 225–241) give the records of Leicestershire players in all first-class county matches (Leicestershire's other opponents being Leeds/Bradford MCCU).

LEICESTERSHIRE RECORDS
FIRST-CLASS CRICKET

Highest Total	For 701-4d		v	Worcs	Worcester	1906
	V 761-6d		by	Essex	Chelmsford	1990
Lowest Total	For 25		v	Kent	Leicester	1912
	V 24		by	Glamorgan	Leicester	1971
	24		by	Oxford U	Oxford	1985
Highest Innings	For 309*	H.D.Ackerman	v	Glamorgan	Cardiff	2006
	V 341	G.H.Hirst	for	Yorkshire	Leicester	1905

Highest Partnership for each Wicket

1st	390	B.Dudleston/J.F.Steele	v	Derbyshire	Leicester	1979
2nd	289*	J.C.Balderstone/D.I.Gower	v	Essex	Leicester	1981
3rd	436*	D.L.Maddy/B.J.Hodge	v	L'boro UCCE	Leicester	2003
4th	360*	J.W.A.Taylor/A.B.McDonald	v	Middlesex	Leicester	2010
5th	330	J.W.A.Taylor/S.J.Thakor	v	L'boro MCCU	Leicester	2011
6th	284	P.V.Simmons/P.A.Nixon	v	Durham	Chester-le-St	1996
7th	219*	J.D.R.Benson/P.Whitticase	v	Hampshire	Bournemouth	1991
8th	195	J.W.A.Taylor/J.K.H.Naik	v	Derbyshire	Leicester	2009
9th	160	R.T.Crawford/ W.W.Odell	v	Worcs	Leicester	1902
10th	228	R.Illingworth/K.Higgs	v	Northants	Leicester	1977

Best Bowling	For 10- 18	G.Geary	v	Glamorgan	Pontypridd	1929
(Innings)	V 10- 32	H.Pickett	for	Essex	Leyton	1895
Best Bowling	For 16- 96	G.Geary	v	Glamorgan	Pontypridd	1929
(Match)	V 16-102	C.Blythe	for	Kent	Leicester	1909

Most Runs – Season	2446	L.G.Berry	(av 52.04)	1937
Most Runs – Career	30143	L.G.Berry	(av 30.32)	1924-51
Most 100s – Season	7	L.G.Berry		1937
	7	W.Watson		1959
	7	B.F.Davison		1982
Most 100s – Career	45	L.G.Berry		1924-51
Most Wkts – Season	170	J.E.Walsh	(av 18.96)	1948
Most Wkts – Career	2131	W.E.Astill	(av 23.18)	1906-39
Most Career W-K Dismissals	905	R.W.Tolchard	(794 ct; 111 st)	1965-83
Most Career Catches in the Field	426	M.R.Hallam		1950-70

LIMITED-OVERS CRICKET

Highest Total	50ov	406-5		v	Berkshire	Leicester	1996
	40ov	344-4		v	Durham	Chester-le-St	1996
	T20	221-3		v	Yorkshire	Leeds	2004
Lowest Total	50ov	56		v	Northants	Leicester	1964
		56		v	Minor Cos	Wellington	1982
	40ov	36		v	Sussex	Leicester	1973
	T20	96		v	Notts	Leicester	2012
Highest Innings	50ov	201	V.J.Wells	v	Berkshire	Leicester	1996
	40ov	154*	B.J.Hodge	v	Sussex	Horsham	2004
	T20	111	D.L.Maddy	v	Yorkshire	Leeds	2004
Best Bowling	50ov	6-16	C.M.Willoughby	v	Somerset	Leicester	2005
	40ov	6-17	K.Higgs	v	Glamorgan	Leicester	1973
	T20	5-13	A.B.McDonald	v	Notts	Nottingham	2010

MIDDLESEX

Formation of Present Club: 2 February 1864
Inaugural First-Class Match: 1864
Colours: Blue
Badge: Three Seaxes
County Champions (since 1890): (10) 1903, 1920, 1921, 1947, 1976, 1980, 1982, 1985, 1990, 1993
Joint Champions: (2) 1949, 1977
Gillette/NatWest Trophy Winners: (4) 1977, 1980, 1984, 1988
Benson and Hedges Cup Winners: (2) 1983, 1986
Sunday League Winners: (1) 1992
Twenty20 Cup Winners: (1) 2008

Secretary: Vincent J.Codrington, Lord's Cricket Ground, London NW8 8QN • Tel: 020 7289 1300 • Fax: 020 7289 5831 • Email: enquiries@middlesexccc.com • Web: www.middlesexccc.com • Twitter: @Middlesex_CCC (10,889 followers)

Managing Director of Cricket: Angus Fraser. **Head Coach**: Richard Scott. **Assistant Coach**: Richard Johnson. **Batting Coach**: Mark Ramprakash. **Captain**: C.J.L.Rogers (f-c) and E.J.G.Morgan (l-o). **Overseas Player**: C.J.L.Rogers. **2014 Beneficiary**: None. **Head Groundsman**: Mick Hunt. **Scorer**: Don K.Shelley. ‡ New registration. NQ Not qualified for England.

NQBALBIRNIE, Andrew (St Andrew's C, Dublin; UWIC), b Dublin, Ireland 28 Dec 1990. 6'2". RHB, OB. Cardiff MCCU 2012-13. Ireland 2012. Middlesex debut 2012. Middlesex 2nd XI debut 2011. MCC YCs 2010. **LOI** (Ire): 4 (2010); HS 17 v Canada (Amstelveen) 2010. HS 36* Ire v South Africa A (Oak Hill) 2012. M HS 14 v Surrey (Oval) 2012. BB 1-5 Ire v Netherlands (Deventer) 2013. LO HS 17 (*see LOI*). LO BB – .

BERG, Gareth Kyle (South African College S), b Cape Town, South Africa 18 Jan 1981. 6'0". RHB, RMF. England qualified through residency. Debut (Middlesex) 2008; cap 2010. WP Academy (1999-00) and WP B (2001-02 to 2002-03). Italy (T20 only). HS 130* v Leics (Leicester) 2011. BB 6-58 v Glamorgan (Cardiff) 2011. LO HS 75 v Glamorgan (Lord's) 2013 (Y40). LO BB 4-24 v Worcs (Worcester) 2011 (CB40). T20 HS 90. T20 BB 4-20.

DENLY, Joseph Liam (Chaucer TC), b Canterbury, Kent 16 Mar 1986. 6'0". RHB, LB. Kent 2004-11; cap 2008. Middlesex debut/cap 2012. MCC 2013. **LOI**: 9 (2009 to 2009-10); HS 67 v Ireland (Belfast) 2009 – on debut. **IT20**: 5 (2009 to 2009-10); HS 14 and BB 1-9 v SA (Centurion) 2009-10. F-c Tours (Eng A): NZ 2008-09; I 2007-08. 1000 runs (2); most – 1024 (2011). HS 199 K v Derbys (Derby) 2011. M HS 134* v Worcs (Lord's) 2012. BB 3-43 K v Surrey (Oval) 2011. M BB 2-47 v Sussex (Lord's) 2013. LO HS 115 K v Warwks (Birmingham) 2009 (FPT). LO BB 3-42 K v Netherlands (Rotterdam) 2011 (CB40). T20 HS 100. T20 BB 1-9.

DEXTER, Neil John (Northwood HS, Durban; Varsity C; U of South Africa), b Johannesburg, South Africa 21 Aug 1984. 6'0". RHB, RM. Kent 2005-08. Essex 2008. Middlesex debut 2009; cap 2010; captain 2010 (*part*) to 2013. Qualified for England in 2010. HS 146 (and 118) v Kent (Uxbridge) 2009. BB 5-27 v Notts (Nottingham) 2013. LO HS 135* K v Glamorgan (Cardiff) 2006 (CGT). LO BB 3-17 K v Leics (Canterbury) 2006 (P40). T20 HS 73. T20 BB 4-21.

ESKINAZI, Stephen Sean (Christ Church GS, Claremont; U of WA), b Johannesburg, South Africa 28 Mar 1994. RHB, WK. Middlesex 2nd XI debut 2013. Awaiting 1st XI debut. British passport.

FINN, Steven Thomas (Parmiter's S, Garston), b Watford, Herts 4 Apr 1989. 6'7½". RHB, RF. Debut (Middlesex) 2005; cap 2009. Otago 2011-12. YC 2010. **ECB central contract 2013-14. Tests:** 23 (2009-10 to 2013); HS 56 v NZ (Dunedin) 2012-13; BB 6-125 v A (Brisbane) 2010-11. **LOI:** 39 (2010-11 to 2013); HS 35 v A (Brisbane) 2010-11; BB 4-34 v P (Abu Dhabi) 2011-12 (twice). **IT20:** 18 (2011 to 2013); HS 8* v I (Colombo, RPS) 2012-13; BB 3-16 v NZ (Pallekele) 2012-13. F-c Tours: A 2010-11, 2013-14; SL 2013-14; I 2012-13; SL 2011-12; B 2009-10; UAE 2011-12 (v P). HS 56 (*see Tests*). M HS 32 v Essex (Lord's) 2011. 50 wkts (2); most – 64 (2010). BB 9-37 (14-106 match) v Worcs (Worcester) 2010. LO HS 35 (*see LOI*). LO BB 5-33 v Derbys (Lord's) 2011 (CB40). T20 HS 8*. T20 BB 3-16.

GUBBINS, Nicholas Richard Trail (Radley C; Leeds U), b Richmond, Surrey 31 Dec 1993. LHB, LB. Leeds/Bradford MCCU 2013. Middlesex 2nd XI debut 2012. Awaiting 1st XI debut. HS 14 LBU v Yorks (Leeds) 2013.

HARRIS, James Alexander Russell (Pontardulais CS; Gorseinon C), b Morriston, Swansea, Glamorgan 16 May 1990. 6'0". RHB, RFM. Glamorgan 2007-12, making debut aged 16y 351d – youngest Glamorgan player to take an f-c wicket; cap 2010. Middlesex debut 2013. Glamorgan 2nd XI debut 2005, aged 14y 353d. Wales MC 2005-08. England U19s 2007. F-c Tours (EL): WI 2010-11; SL 2013-14. HS 87* Gm v Notts (Swansea) 2007. M HS 43* v Cambridge MCCU (Cambridge) 2013. 50 wkts (1): 63 (2010). BB 7-66 (12-118 match) Gm v Glos (Bristol) 2007 – youngest (17y 3d) to take 10 wickets in any CC match. M BB 3-46 v Durham (Chester-le-St) 2013. LO HS 29 EL v Sri Lanka A (Northampton) 2011. LO BB 4-48 Gm v Kent (Canterbury) 2008 (P40). T20 HS 18. T20 BB 4-23.

HELM, Thomas George (Misbourne S, Gt Missenden), b Stoke Mandeville Hospital, Bucks 7 May 1994. RHB, RMF. Debut (Middlesex) 2013. Middlesex 2nd XI debut 2011. Buckinghamshire 2011. HS 18 and BB 3-46 v Yorks (Leeds) 2013 – only f-c match. LO HS – . LO BB 3-27 v Unicorns (Southend) 2013 (Y40).

HIGGINS, Ryan Francis (Bradfield C), b Harare, Zimbabwe 6 Jan 1995. RHB, OB. Middlesex 2nd XI debut 2012. Awaiting 1st XI debut.

MALAN, Dawid Johannes (Paarl HS), b Roehampton, Surrey 3 Sep 1987. Son of D.J.Malan (WP B and Transvaal B 1978-79 to 1981-82), elder brother of C.C.Malan (Loughborough MCCU 2009-10). 6'0". LHB, LB. Boland 2005-06. MCC YC 2006-07. Middlesex debut 2008, scoring 132* v Northants (Uxbridge); cap 2010. MCC 2010-11, 2013. 1000 runs (1): 1001 runs (2010). HS 156* v Cambridge MCCU (Cambridge) 2013. CC HS 143 v Derbys (Lord's) 2011. BB 5-61 v Lancs (Liverpool) 2012. LO HS 134 v Essex (Lord's) 2012 (CB40). LO BB 2-4 v Scotland (Edinburgh) 2009 (FPT). T20 HS 103. T20 BB 2-10.

MORGAN, Eoin Joseph Gerard (Catholic University S), b Dublin, Ireland 10 Sep 1986. 6'0". LHB, RM. British passport. Ireland 2004 to 2007-08. Middlesex debut 2006; cap 2008; l-o captain 2014. *Wisden* 2010. **Tests:** 16 (2010 to 2011-12); HS 130 v P (Nottingham) 2010. **LOI** (E/Ire): 113 (23 for Ire 2006 to 2008-09; 90 for E 2009 to 2013-14, 6 as captain); HS 124* v Ire (Dublin) 2013. **IT20:** 41 (2009 to 2013-14, 3 as captain); HS 85* v SA (Johannesburg) 2009-10. F-c Tours (Ire): A 2010-11 (E); NZ 2008-09 (Eng A); Namibia 2005-06; UAE 2006-07, 2007-08, 2011-12 (E v P). 1000 runs (1): 1085 (2008). HS 209* Ire v UAE (Abu Dhabi) 2006-07. CC HS 137* v Glos (Bristol) 2008. BB 2-24 v Notts (Lord's) 2007. LO HS 161 v Kent (Canterbury) 2009 (FPT). LO BB – . T20 HS 85*.

MURTAGH, Timothy James (John Fisher S; St Mary's C), b Lambeth, London 2 Aug 1981. Elder brother of C.P.Murtagh (Loughborough UCCE and Surrey 2005-09); nephew of A.J.Murtagh (Hampshire and EP 1973-77). 6'0". LHB, RFM. British U 2000-03. Surrey 2001-06. Middlesex debut 2007; cap 2008. MCC 2010. **LOI** (Ire): 9 (2012 to 2013-14); HS 23* v Scotland (Belfast) 2013; BB 3-33 v E (Dublin) 2013. IT20 (Ire): 5 (2012 to 2013-14); HS 3 v B (Belfast) 2012; BB 2-24 v Afghanistan (Abu Dhabi) 2013-14. HS 74* Sy v Middx (Oval) 2004 and 74* Sy v Warwks (Croydon) 2005. M HS 55 v Leics (Leicester) 2011. 50 wkts (5); most – 85 (2011). BB 7-82 v Derbys (Derby) 2009. LO HS 35* v Surrey (Lord's) 2008 (FPT). LO BB 4-14 Sy v Derbys (Derby) 2005 (NL). T20 HS 40*. T20 BB 6-24 Sy v Middx (Lord's) 2005 – Sy record and 4th best UK figs.

PATEL, Ravi Hasmukh (Merchant Taylors' S, Northwood; Loughborough U), b Harrow 4 Aug 1991. RHB, SLA. Debut (Middlesex) 2010. No 1st XI appearances in 2011. Loughborough MCCU 2011. Middlesex 2nd XI debut 2008. HS 26* v Warwks (Uxbridge) 2013. BB 5-69 v Cambridge MCCU (Cambridge) 2013. CC BB 4-72 v Lancs (Lord's) 2012. LO HS – . LO BB 2-41 v Glos (Lord's) 2013 (Y40). T20 HS 1. T20 BB 4-18.

PODMORE, Harry William (Twyford HS), b Hammersmith, London 23 Jul 1994. RHB, RM. Middlesex 2nd XI debut 2011. MCC YC 2013. Awaiting 1st XI debut.

RAYNER, Oliver Philip (St Bede's S, Sussex), b Fallingbostel, W Germany, 1 Nov 1985. 6'5". RHB, OB. Sussex 2006-11, scoring 101 v Sri Lankans (Hove) – first hundred on debut for Sussex since 1920. Middlesex debut 2011. F-c Tour (EL): SL 2013-14. HS 143* v Notts (Nottingham) 2012. BB 8-46 (15-118 match) v Surrey (Oval) 2013. LO HS 61 Sx v Lancs (Hove) 2006 (P40). LO BB 2-20 v Somerset (Lord's) 2013 (Y40). T20 HS 41*. T20 BB 5-18.

ROBSON, Sam David (Marcellin C, Randwick), b Paddington, Sydney, Australia 1 Jul 1989. Elder brother of A.J.Robson (*see LEICESTERSHIRE*). 6'0". RHB, LB. Qualified for England in April 2013. Debut (Middlesex) 2009; cap 2013. Middlesex 2nd XI debut 2008. F-c Tour: SL 2013-14. 1000 runs (1): 1180 (2013). HS 215* v Warwks (Birmingham) 2013. BB 1-4 EL v Sri Lanka A (Dambulla) 2013-14. M BB – . LO HS 65 v Sussex (Lord's) 2011 (CB40). T20 HS 28*.

NO‑ROGERS, Christopher John Llewellyn (Wesley C, Perth; Curtin U, Perth), b St George, Sydney, Australia 31 Aug 1977. Son of W.J.Rogers (NSW 1968-69 to 1969-70). 5'10". LHB, LBG. W Australia 1998-99 to 2007-08. Derbyshire 2004, 2008-10; cap 2008; captain 2008 (*part*) to 2010 (*part*). Leicestershire 2005. Northamptonshire 2006. Victoria 2008-09 to date. Middlesex debut/cap 2011; captain (f-c only) 2013 to date. MCC 2011. Shropshire 2003. Wiltshire 2005. **Tests** (A): 14 (2007-08 to 2013-14); HS 119 v E (Sydney) 2013-14. F-c Tours (A): E 2013; SA 2013-14; P 2007-08 (Aus A). 1000 runs (7+2); most – 1536 (2013). HS 319 Nh v Glos (Northampton) 2006. M HS 214 v Surrey (Lord's) 2013. BB 1-16 Nh v Leics (Northampton) 2006. LO HS 140 Vic v S Aus (Melbourne) 2009-10. LO BB 2-22 Nh v Durham (Northampton) 2006. T20 HS 58.

ROLAND-JONES, Tobias Skelton ('**Toby**') (Hampton S; Leeds U), b Ashford 29 Jan 1988. 6'4". RHB, RMF. Debut (Middlesex) 2010; cap 2012. MCC 2011. Middlesex 2nd XI debut 2008. Leeds/Bradford UCCE 2009 (not f-c). HS 52 v Sussex (Lord's) 2012. 50 wkts (1): 64 (2012). BB 6-63 v Notts (Nottingham) 2013. Hat-trick v Derbys (Lord's) 2013. LO HS 24 EL v Australia A (Sydney) 2012-13. LO BB 4-44 v Yorks (Radlett) 2013 (Y40). T20 HS 12. T20 BB 4-25.

ROSSINGTON, Adam Matthew (Mill Hill S), b Edgware 5 May 1993. 5'11". RHB, WK. Debut (Middlesex) 2010. Middlesex 2nd XI debut 2010. England U19s 2010-11, scoring 113 v SL on debut. Summer contract. HS 103* v Cambridge MCCU (Cambridge) 2013, winning Walter Lawrence Trophy with 55-ball century. CC HS 29 v Warwks (Birmingham) 2012. LO HS 79* v Yorks (Radlett) 2013 (Y40). T20 HS 74.

SANDHU, Gurjit Singh (Isleworth & Syon S; Heathland S), b W Middlesex Hospital 24 Mar 1992. 6'4". RHB, LMF. Middlesex 2nd XI debut 2008, aged 16y 85d. HS 8 v Sri Lankans (Uxbridge) 2011. BB 4-49 v Cambridge MCCU (Cambridge) 2013. CC BB 2-54 v Sussex (Hove) 2013. LO HS 0 and LO BB 3-28 v Essex (Lord's) 2012 (CB40). T20 HS 2*. T20 BB 2-15.

SIMPSON, John Andrew (St Gabriel's RC HS), b Bury, Lancs 13 Jul 1988. 5'10". LHB, WK. Debut (Middlesex) 2009, cap 2011. Cumberland 2007. MCC YCs 2008. HS 143 v Surrey (Lord's) 2011. LO HS 82 v Glos (Cheltenham) 2010 (CB40). T20 HS 60*.

STEEL, Cameron Tate (Scotch C, Perth, Australia), b San Francisco, USA 13 Sep 1995. 5'10". RHB, LB. Middlesex 2nd XI debut 2013. Somerset 2nd XI 2013. Awaiting 1st XI debut; summer contract in 2014.

^{NQ}**STIRLING, Paul** Robert (Belfast HS), b Belfast, N Ireland 3 Sep 1990. Father Brian Stirling was an international rugby referee. 5'10". RHB, OB. Ireland 2007-08 to date. ICC Combined XI 2011-12. Middlesex debut 2013. **LOI** (Ire): 46 (2008 to 2013-14); HS 177 v Canada (Toronto) 2010; BB 4-11 v Netherlands (Amstelveen) 2010. **IT20** (Ire): 23 (2009 to 2013-14); HS 79 v Afghanistan (Dubai, DSC) 2011-12; BB 3-21 v B (Belfast) 2012. F-c Tours (Ire): WI 2009-10; Kenya 2011-12; UAE 2013-14. HS 115 Ire v Australia A (Belfast) 2013. M HS 54 v Cambridge MCCU (Cambridge) 2013. CC HS 1 and BB 2-43 v Surrey (Lord's) 2013. LO HS 177 (*see LOI*). LO BB 4-11 (*see LOI*). T20 HS 82*. T20 BB 4-10.

WILKIN, Oliver (Merchant Taylors' S, Northwood; Loughborough U), b Ealing 6 Apr 1992. RHB, RM. Loughborough MCCU 2011. Middlesex 2nd XI debut 2012. HS 38 LU v Northants (Loughborough) 2011. BB 2-63 v Kent (Canterbury) 2011. LO HS 20 and LO BB 2-44 v Leics (Lord's) 2013 (Y40). T20 HS 28. T20 BB 3-12.

RELEASED/RETIRED

(Having made a County First-Class or List A appearance in 2013)

^{NQ}**COLLYMORE, Corey** Dalanelo (Alexandra SS), b St Peter, Barbados 21 Dec 1977. 6'0". RHB, RFM. Barbados 1998-99 to 2008-09. Warwickshire 2003. Sussex 2008-10; cap 2008. Middlesex 2011-13; cap 2011. Kolpak registration. **Tests** (WI): 30 (1998-99 to 2007); HS 16* v Z (Bulawayo) 2003-04 and 16* v E (Chester-le-St) 2007; BB 7-57 v SL (Kingston) 2003. **LOI** (WI): 84 (1999 to 2006-07); HS 13* v I (Toronto) 1999; BB 5-51 v SL (Colombo) 2001-02. F-c Tours (WI): E 2000, 2004, 2007; A 2005-06; SA 2003-04; P 2006-07; Z 2002, 2003-04; K 2000-01. HS 23 Sx v Notts (Horsham) 2009. M HS 8* v Derbys (Lord's) 2011. 50 wkts (1): 57 (2010). BB 7-57 (*see Tests*). CC BB 6-48 Sx v Leics (Leicester) 2010. M BB 4-28 v Surrey (Guildford) 2011. LO HS 13* (*see LOI*). LO BB 5-27 Barbados v Leeward Is (Weymouth) 2005-06. T20 HS 4. T20 BB 1-21.

DAVEY, Joshua Henry (Culford S), b Aberdeen, Scotland 3 Aug 1990. RHB, RM. Middlesex 2010-12. Scotland 2011-12 to date. Middlesex 2nd XI debut 2008. **LOI** (Scot): 11 (2010 to 2013); HS 64 v Afghanistan (Sharjah) 2012-13; BB 5-9 v Afghanistan (Ayr) 2010. **IT20** (Scot): 1 (2012); HS 7 and BB 3-23 v B (The Hague) 2012. HS 72 and BB 2-41 v Oxford MCCU (Oxford) 2010 – on debut. CC HS 61 v Glos (Bristol) 2010. CC BB – . LO HS 91 Scot v Warwks (Birmingham) 2011 (CB40). LO BB 5-9 (*see LOI*). T20 HS 18*. T20 BB 3-23.

LONDON, Adam Brian (Bishop Wand S, Sunbury), b Ashford 12 Oct 1988. 5'8". LHB, OB. Middlesex 2009-13. No 1st XI appearances in 2011. HS 81 v Cambridge MCCU (Cambridge) 2013. CC HS 77 v Northants (Northampton) 2010. BB 1-15 v Oxford MCCU (Oxford) 2010. CC BB – . LO HS 6 H v Bangladesh A (Southampton) 2013. BB – .

SMITH, T.M.J. – see *GLOUCESTERSHIRE*.

^{NQ}**VOGES, Adam** Charles (Edith Cowan U, Perth), b Perth, Australia 4 Oct 1979. 6'0". RHB, SLC. W Australia 2002-03 to date. Nottinghamshire 2008-12; cap 2008. Middlesex 2013. **LOI** (A): 31 (2006-07 to 2013-14); HS 112* v WI (Melbourne) 2012-13. BB 1-3 v E (Birmingham) 2013. **IT20** (A): 7 (2007-08 to 2012-13); HS 51 v WI (Brisbane) 2012-13; BB 2-5 v I (Melbourne) 2007-08. F-c Tours (Aus A): I 2008-09; P 2007-08. HS 235* WA v Q (Perth) 2013-14. UK HS 165 Nt v Oxford MCCU (Oxford) 2011. CC HS 150 v Warwks (Uxbridge) 2013. BB 4-92 WA v S Aus (Adelaide) 2006-07. UK BB 3-21 Nt v Durham (Nottingham) 2008. M BB 1-10 v Derbys (Derby) 2013. LO HS 112* (*see LOI*). LO BB 3-25 Nt v Sussex (Hove) 2009 (P40). T20 HS 82*. T20 BB 2-4.

K.D.Mills left the staff without making a County First-Class or List A appearance in 2013.

MIDDLESEX 2013

RESULTS SUMMARY

	Place	Won	Lost	Tied	Drew	NR
LV= County Championship (1st Division)	5th	6	5		5	
All First-Class Matches		7	5		5	
Yorkshire Bank 40 (Group C)	3rd	7	4			1
Friends Life t20 (South Group)	4th	5	5			

LV= COUNTY CHAMPIONSHIP AVERAGES

BATTING AND FIELDING

Cap		M	I	NO	HS	Runs	Avge	100	50	Ct/St
2011	C.J.L.Rogers	12	22	3	214	1068	56.21	3	6	11
	A.C.Voges	4	7	–	150	383	54.71	1	2	6
2013	S.D.Robson	16	29	4	215*	1180	47.20	3	4	22
2010	N.J.Dexter	16	26	2	104	772	32.16	1	4	11
2008	E.J.G.Morgan	2	4	1	39*	96	32.00	–	–	2
2011	J.A.Simpson	16	25	4	97*	648	30.85	–	5	55/5
2012	J.L.Denly	16	28	3	77	652	26.08	–	4	6
2010	G.K.Berg	15	23	2	71	501	23.85	–	2	8
2010	D.J.Malan	12	19	1	61	387	21.50	–	2	19
	O.P.Rayner	13	18	3	52*	293	19.53	–	1	19
	J.A.R.Harris	9	12	3	37	146	16.22	–	–	2
	R.H.Patel	3	6	2	26*	47	11.75	–	–	2
2012	T.S.Roland-Jones	8	11	1	21	111	11.10	–	–	4
2008	T.J.Murtagh	13	15	4	29	112	10.18	–	–	4
2011	C.D.Collymore	9	11	5	6*	22	3.66	–	–	3
2009	S.T.Finn	6	7	1	8	15	2.50	–	–	4

Also played: T.G.Helm (1 match) 4, 18; A.B.London (2) 18, 28, 3 (1 ct); G.S.Sandhu (2) did not bat; T.M.J.Smith (2) 17*, 19 (1 ct); P.R.Stirling (1) 0, 1.

BOWLING

	O	M	R	W	Avge	Best	5wI	10wM
T.J.Murtagh	444.1	113	1224	60	20.40	6-49	3	1
N.J.Dexter	163.2	33	415	18	23.05	5-27	1	–
O.P.Rayner	356.1	74	958	41	23.36	8-46	4	1
C.D.Collymore	229.2	49	613	25	24.52	4-61	–	–
S.T.Finn	160.5	38	503	17	29.58	4-46	–	–
T.S.Roland-Jones	219.2	39	694	21	33.04	6-63	1	–
G.K.Berg	324.4	71	942	25	37.68	3-49	–	–
J.A.R.Harris	227.4	31	805	21	38.33	3-46	–	–

Also bowled:

T.G.Helm	18	0	78	5	15.60	3-46		
R.H.Patel	110	24	321	8	40.12	4-89	–	–

J.L.Denly 28.4-3-96-2; A.B.London 1-0-5-0; D.J.Malan 15.5-0-58-0; G.S.Sandhu 28-5-115-2; T.M.J.Smith 22-0-71-1; P.R.Stirling 18-2-47-2; A.C.Voges 9-1-16-1.

The First-Class Averages (pp 225–241) give the records of Middlesex players in all first-class county matches (Middlesex's other opponents being Cambridge MCCU), with the exception of S.T.Finn, C.J.L.Rogers, T.S.Roland-Jones and T.M.J.Smith, whose first-class figures for Middlesex are as above.

MIDDLESEX RECORDS

FIRST-CLASS CRICKET

Highest Total	For 642-3d		v	Hampshire	Southampton	1923
	V 850-7d		by	Somerset	Taunton	2007
Lowest Total	For 20		v	MCC	Lord's	1864
	V 31		by	Glos	Bristol	1924
Highest Innings	For 331*	J.D.B.Robertson	v	Worcs	Worcester	1949
	V 341	C.M.Spearman	for	Glos	Gloucester	2004

Highest Partnership for each Wicket

1st	372	M.W.Gatting/J.L.Langer	v	Essex	Southgate	1998
2nd	380	F.A.Tarrant/J.W.Hearne	v	Lancashire	Lord's	1914
3rd	424*	W.J.Edrich/D.C.S.Compton	v	Somerset	Lord's	1948
4th	325	J.W.Hearne/E.H.Hendren	v	Hampshire	Lord's	1919
5th	338	R.S.Lucas/T.C.O'Brien	v	Sussex	Hove	1895
6th	270	J.D.Carr/P.N.Weekes	v	Glos	Lord's	1994
7th	271*	E.H.Hendren/F.T.Mann	v	Notts	Nottingham	1925
8th	182*	M.H.C.Doll/H.R.Murrell	v	Notts	Lord's	1913
9th	172	G.K.Berg/T.J.Murtagh	v	Leics	Leicester	2011
10th	230	R.W.Nicholls/W.Roche	v	Kent	Lord's	1899

Best Bowling	For 10- 40	G.O.B.Allen	v	Lancashire	Lord's	1929
(Innings)	V 9- 38	R.C.R-Glasgow†	for	Somerset	Lord's	1924
Best Bowling	For 16-114	G.Burton	v	Yorkshire	Sheffield	1888
(Match)	16-114	J.T.Hearne	v	Lancashire	Manchester	1898
	V 16-100	J.E.B.B.P.Q.C.Dwyer	for	Sussex	Hove	1906

Most Runs – Season	2669	E.H.Hendren	(av 83.41)	1923
Most Runs – Career	40302	E.H.Hendren	(av 48.81)	1907-37
Most 100s – Season	13	D.C.S.Compton		1947
Most 100s – Career	119	E.H.Hendren		1907-37
Most Wkts – Season	158	F.J.Titmus	(av 14.63)	1955
Most Wkts – Career	2361	F.J.Titmus	(av 21.27)	1949-82
Most Career W-K Dismissals	1223	J.T.Murray	(1024 ct; 199 st)	1952-75
Most Career Catches in the Field	561	E.H.Hendren		1907-37

LIMITED-OVERS CRICKET

Highest Total	50ov	341-7	v	Somerset	Lord's	2009
	40ov	350-6	v	Lancashire	Lord's	2012
	T20	213-4	v	Glamorgan	Richmond	2010
Lowest Total	50ov	41	v	Essex	Westcliff	1972
	40ov	23	v	Yorkshire	Leeds	1974
	T20	92	v	Surrey	Lords	2013
Highest Innings	50ov	163	A.J.Strauss	v	Surrey	The Oval	2008
	40ov	147*	M.R.Ramprakash	v	Worcs	Lord's	1990
	T20	106	A.C.Gilchrist	v	Kent	Canterbury	2010
Best Bowling	50ov	7-12	W.W.Daniel	v	Minor Cos E	Ipswich	1978
	40ov	6- 6	R.W.Hooker	v	Surrey	Lord's	1969
	T20	5-13	M.Kartik	v	Essex	Lord's	2007

† R.C.Robertson-Glasgow

NORTHAMPTONSHIRE

Formation of Present Club: 31 July 1878
Inaugural First-Class Match: 1905
Colours: Maroon
Badge: Tudor Rose
County Champions: (0); best – 2nd 1912, 1957, 1965, 1976
Gillette/NatWest/C&G/FP Trophy Winners: (2) 1976, 1992
Benson and Hedges Cup Winners: (1) 1980
Twenty20 Cup Winners: (1) 2013

Chief Executive: David Smith, County Ground, Abington Avenue, Northampton, NN1 4PR
• Tel: 01604 514455 • Fax: 01604 609288 • Email: post@nccc.co.uk • Web:
www.nccc.co.uk • Twitter: @NorthantsCCC (9,024 followers)

Head Coach: David Ripley. **Captain**: S.D.Peters (f-c) and A.G.Wakely (l-o). **Vice-Captain**:
A.G.Wakely. **Overseas Players**: J.M.Bird and R.E.Levi (l-o only). **2014 Beneficiary**:
S.D.Peters. **Head Groundsman**: Paul Marshall. **Scorer**: A.C. (Tony) Kingston. ‡ New
registration. ^{NQ} Not qualified for England.

AZHAR ULLAH, Mohammad, b Burewala, Punjab, Pakistan 25 Dec 1983. RHB, RFM.
Multan 2004-05 to 2006-07. WAPDA 2004-05 to 2012-13. Quetta 2005-06. Baluchistan
2007-08 to 2008-09. Northamptonshire debut 2013. UK qualified through residency and
British wife. HS 41 WAPDA v Karachi Whites (Karachi) 2007-08. Nh HS 8 v Essex
(Colchester) 2013. BB 7-74 Quetta v Lahore Ravi (Quetta) 2005-06. Nh BB 4-42 v Lancs
(Manchester) 2013. LO HS 9 (twice). LO BB 5-56 WAPDA v Allied Bank (Karachi)
2004-05. T20 HS 5*. T20 BB 4-14.

‡^{NQ}**BIRD, Jackson** Munro (St Pius C, Sydney; St Ignatius C, Riverview), b Paddington,
Sydney, Australia 11 Dec 1986. RHB, RFM. Tasmania 2011-12 to date. **Tests** (A): 3 (2012-13
to 2013); HS 6* and BB 4-41 v SL (Sydney) 2012-13. F-c Tours (A): E 2012 (Aus A), 2013,
2013 (Aus A). HS 26 and BB 6-25 Tas v WA (Hobart) 2012-13. LO HS 5* Tas v Q (Hobart)
2012-13. LO BB 3-39 Tas v S Aus (Adelaide) 2011-12. T20 HS 0*. T20 BB 4-31.

‡**CHAMBERS, Maurice** Anthony (Homerton TC; Sir George Monoux C), b Port Antonio,
Portland, Jamaica 14 Sep 1987. 6'3". RHB, RFM. Essex 2005-13. No f-c appearances
2006-07 – stress fracture of the back. Warwickshire 2013 (on loan). MCC YC 2004. F-c
Tour (EL): WI 2010-11. HS 58 Wa v Derbys (Derby) 2013. BB 6-68 (10-123 match) Ex v
Notts (Chelmsford) 2010. LO HS 2 Ex v Lancs (Chelmsford) 2012 (CB40). LO BB 1-21 Ex
v Worcs (Worcester) 2012 (CB40). T20 HS 10*. T20 BB 3-31.

COETZER, Kyle James (Aberdeen GS), b Aberdeen, Scotland 14 Apr 1984. 5'11". RHB,
RM. Durham 2004-10. Northamptonshire debut 2011; cap 2013. Scotland 2009 to date. **LOI**
(Scot): 15 (2008 to 2013); HS 133 v Afghanistan (Sharjah) 2012-13; BB 1-35 v Netherlands
(Aberdeen) 2011. **IT20** (Scot): 20 (2008 to 2013-14); HS 62 v Ireland (Dubai, DSC)
2011-12; BB 3-25 v Afghanistan (Abu Dhabi) 2009-10. F-c Tour (Scot): Kenya 2009-10. HS
219 v Leics (Leicester) 2013. BB 2-16 Scot v Kenya (Nairobi) 2009-10. CC BB 1-9 v
Glamorgan (Northampton) 2012. LO HS 133 (*see LOI*). LO BB 1-2 v Notts (Nottingham)
2013 (Y40). T20 HS 71*. T20 BB 3-25.

152

CROOK, Steven Paul (Rostrevor C; Magill U), b Modbury, S Australia 28 May 1983. Younger brother of A.R.Crook (S Australia, Aus Academy, Lancashire, Northamptonshire 1998-99 to 2008). 5'11". RHB, RFM. British passport. Lancashire 2003-05. Northamptonshire debut 2005; cap 2013. Middlesex 2011-12. Aus Academy 2001-02. HS 97 v Yorks (Northampton) 2005. BB 5-48 M v Lancs (Lord's) 2012. Nh BB 5-71 v Essex (Northampton) 2009. LO HS 100 SJD v PDSC (Savar) 2013-14. LO BB 5-36 v Warwks (Northampton) 2013 (Y40). T20 HS 63. T20 BB 3-21.

DUCKETT, Ben Matthew (Stowe S), b Farnborough, Kent 17 Oct 1994. LHB, WK, occ OB. Debut Northamptonshire 2013. Northamptonshire 2nd XI debut 2011. England U19s 2012-13. HS 53* v Leics (Northampton) 2013 – on debut. LO HS 47* v Sussex (Arundel) 2013 (Y40). T20 HS 15*.

[NQ]**HALL, Andrew** James (Alberton HS), b Alberton, Johannesburg, South Africa 31 Jul 1975. 6'0". RHB, RFM. Transvaal/Gauteng 1995-96 to 2000-01. Easterns 2001-02 to 2003-04. Worcestershire 2003-04. Lions 2004-05 to 2005-06. Kent 2005-07; cap 2005. Northamptonshire debut 2008 (Kolpak registration); cap 2009; captain 2010 (part) to 2012. Dolphins 2009-10. ME 2010-11. Durham CB 1999. Suffolk 2002. **Tests** (SA): 21 (2001-02 to 2006-07); HS 163 v I (Kanpur) 2004-05; BB 3-1 v SL (Johannesburg) 2002-03. **LOI** (SA): 88 (1998-99 to 2007); HS 81 v SL (Galle) 2000-01; BB 5-18 v E (Bridgetown) 2004-05. **IT20** (SA): 2 (2005-06); HS 11 v A (Brisbane) 2005-06; BB 3-22 v A Johannesburg) 2005-06. F-c Tours (SA): E 2003; WI 2004-05; I 2004-05; SL 2006; Z 1995-96 (Transvaal B), 2007-08 (SA A). 1000 runs (1): 1161 (2009). HS 163 (see Tests). UK HS 159 v Leics (Northampton) 2009. BB 6-77 (11-99 match) Easterns v WP (Pt Elizabeth) 2002-03. UK BB 5-29 v Essex (Northampton) 2009. LO HS 129* Gauteng v Border (E London) 1999-00. LO BB 5-18 (see LOI). T20 HS 66* and T20 BB 6-21 v Worcs (Northampton) 2008 (Nh record analysis, and 1st man in UK to score 50 and take 5 wkts in a game).

KEOGH, Robert Ian (Queensbury S; Dunstable C), b Luton, Beds 21 Oct 1991. 5'11". RHB, OB. Debut Northamptonshire 2012. Northamptonshire 2nd XI debut 2009. Bedfordshire 2009-10. HS 221 v Hants (Southampton) 2013. BB 1-69 v Glamorgan (Cardiff) 2012. LO HS 61 v Warwks (Birmingham) 2013 (Y40). LO BB –. T20 HS 1. T20 BB –.

KETTLEBOROUGH, James Michael (Bedford S), b Huntingdon 22 Oct 1992. 5'11". RHB, OB. Northamptonshire 2nd XI debut 2012. Middlesex 2nd XI 2011-12. Bedfordshire 2009-13. Awaiting 1st XI debut.

LEVI, Richard Ernst, b Johannesburg, South Africa 14 Jan 1988. RHB, RM. W Province 2006-07 to date. Cape Cobras 2008-09 to 2012-13. Returns to Northamptonshire for l-o only after playing T20 in 2013. **IT20** (SA): 13 (2011-12 to 2012-13); HS 117* v NZ (Hamilton) 2011-12. HS 150* WP v EP (Cape Town) 2006-07. LO HS 166 Cape Cobras v Titans (Paarl) 2012-13. T20 HS 117*.

MIDDLEBROOK, James Daniel (Pudsey Crawshaw S), b Leeds, Yorks 13 May 1977. 6'1". RHB, OB. Yorkshire 1998-2001. Essex 2002-09; cap 2003. Northamptonshire debut 2010, cap 2011. MCC 2010, 2013. HS 127 Ex v Middx (Lord's) 2007. Nh HS 121 and Nh BB 5-63 v Glos (Northampton) 2012. 50 wkts (1): 56 (2003). BB 6-78 v Kent (Northampton) 2013. Took 4 wkts in 5 balls for Y v Hants (Southampton) 2000. Hat-trick Ex v Kent (Canterbury) 2003. LO HS 57* v Derbys (Derby) 2010 (CB40). LO BB 4-27 Ex v Somerset (Taunton) 2006 (CGT). T20 HS 43. T20 BB 3-13.

MURPHY, David (Richard Hale S, Hertford; Loughborough U), b Welwyn Garden City, Herts 24 June 1989. 5'11". RHB, WK. Loughborough MCCU 2009-11. Northamptonshire debut 2009. Northamptonshire 2nd XI debut 2007. **LOI** (Scot): 8 (2012-13 to 2013); HS 20* v Ireland (Belfast) 2013. **IT20** (Scot): 4 (2012-13 to 2013-14); HS 20 v Kenya (Dubai) 2013-14. HS 81 v Hants (Northampton) 2013. LO HS 31* v Netherlands (Northampton) 2010 (CB40). T20 HS 20.

NEWTON, Robert Irving (Framlingham C), b Taunton, Somerset 18 Jan 1990. 5'8". RHB, OB. Debut (Northamptonshire) 2010. Northamptonshire 2nd XI debut 2006. HS 119* v Derbys (Northampton) 2012. BB –. LO HS 88* v Kent (Tunbridge W) 2013 (Y40). T20 HS 38.

PETERS, Stephen David (Coopers Coborn & Co S), b Harold Wood, Essex 10 Dec 1978. 5'11". RHB, occ LB. Essex 1996-2001, scoring 110 and 12* v Cambridge U (Cambridge) on debut. Worcestershire 2002-05. Northamptonshire debut 2006; cap 2007; captain 2013 to date. MCC 2011, 2012. 1000 runs (4); most – 1320 (2010). HS 222 v Glamorgan (Swansea) 2011. BB 1-19 Ex v Oxford U (Chelmsford) 1999. LO HS 107 v Yorks (Leeds) 2007 (FPT). T20 HS 61*.

SALES, David John Grimwood (Caterham S; Cumnor House S), b Carshalton, Surrey 3 Dec 1977. 6'0". RHB, RM. Debut (Northamptonshire) 1996 v Worcs (Kidderminster) scoring 0 and 210* – record Championship score on f-c debut; youngest (18y 237d) to score 200 in a Championship match; cap 1999; captain 2004-07; benefit 2007. Missed entire 2009 season with knee injury. Wellington 2001-02. MCC 2010. F-c Tours (Eng A): NZ 1999-00; SL 1997-98; K 1997-98; B 1999-00. 1000 runs (6); most – 1384 (2007). HS 303* v Essex (Northampton) 1999 – youngest Englishman (21y 240d) to score a f-c 300. BB 4-25 v Sri Lanka A (Northampton) 1999. CC BB 2-7 v Yorks (Scarborough) 1999. LO HS 161 v Yorks (Northampton) 2006 (CGT) – Nh record. LO BB –. T20 HS 78*. T20 BB 1-10.

SPRIEGEL, Matthew Neil William (Whitgift S; Loughborough U), b Epsom, Surrey 4 Mar 1987. 6'3". LHB, OB. Loughborough UCCE 2007-08; captain 2007-08. Surrey 2008-12. Northamptonshire debut 2013. HS 108* Sy v Bangladeshis (Oval) 2010. CC HS 103 Sy v Northants (Oval) 2010. Nh HS 76 v Hants (Southampton) 2013. BB 3-75 v Worcs (Worcester) 2013. LO HS 86 Sy v Durham (Oval) 2011 (CB40). LO BB 3-29 v Worcs (Worcester) 2013 (Y40). T20 HS 53*. T20 BB 4-33.

STONE, Oliver Peter (Thorpe St Andrew HS), b Norwich, Norfolk 9 Oct 1983. 6'1". RHB, RMF. Debut (Northamptonshire) 2012. Northamptonshire 2nd XI debut 2010. Norfolk 2011. Captained England U19s 2012-13. HS 26* and BB 1-6 v Yorks (Northampton) 2012. LO HS 7* v Yorks (Northampton) 2012 (CB40). LO BB 1-12 v Derbys (Northampton) 2012 (CB40). T20 HS 0. T20 BB 2-26.

WAKELY, Alexander George (Bedford S), b Hammersmith, London 3 Nov 1988. 6'2". RHB, OB. Debut (Northamptonshire) 2007; cap 2012; l-o captain 2013 to date. Bedfordshire 2004-05. Suffered ruptured Achilles in pre-season. HS 113* v Glamorgan (Cardiff) 2009. BB 2-62 v Somerset (Taunton) 2007 – on debut. LO HS 102 v Kent (Tunbridge W) 2013 (Y40). LO BB 2-14 v Lancs (Northampton) 2007 (P40). T20 HS 62. T20 BB –.

WHITE, Graeme Geoffrey (Stowe S), b Milton Keynes, Bucks 18 Apr 1987. 5'11". RHB, SLA. Northamptonshire 2006-09, rejoined the county during 2013, initially on loan. Nottinghamshire 2010-13. HS 65 Nh v Glamorgan (Colwyn Bay) 2007. BB 4-72 Nt v Durham (Nottingham) 2011. Nh BB 2-35 v Cambridge UCCE (Cambridge) 2010. LO HS 39* v Somerset (Taunton) 2012 (CB40). LO BB 5-35 v Scotland (Edinburgh) 2010 (CB40). T20 HS 26*. T20 BB 5-22 v Lancs (Nottingham) 2013 – Nt record.

WILLEY, David Jonathan (Northampton S), b Northampton 28 Feb 1990. Son of P.Willey (Northants, Leics and England 1966-91). 6'1". LHB, LFM. Debut (Northamptonshire) 2009; cap 2013. Bedfordshire 2008. England U19s 2009. HS 81 v Glamorgan (Northampton) 2013. BB 5-29 (10-75 match) v Glos (Northampton) 2011. LO HS 167 v Warwks (Birmingham) 2013 (Y40). LO BB 3-28 v Worcs (Worcester) 2013 (Y40). T20 HS 60. T20 BB 4-9.

RELEASED/RETIRED

(Having made a County First-Class or List A appearance in 2013)

[NQ]**COPELAND, Trent** Aaron, b Gosford, NSW, Australia 14 Mar 1986. RHB, RFM. New South Wales 2009-10 to date. Northamptonshire 2013. **Tests** (A): 3 (2011); HS 23* v SL (Galle) 2011; BB 2-24 v SL (Pallekele) 2011. F-c Tours (A): SA 2011-12; SL 2011; Z 2011 (Aus A). HS 106 NSW v Tas (Hobart) 2012-13. Nh HS 70 v Essex (Northampton) 2013. BB 8-92 (10-149 match) NSW v Q (Sydney) 2009-10 – on debut. Nh BB 7-63 v Leics (Northampton) 2013. LO HS 21 NSW v WA (Sydney) 2012-13. LO BB 5-32 v Sussex (Northampton) 2013. T20 HS 1. T20 BB –.

DAGGETT, Lee Martin (Woodhey HS, and Holy Cross C, Bury; Durham U) b Bury, Lancs 1 Oct 1982. 6'0". RHB, RMF. Durham UCCE 2003-05. British U 2004. Warwickshire 2006-08. Leicestershire 2008. Northamptonshire 2009-13; cap 2013. HS 50* v Leics (Leicester) 2011. BB 8-94 DU v Durham (Chester-le-St) 2004. CC BB 6-30 Wa v Durham (Birmingham) 2006. Nh BB 4-25 v Worcs (Worcester) 2010. LO HS 14* and BB 4-17 v Neth (Northampton) 2010 (CB40). T20 HS 3*. T20 BB 2-17.

DAVIS, Christian Arthur Linghorne (Bedford S), b Milton Keynes, Bucks 11 Oct 1992. 6'2". RHB, LFM. Northamptonshire 2nd XI debut 2010. Bedfordshire 2010. England U19s 2010-11. Awaiting f-c debut. LO HS 54 v Kent (Northampton) 2012 (CB40). LO BB –.

[NQ]**WHITE, Cameron** Leon, b Bairnsdale, Victoria, Australia 18 Aug 1983. 6'1½". RHB, LBG. Victoria 2000-01 to date. Somerset 2006-07; captain 2006 (*part*); cap 2007. Northamptonshire 2013 (T20 only in 2012). **Tests** (A): 4 (2008-09); HS 46 v I (Nagpur) 2008-09; BB 2-71 v I (Chandigarh) 2008-09. **LOI** (A): 87 (2005-06 to 2010-11); HS 105 v E (Southampton) 2009 and 105 v P (Brisbane) 2009-10; BB 3-5 v B (Darwin) 2008. **IT20** (A): 41 (2006-07 to 2013-14); HS 85* v SL (Bridgetown) 2010; BB 1-11 v E (Sydney) 2006-07. F-c Tours (A): I 2008-09; P 2005-06 (Aus A), 2007-08 (Aus A). 1000 runs (2); most – 1190 (2006). HS 260* Sm v Derbys (Derby) 2006 – world record score in the fourth innings of a f-c match. Nh HS 90 and Nh BB 1-18 v Lancs (Northampton) 2013. BB 6-66 Vic v WA (Perth) 2002-03. CC BB 5-148 Sm v Surrey (Guildford) 2006. LO HS 126* Vic v NSW (Canberra) 2006-07. LO BB 4-15 Vic v Tas (Melbourne) 2004-05. T20 HS 141* Sm v Worcs (Worcester) 2006 – Sm record. T20 BB 4-10.

C.D.de Lange, L.Evans and S.A.Sweeney left the staff without making a County First-Class or List-A appearance in 2013.

NORTHAMPTONSHIRE 2013

RESULTS SUMMARY

	Place	Won	Lost	Tied	Drew	NR
LV= County Championship (2nd Division)	2nd	5	3		8	
All First-Class Matches		5	3		8	
Yorkshire Bank 40 (Group A)	2nd	8	3			1
Friends Life t20 (Midlands/Wales/West Group)	Winners	10	3			

LV= COUNTY CHAMPIONSHIP AVERAGES

BATTING AND FIELDING

Cap		M	I	NO	HS	Runs	Avge	100	50	Ct/St
2009	A.J.Hall	16	21	4	130*	936	55.05	3	5	13
2007	S.D.Peters	10	15	1	106	735	52.50	2	5	4
1999	D.J.G.Sales	16	23	3	255*	919	45.95	3	1	11
	R.I.Keogh	8	12	2	221	458	45.80	1	1	1
	R.I.Newton	6	8	2	81	251	41.83	–	1	1
2013	S.P.Crook	14	15	3	88*	482	40.16	–	5	3
2013	K.J.Coetzer	10	15	1	219	527	37.64	2	1	3
2011	J.D.Middlebrook	16	21	1	109	711	35.55	1	6	5
	T.A.Copeland	10	10	3	70	247	35.28	–	2	11
	B.M.Duckett	4	6	1	53*	145	29.00	–	1	4
	D.Murphy	14	14	3	81	293	26.63	–	2	51/4
2013	D.J.Willey	13	15	1	81	346	24.71	–	3	3
2012	A.G.Wakely	15	21	1	88	457	22.85	–	2	5
	M.N.W.Spriegel	8	12	2	76	134	13.40	–	1	2
	Azhar Ullah	9	10	6	8	12	3.00	–	–	3

Also batted: J.N.Batty (1 match) 12; L.M.Daggett (3 – cap 2013) 1, 11 (1 ct); C.L.White (2) 90, 1, 16; G.G.White (1) 0, 0.

BOWLING

	O	M	R	W	Avge	Best	5wI	10wM
T.A.Copeland	394.4	139	822	45	18.26	7-63	4	1
D.J.Willey	361.3	66	1122	45	24.93	5-67	2	–
A.J.Hall	325.3	85	937	37	25.32	5-30	1	–
S.P.Crook	326	46	1139	43	26.48	4-30	–	–
Azhar Ullah	225.4	51	717	25	28.68	4-42	–	–
J.D.Middlebrook	249.1	53	775	21	36.90	6-78	1	–

Also bowled:
M.N.W.Spriegel 48 7 183 5 36.60 3-75
K.J.Coetzer 7-1-16-0; L.M.Daggett 59.3-13-203-2; R.I.Keogh 4-1-9-0; A.G.Wakely 1-0-3-0; C.L.White 25.2-4-99-2; G.G.White 4-1-14-0.

Northamptonshire played no first-class fixtures outside the County Championship in 2013. The First-Class Averages (pp 225–241) give the records of their players in all first-class county matches, with the exception of G.G.White, whose first-class figures for Northamptonshire are as above.

NORTHAMPTONSHIRE RECORDS

FIRST-CLASS CRICKET

				v			
Highest Total	For	781-7d		v	Notts	Northampton	1995
	V	673-8d		by	Yorkshire	Leeds	2003
Lowest Total	For	12		v	Glos	Gloucester	1907
	V	33		by	Lancashire	Northampton	1977
Highest Innings	For	331*	M.E.K.Hussey	v	Somerset	Taunton	2003
	V	333	K.S.Duleepsinhji	for	Sussex	Hove	1930

Highest Partnership for each Wicket

1st	375	R.A.White/M.J.Powell	v	Glos	Northampton	2002
2nd	344	G.Cook/R.J.Boyd-Moss	v	Lancashire	Northampton	1986
3rd	393	A.Fordham/A.J.Lamb	v	Yorkshire	Leeds	1990
4th	370	R.T.Virgin/P.Willey	v	Somerset	Northampton	1976
5th	401	M.B.Loye/D.Ripley	v	Glamorgan	Northampton	1998
6th	376	R.Subba Row/A.Lightfoot	v	Surrey	The Oval	1958
7th	293	D.J.G.Sales/D.Ripley	v	Essex	Northampton	1999
8th	179	A.J.Hall/J.D.Middlebrook	v	Surrey	The Oval	2011
9th	156	R.Subba Row/S.Starkie	v	Lancashire	Northampton	1955
10th	148	B.W.Bellamy/J.V.Murdin	v	Glamorgan	Northampton	1925

Best Bowling	For	10-127	V.W.C.Jupp	v	Kent	Tunbridge W	1932
(Innings)	V	10- 30	C.Blythe	for	Kent	Northampton	1907
Best Bowling	For	15- 31	G.E.Tribe	v	Yorkshire	Northampton	1958
(Match)	V	17- 48	C.Blythe	for	Kent	Northampton	1907

Most Runs – Season	2198	D.Brookes	(av 51.11)		1952
Most Runs – Career	28980	D.Brookes	(av 36.13)		1934-59
Most 100s – Season	8	R.A.Haywood			1921
Most 100s – Career	67	D.Brookes			1934-59
Most Wkts – Season	175	G.E.Tribe	(av 18.70)		1955
Most Wkts – Career	1102	E.W.Clark	(av 21.26)		1922-47
Most Career W-K Dismissals	810	K.V.Andrew	(653 ct; 157 st)		1953-66
Most Career Catches in the Field	469	D.S.Steele			1963-84

LIMITED-OVERS CRICKET

Highest Total	50ov	360-2		v	Staffs	Northampton	1990
	40ov	324-6		v	Warwicks	Birmingham	2013
	T20	224-5		v	Glos	Milton Keynes	2005
Lowest Total	50ov	62		v	Leics	Leicester	1974
	40ov	41		v	Middlesex	Northampton	1972
	T20	47		v	Durham	Chester-le-St^2	2011
Highest Innings	50ov	161	D.J.G.Sales	v	Yorkshire	Northampton	2006
	40ov	172*	W.Larkins	v	Warwicks	Luton	1983
	T20	111*	L.Klusener	v	Worcs	Kidderminster	2007
Best Bowling	50ov	7-10	C.Pietersen	v	Denmark	Brondby	2005
	40ov	7-39	A.Hodgson	v	Somerset	Northampton	1976
	T20	6-21	A.J.Hall	v	Worcs	Northampton	2008

NOTTINGHAMSHIRE

Formation of Present Club: March/April 1841
Substantial Reorganisation: 11 December 1866
Inaugural First-Class Match: 1864
Colours: Green and Gold
Badge: Badge of City of Nottingham
County Champions (since 1890): (6) 1907, 1929, 1981, 1987, 2005, 2010
NatWest Trophy Winners: (1) 1987
Benson and Hedges Cup Winners: (1) 1989
Sunday League Winners: (1) 1991
Yorkshire Bank 40 Winners: (1) 2013
Twenty20 Cup Winners: (0); best – Finalist 2006

Chief Executive: Lisa Pursehouse, Trent Bridge, Nottingham NG2 6AG • Tel: 0115 982 3000 • Fax: 0115 982 3037 • Email: administration@nottsccc.co.uk • Webs: www.nottsccc.co.uk • www.trentbridge.co.uk • Twitter: @TrentBridge (15,740 followers)

Director of Cricket: Mick Newell. **Assistant Coach**: Wayne Noon. **Batting Coach**: Paul Johnson. **Bowling Coach**: Andy Pick. **Captains**: C.M.W.Read (f-c) and J.W.A.Taylor (l-o). **Vice-Captain**: J.W.A.Taylor. **Overseas Player**: P.M.Siddle. **2014 Beneficiary**: None. **Head Groundsman**: Steve Birks. **Scorer**: Roger Marshall. ‡ New registration. ᴺᵠ Not qualified for England.

ᴺᵠ**ADAMS, Andre** Ryan (Westlake BHS, Auckland), b Mangere, Auckland, New Zealand 17 Jul 1975. 5'9". RHB, RMF. Auckland 1997-98 to date. Essex 2004-06, scoring 124 on debut (*see below*); cap 2004. Nottinghamshire debut/cap 2007 (Kolpak registration). Herefordshire 2001. **Tests** (NZ): 1 (2001-02); HS 11 and BB 3-44 v E (Auckland) 2001-02. **LOI** (NZ): 42 (2000-01 to 2006-07); HS 45 v P (Rawalpindi) 2001-02; BB 5-22 v I (Queenstown) 2002-03. **IT20** (NZ): 4 (2004-05 to 2005-06); HS 7 v A (Auckland) 2004-05; BB 2-20 v SL (Auckland) 2006-07. HS 124 Ex v Leics (Leicester) 2004 (91 balls, 7 sixes, 13 fours; 100 off 80 balls) on UK debut. Nt HS 84 v Yorks (Scarborough) 2009. 50 wkts (3); most – 68 (2010). BB 7-32 (10-50 match) v Lancs (Manchester) 2012. Hat-trick Ex v Somerset (Taunton) 2005. LO HS 90* North Is Selection XI v Sri Lankans (New Plymouth) 2000-01. LO BB 5-7 Auckland v ND (Auckland) 1999-00. T20 HS 54*. T20 BB 5-20.

BACON, George Peter William (Djanogly City Ac; Bilborough C), b Nottingham 16 Sep 1992. RHB, RFM. Nottinghamshire 2nd XI debut 2011. Bedfordshire 2010-11. Awaiting f-c debut. LO HS 0 and LO BB 2-62 v Bangladesh A (Nottingham) 2013 – only 1st XI game.

BALL, Jacob Timothy ('**Jake**') (Meden CS), b Mansfield 14 Mar 1991. Nephew of B.N.French (Notts and England 1976-95). 6'0". RHB, RM. Debut (Nottinghamshire) 2011. Nottinghamshire 2nd XI debut 2008. England U19s 2010. HS 15 and BB 3-18 v Durham MCCU (Nottingham) 2013. LO HS 19* v Sri Lanka A (Nottingham) 2011. BB 4-25 v Somerset (Nottingham) 2013 (Y40). T20 HS 1*. T20 BB 2-20.

158

BROAD, Stuart Christopher John (Oakham S), b Nottingham 24 Jun 1986. 6'6". LHB, RFM. Son of B.C.Broad (Glos, Notts, OFS and England 1979-94). Debut (Leicestershire) 2005; cap 2007. Nottinghamshire debut/cap 2008. YC 2006. *Wisden* 2009. **ECB central contract 2013-14. Tests:** 67 (2007-08 to 2013-14); HS 169 v P (Lord's) 2010, sharing in record Test and UK f-c 8th-wkt partnership of 332 with I.J.L.Trott; BB 7-44 v NZ (Lord's) 2013. Hat-trick v I (Nottingham) 2011. **LOI:** 108 (2006 to 2013-14, 3 as captain); HS 45* v I (Manchester) 2007; BB 5-23 v SA (Nottingham) 2008. **IT20:** 51 (2006 to 2013-14, 22 as captain); HS 18* v SA (Chester-le-St) 2012 and 18* v A (Melbourne) 2013-14; BB 4-24 v NZ (Auckland) 2012-13. F-c Tours: A 2010-11, 2013-14; SA 2009-10; WI 2005-06 (Eng A), 2008-09; NZ 2007-08, 2012-13; I 2008-09, 2012-13; SL 2007-08, 2011-12; B 2006-07 (Eng A), 2009-10; UAE 2011-12 (v P). HS 169 (*see Tests*). CC HS 91* Le v Derbys (Leicester) 2007. Nt HS 60 v Worcs (Nottingham) 2009. BB 8-52 (11-131 match) v Warwks (Birmingham) 2010. LO HS 45* (*see LOI*). LO BB 5-23 (*see LOI*). T20 HS 18*. T20 BB 4-24.

CARTER, Andrew (Lincoln C), b Lincoln 27 Aug 1988. 6'4". RHB, RM. Debut (Nottinghamshire) 2009. Essex 2010 (on loan). Nottinghamshire 2nd XI debut 2006. Lincolnshire 2007-10. HS 17* v Sussex (Hove) 2012. BB 5-40 Ex v Kent (Canterbury) 2010. Nt BB 4-55 v Warwks (Nottingham) 2012. LO HS 12 v Sussex (Hove) 2010 (P40). LO BB 4-45 v Durham (Nottingham) 2012 (CB40). T20 HS –. T20 BB 4-20.

FLETCHER, Luke Jack (Henry Mellish S, Nottingham), b Nottingham 18 Sep 1988. 6'6". RHB, RMF. Debut (Nottinghamshire) 2008. HS 92 v Hants (Southampton) 2009. BB 5-52 v Warwks (Nottingham) 2013. LO HS 40* v Durham (Chester-le-St) 2009 (P40). LO BB 3-27 v Somerset (Taunton) 2011 (CB40). T20 HS 5. T20 BB 4-30.

FRANKS, Paul John (Southwell Minster CS), b Mansfield 3 Feb 1979. 6'2". LHB, RMF. Debut (Nottinghamshire) 1996; cap 1999; benefit 2007. Canterbury 2002-03. MW Rhinos 2010-11. YC 2000. **LOI:** 1 (2000); HS 4 v WI (Nottingham) 2000. F-c Tours (Eng A): SA 1998-99; WI 2000-01; NZ 1999-00; SL 2004-05; B 1999-00. HS 123* v Leics (Leicester) 2003. 50 wkts (2); most – 63 (1999). BB 7-56 v Middx (Lord's) 2000. Hat-trick v Warwks (Nottingham) 1997. LO HS 84* v Lincs (Lincoln) 2003 (CGT). LO BB 6-27 v Durham (Chester-le-St) 2000 (NL). T20 HS 29*. T20 BB 2-12.

GURNEY, Harry Frederick (Garendon HS; Loughborough GS; Leeds U), b Nottingham 25 Oct 1986. 6'2". RHB, LFM. Leicestershire 2007-11. Nottinghamshire debut 2012. Bradford/Leeds UCCE 2006-07 (not f-c). HS 24* Le v Middx (Leicester) 2009. Nt HS 22* v Somerset (Taunton) 2013. BB 5-81 v Somerset (Nottingham) 2013. Hat-trick v Sussex (Hove) 2013. LO HS 13* v Durham (Chester-le-St) 2012 (CB40). LO BB 5-24 Le v Hants (Leicester) 2010 (CB40). T20 HS 5*. T20 BB 3-21.

HALES, Alexander Daniel (Chesham S), b Hillingdon, Middx 3 Jan 1989. 6'5". RHB, RM, occ WK. Debut (Nottinghamshire) 2008; cap 2011. Buckinghamshire 2006-07. MCC YCs 2006-07. **IT20:** 24 (2011 to 2013-14); HS 99 v WI (Nottingham) 2012. 1000 runs (1): 1127 (2011). HS 184 v Somerset (Nottingham) 2009. BB 2-63 v Yorks (Nottingham) 2009. LO HS 150* v Worcs (Nottingham) 2009 (P40). T20 HS 99.

HUTTON, Brett Alan (Worksop C), b Doncaster, Yorks 6 Feb 1993. 6'2". RHB, RM. Debut (Nottinghamshire) 2011. Nottinghamshire 2nd XI debut 2010. HS 42 and BB 1-31 v Somerset (Nottingham) 2013. LO HS 17* and LO BB 1-60 v Sri Lanka A (Nottingham) 2011.

‡**JAQUES, Philip** Anthony (Fig Tree HS, Wollongong; Australian C of PE, Homebush), b Wollongong, NSW, Australia 3 May 1979. 6'1". LHB, SLC. British passport (English parents) and now UK qualified. NSW 2000-01 to 2011-12. Northamptonshire 2003; cap 2003. Yorkshire 2004-13; cap 2005. Worcestershire 2006-07, 2010. **Tests** (A): 11 (2005-06 to 2008); HS 150 v SL (Hobart) 2007-08. **LOI** (A): 6 (2005-06 to 2006-07); HS 94 v SA (Melbourne) 2005-06. F-c Tours (A): WI 2008; P 2005-06 (Aus A), 2007-08 (Aus A); B 2005-06. 1000 runs (4+2); most – 1409 (2003). HS 244 Wo v Essex (Chelmsford) 2006. BB 1-75 v Sussex (Hove) 2013. LO HS 171* NSW v Q (Sydney) 2009-10. T20 HS 92.

‡**KEEDY, Gary** (Garforth CS), b Wakefield, Yorks 27 Nov 1974. 6'0". LHB, SLA. Yorkshire 1994 (one match). Lancashire debut 1995; cap 2000; benefit 2009. Surrey 2013. MCC 2011. F-c Tour: WI 1995-96 (La). HS 64 La v Sussex (Hove) 2008. 50 wkts (4); most – 72 (2004). BB 7-68 (10-128 match) La v Durham (Manchester) 2010. LO HS 33 La v Derbys (Derby) 2008. LO BB 5-30 La v Sussex (Manchester) 2000 (NL). T20 HS 9*. T20 BB 4-15.

KELSALL, Samuel (Trentham HS, Stoke), b Stoke-on-Trent, Staffs 14 Mar 1993. 5'7". RHB, RM. Debut (Nottinghamshire) 2011. Nottinghamshire 2nd XI debut 2008, aged 15y 158d. No f-c appearances in 2013. HS 35 v Warwks (Nottingham) 2012. LO HS 40 v Sri Lanka A (Nottingham) 2011.

LUMB, Michael John (St Stithians C, Johannesburg), b Johannesburg, South Africa 12 Feb 1980. Son of R.G.Lumb (Yorkshire 1970-84); nephew of A.J.S.Smith (SAU and Natal 1972-73 to 1983-84). 6'0". LHB, RM. Yorkshire 2000-06; ECB qualified and CC debut 2001; cap 2003. Hampshire 2007-11; cap 2008. Nottinghamshire debut/cap 2012. **LOI**: 3 (2013-14); HS 106 v WI (North Sound) 2013-14, becoming only the 2nd England player after D.L.Amiss to score a century on LOI debut. **IT20**: 20 (2009-10 to 2013-14); HS 53* v NZ (Wellington) 2012-13. F-c Tour (Eng A): I 2003-04. 1000 runs (3); most – 1120 (2013). HS 221* v Derbys (Nottingham) 2013. BB 2-10 Y v Kent (Canterbury) 2001. LO HS 110 EL v Pakistan A (Dubai) 2009-10. LO BB –. T20 HS 124* H v Essex (Southampton) 2009 – H record. T20 BB 3-32.

MULLANEY, Steven John (St Mary's RC S, Astley), b Warrington, Cheshire 19 Nov 1986. 5'9". RHB, RM. Lancashire 2006-08. No f-c appearances in 2009. Nottinghamshire debut 2010, scoring 100* v Hants (Southampton) 2007; cap 2013. HS 165* La v Durham UCCE (Durham) 2007. Nt HS 125 v Middx (Lord's) 2013. BB 4-31 v Essex (Nottingham) 2010. LO HS 61 v Sri Lanka A (Nottingham) 2011. LO BB 4-29 v Kent (Nottingham) 2013 (Y40). T20 HS 53. T20 BB 4-19.

PATEL, Samit Rohit (Worksop C), b Leicester 30 Nov 1984. Elder brother of A.Patel (Derbyshire and Notts 2007-11). 5'8". RHB, SLA. Debut (Nottinghamshire) 2002; cap 2008. Nottinghamshire 2nd XI debut 1999, aged 14y 274d. **Tests**: 5 (2011-12 to 2012-13); HS 33 v I (Kolkata) 2012-13; BB 2-27 v SL (Galle) 2011-12. **LOI**: 36 (2008 to 2012-13); HS 70* v I (Mohali) 2011-12; BB 5-41 v SA (Oval) 2008. **IT20**: 18 (2011 to 2012-13); HS 67 v SL (Pallekele) 2012-13; BB 2-6 v Afghanistan (Colombo, RPS) 2012-13. F-c Tours: I 2012-13; SL 2011-12; NZ 2008-09 (Eng A). HS 256 v Durham MCCU (Nottingham) 2013. CC HS 176 v Glos (Nottingham) 2007. BB 7-68 (11-111 match) v Hants (Southampton) 2011. LO HS 129* v Warwks (Nottingham) 2013 (Y40). LO BB 6-13 v Ireland (Dublin) 2009 (FPT). T20 HS 84*. T20 BB 3-11.

READ, Christopher Mark Wells (Torquay GS; Bath U), b Paignton, Devon 10 Aug 1978. 5'8". RHB, WK. Gloucestershire (1-o only) 1997. Debut 1997-98 for England A in Kenya. Nottinghamshire debut 1998; cap 1999; captain 2008 to date; benefit 2009. MCC 2002. Devon 1995-97. *Wisden* 2010. **Tests**: 15 (1999 to 2006-07); HS 55 v P (Leeds) 2006. Made six dismissals twice in successive innings 2006-07 to establish an Ashes record. **LOI**: 36 (1999-00 to 2006-07); HS 30* v SA (Manchester) 2003. **IT20**: 1 (2006); HS 13 v P (Bristol) 2006. F-c Tours: A 2006-07; SA 1998-99 (Eng A), 1999-00; WI 2000-01 (Eng A), 2003-04, 2005-06 (Eng A); SL 1997-98 (Eng A), 2002-03 (ECB Acad), 2003-04; Z 1998-99 (Eng A); B 2003-04; K 1997-98 (Eng A). 1000 runs (1); most – 1203 (2009). HS 240 v Essex (Chelmsford) 2007. BB –. LO HS 135 v Durham (Nottingham) 2006 (CGT). T20 HS 58*.

SHAHZAD, Ajmal (Woodhouse Grove S; Bradford U), b Huddersfield, Yorkshire 27 Jul 1985. 6'0". RHB, RFM. Yorkshire 2006-12 (first British-born Asian to play for Yorkshire); cap 2010. Lancashire 2012 (on loan). Nottinghamshire debut 2013. **Tests**: 1 (2010); HS 5 and BB 3-45 v B (Manchester) 2010. **LOI**: 11 (2009-10 to 2010-11); HS 9 v A (Brisbane) 2010-11; BB 3-41 v B (Bristol) 2010. **IT20**: 3 (2009-10 to 2010-11); HS 0*; BB 2-38 v P (Dubai) 2009-10. F-c Tours: A 2010-11; B 2009-10. HS 88 Y v Sussex (Hove) 2009. Nt HS 77 v Sussex (Nottingham) 2013. BB 5-51 Y v Durham (Chester-le-St) 2010. Nt BB 3-21 v Durham MCCU (Nottingham) 2013. LO HS 59* Y v Kent (Leeds) 2011 (CB40). LO BB 5-51 Y v Sri Lanka A (Leeds) 2007. T20 HS 20. T20 BB 3-30.

^NQ**SIDDLE, Peter** Matthew, b Traralgon, Victoria, Australia 25 Nov 1984. 6'1½". RHB, RFM. Victoria 2005-06 to date. **Tests** (A): 53 (2008-09 to 2013-14); HS 51 v I (Delhi) 2012-13; BB 6-54 v E (Brisbane) 2010-11. **LOI** (A): 17 (2008-09 to 2010-11); HS 9* v SL (Sydney) 2010-11; BB 3-55 v E (Centurion) 2009-10. **IT20** (A): 2 (2008-09 to 2010-11); HS 1* and BB 2-24 v NZ (Sydney) 2008-09. F-c Tours (A): E 2009, 2013; SA 2008-09, 2011-12, 2013-14; WI 2011-12; I 2008-09 (Aus A), 2008-09, 2012-13; SL 2011; Z 2011 (Aus A). HS 103* Aus A v Scotland (Edinburgh) 2013. 50 wkts (0+1): 54 (2011-12). BB 6-43 Vic v S Aus (Melbourne) 2011-12. LO HS 25* Vic v Tas (Hobart) 2010-11. LO BB 4-27 Vic v Tas (Hobart) 2008-09. T20 HS 9*. T20 BB 4-29.

TAYLOR, James William Arthur (Shrewsbury S), b Nottingham 6 Jan 1990. 5'6". RHB, LB. Leicestershire 2008-11; cap 2009. Nottinghamshire debut/cap 2012; 1-o captain 2014. Sussex (1 game) 2013. MCC 2010. Shropshire 2007. England U19s 2008 to 2009. YC 2009. **Tests**: 2 (2012); HS 34 v SA (Leeds) 2012. **LOI**: 1 (2011); HS 1 v Ireland (Dublin) 2011. F-c Tours (EL): WI 2010-11, SL 2013-14. 1000 runs (4); most – 1602 (2011). HS 242 EL v Sri Lanka A (Dambulla) 2013-14. CC HS 207* Le v Surrey (Oval) 2009. Nt HS 204* v Sussex (Nottingham) 2013. BB –. LO HS 115* v Hants (Southampton) 2012 (CB40). LO BB 4-61 Le v Warwks (Leicester) 2010 (CB40). T20 HS 62*. T20 BB 1-10.

^NQ**WESSELS, Mattheus** Hendrik (**'Riki'**) (Woodridge C, Pt Elizabeth; Northampton U), b Marogudoore, Queensland, Australia 12 Nov 1985. Left Australia when 2 months old. Son of K.C.Wessels (OFS, Sussex, WP, NT, Q, EP, GW, Australia and South Africa 1973-74 to 1999-00). 5'11". RHB, WK. MCC 2004. Northamptonshire 2005-09 (Kolpak registration). Nondescripts 2007-08. MWR 2009-10 to 2011-12. Nottinghamshire debut 2011. HS 199 v Sussex (Hove) 2012. BB 1-10 MWR v MT (Bulawayo) 2009-10. LO HS 100 Nh v Surrey (Oval) 2008 (P40). LO BB 1-0 MWR v MT (Bulawayo) 2009-10. T20 HS 86*.

WOOD, Samuel Kenneth William (Colonel Frank Seely S, Nottingham), b Nottingham 3 Apr 1993. 5'11". LHB, OB. Debut (Nottinghamshire) 2011. Nottinghamshire 2nd XI debut 2008, aged 15y 40d. England U19s 2010-11. HS 45 and BB 3-64 v Surrey (Oval) 2012. LO HS 32 v Bangladesh A (Nottingham) 2013. LO BB 2-24 v Lancs (Manchester) 2011 (CB40).

(Having made a County First-Class or List A appearance in 2013)

^{NQ}**COWAN, Edward** James McKenzie (Oxford Brookes U), b Paddington, Sydney, Australia 16 Jun 1982. 5'10". LHB, LB. Oxford UCCE 2003. British Us 2003. NSW 2004-05 to 2008-09. Tasmania 2009-10 to date. Gloucestershire 2012; cap 2012. Nottinghamshire 2013; cap 2013. **Tests** (A): 18 (2011-12 to 2013); HS 136 v SA (Brisbane) 2012-13. F-c Tours (A): WI 2011-12; I 2012-13. 1000 runs (0+1): 1299 (2011-12). HS 225 Tas v SA (Hobart) 2009-10. UK HS 137* Brit Us v Zimbabweans (Birmingham) 2003. CC HS Gs 103 v Essex (Cheltenham) 2012. Nt HS 81 v Sussex (Hove) 2013. BB –. LO HS 131* Tas v NSW (Sydney) 2010-11. T20 HS 70.

^{NQ}**HUSSEY, David** John (Prendiville Catholic C; Edith Cowan U), b Morley, Perth, Australia 15 Jul 1977. Younger brother of M.E.K.Hussey (WA, Northants, Glos, Durham and Australia 1994-95 to 2012-13). 5'11". RHB, OB. Victoria 2002-03 to date. Nottinghamshire 2004-13; cap 2004; scored 107* v Oxford U (Oxford) – on UK debut. **LOI** (A): 69 (2008 to 2012-13); HS 111 v Scotland (Edinburgh) 2009; BB 4-21 v E (Adelaide) 2010-11. **IT20** (A): 39 (2007-08 to 2012-13); HS 88* v SA (Johannesburg) 2008-09; BB 3-25 v SA (Melbourne) 2008-09. F-c Tour (Aus A): P 2007-08. 1000 runs (4+1); most – 1315 (2004). HS 275 v Essex (Nottingham) 2007. Scored 170, 116 and 140 in successive innings 2004. BB 4-105 v Hants (Nottingham) 2005. LO HS 140* Vic v NSW (Sydney) 2012-13. LO BB 4-21 (*see LOI*). T20 HS 100*. T20 BB 3-25.

PHILLIPS, Ben James (Langley Park S and SFC, Beckenham), b Lewisham, London 30 Sep 1974. 6'6". RHB, RFM. Kent 1996-98. Northamptonshire 2002-06; cap 2005. Somerset 2008-10, having joined staff in 2007 but missed entire season through injury. Nottinghamshire 2011-13. HS 100* K v Lancs (Manchester) 1997. Nt HS 71 v Yorks (Nottingham) 2011. BB 6-29 Nh v Cambridge UCCE (Cambridge) 2006. CC BB 5-47 K v Sussex (Horsham) 1997. Nt BB 4-33 v Durham (Chester-le-St) 2012. LO HS 51* Sm v Worcs (Bath) 2010 (CB40). LO BB 4-25 K v Northants (Canterbury) 2000 (NL). T20 HS 41*. T20 BB 4-18.

SWANN, Graeme Peter (Sponne S, Towcester), b Northampton 24 Mar 1979. Son of R.Swann (Northumberland 1969-72; Bedfordshire 1988-95); younger brother of A.J.Swann (Northamptonshire and Lancashire 1996-2004). 6'0". RHB, OB. Northamptonshire 1998-2004; cap 1999. Nottinghamshire 2005-13; cap 2005; benefit 2013. MCC 2005. Bedfordshire 1996. *Wisden* 2009. **ECB central contract 2013-14. Tests**: 60 (2008-09 to 2013-14); HS 85 v SA (Centurion) 2009-10; BB 6-65 v P (Birmingham) 2010. **LOI**: 79 (1999-00 to 2013); HS 34 v SL (Dambulla) 2007-08; BB 5-28 v A (Chester-le-St) 2009. **IT20**: 39 (2007-08 to 2012-13); HS 34 v SL (Pallekele) 2012-13; BB 3-13 v P (Dubai) 2011-12. F-c Tours: A 2010-11, 2013-14; Sa 1998-99 (Eng A), 1999-00, 2009-10; WI 2000-01 (Eng A *part*), 2008-09; NZ 2012-13 (*part*); I 2008-09, 2012-13; SL 2004-05 (Eng A) 2011-12; Z 1998-99 (Eng A); B 2009-10; UAE 2011-12 (v P). HS 183 Nh v Glos (Bristol) 2002 – including 114 before lunch on third day. Nt HS 97 v Essex (Chelmsford) 2007. 50 wkts (1): 57 (1999). BB 7-33 Nh v Derbys (Northampton) 2003. Nt BB 7-100 v Glamorgan (Swansea) 2007. LO HS 83 Nh v Leics (Northampton) 2001 (NL). LO BB 5-17 v Glos (Nottingham) 2007 (P40). T20 HS 90*. T20 BB 3-13.

WHITE, G.G. – *see NORTHAMPTONSHIRE*.

VOGES, A.C. – *see MIDDLESEX*.

I.G.Butler left the staff without making a County First-Class or List A appearance in 2013.

NOTTINGHAMSHIRE 2013

RESULTS SUMMARY

	Place	Won	Lost	Tied	Drew	NR
LV= County Championship (1st Division)	7th	2	5		9	
All First-Class Matches		3	5		9	
Yorkshire Bank 40 (Group A)	**Winners**	11	3			
Friends Life t20 (North Group)	QF	7	4			

LV= COUNTY CHAMPIONSHIP AVERAGES

BATTING AND FIELDING

Cap		M	I	NO	HS	Runs	Avge	100	50	Ct/St
2012	M.J.Lumb	15	25	3	221*	1037	47.13	4	2	4
2012	J.W.A.Taylor	15	21	1	204*	925	46.25	2	5	8
2013	E.J.M.Cowan	7	13	2	81	478	43.45	–	4	4
2013	S.J.Mullaney	14	21	–	125	834	39.71	2	6	8
2004	D.J.Hussey	9	13	–	125	478	36.76	1	3	2
2008	S.R.Patel	16	24	–	157	830	34.58	3	–	17
2007	A.R.Adams	11	15	2	80	354	27.23	–	2	3
2013	A.Shahzad	11	17	2	77	363	24.20	–	2	1
1999	P.J.Franks	8	11	–	78	257	23.36	–	2	3
1999	C.M.W.Read	15	22	2	58	452	22.60	–	2	53/2
	M.H.Wessels	11	16	1	77	316	21.06	–	1	13/1
	L.J.Fletcher	15	22	3	64	368	19.36	–	2	5
2011	A.D.Hales	10	18	–	58	251	13.94	–	2	10
	H.F.Gurney	14	18	11	22*	61	8.71	–	–	4

Also batted: S.C.J.Broad (2 matches – cap 2008) 41, 46, 10 (2 ct); A.Carter (1) 0*, 0*; B.A.Hutton (1) 20*, 42; G.P.Swann (1 – cap 2005) 8*, 57; G.G.White (1) 0.

BOWLING

	O	M	R	W	Avge	Best	5wI	10wM
S.C.J.Broad	80	21	213	12	17.75	4-34	–	–
L.J.Fletcher	460.1	133	1288	43	29.95	5-52	2	–
A.R.Adams	302.5	55	929	31	29.96	4-69	–	–
H.F.Gurney	396.3	65	1334	44	30.31	5-81	1	–
P.J.Franks	128	26	449	11	40.81	3-16	–	–
A.Shahzad	324.1	60	1083	22	49.22	3-43	–	–
S.R.Patel	446.2	120	1293	26	49.73	3-40	–	–

Also bowled:
S.J.Mullaney   75.3   12   254   5   50.80   3-22   –   –
A.Carter 28-5-113-2; E.J.M.Cowan 1-0-3-0; D.J.Hussey 4-1-25-0; B.A.Hutton 22-4-109-1; G.P.Swann 41-7-146-4; M.H.Wessels 2-0-11-0; G.G.White 35-7-85-2.

The First-Class Averages (pp 225–241) give the records of Nottinghamshire players in all first-class county matches (Nottinghamshire's other opponents being Durham MCCU), with the exception of S.C.J.Broad, E.J.M.Cowan and G.P.Swann, whose first-class figures for Nottinghamshire are as above, and:
J.W.A.Taylor 16-23-2-204*-956-45.52-2-5-8ct.
G.G.White 2-2-0-23-23-11.50-0-0-0ct. 39.4-9-100-3-33.33-2/24-0-0.

NOTTINGHAMSHIRE RECORDS

FIRST-CLASS CRICKET

Highest Total	For 791		v	Essex	Chelmsford	2007
	V 781-7d		by	Northants	Northampton	1995
Lowest Total	For 13		v	Yorkshire	Nottingham	1901
	V 16		by	Derbyshire	Nottingham	1879
	16		by	Surrey	The Oval	1880
Highest Innings	For 312*	W.W.Keeton	v	Middlesex	The Oval	1939
	V 345	C.G.Macartney	for	Australians	Nottingham	1921

Highest Partnership for each Wicket

1st	406*	D.J.Bicknell/G.E.Welton	v	Warwicks	Birmingham	2000
2nd	398	A.Shrewsbury/W.Gunn	v	Sussex	Nottingham	1890
3rd	367	W.Gunn/J.R.Gunn	v	Leics	Nottingham	1903
4th	361	A.O.Jones/J.R.Gunn	v	Essex	Leyton	1905
5th	359	D.J.Hussey/C.M.W.Read	v	Essex	Nottingham	2007
6th	372*	K.P.Pietersen/J.E.Morris	v	Derbyshire	Derby	2001
7th	301	C.C.Lewis/B.N.French	v	Durham	Chester-le-St[2]	1993
8th	220	G.F.H.Heane/R.Winrow	v	Somerset	Nottingham	1935
9th	170	J.C.Adams/K.P.Evans	v	Somerset	Taunton	1994
10th	152	E.B.Alletson/W.Riley	v	Sussex	Hove	1911
	152	U.Afzaal/A.J.Harris	for	Worcs	Nottingham	2000

Best Bowling	For 10-66	K.Smales	v	Glos	Stroud	1956
(Innings)	V 10-10	H.Verity	for	Yorkshire	Leeds	1932
Best Bowling	For 17-89	F.C.L.Matthews	v	Northants	Nottingham	1923
(Match)	V 17-89	W.G.Grace	for	Glos	Cheltenham	1877

Most Runs – Season	2620	W.W.Whysall	(av 53.46)		1929
Most Runs – Career	31592	G.Gunn	(av 35.69)		1902-32
Most 100s – Season	9	W.W.Whysall			1928
	9	M.J.Harris			1971
	9	B.C.Broad			1990
Most 100s – Career	65	J.Hardstaff jr			1930-55
Most Wkts – Season	181	B.Dooland	(av 14.96)		1954
Most Wkts – Career	1653	T.G.Wass	(av 20.34)		1896-1920
Most Career W-K Dismissals	957	T.W.Oates	(733 ct; 224 st)		1897-1925
Most Career Catches in the Field	466	A.O.Jones			1892-1914

LIMITED-OVERS CRICKET

Highest Total	50ov	346-9		v	Ireland	Nottingham	2009
	40ov	296-7		v	Somerset	Taunton	2002
	T20	215-6		v	Yorkshire	Nottingham	2011
Lowest Total	50ov	74		v	Leics	Leicester	1987
	40ov	57		v	Glos	Nottingham	2009
	T20	91		v	Lancashire	Manchester	2006
Highest Innings	50ov	167*	P.Johnson	v	Kent	Nottingham	1993
	40ov	150*	A.D.Hales	v	Worcs	Nottingham	2009
	T20	96	M.J.Lumb	v	Durham	Chester-le-St[2]	2004
Best Bowling	50ov	6-10	K.P.Evans	v	Northumb	Jesmond	1994
	40ov	6-12	R.J.Hadlee	v	Lancashire	Nottingham	1980
	T20	5-22	G.G.White	v	Lancashire	Nottingham	2013

SOMERSET

Formation of Present Club: 18 August 1875
Inaugural First-Class Match: 1882
Colours: Black, White and Maroon
Badge: Somerset Dragon
County Champions: (0); best – 2nd (Div 1) 2001, 2010, 2012
Gillette/NatWest/C&G Trophy Winners: (3) 1979, 1983, 2001
Benson and Hedges Cup Winners: (2) 1981, 1982
Sunday League Winners: (1) 1979
Twenty20 Cup Winners: (1) 2005

Chief Executive: Guy Lavender, County Ground, Taunton TA1 1JT • Tel: 0845 337 1875 • Fax: 01823 332395 • Email: enquiries@somersetcountycc.co.uk • Web: www.somersetcricketclub.co.uk • Twitter: @SomersetCCC (18,186 followers)

Director of Cricket: Dave Nosworthy. **Assistant/Batting Coach**: Dave Houghton. **Assistant/Bowling Coach**: Jason Kerr. **Director of High Performance**: Andy Hurry. **Captain**: M.E.Trescothick. **Vice-Captain**: J.C.Hildreth. **Overseas Player**: A.N.Petersen. **2014 Beneficiary**: None. **Groundsman**: Simon Lee. **Scorer**: Gerald A.Stickley. ‡ New registration. NQ Not qualified for England.

BARROW, Alexander William Rodgerson (King's C, Taunton), b Frome 6 May 1992. 5'7". RHB, RM/OB. Debut (Somerset) 2011. Somerset 2nd XI debut 2009. HS 83* v Durham (Taunton) 2013. BB 1-4 v Hants (Southampton) 2011. LO HS 72 v Durham (Chester-le-St) 2012 (CB40).

COMPTON, Nicholas Richard Denis (Harrow S; Durham U), b Durban, South Africa 26 Jun 1983. Son of R.Compton (Natal 1978-79 to 1980-81); grandson of D.C.S.Compton (Middlesex, England, Holkar, Europeans, Commonwealth and Cavaliers 1936-64); great-nephew of L.H.Compton (Middlesex 1938-56). 6'1". RHB, OB. Middlesex 2004-09; cap 2006. Somerset debut 2010; cap 2011. Mashonaland Eagles 2010-11. Worcestershire (1 game) 2013. MCC 2007. PCA 2012. *Wisden* 2012. **Tests**: 9 (2012-13 to 2013); HS 117 v NZ (Dunedin) 2012-13. F-c Tours: NZ 2012-13; I 2012-13. BB 2006-07 (Eng A). 1000 runs (4); most – 1494 (2012). Scored 685 runs in April 2012 – a record for April. HS 254* v Durham (Chester-le-St) 2011. BB 1-1 v Hants (Southampton) 2010. LO HS 131 M v Kent (Canterbury) 2009 (FPT). LO BB 1-0 M v Scotland (Lord's) 2009 (FPT). T20 HS 74.

DIBBLE, Adam John (Taunton S), b Exeter, Devon 9 Mar 1991. 6'4". RHB, RMF. Debut (Somerset) 2011. Missed most of 2012 through injury. Somerset 2nd XI debut 2009. Devon 2009. HS 43 and BB 3-42 v Warwks (Birmingham) 2012. LO HS 15 v Glamorgan (Cardiff) 2013 (Y40). LO BB 4-52 v Yorks (Taunton) 2013 (Y40). T20 HS –. T20 BB 1-20.

DOCKRELL, George Henry (Gonzaga C, Dublin), b Dublin, Ireland 22 Jul 1992. 6'3". RHB, SLA. Ireland 2010 to date. Somerset debut 2011. **LOI** (Ire): 38 (2009-10 to 2013-14); HS 19 v WI (Mohali) 2010-11; BB 4-24 v Scotland (Belfast) 2013. **IT20** (Ire): 23 (2009-10 to 2013-14); HS 2* v Kenya (Mombasa) 2011-12; BB 4-20 v Netherlands (Dubai) 2009-10. HS 53 Ire v Namibia (Belfast) 2011. Sm HS 31 v Durham (Taunton) 2013. BB 6-27 v Middx (Taunton) 2012. LO HS 22* Ire v Namibia (Belfast) 2011. LO BB 4-24 (*see LOI*). T20 HS 2*. T20 BB 4-20.

GREGORY, Lewis (Hele's S, Plympton), b Plymouth, Devon 24 May 1992. 6'0". RHB, RMF. Debut (Somerset) 2011. Somerset 2nd XI debut 2008 along T. HS 52 v Derbys (Taunton) 2013. England U19s 2010 to 2010-11. HS 52 v Derbys (Taunton) 2013. BB 5-38 v Middx (Lord's) 2013. LO HS 39 v Glamorgan (Taunton) 2012 (CB40). LO BB 4-27 v Glos (Taunton) 2011 (CB40). T20 HS 22. T20 BB 4-15.

HILDRETH James Charles (Millfield S), b Milton Keynes, Bucks 9 Sep 1984. 5'10", RHB, RMF. Debut (Somerset) 2003; cap 2007. F-c Tour (EL): WI 2010-11. 1000 runs (4); most – 1440 (2010). HS 303* v Warwks (Taunton) 2009. BB 2-39 v Hants (Taunton) 2004. LO HS 151 v Scotland (Taunton) 2009 (FPT). LO BB 2-26 v Worcs (Worcester) 2008 (FPT). T20 HS 107*. T20 BB 3-24.

JONES, Chris Robert (Poole GS; Richard Huish C, Taunton; Grey C, Durham U), b Harold Wood, Essex 5 Nov 1990. 6'3". RHB, RM. Debut (Somerset) 2010. Durham MCCU 2011-13. Somerset 2nd XI debut 2006, aged 15y 290d. Dorset 2008-11. HS 130 v Australians (Taunton) 2013. CC HS 58 v Middx (Lord's) 2013. BB 1-17 v Surrey (Taunton) 2012. LO HS 45* v Essex (Taunton) 2011 (CB40). T20 HS 53*.

KIESWETTER, Craig (Diocesan C; Millfield S), b Johannesburg, South Africa 18 Nov 1987. 6'1". RHB, WK. Debut (Somerset) 2007; cap 2009. Represented South Africa in U19 World Cup 2006. Qualified for England Feb 2010. **LOI**: 46 (2009-10 to 2012-13); HS 107 v B (Chittagong) 2009-10. **IT20**: 25 (2009-10 to 2012-13); HS 63 v A (Bridgetown) 2009-10. F-c Tour (EL): WI 2010-11. 1000 runs (1): 1242 (2009). HS 164 v Notts (Nottingham) 2011. BB 2-3 v Worcs (Worcester) 2012. LO HS 143 England XI v Bangladesh CB (Fatullah) 2009-10. T20 HS 89*.

KIRBY, Steven Paul (Elton HS; Bury C), b Ainsworth, nr Bolton, Lancs 4 Oct 1977. 6'3½". RHB, RFM. Leicestershire staff 1998 – no f-c appearances. Yorkshire 2001-04, debut as sub for M.J.Hoggard (England duty) taking 7-50; cap 2003. Gloucestershire 2005-10; cap 2005. Somerset debut 2011. MCC 2008, 2010-11, 2013. F-c Tour (Eng A): I 2003-04 (part). HS 57 Y v Hants (Leeds) 2002. Sm HS 19 v Durham (Taunton) 2011. 50 wkts (3); most – 67 (2003). BB 8-80 (13-154 match) Y v Somerset (Taunton) 2003. Sm BB 6-115 v Lancs (Liverpool) 2011. LO HS 15 Y v Leics (Leicester) 2003 (NL). LO BB 5-36 Gs v Middx (Lord's) 2007 (FPT). T20 HS 25. T20 BB 3-17.

LEACH, Matthew Jack (Bishop Fox's Community S, Taunton; Richard Huish C; UWIC), b Taunton 22 Jun 1991. 6'0". LHB, SLA. Cardiff MCCU 2012. Somerset debut 2012. Somerset 2nd XI debut 2009. Dorset 2011. HS 21 v Middx (Taunton) 2013. BB 5-63 v Warwks (Taunton) 2013. LO HS 2 v Hants (Southampton) 2012 (CB40). LO BB 1-30 v Scotland (Uddingston) 2012 (CB40).

MESCHEDE, Craig Anthony Joseph (King's C, Taunton), b Johannesburg, South Africa 21 Nov 1991. 6'1". RHB, RMF. Debut (Somerset) 2011. Somerset 2nd XI debut 2008, aged 16y 244d. HS 62 v Durham (Chester-le-St) 2012. BB 4-43 v Surrey (Taunton) 2013. LO HS 40* v Glamorgan (Taunton) 2013 (Y40). LO BB 4-5 v Leics (Taunton) 2013 (Y40). T20 HS 53. T20 BB 3-9.

‡**NOMYBURGH, Johannes** Gerhardus (Pretoria BHS; U of SA), b Pretoria, South Africa 22 Oct 1980. 5'7". Elder brother of S.J.Myburgh (Northerns, KZN and Netherlands 2005-06 to date); brother-in-law of F.de Wet (Northerns, NW, Lions, Hampshire, Dolphins and South Africa 2001-02 to 2011-12). RHB, OB. Northerns 1997-98 to 2006-07. Titans 2004-05. Canterbury 2007-08 to 2009-10. Hampshire 2011. Durham 2012. EU qualified through wife's visa. HS 203 Northerns B v Easterns (Pretoria) 1997-98. CC HS 80 H v Sussex (Southampton) 2011. BB 4-56 Canterbury v ND (Hamilton) 2008-09. CC BB 1-30 H v Durham (Southampton) 2011. LO HS 112 Canterbury v Auckland (Christchurch) 2009-10. LO BB 2-22 Canterbury v CD (Christchurch) 2009-10. T20 HS 88. T20 BB 3-16.

OVERTON, Craig (West Buckland S), b Barnstaple, Devon 10 Apr 1994. 6'5". RHB, RMF. Debut (Somerset) 2012. Somerset 2nd XI debut 2011. Devon 2010-11. HS 50 v Durham (Taunton) 2012. BB 4-38 v Durham (Chester-le-St) 2012. LO HS 20 v Hants (Taunton) 2012 (CB40). LO BB 2-30 EL v Australia A (Melbourne) 2012-13.

OVERTON, Jamie (West Buckland S), b Barnstaple, Devon 10 Apr 1994. 6'5". RHB, RFM. Debut (Somerset) 2012. Somerset 2nd XI debut 2011. Devon 2011. HS 34* v Surrey (Oval) 2012. BB 6-95 v Middx (Taunton) 2013. LO HS 14 v Glos (Bristol) 2013 (Y40). LO BB 4-42 v Durham (Chester-le-St) 2012 (CB40).

^{NQ}**PETERSEN, Alviro** Nathan, b Port Elizabeth, South Africa 25 November 1980. RHB, RM/OB. Northerns 2000-01 to 2005-06. Titans 2004-05 to 2005-06. Lions 2005-06 to date. North West 2008-09. Glamorgan 2011; cap/captain 2011. Essex 2012. Somerset debut/cap 2013. **Tests** (SA): 30 (2009-10 to 2013-14); HS 182 v E (Leeds) 2012; scored 100 v I (Kolkata) on debut; BB 1-2 v WI (Port-of-Spain) 2010. **LOI** (SA): 21 (2006-07 to 2013); HS 80 v Z (Potchefstroom) 2006-07; BB –. **IT20** (SA): 2 (2010); HS 8 v WI (North Sound) 2010. F-c Tours (SA): E 2012; A 2012-13; WI 2010; NZ 2011-12; I 2007-08 (SA A), 2009-10; Z 2007 (SA A); B 2010 (SA A); UAE (v P) 2010-11, 2013-14. 1000 runs (1+2); most – 1376 (2008-09). HS 210 Gm v Surrey (Oval) 2011. Sm HS 167 v Surrey (Oval) 2013. BB 2-7 Northerns v Easterns (Benoni) 2001-02. CC BB 1-27 v Sussex (Taunton) 2013. LO HS 145* Lions v Dolphins (Potchefstroom) 2011-12. LO BB 2-48 Lions v Cape Cobras (Johannesburg) 2011-12. T20 HS 84*. T20 BB 1-4.

REGAN, James Alan (All Hallows Catholic S; Farnborough SFC), b Frimley, Surrey 30 May 1994. RHB, WK. Debut (Somerset) 2012, without batting or bowling. Somerset 2nd XI debut 2010, aged 16y 81d. No 1st XI appearances in 2013.

^{NQ}**THOMAS, Alfonso** Clive (Ravensmead SS; Parow HS), b Cape Town, South Africa 9 Feb 1977. 5'10". RHB, RFM. W Province 1998-99. North West 2000-01 to 2002-03. Northerns 2003-04 to 2005-06. Titans 2004-05 to 2007-08. Warwickshire 2007. Somerset debut 2008; cap 2008 (Kolpak registration). **IT20** (SA): 1 (2006-07); HS – and BB 3-25 v P (Johannesburg) 2006-07. F-c Tour (SA A): Z 2004. HS 119* NW v Northerns (Pretoria) 2002-03. UK HS 94 v Hants (Taunton) 2011. BB 7-54 Titans v Cape Cobras (Cape Town) 2005-06. UK BB 6-60 (10-88 match) v Sussex (Taunton) 2011 and 6-60 v Warwks (Taunton) 2012. LO HS 28* v Scotland (Edinburgh) 2009 (FPT). LO BB 4-18 v Glos (Bristol) 2009 (P40). T20 HS 30*. T20 BB 5-24.

TREGO, Peter David (Wyvern CS, W-s-M), b Weston-super-Mare 12 Jun 1981. 6'0". RHB, RMF. Somerset 2000-02, 2006 to date; cap 2007. Kent 2003. Middlesex 2005. C Districts 2013-14. MCC 2013. Herefordshire 2005. HS 141 CD v Auckland (Napier) 2013-14. Sm HS 140 v West Indies A (Taunton) 2002. CC HS 135 v Derbys (Taunton) 2006. 50 wkts (1): 50 (2012). BB 6-59 M v Notts (Nottingham) 2005. Sm BB 5-53 v Notts (Nottingham) 2012. LO HS 147 v Glamorgan (Taunton) 2010 (CB40). LO BB 5-40 EL v West Indies A (Worcester) 2010. T20 HS 79. T20 BB 4-27.

TRESCOTHICK, Marcus Edward (Sir Bernard Lovell S), b Keynsham 25 Dec 1975. 6'2". LHB, RM, occ WK. Debut (Somerset) 1993; cap 1999; joint captain 2002; benefit 2008; captain 2010 to date. PCA 2000, 2009, 2011. *Wisden* 2004. MBE 2005. **Tests**: 76 (2000 to 2006, 2 as captain); HS 219 v SA (Oval) 2003; BB 1-34 v P (Karachi) 2000-01. **LOI**: 123 (2000 to 2006, 10 as captain); HS 137 v P (Lord's) 2001; BB 2-7 v Z (Manchester) 2000. **IT20**: 3 (2005 to 2006); HS 72 v SL (Southampton) 2006. F-c Tours: A 2002-03; SA 2004-05; WI 2003-04; NZ 1999-00 (Eng A), 2001-02; I 2001-02, 2005-06 (*part*); P 2000-01, 2005-06; SL 2000-01, 2003-04; B 1999-00 (Eng A), 2003-04. 1000 runs (5); most – 1817 (2009). HS 284 v Northants (Northampton) 2007. BB 4-36 (inc hat-trick) v Young A (Taunton) 1995. CC BB 4-82 v Yorks (Leeds) 1998. Hat-trick 1995 (*see above*). LO HS 184 v Glos (Taunton) 2008 (P40) – Sm l-o record. LO BB 4-50 v Northants (Northampton) 2000 (NL). T20 HS 108*.

WALLER, Maximilian Thomas Charles (Millfield S; Bournemouth U), b Salisbury, Wiltshire 3 March 1988. 6'0". RHB, LB. Debut (Somerset) 2009. Dorset 2007-08. No f-c appearances in 2013. HS 28 v Hants (Southampton) 2009. BB 3-33 v Cardiff MCCU (Taunton Vale) 2012. CC BB 2-27 v Sussex (Hove) 2009. LO HS 25* v Glamorgan (Taunton) 2013 (Y40). LO BB 3-39 v Middx (Taunton) 2010 (Y40). T20 HS 3. T20 BB 4-16.

(Having made a County First-Class or List A appearance in 2013)

BUTTLER, J.C. – *see LANCASHIRE.*

NQ**CHAWLA, Piyush** Pramod, b Aligarh, Uttar Pradesh, India 24 Dec 1988. LHB, LBG. Central Zone 2005-06 to date. Uttar Pradesh 2005-06 to date. Sussex 2009; cap 2009. Somerset 2013. **Tests** (I): 3 (2005-06 to 2012-13); HS 4 v SA (Kanpur) 2007-08; BB 4-69 v E (Nagpur) 2012-13. **LOI** (I): 25 (2007-08 to 2010-11); HS 13* v E (Manchester) 2007; BB 4-23 v Hong Kong (Karachi) 2008. **IT20** (I): 7 (2010 to 2012-13); HS 0; BB 2-13 v E (Colombo, RPS) 2012-13. F-c Tours (I A): A 2006; Z 2007. HS 156 UP v Maharashtra (Gahunje) 2012-13. UK HS 112 v Middx (Lord's) 2013. BB 6-46 (10-58 match) India A v Zimbabwe Select (Bulawayo) 2007. UK BB 6-52 (11-170 match) Sx v Somerset (Hove) 2009. Sm BB 5-97 (10-208 match) v Derbys (Taunton) 2013. LO HS 93 Central Zone v East Zone (Cuttack) 2008-09. LO BB 6-46 Uttar Pradesh v Railways (Indore) 2009-10. T20 HS 39*. T20 BB 4-17.

NQ**ELGAR, Dean**, b Welkom, OFS, South Africa 11 Jun 1987. LHB, SLA. Free State 2005-06 to 2010-11. Eagles 2006-07 to 2009-10. Knights 2010-11 to date. Somerset 2013. **Tests** (SA): 9 (2012-13 to 2013-14); HS 103-* v NZ (Pt Elizabeth) 2012-13; BB 1-3 v P (Dubai) 2013-14. **LOI** (SA): 5 (2012); HS 42 v E (Oval) 2012; BB 1-11 v E (Southampton) 2012. F-c Tours (SA A): A 2012-13 (SA); SL 2010; B 2010; Ire 2012; UAE 2013-14 (SA v P). HS 268 SA A v Aus A (Pretoria) 2013. Sm HS 33 and Sm BB 1-26 v Durham (Taunton) 2013. BB 4-25 Knights v Titans (Centurion) 2011-12. LO HS 117 Knights v Dolphins (Pietermaritzburg) 2011-12. LO BB 2-23 SA A v Zim A (Harare) 2012. T20 HS 66. T20 BB 4-23.

HUSSAIN, Gemaal Maqsood (Top Valley CS, Nottingham; High Pavement SFC, Nottingham), b Whipps Cross, London, 10 Oct 1983. 6'5". RHB, RMF. Gloucestershire 2009-10; cap 2009. Somerset 2011-13. Bradford/Leeds UCCE 2003 (not f-c). HS 42 v Lancs (Liverpool) 2011. 50 wkts (1): 67 (2010). BB 6-33 v Worcs (Taunton) 2011. LO HS 18* v Hants (Southampton) 2012 (CB40). BB 2-17 Gs v Notts (Nottingham) 2009 (P40). T20 HS 8. T20 BB 3-22.

NQ**SUPPIAH, Arul** Vivasvan (Millfield S; Exeter U), b Kuala Lumpur, Malaysia 30 Aug 1983. Son of R.Suppiah (Kuala Lumpur). Brother of R.V.Suppiah (Malaysia 1997-98 to 2006; f-c 2004). 6'0". RHB, SLA. Somerset 2002-13; cap 2009; benefit 2013. Malaysia 2000-01 to 2005 (not f-c). Devon 2003-05. 1000 runs (1): 1201 (2009). HS 156 v Indians (Taunton) 2011. CC HS 151 v Notts (Taunton) 2009. BB 3-46 v West Indies A (Taunton) 2002. CC BB 3-58 v Hants (Taunton) 2009. LO HS 80 v Lancs (Manchester) 2010 (CB40). LO BB 4-39 v Surrey (Oval) 2006 (CGT). T20 HS 32*. T20 BB 6-5 v Glamorgan (Cardiff) 2011 – world record T20 analysis.

SOMERSET 2013

	Place	Won	Lost	Tied	Drew	NR
LV= County Championship (1st Division)	6th	3	5		8	
All First-Class Matches		3	6		8	
Yorkshire Bank 40 (Group C)	SF	8	4			1
Friends Life t20 (Mid/Wales/West Group)	QF	6	5			

LV= COUNTY CHAMPIONSHIP AVERAGES

BATTING AND FIELDING

Cap		M	I	NO	HS	Runs	Avge	100	50	Ct/St
2011	N.R.D.Compton	12	23	3	166	1001	50.05	2	7	6
2013	A.N.Petersen	6	12	–	167	562	46.83	2	2	3
	P.P.Chawla	4	6	–	112	231	38.50	1	–	1
2013	J.C.Buttler	9	15	1	119*	508	36.28	1	2	16
2009	C.Kieswetter	11	19	2	148	584	34.35	1	3	41/3
2007	J.C.Hildreth	16	29	2	161	867	32.11	2	2	16
1999	M.E.Trescothick	16	30	1	74	804	27.72	–	6	30
	A.W.R.Barrow	9	15	1	83*	370	26.42	–	2	9
	D.Elgar	3	5	–	33	123	24.60	–	–	2
	L.Gregory	6	8	1	52	141	20.14	–	1	3
	C.R.Jones	6	11	1	58	198	19.80	–	2	2
2007	P.D.Trego	14	23	1	82	374	17.00	–	1	4
	C.A.J.Meschede	9	13	1	59	192	16.00	–	1	6
2008	A.C.Thomas	13	21	5	54*	239	14.93	–	1	4
	G.H.Dockrell	7	10	2	31	106	13.25	–	–	2
2009	A.V.Suppiah	6	11	–	36	130	11.81	–	–	2
	J.Overton	12	18	6	24	125	10.41	–	–	–
	M.J.Leach	5	9	2	21	66	9.42	–	–	–
	S.P.Kirby	10	15	6	15	75	8.33	–	–	3

Also batted: G.M.Hussain (2 matches) 2*, 0* (1 ct); C.Overton (1) 8.

BOWLING

	O	M	R	W	Avge	Best	5wI	10wM
M.J.Leach	149.4	51	324	13	24.92	5-63	1	–
L.Gregory	119.4	25	358	14	25.57	5-38	1	–
A.C.Thomas	386.4	108	1077	42	25.64	5-69	1	–
C.A.J.Meschede	177.1	33	639	24	26.62	4-43	–	–
P.P.Chawla	122.4	13	453	17	26.64	5-97	2	1
P.D.Trego	340.2	80	1029	31	33.19	4-69	–	–
J.Overton	284.5	48	1121	33	33.96	6-95	1	–
S.P.Kirby	277.5	54	913	26	35.11	4-18	–	–
G.H.Dockrell	210.4	54	568	14	40.57	6-96	1	–

Also bowled:

G.M.Hussain	55.5	4	224	5	44.80	3-99	–	–

D.Elgar 19-4-55-1; C.Kieswetter 6-0-26-0; C.Overton 23-6-67-1; A.N.Petersen 14-4-48-1; A.V.Suppiah 6-1-19-0.

The First-Class Averages (pp 225–241) give the records of Somerset players in all first-class county matches (Somerset's other opponents being the Australians), with the exception of: N.R.D.Compton 13-25-3-166-1116-50.72-2-8-6ct. C.R.Jones 7-13-1-130-329-27.41-1-2-2ct.

SOMERSET RECORDS

FIRST-CLASS CRICKET

Highest Total	For 850-7d		v	Middlesex	Taunton	2007
	V 811		by	Surrey	The Oval	1899
Lowest Total	For 25		v	Glos	Bristol	1947
	V 22		by	Glos	Bristol	1920
Highest Innings	For 342	J.L.Langer	v	Surrey	Guildford	2006
	V 424	A.C.MacLaren	for	Lancashire	Taunton	1895

Highest Partnership for each Wicket

1st	346	L.C.H.Palairet/ H.T.Hewett	v	Yorkshire	Taunton	1892
2nd	450	N.R.D.Compton/J.C.Hildreth	v	Cardiff MCCU	Taunton Vale	2012
3rd	319	P.M.Roebuck/M.D.Crowe	v	Leics	Taunton	1984
4th	310	P.W.Denning/I.T.Botham	v	Glos	Taunton	1980
5th	320	J.D.Francis/I.D.Blackwell	v	Durham UCCE	Taunton	2005
6th	265	W.E.Alley/K.E.Palmer	v	Northants	Northampton	1961
7th	279	R.J.Harden/G.D.Rose	v	Sussex	Taunton	1997
8th	172	I.V.A.Richards/I.T.Botham	v	Leics	Leicester	1983
	172	A.R.K.Pierson/P.S.Jones	v	N Zealanders	Taunton	1999
9th	183	C.H.M.Greetham/H.W.Stephenson	v	Leics	Weston-s-Mare	1963
	183	C.J.Tavaré/N.A.Mallender	v	Sussex	Hove	1990
10th	163	I.D.Blackwell/N.A.M.McLean	v	Derbyshire	Taunton	2003

Best Bowling	For 10- 49	E.J.Tyler	v	Surrey	Taunton	1895
(Innings)	V 10- 35	A.Drake	for	Yorkshire	Weston-s-Mare	1914
Best Bowling	For 16- 83	J.C.White	v	Worcs	Bath	1919
(Match)	V 17-137	W.Brearley	for	Lancashire	Manchester	1905

Most Runs – Season	2761	W.E.Alley	(av 58.74)	1961
Most Runs – Career	21142	H.Gimblett	(av 36.96)	1935-54
Most 100s – Season	11	S.J.Cook		1991
Most 100s – Career	49	H.Gimblett		1935-54
Most Wkts – Season	169	A.W.Wellard	(av 19.24)	1938
Most Wkts – Career	2165	J.C.White	(av 18.03)	1909-37
Most Career W-K Dismissals	1007	H.W.Stephenson	(698 ct; 309 st)	1948-64
Most Career Catches in the Field	381	J.C.White		1909-37

LIMITED-OVERS CRICKET

Highest Total	50ov	413-4		v	Devon	Torquay	1990
	40ov	377-9		v	Sussex	Hove	2003
	T20	250-3		v	Glos	Taunton	2006
Lowest Total	50ov	58		v	Middlesex	Southgate	2000
	40ov	58		v	Essex	Chelmsford	1977
	T20	82		v	Kent	Taunton	2010
Highest Innings	50ov	177	S.J.Cook	v	Sussex	Hove	1990
	40ov	184	M.E.Trescothick	v	Glos	Taunton	2008
	T20	141*	C.L.White	v	Worcs	Worcester	2006
Best Bowling	50ov	8-66	S.R.G.Francis	v	Derbyshire	Derby	2004
	40ov	6-16	Abdur Rehman	v	Notts	Taunton	2012
	T20	6- 5	A.V.Suppiah	v	Glamorgan	Cardiff	2011

SURREY

SURREY CRICKET

Formation of Present Club: 22 August 1845
Inaugural First-Class Match: 1864
Colours: Chocolate
Badge: Prince of Wales' Feathers
County Champions (since 1890): (18) 1890, 1891, 1892, 1894, 1895, 1899, 1914, 1952, 1953, 1954, 1955, 1956, 1957, 1958, 1971, 1999, 2000, 2002
Joint Champions: (1) 1950
NatWest Trophy Winners: (1) 1982
Benson and Hedges Cup Winners: (3) 1974, 1997, 2001
Pro 40/National League (Div 1) Winners: (1) 2003
Sunday League Winners: (1) 1996
Clydesdale Bank 40 Winners: (1) 2011
Twenty20 Cup Winners: (1) 2003

Chief Executive: Richard Gould, The Kia Oval, London, SE11 5SS • Tel: 0844 376 1845 • Fax: 020 7820 5601 • E-mail: enquiries@surreycricket.com • Web: www.kiaoval.com • Twitter: @surreycricket (24, 473 followers)

Head Coach: Graham Ford. **Captain**: G.C.Smith. **Vice-Captain**: tba. **Overseas Player**: G.C.Smith. **2014 Beneficiary**: None. **Head Groundsman**: Lee Fortiss. **Scorer**: Keith R.Booth. ‡ New registration. NQ Not qualified for England.

ANSARI, Zafar Shahaan (Hampton S; Trinity Hall, Cambridge), b Ascot, Berks 10 Dec 1991. Younger brother of A.S.Ansari (Cambridge U 2008-13). 5'11". LHB, SLA. Cambridge MCCU 2011-13. Surrey debut 2011. Surrey 2nd XI debut 2008, aged 16y 133d. HS 83* v Warwks (Birmingham) 2012. BB 5-33 CU v Surrey (Cambridge) 2011. Sy BB 4-70 v Yorks (Oval) 2013. LO HS 62 v Hants (Southampton) 2013 (Y40). LO BB 4-42 v Scotland (Oval) 2013 (Y40). T20 HS 38*. T20 BB 2-7.

BATTY, Gareth Jon (Bingley GS), b Bradford, Yorks 13 Oct 1977. Younger brother of J.D.Batty (Yorkshire and Somerset 1989-96). 5'11". RHB, OB. Yorkshire 1997. Surrey 1999-2001, rejoined in 2010; cap 2011. Worcestershire 2002-09. MCC 2012. **Tests**: 7 (2003-04 to 2005); HS 38 v SL (Kandy) 2003-04; BB 3-55 v SL (Galle) 2003-04. Took wicket with his third ball in Test cricket. **LOI**: 10 (2002-03 to 2008-09); HS 17 v WI (Bridgetown) 2008-09; BB 2-40 v WI (Gros Islet, St Lucia) 2003-04. **IT20**: 1 (2008-09); HS 4 v WI (Port-of-Spain) 2008-09. F-c Tours: WI 2003-04, 2005-06; NZ 2008-09 (Eng A); SL 2002-03 (ECB Acad); SL 2003-04; B 2003-04. HS 133 Wo v Surrey (Oval) 2004. Sy HS 79 v Essex (Croydon) 2011. 50 wkts (2); most – 60 (2003). BB 7-52 (10-113 match) Wo v Northants (Northampton) 2004. Sy BB 6-73 (10-142 match) v Warwks (Oval) 2012. LO HS 83* v Yorks (Oval) 2001 (NL). LO BB 5-35 Wo v Hants (Southampton) 2009 (FPT). T20 HS 87. T20 BB 4-13.

BURNS, Rory Joseph (City of London Freemen's S), b Epsom 26 Aug 1990. 5'9". LHB, WK, occ RM. Debut (Surrey) 2011. Surrey 2nd XI debut 2009. MCC Univs 2010. Hampshire 2nd XI 2010. HS 121 v Middx (Oval) 2012. BB 1-18 v Middx (Lord's) 2013. LO HS 49 v Hants (Southampton) 2013 (Y40). T20 HS 27.

CURRAN, Thomas Kevin (Hilton C, Durban), b Cape Town, South Africa 12 Mar 1995. Son of K.M.Curran (Glos, Natal, Northants, Boland and Zimbabwe 1980-81 to 1999); grandson of K.P.Curran (Rhodesia 1947-48 to 1954-55). RHB, RFM. Surrey 2nd XI debut 2012. Awaiting f-c debut. LO HS 1* v Hants (Southampton) 2013 (Y40). LO BB 5-34 v Scotland (Oval) 2013 (Y40).

DAVIES, Steven Michael (King Charles I S, Kidderminster), b Bromsgrove, Worcs 17 Jun 1986. 5'10". LHB, WK. Worcestershire 2005-09. Surrey debut 2010; cap 2011. MCC 2006-07, 2011. **LOI:** 8 (2009-10 to 2010-11); HS 87 v P (Chester-le-St) 2010. **IT20:** 5 (2008-09 to 2010-11); HS 33 v P (Cardiff) 2010. F-c Tours: A 2010-11; B 2006-07 (Eng A); UAE 2011-12 (v P). 1000 runs (4); most – 1090 (2010). HS 192 Wo v Glos (Bristol) 2006. Sy HS 156 v Northants (Northampton) 2011. LO HS 127* v Hants (Oval) 2013 (Y40). T20 HS 99*.

DERNBACH, Jade Winston (St John the Baptist S), b Johannesburg, South Africa 3 Mar 1986. 6'1½". RHB, RFM. Italian passport. UK resident since 1998. Debut (Surrey) 2003; cap 2011. **LOI:** 24 (2011 to 2013); HS 5 v SL (Leeds) 2011; BB 4-45 v P (Dubai) 2011-12. **IT20:** 28 (2011 to 2013-14); HS 12 v I (Colombo, RPS) 2012-13; BB 4-22 v I (Manchester) 2011. F-c Tour (EL): WI 2010-11. HS 56* v Northants (Northampton) 2010. 50 wkts (1): 51 (2010). BB 6-47 v Leics (Leicester) 2009. LO HS 31 v Somerset (Taunton) 2010 (CB40). LO BB 5-31 v Derbys (Chesterfield) 2008 (P40). T20 HS 12. T20 BB 4-22.

DUNN, Matthew Peter (Bearwood C, Wokingham), b Egham 5 May 1992. 6'2". LHB, RFM. Debut (Surrey) 2010. Surrey 2nd XI debut 2009. England U19s 2010. HS 2* v Cambridge MCCU (Cambridge) 2011. CC HS 0*. BB 5-56 v Derbys (Derby) 2011. LO BB 2-32 England Dev XI v Sri Lanka A (Manchester) 2011. T20 HS and BB –.

EDWARDS, George Alexander (St Joseph C, Croydon), b King's College H, Camberwell, London 29 Jul 1992. 6'3". RHB, RFM. Debut (Surrey) 2011. Surrey 2nd XI debut 2009, aged 16y 322d. HS 19 v Cambridge MCCU (Cambridge) 2011. CC HS 17 and BB 4-44 v Worcs (Worcester) 2012. LO HS 0* and LO BB 1-44 v Durham (Chester-le-St) 2013 (Y40).

HARINATH, Arun (Tiffin Boys GS; Loughborough U), b Sutton 26 Mar 1987. 5'11". LHB, OB. Loughborough UCCE 2007-09. Surrey debut 2009. MCC 2008. Buckinghamshire 2007-08. HS 154 v Derbys (Derby) 2013. BB 1-2 v Middx (Lord's) 2013. LO HS 52 v Derbys (Oval) 2013 (Y40).

JEWELL, Thomas Melvin (Bradfield C), b Reading, Berkshire 13 Jan 1991. 6'1". RHB, RMF. Debut (Surrey) 2008. Surrey 2nd XI debut 2007. HS 70 v Lancs (Liverpool) 2012. BB 5-49 v Cambridge MCCU (Cambridge) 2011. BB 3-100 v Yorks (Oval) 2013. LO HS 13 and LO BB 1-20 v Derbys (Oval) 2013 (Y40).

LINLEY, Timothy Edward (St Mary's RC CS, Menston; Notre Dame SFC; Oxford Brookes U), b Leeds, Yorks 23 Mar 1982. 6'2". RHB, RFM. Oxford UCCE 2003-05. British U 2004. Sussex 2006 (1 match). Surrey debut 2009. HS 42 OU v Derbys (Oxford) 2005. Sy HS 36 v Kent (Canterbury) 2009. 50 wkts (1): 73 (2011). BB 6-57 (9-79 match) v Leics (Leicester) 2011. LO HS 20* v Warwks (Oval) 2009 (P40). LO BB 3-50 v Hants (Croydon) 2011 (CB40). T20 HS 8. T20 BB 2-28.

MEAKER, Stuart Christopher (Cranleigh S), b Durban, South Africa 21 Jan 1989. Moved to UK in 2001. 6'1". RHB, RFM. Debut (Surrey) 2008; cap 2012. England U19s 2007 to 2008. **LOI:** 2 (2011-12); HS 1 and BB 1-45 v I (Mumbai) 2011-12. **IT20:** 2 (2012-13); HS –; BB 1-28 v I (Pune) 2013-14. F-c Tour: I 2012-13. HS 94 v Bangladesh (Oval) 2010. CC HS 72 v Essex (Colchester) 2009. 50 wkts (1): 51 (2012). BB 8-52 (11-167 match) v Somerset (Oval) 2012. LO HS 21* v Glamorgan (Oval) 2012 (CB40). LO BB 4-47 EL v Bangladesh A (Chittagong) 2011-12. T20 HS 17. T20 BB 2-16.

PIETERSEN, Kevin Peter (Maritzburg C; Natal U), b Pietermaritzburg, South Africa 27 Jun 1980. British passport (English mother) – qualified for England Oct 2004. 6'4". RHB, OB. Natal/KZN 1997-98 to 1999-00. Nottinghamshire 2001-04; cap 2002. Hampshire 2005-08; cap 2005 (no f-c appearances 2006-07, 2009-10). Surrey debut 2010 (initially on loan). Dolphins 2010-11. MCC 2004. MBE 2005. *Wisden* 2005. **ECB central contract 2013-14. Tests**: 104 (2005 to 2013-14, 3 as captain); HS 227 v A (Adelaide) 2010-11; BB 3-52 v SA (Leeds) 2012. **LOI**: 136 (2004-05 to 2013, 12 as captain); HS 130 v P (Dubai) 2011-12; scored 454 runs (av 151.33) in 7-match series, including fastest England 100 off 69 balls (E London), v SA 2004-05; BB 3-22 v SA (Leeds) 2008. **IT20**: 37 (2005 to 2013); HS 79 v SA (Cape Town) 2007-08; BB 1-27 v SA (Centurion) 2009-10. F-c Tours: A 2006-07, 2010-11, 2013-14; SA 2009-10; WI 2008-09; NZ 2007-08, 2012-13; I 2003-04 (Eng A), 2005-06, 2008-09 (Captain), 2012-13; P 2005-06; SL 2007-08, 2011-12; B 2009-10; UAE 2011-12 (v P). 1000 runs (3); most – 1546 (2003). HS 254* Nt v Middx (Nottingham) 2002. Sy HS 234* v Lancs (Nottingham) 2012. BB 4-31 Nt v Durham U (Nottingham) 2003. CC BB 3-72 Nt v Hants (Nottingham) 2004. Sy BB 2-24 v Notts (Oval) 2012. LO HS 147 Nt v Somerset (Taunton) 2002 (NL). LO BB 3-14 Nt v Middx (Lord's) 2004 (NL). T20 HS 103*. T20 BB 3-33.

ROY, Jason Jonathan (Whitgift S), b Durban, South Africa 21 Jul 1990. 6'0". RHB, RM. Debut (Surrey) 2010. Surrey 2nd XI debut 2008. HS 106* v Glamorgan (Oval) 2011. BB 3-35 v Warwks (Guildford) 2013. LO HS 131 v Leics (Leicester) 2011 (CB40). LO BB –. T20 HS 101* v Kent (Beckenham) 2010 – Sy record. T20 BB 1-23.

SIBLEY, Dominic Peter (Whitgift S, Croydon), b Epsom 5 Sep 1995. 6'3". RHB, LB. Debut (Surrey) 2013. Surrey 2nd XI debut 2011, aged 15y 302d. England U19s 2012-13. HS 242 v Yorks (Oval) 2013. LO HS 37 v Durham (Chester-le-St) 2013 (Y40).

NQ**SMITH, Graeme** Craig (K Edward VII S, Johannesburg), b Johannesburg, South Africa 1 Feb 1981. 6'3" LHB, OB. W Province 2000-01 to 2003-04. W Province Boland 2004-05. Somerset 2005. Cape Cobras 2010-11. Surrey debut/cap 2013; captain 2013 to date. *Wisden* 2003. **Tests** (SA): 117 (2001-02 to 2013-14, inc 1 for ICC; 109 as captain); HS 277 v E (Birmingham) 2003; BB 2-145 v WI (St John's) 2004-05. **LOI** (SA): 197 (2001-02 to 2013-14, inc 1 for Africa XI; 150 as captain); HS 141 v E (Centurion) 2009-10; BB 3-30 v SL (Perth) 2005-06. **IT20** (SA): 33 (2005-06 to 2011-12; 27 as captain); HS 89* v A (Johannesburg) 2005-06. F-c Tours (SA) (C=Captain): E 2003C, 2008C, 2012C; A 2005-06C, 2008-09C, 2012-13C; WI 2004-05C, 2010C; NZ 2003-04C, 2011-12C; I 2004-05C, 2007-08C, 2009-10C; P 2003-04C, 2007-08C; SL 2004C; B 2002-03C, 2007-08C; UAE (v P) 2010-11C, 2013-14C. HS 311 Sm v Leics (Taunton) 2005. Sy HS 67 v Sussex (Oval) 2013. BB 2-145 (*see Tests*). CC BB 1-34 Sm v Durham (Taunton) 2005. LO HS 141 (*see LOI*). LO BB 3-30 (*see LOI*). T20 HS 105. T20 BB 3-23.

SOLANKI, Vikram Singh (Regis S, Wolverhampton), b Udaipur, India 1 Apr 1976. 6'0". RHB, OB, occ WK. Worcestershire 1995-2012; cap 1998; captain 2005-10; benefit 2007. Rajasthan 2006-07. Surrey debut 2013. **LOI**: 51 (1999-00 to 2006); HS 106 v SA (Oval) 2003; BB 1-17 v SL (Leeds) 2006. **IT20**: 3 (2005 to 2007-08); HS 43 v I (Durban) 2007-08. F-c Tours (Eng A): SA 1998-99, 1999-00 (Eng – *part*); WI 2000-01, 2005-06 (Captain); NZ 1999-00; SL 2004-05; Z 1996-97 (Wo), 1998-99; B 1999-00. 1000 runs (6); most – 1339 (1999). HS 270 Wo v Glos (Cheltenham) 2008, sharing Wo 2nd wkt record partnership of 316 with S.C.Moore. Sy HS 162 v Warwks (Birmingham) 2013. Won Walter Lawrence Trophy in 2009 with 49-ball hundred v Glamorgan (Worcester). BB 5-40 Wo v Middx (Lord's) 2004. Sy BB 2-46 v Sussex (Oval) 2013. LO HS 164* Wo v Worcs CB (Worcester) 2003 (CGT). LO BB 4-14 Wo v Somerset (Taunton) 2006 (P40). T20 HS 100. T20 BB 1-6.

TREMLETT, Christopher Timothy (Thornden S, Chandler's Ford; Taunton's C, Southampton), b Southampton, Hampshire 2 Sep 1981. Son of T.M.Tremlett (Hampshire 1976-91); grandson of M.F.Tremlett (Somerset, CD and England 1947-60). 6'7". RHB, RFM. Hampshire 2000-09, taking wicket of M.H.Richardson (NZ A) with his first ball; cap 2004. Surrey debut 2010. **Tests**: 12 (2007 to 2013-14); HS 25* v I (Oval) 2007; BB 6-48 v SL (Southampton) 2011. **LOI**: 15 (2005 to 2010-11); HS 19* v I (Birmingham) 2007; BB 4-32 v B (Nottingham) 2005 – on debut (hat-trick ball hit stump without dislodging bails). **IT20**: 1 (2007-08); BB 2-45 v I (Durban) 2007-08. F-c Tours: A 2010-11, 2013-14; SL 2002-03 (ECB Acad); UAE 2011-12 (v P). HS 64 H v Glos (Southampton) 2005. Sy HS 54 v Sussex (Arundel) 2013. BB 8-96 v Durham (Chester-le-St) 2013. Hat-trick: H v Notts (Nottingham) 2005. LO HS 38* H v Cheshire (Alderley Edge) 2004 (C&G). LO BB 4-25 H v Essex (Southend) 2002 (NL). T20 HS 13. T20 BB 4-16.

VAN DEN BERGH, Frederick Oliver Edward (Whitgift S, Croydon; Hatfield C, Durham U), b Farnborough, Kent 14 Jun 1992. 6'2". RHB, SLA. Debut (Surrey) 2011. Durham MCCU 2013. Surrey 2nd XI debut 2009, aged 16y 326d. Summer contract. HS 34 and BB 4-84 DU v Notts (Nottingham) 2013. Sy HS 16* v Leeds/Bradford MCCU (Oval) 2012. Sy BB 3-79 v Cambridge MCCU (Cambridge) 2011.

NQWILSON, Gary Craig (Methodist C, Belfast; Manchester Met), b Dundonald, N Ireland 5 Feb 1986. 5'10". RHB, WK. Ireland 2005 to date. Surrey debut 2010. MCC YC 2005. **LOI** (Ire): 47 (2007 to 2013-14); HS 113 v Netherlands (Dublin) 2010. **IT20** (Ire): 31 (2008 to 2013-14); HS 41* v B (Belfast) 2012. HS 125 v Leics (Leicester) 2010. BB –. LO HS 113 (*see LOI*). T20 HS 54*.

WINSLADE, Jack Robert (Whitgift S, Croydon), b Epsom 12 Apr 1995. Younger brother of T.S.Winslade (Loughborough MCCU 2010). 5'10". RHB, RMF. Surrey 2nd XI debut 2011, aged 16y 6d. Awaiting 1st XI debut.

RELEASED/RETIRED

(Having made a County First-Class or List A appearance in 2013)

NQAMLA, Hashim Mahomed, b Durban, South Africa 31 Mar 1983. Younger brother of A.M.Amla (Natal B, KZN, Dolphins 1997-98 to 2012-13). RHB, RM/OB. KZN 1999-00 to 2003-04. Dolphins 2004-05 to 2011-12. Essex 2009. Nottinghamshire 2010; cap 2010. Surrey 2013. *Wisden* 2012. **Tests** (SA): 76 (2004-05 to 2013-14); HS 311* v E (Oval) 2012; BB –. **LOI** (SA): 85 (2007-08 to 2013-14); HS 150 v E (Southampton) 2012. **IT20** (SA): 19 (2008-09 to 2013-14); HS 48 v P (Dubai) 2013-14 and 48 v P (Cape Town) 2013-14. F-c Tours (SA): E 2008, 2012; A 2008-09, 2012-13; WI 2010; NZ 2011-12; I 2004-05, 2007-08 (SA A), 2007-08, 2009-10; P 2007-08; SL 2005-06 (SA A), 2006; Z 2004 (SA A), 2007 (SA A); B 2007-08; UAE 2010-11, 2013-14 (v P). 1000 runs (0+2); most – 1126 (2005-06). HS 311* (*see Tests*). CC HS 181 Ex v Glamorgan (Chelmsford) 2009 – on debut. Sy HS 151 v Yorks (Oval) 2013. BB 1-10 SA A v India A (Kimberley) 2001-02. LO HS 150 (*see LOI*). T20 HS 88*.

NQAZHAR MAHMOOD Sagar (F.G. No. 1 HS, Islamabad), b Rawalpindi, Pakistan 28 Feb 1975. 5'11". RHB, RFM. Islamabad 1993-94 to 2006-07. United Bank 1995-96 to 1996-97. Rawalpindi 1998-99 to 2004-05. PIA 2001-02. Surrey 2002-07; cap 2004. Habib Bank 2006-07 to 2010-11. Kent 2008-12, (British passport holder) scoring 116 v Notts (Canterbury) on debut; cap 2008. MCC 2001. Returned to Surrey in 2013 for l-o and T20 only. **Tests** (P): 21 (1997-98 to 2001); HS 136 v SA (Johannesburg) 1997-98; BB 4-50 v E (Lord's) 2001. Scored 128* and 50* v SA (Rawalpindi) 1997-98 on debut. **LOI** (P): 143 (1996-97 to 2006-07); HS 67 v I (Adelaide) 1999-00; BB 6-18 v WI (Sharjah) 1999-00. F-c Tours (P): E 1997 (Pak A), 2001; A 1999-00; SA 1997-98; I 1998-99; SL 2000; Z 1997-98. HS 204* v Middx (Oval) 2005. 50 wkts (0+1): 59 (1996-97). BB 8-61 v Lancs (Oval) 2002. LO HS 101* v Glamorgan (Oval) 2006 (C&G). LO BB 6-18 (*see LOI*). T20 HS 106*. T20 BB 5-24.

^{NQ}**DE BRUYN, Zander** (Helpmekaar HS; Randburg HS; Rand Afrikaans U, Jo'burg), b Johannesburg, South Africa 5 Jul 1975. 6'0". RHB, RMF. Transvaal B 1995-96 to 1996-97. Gauteng 1996-97 to 2001-02. Easterns 2002-03 to 2005-06. Titans 2004-05 to 2005-06. Worcestershire 2005. Warriors 2006-07 to 2008-09. Somerset 2008-10; cap 2008. Lions 2009-10 to date. Surrey 2011-13 (Kolpak registration). **Tests** (SA): 3 (2004-05); HS 83 v I (Kanpur) 2004-05 – on debut; BB 2-32 v I (Calcutta) 2004-05. F-c Tours (SA): I 2004-05; SL 2005-06 (SA A). 1000 runs (1+1); most – 1383 (2011). HS 266* Easterns v GW (Kimberley) 2003-04. UK HS 179 v Kent (Oval) 2011. BB 7-67 Warriors v Titans (Pt Elizabeth) 2007-08. UK BB 4-23 Sm v Essex (Colchester) 2010. Sy BB 3-28 v Durham (Oval) 2013. LO HS 122* Sm v Pakistanis (Taunton) 2010. LO BB 5-44 Easterns v WP (Cape Town) 2003-04. T20 HS 95*. T20 BB 4-18.

KEEDY, G. – *see NOTTINGHAMSHIRE.*

LEWIS, J. – *see SUSSEX.*

^{NQ}**PONTING, Ricky** Thomas, b Launceston, Tasmania, Australia 19 Dec 1974. 5'10". RHB, RM. Tasmania 1992-93 to 2012-13. Somerset 2004. Surrey 2013; cap 2013. *Wisden* 2005. **Tests** (A): 168 (1995-96 to 2012-13, 77 as captain); HS 257 v I (Melbourne) 2003-04; BB 1-0 v WI (Brisbane) 1996-97. **LOI** (A): 375 (1994-95 to 2011-12, 230 as captain); HS 164 v SA (Johannesburg) 2005-06; BB 1-12 v Z (Sydney) 2000-01. **IT20** (A): 17 (2004-05 to 2009, 17 as captain); HS 98* v NZ (Auckland) 2004-05. F-c Tours (A) (C=Captain): E 1995 (Young A), 1997, 2001, 2005C, 2009C, 2010C (v P); SA 2001-02, 2005-06C, 2008-09C, 2011-12; WI 1994-95, 1998-99, 2003, 2008C; NZ 2004-05C, 2009-10C, 2012; I 1996-97; 1997-98, 2000-01, 2004-05C, 2008-09C, 2010-11C; P 1998-99; SL 1999-00, 2003-04C, 2011; Z 1995-96 (Tas), 1999-00; B 2005-06C; UAE 2002-03 (v P). HS 257 (*see Tests*). CC HS 192 v Derbys (Derby) 2013. BB 2-10 A v Mumbai (Mumbai) 2000-01. LO HS 164 (*see LOI*). LO BB 3-34 Tas v WA (Hobart) 1996-97. T20 HS 98*. T20 BB 1-11.

SURREY 2013

RESULTS SUMMARY

	Place	Won	Lost	Tied	Drew	NR
LV= County Championship (1st Division)	9th	1	6		9	
All First-Class Matches		1	6		9	
Yorkshire Bank 40 (Group B)	5th	4	6			2
Friends Life t20 (South Group)	Finalist	9	4			

LV= COUNTY CHAMPIONSHIP AVERAGES

BATTING AND FIELDING

Cap		M	I	NO	HS	Runs	Avge	100	50	Ct/St
2013	R.T.Ponting	4	6	2	192	493	123.25	2	1	4
	D.P.Sibley	3	4	–	242	264	66.00	1	–	1
	H.M.Amla	6	10	–	151	545	54.50	1	4	1
2011	S.M.Davies	15	23	4	147	867	45.63	2	3	24/3
	V.S.Solanki	16	25	–	162	995	39.80	2	5	18
	R.J.Burns	16	27	1	115	917	35.26	2	4	13
	G.C.Wilson	12	17	4	124	447	34.38	1	1	12
	A.Harinath	12	21	2	154	584	30.73	1	4	4
2013	G.C.Smith	3	5	1	67	120	30.00	–	1	4
	Z.de Bruyn	14	23	–	111	571	24.82	1	1	16
	Z.S.Ansari	6	8	3	27	114	22.80	–	–	3
2011	G.J.Batty	13	18	2	41	313	19.56	–	–	6
2012	S.C.Meaker	8	11	4	30*	80	11.42	–	–	–
	C.T.Tremlett	11	12	1	54	110	10.00	–	1	3
	J.J.Roy	4	7	1	17	49	8.16	–	–	3
	T.E.Linley	12	14	1	22*	84	6.46	–	–	6
2011	J.W.Dernbach	10	14	5	22	58	6.44	–	–	–
	G.Keedy	6	6	4	2*	2	1.00	–	–	2

Also played: M.P.Dunn (1 match) did not bat; G.A.Edwards (1) 0; T.M.Jewell (1) did not bat; J.Lewis (2) 2*; K.P.Pietersen (1) 177* (1 ct).

BOWLING

	O	M	R	W	Avge	Best	5wI	10wM
J.W.Dernbach	315	57	1043	34	30.67	5-57	1	–
Z.S.Ansari	164.1	30	468	15	31.20	4-70	–	–
C.T.Tremlett	349.1	66	1057	32	33.03	8-96	2	–
T.E.Linley	438.1	106	1268	37	34.27	4-59	–	–
S.C.Meaker	195.4	33	840	24	35.00	5-60	1	–
G.Keedy	269	51	796	22	36.18	7-99	2	–
G.J.Batty	395.4	68	1141	27	42.25	5-71	2	–
Z.de Bruyn	253.2	52	824	13	63.38	3-28	–	–

Also bowled: H.M.Amla 5-0-22-0; R.J.Burns 15-0-90-1; M.P.Dunn 35-2-133-4; G.A.Edwards 37-14-80-3; A.Harinath 3-0-6-1; T.M.Jewell 33-5-147-3; J.Lewis 60-14-154-3; K.P.Pietersen 4-1-13-0; J.J.Roy 5.4-0-35-3; D.P.Sibley 1-0-4-0; V.S.Solanki 15-0-90-2; G.C.Wilson 7-0-43-0.

Surrey played no first-class fixtures outside the County Championship in 2013. The First-Class Averages (pp 225–241) give the records of their players in all first-class matches, with the exception of Z.S.Ansari and K.P.Pietersen, whose first-class figures for Surrey are as above.

SURREY RECORDS
FIRST-CLASS CRICKET

Highest Total	For 811		v	Somerset	The Oval	1899
	V 863		by	Lancashire	The Oval	1990
Lowest Total	For 14		v	Essex	Chelmsford	1983
	V 16		by	MCC	Lord's	1872
Highest Innings	For 357*	R.Abel	v	Somerset	The Oval	1899
	V 366	N.H.Fairbrother	for	Lancashire	The Oval	1990

Highest Partnership for each Wicket

1st	428	J.B.Hobbs/A.Sandham	v	Oxford U	The Oval	1926
2nd	371	J.B.Hobbs/E.G.Hayes	v	Hampshire	The Oval	1909
3rd	413	D.J.Bicknell/D.M.Ward	v	Kent	Canterbury	1990
4th	448	R.Abel/T.W.Hayward	v	Yorkshire	The Oval	1899
5th	318	M.R.Ramprakash/Azhar Mahmood	v	Middlesex	The Oval	2005
6th	298	A.Sandham/H.S.Harrison	v	Sussex	The Oval	1913
7th	262	C.J.Richards/K.T.Medlycott	v	Kent	The Oval	1987
8th	205	I.A.Greig/M.P.Bicknell	v	Lancashire	The Oval	1990
9th	168	E.R.T.Holmes/E.W.J.Brooks	v	Hampshire	The Oval	1936
10th	173	A.Ducat/A.Sandham	v	Essex	Leyton	1921

Best Bowling	For 10-43	T.Rushby	v	Somerset	Taunton	1921
(Innings)	V 10-28	W.P.Howell	for	Australians	The Oval	1899
Best Bowling	For 16-83	G.A.R.Lock	v	Kent	Blackheath	1956
(Match)	V 15-57	W.P.Howell	for	Australians	The Oval	1899

Most Runs – Season	3246	T.W.Hayward	(av 72.13)	1906
Most Runs – Career	43554	J.B.Hobbs	(av 49.72)	1905-34
Most 100s – Season	13	T.W.Hayward		1906
	13	J.B.Hobbs		1925
Most 100s – Career	144	J.B.Hobbs		1905-34
Most Wkts – Season	252	T.Richardson	(av 13.94)	1895
Most Wkts – Career	1775	T.Richardson	(av 17.87)	1892-1904
Most Career W-K Dismissals	1221	H.Strudwick	(1035 ct; 186 st)	1902-27
Most Career Catches in the Field	605	M.J.Stewart		1954-72

LIMITED-OVERS CRICKET

Highest Total	50ov	496-4		v	Glos	The Oval	2007
	40ov	386-3		v	Glamorgan	The Oval	2010
	T20	224-5		v	Glos	Bristol	2006
Lowest Total	50ov	74		v	Kent	The Oval	1967
	40ov	64		v	Worcs	Worcester	1978
	T20	88		v	Kent	The Oval	2012
Highest Innings	50ov	268	A.D.Brown	v	Glamorgan	The Oval	2002
	40ov	203	A.D.Brown	v	Hampshire	Guildford	1997
	T20	101*	J.J.Roy	v	Kent	Beckenham	2010
Best Bowling	50ov	7-33	R.D.Jackman	v	Yorkshire	Harrogate	1970
	40ov	7-30	M.P.Bicknell	v	Glamorgan	The Oval	1999
	T20	6-24	T.J.Murtagh	v	Middlesex	Lord's	2005

SUSSEX

Formation of Present Club: 1 March 1839
Substantial Reorganisation: August 1857
Inaugural First-Class Match: 1864
Colours: Dark Blue, Light Blue and Gold
Badge: County Arms of Six Martlets
County Champions: (3) 2003, 2006, 2007
Gillette/NatWest/C&G Trophy Winners: (5) 1963, 1964, 1978, 1986, 2006
Pro 40/National League (Div 1) Winners: (2) 2008, 2009
Sunday League Winners: (1) 1982
Twenty20 Cup Winners: (1) 2009

Chief Executive: Zac Toumazi, The BrightonandHoveJobs.com County Ground, Eaton Road, Hove BN3 3AN • Tel: 0844 264 0202 • Fax: 01273 771549 • Email: info@sussexcricket.co.uk • Web: www.sussexcricket.co.uk • Twitter: @SussexCCC (14,646 followers)

Head Coach: Mark Robinson. **Club Coach**: Mark Davis. **Captain**: E.C.Joyce. **Vice-Captain**: C.D.Nash. **Overseas Players**: S.J.Magoffin and Yasir Arafat (T20 only). **2014 Beneficiary**: M.H.Yardy. **Head Groundsman**: Andy Mackay. **Scorer**: M.J. (Mike) Charman. ‡ New registration. ᴺᴼ Not qualified for England.

ANYON, James Edward (Garstang HS; Preston C; Loughborough U), b Lancaster, Lancs 5 May 1983. 6'1". LHB, RFM. Loughborough U 2003-04. Warwickshire 2005-09. Surrey 2009 (on loan). Sussex debut 2010; cap 2011. Cumberland 2003. HS 64* v Surrey (Horsham) 2012. 50 wkts (1): 55 (2011). BB 6-82 Wa v Glamorgan (Cardiff) 2008. Sx BB 5-36 v Lancs (Liverpool) 2012. LO HS 12 Wa v Worcs (Birmingham) 2006 (CGT). LO BB 3-6 Wa v Notts (Nottingham) 2008 (FPT). T20 HS 8*. T20 BB 3-6.

Syed **ASHAR** Ahmed ZAIDI, b Karachi, Pakistan 13 Jul 1981. LHB, SLA. Islamabad 1999-00 to 2009-10. PTC 2003-04 to 2005-06. Islamabad 2004-05 to 2004-05. KRL 2006-07. Federal Areas 2007-08. Sussex debut 2013. UK citizen. HS 202 Islamabad v Sialkot (Sialkot) 2009-10. Sx HS 45 v Durham (Hove) 2013. BB 4-50 Islamabad v Hyderabad (Islamabad) 2009-10. Sx BB 4-57 v Yorks (Hove) 2013. LO HS 109. LO BB 4-39 Gazi Tank v PDSC (Mirpur) 2013-14. T20 HS 42*. T20 BB 2-16.

BEER, William Andrew Thomas (Reigate GS; Collyer's C, Horsham), b Crawley 8 Oct 1988. RHB, LB. Debut (Sussex) 2008. No f-c appearances in 2009. HS 39 v Middx (Lord's) 2013. BB 3-31 v Worcs (Worcester) 2010. LO HS 27* v Derbys (Derby) 2011 (CB40). LO BB 3-27 v Warwks (Hove) 2012 (CB40). T20 HS 22. T20 BB 3-19.

BROWN, Ben Christopher (Ardingly C), b Crawley 23 Nov 1988. RHB, WK. Debut (Sussex) 2007. No f-c appearances in 2008 or 2009. HS 112 v Derbys (Horsham) 2010 and 112 v Oxford MCCU (Oxford) 2011. LO HS 60 v Yorks (Scarborough) 2011 (CB40). T20 HS 68.

FINCH, Harry Zachariah (St Richard's Catholic C, Bexhill; Eastbourne C), b Hastings 10 Feb 1995. RHB, RMF. Debut (Sussex) 2013. Sussex 2nd XI debut 2011, aged 16y 69d. England U19 2012-13. HS 11 v Durham (Chester-le-St) 2013. BB –. LO HS and LO BB –.

HAMILTON-BROWN, Rory James (Millfield S), b St John's Wood, London 3 Sep 1987. 6'0". RHB, OB. Surrey 2005, 2010-12; captain 2010-12 (*part*); cap 2011. No f-c appearances 2006-07. Sussex debut 2008. 1000 runs (1): 1039 (2011). HS 171* and BB 2-49 v Yorks (Hove) 2009. LO HS 115 Sy v Glamorgan (Oval) 2010 (CB40). LO BB 3-28 Sy v Leics (Leicester) 2007 (P40). T20 HS 87*. T20 BB 4-15.

HATCHETT, Lewis James (Steyning GS), b Shoreham-by-Sea 21 Jan 1990. 6'3". LHB, LMF. Debut (Sussex) 2010. Sussex 2nd XI debut 2009. HS 21 v Yorks (Hove) 2013. BB 5-47 v Leics (Leicester) 2010. LO HS 1 v Northants (Arundel) 2013 (Y40). LO BB 3-65 v Notts (Hove) 2013 (Y40). T20 HS and BB –.

HOBDEN, Matthew Edward (Eastbourne C; UWIC), b Eastbourne 27 Mar 1993. RHB, RFM. Cardiff MCCU 2012-13. Sussex 2nd XI debut 2011. HS 18 CfU v Glamorgan (Cardiff) 2013. BB 5-62 CfU v Warwks (Birmingham) 2012. LO HS 2 and LO BB 1-39 v Notts (Nottingham) 2013 (Y40).

JACKSON, Callum Frederick (St Bede's S, Upper Dicker), b Eastbourne 7 Sep 1994. RHB, WK. Debut (Sussex) 2013. Sussex 2nd XI debut 2011, aged 16y 225d. England U19s 2012-13. HS 26 v Australians (Hove) 2013. LO HS –. T20 HS 3.

NOJORDAN, Christopher James (Comber Mere S, Barbados; Dulwich C), b Christ Church, Barbados 4 Oct 1988. 6'0". RHB, RFM. Surrey 2007-12. Missed entire 2010 season with back injury. Barbados 2011-12 to 2012-13. Sussex debut 2013. **LOI**: 7 (2013 to 2013-14); HS 14 and BB 3-51 v A (Southampton) 2013. **IT20**: 1 (2013-14); HS 10* and BB 1-23 (Sydney) 2013-14. HS 92 v Derbys (Derby) 2013. 50 wkts (1): 61 (2013). BB 7-43 Barbados v CC&C (Bridgetown) 2012-13. Sx BB 6-48 v Yorks (Leeds) 2013. LO HS 38 Sy v Yorks (Guildford) 2008 (P40). LO BB 4-38 EL v Bangladesh A (Taunton) 2013. T20 HS 31. T20 BB 3-39.

JOYCE, Edmund Christopher (Presentation C, Bray, Co Wicklow; Trinity C, Dublin), b Dublin, Ireland 22 Sep 1978. Brother of four Ireland cricketers: Augustine (2000), Dominick (2004-06), Cecilia (2001-07) and Isobel, her twin (1999-2007). 5'11". LHB, RM. Ireland 1997-98. Middlesex 1999-2008; cap 2002. Sussex debut/cap 2009; captain 2013 to date. Qualified for England 2005. MCC 2006, 2008. **LOI** (E/Ire): 40 (17 for E 2006 to 2006-07; 23 for Ire 2010-11 to 2013-14); HS 116* Ire v P (Dublin) 2013. **IT20** (E/Ire): 15 (2 for E 2006 to 2006-07; 13 for Ire 2011-12 to 2013-14); HS 38 Ire v Scotland (Dubai, DSC) 2011-12. F-c Tour (Eng A): WI 2005-06. 1000 runs (7); most – 1668 (2005). HS 211 M v Warwks (Birmingham) 2006. Sx HS 204* v Notts (Nottingham) 2013. BB M 2-34 v Cambridge U (Cambridge) 2004. CC BB 1-4 M v Glamorgan (Cardiff) 2005. Sx BB 1-9 v Hants (Southampton) 2009. LO HS 146 v Glos (Hove) 2009 (FPT). LO BB 2-10 M v Notts (Nottingham) 2003 (NL). T20 HS 78*.

LEWIS, Jonathan (Churchfields S, Swindon; Swindon C), b Aylesbury, Bucks 26 Aug 1975. 6'2". RHB, RMF. Gloucestershire 1995-2011; cap 1998; captain 2006-08; benefit 2007. Surrey 2012-13. MCC 2005, 2010. Wiltshire 1993, 1995. **Tests**: 1 (2006); HS 20 and BB 3-68 v SL (Nottingham) 2006. **LOI**: 13 (2005 to 2007); HS 17 v I (Leeds) 2007; BB 4-36 v A (Brisbane) 2006-07. **IT20**: 2 (2005 to 2006-07); HS 1 v A (Sydney) 2006-07; BB 4-24 v A (Southampton) 2005. F-c Tours (Eng A): WI 2000-01; SL 2004-05. HS 71 Gs v Middx (Uxbridge) 2011. 50 wkts (9); most – 74 (2003). BB 8-95 Gs v Z (Gloucester) 2000. CC BB 7-38 (10-75 match) Gs v Somerset (Bristol) 2006. Hat-trick Gs v Notts (Nottingham) 2000. LO HS 54 Gs v Durham (Cheltenham) 2009 (P40). LO BB 5-19 Gs v Hants (Southampton) 2005 (NL). T20 HS 43. T20 BB 4-24.

LIDDLE, Christopher John (Nunthorpe CS), b Middlesbrough, Yorks 1 Feb 1984. 6'5". RHB, LFM. Leicestershire 2005-06. Sussex debut 2007. Missed entire 2009 season with a stress fracture of the right ankle. HS 53 v Worcs (Hove) 2007. BB 3-42 Le v Somerset (Leicester) 2006. Sx BB 2-24 v Middx (Lord's) 2013. LO HS 15 v Derbys (Derby) 2012 (CB40). LO BB 5-18 v Netherlands (Amstelveen) 2011 (CB40). T20 HS 16. T20 BB 5-17.

MACHAN, Matthew William (Brighton C), b Brighton 15 Feb 1991. 5'8". LHB, RM/OB. Debut (Sussex) 2010. Sussex 2nd XI debut 2006, aged 15y 153d. Scotland 2012-13 to date. **LOI** (Scot): 11 (2012-13 to 2013-14); HS 114 and BB 3-31 v Kenya (Aberdeen) 2013. **IT20** (Scot): 6 (2012-13 to 2013-14); HS 67* v Netherlands (Dubai) 2013-14. BB 3-23 v Afghanistan (Sharjah) 2012-13. HS 103 v Somerset (Taunton) 2013. BB 1-36 Sc v Australia A (Edinburgh) 2013. LO HS 126* v Unicorns (Hove) 2012 (CB40). BB 3-31 (*see LOI*). T20 HS 90*. T20 BB 3-23.

179

NQMAGOFFIN, Stephen James (Indooroopilly HS; Curtin U, Perth), b Corinda, Queensland, Australia 17 Dec 1979. 6'3". LHB, RFM. W Australia 2004-05 to 2010-11. Surrey 2007 (one f-c match). Worcestershire 2008. Queensland 2011-12. Sussex debut 2012; cap 2013. HS 79 WA v Tas (Perth) 2008-09. UK HS 41* v Worcs (Worcester) 2012. 50 wkts (2); most – 65 (2013). BB 8-20 (12-31 match) v Somerset (Horsham) 2013. LO HS 24* Wo v Hants (Southampton) 2008 (FPT). LO BB 4-58 Sy v Kent (Oval) 2007 (FPT). T20 HS 11*. T20 BB 2-15.

NASH, Christopher David (Collyer's SFC; Loughborough U), b Cuckfield 19 May 1983. 5'11". RHB, OB. Debut (Sussex) 2002 – no f-c appearances 2003-04; cap 2008. Loughborough UCCE 2003-04. British U 2004. 1000 runs (3); most – 1321 (2009). HS 184 v Leics (Leicester) 2010. BB 4-12 v Glamorgan (Cardiff) 2010. LO HS 124* v Kent (Canterbury) 2011 (CB40). LO BB 4-40 v Yorks (Hove) 2009 (FPT). T20 HS 80*. T20 BB 4-7.

PIOLET, Steffan Andrew (Warden Park S; Central Sussex C), b Redhill, Surrey 8 Aug 1988. 6'1". RHB, RM. Warwickshire 2009-13. Sussex 2nd XI 2006-08. HS 30 and CC BB 1-59 Wa v Notts (Nottingham) 2013. BB 6-17 (10-43 match) Wa v Durham UCCE (Durham) 2009 – on debut. LO HS 39 Wa v Yorks (Birmingham) 2011 (CB40). LO BB 4-31 Wa v Derbys (Derby) 2012 (CB40). T20 HS 26*. T20 BB 3-24.

PRIOR, Matthew James (Brighton C), b Johannesburg, South Africa 26 Feb 1982. 5'11". RHB, WK. Debut (Sussex) 2001; cap 2003; benefit 2012. MCC 2005. Wisden 2009. ECB central contract 2013-14. Tests: 75 (2007 to 2013-14); HS 131* v WI (Port-of-Spain) 2008-09 (scored 126* v WI on debut – first instance while keeping wicket for England). LOI: 68 (2004-05 to 2010-11); HS 87 v WI (Birmingham) 2009. IT20: 10 (2007 to 2009-10); HS 32 v SA (Cape Town) 2007-08. F-c Tours: A 2010-11, 2013-14; SA 2009-10; WI 2008-09; NZ 2012-13; I 2003-04 (Eng A), 2008-09, 2012-13; SL 2004-05 (Eng A), 2007-08, 2011-12; B 2006-07 (Eng A), 2009-10; UAE 2011-12 (v P). 1000 runs (3); most – 1158 (2004). HS 201* v Loughborough U (Hove) 2004. CC HS 153* v Essex (Colchester) 2003. LO HS 144 v Warwks (Hove) 2005 (NL). T20 HS 117 v Glamorgan (Hove) 2010 – Sx record.

WELLS, Luke William Peter (St Bede's S, Upper Dicker), b Eastbourne 29 Dec 1990. Son of A.P.Wells (Border, Kent, Sussex and England 1981-2000); nephew of C.M.Wells (Border, Derbyshire, Sussex and WP 1979-96). 6'4". LHB, OB. Debut (Sussex) 2010. Colombo CC 2011-12. Sussex 2nd XI debut 2008. England U19s 2009 to 2010. HS 208 v Surrey (Oval) 2013. BB 2-28 v Yorks (Horsham) 2011. LO HS 17 v Yorks (Hove) 2011 (CB40). BB 3-19 v Netherlands (Amstelveen) 2011 (CB40). T20 HS 3.

WRIGHT, Luke James (Belvoir HS; Ratcliffe C; Loughborough U), b Grantham, Lincs 7 Mar 1985. Younger brother of A.S.Wright (Leicestershire 2001-02). 5'11". RHB, RMF. Leicestershire 2003 (one f-c match). Sussex debut 2004; cap 2007. LOI: 50 (2007 to 2013-14); HS 52 v NZ (Birmingham) 2008; BB 2-34 v NZ (Bristol) 2008 and v A (Southampton) 2010. IT20: 49 (2007-08 to 2013-14); HS 99* v Afghanistan (Colombo, RPS) 2012-13 – E record; BB 2-24 v NZ (Hamilton) 2012-13. F-c Tour (EL): NZ 2008-09. HS 187 v Middx (Lord's) 2013. BB 5-65 v Derbys (Derby) 2010. LO HS 143* EL v Bangladesh A (Bristol) 2013. LO BB 4-12 v Middx (Hove) 2004 (NL). T20 HS 117. T20 BB 3-17.

YARDY, Michael Howard (William Parker S, Hastings), b Pembury, Kent 27 Nov 1980. 6'0". LHB, LM/SLA. Debut (Sussex) 2000; cap 2005; captain 2009-12; benefit 2014. LOI: 28 (2006 to 2010-11); HS 60* v A (Perth) 2010-11; BB 3-24 v P (Nottingham) 2006 – on debut. IT20: 14 (2006 to 2010-11); HS 35* v P (Cardiff) 2010; BB 2-19 v P (Bridgetown) 2009-10. F-c Tours (Eng A, C=Captain): WI 2005-06; I 2007-08C; B 2006-07C. 1000 runs (2); most – 1520 (2005). HS 257 (record Sx score v touring team) and BB 5-83 v Bangladeshis (Hove) 2005. CC HS 179 v Middx (Lord's) 2005. CC BB 3-15 v Yorks (Leeds) 2009. LO HS 98* v Surrey (Oval) 2006 (CGT). LO BB 6-27 v Warwks (Birmingham) 2005 (NL). T20 HS 76*. T20 BB 3-21.

^{NQ}**YASIR ARAFAT** Satti (Gordon C, Rawalpindi), b Rawalpindi, Pakistan 12 Mar 1982. 5'9½". RHB, RFM. Rawalpindi 1997-98 to 2012-13. Pakistan Reserves 1999-00. KRL 2000-01 to date. NBP 2005-06. Sussex debut 2006; cap 2006; rejoins in 2014 for T20 only. Kent 2007-08; cap 2007. Federal Areas 2007-08 to 2008-09. Surrey 2011. Scotland (not f-c) 2004-05. **Tests** (P): 3 (2007-08 to 2008-09); HS 50* v SL (Karachi) 2008-09; BB 5-161 v I (Bangalore) 2007-08 – on debut. **LOI** (P): 11 (1999-00 to 2009); HS 27 v SA (Chandigarh) 2006-07; BB 1-28 v SL (Karachi) 1999-00. **IT20** (P): 13 (2007-08 to 2012-13); HS 17 v Scotland (Durban) 2007-08; BB 3-18 v SL (Hambantota) 2012. F-c Tours (P): WI 2010-11 (Pak A); I 2007-08; SL 2001 (Pak A), 2004-05 (Pak A). HS 170 KRL v Multan (Multan) 2011-12. CC HS 122 K v Sussex (Canterbury) 2007. Sx HS 86 v Yorks (Arundel) 2006. 50 wkts (0+4); most – 91 (2001-02). BB 9-35 KRL v SSGC (Rawalpindi) 2008-09. CC BB 6-86 K v Hants (Canterbury) 2008. Sx BB 5-74 v Northants (Hove) 2010. LO HS 110* Otago v Auckland (Oamaru) 2009-10. LO BB 6-24 Pakistan A v England A (Colombo) 2004-05. T20 HS 49. T20 BB 4-5.

RELEASED/RETIRED

(Having made a County First-Class or List A appearance in 2013)

GATTING, J.S. – *see HAMPSHIRE*.

MILLER, Andrew Stephen (St Cecilia's RC HS; Preston C), b Preston, Lancs 27 Sep 1987. 6'4". RHB, RFM. Warwickshire 2008-12. Sussex 2013. HS 35 Wa v Durham (Birmingham) 2010. BB 5-58 Wa v Lancs (Birmingham) 2010. LO HS 2* Wa v Scotland (Birmingham) 2011 (CB40). LO BB 2-24 v Notts (Nottingham) 2013 (Y40). T20 HS 0*. T20 BB 2-16.

PANESAR, M.S. – *see ESSEX*.

^{NQ}**RIPPON, Michael** James Gratton (Rondebosch BHS, Cape Town), b Cape Town, South Africa 14 Sep 1991. RHB, SLC. Dutch passport. Western Province 2011-12. Netherlands 2013. Sussex l-o only. **LOI** (Neth): 4 (2013 to 2013-14); HS 14* v Ireland (Amstelveen) 2013; BB 4-37 v Canada (Maunganui) 2013-14. **IT20** (Neth): 6 (2013 to 2013-14); HS 17 v Kenya (Windhoek) 2013; BB 1-31 v Kenya (Dubai) 2013-14. HS 65 Neth v Namibia (Windhoek) 2013. BB 3-34 WP v KZN Inland (Pietermaritzburg) 2011-12 – on debut. LO HS 44* Neth v Namibia (Maunganui) 2013-14. LO BB 4-15 Neth v Uganda (Maunganui) 2013-14. T20 HS 50*. T20 BB 4-23.

J.A.Glover, A.Khan and S.B.Styris left the staff without making a County First-Class or List A appearance in 2013.

SUSSEX 2013

RESULTS SUMMARY

	Place	Won	Lost	Tied	Drew	NR
LV= County Championship (1st Division)	3rd	5	3		8	
All First-Class Matches		5	3		10	
Yorkshire Bank 40 (Group A)	3rd	6	4			2
Friends Life t20 (South Group)	6th	1	9			

LV= COUNTY CHAMPIONSHIP AVERAGES

BATTING AND FIELDING

Cap		M	I	NO	HS	Runs	Avge	100	50	Ct/St
2009	E.C.Joyce	14	21	4	204*	1118	65.76	2	6	14
2007	L.J.Wright	7	12	–	187	676	56.33	2	2	1
	M.W.Machan	4	5	1	103	193	48.25	1	–	4
2008	C.D.Nash	16	27	3	167*	1072	44.66	3	3	10
	B.C.Brown	15	22	6	93	620	38.75	–	5	58/2
	L.W.P.Wells	16	27	1	208	982	37.76	2	5	7
2005	M.H.Yardy	16	26	2	156	834	34.75	2	1	9
	R.J.Hamilton-Brown	13	19	1	126*	576	32.00	2	2	3
2003	M.J.Prior	7	9	–	62	245	27.22	–	1	15
	C.J.Jordan	14	18	1	92	408	24.00	–	2	22
	W.A.T.Beer	3	6	–	39	106	17.66	–	–	2
2011	J.E.Anyon	13	16	6	24*	134	13.40	–	–	1
	J.S.Gatting	4	5	–	20	58	11.60	–	–	3
2013	S.J.Magoffin	15	19	2	32	187	11.00	–	–	4
2010	M.S.Panesar	11	11	7	17*	40	10.00	–	–	2
	L.J.Hatchett	4	5	–	21	27	5.40	–	–	–

Also played: Ashar Zaidi (2 matches) 17, 45, (1 ct); H.Z.Finch (1) 11, 3 (1 ct); C.J.Liddle (1) 7*, 3*; A.S.Miller (1) did not bat.

BOWLING

	O	M	R	W	Avge	Best	5wI	10wM
S.J.Magoffin	496	128	1354	63	21.49	8-20	3	1
C.J.Jordan	435.3	78	1577	59	26.72	6-48	4	–
J.E.Anyon	386.5	71	1432	50	28.64	5-44	1	–
M.S.Panesar	329.4	72	929	23	40.39	5-95	2	–

Also bowled:

	O	M	R	W	Avge	Best	5wI	10wM
Ashar Zaidi	39.3	6	129	7	18.42	4-57	–	–
L.J.Wright	77.3	15	256	6	42.66	2-36	–	–
C.D.Nash	188.3	30	551	9	61.22	2-51	–	–
L.J.Hatchett	116	15	423	6	70.50	3-56	–	–

W.A.T.Beer 72-8-215-4; H.Z.Finch 4-0-15-0; J.S.Gatting 5-0-14-0; R.J.Hamilton-Brown 7-1-28-0; C.J.Liddle 25-4-98-3; A.S.Miller 28-6-102-0; L.W.P.Wells 45-4-164-2; M.H.Yardy 7-0-27-0.

The First-Class Averages (pp 225–241) give the records of Sussex players in all first-class county matches (Sussex's other opponents being Loughborough MCCU and the Australians), with the exception of M.J.Prior, whose first-class figures for Sussex are as above, and: M.S.Panesar 12-11-7-17*-40-10.00-0-0-2ct. 368.2-81-1039-26-39.96-5/95-2-0.

SUSSEX RECORDS

FIRST-CLASS CRICKET

Highest Total	For 742-5d		v	Somerset	Taunton	2009
	V 726		by	Notts	Nottingham	1895
Lowest Total	For 19		v	Surrey	Godalming	1830
	19		v	Notts	Hove	1873
	V 18		by	Kent	Gravesend	1867
Highest Innings	For 344*	M.W.Goodwin	v	Somerset	Taunton	2009
	V 322	E.Paynter	for	Lancashire	Hove	1937

Highest Partnership for each Wicket

1st	490	E.H.Bowley/J.G.Langridge	v	Middlesex	Hove	1933
2nd	385	E.H.Bowley/M.W.Tate	v	Northants	Hove	1921
3rd	385*	M.H.Yardy/M.W.Goodwin	v	Warwicks	Hove	2006
4th	363	M.W.Goodwin/C.D.Hopkinson	v	Somerset	Taunton	2009
5th	297	J.H.Parks/H.W.Parks	v	Hampshire	Portsmouth	1937
6th	255	K.S.Duleepsinhji/M.W.Tate	v	Northants	Hove	1930
7th	344	K.S.Ranjitsinhji/W.Newham	v	Essex	Leyton	1902
8th	291	R.S.C.Martin-Jenkins/M.J.G.Davis	v	Somerset	Taunton	2002
9th	178	H.W.Parks/A.F.Wensley	v	Derbyshire	Horsham	1930
10th	156	G.R.Cox/H.R.Butt	v	Cambridge U	Cambridge	1908

Best Bowling	For 10- 48	C.H.G.Bland	v	Kent	Tonbridge	1899
(Innings)	V 9- 11	A.P.Freeman	for	Kent	Hove	1922
Best Bowling	For 17-106	G.R.Cox	v	Warwicks	Horsham	1926
(Match)	V 17- 67	A.P.Freeman	for	Kent	Hove	1922

Most Runs – Season	2850	J.G.Langridge	(av 64.77)		1949
Most Runs – Career	34150	J.G.Langridge	(av 37.69)		1928-55
Most 100s – Season	12	J.G.Langridge			1949
Most 100s – Career	76	J.G.Langridge			1928-55
Most Wkts – Season	198	M.W.Tate	(av 13.47)		1925
Most Wkts – Career	2211	M.W.Tate	(av 17.41)		1912-37
Most Career W-K Dismissals	1176	H R Butt	(911 ct; 265 st)		1890-1912
Most Career Catches in the Field	779	J.G.Langridge			1928-55

LIMITED-OVERS CRICKET

Highest Total	50ov	384-9		v	Ireland	Belfast	1996
	40ov	399-4		v	Worcs	Horsham	2011
	T20	239-5		v	Glamorgan	Hove	2010
Lowest Total	50ov	49		v	Derbyshire	Chesterfield	1969
	40ov	59		v	Glamorgan	Hove	1996
	T20	67		v	Hampshire	Hove	2004
Highest Innings	50ov	158*	M.W.Goodwin	v	Essex	Chelmsford	2006
	40ov	163	C.J.Adams	v	Middlesex	Arundel	1999
	T20	117	M.J.Prior	v	Glamorgan	Hove	2010
Best Bowling	50ov	6- 9	A.I.C.Dodemaide	v	Ireland	Downpatrick	1990
	40ov	7-41	A.N.Jones	v	Notts	Nottingham	1986
	T20	5-11	Mushtaq Ahmed	v	Essex	Hove	2005

WARWICKSHIRE

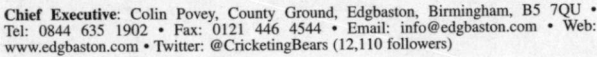

Formation of Present Club: 8 April 1882
Substantial Reorganisation: 19 January 1884
Inaugural First-Class Match: 1894
Colours: Dark Blue, Gold and Silver
Badge: Bear and Ragged Staff
County Champions: (7) 1911, 1951, 1972, 1994, 1995, 2004, 2012
Gillette/NatWest Trophy Winners: (5) 1966, 1968, 1989, 1993, 1995
Benson and Hedges Cup Winners: (2) 1994, 2002
Sunday League Winners: (3) 1980, 1994, 1997
Clydesdale Bank 40 Winners: (1) 2010
Twenty20 Cup Winners: (0); best – Finalist 2003

Chief Executive: Colin Povey, County Ground, Edgbaston, Birmingham, B5 7QU • Tel: 0844 635 1902 • Fax: 0121 446 4544 • Email: info@edgbaston.com • Web: www.edgbaston.com • Twitter: @CricketingBears (12,110 followers)

Director of Cricket: Dougie Brown. **Bowling Coach**: Alan Richardson. **Captain**: J.O.Troughton. **Vice-Captain**: tba. **Overseas Players**: J.S.Patel and Shoaib Malik. **2014 Beneficiary**: I.J.L.Trott. **Head Groundsman**: Gary Barwell. **Scorer**: Mel Smith. New registration. ^NQ Not qualified for England.

AMBROSE, Timothy Raymond (Merewether HS, NSW; TAFE C), b Newcastle, NSW, Australia 1 Dec 1982. ECB qualified – British/EU passport. 5'7". RHB, WK. Sussex 2001-05; cap 2003. Warwickshire debut 2006; cap 2007. **Tests**: 11 (2007-08 to 2008-09); HS 102 v NZ (Wellington) 2007-08. **LOI**: 5 (2008); HS 6 v NZ (Oval) 2008. **IT20**: 1 (2008); HS –. F-c Tours: WI 2008-09; NZ 2007-08. HS 251* v Worcs (Worcester) 2007. LO HS 135 v Durham (Birmingham) 2007 (FPT). T20 HS 77.

BARKER, Keith Hubert Douglas (Moorhead HS; Fulwood C, Preston), b Manchester 21 Oct 1986. Son of K.H.Barker (British Guiana 1960-61 to 1963-64). Played football for Blackburn Rovers and Rochdale. 6'3". LHB, LM. Debut (Warwickshire) 2009; cap 2013. HS 125 v Surrey (Guildford) 2013. 50 wkts (1): 56 (2012). BB 6-40 v Somerset (Taunton) 2012. LO HS 56 v Scotland (Birmingham) 2011 (CB40). LO BB 4-33 v Scotland (Birmingham) 2010 (CB40). T20 HS 46. T20 BB 4-19.

BELL, Ian Ronald (Princethorpe C), b Walsgrave-on-Sowe 11 Apr 1982. 5'9". RHB, RM. Debut (Warwickshire) 1999; cap 2001; benefit 2011. MCC 2004. YC 2004. MBE 2005. *Wisden* 2007. **ECB central contract 2013-14**. **Tests**: 98 (2004 to 2013-14); HS 235 v I (Oval) 2011; BB 1-33 v P (Faisalabad) 2005-06. **LOI**: 140 (2004-05 to 2013-14); HS 126* v I (Southampton) 2007; BB 3-9 v Z (Bulawayo) 2004-05 – taking a wicket with his third ball in LOI. **IT20**: 7 (2006 to 2010-11); HS 60* v NZ (Manchester) 2008. F-c Tours: A 2006-07, 2010-11, 2013-14; SA 2009-10; WI 2000-01 (Eng A – *part*), 2008-09; NZ 2007-08, 2012-13; I 2005-06, 2008-09, 2012-13; P 2005-06; SL 2002-03 (ECB Acad), 2004-05, 2007-08, 2011-12; B 2009-10; UAE 2011-12 (v P). 1000 runs (4); most – 1714 (2004). HS 262* v Sussex (Horsham) 2004. BB 4-4 v Middx (Lord's) 2004. LO HS 158 EL v India A (Worcester) 2010. LO BB 5-41 v Essex (Chelmsford) 2003 (NL). T20 HS 85. T20 BB 1-12.

BEST, Paul Merwood (Bablake S, Coventry; Homerton C, Cambridge), b Nuneaton 8 Mar 1991. LHB, SLA. Cambridge MCCU 2011-12 (blue 2011-12). Warwickshire debut 2011. Northamptonshire 2011. Warwickshire 2nd XI debut 2009. England U19s 2009-10 to 2010. HS 150 CU v Surrey (Cambridge) 2011. CC HS 31* Nh v Glamorgan (Swansea) 2011. Wa HS 2 and CC BB 2-69 v Durham (Chester-le-St) 2011. BB 6-86 (9-131 match) CU v Oxford U (Cambridge) 2011. LO HS 16* and LO BB 3-43 v Yorks (Birmingham) 2012 (CB40). T20 HS –. T20 BB 3-19.

CHOPRA, Varun (Ilford County HS), b Barking, Essex 21 Jun 1987. 6'1". RHB, LB. Essex 2006-09, scoring 106 v Glos (Chelmsford) on CC debut. Warwickshire debut 2010; cap 2012. Tamil Union 2011-12. England U19s 2005 to 2006. F-c Tour (EL): SL 2013-14. 1000 runs (3); most – 1203 (2011). HS 233* Tamil Union v Sinhalese (Colombo, PSS) 2011-12. Wa HS 228 v Worcs (Worcester) 2011 (in 2nd CC game of season, having scored 210 v Somerset in 1st). BB –. LO HS 115 v Leics (Birmingham) 2011 (CB40). T20 HS 75*.

CLARKE, Rikki (Broadwater SS; Godalming C), b Orsett, Essex 29 Sep 1981. 6'4". RHB, RFM. Surrey 2002-07, scoring 107* v Cambridge U (Cambridge) on debut; cap 2005. Derbyshire cap/captain 2008. Warwickshire debut 2008; cap 2011. MCC 2006. YC 2002. **Tests**: 2 (2003-04); HS 55 and BB 2-7 v B (Chittagong) 2003-04. **LOI**: 20 (2003 to 2006); HS 39 v P (Lord's) 2006; BB 2-28 v B (Dhaka) 2003-04. F-c Tours: WI 2003-04, 2005-06; SL 2002-03 (ECB Acad), 2004-05; B 2003-04. 1000 runs (1): 1027 (2006). HS 214 Sy v Somerset (Guildford) 2006. Wa HS 140 v Lancs (Liverpool) 2012. BB 6-63 v Kent (Canterbury) 2010. Took seven catches in an innings v Lancs (Liverpool) 2011 to equal world record. LO HS 98* Sy v Derbys (Derby) 2002 (NL). LO BB 4-28 v Northants (Birmingham) 2011 (CB40). T20 HS 79*. T20 BB 3-11.

COLEMAN, Frederick Robert John (Strathallan S; Oxford Brookes U), b Edinburgh, Scotland 15 Dec 1991. RHB, WK, occ OB. Scotland 2011-12 to date. Oxford MCCU 2012-13. Awaiting Warwickshire f-c debut. Warwickshire 2nd XI debut 2013. **LOI** (Scot): 8 (2013 to 2013-14); HS 40 v Canada (Christchurch) 2013-14. **IT20** (Scot): 1 (2013); HS 9 v Kenya (Aberdeen) 2013. HS 110 OU v Worcs (Oxford) 2012 – on UK debut. LO HS 64* Scot v Nepal (Queenstown) 2013-14. T20 HS 9.

EVANS, Laurie John (Whitgift S; The John Fisher S; St Mary's C, Durham U), b Lambeth, London 12 Oct 1987. 6'0". RHB, RFM. Durham UCCE 2007. MCC 2007. Surrey 2009-10. Warwickshire debut 2010. HS 178 v Notts (Birmingham) 2013. BB 1-30 Sy v Bangladeshis (Oval) 2010. LO HS 47* v Worcs (Birmingham) 2013 (Y40). LO BB –. T20 HS 68*. T20 BB 1-5.

GORDON, Recordo Olton (Aston Manor S; Hamstead Hall SFC), b St Elizabeth, Jamaica 12 Oct 1991. RHB, RFM. Debut (Warwickshire) 2013. Warwickshire 2nd XI debut 2011. HS 13 v Somerset (Birmingham) 2013. BB 2-45 v Sussex (Birmingham) 2013. LO HS 1 v Northants (Birmingham) 2013 (Y40). LO BB 1-46 v Netherlands (Birmingham) 2013 (Y40).

HAIN, Samuel Robert (Southport S, Gold Coast), b Hong Kong 16 July 1995. UK passport (British parents). RHB, OB. Warwickshire 2nd XI debut 2011. Awaiting f-c debut. LO HS 1 v Worcs (Worcester) 2013 (Y40).

HANNON-DALBY, Oliver James (Brooksbank S, Leeds Met U), b Halifax, Yorkshire 20 Jun 1989. 6'7". LHB, RMF. Yorkshire 2008-12. No 1st XI appearances in 2009. Warwickshire debut 2013. HS 13 and Wa BB 4-50 v Oxford MCCU (Oxford) 2013. CC HS 11* Y v Lancs (Manchester) 2010. BB 5-68 v Warwks (Birmingham) and 5-68 v Somerset (Leeds) 2010 – in consecutive matches. LO HS 21* Y v Warwks (Scarborough) 2012 (CB40). LO BB 2-22 Y v Worcs (Worcester) 2011 (CB40). T20 HS –. T20 BB 2-23.

JAVID, Ateeq (Aston Manor S), b Birmingham 15 Oct 1991. RHB, RM. Debut (Warwickshire) 2009. Warwickshire 2nd XI debut 2008. England U19s 2010 to 2010-11. HS 133 v Somerset (Birmingham) 2013. BB 1-27 v Sussex (Birmingham) 2013. LO HS 43 and LO BB 2-34 v Kent (Canterbury) 2013 (Y40). T20 HS 41. T20 BB 4-17.

JONES, Richard Alan (Grange HS and King Edward VI C, Stourbridge; Loughborough U), b Wordsley, Stourbridge, Worcs 6 Nov 1986. 6'2". RHB, RMF. Worcestershire 2007-13; cap 2007. Matabeleland Tuskers 2011-12. HS 62 MT v SR (Bulawayo) 2011-12. UK HS 53* Wo v Durham (Worcester) 2009. BB 7-115 Wo v Sussex (Hove) 2010. LO HS 11* Wo v Sussex (Worcester) 2010 (CB40). LO BB 1-25 MT v ME (Bulawayo) 2011-12. T20 HS 9. T20 BB 1-17.

LEWIS, Thomas Peter (Princethorpe C, Rugby; Castle SFC, Kenilworth), b Coventry 7 Mar 1991. Younger brother of M.F.Lewis (Oxford UCCE 2009). LHB, RM. Warwickshire 2nd XI debut 2008. MCC YC 2010-12. Awaiting 1st XI debut.

McKAY, Peter John (Polesworth Int Language C, Tamworth), b Staffs 12 Oct 1994. LHB, WK. Debut (Warwickshire) 2013. Warwickshire 2nd XI debut 2013. HS 33 v Notts (Nottingham) 2013. LO HS 17* v Northants (Birmingham) 2013 (Y40). T20 HS 2*.

MILNES, Thomas Patrick (Heart of England S, Coventry), b Stourbridge, Worcs 6 Oct 1992. RHB, RFM. Debut (Warwickshire) 2011. Warwickshire 2nd XI debut 2009. England U19s 2010-11. HS 52* and BB 7-39 v Oxford MCCU (Oxford) 2013. CC HS 48 v Sussex (Birmingham) 2013. CC BB 2-64 v Somerset (Birmingham) 2013. LO HS 16 v Worcs (Birmingham) 2013 (Y40). LO BB 2-73 v Northants (Birmingham) 2013 (Y40).

^NQ^**PATEL, Jeetan** Shashi, b Wellington, New Zealand 7 May 1980. RHB, OB. Wellington 1999-00 to date. Warwickshire debut 2009; cap 2012. **Tests** (NZ): 19 (2006-07 to 2012-13); HS 27* v SA (Cape Town) 2006-07; BB 5-110 v WI (Napier) 2008-09. **LOI** (NZ): 39 (2005 to 2009-10); HS 34 v SL (Kingston) 2006-07; BB 3-11 v SA (Mumbai, BS) 2006-07. **IT20** (NZ): 11 (2005-06 to 2008-09); HS 5 v E (Auckland) 2007-08; BB 3-20 v SA (Johannesburg) 2005-06. F-c Tours (NZ): E 2008; SA 2005-06, 2012-13; I 2010-11, 2012; SL 2009, 2012-13; Z 2010-11, 2011-12; B 2008-09. HS 120 v Yorks (Birmingham) 2009. 50 wkts (2); most – 52 (2013). BB 7-75 v Somerset (Taunton) 2012. LO HS 50 v Kent (Birmingham) 2013 (Y40). LO BB 4-16 NZ A v Aus A (Hyderabad) 2008-09. T20 HS 12. T20 BB 4-27.

PORTERFIELD, William Thomas Stuart (Strabane GS; Leeds Met U), b Londonderry, N.Ireland 6 Sep 1984. 5'11". LHB, OB. Ireland 2006-07 to 2008-09. Gloucestershire 2008-10; cap 2008. Warwickshire debut 2011. MCC 2007. **LOI** (Ire): 68 (2006 to 2013-14); HS 112* v Bermuda (Nairobi) 2006-07. **IT20** (Ire): 34 (2008 to 2013-14); HS 56* v Kenya (Dubai, DSC) 2011-12. F-c Tour (Ire, C=Captain): WI 2009-10C; UAE 2013-14C. HS 175 Gs v Worcs (Cheltenham) 2010. Wa HS 87 v Durham (Chester-le-St) 2011. BB 1-29 Ire v Jamaica (Spanish Town) 2009-10. UK BB 1-57 Gs v Loughborough UCCE (Bristol) 2008. LO HS 112* (*see LOI*). T20 HS 127*.

RANKIN, William Boyd (Strabane GS; Harper Adams UC), b Londonderry, Co Derry, N Ireland 5 Jul 1984. Brother of R.J.Rankin (Ireland U19 2003-04). 6'8". LHB, RFM. Ireland 2006-07 to 2008. Derbyshire 2007. Warwickshire debut 2008; cap 2013. Middlesex summer contract 2004-05. Became available for England in 2012. **Test**: 1 (2013-14); HS 13 and BB 1-47 v A (Sydney) 2013-14. **LOI** (E/Ire): 44 (37 for Ire 2006-07 to 2011-12, 7 for E 2013 to 2013-14); HS 7* Ire v SL (St George's) 2006-07; BB 4-46 E v Ire (Dublin) 2013. **IT20** (E/Ire): 17 (15 for Ire 2009 to 2012-13, 2 for E 2013); HS 7* Ire v Kenya (Mombasa) 2011-12; BB 3-20 Ire v Kenya (Dubai, DSC) 2011-12. F-c Tour: A 2013-14. HS 43 ICC Combined XI v England XI (Dubai) 2011-12. Wa HS 28 v Durham (Chester-le-St) 2011. 50 wkts (1): 55 (2011). BB 5-16 v Essex (Birmingham) 2010. LO HS 18* v Northants (Northampton) 2013 (Y40). LO BB 4-34 v Kent (Birmingham) 2010 (CB40). T20 HS 7*. T20 BB 4-9.

‡[NQ]SHOAIB MALIK (Government Arabic SS, Sialkot), b Sialko, Pakistan 1 Feb 1982. 5'6". RHB, OB. Debut (Pakistan A) 1997. Gujranwala (1997-98 to 1998-99). PIA 1998-99 to date. Pakistan Reserves 1999-00. Sialkot 2001-02 to date. Gloucestershire 2003-04. Joins Warwickshire in 2014 for T20 only. **Tests** (P): 32 (2001 to 2010); HS 148* v SL (Colombo, SSC) 2005-06; BB 4-42 v SA (Lahore) 2003-04. **LOI** (P): 216 (1999-00 to 2013); HS 143 v I (Colombo, RPS) 2004; BB 4-19 v Hong Kong (Colombo, SSC) 2004. **IT20** (P): 55 (2006 to 2013-14); HS 57* v I (Bangalore) 2012-13; BB 2-7 v B (Dhaka) 2011-12. F-c Tours (P): E 1997 (Pak A), 2006, 2010; A 2004-05, 2009-10; WI 2005; NZ 2009-10; I 2007-08; SL 2005-06, 2009. HS 200 PIA v Faisalabad (Faisalabad) 2010-11. UK HS 110* P v Leics (Leicester) 2006. CC HS 63 Gs v Northants (Bristol) 2004. BB 7-81 PIA v WAPDA (Faisalabad) 2000-01. CC BB 3-76 Gs v Worcs (Cheltenham) 2003. LO HS 143 (*see LOI*). LO BB 5-35 PIA v Lahore Blues (Karachi) 2002-03. T20 HS 88*. T20 BB 5-13.

TROTT, Ian **Jonathan** Leonard (Rondebosch BHC; Stellenbosch U), b Cape Town, South Africa 22 Apr 1981. Stepbrother of K.C.Jackson (WP and Boland 1988-89 to 2001-02). 6'0". RHB, RM. Boland 2000-01. W Province 2001-02. EU/British passport. Warwickshire debut 2003, scoring 134 v Sussex (Birmingham); cap 2005; benefit 2014. Otago 2009-10. *Wisden* 2010. **ECB central contract 2013-14. Tests**: 49 (2009 to 2013-14); HS 226 v B (Lord's) 2010; scored 119 v A (Oval) 2009 on debut. **LOI**: 68 (2009 to 2013); HS 137 v A (Sydney) 2010-11; BB 2-31 v A (Adelaide) 2010-11. **IT20**: 7 (2007 to 2009-10); HS 51 v SA (Centurion) 2009-10. F-c Tours: A 2010-11, 2013-14 (*part*); SA 2009-10; NZ 2008-09 (EL), 2012-13; I 2007-08 (EL), 2012-13; SL 2011-12. B 2009-10; UAE 2011-12 (v P). 1000 runs (6); most – 1400 (2009). HS 226 (*see Tests*). CC HS 210 v Sussex (Birmingham) 2005. BB 7-39 v Kent (Canterbury) 2003. LO HS 137 (*see LOI*). LO BB 4-55 v Hants (Lord's) 2005 (CGT). T20 HS 86*. T20 BB 2-19.

TROUGHTON, Jamie Oliver (**'Jim'**) (Trinity S, Leamington Spa; Birmingham U), b Camden, London 2 Mar 1979. Great-grandson of H.T.Crichton (Warwicks 1908). 5'11". LHB, SLA. Debut (Warwickshire) 2001; cap 2002; captain 2011 to date; benefit 2013. **LOI**: 6 (2003); HS 20 v P (Lord's) 2003. F-c Tour (ECB Acad): SL 2002-03. 1000 runs (1): 1067 (2002). HS 223 v Hants (Birmingham) 2009. BB 3-1 v Cambridge U (Cambridge) 2004. CC BB 2-26 v Lancs (Birmingham) 2006. LO HS 115* and BB 4-23 Wa CB v Cumberland (Millom) 2001 (CGT). T20 HS 68*. T20 BB 2-10.

WEBB, Jonathon Patrick (Bromsgrove S; Leeds U), b Solihull 12 Jan 1992. RHB, RM. Leeds/Bradford MCCU 2012-13. Warwickshire 2nd XI debut 2008, aged 16y 200d. Awaiting Warwickshire 1st XI debut. HS 38 LBU v Surrey (Oval) 2012.

WESTWOOD, Ian James (Wheelers Lane S; Solihull SFC), b Birmingham 13 Jul 1982. 5'7½". LHB, OB. Debut (Warwickshire) 2003; cap 2008; captain 2009-10. HS 178 v West Indies A (Birmingham) 2006. CC HS 176 v Glamorgan (Cardiff) 2008. BB 2-39 v Hants (Southampton) 2009. LO HS 65 v Northants (Northampton) 2008 (FPT). BB 1-28 Wa CB v Cambs (March) 2001 (CGT). T20 HS 49*. T20 BB 3-29.

WOAKES, Christopher Roger (Barr Beacon Language S, Walsall), b Birmingham 2 March 1989. 6'2". RHB, RMF. Debut (Warwickshire) 2006; cap 2009. MCC 2009. Herefordshire 2006-07. **Test**: 1 (2013); HS 25 and BB 1-96 v A (Oval) 2013. **LOI**: 13 (2010-11 to 2013); HS 36 v NZ (Lord's) 2013; BB 6-45 v A (Brisbane) 2010-11. **IT20**: 4 (2010-11 to 2013); HS 19* v A (Adelaide) 2010-11; BB 1-29 v A (Melbourne) 2010-11. F-c Tours (EL): WI 2010-11, SL 2013-14. HS 152* v Derbys (Derby) 2013. 50 wkts (2); most – 58 (2010). BB 7-20 (10-123 match) v Hants (Birmingham) 2011. LO HS 49* v Leics (Birmingham) 2010 (CB40). LO BB 6-45 (*see LOI*). T20 HS 55*. T20 BB 4-21.

WRIGHT, Christopher Julian Clement (Eggars S, Alton; Anglia Ruskin U), b Chipping Norton, Oxon 14 Jul 1985. 6'3". RHB, RFM. Cambridge UCCE 2004-05. Middlesex 2004-07. Tamil Union 2005-06. Essex 2008-11. Warwickshire debut 2011; cap 2013. HS 77 Ex v Cambridge MCCU (Cambridge) 2011. CC HS 71* Ex v Middx (Chelmsford) 2008. Wa HS 53 v Notts (Birmingham) 2012. 50 wkts (1): 67 (2012). BB 6-22 Ex v Leics (Leicester) 2008. Wa BB 6-31 v Durham (Birmingham) 2013. LO HS 42 Ex v Glos (Cheltenham) 2011 (CB40). LO BB 4-20 Ex v Unicorns (Chelmsford) 2011 (CB40). T20 HS 6*. T20 BB 4-24.

RELEASED/RETIRED

(Having made a County First-Class or List A appearance in 2013)

ALI, Shozair Abbas (Queensbridge S, Moseley; Moseley SFC), b Birmingham 28 Dec 1992. LHB, RMF. Warwickshire 2013. Warwickshire 2nd XI debut 2010. HS 8 and BB 2-76 v Oxford MCCU (Oxford) 2013 – only 1st XI game.

ALLIN, Thomas William (Bideford C; N Devon C; UWIC), b Bideford, Devon 27 Nov 1987. Son of A.W.Allin (Glamorgan 1976), brother of M.L.Allin (Devon 2003). RHB, RMF. Warwickshire 2013. Cardiff UCCE (not f-c) 2008-10. Devon 2007. HS 0 and BB –. LO HS 2* and BB – v Surrey (Birmingham) 2011 (CB40).

ATKINSON, James John (St Mary's C, Durham U), b Hong Kong 24 Aug 1990. RHB, WK. Durham MCCU 2009-11. Warwickshire 2013. Hong Kong. **LOI** (HK): 2 (2008); HS 23 v I (Karachi) 2008. HS 34 DU v Durham (Durham) 2011. LO HS 85 HK v Kenya (Rangiora) 2013-14. T20 HS 87*.

MADDY, Darren Lee (Wreake Valley C), b Leicester 23 May 1974. 5'9". RHB, RM/OB. Leicestershire 1994-2006; cap 1996; benefit 2006. Warwickshire 2007-13; captain 2007-08. **Tests**: 3 (1999 to 1999-00); HS 24 v SA (Durban) 1999-00; BB –. **LOI**: 8 (1998 to 1999-00); HS 53 v Z (Harare) 1999-00. **IT20**: 4 (2007-08); HS 50 and BB 2-6 v NZ (Durban) 2007-08. F-c Tours (Eng A): SA 1996-97 (Le), 1998-99, 1999-00 (Eng); SL 1997-98; Z 1998-99; K 1997-98. 1000 runs (4); most – 1187 (2002). HS 229* Le v Loughborough U (Leicester) 2003. CC HS 162 Le v Durham (Darlington) 1998. Wa HS 148* v Kent (Canterbury) 2007. BB 5-37 Le v Hants (Southampton) 2002. Wa BB 5-63 v Durham (Chester-le-St) 2007. LO HS 167* Le v Scotland (Edinburgh) 2006 (CGT). LO BB 4-16 Le v Somerset (Taunton) 2000 (NL). T20 HS 111 Le v Yorks (Leeds) 2004 – Le record. T20 BB 3-10.

PIOLET, S.A. – *see SUSSEX.*

POYNTER, Stuart William (Teddington S), b Hammersmith, London 18 Oct 1990. RHB, WK. Middlesex 2010. Ireland 2011 to date. Warwickshire 2013. HS 63 Ire v Australia A (Belfast) 2013. Wa HS 0 v Derbys (Derby) 2013. LO HS 0*.

C.L.Metters left the staff without making a County First-Class or List A appearance in 2013.

WARWICKSHIRE 2013

RESULTS SUMMARY

	Place	Won	Lost	Tied	Drew	NR
LV= County Championship (1st Division)	4th	5	2		9	
All First-Class Matches		6	2		9	
Yorkshire Bank 40 (Group A)	7th	2	8			2
Friends Life t20 (Mid/Wales/West Group)	4th	5	5			

LV= COUNTY CHAMPIONSHIP AVERAGES
BATTING AND FIELDING

Cap		M	I	NO	HS	Runs	Avge	100	50	Ct/St
2009	C.R.Woakes	10	16	5	152*	640	58.18	1	4	2
	L.J.Evans	13	19	2	178	943	55.47	3	4	6
2012	V.Chopra	15	25	4	228*	1069	50.90	3	5	26
	A.Javid	11	17	3	133	619	44.21	2	2	5
2007	D.L.Maddy	3	5	1	65	157	39.25	–	1	1
2007	T.R.Ambrose	13	20	2	105	685	38.05	1	5	39/1
2002	J.O.Troughton	7	11	1	84	322	32.20	–	2	5
2011	R.Clarke	13	18	4	92	449	32.07	–	4	19
2013	K.H.D.Barker	11	13	2	125	350	31.81	1	–	4
2012	J.S.Patel	16	18	4	78*	438	31.28	–	5	14
2008	I.J.Westwood	12	20	2	71	481	26.72	–	4	8
	T.P.Milnes	7	7	–	48	160	22.85	–	–	3
	M.A.Chambers	4	4	–	58	80	20.00	–	1	1
	W.T.S.Porterfield	11	16	–	36	235	14.68	–	–	7
2013	W.B.Rankin	9	9	6	12*	32	10.66	–	–	–
2013	C.J.C.Wright	8	8	1	11	30	4.28	–	–	–

Also played: T.W.Allin (1 match) 0; J.J.Atkinson (1) did not bat; I.R.Bell (2 – cap 2001) 56, 62; R.O.Gordon (3) 13, 10 (1 ct); O.J.Hannon-Dalby (2) 5, 10*; P.J.McKay (1) 33, 3*; S.A.Piolet (1) 1, 30 (1 ct); S.W.Poynter 0 (6 ct); I.J.L.Trott (2 – cap 2005) 96, 65 (1 ct).

BOWLING

	O	M	R	W	Avge	Best	5wI	10wM
W.B.Rankin	216.4	20	709	31	22.87	4-29	–	–
K.H.D.Barker	344.1	83	1055	46	22.934	5-55	1	–
C.R.Woakes	245.4	46	711	31	22.935	5-42	1	–
M.A.Chambers	103.2	16	383	14	27.35	5-68	1	–
J.S.Patel	576.1	139	1561	52	30.01	5-56	2	–
R.Clarke	229.3	61	642	19	33.78	4-70	–	–
C.J.C.Wright	209	43	689	19	36.26	6-31	1	–

Also bowled: T.W.Allin 17-3-65-0; V.Chopra 2-0-2-0; L.J.Evans 14-2-37-0; R.O.Gordon 70-9-220-4; O.J.Hannon-Dalby 33-4-164-1; A.Javid 49-10-154-2; D.L.Maddy 26.5-5-71-1; T.P.Milnes 89.1-9-382-4; S.A.Piolet 12-0-59-1; I.J.L.Trott 16-2-47-0; I.J.Westwood 6.5-1-11-1.

The First-Class Averages (pp 225–241) give the records of Warwickshire players in all first-class county matches (Warwickshire's other opponents being Oxford MCCU), with the exception of I.R.Bell, M.A.Chambers, I.J.L.Trott, C.R.Woakes and C.J.C.Wright, whose full first-class figures for Warwickshire are as above, and:
V.Chopra 16-27-4-228*-1095-47.60-3-5-28ct. 4-0-12-0.

WARWICKSHIRE RECORDS

FIRST-CLASS CRICKET

Highest Total	For 810-4d		v	Durham	Birmingham	1994
	V 887		by	Yorkshire	Birmingham	1896
Lowest Total	For 16		v	Kent	Tonbridge	1913
	V 15		by	Hampshire	Birmingham	1922
Highest Innings	For 501*	B.C.Lara	v	Durham	Birmingham	1994
	V 322	I.V.A.Richards	for	Somerset	Taunton	1985

Highest Partnership for each Wicket

1st	377*	N.F.Horner/K.Ibadulla	v	Surrey	The Oval	1960
2nd	465*	J.A.Jameson/R.B.Kanhai	v	Glos	Birmingham	1974
3rd	327	S.P.Kinneir/W.G.Quaife	v	Lancashire	Birmingham	1901
4th	470	A.I.Kallicharran/G.W.Humpage	v	Lancashire	Southport	1982
5th	335	J.O.Troughton/T.R.Ambrose	v	Hampshire	Birmingham	2009
6th	226	T.R.Ambrose/H.H.Streak	v	Worcs	Worcester	2007
7th	289*	I.R.Bell/T.Frost	v	Sussex	Horsham	2004
8th	228	A.J.W.Croom/R.E.S.Wyatt	v	Worcs	Dudley	1925
9th	233	I.J.L.Trott/J.S.Patel	v	Yorkshire	Birmingham	2009
10th	214	N.V.Knight/A.Richardson	v	Hampshire	Birmingham	2002

Best Bowling	For 10-41	J.D.Bannister	v	Comb Servs	Birmingham	1959
(Innings)	V 10-36	H.Verity	for	Yorkshire	Leeds	1931
Best Bowling	For 15-76	S.Hargreave	v	Surrey	The Oval	1903
(Match)	V 17-92	A.P.Freeman	for	Kent	Folkestone	1932

Most Runs – Season	2417	M.J.K.Smith	(av 60.42)	1959
Most Runs – Career	35146	D.L.Amiss	(av 41.64)	1960-87
Most 100s – Season	9	A.I.Kallicharran		1984
	9	B.C.Lara		1994
Most 100s – Career	78	D.L.Amiss		1960-87
Most Wkts – Season	180	W.E.Hollies	(av 15.13)	1946
Most Wkts – Career	2201	W.E.Hollies	(av 20.45)	1932-57
Most Career W-K Dismissals	800	E.J.Smith	(662 ct; 138 st)	1904-30
Most Career Catches in the Field	422	M.J.K.Smith		1956-75

LIMITED-OVERS CRICKET

Highest Total	50ov	392-5		v	Oxfordshire	Birmingham	1984
	40ov	321-7		v	Leics	Birmingham	2010
	T20	205-2		v	Northants	Birmingham	2005
		205-7		v	Glamorgan	Swansea	2005
Lowest Total	50ov	94		v	Glos	Bristol	2000
	40ov	59		v	Yorkshire	Leeds	2001
	T20	73		v	Somerset	Taunton	2013
Highest Innings	50ov	206	A.I.Kallicharran	v	Oxfordshire	Birmingham	1984
	40ov	137	I.R.Bell	v	Yorkshire	Birmingham	2005
	T20	89	N.V.Knight	v	Worcs	Worcester	2003
Best Bowling	50ov	7-32	R.G.D.Willis	v	Yorkshire	Birmingham	1981
	40ov	6-15	A.A.Donald	v	Yorkshire	Birmingham	1995
	T20	5-19	N.M.Carter	v	Worcs	Birmingham	2005

WORCESTERSHIRE

Formation of Present Club: 11 March 1865
Inaugural First-Class Match: 1899
Colours: Dark Green and Black
Badge: Shield Argent a Fess between three Pears Sable
County Championships: (5) 1964, 1965, 1974, 1988, 1989
NatWest Trophy Winners: (1) 1994
Benson and Hedges Cup Winners: (1) 1991
Pro 40/National League (Div 1) Winners: (1) 2007
Sunday League Winners: (3) 1971, 1987, 1988
Twenty20 Cup Winners: (0); best – Quarter-Finalist 2004, 2007, 2012

Chief Executive: David Leatherdale, County Ground, New Road, Worcester, WR2 4QQ • Tel: 01905 748474 • Fax: 01905 748005 • Email: admin@wccc.co.uk • Web: www.wccc.co.uk • Twitter: @WorcsCCC (10,906 followers)

Director of Cricket: Steve Rhodes. **Academy Director/Assistant Coach:** Damian D'Oliveira. **Bowling/Assistant Coach:** Matt Mason. **Captain:** D.K.H.Mitchell. **Vice-Captain:** tba. **Overseas Player:** Saeed Ajmal. **2014 Beneficiary:** None. **Head Groundsman:** Tim Packwood. **Scorer:** Dawn Pugh. ‡ New registration. ^{NQ} Not qualified for England.

Worcestershire revised their capping policy in 2002 and now award players with their County Colours when they make their Championship debut.

ALI, Moeen Munir (Moseley S), b Birmingham, Warwks 18 Jun 1987. Brother of A.K.Ali (Worcestershire, Gloucestershire and Leicestershire 2000-12), cousin of Kabir Ali (*see LANCASHIRE*). 6'0". LHB, OB. Warwickshire 2005-06, having joined staff when aged 15. Worcestershire debut 2007. Moors SC 2011-12. MT 2012-13. MCC 2012. PCA 2013. **LOI:** 3 (2013-14); HS 55 and BB 1-5 v WI (North Sound) 2013-14. F-c Tour (EL): SL 2013-14. 1000 runs (2); most – 1420 (2013). HS 250 v Glamorgan (Worcester) 2013. BB 6-29 (12-96 match) v Lancs (Manchester) 2012. LO HS 158 v Sussex (Horsham) 2011 (CB40). LO BB 3-28 v Notts (Nottingham) 2013 (Y40). T20 HS 85. T20 BB 5-34 v Northants (Northampton) 2013 – Wo record.

ANDREW, Gareth Mark (Ansford Community S; Richard Huish C), b Yeovil, Somerset 27 Dec 1983. 6'0". LHB, RMF. Somerset 2003-05. Worcestershire debut 2008. Canterbury 2012-13. HS 180* Canterbury v Auckland (Auckland) 2012-13. HS 92* v Notts (Worcester) 2009. 50 wkts (1): 52 (2011). BB 5-58 v Middx (Kidderminster) 2008. LO HS 104 v Surrey (Oval) 2010 (CB40). LO BB 5-31 v Yorks (Worcester) 2009 (P40). T20 HS 65*. T20 BB 4-22.

BARNARD, Edward George (Shrewsbury S), b Shrewsbury, Shrops 20 Nov 1995. Younger brother of M.R.Barnard (Oxford MCCU 2010). 6'1". RHB, RM. Shropshire 2012. England U19s 2012-13. Awaiting 1st XI debut.

CESSFORD, Graeme (Queen Elizabeth HS, Hexham; Newcastle C), b Hexham, Northumberland 4 Oct 1983. 6'2". RHB, RFM. Debut (Worcestershire) 2013. Worcestershire 2nd XI debut 2012. HS 20 v Glos (Cheltenham) 2013. BB 4-73 v Lancs (Worcester) 2013. LO HS 0*. LO BB 4-24 v Warwks (Birmingham) 2013 (Y40).

CHOUDHRY, Shaaiq Hussain (Fir Vale S; Bradford U), b Rotherham, Yorkshire 3 Nov 1985. 5'10". RHB, SLA. MCC 2007. Warwickshire 2009. Worcestershire debut 2010. Bradford/Leeds UCCE 2006-08 (not f-c). HS 75 Wa v Durham UCCE (Durham) 2009. CC HS 63 v Sussex (Hove) 2010. BB 4-38 v Lancs (Manchester) 2012. LO HS 39 v Sussex (Hove) 2010 (CB40). LO BB 4-54 v Surrey (Oval) 2010 (CB40). T20 HS 26*. T20 BB 2-21.

CLARKE, Joe Michael (Llanfyllin HS), b Shrewsbury, Shrops 26 May 1996. RHB, WK. Worcestershire 2nd XI debut 2013. Shropshire 2012-13. Awaiting 1st XI debut.

COX, Oliver Ben (Bromsgrove S), b Wordsley, Stourbridge 2 Feb 1992. 5'10". RHB, WK. Debut (Worcestershire) 2009. Worcestershire 2nd XI debut 2009. HS 65 v Hants (Worcester) 2013. LO HS 34* v Netherlands (Rotterdam) 2013 (Y40). T20 HS 37.

D'OLIVEIRA, Brett Louis (Worcester SFC), b Worcester 28 Feb 1992. Son of D.B.D'Oliveira (Worcs 1982-95), grandson of B.L.D'Oliveira (Worcs, EP and England 1964-80). 5'9". RHB, LB. Debut (Worcestershire) 2012. Worcestershire 2nd XI debut 2010. HS 19 v Warwks (Birmingham) 2012. BB –. LO HS 28 v Kent (Worcester) 2013 (Y40). LO BB 3-35 v Warwks (Worcester) 2013 (Y40). T20 HS 9*. T20 BB 3-20.

FELL, Thomas Charles (Oakham S; Oxford Brookes U), b Hillingdon, Middx 17 Oct 1993. RHB, WK, occ OB. Debut (Oxford MCCU) 2013. Worcestershire debut 2013. Worcestershire 2nd XI debut 2010. HS 94* v Kent (Worcester) 2013. LO HS 55 v Northants (Northampton) 2013 (Y40).

HARRISON, Nicholas Luke (Hardenhuish S, Chippenham), b Bath, Somerset 3 Feb 1992. 6'4". RHB, RMF. Debut (Worcestershire) 2012. Worcestershire 2nd XI debut 2010. Wiltshire 2009-10. No 1st XI appearances in 2013. HS 10 v Somerset (Taunton) 2012. BB 2-78 v Oxford MCCU (Oxford) 2012. CC BB 1-62 v Warwks (Worcester) 2012. LO HS 5* v Leics (Worcester) 2012 (CB40). LO BB 2-43 v Yorks (Leeds) 2011 (CB40).

KERVEZEE, Alexei Nicolaas (Duneside HS, Namibia; Grenoobi HS, SA; Segbroek C, Holland), b Walvis Bay, Namibia 11 Sep 1989. 5'8". RHB, OB. Netherlands 2005 to 2009-10. Worcestershire debut 2008. Now qualified for England. **LOI** (Ne): 39 (2006 to 2011-12); HS 92 v Kenya (Voorburg) 2010; BB –. **IT20** (Ne): 10 (2009 to 2011-12); HS 58* v Afghanistan (Dubai, DSC) 2011-12. 1000 runs (1): 1190 (2010). HS 155 v Derbys (Derby) 2010. BB 1-14 Netherlands v Namibia (Windhoek) 2007-08. LO HS 121* Netherlands v Denmark (Potchefstroom) 2008-09. LO BB –. T20 HS 58*.

KOHLER-CADMORE, Tom (Malvern C), b Chatham, Kent 19 Aug 1994. RHB, OB. Worcestershire 2nd XI debut 2010, aged 15y 342d. Awaiting f-c debut. LO HS 47 v Bangladesh A (Worcester) 2013 – only 1st XI appearance.

LEACH, Joseph (Shrewsbury S; Leeds U), b Stafford 30 Oct 1990. 6'1". RHB, RMF. Debut (Leeds/Bradford MCCU) 2012. Worcestershire debut 2012. Worcestershire 2nd XI debut 2008. Staffordshire 2008-09. HS 114 v Glos (Cheltenham) 2013. BB 4-73 LBU v Surrey (Oval) 2012 – on debut. CC BB 2-36 v Glamorgan (Worcester) 2013. LO HS 21* and LO BB 1-45 v Bangladesh A (Worcester) 2013. T20 HS 14*. T20BB 3-20.

MITCHELL, Daryl Keith Henry (Prince Henry's HS; University C, Worcester), b Badsey, near Evesham 25 Nov 1983. 5'10". RHB, RM. Debut (Worcestershire) 2005; captain 2011 to date. Mountaineers 2011-12. 1000 runs (2); most – 1180 (2010). HS 298 v Somerset (Taunton) 2009. BB 4-49 v Yorks (Leeds) 2009. LO HS 107 v Sussex (Hove) 2013 (Y40). LO BB 4-42 v Lancs (Worcester) 2006 (CGT). T20 HS 45. T20 BB 4-11.

MORRIS, Charles Andrew John (King's C, Taunton; Oxford Brookes U), b Hereford 6 Jul 1992. 6'0". RHB, RMF. Debut (Oxford MCCU) 2012. Worcestershire debut 2013. Worcestershire 2nd XI debut 2012. Kent 2nd XI 2012. MCC Univs 2012. Devon 2011-12. HS 33* and BB 3-33 OU v Warwks (Oxford) 2013. Wo HS 25* and Wo BB – v Australians (Worcester) 2013. LO HS 6* v Kent (Worcester) 2013 (Y40). LO BB 2-25 v Notts (Nottingham) 2013 (Y40). T20 BB –.

PARDOE, Matthew Graham (Haybridge HS), b Stourbridge 5 Jan 1991. 6'1". LHB, LM. Debut (Worcestershire) 2011. Southern Rocks 2012-13 to date. Worcestershire 2nd XI debut 2007. HS 102 v Glamorgan (Worcester) 2013. BB 2-34 SR v Mountaineers (Mutare) 2012-13. LO HS 42 SR v MT (Bulawayo) 2012-13. T20 HS 1.

RHODES, George Harry (The Chase HS and SFC, Malvern), b 26 Oct 1993. Son of S.J.Rhodes (Worcestershire, Yorkshire and England 1981-2004), grandson of W.E.Rhodes (Nottinghamshire 1961-64). RHB, RM. Worcestershire 2nd XI debut 2012. Awaiting 1st XI debut.

SHANTRY, Jack David (Priory SS; Shrewsbury SFC; Liverpool U), b Shrewsbury, Shrops 29 Jan 1988. Son of B.K.Shantry (Gloucestershire 1978-79), brother of A.J.Shantry (Northants, Warwicks, Glamorgan 2003-11). 6'4". LHB, LM. Debut (Worcestershire) 2009. Shropshire 2007-09. HS 55* v Northants (Worcester) 2013. BB 7-60 v Oxford MCCU (Oxford) 2013. CC BB 7-69 v Essex (Worcester) 2013. LO HS 18 v Sussex (Hove) 2010 (CB40). Lo BB 4-32 v Middx (Worcester) 2012 (CB40). T20 HS 9*. T20 BB 4-33.

WHITELEY, Ross Andrew (Repton S), b Sheffield, Yorks 13 Sep 1988. 6'2". LHB, LM. Derbyshire 2008-13. Worcestershire debut 2013. No f-c appearances in 2009-10. HS 130* De v Kent (Derby) 2011. Wo HS 56 v Northants (Worcester) 2013. BB 2-6 De v Hants (Derby) 2012. Wo BB 1-23 v Hants (Worcester) 2013. LO HS 40 De v Kent (Canterbury) 2011 (CB40). LO BB 1-17 De v Unicorns (Wormsley) 2012 (CB40). T20 HS 43. T20 BB 1-12.

RELEASED/RETIRED

(Having made a County First-Class or List A appearance in 2013)

[NQ]**JOHNSON, Michael** Anthony, b Perth, Australia 11 Aug 1988. RHB, WK. W Australia 2008-09 to 2011-12. Worcestershire 2013. Has played 2nd XI cricket for Somerset, Hampshire, Northamptonshire, Surrey and Kent. HS 53 WA v Q (Perth) 2011-12. Wo HS 44 v Hants (Southampton) 2013. LO HS 17* v Notts (Worcester) 2013. T20 HS 8*.

JONES, R.A. – *see WARWICKSHIRE*.

KAPIL, Aneesh (Denstone C), b Wolverhampton 3 Aug 1993. 5'8". RHB, RFM. Worcestershire 2011-13. Worcestershire 2nd XI debut 2008, aged 15y 10d. HS 54 v Sussex (Horsham) 2011 – on debut. BB 3-17 v Notts (Worcester) 2012. LO HS 44 v Yorks (Worcester) 2011 (CB40). LO BB 1-18 v Netherlands (Worcester) 2011 (CB40). T20 HS 13. T20 BB 3-9.

LUCAS, David Scott (Djanogly CTC, Nottingham), b Nottingham 19 Aug 1978. 6'2". RHB, LMF. Nottinghamshire 1999-2002. Yorkshire 2005. Northamptonshire 2007-11; cap 2009. Worcestershire 2012-13. Lincolnshire 2006. HS 60 Nh v Leics (Leicester) 2011. Wo HS 19 and Wo BB 4-37 v Surrey (Worcester) 2012. 50 wkts (1): 60 (2009). BB 7-24 (12-73 match) Nh v Glos (Cheltenham) 2009. LO HS 32* Nh v Lancs (Manchester) 2009 (FPT). LO BB 5-48 Nh v Hants (Northampton) 2011 (CB40). T20 HS 5*. T20 BB 3-19.

PINNER, Neil Douglas (RGS Worcester), b Wordsley, Stourbridge 29 Sep 1990. 5'11". RHB, OB. Worcestershire 2011-13. Worcestershire 2nd XI debut 2008. HS 82 v Lancs (Worcester) 2012. BB –. LO HS 37 v Kent (Canterbury) 2011 (CB40). LO BB –.

RICHARDSON, Alan (Alleyne's HS, Stone; Stafford CFE; Durham U), b Newcastle-under-Lyme, Staffs 6 May 1975. 6'2". RHB, RMF. Derbyshire 1995 (one match). Warwickshire 1999-2004; cap 2002. Middlesex 2005-09; cap 2005, taking 7-113 v Notts (Lord's) on debut. Worcestershire 2010-13. MCC 2012. *Wisden* 2011. Staffordshire 1996-98. Minor Counties 1998. HS 91 Wa v Hants (Birmingham) 2002 – adding Wa record 214 for 10th wicket with N.V.Knight. Wo HS 41 v Sussex (Horsham) 2011. 50 wkts (5); most – 73 (2011). BB 8-37 (12-107 match) v Glos (Worcester) 2013. Hat-trick v Leics (Leicester) 2013. LO HS 21* M v Lancs (Lord's) 2005 (NL). LO BB 5-35 Wa v Staffs (Stone) 2002 (CGT). T20 HS 6*. T20 BB 3-13.

RUSSELL, Christopher James (Medina HS), b Newport, IoW 16 Feb 1989. 6'1". RHB, RMF. Worcestershire 2012-13. HS 22 v Middx (Worcester) 2012. BB 4-43 v Warwks (Birmingham) 2012. LO HS 1* v Northants (Worcester) 2013 (Y40). LO BB 4-32 v Netherlands (Rotterdam) 2013 (Y40). T20 HS 3*. T20 BB –.

NQ**SAMARAWEERA, Thilan** Thusara, b Colombo, Sri Lanka 22 Sep 1976. Younger brother of D.P.Samaraweera (Colts and Sri Lanka 1991-92 to 2003-04). RHB, OB. Colts CC 1996-97 to 1997-98. Sinhalese SC 1998-99 to 2012-13. Kandurata 2009-10. Worcestershire 2013. **Tests** (SL): 81 (2001 to 2012-13); HS 231 v P (Karachi) 2008-09; BB 4-49 v B (Colombo, SSC) 2002. **LOI** (SL): 53 (1998-99 to 2010-11); HS 105* v I (Dhaka) 2009-10; BB 3-34 v E (Sydney) 1998-99. F-c Tours (SL): E 2002, 2006, 2007 (SL A), 2011; A 2004, 2007-08, 2012-13; SA 1999-00 (SL A), 2011-12; WI 2003, 2006-07 (SL A), 2007-08; NZ 2004-05; I 2001-02 (Colombo CA), 2005-06, 2006-07 (SL A), 2009-10; P 2001-02, 2002-03 (SL A), 2004-05, 2008-09; Z 2004; B 2005-06, 2008-09. 1000 runs (0+1): 1236 (2003-04). HS 231 (*see Tests*). Wo HS 144* v Leics (Leicester) 2013. BB 6-55 SSC v Singha SC (Colombo, SSC) 2000-01 and 6-55 SL A v Pakistan A (Dambulla) 2001. LO HS 105* (*see LOI*). LO BB 7-30 SL A v ECB Nat Academy (Kurunegala) 2002-03. T20 HS 71. T20 BB 3-17.

WORCESTERSHIRE 2013

RESULTS SUMMARY

	Place	Won	Lost	Tied	Drew	NR
LV= County Championship (2nd Division)	5th	5	6		5	
All First-Class Matches		6	6		6	
Yorkshire Bank 40 (Group A)	5th	5	7			
Friends Life t20 (Mid/Wales/West Group)	5th	4	6			

LV= COUNTY CHAMPIONSHIP AVERAGES
BATTING AND FIELDING

Cap†		M	I	NO	HS	Runs	Avge	100	50	Ct/St
2008	M.M.Ali	16	27	5	250	1375	62.50	4	8	22
2013	T.T.Samaraweera	15	22	4	144*	702	39.00	2	4	6
2012	J.Leach	6	9	2	114	260	37.14	1	1	1
2013	T.C.Fell	7	10	1	94*	333	37.00	–	2	3
2005	D.K.H.Mitchell	16	29	4	156	824	32.96	1	4	21
2011	M.G.Pardoe	16	29	3	102	794	30.53	1	5	3
2009	O.B.Cox	6	9	2	65	180	25.71	–	1	16/1
2013	R.A.Whiteley	4	7	–	56	162	23.14	–	1	2
2009	J.D.Shantry	12	14	1	55*	294	22.61	–	2	3
2010	S.H.Choudhry	6	9	2	61*	146	20.85	–	1	–
2008	G.M.Andrew	10	14	–	66	287	20.50	–	3	5
2011	N.D.Pinner	7	9	–	29	131	14.55	–	–	9
2013	M.A.Johnson	10	14	1	44	184	14.15	–	–	14
2010	A.Richardson	16	18	10	21	109	13.62	–	–	4
2013	G.Cessford	5	6	2	20	45	11.25	–	–	–
2009	A.N.Kervezee	10	14	–	35	148	10.57	–	–	3
2012	D.S.Lucas	3	5	–	12	34	6.80	–	–	1
2012	C.J.Russell	9	11	2	10	42	4.66	–	–	2

Also batted (1 match each): R.A.Jones (cap 2007) 7, 4; A. Kapil (cap 2011) 4, 4.

BOWLING

	O	M	R	W	Avge	Best	5wI	10wM
A.Richardson	541.4	157	1368	69	19.82	8- 37	5	2
J.D.Shantry	323.5	88	949	34	27.91	7- 69	1	–
G.M.Andrew	219	57	698	21	33.23	4- 79	–	–
M.M.Ali	284.4	38	944	28	33.71	6- 77	1	–
G.Cessford	118	13	524	15	34.93	4- 73	–	–
S.H.Choudhry	156.4	21	443	12	36.91	4-111	–	–
C.J.Russell	181.4	32	710	16	44.37	3- 47	–	–

Also bowled:

	O	M	R	W	Avge	Best	5wI	10wM
J.Leach	65	6	293	5	58.60	2- 36	–	–

R.A.Jones 15-3-78-1; A.Kapil 2-0-14-0; D.S.Lucas 55.1-13-183-3; D.K.H.Mitchell 26.2-6-70-2; N.D.Pinner 3-0-15-0; R.A.Whiteley 8-0-42-1.

The First-Class Averages (pp 225–241) give the records of Worcestershire players in all first-class county matches (Worcestershire's other opponents being Oxford MCCU and the Australians), with the exception of R.A.Whiteley, whose full first-class figures for Worcestershire are as above, and:
T.C.Fell 8-12-2-94*-396-39.60-0-3-3ct.

† Worcestershire revised their capping policy in 2002 and now award players with their County Colours when they make their Championship debut.

195

WORCESTERSHIRE RECORDS

FIRST-CLASS CRICKET

Highest Total	For	701-6d		v	Surrey	Worcester	2007
	V	701-4d		by	Leics	Worcester	1906
Lowest Total	For	24		v	Yorkshire	Huddersfield	1903
	V	30		by	Hampshire	Worcester	1903
Highest Innings	For	405*	G.A.Hick	v	Somerset	Taunton	1988
	V	331*	J.D.B.Robertson	for	Middlesex	Worcester	1949

Highest Partnership for each Wicket

1st	309	H.K.Foster/F.L.Bowley	v	Derbyshire	Derby	1901
2nd	316	S.C.Moore/V.S.Solanki	v	Glos	Cheltenham	2008
3rd	438*	G.A.Hick/T.M.Moody	v	Hampshire	Southampton	1997
4th	330	B.F.Smith/G.A.Hick	v	Somerset	Taunton	2006
5th	393	E.G.Arnold/W.B.Burns	v	Warwicks	Birmingham	1909
6th	265	G.A.Hick/S.J.Rhodes	v	Somerset	Taunton	1988
7th	256	D.A.Leatherdale/S.J.Rhodes	v	Notts	Nottingham	2002
8th	184	S.J.Rhodes/S.R.Lampitt	v	Derbyshire	Kidderminster	1991
9th	181	J.A.Cuffe/R.D.Burrows	v	Glos	Worcester	1907
10th	119	W.B.Burns/G.A.Wilson	v	Somerset	Worcester	1906

Best Bowling	For	9- 23	C.F.Root	v	Lancashire	Worcester	1931
(Innings)	V	10- 51	J.Mercer	for	Glamorgan	Worcester	1936
Best Bowling	For	15- 87	A.J.Conway	v	Glos	Moreton-in-M	1914
(Match)	V	17-212	J.C.Clay	for	Glamorgan	Swansea	1937

Most Runs – Season	2654	H.H.I.H.Gibbons	(av 52.03)	1934
Most Runs – Career	34490	D.Kenyon	(av 34.18)	1946-67
Most 100s – Season	10	G.M.Turner		1970
	10	G.A.Hick		1988
Most 100s – Career	106	G.A.Hick		1984-2008
Most Wkts – Season	207	C.F.Root	(av 17.52)	1925
Most Wkts – Career	2143	R.T.D.Perks	(av 23.73)	1930-55
Most Career W-K Dismissals	1095	S.J.Rhodes	(991 ct; 104 st)	1985-2004
Most Career Catches in the Field	528	G.A.Hick		1984-2008

LIMITED-OVERS CRICKET

Highest Total	50ov	404-3		v	Devon	Worcester	1987
	40ov	376-6		v	Surrey	Oval	2010
	T20	227-6		v	Northants	Kidderminster	2007
Lowest Total	50ov	58		v	Ireland	Worcester	2009
	40ov	86		v	Yorkshire	Leeds	1969
	T20	86		v	Northants	Worcester	2006
Highest Innings	50ov	180*	T.M.Moody	v	Surrey	The Oval	1994
	40ov	160	T.M.Moody	v	Kent	Worcester	1991
	T20	116*	G.A.Hick	v	Northants	Luton	2004
Best Bowling	50ov	7-19	N.V.Radford	v	Beds	Bedford	1991
	40ov	6-16	Shoaib Akhtar	v	Glos	Worcester	2005
	T20	5-34	M.M.Ali	v	Northants	Northampton	2013

YORKSHIRE

Formation of Present Club: 8 January 1863
Substantial Reorganisation: 10 December 1891
Inaugural First-Class Match: 1864
Colours: Dark Blue, Light Blue and Gold
Badge: White Rose
County Championships (since 1890): (30) 1893, 1896,
1898, 1900, 1901, 1902, 1905, 1908, 1912, 1919, 1922,
1923, 1924, 1925, 1931, 1932, 1933, 1935, 1937, 1938,
1939, 1946, 1959, 1960, 1962, 1963, 1966, 1967, 1968,
2001
Joint Champions: (1) 1949
Gillette/C&G Trophy Winners: (3) 1965, 1969, 2002
Benson and Hedges Cup Winners: (1) 1987
Sunday League Winners: (1) 1983
Twenty20 Cup Winners: (0); best – Finalist 2012

Chief Executive: Mark Arthur, Headingley Carnegie, Kirkstall Lane, Headingley, Leeds,
LS6 3DP • Tel: 0871 971 1222 • Fax: 0113 278 4099 • Email: cricket@yorkshireccc.com •
Web: www.yorkshireccc.com • Twitter: @Yorkshireccc (34,109 followers)

Director of Professional Cricket: Martyn Moxon. **Senior 1st XI Coach**: Jason Gillespie.
Senior 2nd XI Coach: Richard Dawson. **Captain**: A.W.Gale. **Overseas Players**: A.J.Finch
(T20 only) and K.S.Williamson. **2014 Beneficiary**: T.T.Bresnan. **Head Groundsman**: Andy
Fogarty. **Scorer**: John T.Potter. ‡ New registration. NQ Not qualified for England.

ASHRAF, Moin Aqeeb (Dixons City Academy, Bradford), b Bradford 5 Jan 1992. 6'4".
RHB, RMF. Debut (Yorkshire) 2010. Yorkshire 2nd XI debut 2009. HS 10 and BB 5-32 v
Kent (Leeds) 2010. LO HS 3* v Kent (Leeds) 2012 (CB40). LO BB 3-38 v Glamorgan
(Leeds) 2013 (Y40). T20 HS 4. T20 BB 4-18.

AZEEM Muhammad RAFIQ (Holgate S Sports C; Barnsley C), b Karachi, Pakistan 27 Feb
1991. 5'11". RHB, OB. Debut (Yorkshire) 2009. Derbyshire (on loan) 2011. Yorkshire 2nd
XI debut 2008. England U19s 2009 to 2010. HS 100 v Worcs (Worcester) 2009. BB 5-50 v
Essex (Chelmsford) 2012. LO HS 34* v Unicorns (Leeds) 2012 (CB40). LO BB 5-30 v
Bangladesh A (Leeds) 2013. T20 HS 21*. T20 BB 3-15.

BAIRSTOW, Jonathan Marc (St Peter's S, York; Leeds Met U), b Bradford 26 Sep 1989.
Son of D.L.Bairstow (Yorkshire, GW and England 1970-90), brother of A.D.Bairstow
(Derbyshire 1995). 6'0". RHB, WK. Debut (Yorkshire) 2009; cap 2011. Inaugural winner of
Young Wisden Schools Cricketer of the Year 2008. YC 2011. **Tests**: 14 (2012 to 2013-14);
HS 95 v SA (Lord's) 2012. **LOI**: 7 (2011 to 2012); HS 41* v I (Cardiff) 2011. **IT20**: 18
(2011 to 2012-13); HS 60* v P (Dubai) 2011-12. F-c Tours: A 2013-14; I 2012-13; WI
2010-11 (EL); SL 2013-14 (EL). 1000 runs (1): 1213 (2011). HS 205 v Notts (Nottingham)
2011. LO HS 114 v Middx (Lord's) 2011 (CB40). T20 HS 68*.

BALLANCE, Gary Simon (Peterhouse S, Marondera, Zimbabwe; Harrow S; Leeds Met
U), b Harare, Zimbabwe 22 Nov 1989. Nephew of G.S.Ballance (Rhodesia B 1978-79) and
D.L.Houghton (Rhodesia/Zimbabwe 1978-79 to 1997-98). 6'0". LHB, LB. Debut (York-
shire) 2008; cap 2012. Mid West Rhinos 2010-11 to 2011-12. Derbyshire (List A) 2006-07.
Test: 1 (2013-14); HS 18 v A (Sydney) 2013-14. **LOI**: 5 (2013 to 2013-14); HS 79 v A
(Melbourne) 2013-14. F-c Tour: A 2013-14. 1000 runs (1+1); most – 1363 (2013). HS 210
MWR v SR (Masvingo) 2011-12. Y HS 148 v Surrey (Oval) 2013. BB –. LO HS 139 v
Unicorns (Leeds) 2013. T20 HS 68.

BRESNAN, Timothy Thomas (Castleford HS and TC; Pontefract New C), b Pontefract 28 Feb 1985. 6'0". RHB, RFM. Debut (Yorkshire) 2003; cap 2006; benefit 2014. MCC 2006, 2009. *Wisden* 2011. **ECB central contract 2013-14. Tests**: 23 (2009 to 2013-14); HS 91 v B (Dhaka) 2009-10; BB 5-48 v I (Nottingham) 2011. **LOI**: 84 (2006 to 2012-13); HS 80 v SA (Centurion) 2009-10; BB 5-48 v I (Bangalore) 2010-11. **IT20**: 28 (2006 to 2013-14); HS 23* v NZ (Gros Islet) 2009-10; BB 3-10 v P (Cardiff) 2010. F-c Tours: A 2010-11, 2013-14; I 2012-13; SL 2011-12; B 2006-07 (Eng A), 2009-10. HS 126* Eng A v Indians (Chelmsford) 2007. Y HS 116 v Surrey (Oval) 2007, sharing in Y record 9th wicket partnership of 246 with J.N.Gillespie. BB 5-42 v Worcs (Worcester) 2005. LO HS 80 (*see LOI*). BB 5-48 (*see LOI*). T20 HS 42. T20 BB 3-10.

BROOKS, Jack Alexander (Wheatley Park S), b Oxford 4 Jun 1984. 6'2". RHB, RFM. Northamptonshire 2009-12; cap 2012. Yorkshire debut 2013; cap 2013. Oxfordshire 2004-09. HS 53 Nh v Glos (Bristol) 2010. Y HS 33* v Somerset (Leeds) 2013. BB 5-23 Nh v Leics (Leicester) 2011. Y BB 5-40 v Derbys (Leeds) 2013. LO HS 10 Nh v Middx (Uxbridge) 2009 (P40). LO BB 3-35 EL v Bangladesh A (Sylhet) 2011-12. T20 HS 33*. T20 BB 5-21.

COAD, Benjamin Oliver (Thirsk S and SFC), b Harrogate 10 Jan 1994. 6'2". RHB, RMF. Yorkshire 2nd XI debut 2012. Awaiting f-c debut. LO HS 1* v Somerset (Taunton) 2013 (Y40). LO BB 1-34 v Glos (Bristol) 2013 (Y40).

‡**NOFINCH, Aaron** James, b Colac, Victoria, Australia 17 Nov 1986. RHB, LM. Victoria 2007-08 to date. Joins Yorkshire in 2014 for T20 only. **LOI** (A): 23 (2012-13 to 2013-14; HS 148 v Scotland (Edinburgh) 2013; BB 1-2 v I (Pune) 2013-14. **IT20** (A): 12 (2010-11 to 2013-14); HS 156 v E (Southampton) 2013 – world record IT20 score. F-c Tours (Aus A): SA/Z 2013; Z 2011. HS 122 Aus A v Zimbabwe XI (Harare) 2011. BB 1-0 Vic v WA (Perth) 2013-14. LO HS 154 Vic v Q (Brisbane) 2012-13. LO BB 2-44 Aus A v EL (Hobart) 2012-13. T20 HS 156. T20 BB 1-11.

GALE, Andrew William (Whitcliffe Mount S; Heckmondwike GS), b Dewsbury 28 Nov 1983. 6'2". LHB, LB. Debut (Yorkshire) 2004, 2006 to date; cap 2008; captain 2010 to date. F-c Tour (EL): WI 2010-11. 1000 runs (1): 1076 (2013). HS 272 v Notts (Scarborough) 2013. BB 1-33 v Loughborough UCCE (Leeds) 2007. LO HS 125* v Essex (Chelmsford) 2010 (CB40). T20 HS 91.

GIBSON, Barney Peter (Crawshaw HS, Pudsey), b Leeds 31 Mar 1996. 5'8½". RHB, WK. Debut (Yorkshire) 2011, aged 15y 27d, becoming youngest player to play f-c cricket, beating a record set in 1867. HS 1* v Durham MCCU (Durham) 2011.

HODD, Andrew John (Bexhill C), b Chichester, Sussex 12 Jan 1984. 5'9". RHB, WK. Sussex 2003-11. Surrey 2005 (1 match). Yorkshire debut 2012 (on loan). HS 123 Sx v Yorks (Hove) 2007. Y HS 68* v Somerset (Taunton) 2013. LO HS 91 Sx v Lancs (Hove) 2010 (CB40). T20 HS 26.

HODGSON, Daniel Mark (Richmond S; Leeds U), b Northallerton 26 Feb 1990. RHB, WK. Debut (Leeds/Bradford MCCU) 2012, scoring 64 v Surrey (Oval). Mountaineers 2012-13. Yorkshire 2nd XI debut 2013. Awaiting Y f-c debut. HS 94* Mountaineers v SR (Mutare) 2012-13. LO HS 90 v Glamorgan (Leeds) 2013 (Y40). T20 HS 52*.

LEANING, Jack Andrew (Archbishop Holgate's S, York; York C), b Bristol, Glos 18 Oct 1993. 5'10". RHB, RMF. Debut (Yorkshire) 2013. Yorkshire 2nd XI debut 2011. HS 2 and BB – v Surrey (Leeds) 2013. LO HS 60 v Somerset (Taunton) 2013 (Y40). LO BB 5-22 v Unicorns (Leeds) 2013 (Y40). T20 HS 8. T20 BB –.

LEES, Alexander Zak (Holy Trinity SS, Halifax), b Halifax 14 Apr 1993. 6'3". LHB, LB. Debut (Yorkshire) 2010. Yorkshire 2nd XI debut 2010. HS 275* v Derbys (Chesterfield) 2013 (Y40). LO HS 63 v Unicorns (Leeds) 2013 (Y40). T20 HS 32.

LYTH, Adam (Caedmon S, Whitby; Whitby Community C), b Whitby 25 Sep 1987. 5'8". LHB, RM. Debut (Yorkshire) 2007; cap 2010. F-c Tour (EL): WI 2010-11. 1000 runs (1): 1509 (2010). HS 248* v Leics (Leicester) 2012. BB 2-15 v Somerset (Taunton) 2013. LO HS 109* v Sussex (Scarborough) 2009 (P40). LO BB 1-6 v Middx (Leeds) 2013 (Y40). T20 HS 78. T20 BB 1-16.

PATTERSON, Steven Andrew (Malet Lambert CS; St Mary's SFC, Hull; Leeds U), b Hull 3 Oct 1983. 6'4". RHB, RMF. Debut (Yorkshire) 2005; cap 2012. Bradford/Leeds UCCE 2003 (not f-c). HS 53 v Sussex (Hove) 2011. 50 wkts (2); most – 53 (2012). BB 5-43 v Notts (Nottingham) 2013. LO HS 25* v Worcs (Leeds) 2006 (P40). LO BB 6-32 v Derbys (Leeds) 2010. T20 HS 3*. T20 BB 4-30.

PLUNKETT, Liam Edward (Nunthorpe SS; Teesside Tertiary C), b Middlesbrough, Yorks 6 Apr 1985. 6'3". RHB, RFM. Durham 2003-12. Dolphins 2007-08. Yorkshire debut 2013; cap 2013. **Tests**: 9 (2005-06 to 2007); HS 44* v WI (Leeds) 2007; BB 3-17 v SL (Birmingham) 2006. **LOI**: 29 (2005-06 to 2010-11); HS 56 v P (Lahore) 2005-06; BB 3-24 v A (Sydney) 2006-07. **IT20**: 1 (2006); HS –; BB 1-37 v SL (Southampton) 2006. F-c Tours: WI 2010-11 (EL); NZ 2008-09 (EL); I 2005-06, 2007-08 (EL); P 2005-06; SL 2013-14 (EL). HS 114 EL v Sri Lanka A (Colombo) 2013-14. CC HS 94* Du v Sussex (Hove) 2009. Y HS 68 v Surrey (Leeds) 2013. 50 wkts (3); most – 60 (2009). BB 6-33 v Leeds/Bradford MCCU (Leeds) 2013 on Y debut. CC BB 6-63 (11-119 match) Du v Worcs (Chester-le-St) 2009. LO HS 72 Du v Somerset (Chester-le-St) 2008 (P40). LO BB 4-15 Du v Essex (Chester-le-St) 2007 (FPT). T20 HS 41. T20 BB 5-31.

PYRAH, Richard Michael (Ossett S; Wakefield C), b Dewsbury 1 Nov 1982. 6'0". RHB, RM. Debut (Yorkshire) 2004; cap 2010. HS 134* v Loughborough MCCU (Leeds) 2010. CC HS 117 v Lancs (Leeds) 2011. BB 5-58 v Notts (Leeds) 2011. LO HS 69 v Netherlands (Leeds) 2011 (CB40). LO BB 5-50 Yorks CB v Somerset (Scarborough) 2002 (CGT). T20 HS 42. T20 BB 5-16 v Durham (Scarborough) 2011 – Y record.

RASHID, Adil Usman (Belle Vue S, Bradford), b Bradford 17 Feb 1988. 5'8". RHB, LBG. Debut (Yorkshire) 2006; cap 2008. MCC 2007-09. YC 2007. Match double (114, 48, 8-157 and 2-45) for England U19 v India U19 (Taunton) 2006. **LOI**: 5 (2009 to 2009-10); HS 31* v A (Oval) 2009; BB 1-16 v Ireland (Belfast) 2009. **IT20**: 5 (2009 to 2009-10); HS 9* v SA (Nottingham) 2009; BB 1-11 v WI (Oval) 2009. F-c Tours (EL): WI 2010-11; I 2007-08; B 2006-07 (Eng A). HS 180 v Somerset (Leeds) 2013. 50 wkts (2); most – 65 (2008). BB 7-107 v Hants (Southampton) 2008. LO HS 46* v Middx (Radlett) 2013 (Y40). LO BB 4-38 v Northants (Northampton) 2012 (CB40). T20 HS 36*. T20 BB 4-20.

RHODES, William Michael Henry (Cottingham HS, Cottingham SFC, Hull), b Nottingham 2 Mar 1995. 6'2". LHB, RMF. Yorkshire 2nd XI debut 2012. Awaiting f-c debut. LO HS 19* v Glos (Leeds) 2013 (Y40). LO BB 2-26 v Leics (Scarborough) 2013 (Y40). T20 HS 13. T20 BB –.

ROBINSON, Oliver Edward (King's S, Canterbury), b Margate, Kent 1 Dec 1993. RHB, RM. Kent 2nd XI 2011-12. Leicestershire 2nd XI 2013. Yorkshire 2nd XI debut. Awaiting f-c debut. LO HS 12* v Leics (Leicester) 2013 (Y40). LO BB –.

ROOT, Joseph Edward (King Ecgbert S, Sheffield; Worksop C), b Sheffield 30 Dec 1990. 6'0". RHB, OB. Debut (Yorkshire) 2010; cap 2012. Yorkshire 2nd XI debut 2007. England U19s 2009-10 to 2010. YC 2012. **ECB central contract 2013-14. Tests**: 15 (2012-13 to 2013-14); HS 180 v A (Lord's) 2013; BB 2-9 v A (Lord's) 2013. **LOI**: 26 (2012-13 to 2013-14); HS 107 v WI (North Sound) 2013-14; BB 2-15 v WI (North Sound) 2013-14. **IT20**: 7 (2012-13 to 2013-14); HS 90* v A (Southampton) 2013; BB 1-13 v A (Sydney) 2013-14. F-c Tours: A 2013-14; NZ 2012-13; I 2012-13. 1000 runs (2); most – 1228 (2013). HS 236 v Derbys (Leeds) 2013. BB 3-33 v Warwks (Leeds) 2011. LO HS 110* EL v Sri Lanka A (Colombo, RPS) 2011-12. LO BB 2-10 EL v Bangladesh A (Sylhet) 2011-12. T20 HS 90*. T20 BB 1-12.

SIDEBOTTOM, Ryan Jay (King James's GS, Almondbury), b Huddersfield 15 Jan 1978. Son of A.Sidebottom (Yorkshire, OFS and England 1973-91). 6'3''. LHB, LFM. Yorkshire 1997-2003; cap 2000. Returned to Yorkshire in 2011. Nottinghamshire 2004-10; cap 2004; benefit 2010. *Wisden* 2007. **Tests**: 22 (2001 to 2009-10); HS 31 v SL (Kandy) 2007-08; BB 7-47 v NZ (Napier) 2007-08. Hat-trick v NZ (Hamilton) 2007-08. **LOI**: 25 (2001-02 to 2009-10); HS 24 v A (Southampton) 2009; BB 3-19 v SL (Dambulla) 2007-08. **IT20**: 18 (2007 to 2010); HS 5* and BB 3-16 v NZ (Auckland) 2007-08. F-c Tours: SA 2009-10; WI 2000-01 (Eng A), 2008-09; NZ 2007-08; SL 2007-08. HS 61 v Worcs (Worcester) 2011. 50 wkts (4); most – 62 (2011). BB 7-37 (11-98 match) v Somerset (Leeds) 2011. LO HS 32 Nt v Middx (Nottingham) 2005 (NL). LO BB 6-40 v Glamorgan (Cardiff) 1998 (SL). T20 HS 17*. T20 BB 4-25.

TATTERSALL, Jonathan Andrew (King James S, Knaresborough), b Harrogate 15 Dec 1994. 5'8''. RHB, LB. Yorkshire 2nd XI debut 2012. England U19s 2012-13. Awaiting f-c debut. LO HS 0.

WAINMAN, James Charles (Leeds GS), b Harrogate 25 Jan 1993. 6'4''. RHB, LMF. Yorkshire 2nd XI debut 2010. Awaiting 1st XI debut.

NQ**WILLIAMSON, Kane** Stuart (Tauranga Boys' C), b Tauranga, New Zealand 8 Aug 1990. Cousin of D.Cleaver (C Districts 2010-11 to date). 5'8''. RHB, OB. N Districts 2007-08 to date. Gloucestershire 2011-12; cap 2011. Yorkshire debut 2013. **Tests** (NZ): 31 (2010-11 to 2013-14); HS 135 v SL (Colombo, PSS) 2012-13; scored 131 v I (Ahmedabad) 2010-11 on debut; BB 4-44 v E (Auckland) 2012-13. **LOI** (NZ): 54 (2010 to 2013-14); HS 145* v SA (Kimberley) 2012-13; BB 4-22 v SA (Paarl) 2012-13. **IT20** (NZ): 13 (2011-12 to 2012-13); HS 48 and BB 1-6 v Z (Auckland) 2011-12. F-c Tours (NZ): E 2013; A 2011-12; SA 2012-13; WI 2012; I 2010-11, 2012; SL 2012-13; Z 2011-12; B 2013-14. HS 284* ND v Wellington (Lincoln) 2011-12. CC HS 149 Gs v Leics (Leicester) 2011. Y HS 97 v Durham (Scarborough) 2013. BB 5-75 ND v Canterbury (Christchurch) 2008-09. CC BB 3-58 Gs v Northants (Northampton) 2012. Y BB 2-44 v Sussex (Hove) 2013. LO HS 145* *(see LOI)*. LO BB 5-51 ND v Auckland (Auckland) 2009-10. T20 HS 79*. T20 BB 3-33.

RELEASED/RETIRED

(Having made a County First-Class or List A appearance in 2013)

JAQUES, P.A. – *see NOTTINGHAMSHIRE*.

SAYERS, Joseph John (St Mary's RC CS, Menston; Worcester C, Oxford) b Leeds 5 Nov 1983. 6'0''. LHB, OB. Oxford U 2002-04; blue 2002-03-04. Yorkshire 2004-13; cap 2007. 1000 runs (1): 1150 (2009). HS 187 v Kent (Tunbridge W) 2007. BB 3-15 v Durham MCCU (Durham) 2011. CC BB 3-20 v Warwks (Scarborough) 2009. LO HS 62 v Glos (Leeds) 2003 (NL). LO BB 1-31 v Warwks (Birmingham) 2005 (NL). T20 HS 44.

WARDLAW, Iain (Whitcliffe Mount HS, Cleckheaton; Huddersfield U), b Dewsbury 29 Jun 1985. 6'2''. RHB, RMF. Yorkshire 2011-12. Scotland 2013. **LOI** (Scot): 11 (2012-13 to 2013-14); HS 7* v Ireland (Belfast) 2013. BB 4-43 v Kenya (Aberdeen) 2013. **IT20** (Scot): 4 (2012-13 to 2013-14); HS 1 v Kenya (Dubai, CA) 2013-14; BB 3-40 v Afghanistan (Sharjah) 2013-14. HS 33* and BB 3-101 Scot v Australia A (Edinburgh) 2013. Y HS 17* and BB 1-37 v Hants (Leeds) 2012. LO HS 18 v Bangladesh A (Leeds) 2013. LO BB 4-43 *(see LOI)*. T20 HS 6*. T20 BB 3-40.

A.E.Lilley and G.S.Randhawa left the staff without making a County First-Class or List A appearance in 2013.

YORKSHIRE 2013

RESULTS SUMMARY

	Place	Won	Lost	Tied	Drew	NR
LV= County Championship (1st Division)	2nd	7	2		7	
All First-Class Matches		8	2		7	
Yorkshire Bank 40 (Group C)	6th	3	9			
Friends Life t20 (North Group)	6th	2	7	1		

LV= COUNTY CHAMPIONSHIP AVERAGES
BATTING AND FIELDING

Cap		M	I	NO	HS	Runs	Avge	100	50	Ct/St
2012	G.S.Ballance	14	21	1	148	1251	62.55	5	6	13
2008	A.U.Rashid	15	22	6	180	825	51.56	3	3	7
	K.S.Williamson	5	9	1	97	403	50.37	–	5	4
	A.Z.Lees	8	14	3	275*	500	45.45	2	1	1
2008	A.W.Gale	16	24	–	272	1067	44.45	3	3	4
2011	J.M.Bairstow	8	13	–	186	528	40.61	1	2	27
2005	P.A.Jaques	14	21	–	152	770	36.66	2	3	5
2010	A.Lyth	16	27	4	105	730	31.73	1	4	25
	A.J.Hodd	9	9	2	68*	217	31.00	–	1	17/1
2013	L.E.Plunkett	12	17	2	68	394	26.26	–	2	9
2006	T.T.Bresnan	4	5	1	38	66	16.50	–	–	1
2012	S.A.Patterson	16	17	8	40	147	16.33	–	–	2
	Azeem Rafiq	2	4	–	28	55	13.75	–	–	–
2013	J.A.Brooks	11	13	6	33*	79	11.28	–	–	5
2000	R.J.Sidebottom	14	16	–	48	155	9.68	–	–	3
2007	J.J.Sayers	5	7	–	24	57	8.14	–	–	4

Also played: M.A.Ashraf (2 matches) did not bat; J.A.Leaning (1) 0; R.M.Pyrah (5 – cap 2010) 55, 14*, 1 (5 ct); J.E.Root (2 – cap 2012) 49, 182, 236 (3 ct).

BOWLING

	O	M	R	W	Avge	Best	5wI	10wM
R.J.Sidebottom	369.1	100	995	49	20.30	4-27	–	–
T.T.Bresnan	130.2	31	393	16	24.56	4-41	–	–
S.A.Patterson	413.5	119	1153	46	25.06	5-43	1	–
J.A.Brooks	241	49	859	34	25.26	5-40	1	–
L.E.Plunkett	258.5	42	1020	36	28.33	5-32	1	–
A.U.Rashid	359.5	39	1358	29	46.82	5-78	1	–

Also bowled: M.A.Ashraf 38.3-13-119-4; Azeem Rafiq 16-1-74-1; G.S.Ballance 14-0-98-0; A.W.Gale 9-0-94-0; P.A.Jaques 6-0-75-1; J.A.Leaning 4-0-22-0; A.Z.Lees 1-0-14-0; A.Lyth 36-4-155-4; R.M.Pyrah 77-19-244-2; J.E.Root 9-4-14-0; K.S.Williamson 65.4-13-247-4.

The First-Class Averages (pp 225–241) give the records of Yorkshire players in all first-class county matches (Yorkshire's other opponents being Leeds/Bradford MCCU), with the exception of T.T.Bresnan, J.E.Root and K.S.Williamson, whose first-class figures for Yorkshire are as above, and:
J.M.Bairstow 9-14-0-186-548-39.14-1-2-33ct.

YORKSHIRE RECORDS

FIRST-CLASS CRICKET

Highest Total	For 887		v	Warwicks	Birmingham	1896
	V 681-7d		by	Leics	Bradford	1996
Lowest Total	For 23		v	Hampshire	Middlesbrough	1965
	V 13		by	Notts	Nottingham	1901
Highest Innings	For 341	G.H.Hirst	v	Leics	Leicester	1905
	V 318*	W.G.Grace	for	Glos	Cheltenham	1876

Highest Partnership for each Wicket

1st	555	P.Holmes/H.Sutcliffe	v	Essex	Leyton	1932
2nd	346	W.Barber/M.Leyland	v	Middlesex	Sheffield	1932
3rd	346	J.J.Sayers/A.McGrath	v	Warwicks	Birmingham	2009
4th	358	D.S.Lehmann/M.J.Lumb	v	Durham	Leeds	2006
5th	340	E.Wainwright/G.H.Hirst	v	Surrey	The Oval	1899
6th	276	M.Leyland/E.Robinson	v	Glamorgan	Swansea	1926
7th	254	W.Rhodes/D.C.F.Burton	v	Hampshire	Dewsbury	1919
8th	292	R.Peel/Lord Hawke	v	Warwicks	Birmingham	1896
9th	246	T.T.Bresnan/J.N.Gillespie	v	Surrey	The Oval	2007
10th	149	G.Boycott/G.B.Stevenson	v	Warwicks	Birmingham	1982

Best Bowling	For 10-10	H.Verity	v	Notts	Leeds	1932
(Innings)	V 10-37	C.V.Grimmett	for	Australians	Sheffield	1930
Best Bowling	For 17-91	H.Verity	v	Essex	Leyton	1933
(Match)	V 17-91	H.Dean	for	Lancashire	Liverpool	1913

Most Runs – Season	2883	H.Sutcliffe	(av 80.08)	1932
Most Runs – Career	38558	H.Sutcliffe	(av 50.20)	1919-45
Most 100s – Season	12	H.Sutcliffe		1932
Most 100s – Career	112	H.Sutcliffe		1919-45
Most Wkts – Season	240	W.Rhodes	(av 12.72)	1900
Most Wkts – Career	3597	W.Rhodes	(av 16.02)	1898-1930
Most Career W-K Dismissals	1186	D.Hunter	(863 ct; 323 st)	1888-1909
Most Career Catches in the Field	665	J.Tunnicliffe		1891-1907

LIMITED-OVERS CRICKET

Highest Total	50ov	411-6	v	Devon	Exmouth	2004
	40ov	352-6	v	Notts	Scarborough	2001
	T20	213-7	v	Worcs	Leeds	2010
Lowest Total	50ov	76	v	Surrey	Harrogate	1970
	40ov	54	v	Essex	Leeds	2003
	T20	90-9	v	Durham	Chester-le-St[2]	2009
Highest Innings	50ov	160	M.J.Wood	v	Devon	Exmouth	2004
	40ov	191	D.S.Lehmann	v	Notts	Scarborough	2001
	T20	109	I.J.Harvey	v	Derbyshire	Leeds	2005
Best Bowling	50ov	7-27	D.Gough	v	Ireland	Leeds	1997
	40ov	7-15	R.A.Hutton	v	Worcs	Leeds	1969
	T20	5-16	R.M.Pyrah	v	Durham	Scarborough	2011

FIRST-CLASS UMPIRES 2014

† New appointment. See page 90 for key to abbreviations.

BAILEY, Robert John (Biddulph HS), b Biddulph, Staffs 28 Oct 1963. 6'3". RHB, OB. Northamptonshire 1982-99; cap 1985; benefit 1993; captain 1996-97. Derbyshire 2000-01; cap 2000. Staffordshire 1980. YC 1984. **Tests**: 4 (1988 to 1989-90); HS 43 v WI (Oval) 1988. **LOI**: 4 (1984-85 to 1989-90); HS 43* v SL (Oval) 1988. F-c Tours: SA 1991-92 (Nh); WI 1989-90; Z 1994-95 (Nh). 1000 runs (13); most – 1987 (1990). HS 224* Nh v Glamorgan (Swansea) 1986. BB 5-54 Nh v Notts (Northampton) 1993. F-c career: 374 matches; 21843 runs @ 40.52, 47 hundreds; 121 wickets @ 42.51; 272 ct. Appointed 2006. Umpired 8 LOI (2011 to 2013). **ICC International Panel 2011 to date.**

BAINTON, Neil Laurence, b Romford, Essex 2 October 1970. No f-c appearances. Appointed 2006.

BENSON, Mark Richard (Sutton Valence S), b Shoreham, Sussex 6 Jul 1958. 5'10". LHB, OB. Kent 1980-95; cap 1981; captain 1991-96 (did not play in 1996); benefit 1991. **Tests**: 1 (1986); HS 30 v I (Birmingham) 1986. **LOI**: 1 (1986); HS 24 v NZ (Leeds) 1986. 1000 runs (11); most – 1725 (1987). HS 257 K v Hants (Southampton) 1991. BB 2-55 K v Surrey (Dartford) 1986. F-c career: 292 matches; 18387 runs @ 40.23, 48 hundreds; 5 wickets @ 98.60; 140 ct. Appointed 2000. Umpired 27 Tests (2004-05 to 2009-10) and 72 LOI (2004 to 2008-09). **ICC Elite Panel 2006-09.**

BODENHAM, Martin John Dale, b Brighton, Sussex 23 Apr 1950. No f-c appearances. Former football referee who officiated at the 1997 League Cup final and four internationals. Appointed 2009.

COOK, Nicholas Grant Billson (Lutterworth GS), b Leicester 17 Jun 1956. 6'0". RHB, SLA. Leicestershire 1978-85; cap 1982. Northamptonshire 1986-94; cap 1987; benefit 1995. **Tests**: 15 (1983 to 1989); HS 31 v A (Oval) 1989; BB 6-65 (11-83 match) v P (Karachi) 1983-84. **LOI**: 3 (1983-84 to 1989-90); HS – ; BB 2-18 v P (Peshawar) 1987-88. F-c Tours: NZ 1979-80 (DRH), 1983-84; P 1983-84, 1987-88; SL 1985-86 (Eng B); Z 1980-81 (Le), 1984-85 (EC). HS 75 Le v Somerset (Taunton) 1980. 50 wkts (8); most – 90 (1982). BB 7-34 (10-97 match) Nh v Essex (Chelmsford) 1992. F-c career: 356 matches; 3137 runs @ 11.66; 879 wickets @ 29.01; 197 ct. Appointed 2009.

COWLEY, Nigel Geoffrey Charles (Dutchy Manor SS, Mere), b Shaftesbury, Dorset 1 Mar 1953. 5'7". RHB, OB. Dorset 1972. Hampshire 1974-89; cap 1978; benefit 1988. Glamorgan 1990. 1000 runs (1): 1042 (1984). HS 109* H v Somerset (Taunton) 1977. BB 6-48 H v Leics (Southampton) 1982. F-c career: 271 matches; 7309 runs @ 23.35, 2 hundreds; 437 wickets @ 34.04; 105 ct. Appointed 2000.

EVANS, Jeffery Howard, b Llanelli, Carms 7 Aug 1954. No f-c appearances. Appointed 2001. Umpired in Indian Cricket League 2007-08.

GALE, Stephen Clifford, b Shrewsbury, Shropshire 3 Jun 1952. RHB, LB. No f-c appearances. Shropshire (list A only) 1976-85. Reserve List 2008-10. Appointed 2011.

GARRATT, Steven Arthur, b Nottingham 5 Jul 1953. No f-c appearances. Reserve List 2003-07 standing in 20 f-c matches. Appointed 2008.

GOUGH, Michael Andrew (English Martyrs RCS; Hartlepool SFC), b Hartlepool, Co Durham 18 Dec 1979. Son of M.P.Gough (Durham 1974-77). 6'5". RHB, OB. Durham 1998-2003. F-c Tours (Eng A): NZ 1999-00; B 1999-00. HS 123 Du v CU (Cambridge) 1998. CC HS 103 Du v Essex (Colchester) 2002. BB 5-56 Du v Middx (Chester-le-St) 2001. F-c career: 67 matches; 2952 runs @ 25.44, 2 hundreds; 30 wickets @ 45.00; 57 ct. Reserve List 2006-08. Appointed 2009. Umpired 3 LOI (2013 to 2013-14). **ICC International Panel 2012 to date.**

GOULD, Ian James (Westgate SS, Slough), b Taplow, Bucks 19 Aug 1957. 5'8". LHB, WK. Middlesex 1975 to 1980-81, 1996; cap 1977. Auckland 1979-80. Sussex 1981-90; cap 1981; captain 1987; benefit 1990. MCC YC. **LOI**: 18 (1982-83 to 1983); HS 42 v A (Sydney) 1982-83. F-c Tours: A 1982-83; P 1980-81 (Int); Z 1980-81 (M). HS 128 M v Worcs (Worcester) 1978. BB 3-10 Sx v Surrey (Oval) 1989. Middlesex coach 1991-2000.

Reappeared in one match (v OU) 1996. F-c career: 298 matches; 8756 runs @ 26.05, 4 hundreds; 7 wickets @ 52.14; 603 dismissals (536 ct, 67 st). Appointed 2002. Umpired 37 Tests (2008-09 to 2013-14) and 87 LOI (2006 to 2013-14), including 2010-11 World Cup. **ICC Elite Panel 2009 to date.**

HARTLEY, Peter John (Greenhead GS; Bradford C), b Keighley, Yorks 18 Apr 1960. 6'0''. RHB, RMF. Warwickshire 1982. Yorkshire 1985-97; cap 1987; benefit 1996. Hampshire 1998-2000; cap 1998. F-c Tours (Y): SL 1991-92; WI 1986-87; Z 1995-96. HS 127* Y v Lancs (Manchester) 1988. 50 wkts (7); most – 81 (1995). BB 9-41 (inc hat-trick, 4 wkts in 5 balls and 5 in 9; 11-68 match) Y v Derbys (Chesterfield) 1995. Hat-trick 1995. F-c career: 232 matches; 4321 runs @ 19.91, 2 hundreds; 683 wickets @ 30.21; 68 ct. Appointed 2003. Umpired 6 LOI (2007 to 2009). **ICC International Panel 2006-09.**

ILLINGWORTH, Richard Keith (Salts GS), b Bradford, Yorks 23 Aug 1963. 5'11''. RHB, SLA. Worcestershire 1982-2000; cap 1986; benefit 1997. Natal 1988-89. Derbyshire 2001. Wiltshire 2005. **Tests:** 9 (1991 to 1995-96); HS 28 v SA (Pt Elizabeth) 1995-96; BB 4-96 v WI (Nottingham) 1995. Took wicket of P.V.Simmons with his first ball in Tests – v WI (Nottingham) 1991. **LOI:** 25 (1991 to 1995-96); HS 14 v P (Melbourne) 1991-92; BB 3-33 v Z (Albury) 1991-92. F-c Tours: SA 1995-96; NZ 1991-92; P 1990-91 (Eng A); SL 1990-91 (Eng A); Z 1989-90 (Eng A), 1990-91 (Wo), 1993-94 (Wo), 1996-97 (Wo). HS 120* Wo v Warwks (Worcester) 1987 – as night-watchman. Scored 106 for England A v Z (Harare) 1989-90 – also as night-watchman. 50 wkts (5); most – 75 (1990). BB 7-50 Wo v OU (Oxford) 1985. F-c career: 376 matches; 7027 runs @ 22.45, 4 hundreds; 831 wickets @ 31.54; 161 ct. Appointed 2006. Umpired 7 Tests (2012-13 to 2013-14) and 27 LOI (2010 to 2013-14). **ICC Elite Panel 2013 to date.**

KETTLEBOROUGH, Richard Allan (Worksop C), b Sheffield, Yorks 15 Mar 1973. 6'0''. LHB, RM. Yorkshire 1994-97. Middlesex 1998-99. F-c Tour (Y): Z 1995-96. HS 108 Y v Essex (Leeds) 1996. BB 2-26 Y v Notts (Scarborough) 1996. F-c career: 33 matches; 1258 runs @ 25.16, 1 hundred; 3 wickets @ 81.00; 20 ct. Appointed 2006. Umpired 20 Tests (2010-11 to 2013-14) and 41 LOI (2009 to 2013-14), including 2010-11 World Cup. **ICC Elite Panel 2011 to date.**

LLONG, Nigel James (Ashford North S), b Ashford, Kent 11 Feb 1969. 6'0''. LHB, OB. Kent 1990-98; cap 1993. F-c Tour (K): Z 1992-93. HS 130 K v Hants (Canterbury) 1996. BB 5-21 K v Middx (Canterbury) 1996. F-c career: 68 matches; 3024 runs @ 31.17, 6 hundreds; 35 wickets @ 35.97; 59 ct. Appointed 2002. Umpired 24 Tests (2007-08 to 2013-14) and 78 LOI (2006 to 2013-14), including 2010-11 World Cup. **ICC Elite Panel 2012 to date.**

†**LLOYD, Graham** David (Hollins County HS), b Accrington, Lancs 1 Jul 1969. Son of D.Lloyd (Lancs and England 1965-83). 5'9''. RHB, RM. Lancashire 1988-2002; cap 1992; benefit 2001. **LOI:** 6 (1996 to 1998-99); HS 22 v A (Oval) 1997. F-c Tours: A 1992-93 (Eng A); WI 1995-96 (La). 1000 runs (5); most – 1389 (1992). HS 241 La v Essex (Chelmsford) 1996. BB 1-4. F-c career: 203 matches; 11279 runs @ 38.23, 24 hundreds; 2 wickets @ 220.00; 140 ct. Reserve List 2009-13. Appointed 2014.

LLOYDS, Jeremy William (Blundell's S), b Penang, Malaya 17 Nov 1954. 6'0''. LHB, OB. Somerset 1979-84; cap 1982. Gloucestershire 1985-91; cap 1985. OFS 1983-84 to 1987-88. F-c Tour (Gl): SL 1986-87. 1000 runs (3); most – 1295 (1986). HS 132* Sm v Northants (Northampton) 1982. BB 7-88 Sm v Essex (Chelmsford) 1982. F-c career: 267 matches; 10679 runs @ 31.04, 10 hundreds; 333 wickets @ 38.86; 229 ct. Appointed 1998. Umpired 5 Tests (2003-04 to 2004-05) and 18 LOI (2000 to 2005-06). **ICC International Panel 2003-06.**

MALLENDER, Neil Alan (Beverley GS), b Kirk Sandall, Yorks 13 Aug 1961. 6'0''. RHB, RFM. Northamptonshire 1980-86 and 1995-96; cap 1984. Somerset 1987-94; cap 1987; benefit 1994. Otago 1983-84 to 1992-93; captain 1990-91 to 1992-93. **Tests:** 2 (1992); HS 4 v P (Oval) 1992; BB 5-50 v P (Leeds) 1992 – on debut. F-c Tour (Nh): Z 1994-95. HS 100* Otago v CD (Palmerston N) 1991-92. UK HS 87* Sm v Sussex (Hove) 1990. 50 wkts (6); most – 56 (1983). BB 7-27 Otago v Auckland (Auckland) 1984-85. UK BB 7-41 Nh v Derbys (Northampton) 1982. F-c career: 345 matches; 4709 runs @ 17.18, 1 hundred; 937 wickets @ 26.31; 111 ct. Appointed 1999. Umpired 3 Tests (2003-04) and 22 LOI (2001 to 2003-04), including 2002-03 World Cup. **ICC Elite Panel 2004.**

MILLNS, David James (Garibaldi CS; N Notts C; Nottingham Trent U), b Clipstone, Notts 27 Feb 1965. 6'3''. LHB, RF. Nottinghamshire 1988-89, 2000-01; cap 2000. Leicestershire 1990-99; cap 1991; benefit 1999. Tasmania 1994-95. Boland 1996-97. F-c Tours: A 1992-93 (Eng A); SA 1996-97 (Le). HS 121 Le v Northants (Northampton) 1997. 50 wkts (4); most – 76 (1994). BB 9-37 (12-91 match) Le v Derbys (Derby) 1991. F-c career: 171 matches; 3082 runs @ 22.01, 3 hundreds; 553 wickets @ 27.35; 76 ct. Reserve List 2007-08. Appointed 2009.

O'SHAUGHNESSY, Steven Joseph (Harper Green SS, Franworth), b Bury, Lancs 9 Sep 1961. 5'10½''. RHB, RM. Lancashire 1980-87; cap 1985. Worcestershire 1988-89. Scored 100 in 35 min to equal world record for La v Leics (Manchester) 1983. 1000 runs (1): 1167 (1984). HS 159* La v Somerset (Bath) 1984. BB 4-66 La v Notts (Nottingham) 1982. F-c career: 112 matches; 3720 runs @ 24.31, 5 hundreds; 114 wickets @ 36.03; 57 ct. Reserve list 2009-10. Appointed 2011.

ROBINSON, Robert Timothy (Dunstable GS; High Pavement SFC; Sheffield U), b Sutton in Ashfield, Notts 21 Nov 1958. 6'0''. RHB, RM. Nottinghamshire 1978-99; cap 1983; captain 1988-95; benefit 1992. *Wisden* 1985. **Tests:** 29 (1984-85 to 1989); HS 175 v A (Leeds) 1985. **LOI:** 26 (1984-85 to 1988); HS 83 v P (Sharjah) 1986-87. F-c Tours: A 1987-88; SA 1989-90 (Eng XI), 1996-97 (Nt); NZ 1987-88; WI 1985-86; I/SL 1984-85; P 1987-88. 1000 runs (14) inc 2000 (1): 2032 (1984). HS 220* Nt v Yorks (Nottingham) 1990. BB 1-22. F-c career: 425 matches; 27571 runs @ 42.15, 63 hundreds; 4 wickets @ 72.25; 257 ct. Appointed 2007. Umpired 2 LOI (2013 to 2013-14). **ICC International Panel (Third Umpire) 2012 to date.**

SAGGERS, Martin John (Springwood HS, King's Lynn; Huddersfield U), b King's Lynn, Norfolk 23 May 1972. 6'2''. RHB, RMF. Durham 1996-98. Kent 1999-2009; cap 2001; benefit 2009. MCC 2004. Essex 2007 (on loan). Norfolk 1995-96. **Tests:** 3 (2003-04 to 2004); HS 1 and BB 2-29 v B (Chittagong) 2003-04 – on debut. F-c Tour: B 2003-04. HS 64 K v Worcs (Canterbury) 2004. 50 wkts (4); most – 83 (2002). BB 7-79 K v Durham (Chester-le-St) 2004. F-c career: 119 matches; 1165 runs @ 11.20; 415 wickets @ 25.33; 27 ct. Reserve List 2010-11. Appointed 2012.

SHARP, George (Elwick Road SS, Hartlepool), b West Hartlepool, Co Durham 12 Mar 1950. 5'11''. RHB, WK, occ LM. Northamptonshire 1968-85; cap 1973; benefit 1982. HS 98 Nh v Yorks (Northampton) 1983. BB 1-47. F-c career: 306 matches; 6254 runs @ 19.85; 1 wicket @ 70.00; 655 dismissals (565 ct, 90 st). Appointed 1992. Umpired 15 Tests (1996 to 2001-02) and 31 LOI (1995-96 to 2001-02). **ICC International Panel 1996 to 2001-02.**

†**WHARF, Alexander** George (Buttershaw Upper S; Thomas Danby C), b Bradford, Yorks 4 Jun 1975. 6'5''. RHB, RMF. Yorkshire 1994-97. Nottinghamshire 1998-99. Glamorgan 2000-08, scoring 100* v OU (Oxford) on debut; cap 2000; benefit 2009. **LOI:** 13 (2004 to 2004-05); HS 9 v India (Lord's) 2004; BB 4-24 v Z (Harare) 2004-05. F-c Tour (Eng A): WI 2005-06. HS 128* Gm v Glos (Bristol) 2007. 50 wkts (1): 52 (2003). BB 6-59 Gm v Glos (Bristol) 2005. F-c career: 121 matches; 3570 runs @ 23.03, 6 hundreds; 293 wickets @ 37.34; 63 ct. Reserve List 2011-13. Appointed 2014.

WILLEY, Peter (Seaham SS), b Sedgefield, Co Durham 6 Dec 1949. Father of D.J.Willey (see NORTHAMPTONSHIRE). 6'1''. RHB, OB. Northamptonshire 1966-83; cap 1971; benefit 1981. Leicestershire 1984-91; cap 1984; captain 1987. EP 1982-83 to 1984-85. Northumberland 1992. **Tests:** 26 (1976 to 1986); HS 102* v WI (St John's) 1980-81; BB 2-73 v WI (Lord's) 1980. **LOI:** 26 (1977 to 1985-86); HS 64 v A (Sydney) 1979-80; BB 3-33 v A (Melbourne) 1979-80. F-c Tours: A 1979-80; SA 1972-73 (DHR), 1981-82 (SAB); WI 1980-81, 1985-86; I 1979-80; SL 1977-78 (DHR). 1000 runs (10); most – 1783 (1982). HS 227 Nh v Somerset (Northampton) 1976. 50 wkts (3); most – 52 (1979). BB 7-37 Nh v OU (Oxford) 1975. F-c career: 559 matches; 24361 runs @ 30.56, 44 hundreds; 756 wickets @ 30.95; 235 ct. Appointed 1993. Umpired 25 Tests (1995-96 to 2003-04) and 34 LOI (1996 to 2003), including 1999 and 2002-03 World Cups. **ICC International Panel 1996 to 2001-02 and 2003-04.**

RESERVE FIRST-CLASS LIST: Paul K.Baldwin, Mike Burns, Ismail Dawood, Ben J.Debenham, Russell J.Evans, Paul R.Pollard, Billy V.Taylor.

Test Match and LOI statistics to 5 April 2014.

TOURING TEAMS REGISTER 2013

AUSTRALIA

Full Names	Birthdate	Birthplace	Team	Type	F-C Debut
AGAR, Ashton Charles	14.10.93	Melbourne	W Australia	LHB/SLA	2012-13
BIRD, Jackson Munro	11.12.86	Sydney	Tasmania	RHB/RFM	2011-12
CLARKE, Michael John	02.04.81	Liverpool	NSW	RHB/SLA	1999-00
COWAN, Edward James McKenzie	16.06.82	Paddington	Tasmania	LHB/LB	2003
FAULKNER, James Peter	29.04.90	Launceston	Tasmania	RHB/LFM	2008-09
HADDIN, Bradley James	23.10.77	Cowra	NSW	RHB/WK	1999-00
HARRIS, Ryan James	11.10.79	Sydney	Queensland	RHB/RF	2001-02
HUGHES, Phillip Joel	30.11.88	Macksville	S Australia	LHB/OB	2007-08
JOHNSON, Mitchell Guy	02.11.81	Townsville	W Australia	LHB/LF	2001-02
KHAWAJA, Usman Tariq	18.12.86	Islamabad, Pak	NSW	LHB/RM	2007-08
LYON, Nathan Michael	20.11.87	Young	S Australia	RHB/OB	2010-11
PATTINSON, James Lee	03.05.90	Melbourne	Victoria	RHB/RFM	2008-09
SIDDLE, Peter Matthew	25.11.84	Traralgon	Victoria	RHB/RFM	2005-06
SMITH, Steven Peter Devereux	02.06.89	Sydney	NSW	RHB/LBG	2007-08
STARC, Mitchell Aaron	30.01.90	Sydney	NSW	LHB/LFM	2008-09
TURNER, Ashton James	25.01.93	Perth	W Australia	RHB/OB	2013
WADE, Matthew Scott	26.12.87	Hobart	Victoria	LHB/WK	2007-08
WARNER, David Andrew	27.10.86	Paddington	NSW	LHB/LB	2008-09
WATSON, Shane Robert	17.06.81	Ipswich	NSW	RHB/RMF	2000-01

AUSTRALIA A

Full Names	Birthdate	Birthplace	Team	Type	F-C Debut
AGAR, Ashton Charles	14.10.93	Melbourne	W Australia	LHB/SLA	2012-13
BIRD, Jackson Munro	11.12.86	Sydney	Tasmania	RHB/RFM	2011-12
FAWAD AHMED	05.02.82	Merguz, Pak	Victoria	RHB/LB	2005-06
HARRIS, Ryan James	11.10.79	Sydney	Queensland	RHB/RF	2001-02
HUGHES, Phillip Joel	30.11.88	Macksville	S Australia	LHB/OB	2007-08
KHAWAJA, Usman Tariq	18.12.86	Islamabad, Pak	NSW	LHB/RM	2007-08
MADDINSON, Nicolas James	21.12.91	Nowra	NSW	LHB/SLA	2010-11
SAYERS, Chadd James	31.08.87	Adelaide	S Australia	RHB/RM	2010-11
SILK, Jordan Christopher	13.04.92	Penrith	Tasmania	RHB	2012-13
SMITH, Steven Peter Devereux	02.06.89	Sydney	NSW	RHB/LBG	2007-08
WADE, Matthew Scott	26.12.87	Hobart	Victoria	LHB/WK	2007-08

NEW ZEALAND

Full Names	Birthdate	Birthplace	Team	Type	F-C Debut
BOULT, Trent Alexander	22.07.89	Rotorua	N Districts	RHB/LFM	2008-09
BRACEWELL, Douglas Alexander John	28.09.90	Tauranga	C Districts	RHB/RFM	2008-09
BROWNLIE, Dean Graham	30.07.84	Perth, Australia	Canterbury	RHB/RM	2009-10
FULTON, Peter Gordon	01.02.79	Christchurch	Canterbury	RHB/RM	2000-01
GILLESPIE, Mark Raymond	17.10.79	Wanganui	Wellington	RHB/RFM	1999-00
GUPTILL, Martin James	30.09.86	Auckland	Auckland	RHB/OB	2005-06
LATHAM, Thomas William Maxwell	02.04.92	Christchurch	Canterbury	LHB/RM	2010-11
McCULLUM, Brendon Barrie	27.09.81	Dunedin	Otago	RHB/WK	1999-00
MARTIN, Bruce Philip	25.04.80	Whangarei	Auckland	RHB/SLA	1999-00
RUTHERFORD, Hamish Duncan	27.04.89	Dunedin	Otago	LHB	2008-09
SOUTHEE, Timothy Grant	11.12.88	Whangarei	N Districts	RHB/RMF	2006-07
TAYLOR, Luteru Ross Poutoa Lote	08.03.84	Lower Hutt	C Districts	RHB/OB	2002-03
WAGNER, Neil	13.03.86	Pretoria, SA	Otago	LHB/LMF	2005-06
WATLING, Bradley-John	09.07.85	Durban, SA	N Districts	RHB/WK	2004-05
WILLIAMSON, Kane Stuart	08.08.90	Tauranga	N Districts	RHB/OB	2007-08

UNIVERSITIES REGISTER 2013

CAMBRIDGE († = Blue)

Full Names	Birthdate	Birthplace	College	Bat/Bowl	F-C Debut
ALLCHIN, Alistair Thomas Arthur	12.11.91	Chelmsford	Anglia RU	RHB/RFM	2013
†ANSARI, Akbar Shahzaman	03.07.88	Ascot	Trinity Hall	RHB/LB	2008
ANSARI, Zafar Shahaan	10.12.91	Ascot	Trinity Hall	LHB/SLA	2011
BELL, Dean William	03.05.92	Blackpool	Anglia RU	RHB/WK	2011
COWAN, James Daniel	17.08.89	Cambridge	Anglia RU	LHB/LMF	2011
†ELLIOTT, Tom Christopher	21.11.91	Epsom	Sidney Sussex	RHB/RM	2012
†HEARNE, Alexander Gordon	23.09.93	Kensington	St John's	RHB/LB	2013
†HICKEY, Matthew Robert	23.09.91	Wandsworth	Trinity Hall	LHB/LM	2011
†HUGHES, Philip Heywood	17.06.91	Southampton	Downing	RHB/RM	2010
JOHNSON, James Alexander Michael	25.11.91	Haywards Heath	Anglia RU	RHB/OB	2012
†JOYCE, Jasper Lancaster	02.01.92	Lambeth	Robinson	RHB/WK	2013
NICHOLSON, Grant Frederic	03.01.94	Leeds	Anglia RU	RHB/LMF	2013
†POLLOCK, Alasdair William	24.10.93	High Wycombe	Robinson	RHB/RMF	2013
POYSDEN, Joshua Edward	08.08.91	Shoreham-by-Sea	Anglia RU	LHB/LB	2011
†PROBERT, Thomas John William	26.09.86	Pembury	Peterhouse	LHB/RM	2009
†SADLER, Patrick Thomas	28.09.91	Waltham Forest	Churchill	RHB/RFM	2011
SALISBURY, Matthew Edward Thomas	18.04.93	Chelmsford	Anglia RU	RHB/RMF	2012
†SENARATNE, Nipuna Vikum S.	19.10.93	Leeds	Jesus	RHB/RM	2013
†WYLIE, Benjamin Alexander	24.04.94	Belfast	St Catharine's	LHB/SLA	2013

CARDIFF

Full Names	Birthdate	Birthplace	College	Bat/Bowl	F-C Debut
BALBIRNIE, Andrew	28.12.90	Dublin, Ireland	Cardiff Met	RHB/OB	2012
COWDREY, Fabian Kruuse	30.01.93	Canterbury	Cardiff Met	RHB/SLA	2013
DAVIES, Samuel Llyr	30.01.92	Neath	UWIC	RHB/LM	2012
DENNING, Jonathan Stephen Thomas	03.01.91	Abergavenny	UWIC	RHB/LFM	2013
ELKIN, Zachary	21.06.91	Cape Town, SA	Cardiff	RHB/WK	2012
FRIEND, Thomas Toby	03.05.91	Newport, IoW	UWIC	RHB/RFM	2012
HARRIS, Philip Graham	12.05.90	Worcester	UWIC	RHB/RM	2012
HOBDEN, Matthew Edward	27.03.93	Eastbourne	UWIC	RHB/RFM	2012
MILES, Adam James	19.09.89	Swindon	Cardiff Met	RHB/WK	2012
PHILLIPS, David Scott	31.03.94	Swansea	Cardiff Met	RHB/RFM	2013
QURESHI, Uzair Asad	23.02.93	Lambeth	UWIC	RHB/OB	2012
SIDDIQUE, Hamza Ghani	19.01.91	Stoke-on-Trent	Cardiff	RHB/OB	2012

DURHAM

Full Names	Birthdate	Birthplace	College	Bat/Bowl	F-C Debut
BISHNOI, Chaitanya	25.08.94	Delhi, India	Hatfield	LHB/SLA	2013
COX, Rory Denzil	11.07.91	Winchester	Collingwood	LHB/RM	2013
GREEN, Matthew James Emrys	19.04.93	Wakefield	St Cuthbert's	RHB/RM	2012
HOBSON, Ivo Hamilton	29.12.90	Lambeth	Van Mildert	RHB/OB	2013
JONES, Christopher Robert	05.11.90	Harold Wood	Grey	RHB/RM	2010
PATEL, Luke Adam	06.10.90	Wakefield	Grey	LHB/OB	2010
SHAH, Rishabh Arjun Chandra	11.09.90	Whipps Cross	St Cuthbert's	RHB/LB	2011
STEELE, Oliver James	15.10.93	Worcester	Collingwood	RHB/WK	2013
WALLIS, Charles Alexander	14.10.91	Westminster	Hatfield	RHB/RM	2012
WATKINS, Nathaniel Ashley Thomas	07.11.91	Oxford	Hatfield	RHB/SLA	2011
WILLETT, Ross James David	16.03.92	Farnborough	Hatfield	RHB/RM	2013
van den BERGH, Frederick Oliver Ed	14.06.92	Farnborough	Hatfield	RHB/SLA	2011

LEEDS/BRADFORD

Full Names	Birthdate	Birthplace	College	Bat/Bowl	F-C Debut
GUBBINS, Nicholas Richard Trail	31.12.93	Richmond, Surrey	Leeds	LHB/LB	2012
LEE, James Edward	23.12.88	Sheffield	Leeds	LHB/RMF	2006
MacLEOD, Charles Alastair Roderick	31.10.92	Camden	Leeds	RHB/RMF	2013
MacQUEEN, Alexander	12.01.93	Chertsey	Leeds	RHB/OB	2012
PATEL, Zafir Rashid	14.09.92	Kamboli, India	Bradford	RHB/RMF	2013
REECE, Luis Michael	04.08.90	Taunton	Leeds Met	LHB/LM	2012
ROUSE, Harry Philip	20.10.93	Sheffield	Leeds	RHB/RFM	2013
THOMAS, Ivan Alfred Astley	25.09.91	Greenwich	Leeds	RHB/RMF	2012
THOMPSON, Henry Lester	01.12.92	Preston	Leeds	RHB/OB	2013
VANDERSPAR, William Gordon Rufus	06.10.91	Camden	Leeds	RHB/RFM	2013
WEBB, Jonathon Patrick	12.01.92	Solihull	Leeds	RHB/RM	2012
YOUNG, Daniel Robert	03.10.90	Newcastle upon Tyne	Leeds Met	RHB/RM	2013

LOUGHBOROUGH

Full Names	Birthdate	Birthplace	College	Bat/Bowl	F-C Debut
BAKER, Gavin Charles	03.10.88	Edgware	Loughborough	RHB/RMF	2009
CORNICK, Jack Paris Pattison	24.11.92	Nottingham	Loughborough	RHB/WK	2013
CROSS, Matthew Henry	15.10.92	Aberdeen	Loughborough	RHB/WK	2013
D'SOUZA, Darius Alexander	11.10.89	Bombay, India	Loughborough	RHB/RM	2011
ENDERSBY, Devon Malcolm	12.05.92	East London, SA	Loughborough	RHB/RMF	2012
LESTER, Toby James	05.04.93	Blackpool	Loughborough	LHB/LFM	2012
MacVICAR, William Angus	16.01.92	Lambeth	Loughborough	RHB/RM	2013
MORRIS, Aiden Joseph	25.04.93	Nottingham	Loughborough	RHB/RMF	2012
PATEL, Anish Kirtesh	26.05.90	Manchester	Loughborough	RHB/OB	2013
RATNAYAKE, Dimitri Eranga Mahen	09.03.90	Kandy, Sri Lanka	Loughborough	RHB/RM	2011
RILEY, Adam Edward Nicholas	23.03.92	Sidcup	Loughborough	RHB/OB	2011
SOILLEUX, Adam Charles	29.11.91	Southend	Loughborough	RHB/RMF	2011

OXFORD († = Blue)

Full Names	Birthdate	Birthplace	College	Bat/Bowl	F-C Debut
†AGARWAL, Samridh Sunil	13.07.90	Agra, India	Queen's	RHB/OB	2010
BODENSTEIN, Cornelis Johannes	03.11.92	Pretoria, SA	Brookes U	LHB/LMF	2013
†CATO, Samuel John	23.11.92	Chiswick	New	RHB/OB	2013
†CHADWICK, Thomas Robert	21.10.91	Norwich	Worcester	RHB/RM	2011
COLEMAN, Frederick Robert John	15.12.91	Edinburgh	Brookes U	RHB/OB	2011-12
DAVISON, Stewart Richard	06.04.91	Basingstoke	Brookes U	RHB/RM	2013
ELLISON, Charles Peter	26.01.91	Canterbury	Brookes U	RHB/RMF	2011
FELL, Thomas Charles	17.10.93	Hillingdon	Brookes U	RHB/OB	2013
†JEFFERY, Benjamin Anthony	31.07.91	Camden	St John's	RHB/LB	2011
JONES, Owain James	24.09.92	Brighton	St Edmund Hall	LHB/RM	2012
KEMP, Benedict William	26.05.93	Canterbury	Brookes U	RHB/RMF	2012
†KENNEDY, Augustus Damian John	10.08.90	London	Wycliffe	RHB/WK	2010
MARRIOTT, Wilfred William John	11.04.94	Westminster	Brooks U	RHB/OB	2013
†MARSDEN, Jonathan	07.04.93	Sevenoaks	St Hilda's	RHB/RFM	2013
MORRIS, Charles Andrew John	06.07.92	Hereford	Brookes U	RHB/RMF	2012
†MYLAVARAPU, Sachin Venkata S.	21.06.91	Singapore	St Hugh's	RHB/SLA	2013
SABIN, Lloyd Michael	22.06.94	Banbury	Brookes U	RHB/OB	2013
THOMPSON, James Scott	11.03.91	Shrewsbury	Brookes U	RHB/RMF	2012
†WESTAWAY, Samuel Alexander	29.07.92	Welwyn Garden City	Pembroke	RHB/WK	2011
†WILLIAMS, Ben	24.06.92	Whiston	Hertford	RHB/RSM	2011
†WILLIAMS, Thomas J.	–	Epsom	Balliol	RHB/RMF	2013
†WINTER, Matthew J.	–	Crewe	Lady Margaret	–	2013

THE 2013 FIRST-CLASS SEASON
STATISTICAL HIGHLIGHTS

FIRST TO INDIVIDUAL TARGETS

1000 RUNS	J.E.Root	Yorkshire, England, England Lions	20 July
2000 RUNS	–	Most – 1536 C.J.L.Rogers (Australia, Middlesex)	
50 WICKETS	C.J.Jordan	Sussex	3 August
100 WICKETS	–	Most – 73 G.Onions (Durham, England Lions)	

TEAM HIGHLIGHTS
HIGHEST INNINGS TOTALS

677-7d	Yorkshire v Derbyshire	Leeds
634-5d	Surrey v Yorkshire	The Oval
631-9d	Warwickshire v Surrey	Guildford
617-5d	Yorkshire v Derbyshire	Chesterfield

HIGHEST FOURTH INNINGS TOTAL

418-8	Kent (set 418) v Lancashire	Canterbury
411-8	Kent (set 411) v Gloucestershire	Cheltenham

LOWEST INNINGS TOTALS († *County record*)

20†	Essex v Lancashire	Chelmsford
60	Derbyshire v Middlesex	Lord's
62	Northamptonshire v Lancashire	Manchester
63	Derbyshire v Durham	Derby
63	Kent v Worcestershire	Canterbury
68	New Zealand v England (*1st Test*)	Lord's
76	Somerset v Sussex	Horsham
78	Nottinghamshire v Durham	Chester-le-Street
94	Derbyshire v Somerset	Derby
94	Durham v Warwickshire	Birmingham
96	Yorkshire v Sussex	Leeds
99	Cambridge MCCU v Essex	Cambridge

MATCH AGGREGATES OF 1500 RUNS

1599-19	Gloucestershire (562-5d & 237-1d) v Kent (389-5d & 411-8)	Cheltenham

BATSMEN'S MATCH (Qualification: 1200 runs, average 60 per wicket)

84.15 (1599-19)	Gloucestershire (562-5d & 237-1d) v Kent (389-5d & 411-8)	Cheltenham
63.47 (1333-21)	Surrey (634-5d) v Yorkshire (434 & 265-6)	The Oval

LARGE MARGINS OF VICTORY

Inns & 186 runs	Oxford U (550-7d) beat Cambridge U (119 & 245)	Cambridge
Inns & 179 runs	Somerset (449) beat Middlesex (106 & 164)	Lord's
Inns & 168 runs	Warwickshire (391-9d) beat Derbyshire (103 & 120)	Derby
541 runs	Notts (396-3d & 408-9d) beat Durham MCCU (142 & 121)	Nottingham
347 runs	England (361 & 349-7d) beat Australia (128 & 235)	Lord's
318 runs	Warwickshire (345 & 351-8d) beat Durham (284 & 94)	Birmingham

NARROW MARGINS OF VICTORY

11 runs	Durham (267 & 198) beat Warwickshire (209 & 245)	Chester-le-Street
14 runs	Lancashire (123 & 272) beat Glamorgan (242 & 139)	Colwyn Bay
14 runs	England (215 & 375) beat Australia (280 & 296)	Nottingham
2 wkts	Derbyshire (298 & 244-8) beat Somerset (103 & 438)	Taunton
2 wkts	Kent (389-5d & 411-8) beat Gloucestershire (562-5d & 237-1d)	Cheltenham
2 wkts	Kent (260 & 418-8) beat Lancashire (284 & 393-5d)	Canterbury

ALL ELEVEN SCORING DOUBLE FIGURES

Durham (471) v Nottinghamshire   Nottingham

MOST EXTRAS IN AN INNINGS

B	LB	W	NB	P		
56	19	19	5	8	5 Hampshire (545) v Northamptonshire	Southampton

Under ECB regulations, Test matches excluded, two penalty extras were scored for each no-ball.

BATTING HIGHLIGHTS
TRIPLE HUNDREDS († *Team record*)

S.S.Agarwal	313*†	Oxford U v Cambridge U	Cambridge

DOUBLE HUNDREDS

J.H.K.Adams (2)	219*	Hampshire v Worcestershire	Southampton
	218	Hampshire v Northamptonshire	Southampton
M.M.Ali	250	Worcestershire v Glamorgan	Worcester
V.Chopra	228*	Warwickshire v Middlesex	Uxbridge
K.J.Coetzer	219	Northamptonshire v Leicestershire	Leicester
A.W.Gale	272	Yorkshire v Nottinghamshire	Scarborough
A.P.R.Gidman	211	Gloucestershire v Kent	Cheltenham
C.F.Hughes	270*	Derbyshire v Yorkshire	Leeds
E.C.Joyce	204*	Sussex v Nottinghamshire	Nottingham
S.M.Katich	200	Lancashire v Northamptonshire	Northampton
R.I.Keogh	221	Northamptonshire v Hampshire	Southampton
A.Z.Lees	275*	Yorkshire v Derbyshire	Chesterfield
M.J.Lumb	221*	Nottinghamshire v Derbyshire	Nottingham
J.C.Mickleburgh	243	Essex v Leicestershire	Chelmsford
S.R.Patel	256	Nottinghamshire v Durham MCCU	Nottingham
S.D.Robson	215*	Middlesex v Warwickshire	Birmingham
C.J.L.Rogers	214	Middlesex v Surrey	Lord's
J.E.Root	236	Yorkshire v Derbyshire	Leeds
D.J.G.Sales	255*	Northamptonshire v Gloucestershire	Northampton
D.P.Sibley	242	Surrey v Yorkshire	The Oval
D.I.Stevens	205*	Kent v Lancashire	Canterbury
J.W.A.Taylor	204*	Nottinghamshire v Sussex	Nottingham
L.W.P.Wells	208	Sussex v Surrey	The Oval

HUNDREDS IN THREE CONSECUTIVE INNINGS

A.W.Gale	272	Yorkshire v Nottinghamshire	Scarborough
	103	Yorkshire v Middlesex	Lord's
	148	Yorkshire v Surrey	Leeds
A.U.Rashid	180	Yorkshire v Somerset	Leeds
	110*	Yorkshire v Warwickshire	Birmingham
	103*	Yorkshire v Somerset	Taunton
J.E.Root	182	Yorkshire v Durham	Chester-le-Street
	236	Yorkshire v Derbyshire	Leeds
	179	England Lions v New Zealanders	Leicester

HUNDRED IN EACH INNINGS OF A MATCH

M.M.Ali	104	109	Worcestershire v Lancashire	Worcester
G.S.Ballance	148	108*	Yorkshire v Surrey	The Oval
E.J.H.Eckersley	106	119	Leicestershire v Worcestershire	Leicester
A.G.Prince	134	108	Lancashire v Kent	Canterbury

FASTEST HUNDRED AGAINST GENUINE BOWLING

A.M.Rossington (103*)   55 balls   Middlesex v Cambridge MCCU   Cambridge

MOST SIXES IN AN INNINGS

12   S.R.Patel (256)   Nottinghamshire v Durham MCCU   Nottingham

150 OR MORE RUNS FROM BOUNDARIES IN AN INNINGS

Runs	6s	4s			
188	12	29	S.R.Patel	Nottinghamshire v Durham MCCU	Nottingham
182	3	41	S.S.Agarwal	Oxford U v Cambridge U	Cambridge
178	3	40	C.F.Hughes	Derbyshire v Yorkshire	Leeds
162	3	36	D.J.G.Sales	Northamptonshire v Gloucestershire	Northampton
158	1	38	A.Z.Lees	Yorkshire v Derbyshire	Chesterfield
150	1	36	K.J.Coetzer	Northamptonshire v Leicestershire	Leicester

HUNDRED ON FIRST-CLASS DEBUT IN BRITAIN

N.J.Maddinson   181   Australia A v Gloucestershire   Bristol
He had scored 113* v Ireland in Belfast in his previous match.
R.J.Quiney   112   Essex v Cambridge MCCU   Cambridge

CARRYING BAT THROUGH COMPLETED INNINGS

J.H.K.Adams   138*   Hampshire (274) v Gloucestershire   Bristol
C.F.Hughes   270*   Derbyshire (475) v Yorkshire   Leeds

LONG INNINGS (Qualification 600 mins and/or 400 balls)

Mins	Balls			
575	444	J.H.K.Adams (218)	Hampshire v Northamptonshire	Southampton
569	428	V.Chopra (228*)	Warwickshire v Middlesex	Uxbridge
503	402	K.J.Coetzer (219)	Northamptonshire v Leics	Leicester
535	404	A.W.Gale (272)	Yorkshire v Nottinghamshire	Scarborough
544	415	C.F.Hughes (270*)	Derbyshire v Yorkshire	Leeds
555	436	A.Z.Lees (275*)	Yorkshire v Derbyshire	Chesterfield
508	434	J.C.Mickleburgh (243)	Essex v Leicestershire	Chelmsford
599	536	D.P.Sibley (242)	Surrey v Yorkshire	The Oval
526	412	L.W.P.Wells (208)	Sussex v Surrey	The Oval

FIRST-WICKET PARTNERSHIP OF 100 IN EACH INNINGS

106/110*   C.J.L.Rogers/S.D.Robson   Middlesex v Nottinghamshire   Nottingham

OTHER NOTABLE PARTNERSHIPS († Team record)

Qualifications: 1st-4th wkts: 250 runs; 5th-6th: 225; 7th: 200; 8th: 175; 9th: 150; 10th: 100.

First Wicket
259   C.J.L.Rogers/S.D.Robson   Middlesex v Surrey   Lord's

Second Wicket
311   A.Z.Lees/P.A.Jaques   Yorkshire v Derbyshire   Chesterfield

264	P.A.Jaques/K.S.Williamson	Yorkshire v Durham	Scarborough
258	C.F.Hughes/W.L.Madsen	Derbyshire v Yorkshire	Leeds

Third Wicket

275	M.H.Yardy/M.W.Machan	Sussex v Somerset	Taunton
267	C.D.J.Dent/A.P.R.Gidman	Gloucestershire v Kent	Cheltenham
265	W.L.Madsen/S.Chanderpaul	Derbyshire v Surrey	Derby
250*	L.A.Dawson/J.M.Vince	Hampshire v Leicestershire	Leicester

Fourth Wicket

280	D.M.Housego/H.J.H.Marshall	Gloucestershire v Essex	Chelmsford
269	A.Javid/L.J.Evans	Warwickshire v Somerset	Birmingham
260*	C.D.Nash/R.J.Hamilton-Brown	Sussex v Yorkshire	Hove

Fifth Wicket

297	A.W.Gale/G.S.Ballance	Yorkshire v Nottinghamshire	Scarborough
270	J.C.Mickleburgh/B.T.Foakes	Essex v Leicestershire	Chelmsford
232	E.C.Joyce/R.J.Hamilton-Brown	Sussex v Nottinghamshire	Nottingham

Seventh Wicket

218	K.K.Jennings/M.J.Richardson	Durham v Sussex	Hove
211	A.Javid/K.H.D.Barker	Warwickshire v Surrey	Guildford
200	J.W.A.Taylor/A.Shahzad	Nottinghamshire v Sussex	Nottingham

Eighth Wicket

191	A.J.Wheater/M.T.Coles	Hampshire v Lancashire	Southport

Ninth Wicket

166	C.R.Woakes/M.A.Chambers	Warwickshire v Derbyshire	Derby

Tenth Wicket

163*	P.J.Hughes/A.C.Agar	Australia v England (*1st Test*)	Nottingham
117	S.P.Crook/T.A.Copeland	Northamptonshire v Essex	Northampton
114	G.Chapple/S.C.Kerrigan	Lancashire v Hampshire	Southport

BOWLING HIGHLIGHTS
EIGHT OR MORE WICKETS IN AN INNINGS

S.J.Magoffin	8-20	Sussex v Somerset	Horsham
O.P.Rayner	8-46	Middlesex v Surrey	The Oval
A.Richardson	8-37	Worcestershire v Gloucestershire	Worcester
C.T.Tremlett	8-96	Surrey v Durham	Chester-le-Street

TEN OR MORE WICKETS IN A MATCH

J.M.Anderson	10-158	England v Australia (*1st Test*)	Nottingham
S.C.J.Broad	11-121	England v Australia (*4th Test*)	Chester-le-Street
P.P.Chawla	10-208	Somerset v Derbyshire	Taunton
M.T.Coles	10-154	Hampshire v Essex	Southampton
T.A.Copeland	10-113	Northamptonshire v Kent	Canterbury
W.R.S.Gidman	10- 43	Gloucestershire v Leicestershire	Bristol
S.C.Kerrigan	12-252	Lancashire v Glamorgan	Manchester
S.J.Magoffin	12- 31	Sussex v Somerset	Horsham
T.J.Murtagh	10- 77	Middlesex v Somerset	Taunton
O.P.Rayner	15-118	Middlesex v Surrey	The Oval
A.Richardson (2)	12- 63	Worcestershire v Kent	Canterbury
	12-107	Worcestershire v Gloucestershire	Worcester
C.Rushworth	10-103	Durham v Derbyshire	Chester-le-Street
T.G.Southee	10-108	New Zealand v England (*1st Test*)	Lord's
G.P.Swann	10-132	England v New Zealand (*2nd Test*)	Leeds
R.J.W.Topley	11- 85	Essex v Worcestershire	Chelmsford

BOWLING UNCHANGED THROUGHOUT INNINGS

J.M.Anderson (11.3-5-23-2)/S.C.J.Broad (11-0-44-7)	England v New Zealand	Lord's
G.Chapple (7.2-4-9-5)/K.W.Hogg (7-3-11-4)	Lancashire v Essex	Chelmsford
G.Chapple (15-4-34-3)/K.W.Hogg (14.5-5-27-7)	Lancashire v Northants	Manchester

They achieved these feats in successive innings.

HAT-TRICKS

J.K.Fuller	Gloucestershire v Worcestershire	Cheltenham
H.F.Gurney	Nottinghamshire v Sussex	Hove
A.Richardson	Worcestershire v Leicestershire	Leicester
T.S.Roland-Jones	Middlesex v Derbyshire	Lord's

MOST RUNS CONCEDED IN AN INNINGS

A.U.Rashid	55-6-227-2	Yorkshire v Surrey	The Oval

MOST OVERS BOWLED IN AN INNINGS

P.I.Burgoyne	55-8-149-1	Derbyshire v Yorkshire	Chesterfield
A.U.Rashid	55-6-227-2	Yorkshire v Surrey	The Oval

ALL-ROUND HIGHLIGHTS

MATCH DOUBLE (100 RUNS AND TEN WICKETS IN MATCH)

W.R.S.Gidman (143 & 6-15, 4-28)	Gloucestershire v Leicestershire	Bristol

Gidman was the fifth Gloucestershire player to score a century and take ten wickets in a match, and the first since M.J.Procter in 1980.

MATCH DOUBLE (CENTURY AND FIVE WICKETS IN AN INNINGS)

W.R.S.Gidman (143 & 6-15)	Gloucestershire v Leicestershire	Bristol
J.D.Middlebrook (109 & 6-78)	Northamptonshire v Kent	Northampton

WICKET-KEEPING HIGHLIGHTS

SIX OR MORE WICKET-KEEPING DISMISSALS IN AN INNINGS

O.B.Cox	7ct	Worcestershire v Oxford MCCU	Oxford
J.M.Bairstow	6ct	Yorkshire v Middlesex	Leeds
M.D.Bates	6ct	Hampshire v Northamptonshire	Southampton
P.Mustard	6ct	Durham v Surrey	Chester-le-Street
M.J.Prior	6ct	Sussex v Warwickshire	Hove
C.M.W.Read	6ct	Nottinghamshire v Yorkshire	Nottingham
J.A.Simpson	6ct	Middlesex v Yorkshire	Leeds

NINE OR MORE WICKET-KEEPING DISMISSALS IN A MATCH

S.A.Westaway	10ct	Oxford U v Cambridge U	Cambridge
B.C.Brown	9ct	Sussex v Somerset	Taunton
O.B.Cox	9ct	Worcestershire v Oxford MCCU	Oxford
D.Murphy	9ct	Northamptonshire v Glamorgan	Northampton

FIELDING HIGHLIGHTS

FIVE OR MORE CATCHES IN THE FIELD IN AN INNINGS

M.E.Trescothick	5ct	Somerset v Middlesex	Lord's

COUNTY CHAMPIONSHIP 2013
LV= FINAL TABLES

DIVISION 1

	P	W	L	D	Bonus Points Bat	Bowl	Deduct Points	Total Points
1 DURHAM (6)	16	10	4	2	36	46	2.5	245.5
2 Yorkshire (-)	16	7	2	7	49	39	–	221
3 Sussex (4)	16	5	3	8	45	39	–	188
4 Warwickshire (1)	16	5	2	9	37	42	–	186
5 Middlesex (3)	16	6	5	5	32	39	–	182
6 Somerset (2)	16	3	5	8	33	41	–	146
7 Nottinghamshire (5)	16	2	5	9	47	40	–	146
8 Derbyshire (-)	16	3	10	3	31	34	–	122
9 Surrey (7)	16	1	6	9	36	37	–	116

DIVISION 2

	P	W	L	D	Bonus Points Bat	Bowl	Deduct Points	Total Points
1 Lancashire (-)	16	8	1	7	45	45	1	238
2 Northamptonshire (8)	16	5	3	8	55	43	–	202
3 Essex (5)	16	5	4	7	43	41	3	182
4 Hampshire (4)	16	4	3	9	45	35	–	171
5 Worcestershire (-)	16	5	6	5	29	43	–	167
6 Gloucestershire (9)	16	4	4	8	43	36	–	167
7 Kent (3)	16	3	2	11	39	31	–	151
8 Glamorgan (6)	16	3	6	7	41	39	–	149
9 Leicestershire (7)	16	0	8	8	23	32	–	79

Durham deducted 2.5 points for breach of team salary payments.
Essex deducted 3 points for slow over rates; Lancashire deducted 1 point for slow over rate.

SCORING OF CHAMPIONSHIP POINTS 2013 and 2014

(a) For a win, 16 points, plus any points scored in the first innings.
(b) In a tie, each side to score eight points, plus any points scored in the first innings.
(c) In a drawn match, each side to score three points, plus any points scored in the first innings (see also paragraph (f) below).
(d) If the scores are equal in a drawn match, the side batting in the fourth innings to score eight points plus any points scored in the first innings, and the opposing side to score three points plus any points scored in the first innings.
(e) **First Innings Points** (awarded only for performances **in the first 110 overs** of each first innings and retained whatever the result of the match).
　　(i) A maximum of five batting points to be available as under:
　　　　200 to 249 runs – 1 point; 250 to 299 runs – 2 points; 300 to 349 runs – 3 points; 350 to 399 runs – 4 points; 400 runs or over – 5 points.
　　(ii) A maximum of three bowling points to be available as under:
　　　　3 to 5 wickets taken – 1 point; 6 to 8 wickets taken – 2 points; 9 to 10 wickets taken – 3 points.
(f) If a match is abandoned without a ball being bowled, each side to score three points.
(g) The side which has the highest aggregate of points gained at the end of the season shall be the Champion County of their respective Division. Should any sides in the Championship table be equal on points, the following tie-breakers will be applied in the order stated: most wins, fewest losses, team achieving most points in contests between teams level on points, most wickets taken, most runs scored. At the end of the season, the top two teams from the Second Division will be promoted and the bottom two teams from the First Division will be relegated.

COUNTY CHAMPIONS

The English County Championship was not officially constituted until December 1889. Prior to that date there was no generally accepted method of awarding the title; although the 'least matches lost' method existed, it was not consistently applied. Rules governing playing qualifications were agreed in 1873 and the first unofficial points system 15 years later.

Research has produced a list of champions dating back to 1826, but at least seven different versions exist for the period from 1864 to 1889 (see *The Wisden Book of Cricket Records*). Only from 1890 can any authorised list of county champions commence.

That first official Championship was contested between eight counties: Gloucestershire, Kent, Lancashire, Middlesex, Nottinghamshire, Surrey, Sussex and Yorkshire. The remaining counties were admitted in the following seasons: 1891 – Somerset, 1895 – Derbyshire, Essex, Hampshire, Leicestershire and Warwickshire, 1899 – Worcestershire, 1905 – Northamptonshire, 1921 – Glamorgan, and 1992 – Durham.

The Championship pennant was introduced by the 1951 champions, Warwickshire, and the Lord's Taverners' Trophy was first presented in 1973. The first sponsors, Schweppes (1977-83), were succeeded by Britannic Assurance (1984-98), PPP Healthcare (1999-2000), CricInfo (2001), Frizzell (2002-05) and Liverpool Victoria (2006 to date). Based on their previous season's positions, the 18 counties were separated into two divisions in 2000. From 2000 to 2005 the bottom three Division 1 teams were relegated and the top three Division 2 sides promoted. This was reduced to two teams from the end of the 2006 season.

1890	Surrey	1933	Yorkshire	1976	Middlesex
1891	Surrey	1934	Lancashire	1977	Kent
1892	Surrey	1935	Yorkshire		Middlesex
1893	Yorkshire	1936	Derbyshire	1978	Kent
1894	Surrey	1937	Yorkshire	1979	Essex
1895	Surrey	1938	Yorkshire	1980	Middlesex
1896	Yorkshire	1939	Yorkshire	1981	Nottinghamshire
1897	Lancashire	1946	Yorkshire	1982	Middlesex
1898	Yorkshire	1947	Middlesex	1983	Essex
1899	Surrey	1948	Glamorgan	1984	Essex
1900	Yorkshire	1949	Middlesex	1985	Middlesex
1901	Yorkshire		Yorkshire	1986	Essex
1902	Yorkshire	1950	Lancashire	1987	Nottinghamshire
1903	Middlesex		Surrey	1988	Worcestershire
1904	Lancashire	1951	Warwickshire	1989	Worcestershire
1905	Yorkshire	1952	Surrey	1990	Middlesex
1906	Kent	1953	Surrey	1991	Essex
1907	Nottinghamshire	1954	Surrey	1992	Essex
1908	Yorkshire	1955	Surrey	1993	Middlesex
1909	Kent	1956	Surrey	1994	Warwickshire
1910	Kent	1957	Surrey	1995	Warwickshire
1911	Warwickshire	1958	Surrey	1996	Leicestershire
1912	Yorkshire	1959	Yorkshire	1997	Glamorgan
1913	Kent	1960	Yorkshire	1998	Leicestershire
1914	Surrey	1961	Hampshire	1999	Surrey
1919	Yorkshire	1962	Yorkshire	2000	Surrey
1920	Middlesex	1963	Yorkshire	2001	Yorkshire
1921	Middlesex	1964	Worcestershire	2002	Surrey
1922	Yorkshire	1965	Worcestershire	2003	Sussex
1923	Yorkshire	1966	Yorkshire	2004	Warwickshire
1924	Yorkshire	1967	Yorkshire	2005	Nottinghamshire
1925	Yorkshire	1968	Yorkshire	2006	Sussex
1926	Lancashire	1969	Glamorgan	2007	Sussex
1927	Lancashire	1970	Kent	2008	Durham
1928	Lancashire	1971	Surrey	2009	Durham
1929	Nottinghamshire	1972	Warwickshire	2010	Nottinghamshire
1930	Lancashire	1973	Hampshire	2011	Lancashire
1931	Yorkshire	1974	Worcestershire	2012	Warwickshire
1932	Yorkshire	1975	Leicestershire	2013	Durham

COUNTY CHAMPIONSHIP RESULTS 2013

DIVISION 1

	DERBYS	DURHAM	MIDDX	NOTTS	SOM'T	SURREY	SUSSEX	WARWKS	YORKS
DERBYS	–	Derby Du 9w	Derby De 56	Derby N 9w	Derby Sm 4w	Derby Drawn	Derby Sx 9w	Derby W I/168	C'field Y I/113
DURHAM	C-le-St Du 279	–	C-le-St Drawn	C-le-St Du 8w	C-le-St Du 48	C-le-St Du I/144	C-le-St Du 285	C-le-St Du 11	C-le-St Y 4w
MIDDX	Lord's M 9w	Lord's M 6w	–	Lord's Drawn	Lord's Sm I/179	Lord's Drawn	Lord's Drawn	Uxbridge W 5w	Lord's Y 10w
NOTTS	N'ham Drawn	N'ham Du 6w	N'ham M 10w	–	N'ham Drawn	N'ham N 114	N'ham Drawn	N'ham Drawn	N'ham Y 10w
SOM'T	Taunton De 2w	Taunton Drawn	Taunton M 9w	Taunton Drawn	–	Taunton Sm 7w	Taunton Sx 9w	Taunton Drawn	Taunton Drawn
SURREY	Oval Sy 4w	Oval Du 5w	Oval M 146	Oval Drawn	Oval Drawn	–	Oval Drawn	Guildford Drawn	Oval Drawn
SUSSEX	Hove De 9w	Hove Sx 6w	Hove M 10w	Hove Drawn	Horsham Sx I/116	Arundel Drawn	–	Hove Drawn	Hove Drawn
WARWKS	B'ham Drawn	B'ham W 318	B'ham Drawn	B'ham W 216	B'ham Drawn	B'ham W 6w	B'ham Drawn	–	B'ham Y I/139
YORKS	Leeds Y I/39	Scar Du 7w	Leeds Y 80	Scar Drawn	Leeds Drawn	Leeds Drawn	Leeds Sx I/12	Leeds Drawn	–

DIVISION 2

	ESSEX	GLAM	GLOS	HANTS	KENT	LANCS	LEICS	N'HANTS	WORCS
Essex	–	C'ford Drawn	C'ford Drawn	C'ford E 4w	C'ford Drawn	C'ford La I/105	C'ford E I/25	Colch'r Drawn	C'ford E 8w
GLAM	Cardiff E 5w	–	Cardiff Gm 8w	Cardiff H 43	Cardiff K 7w	Col B La 14	Swansea Gm I/37	Cardiff Drawn	Cardiff Gm 10w
GLOS	Bristol Drawn	Bristol Drawn	–	Bristol Drawn	Chelt'm K 2w	Bristol Drawn	Bristol Gs I/138	Bristol N 7w	Chelt'm Gs 6w
HANTS	So'ton H I/31	So'ton Drawn	So'ton Gs 198	–	So'ton Drawn	So'ton Drawn	So'ton Drawn	So'ton Drawn	So'ton H I/42
KENT	Cant Drawn	Cant Drawn	Cant Drawn	Cant Drawn	–	Cant K 2w	Tun W Drawn	Cant N 7w	Cant W 10w
LANCS	Man La 3w	Man Drawn	L'pool Drawn	S'port La 122	Man Drawn	–	Man Drawn	Man La 8w	Man Drawn
LEICS	Leics E 4w	Leics Drawn	Leics Gs 9w	Leics H 180	Leics Drawn	Leics La I/52	–	Leics Drawn	Leics W 9w
N'HANTS	No'ton N I/9	No'ton N I/25	No'ton Drawn	No'ton Drawn	No'ton Drawn	No'ton La 8w	No'ton Drawn	–	No'ton N 10w
WORCS	Worcs Drawn	Worcs W 8w	Worcs W 10w	Worcs Drawn	Worcs Drawn	Worcs La 9w	Worcs Drawn	Worcs W 115	–

KEEP YOUR OWN RECORD (see page 216)

DIVISION 1

	DURHAM	LANCS	MIDDX	N'HANTS	NOTTS	SOM'T	SUSSEX	WARWKS	YORKS
DURHAM	–	C-le-St	C-le-St	C-le-St	C-le-St	C-le-St	C-le-St	C-le-St	C-le-St
LANCS	Man	–	Man	Man	L'pool	Man	Man	Man	Man
MIDDX	Lord's	Lord's	–	Lord's	Lord's	Uxbridge	N'wood	Lord's	Lord's
N'HANTS	No'ton	No'ton	No'ton	–	No'ton	No'ton	No'ton	No'ton	No'ton
NOTTS	N'ham	N'ham	N'ham	N'ham	–	N'ham	N'ham	N'ham	N'ham
SOM'T	Taunton	Taunton	Taunton	Taunton	Taunton	–	Taunton	Taunton	Taunton
SUSSEX	Hove	Hove	Hove	Hove	Hove	Hove	–	Horsham	Arundel
WARWKS	B'ham	B'ham	B'ham	B'ham	B'ham	B'ham	B'ham	–	B'ham
YORKS	Leeds	Leeds	Scar	Leeds	Leeds	Leeds	Scar	Leeds	–

DIVISION 2

	DERBYS	ESSEX	GLAM	GLOS	HANTS	KENT	LEICS	SURREY	WORCS
DERBYS	–	C'field	Derby	Derby	Derby	Derby	Derby	Derby	Derby
ESSEX	C'ford	–	C'ford	C'ford	Colch'r	C'ford	C'ford	C'ford	C'ford
GLAM	Cardiff	Swansea	–	Cardiff	Cardiff	Cardiff	Cardiff	Col B	Cardiff
GLOS	Chelt'm	Bristol	Bristol	–	Bristol	Bristol	Bristol	Bristol	Chelt'm
HANTS	So'ton	So'ton	So'ton	So'ton	–	So'ton	So'ton	So'ton	So'ton
KENT	Cant	Cant	Cant	Cant	Cant	–	Cant	Cant	Tun W
LEICS	Leics	Leics	Leics	Leics	Leics	Leics	–	Leics	Leics
SURREY	Oval	Oval	Oval	Oval	Oval	Guildford	Oval	–	Oval
WORCS	Worcs	Worcs	Worcs	Worcs	Worcs	Worcs	Worcs	Worcs	–

YORKSHIRE BANK 40 2013

This latest format of the 40-over competition was launched in 2010, and is now the only List-A tournament played in the UK. The three Group winners, plus the runner-up with the most points, met in the semi-finals, with the winner decided in the final at Lord's.

GROUP A	P	W	L	T	NR	Pts	Net RR
1 Nottinghamshire (4)	12	9	3	–	–	18	+0.45
2 Northamptonshire (6)	12	8	3	–	1	17	+0.39
3 Sussex (1)	12	6	4	–	2	14	+0.46
4 Kent (3)	12	6	6	–	–	12	+0.22
5 Worcestershire (7)	12	5	7	–	–	10	+0.24
6 Netherlands (4)	12	2	7	–	3	7	–1.15
7 Warwickshire (2)	12	2	8	–	2	6	–0.92

GROUP B	P	W	L	T	NR	Pts	Net RR
1 Hampshire (1)	12	9	3	–	–	18	+0.73
2 Essex (5)	12	8	4	–	–	16	+0.97
3 Lancashire (1)	12	7	4	–	1	15	–0.02
4 Durham (5)*	12	7	4	–	1	14.75	+0.65
5 Surrey (2)	12	4	6	–	2	10	–0.52
6 Scotland (7)	12	–	11	–	1	1	–1.94
7 Derbyshire (4)	12	3	6	–	3	9	–0.25

GROUP B	P	W	L	T	NR	Pts	Net RR
1 Somerset (3)	12	8	3	–	1	17	+1.00
2 Glamorgan (6)	12	8	3	–	1	17	+0.57
3 Middlesex (2)	12	7	4	–	1	15	+0.31
4 Gloucestershire (3)	12	7	4	–	1	15	+0.16
5 Leicestershire (6)	12	5	7	–	–	10	–0.35
6 Yorkshire (5)	12	3	9	–	–	6	–0.46
7 Unicorns (7)	12	1	9	–	2	4	–1.19

Win = 2 points. Tie (T)/No Result (NR) = 1 point. (Last year's positions in brackets.)

* Durham were deducted 0.25 points for a breach of the salary cap in 2012.

Positions of counties finishing equal on points are decided by most wins or, if equal, the team that achieved the most points in the matches played between them; if still equal, the team with the higher net run rate (ie deducting from the average runs per over scored by that team in matches where a result was achieved, the average runs per over scored against that team).

Statistical Highlights in 2013

Highest total	368-7		Essex v Scotland	Chelmsford
Biggest victory (runs)	178		Essex beat Surrey	Chelmsford
Biggest victory (wkts)	10		Middlesex beat Leicestershire	Leicester
Most runs	745 (ave 82.77)	P.D.Trego (Somerset)		
Highest innings	180	R.N.ten Doeschate	Essex v Scotland	Chelmsford
Most sixes	15	R.N.ten Doeschate	Essex v Scotland	Chelmsford
Highest partnership	235	J.J.Cobb/G.P.Smith	Leicestershire v Somerset	Leicester
Most wickets	28 (ave 17.42)	M.G.Hogan (Glamorgan)		
Best bowling	7-32	G.R.Napier	Essex v Surrey	Chelmsford
Most economical	8-1-15-2	C.A.J.Meschede	Somerset v Unicorns	Taunton
	8-2-15-0	G.Onions	Durham v Scotland	Glasgow
Most expensive	8-0-97-2	C.J.Haggett	Kent v Sussex	Canterbury
Most w/k dismissals	17	G.D.Cross (Lancashire)		
	17	C.M.W.Read (Nottinghamshire)		
Most w/k dismissals (inns)	6 (5 ct, 1 st)		Essex v Hampshire	
Most catches	13	S.J.Mullaney (Nottinghamshire)		

218

2013 YORKSHIRE BANK 40 FINAL

GLAMORGAN v NOTTINGHAMSHIRE

At Lord's, London, on 21 September.
Result: NOTTINGHAMSHIRE won by 87 runs.
Toss: Glamorgan. Award: S.R.Patel.

NOTTINGHAMSHIRE		Runs	Balls	4/6	Fall
M.J.Lumb	c and b Salter	28	27	3/1	1- 52
A.D.Hales	c Goodwin b Jones	18	33	1	2- 58
J.W.A.Taylor	c Wallace b Jones	22	28	2	4- 90
S.R.Patel	c Rees b Salter	10	21	–	3- 80
D.J.Hussey	run out	42	46	3	5-189
*†C.M.W.Read	c Cooke b Hogan	53	53	4/2	6-195
G.P.Swann	not out	29	19	4	
S.J.Mullaney	b Wagg	21	12	4	7-237
S.C.J.Broad	b Hogan	0	1	–	8-244
A.Shahzad					
H.F.Gurney					
Extras	(LB 12, W 9)	21			
Total	(8 wkts; 40 overs)	**244**			

GLAMORGAN		Runs	Balls	4/6	Fall
G.P.Rees	b Shahzad	29	36	4	2- 42
*†M.A.Wallace	c Taylor b Gurney	2	3	–	1- 4
C.B.Cooke	b Patel	46	45	4	3-108
J.Allenby	b Patel	34	40	1	4-115
M.W.Goodwin	lbw b Patel	6	9	–	5-118
B.J.Wright	c Lumb b Shahzad	14	22	–	6-144
G.G.Wagg	c Read b Broad	18	31	2	9-157
A.G.Salter	lbw b Shahzad	2	2	–	7-147
D.A.Cosker	c Mullaney b Broad	3	7	–	8-155
M.G.Hogan	b Broad	0	3	–	10-157
S.P.Jones	not out	0			
Extras	(B 2, W 1)	3			
Total	(33 overs)	**157**			

GLAMORGAN	O	M	R	W	NOTTINGHAMSHIRE	O	M	R	W
Hogan	8	0	49	2	Broad	7	0	29	3
Allenby	6	0	38	2	Gurney	5	0	22	1
Jones	8	0	36	2	Shahzad	6	0	33	3
Salter	7	1	41	2	Swann	6	0	36	0
Cosker	7	0	37	0	Mullaney	2	0	14	0
Wagg	4	0	31	1	Patel	7	0	21	3

Umpires: P.J.Hartley and R.A.Kettleborough

SEMI-FINALS

At The Rose Bowl, Southampton, on 7 September. Toss: Hampshire. **GLAMORGAN** won by 31 runs. Glamorgan 234-4 (40; J.Allenby 74*). Hampshire 203-8 (40; J.H.K.Adams 59, S.M.Ervine 54, M.G.Hogan 4-51). Award: J.Allenby.

At Trent Bridge, Nottingham, on 9 September. Toss: Nottinghamshire. **NOTTINGHAM-SHIRE** won by eight wickets. Somerset 119 (25.4; J.T.Ball 4-25, S.J.Mullaney 3-35). Nottinghamshire 122-2 (16.2). Award: J.T.Ball.

1969	Lancashire	1984	Essex	1999	Lancashire
1970	Lancashire	1985	Essex	2000	Gloucestershire
1971	Worcestershire	1986	Hampshire	2001	Kent
1972	Kent	1987	Worcestershire	2002	Glamorgan
1973	Kent	1988	Worcestershire	2003	Surrey
1974	Leicestershire	1989	Lancashire	2004	Glamorgan
1975	Hampshire	1990	Derbyshire	2005	Essex
1976	Kent	1991	Nottinghamshire	2006	Essex
1977	Leicestershire	1992	Middlesex	2007	Worcestershire
1978	Hampshire	1993	Glamorgan	2008	Sussex
1979	Somerset	1994	Warwickshire	2009	Sussex
1980	Warwickshire	1995	Kent	2010	Warwickshire
1981	Essex	1996	Surrey	2011	Surrey
1982	Sussex	1997	Warwickshire	2012	Hampshire
1983	Yorkshire	1998	Lancashire	2013	Nottinghamshire

PRINCIPAL 40-OVER RECORDS 1969-2013

Highest Total		399-4	Sussex v Worcs	Horsham	2011
Highest Total Batting Second		337-7	Kent v Sussex	Canterbury	2013
Lowest Total		23	Middlesex v Yorks	Leeds	1974
Largest Victory (Runs)		249	Somerset beat Glamorgan	Taunton	2010
Highest Scores	203	A.D.Brown	Surrey v Hampshire	Guildford	1997
	191	D.S.Lehmann	Yorkshire v Notts	Scarborough	2001
	184	M.E.Trescothick	Somerset v Glos	Taunton	2008
	180	R.N.ten Doeschate	Essex v Scotland	Chelmsford	2013
Fastest Hundred	44balls	M.A.Ealham	Kent v Derbyshire	Maidstone	1995
	44balls	T.C.Smith	Lancashire v Worcestershire	Worcester	2012
	44balls	D.I.Stevens	Kent v Sussex	Canterbury	2013
Most Sixes (Inns)	15	R.N.ten Doeschate	Essex v Scotland	Chelmsford	2013

Highest Partnership for each Wicket

1st	239	G.A.Gooch/B.R.Hardie	Essex v Notts	Nottingham	1985
2nd	302	M.E.Trescothick/C.Kieswetter	Somerset v Glos	Taunton	2008
3rd	228*	M.W.Goodwin/C.J.Adams	Sussex v Middlesex	Hove	2003
4th	230	H.D.Rutherford/R.N.ten Doeschate	Essex v Scotland	Chelmsford	2013
5th	221*	R.R.Sarwan/M.A.Hardinges	Glos v Lancashire	Manchester	2005
6th	167	C.L.Cairns/C.M.W.Read	Notts v Sussex	Nottingham	2003
7th	164	J.N.Snape/M.A.Hardinges	Glos v Notts	Nottingham	2001
8th	116*	N.D.Burns/P.A.J.DeFreitas	Leics v Northants	Leicester	2001
9th	105	D.G.Moir/R.W.Taylor	Derbyshire v Kent	Derby	1984
10th	82	G.Chapple/P.J.Martin	Lancashire v Worcs	Manchester	1996

Best Bowling	8-26	K.D.Boyce	Essex v Lancashire	Manchester	1971
	7-15	R.A.Hutton	Yorkshire v Worcs	Leeds	1969
	7-16	S.D.Thomas	Glamorgan v Surrey	Swansea	1998
	7-29	D.A.Payne	Gloucestershire v Essex	Chelmsford	2010
	7-30	M.P.Bicknell	Surrey v Glamorgan	The Oval	1999
	7-32	G.R.Napier	Essex v Surrey	Chelmsford	2013
	7-39	A.Hodgson	Northants v Somerset	Northampton	1976
	7-41	A.N.Jones	Sussex v Notts	Nottingham	1986
Four Wkts in Four Balls		A.Ward	Derbyshire v Sussex	Derby	1970
		V.C.Drakes	Notts v Derbys	Nottingham	1999
		D.A.Payne	Gloucestershire v Essex	Chelmsford	2010

Most Economical Analysis

8-8-0-0	B.A.Langford	Somerset v Essex	Yeovil	1969

Most Expensive Analysis

8-0-100-0	D.S.Harrison	Glamorgan v Somerset	Taunton	2010

Most Wicket-Keeping Dismissals in an Innings

7 (6 ct, 1 st)	R.W.Taylor	Derbyshire v Lancs	Manchester	1975

Most Catches in an Innings by a Fielder

5	J.M.Rice	Hampshire v Warwicks	Southampton	1978
5	D.J.G.Sales	Northants v Essex	Northampton	2007

FRIENDS LIFE t20 2013

In 2013, the Twenty20 competition was sponsored by Friends Life. Between 2003 and 2009, three regional leagues competed to qualify for the knockout stages, but this was reduced to two leagues in 2010, before returning to the three-division format in 2012. (2012's positions in brackets.)

MIDLANDS/WALES/WEST GROUP

	P	W	L	T	NR	Pts	Net RR
Northamptonshire (6)	10	7	3	–	–	14	+0.32
Somerset (1)	10	6	4	–	–	12	+0.84
Glamorgan (5)	10	5	5	–	–	10	–0.16
Warwickshire (4)	10	5	5	–	–	10	–0.41
Worcestershire (3)	10	4	6	–	–	8	–0.32
Gloucestershire (2)	10	3	7	–	–	6	–0.24

NORTH GROUP

	P	W	L	T	NR	Pts	Net RR
Nottinghamshire (2)	10	7	3	–	–	14	+1.00
Lancashire (4)	10	5	3	2	–	12	+0.17
Durham (3)*	10	6	4	–	–	11.75	+0.31
Leicestershire (6)	10	4	5	1	–	9	+0.41
Derbyshire (5)	10	4	6	–	–	8	–0.60
Yorkshire (1)	10	2	7	1	–	5	–1.22

SOUTH

	P	W	L	T	NR	Pts	Net RR
Hampshire (2)	10	8	1	–	1	17	+0.81
Surrey (6)	10	7	3	–	–	14	+0.91
Essex (3)	10	5	4	–	1	11	–0.04
Middlesex (5)	10	5	5	–	–	10	–0.19
Kent (4)	10	3	7	–	–	6	–0.94
Sussex (1)	10	1	9	–	–	2	–0.52

* Durham were deducted 0.25 points for a breach of the salary cap in 2012.

QUARTER-FINALS: SURREY beat Somerset by three wickets at The Oval.
NORTHAMPTONSHIRE beat Durham by 36 runs at Northampton.
HAMPSHIRE beat Lancashire by 1 run at Southampton.
NOTTINGHAMSHIRE beat Essex by 47 runs at Nottingham.

SEMI-FINALS: NORTHAMPTONSHIRE beat Essex by seven wickets at Birmingham.
SURREY beat Hampshire by four wickets at Birmingham.

LEADING AGGREGATES AND RECORDS 2013

BATTING (500 runs)

		M	I	NO	HS	Runs	Avg	100	50	R/100b	Sixes
C.Kieswetter	(Somerset)	11	11	3	89*	517	64.62	–	5	137.1	19
M.A.Carberry	(Hampshire)	12	11	2	100*	502	55.77	1	4	142.6	16

BOWLING (20 wkts)

		O	M	R	W	Avge	BB	4w	R/Over
Azhar Ullah	(Northants)	45.5	1	341	27	12.62	4-14	3	7.44
R.J.W.Topley	(Essex)	37.0	–	278	21	13.23	4-26	2	7.51
D.J.Willey	(Northants)	42.3	1	280	21	13.33	4- 9	2	6.58
Yasir Arafat	(Somerset)	41.1	1	292	20	14.60	4- 5	1	7.09

Highest total	215-6	Durham v Yorkshire	Chester-le-Street
Highest innings	110*	R.E.Levi	Northamptonshire v Glos	Bristol
Best bowling	5-14	G.G.Wagg	Glamorgan v Worcestershire	Worcester
Most economical	4-0-9-3	J.J.Cobb	Leicestershire v Yorkshire	Leicester
	4-1-9-2	Azhar Mahmood	Surrey v Hampshire	Birmingham
Most expensive	4-0-57-0	D.T.Christian	Gloucestershire v Somerset	Taunton
Most w/k dismissals	4	A.M.Rossington	Middlesex v Essex	Chelmsford

2013 FRIENDS LIFE t20 FINAL

NORTHAMPTONSHIRE v SURREY

At Edgbaston, Birmingham, on 17 August (floodlit).

Result: NORTHAMPTONSHIRE won by 102 runs (D/L method).

Toss: Surrey. Award: D.J.Willey.

NORTHAMPTONSHIRE		Runs	Balls	4/6	Fall
R.E.Levi	b Mahmood	14	13	1/1	1-37
D.J.Willey	c Wilson b Lewis	60	27	6/4	2-87
C.L.White	not out	54	39	2/2	
* A.G.Wakely	not out	59	30	7/2	
S.P.Crook					
B.M.Duckett					
M.N.W.Spriegel					
J.D.Middlebrook					
† D.Murphy					
L.M.Daggett					
Azhar Ullah					
Extras	(LB 1, W 4, NB 2)	7			
Total	**(2 wkts; 18 overs)**	**194**			

SURREY		Runs	Balls	4/6	Fall
J.J.Roy	b Willey	13	12	2	1-17
† S.M.Davies	run out	8	7	1	2-39
G.J.Maxwell	c Murphy b Crook	29	17	2/3	3-53
* V.S.Solannki	c Duckett b Middlebrook	12	15	1	6-72
Azhar Mahmood	c Willey b Azhar Ullah	2	4	–	4-59
Z.de Bruyn	c White b Daggett	4	4	–	5-70
G.C.Wilson	b Crook	14	11	1/1	7-92
Z.S.Ansari	c Crook b Willey	6	8	-	8-92
J.Lewis	c Middlebrook b Willey	0	2	–	9-92
C.T.Tremlett	c Murphy b Willey	0	1	–	10-92
J.W.Dernbach	not out	0	–	–	
Extras	(LB 3, W 1)	4			
Total	**(13.3 overs)**	**92**			

SURREY	O	M	R	W	NORTHAMPTONSHIRE	O	M	R	W
Ansari	1	0	1	0	Willey	2.3	0	9	4
Azhar Mahmood	4	0	53	0	Crook	3	0	26	2
Tremlett	3	0	29	0	Azhar Ullah	3	0	30	1
Dernbach	4	0	55	0	Daggett	2	0	5	1
Lewis	3	0	24	1	Middlebrook	3	0	19	1
De Bruyn	3	0	31	0					

Umpires: M.A.Gough and N.A.Mallender

TWENTY20 CUP WINNERS

2003	Surrey	2007	Kent	2011	Leicestershire
2004	Leicestershire	2008	Middlesex	2012	Hampshire
2005	Somerset	2009	Sussex	2013	Northamptonshire
2006	Leicestershire	2010	Hampshire		

PRINCIPAL TWENTY20 CUP RECORDS 2003-13

Highest Total	254-3		Gloucestershire v Middx	Uxbridge	2011
Highest Total Batting 2nd	222-3		Northants v Worcs	Kidderminster	2007
Lowest Total	47		Northants v Durham	Chester-le-St	2011
Largest Victory (Runs)	143		Somerset v Essex	Chelmsford	2011
Largest Victory (Balls)	75		Hampshire v Glos	Bristol	2010
Highest Scores	152*	G.R.Napier	Essex v Sussex	Chelmsford	2008
	141*	C.L.White	Somerset v Worcs	Worcester	2006
	124*	M.J.Lumb	Hampshire v Essex	Southampton	2009
	119	K.J.O'Brien	Gloucestershire v Middx	Uxbridge	2011
Fastest Hundred	34 balls	A.Symonds	Kent v Middlesex	Maidstone	2004
Most Sixes (Innings)	16	G.R.Napier	Essex v Sussex	Chelmsford	2008
Most Runs in Career	2476	D.I.Stevens	Kent, Leicestershire		2003-13

Highest Partnership for each Wicket

1st	192	K.J.O'Brien/H.J.H.Marshall	Gloucestershire v Middx	Uxbridge	2011
2nd	186	J.L.Langer/C.L.White	Somerset v Glos	Taunton	2006
3rd	144*	J.H.K.Adams/S.M.Ervine	Hampshire v Surrey	Southampton	2010
4th	139	M.R.Ramprakash/R.Clarke	Surrey v Glos	Bristol	2006
5th	117*	M.N.W.Spriegel/G.C.Wilson	Surrey v Middlesex	Lord's	2012
6th	98*	R.W.T.Key/M.J.Walker	Kent v Middlesex	Beckenham	2006
7th	67	O.A.C.Banks/B.J.Phillips	Somerset v Northants	Northampton	2008
8th	68	M.W.Alleyne/J.Lewis	Glos v Glamorgan	Cardiff	2005
9th	59*	G.Chapple/P.J.Martin	Lancashire v Leics	Leicester	2003
9th	59*	D.J.Willey/J.A.Brooks	Northants v Warwickshire	Birmingham	2011
10th	59	H.H.Streak/J.E.Anyon	Warwickshire v Worcs	Birmingham	2005
Best Bowling	6-5	A.V.Suppiah	Somerset v Glamorgan	Cardiff	2011
	6-16	T.G.Southee	Essex v Glamorgan	Chelmsford	2011
	6-21	A.J.Hall	Northants v Worcs	Northampton	2008
	6-24	T.J.Murtagh	Surrey v Middlesex	Lord's	2005
Most Wkts in Career	121	Yasir Arafat	Kent, Lancashire, Somerset, Surrey, Sussex		2003-13

Most Economical Innings Analyses (Qualification: 4 overs)

4-2-5-2	A.C.Thomas	Somerset v Hampshire	Southampton	2010
4-0-5-3	D.R.Briggs	Hampshire v Kent	Canterbury	2010
4-1-6-2	J.Louw	Northants v Warwicks	Birmingham	2004
4-0-6-1	M.W.Alleyne	Glos v Worcs	Worcester	2005

Most Maiden Overs in an Innings

4-2-9-1	M.Morkel	Kent v Surrey	Beckenham	2007
4-2-5-2	A.C.Thomas	Somerset v Hampshire	Southampton	2010

Most Expensive Innings Analyses

4-0-67-1	R.J.Kirtley	Sussex v Essex	Chelmsford	2008
4-0-65-2	M.J.Hoggard	Yorkshire v Lancs	Leeds	2005
4-0-64-0	Abdul Razzaq	Hampshire v Somerset	Taunton	2010
4-0-63-1	R.J.Kirtley	Sussex v Surrey	Hove	2004

Most Wicket-Keeping Dismissals in an Innings

5 (5 ct)	M.J.Prior	Sussex v Middlesex	Richmond	2006
5 (4 ct, 1 st)	G.L.Brophy	Yorkshire v Durham	Chester-le-St	2008
5 (3 ct, 2 st)	B.J.M.Scott	Worcs v Yorkshire	Worcester	2011

Most Catches in an Innings by a Fielder

4	D.Pretorius	Warwicks v Glamorgan	Swansea	2005
4	W.R.Smith	Notts v Surrey	Nottingham	2006
4	D.J.G.Sales	Northants v Worcs	Northampton	2008
4	G.D.Elliott	Surrey v Kent	The Oval	2009
4	G.R.Breese	Durham v Yorkshire	Scarborough	2011

YOUNG CRICKETER OF THE YEAR

This annual award, made by The Cricket Writers' Club, is currently restricted to players qualified for England, Andrew Symonds meeting that requirement at the time of his award, and under the age of 23 on 1st May. In 1986 their ballot resulted in a dead heat. Up to 1 April 2014 their selections have gained a tally of 2,328 international Test match caps (shown in brackets).

Year	Name	Year	Name	Year	Name
1950	R.Tattersall (16)	1972	D.R.Owen-Thomas	1993	M.N.Lathwell (2)
1951	P.B.H.May (66)	1973	M.Hendrick (30)	1994	J.P.Crawley (37)
1952	F.S.Trueman (67)	1974	P.H.Edmonds (51)	1995	A.Symonds (26 – Australia)
1953	M.C.Cowdrey (114)	1975	A.Kennedy	1996	C.E.W.Silverwood (6)
1954	P.J.Loader (13)	1976	G.Miller (34)	1997	B.C.Hollioake (2)
1955	K.F.Barrington (82)	1977	I.T.Botham (102)	1998	A.Flintoff (79)
1956	B.Taylor	1978	D.I.Gower (117)	1999	A.J.Tudor (10)
1957	M.J.Stewart (8)	1979	P.W.G.Parker (1)	2000	P.J.Franks
1958	A.C.D.Ingleby-Mackenzie	1980	G.R.Dilley (41)	2001	O.A.Shah (6)
1959	G.Pullar (28)	1981	M.W.Gatting (79)	2002	R.Clarke (2)
1960	D.A.Allen (39)	1982	N.G.Cowans (19)	2003	J.M.Anderson (92)
1961	P.H.Parfitt (37)	1983	N.A.Foster (29)	2004	I.R.Bell (98)
1962	P.J.Sharpe (12)	1984	R.J.Bailey (4)	2005	A.N.Cook (102)
1963	G.Boycott (108)	1985	D.V.Lawrence (5)	2006	S.C.J.Broad (67)
1964	J.M.Brearley (39)	1986 {	A.A.Metcalfe	2007	A.U.Rashid
1965	A.P.E.Knott (95)		J.J.Whitaker (1)	2008	R.S.Bopara (13)
1966	D.L.Underwood (86)	1987	R.J.Blakey (2)	2009	J.W.A.Taylor (2)
1967	A.W.Greig (58)	1988	M.P.Maynard (4)	2010	S.T.Finn (23)
1968	R.M.H.Cottam (4)	1989	N.Hussain (96)	2011	J.M.Bairstow (14)
1969	A.Ward (5)	1990	M.A.Atherton (115)	2012	J.E.Root (15)
1970	C.M.Old (46)	1991	M.R.Ramprakash (52)	2013	B.A.Stokes (4)
1971	J.Whitehouse	1992	I.D.K.Salisbury (15)		

THE PROFESSIONAL CRICKETERS' ASSOCIATION

PLAYER OF THE YEAR

Founded in 1967, the Professional Cricketers' Association introduced this award, decided by their membership, in 1970. The NatWest-sponsored award is presented at the PCA's Annual Awards Dinner in London.

Year	Name	Year	Name	Year	Name
1970 {	M.J.Procter	1984	R.J.Hadlee	1999	S.G.Law
	J.D.Bond	1985	N.V.Radford	2000	M.E.Trescothick
1971	L.R.Gibbs	1986	C.A.Walsh	2001	D.P.Fulton
1972	A.M.E.Roberts	1987	R.J.Hadlee	2002	M.P.Vaughan
1973	P.G.Lee	1988	G.A.Hick	2003	Mushtaq Ahmed
1974	B.Stead	1989	S.J.Cook	2004	A.Flintoff
1975	Zaheer Abbas	1990	G.A.Gooch	2005	A.Flintoff
1976	P.G.Lee	1991	Waqar Younis	2006	M.R.Ramprakash
1977	M.J.Procter	1992	C.A.Walsh	2007	O.D.Gibson
1978	J.K.Lever	1993	S.L.Watkin	2008	M.van Jaarsveld
1979	J.K.Lever	1994	B.C.Lara	2009	M.E.Trescothick
1980	R.D.Jackman	1995	D.G.Cork	2010	N.M.Carter
1981	R.J.Hadlee	1996	P.V.Simmons	2011	M.E.Trescothick
1982	M.D.Marshall	1997	S.P.James	2012	N.R.D.Compton
1983	K.S.McEwan	1998	M.B.Loye	2013	M.M.Ali

2013 FIRST-CLASS AVERAGES

These averages involve the 495 players who appeared in the 169 first-class matches played by 29 teams in England and Wales during the 2013 season.

'Cap' denotes the season in which the player was awarded a 1st XI cap by the county he represented in 2013. If he played for more than one county in 2013, the county(ies) who awarded him his cap is (are) underlined. Durham abolished both their capping and 'awards' system after the 2005 season. Glamorgan's capping system is based on a player's number of appearances. Gloucestershire now cap players on first-class debut. Worcestershire now award county colours when players make their Championship debut.

Team abbreviations: A – Australia(ns); AA – Australia A; CU – Cambridge University/ Cambridge MCCU; CfU – Cardiff MCCU; De – Derbyshire; Du – Durham; DU – Durham MCCU; E – England; EL – England Lions; Ex – Essex; Gm – Glamorgan; Gs – Gloucestershire; H – Hampshire; K – Kent; La – Lancashire; LBU – Leeds/Bradford MCCU; Le – Leicestershire; LU – Loughborough MCCU; M – Middlesex; Nh – Northamptonshire; Nt – Nottinghamshire; NZ – New Zealand(ers); OU – Oxford University/Oxford MCCU; Sm – Somerset; Sy – Surrey; Sx – Sussex; Wa – Warwickshire; Wo – Worcestershire; Y – Yorkshire.

† Left-handed batsman. Cap: a dash (–) denotes a non-county player. A blank denotes uncapped by his current county.

BATTING AND FIELDING

	Cap	M	I	NO	HS	Runs	Avge	100	50	Ct/St
A.R.Adams (Nt)	2007	11	15	2	80	354	27.23	–	2	3
† J.H.K.Adams (H)	2006	17	26	4	213*	990	45.00	3	3	7
† A.C.Agar (A/AA)	–	5	7	2	98	175	35.00	–	1	1
S.S.Agarwal (OU)	–	3	5	1	313*	460	115.00	2	–	2
A.P.Agathangelou (La)		11	6	2	121	497	35.50	1	2	24
† M.M.Ali (Wo)	2007	17	29	5	250	1420	59.16	4	8	22
† S.A.Ali (Wa)		1	2	–	8	10	5.00	–	–	–
A.T.A.Allchin (CU)	–	1	1	–	0	0	0.00	–	–	–
J.Allenby (Gm)	2010	16	25	3	138*	1202	60.10	2	8	28
T.W.Allin (Wa)		1	1	–	0	0	0.00	–	–	–
T.R.Ambrose (Wa)	2007	14	22	2	105	747	37.35	1	6	42/1
H.M.Amla (Sy)		6	10	–	151	545	54.50	1	4	1
† J.M.Anderson (E/La)	2003	9	13	4	26	80	8.88	–	–	6
† G.M.Andrew (Wo)	2008	11	15	–	66	311	20.73	–	3	6
A.S.Ansari (CU)	–	3	6	–	31	72	12.00	–	–	1
† Z.S.Ansari (CU/Sy)		8	12	3	72	222	24.66	–	1	3
† J.E.Anyon (Sx)	2011	14	17	6	25	159	14.45	–	–	1
U.Arshad (Du)		5	6	–	83	170	28.33	–	1	1
† Ashar Zaidi (Sx)		2	2	–	45	62	31.00	–	–	1
M.A.Ashraf (Y)		2	–	–				–	–	–
J.J.Atkinson (Wa)		1	–	–				–	–	–
Azeem Rafiq (Y)		3	5	–	28	58	11.60	–	–	–
Azhar Ullah (Nh)		9	10	6	8	12	3.00	–	–	3
G.J.Bailey (H)		5	7	–	93	263	37.57	–	2	3
J.M.Bairstow (E/EL/Y)	2011	16	26	1	186	955	38.20	1	5	34
G.C.Baker (LU)	–	2	3	–	52	131	43.66	–	1	–
A.Balbirnie (CfU)	–	2	2	–	15	19	9.50	–	1	2
D.J.Balcombe (H)		12	13	2	30*	106	9.63	–	–	1
A.J.Ball (K)		2	3	–	69	108	36.00	–	1	–
J.T.Ball (Nt)		1	1	–	15	15	15.00	–	–	–
† G.S.Ballance (Y)	2012	15	22	1	148	1363	64.90	6	6	13

225

	Cap	M	I	NO	HS	Runs	Avge	100	50	Ct/St
† K.H.D.Barker (Wa)	2013	11	13	2	125	350	31.81	1	–	4
A.W.R.Barrow (Sm)		10	17	1	83*	378	23.62	–	2	12
M.D.Bates (H)		6	4	–	71	117	29.25	–	1	18
G.J.Batty (Sy)	2011	13	18	2	41	313	19.56	–	–	6
J.N.Batty (Nh)		1	1	–	12	12	12.00	–	–	–
W.A.T.Beer (Sx)		3	6	–	39	106	17.66	–	–	2
D.W.Bell (CU)		2	4	1	47	58	19.33	–	–	5/1
I.R.Bell (E/Wa)	2001	9	16	1	113	753	50.20	3	4	7
D.J.Bell-Drummond (K)		14	21	1	102*	568	28.40	1	4	7
D.M.Benkenstein (Du)	2005	6	11	2	74*	267	29.66	–	2	5
G.K.Berg (M)	2010	15	23	2	71	501	23.85	–	2	8
S.W.Billings (K)		2	3	–	24	45	15.00	–	–	4/1
J.M.Bird (A/AA)	–	4	3	2	6	7	7.00	–	–	–
† C.Bishnoi (DU)	–	2	4	–	60	139	34.75	–	2	2
† C.J.Bodenstein (OU)	–	2	4	–	27	32	8.00	–	–	1
R.S.Bopara (EL/Ex)	2005	9	14	1	145	443	34.07	1	2	6
P.M.Borrington (De)		4	8	–	75	209	26.12	–	1	2
S.G.Borthwick (Du)		17	29	3	135	1121	41.51	3	6	29
T.A.Boult (NZ)	–	3	5	2	24*	28	9.66	–	–	1
† M.A.G.Boyce (Le)	2013	15	23	1	135	677	30.77	1	2	8
D.A.J.Bracewell (NZ)	–	3	3	–	19	24	8.00	–	–	1
† W.D.Bragg (Gm)		15	26	2	71*	660	27.50	–	4	4
R.M.R.Brathwaite (H)		3	2	–	17	26	13.00	–	–	1
G.R.Breese (Du)		3	6	2	44	110	27.50	–	–	7
T.T.Bresnan (E/Y)	2006	7	10	3	45	169	21.12	–	–	1
D.R.Briggs (H)	2012	13	12	3	54	244	27.11	–	1	6
† S.C.J.Broad (E/Nt)	2008	9	13	1	65	302	25.16	–	1	4
J.A.Brooks (Y)	2013	12	14	7	33*	100	14.28	–	–	6
B.C.Brown (Sx)		16	23	6	93	705	41.47	–	6	61/3
† K.R.Brown (La)		10	16	–	87	428	26.75	–	3	8
† N.L.J.Browne (Ex)		3	5	1	22*	26	6.50	–	–	1
D.G.Brownlie (NZ)	–	4	7	1	71	176	29.33	–	1	8
N.L.Buck (Le)	2011	4	3	2	16*	37	37.00	–	–	–
R.S.Buckley (Du)		2	2	–	6	10	5.00	–	–	1
P.I.Burgoyne (De)		5	9	1	62*	168	21.00	–	1	2
J.A.Burns (Le)		5	8	1	77	214	30.57	–	1	4
† R.J.Burns (Sy)		16	27	1	115	917	35.26	2	4	13
J.C.Buttler (Sm)	2013	9	15	1	119*	508	36.28	1	2	16
† M.A.Carberry (EL/H)	2006	13	19	–	154	889	46.78	2	6	6
A.Carter (Nt)		1	2	2	0*	0	–	–	–	–
S.J.Cato (OU)	–	1	1	–	33	33	33.00	–	–	–
G.Cessford (Wo)	2013	6	6	2	20	45	11.25	–	–	1
T.R.Chadwick (OU)	–	1	1	–	15	15	15.00	–	–	2
M.A.Chambers (Ex/Wa)		7	6	–	58	84	14.00	–	1	2
† S.Chanderpaul (De)		15	27	4	129	884	38.43	1	7	8
G.Chapple (La)	1994	14	16	3	63	308	23.69	–	3	9
† P.P.Chawla (Sm)		4	6	–	112	231	38.50	1	–	1
V.Chopra (EL/Wa)	2012	17	28	4	228*	1099	45.79	3	5	29
S.H.Choudhry (Wo)	2010	7	10	3	61*	167	23.85	–	1	1
D.T.Christian (Gs)	2013	1	2	–	46	47	23.50	–	–	1
J.L.Clare (De)	2012	6	12	1	49	130	11.81	–	–	8
M.J.Clarke (A)	–	7	14	2	187	638	53.16	2	2	10

	Cap	M	I	NO	HS	Runs	Avge	100	50	Ct/St
R.Clarke (Wa)	2011	13	18	4	92	449	32.07	–	4	19
† M.E.Claydon (Du/K)		4	6	2	40	123	30.75	–	–	2
J.J.Cobb (Le)		12	20	2	46*	258	14.33	–	–	6
I.A.Cockbain (Gs)	2011	1	2	–	2	2	1.00	–	–	1
† K.J.Coetzer (Nh)	2013	10	15	1	219	527	37.64	2	1	3
F.R.J.Coleman (OU)		2	4	–	46	62	15.50	–	–	–
M.T.Coles (H/K)	2012	12	14	2	68	254	21.16	–	3	7
P.D.Collingwood (Du)	1998	15	25	3	88*	646	29.36	–	5	20
C.D.Collymore (M)	2011	10	11	5	6*	22	3.66	–	–	3
N.R.D.Compton (E/Sm/Wo)	2011	16	31	3	166	1260	45.00	2	9	6
† A.N.Cook (E/Ex)	2005	9	18	–	130	651	36.16	1	5	12
C.B.Cooke (Gm)		7	11	1	92	394	39.40	–	3	2
T.A.Copeland (Nh)		10	10	3	70	247	35.28	–	2	11
J.P.P.Cornick (LU)	–	2	3	–	10	11	3.66	–	–	1
D.A.Cosker (Gm)	2000	16	22	7	44*	286	19.06	–	–	7
† E.J.M.Cowan (A/Nt)	2013	11	21	3	81	776	43.11	–	7	5
† J.D.Cowan (CU)		1	2	–	7	8	4.00	–	–	–
F.K.Cowdrey (CfU)		2	3	1	62	100	50.00	–	1	–
O.B.Cox (Wo)	2009	8	13	5	65	287	35.87	–	2	25/1
† R.D.Cox (DU)		2	2	–	15	20	10.00	–	–	–
T.R.Craddock (Ex)		3	3	–	20	24	8.00	–	–	–
S.J.Croft (La)	2010	8	13	3	101*	379	37.90	1	2	4
S.P.Crook (Nh)	2013	14	15	3	88*	482	40.16	–	5	3
G.D.Cross (La)		13	17	–	100	409	24.05	1	2	35/2
M.H.Cross (LU)	–	2	3	–	29	61	20.33	–	–	5
L.M.Daggett (Nh)	2013	3	2	–	11	12	6.00	–	–	1
A.L.Davies (La)		3	3	1	30*	58	29.00	–	–	3
M.Davies (K)		11	15	4	41	158	14.36	–	–	–
S.L.Davies (CfU)	–	2	2	–	31	35	17.50	–	–	2
† S.M.Davies (Sy)	2011	15	23	4	147	867	45.63	2	3	24/3
S.R.Davison (OU)	–	2	4	–	13	26	6.50	–	–	7
L.A.Dawson (H)	2013	17	26	4	136*	1060	48.18	1	8	24
Z.de Bruyn (Sy)		14	23	–	111	571	24.82	1	1	16
J.L.Denly (M)	2012	17	30	3	97	662	24.51	–	4	6
J.S.T.Denning (CfU)	–	2	2	2	22*	28	–	–	–	1
† C.D.J.Dent (Gs)	2010	16	27	2	153	1128	45.12	2	7	20
J.W.Dernbach (Sy)	2011	10	14	5	22	58	6.44	–	–	–
N.J.Dexter (M)	2010	17	28	2	104	807	31.03	1	4	12
G.H.Dockrell (Sm)		8	12	2	31	106	10.60	–	–	2
D.A.D'Souza (LU)	–	2	3	–	23	37	12.33	–	–	–
† B.M.Duckett (Nh)		4	6	1	53*	145	29.00	–	1	4
† M.P.Dunn (Sy)		1	–	–	–	–	–	–	–	–
W.J.Durston (De)	2012	10	18	1	50	317	18.64	–	1	8
E.J.H.Eckersley (Le)	2013	17	29	3	147	1302	50.07	4	4	8
G.A.Edwards (Sy)		1	1	–	0	0	0.00	–	–	–
† D.Elgar (Sm)		3	5	–	33	123	24.60	–	–	2
Z.W.Elkin (CfU)	–	2	3	–	23	28	9.33	–	–	2
T.C.Elliott (CU)	–	3	6	1	101	183	36.60	1	–	4
C.P.Ellison (OU)	–	1	2	–	36	43	21.50	–	–	1
D.M.Endersby (LU)	–	2	3	–	22	36	12.00	–	–	1
† S.M.Ervine (H)	2005	15	19	1	86	458	25.44	–	4	20
A.C.Evans (De)		2	4	3	6*	13	13.00	–	–	–

227

	Cap	M	I	NO	HS	Runs	Avge	100	50	Ct/St
L.J.Evans (Wa)		14	21	2	178	950	50.00	3	4	8
J.P.Faulkner (A)	–	4	6	3	48	127	42.33	–	–	1
Fawad Ahmed (AA)	–	1	1	1	4*	4	–	–	–	2
T.C.Fell (OU/Wo)	2013	10	16	2	94*	477	34.07	–	3	3
H.Z.Finch (Sx)		1	2	–	11	14	7.00	–	–	1
S.T.Finn (E/M)	2009	9	12	2	8	33	3.30	–	–	4
L.J.Fletcher (Nt)		15	22	3	64	368	19.36	–	2	5
B.T.Foakes (Ex)		15	20	2	120	639	35.50	2	3	11
M.H.A.Footitt (De)		13	22	5	24	153	9.00	–	–	3
J.S.Foster (Ex)	2001	17	26	3	143	883	38.39	1	6	49/1
† P.J.Franks (Nt)	1999	9	12	–	78	323	26.91	–	3	3
O.H.Freckingham (Le)		15	21	2	30	204	10.73	–	–	4
J.K.Fuller (Gs)	2011	8	8	–	42	122	15.25	–	–	2
P.G.Fulton (NZ)	–	4	7	–	28	67	9.57	–	–	1
† A.W.Gale (Y)	2008	17	26	1	272	1076	43.04	3	3	5
† G.Gambhir (Ex)		5	7	–	106	239	34.14	1	–	4
J.S.Gatting (Sx)		5	6	–	61	119	19.83	–	1	3
A.P.R.Gidman (Gs)	2004	16	22	–	211	1125	51.13	3	5	12
† W.R.S.Gidman (Gs)	2011	14	17	4	143	439	33.76	1	1	3
M.R.Gillespie (NZ)	–	1	1	–	–	–	–	–	–	1
J.C.Glover (Gm)		8	10	2	51*	127	15.87	–	1	1
† B.A.Godleman (De)		9	16	–	55	275	17.18	–	1	3
M.W.Goodwin (Gm)		16	26	4	194	1263	57.40	4	7	7
R.O.Gordon (Wa)		4	4	1	13	38	12.66	–	–	2
M.J.E.Green (DU)	–	1	1	1	0*	0	–	–	–	
L.Gregory (Sm)		6	8	1	52	141	20.14	–	1	3
† D.A.Griffiths (H)		3	2	–	14	15	7.50	–	–	–
T.D.Groenewald (De)	2011	15	26	5	49	231	11.00	–	–	7
† N.R.T.Gubbins (LBU)	–	2	4	–	14	40	10.00	–	–	1
† M.J.Guptill (NZ)	–	2	4	–	25	37	9.25	–	–	3
H.F.Gurney (Nt)		15	19	11	22*	62	7.75	–	–	4
B.J.Haddin (A)	–	7	12	2	71	296	29.60	–	3	33/1
† C.J.Haggett (K)		12	14	7	44*	249	35.57	–	–	3
A.D.Hales (Nt)	2011	10	18	–	58	251	13.94	–	2	10
A.J.Hall (Nh)	2009	16	21	4	130*	936	55.05	3	5	13
R.J.Hamilton-Brown (Sx)		15	21	1	126*	683	34.15	2	3	3
† M.A.H.Hammond (Gs)	2013	2	2	–	4	4	2.00	–	–	1
† O.J.Hannon-Dalby (Wa)		3	4	2	13	37	18.50	–	–	–
A.Harinath (Sy)		12	21	2	154	584	30.73	1	4	4
† B.W.Harmison (K)		13	19	3	106	712	44.50	2	5	8
J.A.R.Harris (M)		10	13	4	43*	189	21.00	–	–	2
P.G.Harris (CfU)		2	2	1	11*	11	11.00	–	–	–
R.J.Harris (A/AA)	–	6	8	2	33	102	17.00	–	–	2
J.Harrison (Du)		4	4	–	35	60	15.00	–	–	–
† L.J.Hatchett (Sx)		5	6	1	21	42	8.40	–	–	–
A.G.Hearne (CU)	–	2	3	–	39	47	15.66	–	–	–
T.G.Helm (M)		1	2	–	18	22	11.00	–	–	–
C.W.Henderson (Le)	2004	2	4	–	33	48	12.00	–	–	–
C.L.Herring (Gs)	2013	6	7	–	43	122	17.42	–	–	14
M.R.Hickey (CU)	–	1	2	–	5	5	2.50	–	–	–
† M.Higginbottom (De)		4	7	1	9	29	4.83	–	–	–
J.C.Hildreth (Sm)	2007	17	31	2	161	1008	34.75	2	4	17

	Cap	M	I	NO	HS	Runs	Avge	100	50	Ct/St
M.E.Hobden (CfU)	–	2	1	–	18	18	18.00	–	–	–
I.H.Hobson (DU)	–	2	4	–	13	17	4.25	–	–	2
A.J.Hodd (Y)		9	9	2	68*	217	31.00	–	1	17/1
M.G.Hogan (Gm)	2013	14	18	3	51	297	19.80	–	1	5
† K.W.Hogg (La)	2010	15	16	5	58	241	21.90	–	1	2
M.J.Hoggard (Le)	2010	7	11	3	24	75	9.37	–	–	1
P.J.Horton (La)	2007	10	16	–	156	645	40.31	3	3	1
D.M.Housego (Gs)	2012	10	16	2	150	463	33.07	1	3	6
B.A.C.Howell (Gs)	2012	17	24	4	60	596	29.80	–	4	8
A.L.Hughes (De)		6	11	–	33	136	12.36	–	–	3
† C.F.Hughes (De)		12	22	1	270*	636	30.28	1	2	7
P.H.Hughes (CU)	–	1	2	–	92	113	56.50	–	1	–
† P.J.Hughes (A/AA)	–	6	12	3	86	494	54.88	–	5	5
M.D.Hunn (K)		1	1	–	0	0	0.00	–	–	1
G.M.Hussain (Sm)		4	4	4	12*	20	–	–	–	1
D.J.Hussey (Nt)	2004	9	13	–	125	478	36.76	1	3	2
B.A.Hutton (Nt)		1	2	1	42	62	62.00	–	–	1
A.J.Ireland (Le)		2	3	1	15*	28	14.00	–	–	1
C.F.Jackson (Sx)		1	1	–	26	26	26.00	–	–	1
P.A.Jaques (Y)	2005	14	21	–	152	770	36.66	2	3	5
K.M.Jarvis (La)		1	1	1	3*	3	–	–	–	1
A.Javid (Wa)		11	17	3	133	619	44.21	2	2	5
B.A.Jeffery (OU)	–	1	1	–	17	17	17.00	–	–	1
† K.K.Jennings (Du)		15	28	2	127	822	31.61	3	1	8
T.M.Jewell (Sy)		1	–	–	–	–	–	–	–	–
J.A.M.Johnson (CU)	–	2	4	–	22	38	9.50	–	–	2
M.A.Johnson (Wo)	2013	10	14	1	44	184	14.15	–	–	14
R.M.Johnson (De)		13	23	1	72	556	25.27	–	4	12
Alex J.Jones (Gm)		1	1	1	5*	5	–	–	–	–
C.R.Jones (DU/Sm)		9	17	1	130	394	24.62	1	2	4
G.O.Jones (K)	2003	15	20	2	67	404	22.44	–	2	40/1
† O.J.Jones (OU)	–	2	4	–	11	24	6.00	–	–	–
R.A.Jones (Wo)	2007	2	2	–	7	11	5.50	–	–	1
C.J.Jordan (Sx)		16	20	1	92	472	24.84	–	2	24
† E.C.Joyce (Sx)	2009	15	23	5	204*	1152	64.00	2	6	15
J.L.Joyce (CU)	–	1	2	1	25	27	27.00	–	–	1
A.Kapil (Wo)	2011	1	2	–	4	8	4.00	–	–	–
† S.M.Katich (La)	2013	12	16	1	200	1097	73.13	4	6	7
† G.Keedy (Sy)		6	6	4	2*	1	1.00	–	–	1
B.W.Kemp (OU)	–	2	4	2	11	20	10.00	–	–	1
A.D.J.Kennedy (OU)	–	1	1	–	25	25	25.00	–	–	–
R.I.Keogh (Nh)		8	12	2	221	458	45.80	1	1	1
S.C.Kerrigan (E/EL/La)	2013	15	12	6	62*	147	24.50	–	1	4
A.N.Kervezee (Wo)	2009	12	18	–	47	204	11.33	–	–	5
R.W.T.Key (K)	2001	17	28	3	180	1169	46.76	5	3	5
† U.T.Khawaja (A/AA)	–	6	12	1	73	290	26.36	–	2	5
C.Kieswetter (Sm)	2009	12	21	2	148	606	31.89	1	3	41/3
S.P.Kirby (Sm)		10	15	6	15	75	8.33	–	–	3
M.Klinger (Gs)	2013	16	26	3	163	1140	49.56	4	4	16
† T.W.M.Latham (NZ)		1	2	–	47*	68	–	–	–	1/1
J.Leach (Wo)	2012	7	10	3	114	315	45.00	1	2	1
† M.J.Leach (Sm)		5	9	2	21	66	9.42	–	–	–

	Cap	M	I	NO	HS	Runs	Avge	100	50	Ct/St
J.A.Leaning (Y)		1	1	–	0	0	0.00	–	–	–
† J.E.Lee (LBU)	–	2	4	–	34	63	15.75	–	–	1
† A.Z.Lees (Y)		9	16	3	275*	621	47.76	3	1	2
† T.J.Lester (LU)		2	3	2	1	1	1.00	–	–	–
J.Lewis (Sy)		2	1	1	2*	2	–	–	–	–
C.J.Liddle (Sx)		3	3	3	7*	12	–	–	–	1
A.M.Lilley (La)		2	2	2	35*	39	–	–	–	–
T.E.Linley (Sy)		12	14	1	22*	84	6.46	–	–	6
D.L.Lloyd (Gm)		1	1	–	16	16	16.00	–	–	–
† A.B.London (M)		3	4	–	81	130	32.50	–	1	5
D.S.Lucas (Wo)	2012	3	5	–	12	34	6.80	–	–	1
† M.J.Lumb (Nt)	2012	16	26	3	221*	1120	48.69	4	3	4
N.M.Lyon (A)	–	5	3	1	8	12	6.00	–	–	2
† A.Lyth (Y)	2010	17	29	4	111	850	34.00	2	4	27
G.J.McCarter (Gs)	2012	4	6	1	20	51	10.20	–	–	–
B.B.McCullum (NZ)	–	3	5	–	20	32	6.40	–	–	8
N.L.McCullum (Gm)		1	2	1	35*	49	49.00	–	–	–
† P.J.McKay (Wa)		2	4	1	33	45	15.00	–	–	–
N.D.McKenzie (H)	2010	6	10	1	146	433	48.11	1	2	1
C.A.R.Macleod (LBU)	–	2	4	–	15	27	6.75	–	–	5
A.MacQueen (LBU)	–	2	4	–	36	69	17.25	–	–	2
W.A.MacVicar (LU)	–	2	3	–	41	61	20.33	–	–	2
† M.W.Machan (Sx)		5	6	1	103	209	41.80	1	–	4
N.J.Maddinson (AA)	–	1	2	–	181	181	90.50	1	–	4
D.L.Maddy (Wa)	2007	3	5	1	65	157	39.25	–	1	1
W.L.Madsen (De)	2011	17	32	2	152	1239	41.30	3	8	11
† S.J.Magoffin (Sx)	2013	16	20	2	32	192	10.66	–	–	4
S.I.Mahmood (Ex)		4	6	–	54	112	18.66	–	1	3
† D.J.Malan (M)	2010	13	20	2	156*	543	30.16	1	2	19
W.W.J.Marriott (OU)	–	1	2	–	81	86	43.00	–	1	–
J.Marsden (OU)		1	–	–	–	–	–	–	–	–
H.J.H.Marshall (Gs)	2006	16	21	1	149	1007	50.35	4	2	5
B.P.Martin (NZ)	–	3	3	–	6	7	2.33	–	–	–
A.D.Mascarenhas (H)	1998	1	1	–	41	41	41.00	–	–	–
D.D.Masters (Ex)	2008	14	12	3	37*	95	10.55	–	–	3
S.C.Meaker (Sy)	2012	8	11	4	30*	80	11.42	–	–	–
C.A.J.Meschede (Sm)		10	15	1	59	192	13.71	–	1	6
J.C.Mickleburgh (Ex)	2013	13	21	1	243	829	41.45	2	4	3
J.D.Middlebrook (Nh)	2011	16	21	1	109	711	35.55	1	6	5
A.J.Miles (CfU)	–	2	2	1	29*	39	39.00	–	–	2
C.N.Miles (Gs)	2011	13	13	1	50*	161	13.41	–	1	1
A.S.Miller (Sx)		1	–	–	–	–	–	–	–	–
T.S.Mills (Ex)		6	6	3	17	53	17.66	–	–	1
T.P.Milnes (Wa)		8	9	1	52*	215	26.87	–	1	3
D.K.H.Mitchell (Wo)	2005	18	32	4	156	1061	37.89	2	6	21
S.C.Moore (La)	2011	2	4	–	34	81	20.25	–	–	–
† E.J.G.Morgan (M)	2008	2	4	1	39*	96	32.00	–	–	2
A.J.Morris (LU)	–	1	2	1	18*	26	26.00	–	–	1
C.A.J.Morris (OU/Wo)		3	5	3	33*	71	35.50	–	–	1
S.J.Mullaney (Nt)	2013	15	23	1	125	965	41.95	3	6	8
D.Murphy (Nh)		14	14	3	81	293	26.63	–	2	51/4
† T.J.Murtagh (M)	2008	13	15	4	29	112	10.18	–	–	4

	Cap	M	I	NO	HS	Runs	Avge	100	50	Ct/St
† P.Mustard (Du)		17	27	4	77	823	35.78	–	7	67/1
S.V.S.Mylavarapu (OU)		1	–							
J.K.H.Naik (Le)	2013	10	13	2	47*	127	11.54	–	–	8
G.R.Napier (Ex)	2003	17	23	7	102*	796	49.75	1	7	5
B.P.Nash (K)	2013	17	27	4	199*	1110	48.26	5	5	4
C.D.Nash (Sx)	2008	18	30	4	167*	1211	46.57	3	5	11
O.J.Newby (La)		3	2	1	9*	10	10.00	–	–	–
R.I.Newton (Nh)		6	8	2	81	251	41.83	–	1	1
G.F.Nicholson (CU)	–	1	1	–	1	1	1.00	–	–	–
M.J.North (Gm)		11	18	1	68	392	23.05	–	1	7
S.A.Northeast (K)	2012	16	27	1	94	664	25.53	–	6	11
L.C.Norwell (Gs)	2011	6	9	6	16	25	8.33	–	–	1
† N.J.O'Brien (Le)	2011	14	23	–	67	695	30.21	–	6	25/3
G.Onions (Du/EL)		14	18	6	27	169	14.08	–	–	3
C.Overton (Sm)		1	1	–	8	8	8.00	–	–	–
J.Overton (Sm)		13	20	6	24	131	9.35	–	–	–
W.T.Owen (Gm)		2	3	–	40	45	15.00	–	–	2
A.P.Palladino (De)	2012	8	14	1	68	233	17.92	–	1	1
† M.S.Panesar (Ex/Sx)	2010	18	17	7	22	95	9.50	–	–	2
† M.G.Pardoe (Wo)	2011	18	32	3	102	956	32.96	1	7	4
S.D.Parry (La)		3	3	1	20	37	18.50	–	–	–
A.K.Patel (LU)	–	2	3	–	38	61	20.33	–	–	1
J.S.Patel (Wa)	2012	16	18	4	78*	438	31.28	–	5	14
† L.A.Patel (DU)	–	2	4	–	28	72	18.00	–	–	3
R.H.Patel (M)		4	6	2	26*	47	11.75	–	–	–
S.R.Patel (Nt)	2008	17	26	–	256	1104	42.46	4	–	17
Z.R.Patel (LBU)	–	1	2	–	0	0	0.00	–	–	–
S.A.Patterson (Y)	2012	17	18	8	40	147	14.70	–	–	2
† J.L.Pattinson (A)	–	3	4	2	35	72	36.00	–	–	1
D.A.Payne (Gs)	2011	10	9	2	16	42	6.00	–	–	2
S.D.Peters (Nh)	2007	10	15	1	106	735	52.50	2	5	4
A.N.Petersen (Sm)	2013	6	12	–	167	562	46.83	2	2	3
M.L.Pettini (Ex)	2006	9	15	4	100*	419	38.09	1	1	10
V.D.Philander (K)		2	2	–	23	25	12.50	–	–	–
B.J.Phillips (Nt)		1	1	1	53*	53	–	–	1	1
D.S.Phillips (CfU)		1	1	–	7	7	7.00	–	–	–
† T.J.Phillips (E)	2006	3	3	1	40*	47	23.50	–	–	1
K.P.Pietersen (E/Sy)		6	11	1	177*	565	56.50	2	3	6
N.D.Pinner (Wo)	2011	8	11	–	80	265	24.09	–	2	10
S.A.Piolet (Wa)		1	2	–	30	31	15.50	–	–	1
L.E.Plunkett (Y)	2013	13	18	2	68	394	24.62	–	2	9
A.W.Pollock (CU)	–	2	3	1	44*	44	22.00	–	–	1
R.T.Ponting (Sy)	2013	4	6	2	192	493	123.25	2	1	4
† W.T.S.Porterfield (Wa)		12	18	–	43	288	16.00	–	–	8
M.J.Powell (K)		7	10	3	70	265	37.85	–	3	–
S.W.Poynter (Wa)		1	1	–	0	0	0.00	–	–	6
T.Poynton (De)		12	22	2	63*	443	22.15	–	3	27/3
† J.E.Poysden (CU)	–	1	2	–	9	9	4.50	–	–	–
† A.G.Prince (La)	2010	16	26	2	134	1169	48.70	3	7	16
M.J.Prior (E/Sx)	2003	14	22	3	62	421	22.15	–	1	39
† T.J.W.Probert (CU)	–	1	2	1	3	3	3.00	–	–	–
† L.A.Procter (La)		15	21	–	106	718	34.19	1	7	5

	Cap	M	I	NO	HS	Runs	Avge	100	50	Ct/St
R.M.Pyrah (Y)	2010	5	3	1	55	70	35.00	–	1	5
R.G.Querl (H)		1	–	–	–	–	–	–	–	–
† R.J.Quiney (Ex)		5	9	–	112	267	29.66	1	1	7
U.A.Qureshi (CfU)	–	2	2	–	13	13	6.50	–	–	–
B.A.Raine (Le)		5	8	1	72	190	27.14	–	1	–
† W.B.Rankin (Wa)	2013	9	9	6	12*	32	10.66	–	–	–
A.U.Rashid (Y)	2008	15	22	6	180	825	51.56	3	3	7
D.E.M.Ratnayake (LU)	–	2	3	–	46	60	20.00	–	–	1
O.P.Rayner (M)		14	19	3	52*	303	18.93	–	1	20
C.M.W.Read (Nt)	1999	16	23	2	80	532	25.33	–	3	59/2
† D.J.Redfern (De)	2012	8	15	–	61	252	16.80	–	2	6
† L.M.Reece (La/LBU)		12	20	4	114*	877	54.81	1	8	10
M.T.Reed (Gm)		12	15	7	27	71	8.87	–	–	2
† G.P.Rees (Gm)	2009	9	16	1	112	564	37.60	2	3	5
H.Riazuddin (H)		1	–	–	–	–	–	–	–	2
A.Richardson (Wo)	2010	16	18	10	21	109	13.62	–	–	4
M.J.Richardson (Du)		11	16	–	129	530	33.12	2	2	13
A.E.N.Riley (K/LU)		7	9	2	21*	63	9.00	–	–	2
M.D.T.Roberts (H)		6	9	1	44	159	19.87	–	–	2
A.J.Robson (Le)		3	4	–	49	59	14.75	–	–	–
S.D.Robson (M)	2013	16	29	4	215*	1180	47.20	3	4	22
G.H.Roderick (Gs)	2013	13	19	4	152*	665	44.33	2	2	43
C.J.L.Rogers (A/M)	2011	18	33	3	214	1536	51.20	4	9	15
T.S.Roland-Jones (EL/M)	2012	9	12	2	22*	133	13.30	–	–	4
J.E.Root (E/EL/Y)	2012	10	18	1	236	1228	72.23	5	2	8
A.M.Rossington (M)		1	2	2	103*	160	–	–	–	5
A.P.Rouse (H)		1	1	–	9	9	9.00	–	–	–
H.P.Rouse (LBU)	–	1	2	–	15	29	14.50	–	–	–
J.J.Roy (Sy)		4	7	1	17	49	8.16	–	–	3
C.Rushworth (Du)		15	20	8	18*	107	8.91	–	–	4
C.J.Russell (Wo)	2012	11	12	2	10	46	4.60	–	–	2
† H.D.Rutherford (Ex/NZ)		6	10	–	126	250	25.00	1	–	2
L.M.Sabin (OU)	–	2	4	–	50	91	22.75	–	1	1
P.T.Sadler (CU)	–	2	4	1	8	18	6.00	–	–	2
D.J.G.Sales (Nh)	1999	16	23	3	255*	919	45.95	3	1	11
M.E.T.Salisbury (CU)	–	2	3	–	5	9	3.00	–	–	–
A.G.Salter (CfU/Gm)		5	6	–	16	57	9.50	–	–	1
T.T.Samaraweera (Wo)	2013	15	22	4	144*	702	39.00	2	4	6
G.S.Sandhu (M)		3	–	–	–	–	–	–	–	–
R.R.Sarwan (Le)		5	8	1	79	255	36.42	–	2	4
C.J.Sayers (AA)	–	1	1	–	15	15	15.00	–	–	–
† J.J.Sayers (Y)	2007	6	9	1	25*	83	10.37	–	–	4
N.V.S.Senaratne (CU)	–	3	6	–	82	118	19.66	–	1	–
O.A.Shah (Ex)	2013	7	11	1	120	307	30.70	1	1	10
R.A.C.Shah (DU)	–	2	4	1	57*	113	37.66	–	1	–
A.Shahzad (Nt)	2013	12	18	2	77	379	23.68	–	2	1
† J.D.Shantry (Wo)	2009	14	15	1	55*	307	21.92	–	2	4
C.E.Shreck (K)		15	15	8	19*	82	11.71	–	–	1
T.W.Shrewsbury (Gs)	2013	1	1	1	2*	2	–	–	–	–
D.P.Sibley (Sy)		3	4	–	242	264	66.00	1	–	1
H.G.Siddique (CfU)	–	1	–	–	–	–	–	–	–	1
P.M.Siddle (A)	–	6	8	–	23	84	10.50	–	–	–

232

	Cap	M	I	NO	HS	Runs	Avge	100	50	Ct/St
† R.J.Sidebottom (Y)	2000	15	17	–	48	195	11.47	–	–	4
J.C.Silk (AA)	–	1	2	–	41	50	25.00	–	–	4
J.A.Simpson (M)	2011	16	25	4	97*	648	30.85	–	5	55/5
† B.T.Slater (De)		10	18	1	66*	335	19.70	–	3	3
† G.C.Smith (Sy)	2013	3	5	1	67	120	30.00	–	1	4
G.M.Smith (Ex)		11	16	3	177	555	42.69	1	2	2
G.P.Smith (Le)		13	23	1	70	500	22.72	–	4	13
R.A.J.Smith (Gm)		3	4	1	39	100	33.33	–	–	–
S.P.D.Smith (A/AA)	–	8	15	3	138*	568	47.33	2	3	7
† T.C.Smith (La)	2010	7	8	2	88	289	48.16	–	2	9
T.M.J.Smith (Gs/M)	2013	11	13	–	50	234	26.00	–	1	3
W.R.Smith (Du)		17	30	3	153	889	32.92	2	2	15
† Sohail Tanvir (H)		4	5	–	38	133	26.60	–	–	–
A.C.Soilleux (LU)	–	1	1	–	9	9	9.00	–	–	–
V.S.Solanki (Sy)		16	25	–	162	995	39.80	2	5	18
T.G.Southee (NZ)	–	3	5	–	38	87	17.40	–	–	5
† M.N.W.Spriegel (Nh)		8	12	2	76	134	13.40	–	1	2
† M.A.Starc (A)	–	5	6	2	66*	104	26.00	–	1	2
O.J.Steele (DU)	–	2	4	1	14	22	7.33	–	–	1
D.I.Stevens (K)	2005	16	22	1	205*	1304	62.09	4	7	13
P.R.Stirling (M)		2	3	–	54	55	18.33	–	1	1
B.A.Stokes (Du)		14	25	2	127	726	31.56	2	3	11
† M.D.Stoneman (Du)		17	32	1	122	1068	34.45	3	6	6
A.V.Suppiah (Sm)	2009	6	11	–	36	130	11.81	–	–	2
G.P.Swann (E/Nt)	2005	8	12	4	57	223	27.87	–	1	6
† J.S.Sykes (Le)		7	12	2	34	139	13.90	–	–	3
B.J.Taylor (H)		1	2	1	20	20	20.00	–	–	1
J.M.R.Taylor (Gs)	2010	4	5	1	61*	178	44.50	–	1	4
J.W.A.Taylor (EL/Nt/Sx)	2012	18	25	3	204*	1079	49.04	3	5	9
L.R.P.L.Taylor (NZ)	–	3	5	–	70	177	35.40	–	2	1
M.D.Taylor (Gs)	2013	3	3	2	26*	31	31.00	–	–	–
† R.M.L.Taylor (Le)		3	4	–	25	37	9.25	–	–	1
R.N.ten Doeschate (Ex)	2006	9	13	2	103	391	35.54	1	1	3
S.P.Terry (H)		2	2	–	58	115	57.50	–	2	2
S.J.Thakor (De)		15	24	3	114	671	31.95	1	5	4
A.C.Thomas (Sm)	2008	13	21	5	54*	239	14.93	–	1	4
I.A.A.Thomas (LBU)	–	2	4	3	10*	19	19.00	–	–	1
H.L.Thompson (LBU)	–	2	4	–	40	67	16.75	–	–	–
J.S.Thompson (OU)	–	1	2	–	15	23	11.50	–	–	–
M.A.Thornely (Le)		11	17	–	53	282	16.58	–	1	10
C.D.Thorp (Du)		8	12	2	27	157	15.70	–	–	2
† J.A.Tomlinson (H)	2008	15	15	8	30*	72	10.28	–	–	1
R.J.W.Topley (Ex)	2013	13	14	7	8*	12	1.71	–	–	6
† J.C.Tredwell (K)	2007	12	15	1	48	238	17.00	–	–	9
P.D.Trego (Sm)	2007	15	25	1	82	434	18.08	–	2	5
C.T.Tremlett (Sy)		11	12	1	54	110	10.00	–	1	3
† M.E.Trescothick (Sm)	1999	17	32	1	74	843	27.19	–	6	31
I.J.L.Trott (E/Wa)	2005	9	16	–	96	653	40.81	–	6	10
† J.O.Troughton (Wa)	2002	8	13	1	84	404	33.66	–	3	5
A.J.Turner (A)	–	1	–	–	–	–	–	–	–	–
M.L.Turner (De)		5	7	3	23*	79	19.75	–	–	–
F.O.E.van den Bergh (DU)	–	2	3	–	34	37	12.33	–	–	–

Name	Cap	M	I	NO	HS	Runs	Avge	100	50	Ct/St
W.G.R.Vanderspar (LBU)	–	2	4	–	37	78	19.50	–	–	1
K.S.Velani (Ex)		1	2	–	13	22	11.00	–	–	–
J.M.Vince (H)	2013	16	23	4	148	1215	63.94	5	6	17
A.C.Voges (M)		4	7	–	150	383	54.71	1	2	6
† M.S.Wade (A/AA)	–	2	4	2	30*	61	30.50	–	–	6
G.G.Wagg (Gm)	2013	10	12	1	58	308	28.00	–	2	1
† N.Wagner (NZ)	–	3	4	2	27	50	25.00	–	–	–
† D.J.Wainwright (De)	2012	9	16	4	54*	241	20.08	–	1	–
A.G.Wakely (Nh)	2012	15	21	1	88	457	22.85	–	2	5
† M.A.Wallace (Gm)	2003	17	24	–	101	656	27.33	1	2	44/3
C.A.Wallis (DU)	–	2	3	–	10	11	3.66	–	–	–
S.J.Walters (Gm)		10	17	–	98	398	23.41	–	2	13
† D.A.Warner (A)	–	3	6	–	71	138	23.00	–	1	3
H.T.Waters (Gm)	2012	1	–	–	–	–	–	–	–	–
N.A.T.Watkins (DU)	–	2	3	–	15	28	9.33	–	–	1
B.J.Watling (NZ)	–	3	5	2	77*	191	63.66	–	2	11
S.R.Watson (A)	–	7	12	–	176	617	51.41	2	2	7
J.P.Webb (LBU)	–	2	4	–	8	15	3.75	–	–	2
† L.W.P.Wells (Sx)		18	30	1	208	994	34.27	2	5	7
T.J.Wells (Le)		5	8	–	82	177	22.12	–	1	2
M.H.Wessels (Nt)		11	16	1	77	316	21.06	–	1	13/1
S.A.Westaway (OU)	–	1	1	–	17	17	17.00	–	–	10
T.Westley (Ex)		11	20	–	163	774	38.70	2	3	7
† I.J.Westwood (Wa)	2008	13	22	2	71	543	27.15	–	4	8
A.J.A.Wheater (H)		16	19	3	140	687	42.93	3	1	19/2
C.L.White (Nh)		2	3	–	90	107	35.66	–	1	–
G.G.White (Nh/Nt)		3	4	–	23	23	5.75	–	–	–
W.A.White (La)		6	9	3	61	133	22.16	–	1	2
R.A.Whiteley (De/Wo)	2013	8	14	–	56	189	13.50	–	1	5
R.J.D.Willett (DU)	–	1	2	2	2*	2	–	–	–	1
D.J.Willey (Nh)	2013	13	15	1	81	346	24.71	–	3	3
B.Williams (OU)	–	2	3	–	43	120	40.00	–	–	–
R.E.M.Williams (Le)		6	7	2	13*	41	8.20	–	–	1
T.J.Williams (OU)	–	1	1	1	9*	9	–	–	–	–
K.S.Williamson (NZ/Y)		9	16	1	97	584	38.93	–	6	5
G.C.Wilson (Sy)		12	17	4	124	447	34.38	1	1	12
M.J.Winter (OU)	–	1	1	–	51	51	51.00	–	1	–
C.R.Woakes (E/EL/Wa)	2009	12	19	6	152*	683	52.53	1	4	2
C.P.Wood (H)		9	12	1	69	256	23.27	–	2	6
M.A.Wood (Du)		8	10	2	58*	153	19.12	–	1	1
B.J.Wright (Gm)	2011	14	25	3	68*	604	27.45	–	3	10
C.J.C.Wright (EL/Wa)	2013	9	9	1	11	35	4.37	–	–	–
L.J.Wright (Sx)	2007	7	12	–	187	676	56.33	2	2	1
A.C.F.Wyatt (Le)		11	17	7	28	117	11.70	–	–	1
† B.A.Wylie (CU)	–	2	4	1	29	35	11.66	–	–	–
† M.H.Yardy (Sx)	2005	18	29	2	156	834	30.88	2	1	9
D.R.Young (LBU)	–	2	4	–	14	26	6.50	–	–	3
E.G.C.Young (Gs)	2010	1	2	2	2*	2	–	–	–	–

BOWLING

See BATTING AND FIELDING section for details of matches and caps

	Cat	O	M	R	W	Avge	Best	5wI	10wM
A.R.Adams (Nt)	RMF	302.5	55	929	31	29.96	4- 69	–	–
J.H.K.Adams (H)	LM	14	1	52	1	52.00	1- 26	–	–
A.C.Agar (A/AA)	SLA	159	33	517	8	64.62	2- 79	–	–
S.S.Agarwal (OU)	OB	73	18	201	5	40.20	3- 26	–	–
A.P.Agathangelou (La)	LB	43	12	125	3	41.66	2- 18	–	–
M.M.Ali (Wo)	OB	324.4	41	1127	31	36.35	6- 77	1	–
S.A.Ali (Wa)	RFM	29	5	103	2	51.50	2- 76	–	–
A.T.A.Allchin (CU)	RFM	38	1	178	1	178.00	1- 98	–	–
J.Allenby (Gm)	RM	391.5	109	951	30	31.70	4- 16	–	–
T.W.Allin (Wa)	RMF	17	3	65	0			–	–
H.M.Amla (Sy)	RM	5	0	22	0			–	–
J.M.Anderson (E/La)	RFM	332.3	85	963	39	24.69	5- 47	3	1
G.M.Andrew (Wo)	RMF	242.3	59	818	21	38.95	4- 79	–	–
A.S.Ansari (CU)	LB	16	0	129	2	64.50	2- 86	–	–
Z.S.Ansari (CU/Sy)	SLA	204.1	32	602	17	35.41	4- 70	–	–
J.E.Anyon (Sx)	RFM	399.5	77	1454	52	27.96	5- 44	1	–
U.Arshad (Du)	RMF	73.1	16	249	16	15.56	3- 16	–	–
Ashar Zaidi (Sx)	SLA	39.3	6	129	7	18.42	4- 57	–	–
M.A.Ashraf (Y)	RMF	38.3	13	119	4	29.75	3- 60	–	–
Azeem Rafiq (Y)	OB	40	9	141	3	47.00	1- 17	–	–
Azhar Ullah (Nh)	RFM	225.4	51	717	25	28.68	4- 42	–	–
G.C.Baker (LU)	RMF	38	5	203	2	101.50	2- 57	–	–
A.Balbirnie (CfU)	OB	10	1	41	0			–	–
D.J.Balcombe (H)	RFM	349	80	1101	22	50.04	5-104	1	–
A.J.Ball (K)	LFM	37	4	170	3	56.66	2- 42	–	–
J.T.Ball (Nt)	RM	14	5	39	3	13.00	3- 18	–	–
G.S.Ballance (Y)	LB	14	0	98	0			–	–
K.H.D.Barker (Wa)	LM	345	83	1055	46	22.93	5- 55	1	–
G.J.Batty (Sy)	OB	395.4	68	1141	27	42.25	5- 71	2	–
W.A.T.Beer (Sx)	LB	72	8	215	4	53.75	3- 89	–	–
D.J.Bell-Drummond (K)	RMF	6.5	0	54	0			–	–
D.M.Benkenstein (Du)	RM/OB	5	0	19	0			–	–
G.K.Berg (M)	RMF	324.4	71	942	25	37.68	3- 49	–	–
J.M.Bird (A/AA)	RFM	127.3	42	370	11	33.63	4- 48	–	–
C.Bishnoi (DU)	SLA	30	1	152	1	152.00	1- 52	–	–
C.J.Bodenstein (OU)	LMF	44.4	13	141	5	28.20	3- 53	–	–
R.S.Bopara (EL/Ex)	RM	148	26	427	16	26.68	3- 41	–	–
S.G.Borthwick (Du)	LBG	297.4	43	1140	34	33.52	6- 70	1	–
T.A.Boult (NZ)	LFM	91	23	249	11	22.63	5- 57	1	–
D.A.J.Bracewell (NZ)	RFM	93	26	311	10	31.10	4- 28	–	–
W.D.Bragg (Gm)	RM	22	2	111	2	55.50	2- 10	–	–
R.M.R.Brathwaite (Du)	RFM	58	13	222	6	37.00	3-112	–	–
G.R.Breese (Du)	OB	53	18	117	4	29.25	2- 40	–	–
T.T.Bresnan (E/Y)	RFM	221.2	51	689	26	26.50	4- 41	–	–
D.R.Briggs (H)	SLA	300.4	76	857	25	34.28	3- 33	–	–
S.C.J.Broad (E/Nt)	RFM	323.5	68	1008	46	21.91	7- 44	3	1
J.A.Brooks (Nh)	RFM	261.2	55	908	37	24.54	5- 40	1	–
N.L.J.Browne (Ex)	LB	16.5	4	59	0			–	–
N.L.Buck (Le)	RMF	94.3	19	365	6	60.83	3- 83	–	–
R.S.Buckley (Du)	OB	114.2	21	344	10	34.40	5- 86	1	–

235

	Cat	O	M	R	W	Avge	Best	5wI	10wM
P.I.Burgoyne (De)	OB	165.1	26	487	6	81.16	3- 66	–	–
R.J.Burns (Sy)	RM	15	0	90	1	90.00	1- 18	–	–
M.A.Carberry (EL/H)	OB	23.3	2	100	2	50.00	1- 13	–	–
A.Carter (Nt)	RM	28	5	113	2	56.50	2- 87	–	–
S.J.Cato (OU)	OB	2.1	2	0	0			–	–
G.Cessford (Wo)	RFM	145.4	26	591	17	34.76	4- 73	–	–
M.A.Chambers (Ex/Wa)	RFM	157.2	25	581	18	32.27	5- 68	1	–
S.Chanderpaul (De)	LB	18.4	4	40	3	13.33	2- 32	–	–
G.Chapple (La)	RMF	430.4	110	1099	53	20.73	5- 0	2	–
P.P.Chawla (Sm)	LB	122.4	13	453	17	26.64	5- 97	2	1
V.Chopra (EL/Wa)	LB	4	0	12	0			–	–
S.H.Choudhry (Wo)	SLA	173.4	26	484	13	37.23	4-111	–	–
D.T.Christian (Gs)	RFM	13	3	65	2	32.50	1- 19	–	–
J.L.Clare (De)	RMF	124	7	554	17	32.58	5- 29	1	–
M.J.Clarke (A)	SLA	3	0	6	0			–	–
R.Clarke (Wa)	RFM	229.3	61	642	19	33.78	4- 70	–	–
M.E.Claydon (Du/K)	RMF	83.3	14	282	10	28.20	3- 25	–	–
J.J.Cobb (Le)	LB	58.1	5	202	0			–	–
K.J.Coetzer (Nh)	RM	7	1	16	0			–	–
M.T.Coles (H/K)	RMF	289	55	1053	34	30.97	6- 71	3	1
P.D.Collingwood (Du)	RM	35.4	14	73	1	73.00	1- 14	–	–
C.D.Collymore (M)	RFM	247.2	53	668	26	25.69	4- 61	–	–
T.A.Copeland (Nh)	RFM	394.4	139	822	45	18.26	7- 63	4	1
D.A.Cosker (Gm)	SLA	462.2	93	1318	37	35.62	5-120	1	–
E.J.M.Cowan (A/Nt)	LB	1	0	3	0			–	–
J.D.Cowan (CU)	LMF	30	8	102	4	25.50	2- 29	–	–
F.C.Cowdrey (CfU)	SLA	16	1	70	0			–	–
R.D.Cox (DU)	RM	18	4	71	3	23.66	3- 49	–	–
T.R.Craddock (Ex)	LB	43	9	132	3	44.00	2- 77	–	–
S.J.Croft (La)	RMF	41	6	132	1	132.00	1- 11	–	–
S.P.Crook (Nh)	RFM	326	46	1139	43	26.48	4- 30	–	–
L.M.Daggett (Nh)	RMF	59.3	13	203	2	101.50	1- 34	–	–
M.Davies (K)	RMF	272.3	76	639	26	24.57	4- 36	–	–
L.A.Dawson (H)	SLA	216.2	55	647	11	58.81	2- 36	–	–
Z.de Bruyn (Sy)	RMF	253.2	52	824	13	63.38	3- 28	–	–
J.L.Denly (M)	LB	28.4	3	96	2	48.00	2- 47	–	–
J.S.T.Denning (CfU)	LFM	56	12	156	3	52.00	2- 46	–	–
C.D.J.Dent (Gs)	SLA	19.1	5	60	1	60.00	1- 12	–	–
J.W.Dernbach (Sy)	RFM	315	57	1043	34	30.67	5- 57	1	–
N.J.Dexter (M)	RM	176.2	40	445	18	24.72	5- 27	1	–
G.H.Dockrell (Sm)	SLA	254.4	60	722	17	42.47	6- 96	1	–
M.P.Dunn (Sy)	RFM	35	2	133	4	33.25	3- 97	–	–
W.J.Durston (De)	OB	180	23	586	10	58.60	2- 29	–	–
E.J.H.Eckersley (Le)	OB	8.1	1	42	2	21.00	2- 29	–	–
G.A.Edwards (Sy)	RFM	37	14	80	3	26.66	3- 29	–	–
D.Elgar (Sm)	SLA	19	4	55	1	55.00	1- 26	–	–
C.P.Ellison (OU)	RM	32.2	3	126	2	63.00	2- 50	–	–
D.M.Endersby (LU)	RMF	33	7	135	1	135.00	1- 52	–	–
S.M.Ervine (H)	RM	179.1	39	577	17	33.94	2- 17	–	–
A.C.Evans (De)	RMF	38	5	174	2	87.00	1- 30	–	–
L.J.Evans (Wa)	RFM	22	3	63	0			–	–
J.P.Faulkner (A)	LFM	102.5	23	325	13	25.00	4- 51	–	–
Fawad Ahmed (AA)	LB	31.2	9	100	1	100.00	1- 20	–	–

	Cat	O	M	R	W	Avge	Best	5wI	10wM
H.Z.Finch (Sx)	RMF	4	0	15	0			–	–
S.T.Finn (E/M)	RF	231.5	52	781	27	28.92	4- 46	–	–
L.J.Fletcher (Nt)	RMF	460.1	133	1288	43	29.95	5- 52	2	–
M.H.A.Footitt (De)	LFM	380.5	57	1377	42	32.78	6- 53	2	–
P.J.Franks (Nt)	RMF	149	34	494	12	41.16	3- 16	–	–
O.H.Freckingham (Le)	RMF	399	61	1584	36	44.00	6-125	1	–
J.K.Fuller (Gs)	RFM	228.4	44	793	16	49.56	5- 43	1	–
A.W.Gale (Y)	LB	9	0	94	0			–	–
J.S.Gatting (Sx)	OB	6	0	19	0			–	–
A.P.R.Gidman (Gs)	RM	28.3	6	93	1	93.00	1- 5	–	–
W.R.S.Gidman (Gs)	RM	407.2	88	1209	55	21.98	6- 15	2	1
M.R.Gillespie (NZ)	RFM	29	5	107	0			–	–
J.C.Glover (Gm)	RMF	174.1	35	558	14	39.85	4- 51	–	–
R.O.Gordon (Wa)	RFM	95	18	288	7	41.14	2- 45	–	–
M.J.E.Green (DU)	RM	33	8	93	3	31.00	2- 60	–	–
L.Gregory (Sm)	RMF	119.4	25	358	14	25.57	5- 38	1	–
D.A.Griffiths (H)	RFM	85.3	11	362	11	32.90	5- 68	1	–
T.D.Groenewald (De)	RFM	437.5	86	1404	45	31.20	5- 30	3	–
M.J.Guptill (NZ)	OB	5	0	41	0			–	–
H.F.Gurney (Nt)	LFM	412.3	70	1376	48	28.66	5- 81	1	–
C.J.Haggett (K)	RMF	298	72	907	26	34.88	4- 94	–	–
A.J.Hall (Nh)	RFM	325.3	85	937	37	25.32	5- 30	1	–
R.J.Hamilton-Brown (Sx)	OB	11	1	52	0			–	–
M.A.H.Hammond (Gs)	OB	49	3	196	1	196.00	1- 96	–	–
O.J.Hannon-Dalby (Wa)	RMF	70	13	257	7	36.71	4- 50	–	–
A.Harinath (Sy)	OB	3	0	6	1	6.00	1- 2	–	–
B.W.Harmison (K)	RMF	37	1	161	1	161.00	1- 21	–	–
J.A.R.Harris (M)	RFM	251.4	37	854	25	34.16	3- 46	–	–
P.G.Harris (CfU)	RM	32	5	108	4	27.00	2- 22	–	–
R.J.Harris (A/AA)	RF	235.1	60	676	33	20.48	7-117	2	–
J.Harrison (Du)	LMF	96.1	20	336	14	24.00	5- 31	1	–
L.J.Hatchett (Sx)	LMF	141.4	23	489	10	48.90	3- 56	–	–
T.G.Helm (M)	RMF	18	0	78	5	15.60	3- 46	–	–
C.W.Henderson (Le)	SLA	56	13	134	6	22.33	3- 40	–	–
M.R.Hickey (CU)	LM	16	3	68	0			–	–
M.Higginbottom (De)	RMF	92.5	20	364	10	36.40	3- 59	–	–
M.E.Hobden (CfU)	RFM	56	11	238	8	29.75	5- 89	1	–
I.H.Hobson (DU)	OB	4	0	27	0			–	–
M.G.Hogan (Gm)	RFM	512	133	1376	67	20.53	7- 92	4	–
K.W.Hogg (La)	RFM	436	105	1105	60	18.41	7- 27	3	–
M.J.Hoggard (Le)	RMF	171	35	545	16	34.06	6- 66	1	–
D.M.Housego (Gs)	LB	3	0	15	0			–	–
B.A.C.Howell (Gs)	RMF	355	85	1029	30	34.30	5- 57	1	–
A.L.Hughes (De)	RM	71	12	230	6	38.33	3- 49	–	–
C.F.Hughes (De)	SLA	5	1	19	1	19.00	1- 19	–	–
P.J.Hughes (A/AA)	OB	1	0	5	0			–	–
M.D.Hunn (K)	RFM	31.4	6	118	3	39.33	2- 51	–	–
G.M.Hussain (Sm)	RMF	89.5	7	389	7	55.57	3- 99	–	–
D.J.Hussey (Nt)	OB	4	1	25	0			–	–
B.A.Hutton (Nt)	RM	22	4	109	1	109.00	1- 31	–	–
A.J.Ireland (Le)	RM	54	7	192	2	96.00	1- 83	–	–
P.A.Jaques (Y)	SLC	6	0	75	1	75.00	1- 75	–	–
K.M.Jarvis (La)	RFM	34	1	179	4	44.75	3- 72	–	–

	Cat	O	M	R	W	Avge	Best	5wI	10wM
A.Javid (Wa)	RM	49	10	154	2	77.00	1- 27	–	–
K.K.Jennings (Du)	RMF	11.2	0	48	2	24.00	1- 5	–	–
T.M.Jewell (Sy)	RMF	33	5	147	3	49.00	3-100	–	–
Alex J.Jones (Gm)	LMF	12	0	53	0				
O.J.Jones (OU)	RM	30	2	125	1	125.00	1- 58	–	–
R.A.Jones (Wo)	RMF	33	7	150	7	21.42	5- 45	1	–
C.J.Jordan (Sx)	RFM	471.3	88	1719	61	28.18	6- 48	4	–
A.Kapil (Wo)	RFM	2	0	14	0				
G.Keedy (Sy)	SLA	269	51	796	22	36.18	7- 99	2	–
B.W.Kemp (OU)	RFM	66	17	214	6	35.66	3- 31	–	–
R.I.Keogh (Nh)	OB	4	1	9	0				
S.C.Kerrigan (E/EL/La)	SLA	474.2	108	1275	58	21.98	7- 63	5	1
R.W.T.Key (K)	RM/OB	9.2	0	86	0				
U.T.Khawaja (A/AA)	RM	1	0	7	0				
C.Kieswetter (Sm)	OB	6	0	26	0				
S.P.Kirby (Sm)	RFM	277.5	54	913	26	35.11	4- 18	–	–
J.Leach (Wo)	RMF	69	6	306	6	51.00	2- 36	–	–
M.J.Leach (Sm)	SLA	149.4	51	324	13	24.92	5- 63	1	–
J.A.Leaning (Y)	RMF	4	0	22	0				
J.E.Lee (LBU)	RFM	52	9	165	15	11.00	7- 45	2	–
A.Z.Lees (Y)	LB	1	0	14	0				
T.Lester (LU)	LFM	44	10	147	3	49.00	2- 58	–	–
J.Lewis (Sy)	RMF	60	14	154	3	51.33	3- 80	–	–
C.J.Liddle (LU)	LFM	66.2	13	236	5	47.20	2- 24	–	–
A.M.Lilley (La)	OB	69	9	212	2	106.00	1- 41	–	–
T.E.Linley (Sy)	RFM	438.1	106	1268	37	34.27	4- 59	–	–
A.B.London (M)	OB	1	0	5	0				
D.S.Lucas (Wo)	LMF	55.1	13	183	3	61.00	1- 40	–	–
N.M.Lyon (A)	OB	186.1	45	550	14	39.28	4- 42	–	–
A.Lyth (Y)	RM	36	4	155	4	38.75	2- 15	–	–
G.J.McCarter (Gs)	RFM	110	19	431	9	47.88	4- 95	–	–
N.L.McCullum (Gm)	OB	47.4	6	191	5	38.20	5-191	1	–
N.D.McKenzie (H)	RM	10	4	17	1	17.00	1- 10	–	–
A.MacQueen (LBU)	OB	41	13	94	1	94.00	1- 45	–	–
W.A.MacVicar (LU)	RM	38	5	153	2	76.50	2- 46	–	–
D.L.Maddy (Wa)	RM/OB	26	5	71	1	71.00	1- 50	–	–
W.L.Madsen (De)	OB	43	10	121	3	40.33	2- 9	–	–
S.J.Magoffin (Sx)	RFM	512	134	1379	65	21.21	8- 20	3	1
S.I.Mahmood (Ex)	RF	66	4	329	3	109.66	2-112	–	–
D.J.Malan (M)	LB	15.5	0	58	0				
W.W.J.Marriott (OU)	OB	1	0	6	0				
J.Marsden (OU)	RFM	25.2	9	64	3	21.33	3- 32	–	–
B.P.Martin (NZ)	SLA	86.4	27	243	7	34.71	3- 13	–	–
A.D.Mascarenhas (H)	RMF	25	7	61	4	15.25	4- 61	–	–
D.D.Masters (Ex)	RMF	489.4	129	1209	51	23.70	6- 41	4	–
S.C.Meaker (Sy)	RMF	195.4	33	840	24	35.00	5- 60	1	–
C.A.J.Meschede (Sm)	RMF	204.1	38	738	26	28.38	4- 43	–	–
J.D.Middlebrook (Nh)	OB	249.1	53	775	21	36.90	6- 78	1	–
C.N.Miles (Gs)	RMF	358	69	1315	43	30.58	6- 88	3	–
A.S.Miller (Sx)	RFM	28	6	102	0				
T.S.Mills (Ex)	LFM	120.4	19	477	11	43.36	3- 42	–	–
T.P.Milnes (Wa)	RFM	128.1	21	476	13	36.61	7- 39	1	–
D.K.H.Mitchell (Wo)	RM	31.2	7	104	2	52.00	1- 1	–	–

	Cat	O	M	R	W	Avge	Best	5wI	10wM
A.J.Morris (LU)	RMF	18	1	60	1	60.00	1- 47	–	–
C.A.J.Morris (OU/Wo)	RMF	95	26	289	6	48.16	3- 33	–	–
S.J.Mullaney (Nt)	RM	80.3	13	264	6	44.00	3- 22	–	–
T.J.Murtagh (M)	RFM	444.1	113	1224	60	20.40	6- 49	3	1
P.Mustard (Du)	LB	1.1	0	9	1	9.00	1- 9	–	–
S.V.S.Mylavarapu (OU)	SLA	43.1	12	110	8	13.75	5- 23	1	–
J.K.H.Naik (Le)	OB	326.3	67	934	26	35.92	5- 70	2	–
G.R.Napier (Ex)	RM	479.1	86	1572	51	30.82	7- 90	3	–
B.P.Nash (K)	LM	9	0	43	1	43.00	1- 9	–	–
C.D.Nash (Sx)	OB	209.2	35	613	11	55.72	2- 27	–	–
O.J.Newby (La)	RMF	68.2	12	264	12	22.00	4- 71	–	–
G.F.Nicholson (CU)	LMF	32	1	174	0			–	–
M.J.North (Gm)	OB	48.2	6	143	7	20.42	5- 30	1	–
S.A.Northeast (K)	OB	20	0	131	1	131.00	1- 60	–	–
L.C.Norwell (Gs)	RMF	139	16	599	14	42.78	3- 80	–	–
G.Onions (Du/EL)	RFM	452.1	94	1382	73	18.93	7- 62	5	–
C.Overton (Sm)	RMF	23	6	67	1	67.00	1- 7	–	–
J.Overton (Sm)	RFM	304.5	48	1221	35	34.88	6- 95	1	–
W.T.Owen (Gm)	RMF	47	8	170	1	170.00	1- 51	–	–
A.P.Palladino (De)	RMF	214.5	43	644	23	28.00	6- 90	2	–
M.S.Panesar (Ex/Sx)	SLA	558	131	1543	40	38.57	5- 95	2	–
S.D.Parry (La)	SLA	65.3	5	197	5	39.40	3- 51	–	–
J.S.Patel (Wa)	OB	576.1	139	1561	52	30.01	5- 56	2	–
L.A.Patel (DU)	OB	15.4	0	106	1	106.00	1- 12	–	–
R.H.Patel (M)	SLA	134.5	30	395	14	28.21	5- 69	1	–
S.R.Patel (Nt)	SLA	460.2	126	1316	28	47.00	3- 40	–	–
Z.R.Patel (LBU)	RMF	19	8	53	3	17.66	2- 32	–	–
S.A.Patterson (Y)	RMF	435.5	130	1197	51	23.47	5- 43	1	–
J.L.Pattinson (A)	RMF	120.1	27	424	14	30.28	4- 56	–	–
D.A.Payne (Gs)	LMF	275.4	59	917	18	50.94	3- 75	–	–
A.N.Petersen (Sm)	RM/OB	14	4	48	1	48.00	1- 27	–	–
V.D.Philander (K)	RMF	64	9	170	0			–	–
B.J.Phillips (Nt)	RFM	13	3	31	1	31.00	1- 6	–	–
D.S.Phillips (CfU)	RM	23	2	95	2	47.50	2- 45	–	–
T.J.Phillips (Ex)	SLA	39.4	10	98	6	16.33	3- 20	–	–
K.P.Pietersen (E/Sy)	OB	4	1	13	0			–	–
N.D.Pinner (Wo)	OB	4	0	19	0			–	–
S.A.Piolet (Wa)	RM	12	0	59	1	59.00	1- 59	–	–
L.E.Plunkett (Y)	RMF	278.4	49	1065	42	25.35	6- 33	2	–
A.W.Pollock (CU)	RMF	65	11	218	4	54.50	3-105	–	–
J.E.Poysden (CU)	LB	12	0	48	0				
T.J.W.Probert (CU)	RM	26.5	2	125	2	62.50	2-125	–	–
L.A.Procter (La)	RM	194	31	633	15	42.20	4- 39	–	–
R.M.Pyrah (Y)	RM	77	19	244	2	122.00	1- 45	–	–
R.G.Querl (H)	RMF	27	8	47	1	47.00	1- 20	–	–
B.A.Raine (Le)	RMF	98.3	17	349	9	38.77	4- 98	–	–
W.B.Rankin (Wa)	RMF	216.4	20	709	31	22.87	4- 29	–	–
A.U.Rashid (Y)	LB	359.5	39	1358	29	46.82	5- 78	1	–
D.E.M.Ratnayake (LU)	RM	5	0	30	1	30.00	1- 22	–	–
O.P.Rayner (M)	OB	376.3	78	1014	46	22.04	8- 46	4	1
D.J.Redfern (De)	OB	32.1	2	119	4	29.75	3- 33	–	–
L.M.Reece (La/LBU)	LM	80	8	258	9	28.66	4- 28	–	–
M.T.Reed (Gm)	RFM	330.3	63	1120	38	29.47	6- 34	2	–

	Cat	O	M	R	W	Avge	Best	5wI	10wM
G.P.Rees (Gm)	LM	1	0	2	0				
H.Riazuddin (H)	RMF	23	10	51	1	51.00	1- 12	–	–
A.Richardson (Wo)	RMF	541.4	157	1368	69	19.82	8- 37	5	2
A.E.N.Riley (K/LU)	OB	130.4	12	489	19	25.73	7-150	1	–
M.D.T.Roberts (H)	OB	3.5	1	19	0				
A.J.Robson (Le)	LB	1	0	11	0				
T.S.Roland-Jones (EL/M)	RMF	232.1	42	748	25	29.92	6- 63	1	–
J.E.Root (E/EL/Y)	OB	28	11	49	3	16.33	2- 9	–	–
H.P.Rouse (LBU)	RFM	30	4	105	1	105.00	1- 64	–	–
J.J.Roy (Sy)	RM	5.4	0	35	3	11.66	3- 35	–	–
C.Rushworth (Du)	RMF	423.2	105	1240	55	22.54	6- 58	3	1
C.J.Russell (Wo)	RMF	235.4	40	930	19	48.94	3- 47	–	–
P.T.Sadler (CU)	RFM	58	7	244	1	244.00	1-122	–	–
M.E.T.Salisbury (CU)	RMF	69	11	218	6	36.33	3- 64	–	–
A.G.Salter (CfU/Gm)	OB	91.2	17	301	9	33.44	3- 66	–	–
G.S.Sandhu (M)	LMF	50	10	170	6	28.33	4- 49	–	–
R.R.Sarwan (Le)	LB	2	0	11	0				
C.J.Sayers (AA)	RM	30.3	6	92	8	11.50	5- 24	1	–
O.A.Shah (Ex)	OB	2	0	12	0				
A.Shahzad (Nt)	RFM	343.4	66	1125	26	43.26	3- 21	–	–
J.D.Shantry (Wo)	LM	396.2	106	1183	45	26.28	7- 60	2	–
C.E.Shreck (K)	RFM	435.2	98	1316	33	39.87	4- 65	–	–
T.W.Shrewsbury (Gs)	OB	23	0	94	1	94.00	1- 94	–	–
D.P.Sibley (Sy)	LB	1	0	4	0				
P.M.Siddle (A)	RFM	216.5	55	654	18	36.33	5- 50	1	–
R.J.Sidebottom (Y)	LFM	385.1	107	1012	53	19.09	4- 27	–	–
G.M.Smith (Ex)	OB/RM	114.5	23	365	17	21.47	5- 42	–	–
R.A.J.Smith (Gm)	RM	61	6	274	10	27.40	3- 50	–	–
S.P.D.Smith (A/AA)	LBG	39	4	137	4	34.25	3- 18	–	–
T.C.Smith (La)	RMF	150.5	35	498	22	22.63	4- 49	–	–
T.M.J.Smith (Gs/M)	SLA	263.5	38	840	17	49.41	4- 91	–	–
W.R.Smith (Du)	OB	55.4	12	176	6	29.33	2- 30	–	–
Sohail Tanvir (H)	LMF	107.2	19	348	10	34.80	3- 62	–	–
A.C.Soilleux (LU)	RMF	19	2	80	2	40.00	2- 36	–	–
V.S.Solanki (Sy)	OB	15	0	90	2	45.00	2- 46	–	–
T.G.Southee (NZ)	RMF	107.2	25	300	13	23.07	6- 50	1	1
M.N.W.Spriegel (Nh)	OB	48	7	183	5	36.60	3- 75	–	–
M.A.Starc (A)	LFM	167.1	39	474	19	24.94	4- 33	–	–
D.I.Stevens (K)	RM	403.4	111	1051	32	32.84	5- 39	1	–
P.R.Stirling (M)	OB	18	2	47	2	23.50	2- 43	–	–
B.A.Stokes (Du)	RFM	351.4	59	1171	44	26.61	4- 49	–	–
A.V.Suppiah (Sm)	SLA	6	1	19	0				
G.P.Swann (E/Nt)	OB	339	61	1052	40	26.30	6- 90	3	1
J.S.Sykes (Le)	SLA	199.3	30	733	12	61.08	4-176	–	–
B.J.Taylor (H)	OB	22	3	106	4	26.50	4- 64	–	–
J.M.R.Taylor (Gs)	OB	89.1	17	247	6	41.16	2- 39	–	–
M.D.Taylor (Gs)	LMF	75	19	246	4	61.50	3-108	–	–
R.M.L.Taylor (Le)	LM	61.1	14	208	4	52.00	2- 49	–	–
R.N.ten Doeschate (Ex)	RMF	77	9	267	8	33.37	4- 28	–	–
S.J.Thakor (Le)	RM	139.1	22	563	9	62.55	2- 24	–	–
A.C.Thomas (Sm)	RFM	386.4	108	1077	42	25.64	5- 69	1	–
I.A.A.Thomas (LBU)	RMF	58	14	177	4	44.25	2- 37	–	–
H.L.Thompson (LBU)	OB	3	2	6	0				

	Cat	O	M	R	W	Avge	Best	5wI	10wM
J.S.Thompson (OU)	RMF	12	5	26	0			–	–
M.A.Thornely (Le)	RM	67.2	13	277	3	92.33	1- 14	–	–
C.D.Thorp (Du)	RMF	190.5	68	378	18	21.00	3- 29	–	–
J.A.Tomlinson (H)	LMF	454.5	126	1281	53	24.16	5- 44	1	–
R.J.W.Topley (Ex)	LMF	411.4	78	1364	48	28.41	6- 29	3	1
J.C.Tredwell (K)	OB	331.3	67	965	17	56.76	5- 51	1	–
P.D.Trego (Sm)	RMF	354.2	83	1071	31	34.54	4- 69	–	–
C.T.Tremlett (Sy)	RFM	349.1	66	1057	32	33.03	8- 96	2	–
I.J.L.Trott (E/Wa)	RM	24	2	77	1	77.00	1- 12	–	–
A.J.Turner (A)	OB	4	0	16	0				
M.L.Turner (De)	RMF	91.4	9	407	6	67.83	3- 51	–	–
F.O.E.van den Bergh (DU)	SLA	66.1	10	251	6	41.83	4- 84	–	–
W.G.R.Vanderspar (LBU)	RFM	10	1	35	1	35.00	1- 26	–	–
K.S.Velani (Ex)	RM	2	0	8	0				
J.M.Vince (H)	RM	119.4	17	452	15	30.13	5- 41	1	–
A.C.Voges (M)	SLC	9	1	16	1	16.00	1- 10	–	–
G.G.Wagg (Gm)	LM	295.2	63	971	18	53.94	3- 78	–	–
N.Wagner (NZ)	LMF	108	26	332	15	22.13	5- 45	1	–
D.J.Wainwright (De)	SLA	296	42	924	17	54.35	3- 46	–	–
A.G.Wakely (Nh)	OB	1	0	3	0				
C.A.Wallis (DU)	RM	63	4	317	4	79.25	2- 63	–	–
H.T.Waters (Gm)	RMF	30	5	89	3	29.66	2- 35	2	–
N.A.T.Watkins (DU)	SLA	54	4	270	3	90.00	2- 76	–	–
S.R.Watson (A)	RMF	100.3	45	205	2	102.50	1- 31	–	–
L.W.P.Wells (Sx)	OB	55	6	199	2	99.50	2- 44	–	–
T.J.Wells (Le)	RMF	37	5	129	1	129.00	1- 36	–	–
M.H.Wessels (Nt)	(WK)	2	0	11	0				
T.Westley (Ex)	OB	48	8	151	1	151.00	1- 7	–	–
I.J.Westwood (Wa)	OB	6.5	1	11	1	11.00	1- 11	–	–
C.L.White (Nh)	LBG	25.2	4	99	2	49.50	1- 18	–	–
G.G.White (Nh/Nt)	SLA	43.4	10	114	3	38.00	2- 24	–	–
W.A.White (La)	RMF	131	16	452	8	56.50	2- 69	–	–
R.A.Whiteley (De/Wo)	LMF	40	1	189	2	94.50	1- 23	–	–
R.J.D.Willett (DU)	RM	34	5	141	1	141.00	1- 80	–	–
D.J.Willey (Nh)	LFM	361.3	66	1122	45	24.93	5- 67	2	–
B.Williams (OU)	RSM	6	1	30	0				
R.E.M.Williams (Le)	RMF	145.1	22	521	10	52.10	4- 69	–	–
T.J.Williams (OU)	RMF	27	9	69	8	8.62	5- 34	1	–
K.S.Williamson (NZ/Y)	OB	135.1	24	472	10	47.20	3- 68	–	–
G.C.Wilson (Sy)	(WK)	7	0	43	0				
C.R.Woakes (E/EL/Wa)	RMF	287.4	58	863	33	26.15	5- 42	1	–
C.P.Wood (H)	LM	231.3	65	659	15	43.93	3- 30	–	–
M.A.Wood (Du)	RMF	209.4	38	650	27	24.07	5- 44	1	–
B.J.Wright (Gm)	RM	1	0	7	0				
C.J.C.Wright (EL/Wa)	RFM	224	44	748	19	39.36	6- 31	1	–
L.J.Wright (Sx)	RM	77.3	15	256	6	42.66	2- 36	–	–
A.C.F.Wyatt (Le)	RMF	312.1	74	974	24	40.58	3- 35	–	–
B.A.Wylie (CU)	SLA	34	5	182	1	182.00	1-111	–	–
M.H.Yardy (Sx)	LM/SLA	10	0	41	0				
D.R.Young (LBU)	RM	1	0	2	0				
E.G.C.Young (Gs)	SLA	5	0	25	0				

FIRST-CLASS CAREER RECORDS

Compiled by Philip Bailey

The following career records are for all players who appeared in first-class cricket during the 2013 season, and are complete to the end of that season. Some players who did not appear in 2013 but may do so in 2014 are included.

BATTING AND FIELDING

'1000' denotes instances of scoring 1000 runs in a season. Where these have been achieved outside the British Isles they are shown after a plus sign.

	M	I	NO	HS	Runs	Avge	100	50	1000	Ct/St
Abbott, K.J.	42	61	11	80	956	19.12	–	4	–	11
Adams, A.R.	160	220	23	124	4421	22.44	3	20	–	103
Adams, J.H.K.	159	279	26	262*	9810	38.77	19	49	4	135
Agar, A.C.	13	21	7	98	474	33.85	–	4	–	4
Agarwal, S.S.	13	21	3	313*	899	49.94	3	3	–	4
Agathangelou, A.P.	41	72	4	158	2364	34.76	5	13	0+1	66
Ali, K.	130	182	28	84*	2621	17.01	–	7	–	33
Ali, M.M.	107	186	17	250	6388	37.79	12	38	2	68
Ali, S.A.	1	2	–	8	10	5.00	–	–	–	–
Allchin, A.T.A.	1	1	–	0	0	0.00	–	–	–	–
Allenby, J.	103	160	25	138*	5627	41.68	9	40	1	105
Allin, T.W.	1	1	–	0	0	0.00	–	–	–	–
Ambrose, T.R.	165	249	24	251*	7715	34.28	11	48	–	406/23
Amla, H.M.	168	278	25	311*	13127	51.88	40	66	0+2	124
Anderson, J.M.	156	190	70	37*	1189	9.90	–	–	–	83
Andrew, G.M.	83	126	16	180*	2649	24.08	1	15	–	30
Ansari, A.S.	17	27	5	193	675	30.68	2	1	–	5
Ansari, Z.S.	23	37	5	83*	630	19.68	–	3	–	11
Anyon, J.E.	102	132	42	64*	1282	14.24	–	4	–	30
Arshad, U.	5	6	–	83	170	28.33	–	1	–	1
Ashar Zaidi	90	149	12	202	5242	38.26	11	26	0+1	76
Ashraf, M.A.	21	19	5	10	56	4.00	–	–	–	2
Atkinson, J.J.	7	10	–	34	126	12.60	–	–	–	6/1
Azeem Rafiq	24	28	3	100	549	21.96	1	2	–	8
Azhar Ullah	62	80	44	41	497	13.80	–	–	–	16
Bailey, G.J.	96	170	15	160*	5936	38.29	14	30	–	86
Bairstow, J.M.	79	131	20	205	4834	43.54	8	31	1	160/5
Baker, G.C.	7	10	1	66	327	36.33	–	3	–	1
Balbirnie, A.	9	13	1	38	181	15.08	–	–	–	6
Balcombe, D.J.	63	79	18	73	867	14.21	–	2	–	14
Ball, A.J.	11	18	1	69	292	17.17	–	1	–	5
Ball, J.T.	2	3	1	15	19	9.50	–	–	–	–
Ballance, G.S.	65	101	14	210	4743	54.51	18	22	1+1	62
Barker, K.H.D.	43	50	7	125	1212	28.18	3	2	–	15
Barrow, A.W.R.	26	43	1	83*	782	18.61	–	3	–	30
Bates, M.D.	39	50	4	103	943	20.50	1	4	–	120/5
Batty, G.J.	194	296	46	133	5990	23.96	2	28	–	145
Batty, J.N.	221	346	38	168*	9685	31.44	20	41	1	605/68
Beer, W.A.T.	8	10	2	39	182	22.75	–	–	–	3
Bell, D.W.	7	11	2	47	134	14.88	–	–	–	13/7
Bell, I.R.	228	383	43	262*	15580	45.82	44	80	4	164
Bell-Drummond, D.J.	20	32	2	102*	838	27.93	1	5	–	11
Benkenstein, D.M.	264	408	47	259	15962	44.21	38	86	5	169

242

F-C	M	I	NO	HS	Runs	Avge	100	50	1000	Ct/St
Berg, G.K.	70	112	12	130*	2980	29.80	2	17	–	45
Billings, S.W.	8	12	–	131	398	33.16	1	1	–	10/1
Bird, J.M.	23	22	11	26	87	7.90	–	–	–	10
Bishnoi, C.	2	4	–	60	139	34.75	–	2	–	2
Blake, A.J.	28	47	2	105*	993	22.06	1	4	–	17
Bodenstein, C.J.	2	4	–	27	32	8.00	–	–	–	1
Bollinger, D.E.	80	89	37	31*	362	6.96	–	–	–	27
Bopara, R.S.	138	229	28	229	8338	41.48	23	32	1	80
Borrington, P.M.	42	72	8	105	1753	27.39	2	8	–	24
Borthwick, S.G.	59	90	15	135	2322	30.96	4	12	1	73
Boult, T.A.	42	57	18	46	471	12.07	–	–	–	17
Boyce, M.A.G.	93	163	9	135	4413	28.65	6	21	–	56
Bracewell, D.A.J.	41	65	8	97	1161	20.36	–	7	–	15
Bragg, W.D.	60	103	2	110	2815	27.87	1	19	1	25/1
Brathwaite, R.M.R.	26	28	10	76*	226	12.55	–	1	–	3
Breese, G.R.	120	193	22	165*	4511	26.38	4	27	–	106
Bresnan, T.T.	128	166	29	126*	3731	27.23	3	17	–	50
Briggs, D.R.	50	58	11	54	615	13.08	–	1	–	17
Broad, S.C.J.	115	153	25	169	3033	23.69	1	17	–	38
Brooks, J.A.	49	56	21	53	427	12.20	–	1	–	14
Brown, B.C.	51	79	13	112	2291	34.71	4	15	–	122/10
Brown, K.R.	55	92	5	114	2290	26.32	1	13	–	28
Browne, N.L.J.	3	5	1	22*	26	6.50	–	–	–	1
Brownlie, D.G.	47	84	10	171	3042	41.10	8	14	0+1	60
Buck, N.L.	51	67	18	27	421	8.59	–	–	–	6
Buckley, R.S.	2	2	–	6	10	5.00	–	–	–	1
Burgoyne, P.I.	12	21	2	104	538	28.31	2	1	–	9
Burns, J.A.	32	55	5	140*	1976	39.52	5	9	–	23
Burns, R.J.	27	46	3	121	1693	39.37	4	8	–	22
Buttler, J.C.	48	70	6	144	2031	31.73	3	9	–	82/2
Carberry, M.A.	146	254	22	300*	10086	43.47	28	47	3	66
Carter, A.	18	19	8	17*	107	9.72	–	–	–	4
Cato, S.J.	1	1	–	33	33	33.00	–	–	–	–
Cessford, G.	6	6	2	20	45	11.25	–	–	–	1
Chadwick, T.R.	3	4	–	21	37	9.25	–	–	–	2
Chambers, M.A.	50	62	21	58	281	6.85	–	1	–	14
Chanderpaul, S.	310	505	93	303*	22820	55.38	67	115	1+1	175
Chapple, G.	295	408	70	155	8215	24.30	6	37	–	98
Chawla, P.P.	88	126	12	156	3596	31.54	4	25	–	44
Chopra, V.	114	189	13	233*	6642	37.73	14	31	3	127
Choudhry, S.H.	16	25	6	75	420	22.10	–	4	–	6
Christian, D.T.	38	66	5	131*	1755	28.77	3	8	–	40
Clare, J.L.	55	80	9	130	1720	24.22	2	8	–	27
Clarke, M.J.	164	283	27	329*	12446	48.61	41	45	0+1	176
Clarke, R.	164	251	29	214	7880	35.49	16	37	1	251
Claydon, M.E.	53	67	14	55	816	15.39	–	1	–	8
Cobb, J.J.	63	109	8	148*	2330	23.06	2	12	–	30
Cockbain, I.A.	28	47	3	127	1308	29.72	2	8	–	23
Coetzer, K.J.	74	124	11	219	3833	33.92	8	16	–	36
Coleman, F.R.J.	7	12	–	110	219	18.25	1	–	–	4
Coles, M.T.	55	74	13	103*	1296	21.24	1	6	–	18
Collingwood, P.D.	233	400	34	206	13139	35.89	26	69	2	271
Collymore, C.D.	167	223	103	23	913	7.60	–	–	–	49
Compton, N.R.D.	122	213	28	254*	8129	43.94	20	39	4	61
Cook, A.N.	191	340	26	294	14899	47.44	44	71	5+1	179
Cooke, C.B.	13	22	2	92	580	29.00	–	3	–	14/1

F-C	M	I	NO	HS	Runs	Avge	100	50	1000	Ct/St
Copeland, T.A.	47	56	10	106	993	21.58	1	5	–	43
Cornick, J.P.P.	2	3	–	10	11	3.66	–	–	–	1
Cosker, D.A.	225	295	85	52	3017	14.36	–	1	–	133
Cowan, E.J.M.	100	180	12	225	6712	39.95	16	30	0+1	77
Cowan, J.D.	2	4	–	11	26	6.50	–	–	–	–
Cowdrey, F.K.	2	3	1	62	100	50.00	–	1	–	–
Cox, O.B.	25	44	11	65	719	21.78	–	4	–	67/3
Cox, R.D.	2	2	–	15	20	10.00	–	–	–	–
Craddock, T.R.	17	22	7	21	135	9.00	–	–	–	3
Croft, S.J.	102	159	15	154*	4507	31.29	6	27	–	88
Crook, S.P.	65	81	11	97	2092	29.88	–	16	–	21
Cross, G.D.	62	94	5	125	2196	24.67	3	11	–	155/23
Cross, M.H.	3	5	–	29	79	15.80	–	–	–	7
Daggett, L.M.	71	83	35	50*	613	12.77	–	1	–	13
Davies, A.L.	4	3	1	30*	58	29.00	–	–	–	5
Davies, M.	109	138	49	62	1118	12.56	–	2	–	21
Davies, S.L.	3	4	–	42	91	22.75	–	–	–	3
Davies, S.M.	137	227	24	192	7872	38.77	13	38	4	384/20
Davison, S.R.	2	4	–	13	26	6.50	–	–	–	–
Dawson, L.A.	79	125	14	169	3889	35.03	6	22	1	96
de Bruyn, Z.	237	399	35	266*	14154	38.88	29	78	1+1	149
Denly, J.L.	118	209	13	199	6625	33.80	15	32	2	50
Denning, J.S.T.	2	2	–	22*	28	–	–	–	–	1
Dent, C.D.J.	52	94	8	153	2926	34.02	4	16	1	72
Dernbach, J.W.	83	107	39	56*	619	9.10	–	1	–	10
Dexter, N.J.	94	154	19	146	5024	37.21	11	26	–	77
Dibble, A.J.	3	6	2	43	84	21.00	–	–	–	–
Dockrell, G.H.	29	34	9	53	291	11.64	–	1	–	11
D'Oliveira, B.L.	3	6	–	19	62	10.33	–	–	–	–
D'Souza, D.A.	3	5	–	23	56	11.20	–	–	–	–
Duckett, B.M.	4	6	1	53*	145	29.00	–	1	–	4
Dunn, M.P.	7	6	6	2*	3	–	–	–	–	–
Durston, W.J.	83	144	19	151	4299	34.39	6	25	1	84
Eckersley, E.J.H.	41	71	7	147	2495	38.98	6	10	1	80/3
Edwards, G.A.	4	5	1	19	56	14.00	–	–	–	1
Elgar, D.	89	154	14	268	6177	44.12	18	24	0+1	63
Elkin, Z.W.	4	7	–	138	197	28.14	1	–	–	3
Elliott, T.C.	5	8	1	101	257	36.71	1	–	–	–
Ellison, C.P.	4	5	–	36	46	9.20	–	–	–	1
Endersby, D.M.	4	6	–	22	49	8.16	–	–	–	5
Ervine, S.M.	168	262	29	237*	8139	34.93	14	43	–	141
Evans, A.C.	8	10	7	14*	34	11.33	–	–	–	1
Evans, L.J.	28	46	3	178	1702	39.58	4	9	–	16
Faulkner, J.P.	38	56	10	89	1379	29.97	–	8	–	18
Fawad Ahmed	18	27	10	23	170	10.00	–	–	–	8
Fell, T.C.	10	16	2	94*	477	34.07	–	3	–	3
Finch, A.J.	33	58	1	122	1685	29.56	2	11	–	31
Finch, H.Z.	1	2	–	11	14	7.00	–	–	–	1
Finn, S.T.	91	110	34	56	552	7.26	–	1	–	29
Fletcher, L.J.	53	76	19	92	890	15.61	–	3	–	12
Foakes, B.T.	20	25	2	120	758	32.95	2	4	–	15
Footitt, M.H.A.	40	54	17	30	318	8.59	–	–	–	12
Foster, J.S.	223	336	44	212	10829	37.08	19	55	1	624/52
Franks, P.J.	215	313	56	123*	7185	27.95	4	41	–	69
Freckingham, O.H.	15	21	2	30	204	10.73	–	–	–	4
Fuller, J.K.	20	25	2	57	299	13.00	–	1	–	7

F-C	M	I	NO	HS	Runs	Avge	100	50	1000	Ct/St
Fulton, P.G.	119	208	16	301*	8079	42.07	14	48	0+1	90
Gale, A.W.	111	174	13	272	6033	37.47	15	25	1	41
Gambhir, G.	146	247	21	233*	11513	50.94	34	50	–	91
Gatting, J.S.	35	50	4	152	1376	29.91	3	6	–	17
Gidman, A.P.R.	174	298	24	211	9904	36.14	20	54	5	114
Gidman, W.R.S.	42	64	11	143	1900	35.84	2	12	1	9
Gillespie, M.R.	78	96	13	81*	1367	16.46	–	5	–	18
Glover, J.C.	26	34	9	55	328	13.12	–	2	–	7
Godleman, B.A.	78	134	4	130	3722	28.63	5	18	–	55
Goodwin, M.W.	312	539	46	344*	23376	47.41	71	97	10+1	162
Gordon, R.O.	4	4	1	13	38	12.66	–	–	–	2
Green, M.J.E.	3	4	2	4	4	2.00	–	–	–	–
Gregory, L.	16	22	3	52	282	14.84	–	1	–	3
Griffiths, D.A.	36	50	19	31*	202	6.51	–	–	–	4
Groenewald, T.D.	82	113	31	78	1515	18.47	–	4	–	29
Gubbins, N.R.T.	2	4	–	14	40	10.00	–	–	–	1
Guptill, M.J.	75	137	8	195*	4300	33.33	7	24	–	73
Gurney, H.F.	42	46	20	24*	135	5.19	–	–	–	6
Haddin, B.J.	162	265	33	169	9032	38.93	16	49	–	528/37
Haggett, C.J.	12	14	7	44*	249	35.57	–	–	–	3
Hales, A.D.	61	104	3	184	3367	34.01	6	22	1	57
Hall, A.J.	226	332	44	163	10379	36.03	15	62	1	213
Hamilton-Brown, R.J.	66	112	7	171*	3576	34.05	8	16	1	39
Hammond, M.A.H.	2	2	–	4	4	2.00	–	–	–	1
Hannon-Dalby, O.J.	28	29	12	13	82	4.82	–	–	–	3
Harinath, A.	44	76	4	154	2081	28.90	3	13	–	11
Harmison, B.W.	62	98	9	110	2525	28.37	5	12	–	34
Harris, J.A.R.	75	102	21	87*	1721	21.24	–	7	–	18
Harris, P.G.	4	4	2	20	34	17.00	–	–	–	–
Harris, R.J.	66	103	17	94	1638	19.04	–	8	–	32
Harrison, J.	7	10	1	35	120	13.33	–	–	–	–
Hatchett, L.J.	13	16	4	21	104	8.66	–	–	–	2
Hearne, A.G.	2	3	–	39	47	15.66	–	–	–	–
Helm, T.G.	1	2	–	18	22	11.00	–	–	–	–
Henderson, C.W.	273	377	79	81	5637	18.91	–	20	–	88
Herring, C.L.	6	7	–	43	122	17.42	–	–	–	14
Hickey, M.R.	4	7	1	53	125	20.83	–	1	–	–
Higginbottom, M.	6	11	4	31*	108	15.42	–	–	–	–
Hildreth, J.C.	168	274	22	303*	10880	43.17	29	50	4	145
Hobden, M.E.	4	2	1	18	33	33.00	–	–	–	–
Hobson, I.H.	2	4	–	13	17	4.25	–	–	–	2
Hodd, A.J.	70	98	17	123	2314	28.56	4	11	–	148/13
Hodgson, D.M.	10	19	2	94*	431	25.35	–	4	–	32/1
Hogan, M.G.	50	74	24	51	899	17.98	–	1	–	20
Hogg, K.W.	105	132	26	88	2596	24.49	–	16	–	21
Hoggard, M.J.	239	305	94	89*	1908	9.04	–	4	–	63
Horton, P.J.	136	227	19	209	8019	38.55	18	43	3	136/1
Housego, D.M.	35	61	5	150	1616	28.85	3	7	–	18
Howell, B.A.C.	31	50	7	83*	1164	27.06	–	8	–	13
Hughes, A.L.	6	11	–	33	136	12.36	–	–	–	3
Hughes, C.F.	39	71	3	270*	2189	32.19	5	8	–	32
Hughes, P.H.	8	15	2	92	396	30.46	–	3	–	1
Hughes, P.J.	101	187	12	198	7832	44.75	21	43	–	63
Hunn, M.D.	1	1	–	0	0	0.00	–	–	–	1
Hussain, G.M.	34	53	20	42	319	9.66	–	–	–	5
Hussey, D.J.	178	279	26	275	13175	52.07	43	59	4+1	229

F-C	M	I	NO	HS	Runs	Avge	100	50	1000	Ct/St
Hutton, B.A.	2	4	1	42	71	23.66	–	–	–	1
Ireland, A.J.	43	64	18	29	285	6.19	–	–	–	9
Jackson, C.F.	1	1	–	26	26	26.00	–	–	–	1
Jaques, P.A.	189	326	12	244	15141	48.21	42	70	4+2	146
Jarvis, K.M.	30	42	15	48	355	13.14	–	–	–	10
Javid, A.	20	32	4	133	821	29.32	2	2	–	11
Jeffery, B.A.	5	8	–	39	127	15.87	–	–	–	6
Jennings, K.K.	26	46	2	127	1263	28.70	3	5	–	10
Jewell, T.M.	9	7	1	70	185	30.83	–	2	–	2
Johnson, J.A.M.	4	7	1	61	131	21.83	–	1	–	2
Johnson, M.A.	20	30	1	53	384	13.24	–	1	–	48/2
Johnson, R.M.	26	43	3	72	881	22.02	–	5	–	48/2
Jones, A.J.	3	4	1	26	39	13.00	–	–	–	2
Jones, C.R.	28	46	2	130	883	20.06	1	6	–	14
Jones, G.O.	190	289	27	178	8479	32.36	15	45	2	580/36
Jones, O.J.	4	7	1	83	240	40.00	–	3	–	–
Jones, R.A.	44	67	12	62	633	11.50	–	2	–	18
Jordan, C.J.	59	78	12	92	1473	22.31	–	6	–	53
Joyce, E.C.	199	330	30	211	13829	46.09	31	77	7	172
Joyce, J.L.	1	2	1	25	27	27.00	–	–	–	1
Kapil, A.	10	16	1	54	240	16.00	–	1	–	2
Katich, S.M.	266	448	52	306	20926	52.84	58	111	4+4	227
Keedy, G.	223	256	125	64	1429	10.90	–	2	–	54
Kelsall, S.	2	4	–	35	50	12.50	–	–	–	1
Kemp, B.W.	3	5	2	11	23	7.66	–	–	–	2
Kennedy, A.D.J.	4	6	1	61	183	36.60	–	1	–	11
Keogh, R.I.	9	13	2	221	464	42.18	1	1	–	1
Kerrigan, S.C.	52	57	22	62*	388	11.08	–	1	–	15
Kervezee, A.N.	71	121	7	155	3413	29.93	4	20	1	37
Key, R.W.T.	270	466	36	270*	17900	41.62	51	69	7	148
Khawaja, U.T.	69	120	11	214	4425	40.59	11	23	–	46
Kieswetter, C.	101	152	21	164	5219	39.83	11	26	1	292/8
Kirby, S.P.	167	234	72	57	1320	8.14	–	1	–	37
Klinger, M.	118	209	21	255	7082	37.67	15	32	1+1	113
Knight, T.C.	2	3	1	14	15	7.50	–	–	–	1
Latham, T.W.M.	27	46	5	145	1477	36.02	2	10	–	45/1
Leach, J.	14	23	3	114	474	23.70	1	3	–	3
Leach, M.J.	8	10	3	21	66	9.42	–	–	–	–
Leaning, J.A.	1	1	–	0	0	0.00	–	–	–	–
Lee, J.E.	4	7	1	34	87	14.50	–	–	–	2
Lees, A.Z.	11	18	3	275*	659	43.93	3	1	–	2
Lester, T.J.	4	6	4	1	1	0.50	–	–	–	–
Levi, R.E.	39	62	8	150*	2105	38.98	5	12	–	28
Lewis, J.	243	347	70	71	4519	16.31	–	13	–	61
Liddle, C.J.	19	17	8	53	125	13.88	–	1	–	6
Lilley, A.M.	2	2	2	35*	39	–	–	–	–	–
Linley, T.E.	54	73	15	42	477	8.22	–	–	–	20
Lloyd, D.L.	3	5	1	16	27	6.75	–	–	–	–
London, A.B.	12	21	3	81	497	27.61	–	4	–	9
Lucas, D.S.	95	124	27	60	1698	17.50	–	2	–	18
Lumb, M.J.	166	277	18	221*	9374	36.19	19	51	3	103
Lyon, N.M.	46	60	19	40*	450	10.97	–	–	–	10
Lyth, A.	82	133	6	248*	4777	37.61	7	33	1	84
McCarter, G.J.	7	9	2	29*	97	13.85	–	–	–	1
McCullum, B.B.	124	217	12	225	7169	34.97	11	43	–	290/19
McCullum, N.L.	58	90	8	106*	2114	25.78	1	13	–	67

F-C	M	I	NO	HS	Runs	Avge	100	50	1000	Ct/St
McKay, P.J.	2	4	1	33	45	15.00	–	–	–	–
McKenzie, N.D.	263	448	57	237	17856	45.66	49	83	1	229
MacLeod, C.A.R.	2	4	–	15	27	6.75	–	–	–	5
MacLeod, C.S.	11	15	3	67	277	23.08	–	2	–	5
MacQueen, A.	3	6	–	69	141	23.50	–	1	–	2
MacVicar, W.A.	2	3	–	41	61	20.33	–	–	–	2
Machan, M.W.	12	16	1	103	442	29.46	1	2	–	6
Maddinson, N.J.	27	50	4	181	1863	40.50	5	8	–	20
Maddy, D.L.	284	460	32	229*	13796	32.23	27	63	4	290
Madsen, W.L.	97	172	11	231*	5951	36.96	16	29	1	78
Magoffin, S.J.	104	144	35	79	2012	18.45	–	4	–	29
Mahmood, S.I.	119	154	19	94	2148	15.91	–	10	–	29
Malan, D.J.	95	161	12	156*	5185	34.79	10	27	1	117
Marriott, W.W.J.	1	2	–	81	86	43.00	–	1	–	–
Marsden, J.	1	–	–	–	–	–	–	–	–	–
Marshall, H.J.H.	208	346	23	170	11831	36.62	24	58	2	110
Martin, B.P.	121	165	38	114	2306	18.15	2	5	–	45
Mascarenhas, A.D.	195	291	32	131	6495	25.07	8	23	–	76
Masters, D.D.	176	213	32	119	2533	13.99	1	6	–	55
Maxwell, G.J.	20	34	3	155*	1221	39.38	2	9	–	20
Meaker, S.C.	51	66	11	94	857	15.58	–	4	–	6
Meschede, C.A.J.	22	30	3	62	513	19.00	–	3	–	9
Mickleburgh, J.C.	70	124	2	243	3523	28.87	6	17	–	47
Middlebrook, J.D.	204	290	43	127	6999	28.33	10	30	–	97
Miles, A.J.	3	4	2	29*	45	22.50	–	–	–	2
Miles, C.N.	14	15	1	50*	185	13.21	–	1	–	1
Miller, A.S.	19	26	12	35	85	6.07	–	–	–	5
Mills, T.S.	18	22	9	20*	102	7.84	–	–	–	8
Milnes, T.P.	13	13	2	52*	278	25.27	–	1	–	3
Mitchell, D.K.H.	115	211	25	298	6986	37.55	14	32	3	157
Moore, S.C.	145	262	19	246	8843	36.39	17	41	4	72
Morgan, E.J.G.	78	127	15	209*	3859	34.45	9	18	1	63/1
Morris, A.J.	2	4	1	18*	33	11.00	–	–	–	1
Morris, C.A.J.	5	8	3	33*	79	15.80	–	–	–	2
Muchall, G.J.	137	237	11	219	6537	28.92	11	33	–	93
Mullaney, S.J.	54	87	6	165*	2774	34.24	5	16	–	38
Murphy, D.	48	61	13	81	1351	28.14	–	10	–	139/9
Murtagh, T.J.	144	195	59	74*	2940	21.61	–	10	–	43
Mustard, P.	165	255	32	130	6953	31.17	6	42	–	553/18
Myburgh, J.G.	80	145	18	203	5509	43.37	13	32	–	52
Mylavarapu, S.V.S.	1	–	–	–	–	–	–	–	–	–
Naik, J.K.H.	53	80	18	109*	1332	21.48	1	3	–	28
Napier, G.R.	139	189	40	196	4864	32.64	6	28	–	51
Nash, B.P.	119	195	28	207	6597	39.50	17	27	1	42
Nash, C.D.	129	220	17	184	7857	38.70	16	38	3	61
Newby, O.J.	51	44	12	38*	323	10.09	–	–	–	8
Newton, R.I.	33	53	6	119*	1837	39.08	5	7	–	8
Nicholson, G.F.	1	1	–	1	1	1.00	–	–	–	–
North, M.J.	199	345	29	239*	12730	40.28	34	64	0+1	147
Northeast, S.A.	75	132	5	176	4000	31.49	6	24	–	42
Norwell, L.C.	18	25	12	26	121	9.30	–	–	–	4
O'Brien, N.J.	125	193	20	182	6138	35.47	12	29	–	325/34
Onions, G.J.	115	149	52	41	1261	13.00	–	–	–	25
Overton, C.	8	9	1	50	83	10.37	–	1	–	4
Overton, J.	16	24	8	34*	186	11.62	–	–	–	1
Owen, W.T.	18	21	6	69	270	18.00	–	1	–	5

247

F-C	M	I	NO	HS	Runs	Avge	100	50	1000	Ct/St
Palladino, A.P.	90	123	27	106	1438	14.97	1	5	–	26
Panesar, M.S.	195	239	80	46*	1366	8.59	–	–	–	38
Pardoe, M.G.	46	85	5	102	2007	25.08	1	13	–	19
Parry, S.D.	6	5	1	20	40	10.00	–	–	–	1
Patel, A.K.	2	3	–	38	61	20.33	–	–	–	1
Patel, J.S.	154	191	51	120	3004	21.45	1	16	–	73
Patel, L.A.	7	12	–	32	167	13.91	–	–	–	4
Patel, R.H.	11	17	7	26*	135	13.50	–	–	–	3
Patel, S.R.	129	201	13	256	7420	39.46	18	36	2	79
Patel, Z.R.	1	2	–	0	0	0.00	–	–	–	–
Patterson, S.A.	73	82	28	53	807	14.94	–	1	–	13
Pattinson, J.L.	29	38	9	66	620	21.37	–	1	–	7
Payne, D.A.	32	40	11	62	372	12.82	–	1	–	9
Peters, S.D.	236	397	31	222	13168	35.97	31	64	4	184
Petersen, A.N.	163	289	14	210	10915	39.69	33	43	1+2	126
Pettini, M.L.	137	231	36	208*	6746	34.59	8	41	1	97
Philander, V.D.	99	128	19	168	2765	25.36	2	8	–	26
Phillips, B.J.	124	172	32	100*	2991	21.36	1	16	–	38
Phillips, D.S.	1	1	–	7	7	7.00	–	–	–	–
Phillips, T.J.	76	106	17	89	1836	20.62	–	7	–	49
Pietersen, K.P.	206	339	23	254*	15688	49.64	49	67	3	147
Pinner, N.D.	13	19	–	82	397	20.89	–	3	–	12
Piolet, S.A.	4	7	1	30	78	13.00	–	–	–	4
Plunkett, L.E.	120	164	30	107*	3039	22.67	1	14	–	73
Pollock, A.W.	2	3	1	44*	44	22.00	–	–	–	1
Ponting, R.T.	289	494	62	257	24150	55.90	82	106	0+1	309
Porterfield, W.T.S.	92	151	6	175	4371	30.14	6	24	–	98
Powell, M.J.	236	389	40	299	13421	38.45	27	70	5	136
Poynter, S.W.	8	9	–	63	201	22.33	–	1	–	23/2
Poynton, T.	33	50	6	106	941	21.38	1	5	–	81/6
Poysden, J.E.	4	4	–	47	63	15.75	–	–	–	2
Prince, A.G.	248	400	47	254	15239	43.16	36	79	2+1	187
Prior, M.J.	237	361	42	201*	12695	39.79	27	73	3	598/41
Probert, T.J.W.	4	6	4	4*	9	4.50	–	–	–	2
Procter, L.A.	39	57	4	106	1704	32.15	1	10	–	7
Pyrah, R.M.	42	51	6	134*	1256	27.91	3	6	–	20
Querl, R.G.	15	19	9	188*	490	49.00	1	1	–	5
Quiney, R.J.	64	110	8	153	3595	35.24	8	19	–	55
Qureshi, U.A.	4	6	–	47	92	15.33	–	–	–	–
Raine, B.A.	6	10	1	72	201	22.33	–	1	–	1
Rankin, W.B.	63	73	32	43	345	8.41	–	–	–	18
Rashid, A.U.	114	159	30	180	4534	35.14	7	26	–	54
Ratnayake, D.E.M.	5	9	–	46	164	18.22	–	–	–	2
Rayner, O.P.	77	98	20	143*	1953	25.03	2	10	–	92
Read, C.M.W.	290	435	71	240	13239	36.37	21	73	3	863/47
Redfern, D.J.	70	116	7	133	3213	29.47	2	23	–	37
Reece, L.M.	14	24	4	114*	1011	50.55	1	9	–	11
Reed, M.T.	16	22	9	27	89	6.84	–	–	–	2
Rees, G.P.	101	175	9	154	5514	33.21	13	30	2	79
Riazuddin, H.	9	9	2	55*	130	18.57	–	1	–	3
Richardson, A.	169	194	83	91	1176	10.59	–	1	–	50
Richardson, M.J.	22	33	1	129	883	27.59	2	5	–	53/1
Riley, A.E.N.	20	24	6	21*	118	6.55	–	–	–	8
Roberts, M.D.T.	6	9	1	44	159	19.87	–	–	–	2
Robson, A.J.	3	4	–	49	59	14.75	–	–	–	–
Robson, S.D.	59	106	9	215*	3851	39.70	8	16	1	66

F-C	M	I	NO	HS	Runs	Avge	100	50	1000	Ct/St
Roderick, G.H.	25	36	9	152*	1117	41.37	2	5	–	53/1
Rogers, C.J.L.	249	442	32	319	20498	49.99	62	95	7+2	212
Roland-Jones, T.S.	40	55	12	52	692	16.09	–	1	–	13
Root, J.E.	51	88	10	236	3490	44.74	9	11	2	28
Rossington, A.M.	6	10	2	103*	227	28.37	1	1	–	16/1
Rouse, A.P.	1	1	–	9	9	9.00	–	–	–	–
Rouse, H.P.	1	2	–	15	29	14.50	–	–	–	–
Roy, J.J.	32	57	4	106*	1486	28.03	1	6	–	25
Rudolph, J.A.	234	400	26	228*	16629	44.46	46	77	4+1	205
Rushworth, C.	37	50	19	28	359	11.58	–	–	–	7
Russell, C.J.	17	22	4	22	129	7.16	–	–	–	4
Rutherford, H.D.	29	51	–	239	2065	40.49	6	7	0+1	20
Sabin, L.M.	2	4	–	50	91	22.75	–	1	–	1
Sadler, P.T.	6	9	2	34	65	9.28	–	–	–	4
Saeed Ajmal	118	161	46	53	1381	12.00	–	3	–	38
Sales, D.J.G.	246	389	35	303*	14037	39.65	29	64	6	219
Salisbury, M.E.T.	4	5	2	5	10	3.33	–	–	–	1
Salter, A.G.	7	10	3	21	98	14.00	–	–	–	2
Samaraweera, T.T.	271	389	70	231	15501	48.59	43	76	0+1	201
Sandhu, G.S.	4	2	1	8	15	15.00	–	–	–	–
Sarwan, R.R.	215	364	26	291	13221	39.11	33	70	–	152
Sayers, C.J.	16	25	2	38*	293	12.73	–	–	–	5
Sayers, J.J.	108	179	14	187	5457	33.07	11	28	1	63
Senaratne, N.V.S.	3	6	–	82	118	19.66	–	1	–	–
Shah, O.A.	252	428	38	203	16357	41.94	45	79	8	200
Shah, R.A.C.	7	14	2	57*	288	24.00	–	2	–	3
Shahzad, A.	71	95	23	88	1702	23.63	–	5	–	10
Shantry, J.D.	41	51	13	55*	589	15.50	–	2	–	12
Shreck, C.E.	128	144	84	19*	351	5.85	–	–	–	34
Shrewsbury, T.W.	1	1	1	2*	2	–	–	–	–	–
Sibley, D.P.	3	4	–	242	264	66.00	1	–	–	1
Siddique, H.G.	3	4	–	37	53	13.25	–	–	–	2
Siddle, P.M.	84	112	17	103*	1634	17.20	1	4	–	33
Sidebottom, R.J.	189	236	67	61	2340	13.84	–	3	–	56
Silk, J.C.	5	10	–	127	423	42.30	2	1	–	5
Simpson, J.A.	67	105	14	143	2687	29.52	2	15	–	212/13
Slater, B.T.	16	29	1	89	584	20.85	–	4	–	3
Smith, G.C.	153	263	18	311	12141	49.55	35	49	–	222
Smith, G.M.	108	178	16	177	5172	31.92	7	31	–	33
Smith, G.P.	65	120	8	158*	3096	27.64	5	15	–	52
Smith, R.A.J.	3	4	1	39	100	33.33	–	–	–	–
Smith, S.P.D.	50	88	10	177	3365	43.14	8	18	–	60
Smith, T.C.	83	118	21	128	2743	28.27	3	15	–	91
Smith, T.M.J.	22	31	5	50	430	16.53	–	1	–	6
Smith, W.R.	122	204	12	201*	6004	31.27	14	19	–	67
Sohail Tanvir	59	94	9	132	2389	28.10	4	12	–	24
Soilleux, A.C.	4	6	1	22	44	8.80	–	–	–	–
Solanki, V.S.	313	526	32	270	17738	35.90	33	93	6	335
Southee, T.G.	55	76	8	156	1337	19.66	1	4	–	21
Spriegel, M.N.W.	43	69	5	108*	1444	22.56	3	4	–	26
Starc, M.A.	39	47	17	99	742	24.73	–	4	–	18
Steele, O.J.	2	4	1	14	22	7.33	–	–	–	1
Stevens, D.I.	218	349	21	208	11578	35.29	28	55	3	161
Stirling, P.R.	19	30	–	115	907	30.23	3	5	–	12
Stokes, B.A.	58	95	7	185	3168	36.00	8	14	–	36
Stone, O.P.	3	3	1	26*	47	23.50	–	–	–	3

F-C	M	I	NO	HS	Runs	Avge	100	50	1000	Ct/St
Stoneman, M.D.	83	144	5	128	4074	29.30	7	22	1	49
Suppiah, A.V.	100	167	8	156	5156	32.42	8	29	1	56
Swann, G.P.	247	336	36	183	7764	25.88	4	37	–	190
Sykes, J.S.	7	12	2	34	139	13.90	–	–	–	3
Taylor, B.J.	1	2	1	20	20	20.00	–	–	–	1
Taylor, J.M.R.	12	19	2	63	451	26.52	–	2	–	8
Taylor, J.W.A.	99	159	22	237	6488	47.35	16	29	4	67
Taylor, L.R.P.L.	101	172	7	217	6708	40.65	14	38	–	128
Taylor, M.D.	3	3	2	26*	31	31.00	–	–	–	–
Taylor, R.M.L.	16	26	2	101*	488	20.33	1	1	–	8
ten Doeschate, R.N.	109	159	22	259*	6426	46.90	20	25	–	64
Terry, S.P.	6	7	1	59*	208	34.66	–	3	–	5
Thakor, S.J.	24	39	6	134	1288	39.03	2	9	–	6
Thomas, A.C.	142	200	39	119*	3826	23.76	2	13	–	36
Thomas, I.A.A.	6	10	5	11	49	9.80	–	–	–	1
Thompson, H.L.	2	4	–	40	67	16.75	–	–	–	–
Thompson, J.S.	2	4	–	15	32	8.00	–	–	–	–
Thornely, M.A.	39	67	2	131	1434	22.06	2	6	–	32
Thorp, C.D.	94	127	16	79*	1664	14.99	–	3	–	53
Tomlinson, J.A.	98	124	56	42	683	10.04	–	–	–	22
Topley, R.J.W.	25	29	13	9	34	2.12	–	–	–	7
Tredwell, J.C.	140	197	24	123*	3836	22.17	3	14	–	145
Trego, P.D.	152	222	30	140	6326	32.94	9	39	–	65
Tremlett, C.T.	130	164	42	64	2089	17.12	–	8	–	35
Trescothick, M.E.	310	534	30	284	21064	41.79	51	104	5	426
Trott, I.J.L.	205	344	37	226	13796	44.93	32	69	6	183
Troughton, J.O.	165	256	21	223	8390	35.70	19	43	1	86
Turner, A.J.	1	–	–	–	–	–	–	–	–	–
Turner, M.L.	28	33	15	57	324	18.00	–	1	–	10
van den Bergh, F.O.E.	4	5	1	34	53	13.25	–	–	–	–
Vanderspar, W.G.R.	2	4	–	37	78	19.50	–	–	–	1
Velani, K.S.	1	2	–	13	22	11.00	–	–	–	–
Vince, J.M.	69	109	12	180	3675	37.88	10	13	1	53
Voges, A.C.	135	230	28	180	8204	40.61	16	46	–	179
Wade, M.S.	68	106	20	113*	3403	39.56	6	22	–	238/8
Wagg, G.G.	101	142	13	108	3041	23.57	1	17	–	32
Wagner, N.	73	96	26	70	1411	20.15	–	6	–	21
Wainwright, D.J.	63	86	20	104*	1706	25.84	2	6	–	24
Wakely, A.G.	79	122	5	113*	3387	28.94	2	21	–	43
Wallace, M.A.	216	342	26	139	9299	29.42	15	42	1	543/49
Waller, M.T.C.	8	9	1	28	91	11.37	–	–	–	5
Wallis, C.A.	4	6	1	10	21	4.20	–	–	–	2
Walters, S.J.	65	108	7	188	3055	30.24	5	14	–	69
Warner, D.A.	36	63	3	211	2645	44.08	7	11	–	27
Waters, H.T.	51	69	36	54	411	12.45	–	1	–	12
Watkins, N.A.T.	5	8	1	38*	82	11.71	–	–	–	3
Watling, B.J.	74	132	15	164*	4361	37.27	8	26	–	117
Watson, S.R.	119	211	18	203*	8477	43.92	19	47	–	92
Webb, J.P.	4	8	–	38	77	9.62	–	–	–	3
Wells, L.W.P.	51	86	7	208	2658	33.64	7	9	–	27
Wells, T.J.	5	8	–	82	177	22.12	–	1	–	2
Wessels, M.H.	123	201	16	199	6321	34.16	14	30	–	209/14
Westaway, S.A.	3	5	2	63*	120	40.00	–	1	–	17
Westley, T.	76	130	11	185	3777	31.73	7	18	–	43
Westwood, I.J.	122	206	20	178	6156	33.09	12	34	–	70
Wheater, A.J.A.	66	92	13	164	3150	39.87	6	18	–	94/3

F-C	M	I	NO	HS	Runs	Avge	100	50	1000	Ct/St
White, C.L.	131	221	27	260*	7801	40.21	17	36	2	134
White, G.G.	24	36	5	65	441	14.22	–	2	–	8
White, W.A.	68	109	16	101*	2418	26.00	1	13	–	22
Whiteley, R.A.	35	57	7	130*	1387	27.74	2	6	–	19
Wilkin, O.	3	6	–	38	138	23.00	–	–	–	1
Willett, R.J.D.	1	2	2	2*	2	–	–	–	–	1
Willey, D.J.	43	56	9	81	1325	28.19	–	10	–	10
Williams, B.	9	15	2	92	399	30.69	–	2	–	5
Williams, R.E.M.	15	22	7	31	160	10.66	–	–	–	5
Williams, T.J.	1	1	1	9*	9	–	–	–	–	–
Williamson, K.S.	74	130	7	284*	5049	41.04	12	26	–	65
Wilson, G.C.	44	64	8	125	1709	30.51	2	8	–	65/1
Winter, M.J.	1	1	–	51	51	51.00	–	1	–	–
Woakes, C.R.	86	117	32	152*	3386	39.83	7	14	–	38
Wood, C.P.	30	42	3	105*	907	23.25	1	4	–	11
Wood, M.A.	13	19	3	58*	347	21.68	–	1	–	7
Wood, S.K.W.	2	2	–	45	47	23.50	–	–	–	–
Wright, B.J.	77	128	10	172	3252	27.55	5	14	–	41
Wright, C.J.C.	89	107	26	77	1388	17.13	–	5	–	15
Wright, L.J.	86	126	16	187	4136	37.60	11	20	–	37
Wyatt, A.C.F.	23	30	12	28	145	8.05	–	–	–	3
Wylie, B.A.	2	4	1	29*	35	11.66	–	–	–	–
Yardy, M.H.	173	287	27	257	9631	37.04	20	45	2	157
Yasir Arafat	193	281	41	170	6664	27.76	5	35	–	51
Young, D.R.	2	4	–	14	26	6.50	–	–	–	3
Young, E.G.C.	21	32	7	133	846	33.84	1	5	–	11

BOWLING

'50wS' denotes instances of taking 50 or more wickets in a season. Where these have been achieved outside the British Isles they are shown after a plus sign.

	Runs	Wkts	Avge	Best	5wI	10wM	50wS
Abbott, K.J.	3513	157	22.37	8-45	8	1	0+1
Adams, A.R.	15148	645	23.48	7-32	31	6	3
Adams, J.H.K.	718	13	55.23	2-16	–	–	–
Agar, A.C.	1225	34	36.02	5-65	1	–	–
Agarwal, S.S.	998	20	49.90	5-78	1	–	–
Agathangelou, A.P.	436	9	48.44	2-18	–	–	–
Ali, K.	13214	483	27.35	8-50	23	4	5
Ali, M.M.	5290	125	42.32	6-29	4	1	–
Ali, S.A.	103	2	51.50	2-76	–	–	–
Allchin, A.T.A.	178	1	178.00	1-98	–	–	–
Allenby, J.	5374	196	27.41	5-44	3	–	–
Allin, T.W.	65	0	–		–	–	–
Ambrose, T.R.	1	0	–		–	–	–
Amla, H.M.	275	1	275.00	1-10	–	–	–
Anderson, J.M.	16132	589	27.38	7-43	28	4	2
Andrew, G.M.	7163	201	35.63	5-58	4	–	1
Ansari, A.S.	605	14	43.21	4-50	–	–	–
Ansari, Z.S.	1154	29	39.79	5-33	1	–	–
Anyon, J.E.	10161	290	35.03	6-82	6	–	2
Arshad, U.	249	16	15.56	3-16	–	–	–
Ashar Zaidi	1619	56	28.91	4-50	–	–	–
Ashraf, M.A.	1268	43	29.48	5-32	1	–	–
Azeem Rafiq	1900	54	35.18	5-50	1	–	–
Azhar Ullah	5774	215	26.85	7-74	11	1	0+1

F-C	Runs	Wkts	Avge	Best	5wI	10wM	50wS
Bailey, G.J.	46	0	–				–
Baker, G.C.	593	7	84.71	2-35	–	–	–
Balbirnie, A.	95	2	47.50	1- 5	–	–	–
Balcombe, D.J.	6192	191	32.41	8-71	9	2	1
Ball, A.J.	730	18	40.55	3-36	–	–	–
Ball, J.T.	145	6	24.16	3-18	–	–	–
Ballance, G.S.	138	0	–				–
Barker, K.H.D.	3334	130	25.64	6-40	7	1	1
Barrow, A.W.R.	36	1	36.00	1- 4	–	–	–
Batty, G.J.	17271	505	34.20	7-52	21	2	2
Batty, J.N.	61	1	61.00	1-21	–	–	–
Beer, W.A.T.	443	13	34.07	3-31	–	–	–
Bell, I.R.	1598	47	34.00	4- 4	–	–	–
Bell-Drummond, D.J.	54	0	–				–
Benkenstein, D.M.	3615	100	36.15	4-16	–	–	–
Berg, G.K.	4454	140	31.81	6-58	3	–	–
Bird, J.M.	2264	109	20.77	6-25	6	2	0+1
Bishnoi, C.	152	1	152.00	1-52	–	–	–
Blake, A.J.	129	3	43.00	2- 9	–	–	–
Bodenstein, C.J.	141	5	28.20	3-53	–	–	–
Bollinger, D.E.	7714	273	28.25	6-47	12	2	–
Bopara, R.S.	6263	150	41.75	5-75	1	–	–
Borrington, P.M.	7	0	–				–
Borthwick, S.G.	3442	110	31.29	6-70	2	–	–
Boult, T.A.	3560	131	27.17	6-68	7	–	–
Boyce, M.A.G.	72	0	–				–
Bracewell, D.A.J.	4237	125	33.89	7-35	4	–	–
Bragg, W.D.	268	4	67.00	2-10	–	–	–
Brathwaite, R.M.R.	2309	71	32.52	5-54	3	–	–
Breese, G.R.	8507	285	29.84	7-60	12	3	–
Bresnan, T.T.	11295	363	31.11	5-42	6	–	–
Briggs, D.R.	4711	143	32.94	6-45	5	–	–
Broad, S.C.J.	11917	420	28.37	8-52	20	3	–
Brooks, J.A.	4325	155	27.90	5-23	5	–	–
Browne, N.L.J.	59	0	–				–
Brown, K.R.	49	2	24.50	2-30	–	–	–
Brownlie, D.G.	180	1	180.00	1-13	–	–	–
Buck, N.L.	4377	108	40.52	5-99	1	–	–
Buckley, R.S.	344	10	34.40	5-86	1	–	–
Burgoyne, P.I.	814	16	50.87	3-27	–	–	–
Burns, R.J.	90	1	90.00	1-18	–	–	–
Buttler, J.C.	11	0	–				–
Carberry, M.A.	1010	16	63.12	2-85	–	–	–
Carter, A.	1622	49	33.10	5-40	1	–	–
Cato, S.J.	0	0	–				–
Cessford, G.	591	17	34.76	4-73	–	–	–
Chambers, M.A.	4154	128	32.45	6-68	3	1	–
Chanderpaul, S.	2537	60	42.28	4-48	–	–	–
Chapple, G.	24410	936	26.07	7-53	38	3	7
Chawla, P.P.	10036	330	30.41	6-46	19	3	–
Chopra, V.	111	0	–				–
Choudhry, S.H.	805	25	32.20	4-38	–	–	–
Christian, D.T.	3559	100	35.59	5-24	2	–	–
Clare, J.L.	4166	152	27.40	7-74	6	1	–
Clarke, M.J.	1831	41	44.65	6- 9	2	–	–
Clarke, R.	9090	264	34.43	6-63	2	–	–

F-C	Runs	Wkts	Avge	Best	5wI	10wM	50wS
Claydon, M.E.	4149	130	31.91	6-104	2	–	–
Cobb, J.J.	732	9	81.33	2- 11	–	–	–
Coetzer, K.J.	247	4	61.75	2- 16	–	–	–
Coles, M.T.	4584	154	29.76	6- 51	7	1	1
Collingwood, P.D.	5317	134	39.67	5- 52	1	–	–
Collymore, C.D.	13214	492	26.85	7- 57	12	2	1
Compton, N.R.D.	215	3	71.66	1- 1	–	–	–
Cook, A.N.	205	6	34.16	3- 13	–	–	–
Copeland, T.A.	4498	186	24.18	8- 92	9	2	–
Cosker, D.A.	19849	547	36.28	6- 91	9	1	1
Cowan, E.J.M.	36	0	–		–	–	–
Cowan, J.D.	167	5	33.40	2- 29	–	–	–
Cowdrey, F.K.	70	0	–		–	–	–
Cox, R.D.	71	3	23.66	3- 49	–	–	–
Craddock, T.R.	1198	40	29.95	5- 96	1	–	–
Croft, S.J.	2047	51	40.13	6- 41	1	–	–
Crook, S.P.	5327	146	36.48	5- 48	3	–	–
Daggett, L.M.	6300	166	37.95	8- 94	2	–	–
Davies, M.	7064	315	22.42	8- 24	13	2	1
Dawson, L.A.	2540	64	39.68	7- 51	2	–	–
de Bruyn, Z.	10947	276	39.66	7- 67	4	–	–
Denly, J.L.	1167	23	50.73	3- 43	–	–	–
Denning, J.S.T.	156	3	52.00	2- 46	–	–	–
Dent, C.D.J.	143	1	143.00	1- 12	–	–	–
Dernbach, J.W.	7581	237	31.98	6- 47	10	–	1
Dexter, N.J.	2355	67	35.14	5- 27	1	–	–
Dibble, A.J.	184	5	36.80	3- 42	–	–	–
Dockrell, G.H.	2561	92	27.83	6- 27	6	–	–
D'Oliveira, B.L.	198	0	–		–	–	–
D'Souza, D.A.	7	0	–		–	–	–
Dunn, M.P.	510	17	30.00	5- 56	1	–	–
Durston, W.J.	3001	65	46.16	5- 34	1	–	–
Eckersley, E.J.H.	42	2	21.00	2- 29	–	–	–
Edwards, G.A.	346	8	43.25	4- 44	–	–	–
Elgar, D.	1602	31	51.67	4- 25	–	–	–
Ellison, C.P.	350	9	38.88	3- 69	–	–	–
Endersby, D.M.	256	4	64.00	1- 38	–	–	–
Ervine, S.M.	10121	243	41.65	6- 82	5	–	–
Evans, A.C.	567	15	37.80	6- 30	1	–	–
Evans, L.J.	213	1	213.00	1- 30	–	–	–
Faulkner, J.P.	3118	138	22.59	5- 5	4	–	–
Fawad Ahmed	1761	56	31.44	6-109	2	–	–
Finch, A.J.	132	1	132.00	1- 9	–	–	–
Finch, H.Z.	15	0	–		–	–	–
Finn, S.T.	9168	326	28.12	9- 37	8	1	2
Fletcher, L.J.	4807	161	29.85	5- 52	3	–	–
Footitt, M.H.A.	3611	114	31.67	6- 53	5	–	–
Foster, J.S.	128	1	128.00	1-122	–	–	–
Franks, P.J.	17322	524	33.05	7- 56	11	–	2
Freckingham, O.H.	1584	36	44.00	6-125	1	–	–
Fuller, J.K.	1818	53	34.30	6- 24	3	1	–
Fulton, P.G.	445	11	40.45	4- 49	–	–	–
Gale, A.W.	238	1	238.00	1- 33	–	–	–
Gambhir, G.	281	7	40.14	3- 12	–	–	–
Gatting, J.S.	130	2	65.00	1- 8	–	–	–
Gidman, A.P.R.	4521	102	44.32	4- 47	–	–	–

F-C	Runs	Wkts	Avge	Best	5wI	10wM	50wS
Gidman, W.R.S.	3326	154	21.59	6- 15	7	1	2
Gillespie, M.R.	8838	326	27.11	6- 41	17	2	0+1
Glover, J.C.	1945	53	36.69	5- 38	1	–	–
Godleman, B.A.	35	0	–				
Goodwin, M.W.	376	7	53.71	2- 23	–	–	–
Gordon, R.O.	288	7	41.14	2- 45	–	–	–
Green, M.J.E.	230	4	57.50	2- 60	–	–	–
Gregory, L.	770	25	30.80	5- 38	1	–	–
Griffiths, D.A.	3654	105	34.80	6- 85	3	–	–
Groenewald, T.D.	7257	233	31.14	6- 50	9	–	–
Guptill, M.J.	387	6	64.50	3- 37	–	–	–
Gurney, H.F.	3536	100	35.36	5- 81	2	–	–
Haggett, C.J.	907	26	34.88	4- 94	–	–	–
Hales, A.D.	167	3	55.66	2- 63	–	–	–
Hall, A.J.	16337	604	27.04	6- 77	17	1	–
Hamilton-Brown, R.J.	594	9	66.00	2- 49	–	–	–
Hammond, M.A.H.	196	1	196.00	1- 96	–	–	–
Hannon-Dalby, O.J.	2328	55	42.32	5- 68	2	–	–
Harinath, A.	36	1	36.00	1- 2	–	–	–
Harmison, B.W.	1371	34	40.32	4- 27	–	–	–
Harris, J.A.R.	7148	253	28.25	7- 66	9	1	1
Harris, P.G.	245	5	49.00	2- 22	–	–	–
Harris, R.J.	6489	245	26.48	7- 60	9	–	–
Harrison, J.	596	24	24.83	5- 31	1	–	–
Hatchett, L.J.	1070	32	33.43	5- 47	1	–	–
Helm, T.G.	78	5	15.60	3- 46	–	–	–
Henderson, C.W.	27841	905	30.76	7- 57	34	2	1
Hickey, M.R.	223	4	55.75	2- 63	–	–	–
Higginbottom, M.	484	14	34.57	3- 59	–	–	–
Hildreth, J.C.	444	5	88.80	2- 39	–	–	–
Hobden, M.E.	433	13	33.30	5- 62	2	–	–
Hobson, I.H.	27	0	–				–
Hodd, A.J.	7	0	–				–
Hogan, M.G.	4972	197	25.23	7- 92	9	–	1
Hogg, K.W.	7259	253	28.69	7- 27	7	1	2
Hoggard, M.J.	21739	786	27.65	7- 49	26	1	3
Horton, P.J.	16	0	–				–
Housego, D.M.	32	0	–				–
Howell, B.A.C.	1295	36	35.97	5- 57	1	–	–
Hughes, A.L.	230	6	38.33	3- 49	–	–	–
Hughes, C.F.	470	11	42.72	2- 9	–	–	–
Hughes, P.J.	14	0	–				–
Hunn, M.D.	118	3	39.33	2- 51	–	–	–
Hussain, G.M.	3365	111	30.31	6- 33	4	–	1
Hussey, D.J.	1699	28	60.67	4-105	–	–	–
Hutton, B.A.	178	1	178.00	1- 31	–	–	–
Ireland, A.J.	3907	124	31.50	7- 36	4	1	–
Jaques, P.A.	162	1	162.00	1- 75	–	–	–
Jarvis, K.M.	3080	127	24.25	7- 35	8	1	–
Javid, A.	233	2	116.50	1- 27	–	–	–
Jennings, K.K.	84	4	21.00	2- 8	–	–	–
Jewell, T.M.	521	19	27.42	5- 49	1	–	–
Jones, A.J.	211	2	105.50	1- 50	–	–	–
Jones, C.R.	17	1	17.00	1- 17	–	–	–
Jones, G.O.	26	0	–				–
Jones, O.J.	232	3	77.33	1- 7	–	–	–

F-C	Runs	Wkts	Avge	Best	5wI	10wM	50wS
Jones, R.A.	4153	133	31.22	7-115	5	–	–
Jordan, C.J.	5194	161	32.26	7- 43	6	–	1
Joyce, E.C.	1025	11	93.18	2- 34	–	–	–
Kapil, A.	288	8	36.00	3- 17	–	–	–
Katich, S.M.	3778	107	35.30	7-130	3	–	–
Keedy, G.	21279	678	31.38	7- 68	34	7	4
Kemp, B.W.	295	7	42.14	3- 31	–	–	–
Keogh, R.I.	78	1	78.00	1- 69	–	–	–
Kerrigan, S.C.	4643	174	26.68	9- 51	11	2	2
Kervezee, A.N.	145	2	72.50	1- 14	–	–	–
Key, R.W.T.	319	3	106.33	2- 31	–	–	–
Khawaja, U.T.	69	1	69.00	1- 21	–	–	–
Kieswetter, C.	29	2	14.50	2- 3	–	–	–
Kirby, S.P.	16442	572	28.74	8- 80	17	4	3
Klinger, M.	3	0	–		–	–	–
Knight, T.C.	143	2	71.50	2- 32	–	–	–
Latham, T.W.M.	6	0	–		–	–	–
Leach, J.	532	18	29.55	4- 73	–	–	–
Leach, M.J.	518	15	34.53	5- 63	1	–	–
Leaning, J.A.	22	0	–		–	–	–
Lee, J.E.	314	17	18.47	7- 45	2	–	–
Lees, A.Z.	14	0	–		–	–	–
Lester, T.J.	360	5	72.00	2- 58	–	–	–
Lewis, J.	21757	832	26.15	8- 95	35	5	9
Liddle, C.J.	1222	24	50.91	3- 42	–	–	–
Lilley, A.M.	212	2	106.00	1- 41	–	–	–
Linley, T.E.	4638	170	27.28	6- 57	5	1	1
London, A.B.	59	1	59.00	1- 15	–	–	–
Lucas, D.S.	8564	264	32.43	7- 24	9	1	1
Lumb, M.J.	255	6	42.50	2- 10	–	–	–
Lyon, N.M.	5214	136	38.33	7- 94	3	–	–
Lyth, A.	452	7	64.57	2- 15	–	–	–
McCarter, G.J.	618	15	41.20	4- 95	–	–	–
McCullum, B.B.	18	0	–		–	–	–
McCullum, N.L.	5019	122	41.13	6- 90	3	–	–
McKenzie, N.D.	536	11	48.72	2- 13	–	–	–
MacLeod, C.S.	342	15	22.80	4- 66	–	–	–
MacQueen, A.	99	1	99.00	1- 45	–	–	–
MacVicar, W.A.	153	2	76.50	2- 46	–	–	–
Machan, M.W.	72	1	72.00	1- 36	–	–	–
Maddinson, N.J.	82	4	20.50	2- 22	–	–	–
Maddy, D.L.	7969	253	31.49	5- 37	5	–	–
Madsen, W.L.	494	10	49.40	3- 45	–	–	–
Magoffin, S.J.	9098	369	24.65	8- 20	13	2	2
Mahmood, S.I.	10726	326	32.90	6- 30	9	2	–
Malan, D.J.	1697	38	44.65	5- 61	1	–	–
Marriott, W.W.J.	6	0	–		–	–	–
Marsden, J.	64	3	21.33	3- 32	–	–	–
Marshall, H.J.H.	1768	37	47.78	4- 24	–	–	–
Martin, B.P.	11934	330	36.16	7- 33	18	2	–
Mascarenhas, A.D.	12701	450	28.22	6- 25	17	–	1
Masters, D.D.	14729	573	25.70	8- 10	28	–	4
Maxwell, G.J.	1233	35	35.22	4- 42	–	–	–
Meaker, S.C.	4865	169	28.78	8- 52	9	1	1
Meschede, C.A.J.	1297	40	32.42	4- 43	–	–	–
Mickleburgh, J.C.	50	0	–		–	–	–

255

F-C	Runs	Wkts	Avge	Best	5wI	10wM	50wS
Middlebrook, J.D.	16375	429	38.17	6- 78	12	1	1
Miles, C.N.	1395	45	31.00	6- 88	3	–	–
Miller, A.S.	1364	35	38.97	5- 58	2	–	–
Mills, T.S.	1143	32	35.71	4- 25	–	–	–
Milnes, T.P.	717	22	32.59	7- 39	1	–	–
Mitchell, D.K.H.	814	19	42.84	4- 49	–	–	–
Moore, S.C.	321	5	64.20	1- 13	–	–	–
Morgan, E.J.G.	83	2	41.50	2- 24	–	–	–
Morris, A.J.	107	2	53.50	1- 47	–	–	–
Morris, C.A.J.	495	10	49.50	3- 33	–	–	–
Muchall, G.J.	617	15	41.13	3- 26	–	–	–
Mullaney, S.J.	1146	22	52.09	4- 31	–	–	–
Murphy, D.	3	0	–		–	–	–
Murtagh, T.J.	13122	487	26.94	7- 82	21	3	5
Mustard, P.	9	1	9.00	1- 9	–	–	–
Myburgh, J.G.	1392	31	44.90	4- 56	–	–	–
Mylavarapu, S.V.S.	110	8	13.75	5- 23	1	–	–
Naik, J.K.H.	4285	130	32.96	7- 96	5	–	–
Napier, G.R.	11429	334	34.21	7- 90	10	–	1
Nash, B.P.	695	22	31.59	2- 7	–	–	–
Nash, C.D.	2517	70	35.95	4- 12	–	–	–
Newby, O.J.	4151	130	31.93	5- 69	1	–	–
Newton, R.I.	19	0	–		–	–	–
Nicholson, G.F.	174	0	–				
North, M.J.	5706	143	39.90	6- 55	3	–	–
Northeast, S.A.	141	1	141.00	1- 60	–	–	–
Norwell, L.C.	1572	48	32.75	6- 46	2	–	–
O'Brien, N.J.	19	2	9.50	1- 4	–	–	–
Onions, G.	11248	434	25.91	9- 67	21	3	5
Overton, C.	430	13	33.07	4- 38	–	–	–
Overton, J.	1450	41	35.36	6- 95	1	–	–
Owen, W.T.	1718	41	41.90	5-124	1	–	–
Palladino, A.P.	7448	248	30.03	7- 53	10	–	2
Panesar, M.S.	19910	641	31.06	7- 60	34	5	6
Pardoe, M.G.	100	2	50.00	2- 34	–	–	–
Parry, S.D.	453	14	32.35	5- 23	1	–	–
Patel, J.S.	14973	393	38.09	7- 75	15	1	2
Patel, L.A.	271	3	90.33	1- 12	–	–	–
Patel, R.H.	1119	40	27.97	5- 69	1	–	–
Patel, S.R.	7491	185	40.49	7- 68	3	1	–
Patel, Z.R.	53	3	17.66	2- 32	–	–	–
Patterson, S.A.	5469	192	28.48	5- 43	3	–	2
Pattinson, J.L.	2861	120	23.84	6- 32	4	–	–
Payne, D.A.	2719	82	33.15	6- 26	2	–	–
Peters, S.D.	31	1	31.00	1- 19	–	–	–
Petersen, A.N.	660	12	55.00	2- 7	–	–	–
Pettini, M.L.	263	1	263.00	1- 72	–	–	–
Philander, V.D.	7723	382	20.21	7- 61	20	2	0+2
Phillips, B.J.	8132	271	30.00	6- 29	5	–	–
Phillips, D.S.	95	2	47.50	2- 45	–	–	–
Phillips, T.J.	5896	128	46.06	5- 41	1	–	–
Pietersen, K.P.	3735	73	51.16	4- 31	–	–	–
Pinner, N.D.	32	0	–		–	–	–
Piolet, S.A.	241	14	17.21	6- 17	1	1	–
Plunkett, L.E.	11257	363	31.01	6- 33	10	1	3
Pollock, A.W.	218	4	54.50	3-105	–	–	–

F-C	Runs	Wkts	Avge	Best	5wI	10wM	50wS
Ponting, R.T.	813	14	58.07	2- 10	–	–	–
Porterfield, W.T.S.	138	2	69.00	1- 29	–	–	–
Powell, M.J.	132	2	66.00	2- 39	–	–	–
Poynton, T.	96	2	48.00	2- 96	–	–	–
Poysden, J.E.	264	5	52.80	3- 20	–	–	–
Prince, A.G.	171	4	42.75	2- 11	–	–	–
Probert, T.J.W.	383	12	31.91	4- 20	–	–	–
Procter, L.A.	1678	53	31.66	7- 71	2	–	–
Pyrah, R.M.	2145	49	43.77	5- 58	1	–	–
Querl, R.G.	1241	83	14.95	6- 20	8	–	–
Quiney, R.J.	425	3	141.66	2- 22	–	–	–
Raine, B.A.	356	9	39.55	4- 98	–	–	–
Rankin, W.B.	5617	206	27.26	5- 16	6	–	1
Rashid, A.U.	11664	325	35.88	7-107	17	1	2
Ratnayake, D.E.M.	76	2	38.00	1- 22	–	–	–
Rayner, O.P.	5497	172	31.95	8- 46	7	1	–
Read, C.M.W.	90	0	–		–	–	–
Redfern, D.J.	460	10	46.00	3- 33	–	–	–
Reece, L.M.	378	14	27.00	4- 28	–	–	–
Reed, M.T.	1430	46	31.08	6- 34	2	–	–
Rees, G.P.	27	0	–		–	–	–
Riazuddin, H.	520	18	28.88	5- 61	1	–	–
Richardson, A.	15007	569	26.37	8- 37	23	4	5
Riley, A.E.N.	1449	42	34.50	7-150	2	–	–
Roberts, M.D.T.	19	0	–		–	–	–
Robson, A.J.	11	0	–		–	–	–
Robson, S.D.	47	0	–		–	–	–
Rogers, C.J.L.	131	1	131.00	1- 16	–	–	–
Roland-Jones, T.S.	3491	157	22.23	6- 63	8	1	1
Root, J.E.	645	13	49.61	3- 33	–	–	–
Rouse, H.P.	105	1	105.00	1- 64	–	–	–
Roy, J.J.	97	5	19.40	3- 35	–	–	–
Rudolph, J.A.	2572	58	44.34	5- 80	3	–	–
Rushworth, C.	2946	122	24.14	6- 58	6	1	1
Russell, C.J.	1493	36	41.47	4- 43	–	–	–
Sadler, P.T.	492	4	123.00	2- 38	–	–	–
Saeed Ajmal	12043	452	26.64	7- 55	29	5	0+1
Sales, D.J.G.	184	9	20.44	4- 25	–	–	–
Salisbury, M.E.T.	443	10	44.30	3- 64	–	–	–
Salter, A.G.	512	13	39.38	3- 66	–	–	–
Samaraweera, T.T.	8366	356	23.50	6- 55	15	2	0+1
Sandhu, G.S.	239	6	39.83	4- 49	–	–	–
Sarwan, R.R.	2351	56	41.98	6- 62	1	–	–
Sayers, C.J.	1473	73	20.17	6- 49	5	–	–
Sayers, J.J.	178	6	29.66	3- 15	–	–	–
Shah, O.A.	1505	26	57.88	3- 33	–	–	–
Shahzad, A.	6398	181	35.34	5- 51	3	–	–
Shantry, J.D.	3567	109	32.72	7- 60	4	–	–
Shreck, C.E.	13265	432	30.70	8- 31	21	2	3
Shrewsbury, T.W.	94	1	94.00	1- 94	–	–	–
Sibley, D.P.	4	0	–		–	–	–
Siddle, P.M.	8232	300	27.44	6- 43	15	–	0+1
Sidebottom, R.J.	15280	614	24.88	7- 37	24	3	4
Slater, B.T.	28	0	–		–	–	–
Smith, G.C.	1132	11	102.90	2-145	–	–	–
Smith, G.M.	6001	169	35.50	5- 42	4	–	–

F-C	Runs	Wkts	Avge	Best	5wI	10wM	50wS
Smith, G.P.	73	1	73.00	1- 64	–	–	–
Smith, R.A.J.	274	10	27.40	3- 50	–	–	–
Smith, S.P.D.	2795	51	54.80	7- 64	1	–	–
Smith, T.C.	5328	172	30.97	6- 46	2	–	–
Smith, T.M.J.	1691	29	58.31	4- 91	–	–	–
Smith, W.R.	768	15	51.20	3- 34	–	–	–
Sohail Tanvir	6519	265	24.60	8- 54	17	3	0+1
Soilleux, A.C.	399	11	36.27	3- 67	–	–	–
Solanki, V.S.	4210	88	47.84	5- 40	4	1	–
Southee, T.G.	5541	195	28.41	8- 27	11	1	–
Spiegel, M.N.W.	1042	24	43.41	3- 75	–	–	–
Starc, M.A.	3700	117	31.62	6-154	4	–	–
Stevens, D.I.	6160	202	30.49	7- 21	4	1	–
Stirling, P.R.	345	6	57.50	2- 43	–	–	–
Stokes, B.A.	3033	109	27.82	6- 68	1	–	–
Stone, O.P.	202	5	40.40	1- 6	–	–	–
Suppiah, A.V.	2630	45	58.44	3- 46	–	–	–
Swann, G.P.	23019	729	31.57	7- 33	32	6	1
Sykes, J.S.	733	12	61.08	4-176	–	–	–
Taylor, B.J.	106	4	26.50	4- 64	–	–	–
Taylor, J.M.R.	892	21	42.47	2- 28	–	–	–
Taylor, J.W.A.	176	0	–				
Taylor, L.R.P.L.	359	6	59.83	2- 4	–	–	–
Taylor, M.D.	246	4	61.50	3-108	–	–	–
Taylor, R.M.L.	1408	31	45.41	5- 91	1	–	–
ten Doeschate, R.N.	6171	182	33.90	6- 20	7	–	–
Thakor, S.J.	796	16	49.75	3- 57	–	–	–
Thomas, A.C.	12312	461	26.70	7- 54	21	2	–
Thomas, I.A.A.	365	12	30.41	2- 24	–	–	–
Thompson, H.L.	6	0	–				
Thompson, J.S.	39	1	39.00	1- 13	–	–	–
Thornely, M.A.	527	10	52.70	2- 14	–	–	–
Thorp, C.D.	6776	267	25.37	7- 88	9	1	1
Tomlinson, J.A.	9720	301	32.29	8- 46	11	1	2
Topley, R.J.W.	2515	93	27.04	6- 29	5	1	–
Tredwell, J.C.	12585	352	35.75	8- 66	12	3	1
Trego, P.D.	10367	282	36.76	6- 59	3	–	1
Tremlett, C.T.	11862	423	28.04	8- 96	11	–	–
Trescothick, M.E.	1551	36	43.08	4- 36	–	–	–
Trott, I.J.L.	2928	61	48.00	7- 39	1	–	–
Troughton, J.O.	1416	22	64.36	3- 1	–	–	–
Turner, A.J.	16	0	–				
Turner, M.L.	2526	59	42.81	5- 32	1	–	–
van den Bergh, F.O.E.	399	10	39.90	4- 84	–	–	–
Vanderspar, W.G.R.	35	1	35.00	1- 26	–	–	–
Velani, K.S.	8	0	–				
Vince, J.M.	519	15	34.60	5- 41	1	–	–
Voges, A.C.	1465	43	34.06	4- 92	–	–	–
Wade, M.S.	0	0	–				
Wagg, G.G.	10144	299	33.92	6- 35	9	1	2
Wagner, N.	7707	309	24.94	7- 46	13	1	0+2
Wainwright, D.J.	5572	151	36.90	6- 33	5	–	1
Wakely, A.G.	322	6	53.66	2- 62	–	–	–
Wallace, M.A.	3	0	–				
Waller, M.T.C.	493	10	49.30	3- 33	–	–	–
Wallis, C.A.	506	5	101.20	2- 63	–	–	–

F-C	Runs	Wkts	Avge	Best	5wI	10wM	50wS
Walters, S.J.	245	3	81.66	1- 4	–	–	–
Warner, D.A.	370	6	61.66	2- 45	–	–	–
Waters, H.T.	3425	110	31.13	7- 53	3	–	–
Watkins, N.A.T.	598	13	46.00	5- 88	1	–	–
Watling, B.J.	8	0	–				–
Watson, S.R.	5690	198	28.73	7- 69	7	1	–
Wells, L.W.P.	496	7	70.85	2- 28	–	–	–
Wells, T.J.	129	1	129.00	1- 36	–	–	–
Wessels, M.H.	96	3	32.00	1- 10	–	–	–
Westley, T.	1415	31	45.64	4- 55	–	–	–
Westwood, I.J.	300	7	42.85	2- 39	–	–	–
Wheater, A.J.A.	86	1	86.00	1- 86	–	–	–
White, C.L.	7443	186	40.01	6- 66	3	1	–
White, G.G.	1607	37	43.43	4- 72	–	–	–
White, W.A.	5455	147	37.10	5- 54	4	–	–
Whiteley, R.A.	1348	28	48.14	2- 6	–	–	–
Wilkin, O.	213	4	53.25	2- 63	–	–	–
Willett, R.J.D.	141	1	141.00	1- 80	–	–	–
Willey, D.J.	3277	113	29.00	5- 29	5	1	–
Williams, B.	130	1	130.00	1- 55	–	–	–
Williams, R.E.M.	1276	33	38.66	5- 70	2	–	–
Williams, T.J.	69	8	8.62	5- 34	1	–	–
Williamson, K.S.	2861	69	41.46	5- 75	1	–	–
Wilson, G.C.	89	0	–				–
Woakes, C.R.	7490	290	25.82	7- 20	13	3	2
Wood, C.P.	2302	78	29.51	5- 41	2	–	–
Wood, M.A.	1061	46	23.06	5- 44	2	–	–
Wood, S.K.W.	92	3	30.66	3- 64	–	–	–
Wright, B.J.	174	2	87.00	1- 14	–	–	–
Wright, C.J.C.	8586	251	34.20	6- 22	8	–	1
Wright, L.J.	4653	117	39.76	5- 65	3	–	–
Wyatt, A.C.F.	1861	53	35.11	3- 35	–	–	–
Wylie, B.A.	182	1	182.00	1-111	–	–	–
Yardy, M.H.	2119	28	75.67	5- 83	1	–	–
Yasir Arafat	18149	752	24.13	9- 35	43	5	0+4
Young, D.R.	2	0	–				–
Young, E.G.C.	1058	15	70.53	2- 23	–	–	–

LIMITED-OVERS CAREER RECORDS

Compiled by Philip Bailey

The following career records, to the end of the 2013 season, include all players currently registered with first-class counties. These records are restricted to performances in limited-overs matches of 'List A' status as defined by the Association of Cricket Statisticians and Historians now incorporated by ICC into their Classification of Cricket. The following matches qualify for List A status and are included in the figures that follow: Limited-Overs Internationals; Other International matches (e.g. Commonwealth Games, 'A' team internationals); Premier domestic limited-overs tournaments in Test status countries; Official tourist matches against the main first-class teams.

The following matches do NOT qualify for inclusion: World Cup warm-up games; Tourist matches against first-class teams outside the major domestic competitions (e.g. Universities, Minor Counties etc.); Festival, pre-season friendly games and Twenty20 Cup matches.

	M	Runs	Avge	HS	100	50	Wkts	Avge	Best	Econ
Abbott, K.J.	48	212	15.14	29	–	–	62	29.37	4-36	5.40
Adams, A.R.	165	1504	16.71	90*	–	1	209	28.50	5- 7	4.72
Adams, J.H.K.	83	2720	39.42	131	2	21	1	105.00	1-34	7.97
Agathangelou, A.P.	25	679	33.95	94	–	5	0	–	–	9/1
Ali, K.	172	1240	15.89	92	–	4	255	25.04	5-36	5.26
Ali, M.M.	100	2794	30.04	158	7	12	51	40.98	3-28	5.76
Allenby, J.	88	1942	26.60	91*	–	9	78	29.79	5-43	5.02
Ambrose, T.R.	136	2797	29.13	135	3	12	–	–	–	130/23
Anderson, J.M.	227	330	9.16	28	–	–	319	27.98	5-23	4.86
Andrew, G.M.	110	1167	18.52	104	1	2	104	35.25	5-31	6.24
Ansari, Z.S.	23	388	29.84	62	–	2	20	29.55	4-42	5.79
Anyon, J.E.	43	43	5.37	12	–	–	47	30.55	3- 6	5.53
Arshad, U.	1	–	–	–	–	–	0	–	–	4.33
Ashar Zaidi	54	1696	34.61	109	3	9	38	26.84	4-42	4.23
Ashraf, M.A.	23	3	1.50	3*	–	–	25	36.80	3-38	5.93
Atkinson, J.J.	2	41	20.50	23	–	–	–	–	–	1/1
Azeem Rafiq	20	146	18.25	34*	–	–	19	31.47	5-30	5.20
Azhar Ullah	34	57	9.50	9	–	–	55	24.89	5-56	5.33
Bacon, G.P.W.	1	–	–	–	–	–	2	31.00	2-62	6.20
Bairstow, J.M.	50	1099	27.47	114	1	5	–	–	–	31/3
Balbirnie, A.	6	30	6.00	17	–	–	0	–	–	6.75
Balcombe, D.J.	13	10	2.00	6	–	–	18	27.33	4-38	5.68
Ball, A.J.	24	131	13.10	28	–	–	21	34.42	3-36	5.67
Ball, J.T.	27	62	8.85	19*	–	–	30	28.00	4-25	5.63
Ballance, G.S.	57	2469	56.11	139	6	14	–	–	–	–
Barker, K.H.D.	43	397	17.26	56	–	1	48	30.58	4-33	5.87
Barrow, A.W.R.	9	144	36.00	72	–	1	–	–	–	–
Bates, M.D.	32	73	8.11	24*	–	–	–	–	–	21/4
Batty, G.J.	223	2203	16.19	83*	–	5	205	31.65	5-35	4.57
Batty, J.N.	209	2992	21.83	158*	1	14	–	–	–	220/40
Beer, W.A.T.	29	137	17.12	27*	–	–	28	34.96	3-27	5.02
Bell, I.R.	264	9128	39.86	158	10	64	33	34.48	5-41	5.29
Bell-Drummond, D.J.	5	111	22.20	42	–	–	–	–	–	–
Berg, G.K.	59	999	25.61	75	–	5	40	35.17	4-24	5.57
Billings, S.W.	19	449	29.93	143	1	2	–	–	–	11/2

L-O	M	Runs	Avge	HS	100	50	Wkts	Avge	Best	Econ
Bird, J.M.	7	7	7.00	5*	–	–	8	34.62	3-39	4.35
Blake, A.J.	35	491	23.38	81*	–	2	3	24.66	2-13	5.28
Bollinger, D.E.	103	117	7.80	30	–	–	150	27.48	5-35	4.73
Bopara, R.S.	235	6858	39.41	201*	10	39	170	26.74	5-63	5.23
Borrington, P.M.	13	262	26.20	72	–	1	–	–	–	–
Borthwick, S.G.	52	386	14.84	80	–	1	40	38.07	4-51	5.90
Boyce, M.A.G.	61	1339	25.26	80	–	8	–	–	–	–
Bragg, W.D.	20	486	27.00	78	–	3	1	40.00	1-11	7.50
Brathwaite, R.M.R.	2	–	–	–	–	–	1	68.00	1-19	7.55
Breese, G.R.	176	2048	20.89	68*	–	3	184	27.74	5-41	4.69
Bresnan, T.T.	216	2006	18.23	80	–	4	240	34.43	5-48	5.17
Briggs, D.R.	57	145	9.66	25	–	–	65	33.27	4-32	4.97
Broad, S.C.J.	120	476	11.60	45*	–	–	188	27.75	5-23	5.22
Brooks, J.A.	23	34	5.66	10	–	–	19	40.00	3-35	4.96
Brown, B.C.	38	421	22.15	60	–	3	–	–	–	34/9
Brown, K.R.	46	1283	36.65	101*	1	7	–	–	–	–
Buck, N.L.	34	78	9.75	21	–	–	42	34.47	4-39	6.09
Burgoyne, P.I.	16	129	16.12	43	–	–	13	39.46	3-31	5.42
Burns, J.A.	22	615	30.75	114	1	4	–	–	–	–
Burns, R.J.	8	171	24.42	49	–	–	–	–	–	–
Buttler, J.C.	80	2296	51.02	119	2	17	–	–	–	74/6
Carberry, M.A.	153	4289	33.24	150*	6	30	11	27.00	3-37	5.53
Carter, A.	20	35	5.83	12	–	–	26	27.00	4-45	6.41
Cessford, G.	4	0	0.00	0*	–	–	6	29.33	4-24	6.32
Chambers, M.A.	6	3	3.00	2	–	–	5	35.80	1-21	5.96
Chanderpaul, S.	394	12502	41.67	150	12	90	56	24.78	4-22	4.95
Chapple, G.	284	2062	17.77	81*	–	9	320	28.55	6-18	4.50
Chopra, V.	76	2818	39.69	115	6	19	0	–	–	6.00
Choudhry, S.H.	23	163	18.11	39	–	–	17	40.05	4-54	6.02
Clare, J.L.	41	321	11.46	57	–	1	30	40.13	3-39	5.59
Clark, J.	13	185	30.83	72	–	1	3	64.33	2-45	6.89
Clarke, R.	186	3505	26.15	98*	–	18	103	39.21	4-28	5.62
Claydon, M.E.	67	187	8.13	19	–	–	83	30.36	4-39	5.41
Coad, B.O.	6	1	–	1*	–	–	3	81.33	1-34	6.90
Cobb, J.J.	50	1582	36.79	137	4	7	20	50.50	3-34	5.97
Cockbain, I.A.	36	781	31.24	79	–	6	–	–	–	–
Coetzer, K.J.	102	3148	35.77	133	5	19	3	97.66	1-2	5.86
Coleman, F.R.J.	22	384	19.20	64	–	3	–	–	–	–
Coles, M.T.	36	157	12.07	47	–	–	55	22.50	6-32	6.09
Collingwood, P.D.	394	10189	33.62	120*	8	57	242	34.11	6-31	4.86
Compton, N.R.D.	101	2802	38.91	131	6	17	1	53.00	1-0	5.21
Cook, A.N.	128	4556	38.94	137	9	28	0	–	–	3.33
Cooke, C.B.	45	1336	36.10	137*	2	7	–	–	–	20/2
Cosker, D.A.	235	804	11.32	50*	–	1	240	32.92	5-54	4.81
Cowdrey, F.K.	4	110	55.00	52*	–	1	0	–	–	4.50
Cox, O.B.	26	164	13.66	34*	–	–	–	–	–	18/3
Craddock, T.R.	7	13	–	5*	–	–	5	44.00	2-38	4.68
Croft, S.J.	114	2888	34.79	107	1	21	51	34.96	4-24	5.45

L-O	M	Runs	Avge	HS	100	50	Wkts	Avge	Best	Econ
Crook, S.P.	55	540	16.36	72	–	3	58	32.72	5-36	5.83
Cross, M.H.	11	192	21.33	54*	–	1	–	–	–	3/3
Curran, T.K.	5	3	1.00	1*	–	–	9	22.44	5-34	6.27
Davies, A.L.	2	19	19.00	13	–	–	–	–	–	–
Davies, M.	90	170	7.39	31*	–	–	86	30.48	4-13	4.24
Davies, S.M.	143	4267	35.85	127*	6	26	–	–	–	126/41
Dawson, L.A.	78	1446	29.51	97	–	6	48	39.56	4-45	5.23
Denly, J.L.	103	3051	33.90	115	4	16	5	26.40	3-42	6.18
Dent, C.D.J.	24	509	29.94	151*	1	1	9	27.22	4-43	5.32
Dernbach, J.W.	114	197	7.29	31	–	–	172	28.58	5-31	6.11
Dexter, N.J.	84	1785	31.87	135*	2	8	30	54.23	3-17	5.57
Dibble, A.J.	7	15	15.00	15	–	–	11	26.81	4-52	6.14
Dockrell, G.H.	56	142	11.83	22*	–	–	58	30.89	4-24	4.33
D'Oliveira, B.L.	20	149	21.28	28	–	–	15	35.80	3-35	5.53
Duckett, B.M.	5	94	31.33	47*	–	–	–	–	–	3/–
Dunn, M.P.	1	–	–	–	–	–	2	16.00	2-32	5.33
Durston, W.J.	101	2266	32.84	120*	2	13	45	36.66	3- 7	5.60
Eckersley, E.J.H.	21	493	29.00	108	1	2	–	–	–	17/1
Edwards, G.A.	1	0	–	0*	–	–	1	44.00	1-44	7.33
Elstone, S.L.	25	512	24.38	75*	–	1	1	32.00	1-22	5.64
Ervine, S.M.	213	5033	31.65	167*	7	23	198	32.98	5-50	5.56
Evans, L.J.	10	164	23.42	47*	–	–	0	–		8.20
Fell, T.C.	7	142	23.66	55	–	1	–	–	–	–
Finch, A.J.	70	2661	40.93	154	5	14	5	33.20	2-44	5.10
Finch, H.Z.	1	–	–	–	–	–	0	–	–	2.00
Finn, S.T.	87	170	9.44	35	–	–	119	27.60	5-33	4.88
Fisher, M.D.	2	10	10.00	10	–	–	1	85.00	1-40	6.07
Fletcher, L.J.	32	99	9.00	40*	–	–	29	39.89	3-27	5.47
Foakes, B.T.	8	86	12.28	56	–	1	–	–	–	2/1
Footitt, M.H.A.	20	5	2.50	4	–	–	21	29.09	5-28	6.50
Foster, J.S.	193	3044	28.44	83*	–	15	–	–	–	216/56
Franks, P.J.	184	2039	21.69	84*	–	7	198	28.79	6-27	5.06
Fuller, J.K.	26	295	21.07	43	–	–	43	23.53	6-35	5.79
Gale, A.W.	123	3270	31.44	125*	2	18	–	–	–	–
Gatting, J.S.	43	975	27.85	122	1	4	0	–		6.60
Gibson, R.	4	10	5.00	6	–	–	4	28.75	1-17	5.75
Gidman, A.P.R.	190	4367	27.46	116	5	21	71	39.23	5-42	5.13
Gidman, W.R.S.	38	379	19.94	76	–	1	30	34.80	4-36	4.94
Glover, J.C.	5	16	8.00	10	–	–	7	32.85	3-34	6.38
Godleman, B.A.	22	434	24.11	82	–	2	–	–	–	–
Goodwin, M.W.	375	11170	35.57	167	14	67	7	43.71	1- 9	5.23
Gordon, R.O.	2	1	1.00	1	–	–	2	61.00	1-46	8.71
Gregory, L.	23	128	11.63	39	–	–	25	22.84	4-27	6.28
Griffiths, D.A.	22	15	15.00	7	–	–	27	29.44	4-29	6.11
Groenewald, T.D.	69	391	13.96	36	–	–	71	31.81	4-22	5.46
Gurney, H.F.	39	25	3.57	13*	–	–	40	33.87	5-24	5.48
Haggett, C.J.	3	2	1.00	2	–	–	4	40.25	2-97	8.05
Hain, S.R.	1	1	1.00	1	–	–	–	–	–	–

L-O	M	Runs	Avge	HS	100	50	Wkts	Avge	Best	Econ
Hales, A.D.	72	2262	33.26	150*	4	13	0	–		15.00
Hall, A.J.	314	5933	29.81	129*	6	33	360	27.51	5-18	4.77
Hamilton-Brown, R.J.	83	1720	24.92	115	2	7	32	37.84	3-28	5.73
Hammond, M.A.H.	2	–	–	–	–	–	3	26.33	2-29	6.07
Hannon-Dalby, O.J.	6	21	–	21*	–	–	6	41.16	2-22	7.52
Harinath, A.	3	74	37.00	52	–	1	–	–		–
Harmison, B.W.	61	1049	24.39	67	–	3	24	35.62	3-43	5.93
Harris, J.A.R.	43	200	10.00	29	–	–	59	27.06	4-48	5.66
Harrison, J.	2	7	–	7*	–	–	2	41.50	2-51	6.91
Hatchett, L.J.	7	1	1.00	1	–	–	10	23.90	3-65	5.73
Helm, T.G.	2	–	–	–	–	–	3	9.00	3-27	3.37
Higginbottom, M.	1	–	–	–	–	–	0	–		8.60
Hildreth, J.C.	160	3996	32.48	151	5	16	6	30.83	2-26	7.40
Hobden, M.E.	1	2	2.00	2	–	–	1	39.00	1-39	4.87
Hodd, A.J.	49	622	21.44	91	–	1	–	–		42/9
Hodgson, D.M.	13	245	27.22	90	–	2	–	–		12/3
Hogan, M.G.	37	90	11.25	27	–	–	63	25.68	5-44	4.91
Hogg, K.W.	139	966	16.10	66*	–	1	141	30.41	4-20	4.86
Horton, P.J.	92	2239	31.09	111*	2	12	–	–		–
Housego, D.M.	7	269	44.83	132	1	1	–	–		–
Howell, B.A.C.	36	889	37.04	122	1	5	16	42.37	2-26	5.55
Hughes, A.L.	16	168	24.00	59*	–	1	13	36.00	3-56	6.01
Hughes, C.F.	64	1435	24.74	81	–	12	22	34.27	5-29	5.15
Hutton, B.A.	3	24	24.00	17*	–	–	2	84.50	1-60	7.04
Ireland, A.J.	78	179	7.78	27	–	–	95	31.67	4-16	5.51
Jackson, C.F.	3	–	–	–	–	–	–	–		1/2
James, N.A.	20	212	19.27	43	–	–	15	21.60	3-36	4.90
Jaques, P.A.	165	6179	40.65	171*	14	33	0	–		6.33
Jarvis, K.M.	34	57	4.75	13	–	–	42	36.30	4-35	5.69
Javid, A.	12	256	32.00	43	–	–	5	63.80	2-34	6.51
Jennings, K.K.	6	286	57.20	71*	–	4	0	–		3.66
Jewell, T.M.	8	31	5.16	13	–	–	1	158.00	1-20	8.31
Johnson, R.M.	26	215	21.50	79	–	2	–	–		19/4
Jones, A.J.	6	9	4.50	5	–	–	5	51.80	1-26	7.61
Jones, C.R.	5	126	42.00	45*	–	–	–	–		–
Jones, G.O.	193	3168	24.55	86	–	12	–	–		205/42
Jones, R.A.	10	23	7.66	11*	–	–	3	126.66	1-25	6.84
Jordan, C.J.	32	217	12.76	38	–	–	50	24.62	4-38	5.47
Joyce, E.C.	248	8047	38.50	146	13	48	6	51.50	2-10	7.02
Keedy, G.	97	161	8.94	33	–	–	119	26.47	5-30	4.80
Kelsall, S.	2	49	24.50	40	–	–	–	–		–
Keogh, R.I.	9	168	24.00	61	–	1	0	–		6.05
Kerrigan, S.C.	30	28	3.11	10	–	–	21	51.52	3-21	5.29
Kervezee, A.N.	91	2294	29.03	121*	2	10	0	–		9.12
Key, R.W.T.	221	6381	32.39	144*	8	37	–	–		–
Kieswetter, C.	134	4254	39.38	143	11	17	1	19.00	1-19	136/26
King, M.J.	1	8	8.00	8	–	–	0	–		3.00
Kirby, S.P.	104	88	4.00	15	–	–	142	27.90	5-36	5.63

263

L-O	M	Runs	Avge	HS	100	50	Wkts	Avge	Best	Econ
Klinger, M.	116	4545	45.00	133*	10	30	–	–	–	–
Knight, T.C.	8	16	8.00	10	–	–	9	35.66	3-36	5.35
Kohler-Cadmore, T.	1	47	47.00	47	–	–	–	–	–	–
Leach, J.	2	21	–	21*	–	–	1	92.00	1-45	8.36
Leach, M.J.	3	2	2.00	2	–	–	1	90.00	1-30	4.73
Leaning, J.A.	5	114	28.50	60	–	1	6	12.66	5-22	5.84
Lees, A.Z.	7	229	38.16	63	–	2	–	–	–	–
Lewis, J.	232	1000	11.49	54	–	1	302	26.45	5-19	4.62
Liddle, C.J.	50	74	5.69	15	–	–	69	25.47	5-18	5.83
Lilley, A.M.	6	10	5.00	10	–	–	10	17.20	4-30	4.52
Linley, T.E.	22	73	24.33	20*	–	–	17	43.58	3-50	5.85
Lumb, M.J.	188	5337	31.21	110	3	41	0	–	–	14.00
Lyth, A.	74	1899	30.62	109*	1	9	1	100.00	1- 6	6.25
McCarter, G.J.	7	18	–	18*	–	–	10	18.30	3-15	5.01
McKay, P.J.	5	26	13.00	17*	–	–	–	–	–	4/1
MacLeod, C.S.	55	860	19.11	99*	–	4	14	41.21	2-26	5.45
Machan, M.W.	21	781	43.38	126*	2	4	8	30.25	3-31	5.37
Madsen, W.L.	57	1516	36.09	78	–	11	9	15.22	3-27	4.41
Magoffin, S.J.	51	225	22.50	24*	–	–	65	30.92	4-58	4.71
Mahmood, S.I.	153	541	9.16	29	–	–	210	28.50	5-16	5.37
Malan, D.J.	77	2270	33.88	134	3	11	15	38.13	2- 4	6.22
Marshall, H.J.H.	278	6749	28.12	122	6	45	4	73.75	2-21	6.23
Masters, D.D.	153	532	12.37	39	–	–	148	32.37	5-17	4.52
Maxwell, G.J.	36	877	35.08	145*	1	6	20	42.90	4-63	5.03
Meaker, S.C.	43	73	5.61	21*	–	–	40	37.35	4-47	5.90
Meschede, C.A.J.	28	256	19.69	40*	–	–	36	23.22	4- 5	5.63
Mickleburgh, J.C.	19	393	32.75	73	–	2	–	–	–	–
Middlebrook, J.D.	187	1686	20.07	57*	–	1	142	36.33	4-27	4.71
Miles, C.N.	6	0	–	0*	–	–	9	27.66	2-32	6.49
Mills, T.S.	20	4	2.00	2*	–	–	19	33.63	3-23	5.68
Milnes, T.P.	3	22	11.00	16	–	–	3	59.00	2-73	7.69
Mitchell, D.K.H.	92	2170	33.38	107	2	13	53	36.43	4-42	5.60
Moore, S.C.	141	3774	30.68	118	5	25	1	53.00	1- 1	7.75
Morgan, E.J.G.	200	5859	38.29	161	10	34	0	–	–	7.00
Morris, C.A.J.	5	7	–	6*	–	–	6	35.00	2-25	6.49
Muchall, G.J.	129	3195	34.35	101*	1	20	1	144.00	1-15	5.14
Mullaney, S.J.	57	620	20.00	61	–	2	54	26.42	4-29	4.98
Murphy, D.	36	214	19.45	31*	–	–	–	–	–	21/11
Murtagh, T.J.	142	665	11.87	35*	–	–	188	28.78	4-14	5.24
Mustard, P.	165	4366	30.96	143	7	27	–	–	–	163/41
Myburgh, J.G.	97	2344	28.58	112	1	14	24	60.41	2-22	5.06
Naik, J.K.H.	32	154	11.00	22*	–	–	26	41.65	3-21	5.38
Napier, G.R.	229	2861	18.82	79	–	14	269	25.75	7-32	5.26
Nash, B.P.	83	1557	33.84	98*	–	8	16	35.12	4-20	4.22
Nash, C.D.	86	2539	32.97	124*	2	16	42	26.00	4-40	5.24
Newby, O.J.	36	124	13.77	36*	–	–	35	34.48	5-35	6.15
Newton, R.I.	24	616	28.00	88*	–	2	–	–	–	–
Northeast, S.A.	44	1047	29.91	115	1	6	–	–	–	–

L-O	M	Runs	Avge	HS	100	50	Wkts	Avge	Best	Econ
Norwell, L.C.	4	1	–	1*	–	–	9	19.66	6-52	6.55
O'Brien, N.J.	163	3739	29.91	121	2	24	–	–	–	133/32
Onions, G.	71	122	6.42	19	–	–	80	31.51	4-45	5.07
Overton, C.	7	69	11.50	20	–	–	4	65.50	2-30	4.85
Overton, J.	14	47	15.66	14	–	–	20	27.00	4-42	6.27
Owen, W.T.	25	78	13.00	13*	–	–	37	21.13	5-49	6.08
Palladino, A.P.	44	195	9.28	31	–	–	41	35.75	4-32	5.33
Panesar, M.S.	84	141	8.81	17*	–	–	81	35.37	5-20	4.64
Pardoe, M.G.	3	69	23.00	42	–	–	–	–	–	–
Parry, S.D.	54	222	14.80	31	–	–	65	28.93	5-17	4.98
Patel, J.S.	146	516	9.92	50	–	1	158	33.57	4-16	4.67
Patel, R.H.	3	–	–	–	–	–	4	32.00	2-41	6.73
Patel, S.R.	181	4294	33.03	129*	3	22	163	30.76	6-13	5.28
Patterson, S.A.	52	128	21.33	25*	–	–	65	29.61	6-32	5.16
Payne, D.A.	36	56	18.66	18	–	–	64	21.59	7-29	5.88
Peters, S.D.	173	3386	22.57	107	2	20	–	–	–	–
Petersen, A.N.	160	4798	33.78	145*	7	29	8	41.62	2-48	5.48
Pettini, M.L.	151	3653	28.10	144	6	22	–	–	–	–
Phillips, T.J.	81	489	19.56	58*	–	1	90	24.72	5-28	5.22
Pietersen, K.P.	253	8112	40.76	147	15	46	41	51.75	3-14	5.32
Piolet, S.A.	34	210	14.00	39	–	–	33	32.90	4-31	5.78
Plunkett, L.E.	124	1081	20.01	72	–	3	147	31.80	4-15	5.42
Porterfield, W.T.S.	159	5164	33.97	112*	7	32	–	–	–	–
Poynter, S.W.	1	0	–	0*	–	–	–	–	–	–
Poynton, T.	20	138	12.54	40	–	–	–	–	–	11/3
Prince, A.G.	247	5789	32.16	128	3	30	0	–	–	5.67
Pringle, R.D.	11	48	9.60	26	–	–	3	50.00	1-12	5.00
Prior, M.J.	222	5072	27.26	144	4	28	–	–	–	187/31
Procter, L.A.	19	252	28.00	97	–	2	11	39.18	3-29	6.33
Pyrah, R.M.	105	1020	18.54	69	–	2	125	26.07	5-50	5.77
Querl, R.G.	48	454	18.91	44	–	–	61	29.42	5-26	5.15
Raine, B.A.	3	7	7.00	7	–	–	2	50.50	2-59	6.73
Rankin, W.B.	85	90	7.50	18*	–	–	102	27.98	4-34	4.89
Rashid, A.U.	82	736	18.40	46*	–	–	81	33.83	4-38	5.20
Rayner, O.P.	40	365	26.07	61	–	1	29	40.27	3-31	5.43
Read, C.M.W.	299	5056	29.05	135	2	21	–	–	–	284/68
Redfern, D.J.	43	655	19.84	57*	–	3	5	45.60	2-10	4.88
Reece, L.M.	20	348	24.85	59	–	1	6	69.66	4-35	6.20
Reed, M.T.	3	–	–	–	–	–	0	–	–	7.09
Rees, G.P.	51	1535	35.69	123*	3	10	0	–	–	4.00
Rhodes, W.M.H.	7	53	10.60	19*	–	–	4	33.25	2-26	6.65
Richardson, M.J.	2	45	45.00	45	–	–	–	–	–	–
Riley, A.E.N.	19	6	6.00	3*	–	–	15	39.53	2-32	5.70
Rippon, M.J.G.	8	41	8.20	14*	–	–	2	119.00	1-30	5.06
Robinson, O.E.	3	16	–	12*	–	–	0	–	–	6.60
Robson, S.D.	8	169	28.16	65	–	1	–	–	–	–
Roderick, G.H.	16	191	23.87	63	–	1	–	–	–	12/2
Roland-Jones, T.S.	30	122	10.16	24	–	–	52	23.44	4-44	5.71

L-O	M	Runs	Avge	HS	100	50	Wkts	Avge	Best	Econ
Root, J.E.	48	1384	34.60	110*	1	8	15	47.13	2-10	5.57
Rossington, A.M.	8	161	32.20	79*	–	1	–	–	–	8/2
Rowe, T.C.	1	10	10.00	10	–	–	–	–	–	–
Roy, J.J.	49	1251	29.09	131	4	6	0	–	–	12.00
Rudolph, J.A.	220	8652	48.33	134*	13	60	12	32.41	4-40	5.58
Rushworth, C.	33	49	7.00	12*	–	–	57	19.10	5-31	5.30
Russell, C.J.	6	1	–	1*	–	–	5	34.00	4-32	5.86
Saeed Ajmal	198	490	8.03	33	–	–	300	25.09	5-18	4.37
Sales, D.J.G.	267	7406	33.81	161	4	53	0	–	–	4.78
Salter, A.G.	6	6	3.00	3	–	–	6	38.00	2-41	5.06
Sandhu, G.S.	1	0	0.00	0	–	–	3	9.33	3-28	4.66
Sarwan, R.R.	262	8337	40.27	120*	11	48	35	28.60	5-10	5.31
Shah, O.A.	360	10529	35.45	134	14	68	27	33.70	4-11	5.90
Shahzad, A.	68	368	12.68	59*	–	1	101	26.71	5-51	5.31
Shantry, J.D.	52	111	11.10	18	–	–	73	27.65	4-32	5.90
Shreck, C.E.	53	45	6.42	9*	–	–	63	32.33	5-19	5.25
Sibley, D.P.	2	39	39.00	37	–	–	–	–	–	–
Siddle, P.M.	38	94	10.44	25*	–	–	41	34.39	4-27	4.65
Sidebottom, R.J.	186	552	11.04	32	–	–	198	30.97	6-40	4.47
Simpson, J.A.	42	567	25.77	82	–	3	–	–	–	26/5
Slater, B.T.	7	109	18.16	46	–	–	–	–	–	–
Smith, G.C.	255	9284	39.67	141	14	67	47	38.21	3-30	5.47
Smith, G.M.	96	2077	23.87	88	–	9	68	36.42	4-53	5.66
Smith, G.P.	32	639	22.03	135*	1	3	–	–	–	–
Smith, R.A.J.	5	9	4.50	7	–	–	3	39.00	3-48	7.80
Smith, T.C.	62	1359	32.35	117	2	8	73	27.54	4-48	5.21
Smith, T.M.J.	40	199	16.58	65	–	1	31	41.22	3-26	5.59
Smith, W.R.	89	1865	27.02	120*	2	14	8	18.50	2-19	5.72
Solanki, V.S.	394	10844	32.56	164*	16	62	28	35.25	4-14	5.27
Spriegel, M.N.W.	71	1530	34.77	86	–	10	48	35.85	3-29	5.20
Stevens, D.I.	259	6532	30.52	133	5	42	97	31.75	5-32	4.97
Stirling, P.R.	99	3156	33.93	177	8	11	44	32.47	4-11	4.89
Stokes, B.A.	62	1255	26.70	150*	1	5	45	24.26	5-61	5.38
Stone, O.P.	9	10	3.33	7*	–	–	2	114.00	1-12	6.21
Stoneman, M.D.	32	1084	40.14	136*	3	5	–	–	–	–
Suppiah, A.V.	94	1722	26.90	90	–	10	46	33.95	4-39	5.53
Sykes, J.S.	15	30	7.50	15	–	–	11	42.18	3-39	5.52
Tattersall, J.A.	1	0	0.00	0	–	–	–	–	–	–
Taylor, B.J.	2	2	–	2*	–	–	4	18.25	2-23	4.86
Taylor, J.M.R.	7	53	26.50	22*	–	–	9	23.00	3-37	4.96
Taylor, J.W.A.	90	3401	50.76	115*	8	19	5	34.00	4-61	7.39
Taylor, M.D.	2	7	–	7*	–	–	4	22.25	2-43	6.43
Taylor, R.M.L.	25	305	20.33	48*	–	–	32	30.12	3-39	5.63
ten Doeschate, R.N.	156	4222	46.39	180	8	23	143	29.11	5-50	5.61
Terry, S.P.	3	35	17.50	33	–	–	–	–	–	–
Thakor, S.J.	18	342	22.80	83*	–	3	9	46.22	3-39	7.65
Thomas, A.C.	156	586	14.29	28*	–	–	206	27.04	4-18	5.12
Thornely, M.A.	46	1171	29.27	105*	1	6	5	73.00	1-20	6.71

L-O	M	Runs	Avge	HS	100	50	Wkts	Avge	Best	Econ
Tillcock, A.D.	1	97	–	97*	–	1	–	–	–	–
Tomlinson, J.A.	29	35	3.88	14	–	–	30	32.43	4-47	5.10
Topley, R.J.W.	16	25	6.25	19	–	–	24	26.04	4-26	5.69
Tredwell, J.C.	208	1529	17.37	88	–	4	220	30.48	6-27	4.71
Trego, P.D.	145	3015	29.85	147	4	15	142	32.37	5-40	5.64
Tremlett, C.T.	131	550	10.18	38*	–	–	175	28.10	4-25	4.89
Trescothick, M.E.	364	11985	37.45	184	28	61	57	28.84	4-50	4.90
Trott, I.J.L.	234	8342	46.86	137	15	57	54	27.01	4-55	5.64
Troughton, J.O.	169	3654	27.06	115*	2	21	25	25.76	4-23	5.25
Turner, M.L.	41	67	8.37	15*	–	–	57	27.54	4-36	6.33
Vince, J.M.	67	2219	36.98	131	3	11	1	56.00	1-18	5.09
Wagg, G.G.	105	1332	18.00	54	–	1	121	32.48	4-35	5.91
Wainwright, D.J.	70	294	19.60	40	–	–	57	36.19	4-11	4.93
Wakely, A.G.	52	1364	31.00	102	1	9	5	21.40	2-14	4.86
Wallace, M.A.	189	2589	20.71	118*	2	7	–	–	–	166/44
Waller, M.T.C.	39	71	17.75	25*	–	–	28	40.21	3-39	5.66
Walters, S.J.	67	1485	29.11	91	–	10	3	59.66	1-12	6.50
Waters, H.T.	22	24	4.80	8	–	–	14	60.28	3-47	6.20
Wells, L.W.P.	11	35	5.00	17	–	–	3	20.33	3-19	4.75
Wells, T.J.	4	92	92.00	32*	–	–	–	–	–	–
Wessels, M.H.	121	2749	27.49	100	1	15	1	48.00	1- 0	5.87
Westley, T.	28	733	29.32	82	–	7	4	50.25	1- 9	5.58
Westwood, I.J.	60	941	22.95	65	–	3	3	75.66	1-28	5.15
Wheater, A.J.A.	48	651	21.70	70	–	3	–	–	–	17/4
White, G.G.	41	161	13.41	39*	–	–	40	27.67	5-35	5.41
White, W.A.	62	702	19.50	46*	–	–	56	37.64	6-29	6.45
Whiteley, R.A.	25	254	13.36	40	–	–	5	44.60	1-17	6.37
Wilkin, O.	1	20	20.00	20	–	–	2	22.00	2-44	5.50
Willey, D.J.	47	669	20.90	167	1	2	33	36.27	3-28	5.52
Williamson, K.S.	91	3006	42.33	145*	7	16	43	36.39	5-51	5.16
Wilson, G.C.	117	2190	23.80	113	1	14	–	–	–	73/20
Woakes, C.R.	80	630	18.52	49*	–	–	82	34.65	6-45	5.51
Wood, C.P.	47	169	10.56	41	–	–	72	24.58	5-22	5.53
Wood, M.A.	14	28	7.00	15*	–	–	17	25.82	3-23	5.28
Wood, S.K.W.	6	40	10.00	32	–	–	5	25.60	2-24	5.33
Wright, B.J.	71	1332	25.13	79	–	7	1	126.00	1-19	5.72
Wright, C.J.C.	90	219	10.42	42	–	–	91	35.35	4-20	5.58
Wright, L.J.	168	3404	30.12	143*	8	8	108	38.87	4-12	5.33
Wyatt, A.C.F.	14	13	3.25	9*	–	–	11	43.45	2-36	6.34
Yardy, M.H.	205	3639	25.27	98*	–	23	138	38.66	6-27	5.09
Yasir Arafat	234	2579	21.13	110*	1	8	366	25.05	6-24	4.98

FIRST-CLASS CRICKET RECORDS

To the end of the 2013 season

TEAM RECORDS
HIGHEST INNINGS TOTALS

1107	Victoria v New South Wales	Melbourne	1926-27
1059	Victoria v Tasmania	Melbourne	1922-23
952-6d	Sri Lanka v India	Colombo	1997-98
951-7d	Sind v Baluchistan	Karachi	1973-74
944-6d	Hyderabad v Andhra	Secunderabad	1993-94
918	New South Wales v South Australia	Sydney	1900-01
912-8d	Holkar v Mysore	Indore	1945-46
910-6d	Railways v Dera Ismail Khan	Lahore	1964-65
903-7d	England v Australia	The Oval	1938
900-6d	Queensland v Victoria	Brisbane	2005-06
887	Yorkshire v Warwickshire	Birmingham	1896
863	Lancashire v Surrey	The Oval	1990
860-6d	Tamil Nadu v Goa	Panjim	1988-89
850-7d	Somerset v Middlesex	Taunton	2007

Excluding penalty runs in India, there have been 34 innings totals of 800 runs or more in first-class cricket. Tamil Nadu's total of 860-6d was boosted to 912 by 52 penalty runs.

HIGHEST SECOND INNINGS TOTAL

770	New South Wales v South Australia	Adelaide	1920-21

HIGHEST FOURTH INNINGS TOTAL

654-5	England (set 696 to win) v South Africa	Durban	1938-39

HIGHEST MATCH AGGREGATE

2376-37	Maharashtra v Bombay	Poona	1948-49

RECORD MARGIN OF VICTORY

Innings and 851 runs: Railways v Dera Ismail Khan	Lahore	1964-65

MOST RUNS IN A DAY

721	Australians v Essex	Southend	1948

MOST HUNDREDS IN AN INNINGS

6	Holkar v Mysore	Indore	1945-46

LOWEST INNINGS TOTALS

12	†Oxford University v MCC and Ground	Oxford	1877
12	Northamptonshire v Gloucestershire	Gloucester	1907
13	Auckland v Canterbury	Auckland	1877-78
13	Nottinghamshire v Yorkshire	Nottingham	1901
14	Surrey v Essex	Chelmsford	1983
15	MCC v Surrey	Lord's	1839
15	†Victoria v MCC	Melbourne	1903-04
15	†Northamptonshire v Yorkshire	Northampton	1908
15	Hampshire v Warwickshire	Birmingham	1922

† Batted one man short

There have been 28 instances of a team being dismissed for under 20.

LOWEST MATCH AGGREGATE BY ONE TEAM

34 (16 and 18)	Border v Natal	East London	1959-60

LOWEST COMPLETED MATCH AGGREGATE BY BOTH TEAMS

105	MCC v Australians	Lord's	1878

TIED MATCHES

Before 1949 a match was considered to be tied if the scores were level after the fourth innings, even if the side batting last had wickets in hand when play ended. Law 22 was amended in 1948 and since then a match has been tied only when the scores are level after the fourth innings has been completed. There have been 56 tied first-class matches, five of which would not have qualified under the current law. The most recent are:

Warwickshire (446-7d & forfeit) v Essex (66-0d & 380)	Birmingham	2003
Worcestershire (262 & 247) v Zimbabweans (334 & 175)	Worcester	2003
Habib Bank (245 & 178) v WAPDA (233 & 190)	Lahore	2011-12
Border (210 & 210) v Boland (219 & 201)	East London	2012-13

BATTING RECORDS
35,000 RUNS IN A CAREER

	Career	I	NO	HS	Runs	Avge	100
J.B.Hobbs	1905-34	1315	106	316*	61237	50.65	197
F.E.Woolley	1906-38	1532	85	305*	58969	40.75	145
E.H.Hendren	1907-38	1300	166	301*	57611	50.80	170
C.P.Mead	1905-36	1340	185	280*	55061	47.67	153
W.G.Grace	1865-1908	1493	105	344	54896	39.55	126
W.R.Hammond	1920-51	1005	104	336*	50551	56.10	167
H.Sutcliffe	1919-45	1088	123	313	50138	51.95	149
G.Boycott	1962-86	1014	162	261*	48426	56.83	151
T.W.Graveney	1948-71/72	1223	159	258	47793	44.91	122
G.A.Gooch	1973-2000	990	75	333	44846	49.01	128
T.W.Hayward	1893-1914	1138	96	315*	43551	41.79	104
D.L.Amiss	1960-87	1139	126	262*	43423	42.86	102
M.C.Cowdrey	1950-76	1130	134	307	42719	42.89	107
A.Sandham	1911-37/38	1000	79	325	41284	44.82	107
G.A.Hick	1983/84-2008	871	84	405*	41112	52.23	136
L.Hutton	1934-60	814	91	364	40140	55.51	129
M.J.K.Smith	1951-75	1091	139	204	39832	41.84	69
W.Rhodes	1898-1930	1528	237	267*	39802	30.83	58
J.H.Edrich	1956-78	979	104	310*	39790	45.47	103
R.E.S.Wyatt	1923-57	1141	157	232	39405	40.04	85
D.C.S.Compton	1936-64	839	88	300	38942	51.85	123
G.E.Tyldesley	1909-36	961	106	256*	38874	45.46	102
J.T.Tyldesley	1895-1923	994	62	295*	37897	40.60	86
K.W.R.Fletcher	1962-88	1167	170	228*	37665	37.77	63
C.G.Greenidge	1970-92	889	75	273*	37354	45.88	92
J.W.Hearne	1909-36	1025	116	285*	37252	40.98	96
L.E.G.Ames	1926-51	951	95	295	37248	43.51	102
D.Kenyon	1946-67	1159	59	259	37002	33.63	74
W.J.Edrich	1934-58	964	92	267*	36965	42.39	86
J.M.Parks	1949-76	1227	172	205*	36673	34.76	51
M.W.Gatting	1975-98	861	123	258	36549	49.52	94
D.Denton	1894-1920	1163	70	221	36479	33.37	69
G.H.Hirst	1891-1929	1215	151	341	36323	34.13	60
I.V.A.Richards	1971/72-93	796	63	322	36212	49.40	114
A.Jones	1957-83	1168	72	204*	36049	32.89	56
W.G.Quaife	1894-1928	1203	185	255*	36012	35.37	72
R.E.Marshall	1945/46-72	1053	59	228*	35725	35.94	68
M.R.Ramprakash	1987-2012	764	93	301*	35659	53.14	114
G.Gunn	1902-32	1061	82	220	35208	35.96	62

HIGHEST INDIVIDUAL INNINGS

501*	B.C.Lara	Warwickshire v Durham	Birmingham	1994
499	Hanif Mohammed	Karachi v Bahawalpur	Karachi	1958-59
452*	D.G.Bradman	New South Wales v Queensland	Sydney	1929-30
443*	B.B.Nimbalkar	Maharashtra v Kathiawar	Poona	1948-49
437	W.H.Ponsford	Victoria v Queensland	Melbourne	1927-28
429	W.H.Ponsford	Victoria v Tasmania	Melbourne	1922-23
428	Aftab Baloch	Sind v Baluchistan	Karachi	1973-74
424	A.C.MacLaren	Lancashire v Somerset	Taunton	1895
405*	G.A.Hick	Worcestershire v Somerset	Taunton	1988
400*	B.C.Lara	West Indies v England	St John's	2003-04
394	Naved Latif	Sargodha v Gujranwala	Gujranwala	2000-01
390	S.C.Cook	Lions v Warriors	East London	2009-10
385	B.Sutcliffe	Otago v Canterbury	Christchurch	1952-53
383	C.W.Gregory	New South Wales v Queensland	Brisbane	1906-07
380	M.L.Hayden	Australia v Zimbabwe	Perth	2003-04
377	S.V.Manjrekar	Bombay v Hyderabad	Bombay	1990-91
375	B.C.Lara	West Indies v England	St John's	1993-94
374	D.P.M.D.Jayawardena	Sri Lanka v South Africa	Colombo	2006
369	D.G.Bradman	South Australia v Tasmania	Adelaide	1935-36
366	N.H.Fairbrother	Lancashire v Surrey	The Oval	1990
366	M.V.Sridhar	Hyderabad v Andhra	Secunderabad	1993-94
365*	C.Hill	South Australia v NSW	Adelaide	1900-01
365*	G.St A.Sobers	West Indies v Pakistan	Kingston	1957-58
364	L.Hutton	England v Australia	The Oval	1938
359*	V.M.Merchant	Bombay v Maharashtra	Bombay	1943-44
359	R.B.Simpson	New South Wales v Queensland	Brisbane	1963-64
357*	R.Abel	Surrey v Somerset	The Oval	1899
357	D.G.Bradman	South Australia v Victoria	Melbourne	1935-36
356	B.A.Richards	South Australia v W Australia	Perth	1970-71
355*	G.R.Marsh	W Australia v S Australia	Perth	1989-90
355	B.Sutcliffe	Otago v Auckland	Dunedin	1949-50
353	V.V.S.Laxman	Hyderabad v Karnataka	Bangalore	1999-00
352	W.H.Ponsford	Victoria v New South Wales	Melbourne	1926-27
352	C.A.Pujara	Saurashtra v Karnataka	Rajkot	2012-13
350	Rashid Israr	Habib Bank v National Bank	Lahore	1976-77

There have been 193 triple hundreds in first-class cricket, W.V.Raman (313) and Arjan Kripal Singh (302*) for Tamil Nadu v Goa at Panjim in 1988-89 providing the only instance of two batsmen scoring 300 in the same innings.

MOST HUNDREDS IN SUCCESSIVE INNINGS

6	C.B.Fry	Sussex and Rest of England	1901
6	D.G.Bradman	South Australia and D.G.Bradman's XI	1938-39
6	M.J.Procter	Rhodesia	1970-71

TWO DOUBLE HUNDREDS IN A MATCH

244	202*	A.E.Fagg	Kent v Essex	Colchester	1938

TRIPLE HUNDRED AND HUNDRED IN A MATCH

333	123	G.A.Gooch	England v India	Lord's	1990

DOUBLE HUNDRED AND HUNDRED IN A MATCH MOST TIMES

4	Zaheer Abbas	Gloucestershire	1976-81

TWO HUNDREDS IN A MATCH MOST TIMES

8	Zaheer Abbas	Gloucestershire and PIA	1976-82
8	R.T.Ponting	Tasmania, Australia and Australians	1992-2006
7	W.R.Hammond	Gloucestershire, England and MCC	1927-45
7	M.R.Ramprakash	Middlesex, Surrey	1990-2010

MOST HUNDREDS IN A SEASON

18   D.C.S.Compton   1947   16   J.B.Hobbs   1925

100 HUNDREDS IN A CAREER

	Total		100th Hundred	
	Hundreds	Inns	Season	Inns
J.B.Hobbs	197	1315	1923	821
E.H.Hendren	170	1300	1928-29	740
W.R.Hammond	167	1005	1935	679
C.P.Mead	153	1340	1927	892
G.Boycott	151	1014	1977	645
H.Sutcliffe	149	1088	1932	700
F.E.Woolley	145	1532	1929	1031
G.A.Hick	136	871	1998	574
L.Hutton	129	814	1951	619
G.A.Gooch	128	990	1992-93	820
W.G.Grace	126	1493	1895	1113
D.C.S.Compton	123	839	1952	552
T.W.Graveney	122	1223	1964	940
D.G.Bradman	117	338	1947-48	295
I.V.A.Richards	114	796	1988-89	658
M.R.Ramprakash	114	764	2008	676
Zaheer Abbas	108	768	1982-83	658
A.Sandham	107	1000	1935	871
M.C.Cowdrey	107	1130	1973	1035
T.W.Hayward	104	1138	1913	1076
G.M.Turner	103	792	1982	779
J.H.Edrich	103	979	1977	945
L.E.G.Ames	102	951	1950	915
G.E.Tyldesley	102	961	1934	919
D.L.Amiss	102	1139	1986	1081

MOST 400s: 2 – B.C.Lara, W.H.Ponsford

MOST 300s or more: 6 – D.G.Bradman; 4 – W.R.Hammond, W.H.Ponsford

MOST 200s or more: 37 – D.G.Bradman; 36 – W.R.Hammond; 22 – E.H.Hendren

MOST RUNS IN A MONTH

1294 (avge 92.42)   L.Hutton   Yorkshire   June 1949

MOST RUNS IN A SEASON

Runs			I	NO	HS	Avge	100	Season
3816	D.C.S.Compton	Middlesex	50	8	246	90.85	18	1947
3539	W.J.Edrich	Middlesex	52	8	267*	80.43	12	1947
3518	T.W.Hayward	Surrey	61	8	219	66.37	13	1906

The feat of scoring 3000 runs in a season has been achieved 28 times, the most recent instance being by W.E.Alley (3019) in 1961. The highest aggregate in a season since 1969 is 2755 by S.J.Cook in 1991.

1000 RUNS IN A SEASON MOST TIMES

28   W.G.Grace (Gloucestershire), F.E.Woolley (Kent)

HIGHEST BATTING AVERAGE IN A SEASON

(Qualification: 12 innings)

Avge			I	NO	HS	Runs	100	Season
115.66	D.G.Bradman	Australians	26	5	278	2429	13	1938
104.66	D.R.Martyn	Australians	14	5	176*	942	5	2001
103.54	M.R.Ramprakash	Surrey	24	2	301*	2278	8	2006
102.53	G.Boycott	Yorkshire	20	5	175*	1538	6	1979

Avge			I	NO	HS	Runs	100	Season
102.00	W.A.Johnston	Australians	17	16	28*	102	–	1953
101.70	G.A.Gooch	Essex	30	3	333	2746	12	1990
101.30	M.R.Ramprakash	Surrey	25	5	266*	2026	10	2007
100.12	G.Boycott	Yorkshire	30	5	233	2503	13	1971

FASTEST HUNDRED AGAINST AUTHENTIC BOWLING

35 min	P.G.H.Fender	Surrey v Northamptonshire	Northampton	1920

FASTEST DOUBLE HUNDRED

113 min	R.J.Shastri	Bombay v Baroda	Bombay	1984-85

FASTEST TRIPLE HUNDRED

181 min	D.C.S.Compton	MCC v NE Transvaal	Benoni	1948-49

MOST SIXES IN AN INNINGS

16	A.Symonds	Gloucestershire v Glamorgan	Abergavenny	1995
16	G.R.Napier	Essex v Surrey	Croydon	2011
16	J.D.Ryder	New Zealanders v Australia A	Brisbane	2011-12

MOST SIXES IN A MATCH

20	A.Symonds	Gloucestershire v Glamorgan	Abergavenny	1995

MOST SIXES IN A SEASON

80	I.T.Botham	Somerset and England	1985

MOST FOURS IN AN INNINGS

72	B.C.Lara	Warwickshire v Durham	Birmingham	1994

MOST RUNS OFF ONE OVER

36	G.St A.Sobers	Nottinghamshire v Glamorgan	Swansea	1968
36	R.J.Shastri	Bombay v Baroda	Bombay	1984-85

Both batsmen hit for six all six balls of overs bowled by M.A.Nash and Tilak Raj respectively.

MOST RUNS IN A DAY

390*	B.C.Lara	Warwickshire v Durham	Birmingham	1994

There have been 19 instances of a batsman scoring 300 or more runs in a day.

LONGEST INNINGS

1015 min	R.Nayyar (271)	Himachal Pradesh v Jammu & Kashmir Chamba	1999-00

HIGHEST PARTNERSHIPS FOR EACH WICKET

First Wicket

561	Waheed Mirza/Mansoor Akhtar	Karachi W v Quetta	Karachi	1976-77
555	P.Holmes/H.Sutcliffe	Yorkshire v Essex	Leyton	1932
554	J.T.Brown/J.Tunnicliffe	Yorkshire v Derbys	Chesterfield	1898

Second Wicket

580	Rafatullah Mohmand/Aamer Sajjad	WAPDA v SSGC	Sheikhupura	2009-10
576	S.T.Jayasuriya/R.S.Mahanama	Sri Lanka v India	Colombo	1997-98
480	E.Elgar/R.R.Rossouw	Eagles v Titans	Centurion	2009-10
475	Zahir Alam/L.S.Rajput	Assam v Tripura	Gauhati	1991-92
465*	J.A.Jameson/R.B.Kanhai	Warwickshire v Glos	Birmingham	1974

Third Wicket

624	K.C.Sangakkara/D.P.M.D.Jayawardena	Sri Lanka v South Africa	Colombo	2006
539	S.D.Jogiyani/R.A.Jadeja	Saurashtra v Gujarat	Surat	2012-13
523	M.A.Carberry/N.D.McKenzie	Hampshire v Yorkshire	Southampton	2011

Fourth Wicket

577	V.S.Hazare/Gul Mahomed	Baroda v Holkar	Baroda	1946-47
574*	C.L.Walcott/F.M.M.Worrell	Barbados v Trinidad	Port-of-Spain	1945-46
502*	F.M.M.Worrell/J.D.C.Goddard	Barbados v Trinidad	Bridgetown	1943-44
470	A.I.Kallicharran/G.W.Humpage	Warwickshire v Lancs	Southport	1982

Fifth Wicket

520*	C.A.Pujara/R.A.Jadeja	Saurashtra v Orissa	Rajkot	2008-09
494	Marchall Ayub/Mehrab Hossain Jr	Central Zone v East Zone	Bogra	2012-13
479	Misbah-ul-Haq/Usman Arshad	Sui NGP v Lahore Shalimar	Lahore	2009-10
464*	M.E.Waugh/S.R.Waugh	NSW v W Australia	Perth	1990-91
420	Mohd. Ashraful/Marshall Ayub	Dhaka v Chittagong	Chittagong	2006-07
410*	A.S.Chopra/S.Badrinath	India A v South Africa A	Delhi	2007-08
405	S.G.Barnes/D.G.Bradman	Australia v England	Sydney	1946-47
401	M.B.Loye/D.Ripley	Northants v Glamorgan	Northampton	1998

Sixth Wicket

487*	G.A.Headley/C.C.Passailaigue	Jamaica v Tennyson's	Kingston	1931-32
428	W.W.Armstrong/M.A.Noble	Australians v Sussex	Hove	1902
417	W.P.Saha/L.R.Shukla	Bengal v Assam	Kolkata	2010-11
411	R.M.Poore/E.G.Wynyard	Hampshire v Somerset	Taunton	1899

Seventh Wicket

460	Bhupinder Singh jr/P.Dharmani	Punjab v Delhi	Delhi	1994-95
347	D.St E.Atkinson/C.C.Depeiza	W Indies v Australia	Bridgetown	1954-55
344	K.S.Ranjitsinhji/W.Newham	Sussex v Essex	Leyton	1902

Eighth Wicket

433	V.T.Trumper/A.Sims	Australians v C'bury	Christchurch	1913-14
392	A.Mishra/J.Yadav	Haryana v Karnataka	Hubli	2012-13
332	I.J.L.Trott/S.C.J.Broad	England v Pakistan	Lord's	2010

Ninth Wicket

283	J.Chapman/A.Warren	Derbys v Warwicks	Blackwell	1910
268	J.B.Commins/N.Boje	SA 'A' v Mashonaland	Harare	1994-95
261	W.L.Madsen/T.Poynton	Derbys v Northants	Northampton	2012
251	J.W.H.T.Douglas/S.N.Hare	Essex v Derbyshire	Leyton	1921

Tenth Wicket

307	A.F.Kippax/J.E.H.Hooker	NSW v Victoria	Melbourne	1928-29
249	C.T.Sarwate/S.N.Banerjee	Indians v Surrey	The Oval	1946
239	Aqil Arshad/Ali Raza	Lahore Whites v Hyderabad	Lahore	2004-05

BOWLING RECORDS
2000 WICKETS IN A CAREER

	Career	Runs	Wkts	Avge	100w
W.Rhodes	1898-1930	69993	**4187**	16.71	23
A.P.Freeman	1914-36	69577	**3776**	18.42	17
C.W.L.Parker	1903-35	63817	**3278**	19.46	16
J.T.Hearne	1888-1923	54352	**3061**	17.75	15
T.W.J.Goddard	1922-52	59116	**2979**	19.84	16
W.G.Grace	1865-1908	51545	**2876**	17.92	10
A.S.Kennedy	1907-36	61034	**2874**	21.23	15
D.Shackleton	1948-69	53303	**2857**	18.65	20
G.A.R.Lock	1946-70/71	54709	**2844**	19.23	14
F.J.Titmus	1949-82	63313	**2830**	22.37	16
M.W.Tate	1912-37	50571	**2784**	18.16	13+1
G.H.Hirst	1891-1929	51282	**2739**	18.72	15
C.Blythe	1899-1914	42136	**2506**	16.81	14
D.L.Underwood	1963-87	49993	**2465**	20.28	10
W.E.Astill	1906-39	57783	**2431**	23.76	9
J.C.White	1909-37	43759	**2356**	18.57	14

	Career	Runs	Wkts	Avge	100w
W.E.Hollies	1932-57	48656	**2323**	20.94	14
F.S.Trueman	1949-69	42154	**2304**	18.29	12
J.B.Statham	1950-68	36999	**2260**	16.37	13
R.T.D.Perks	1930-55	53771	**2233**	24.07	16
J.Briggs	1879-1900	35431	**2221**	15.95	12
D.J.Shepherd	1950-72	47302	**2218**	21.32	12
E.G.Dennett	1903-26	42571	**2147**	19.82	12
T.Richardson	1892-1905	38794	**2104**	18.43	10
T.E.Bailey	1945-67	48170	**2082**	23.13	9
R.Illingworth	1951-83	42023	**2072**	20.28	10
F.E.Woolley	1906-38	41066	**2068**	19.85	8
N.Gifford	1960-88	48731	**2068**	23.56	4
G.Geary	1912-38	41339	**2063**	20.03	11
D.V.P.Wright	1932-57	49307	**2056**	23.98	10
J.A.Newman	1906-30	51111	**2032**	25.15	9
A.Shaw	1864-97	24580	**2026+1**	12.12	9
S.Haigh	1895-1913	32091	**2012**	15.94	11

ALL TEN WICKETS IN AN INNINGS

This feat has been achieved 81 times in first-class matches (excluding 12-a-side fixtures).
Three Times: A.P.Freeman (1929, 1930, 1931).
Twice: V.E.Walker (1859, 1865); H.Verity (1931, 1932); J.C.Laker (1956)

Instances since 1945:

W.E.Hollies	Warwickshire v Notts	Birmingham	1946
J.M.Sims	East v West	Kingston on Thames	1948
J.K.R.Graveney	Gloucestershire v Derbyshire	Chesterfield	1949
T.E.Bailey	Essex v Lancashire	Clacton	1949
R.Berry	Lancashire v Worcestershire	Blackpool	1953
S.P.Gupte	President's XI v Combined XI	Bombay	1954-55
J.C.Laker	Surrey v Australians	The Oval	1956
K.Smales	Nottinghamshire v Glos	Stroud	1956
G.A.R.Lock	Surrey v Kent	Blackheath	1956
J.C.Laker	England v Australia	Manchester	1956
P.M.Chatterjee	Bengal v Assam	Jorhat	1956-57
J.D.Bannister	Warwicks v Combined Services	Birmingham (M & B)	1959
A.J.G.Pearson	Cambridge U v Leicestershire	Loughborough	1961
N.I.Thomson	Sussex v Warwickshire	Worthing	1964
P.J.Allan	Queensland v Victoria	Melbourne	1965-66
I.J.Brayshaw	Western Australia v Victoria	Perth	1967-68
Shahid Mahmood	Karachi Whites v Khairpur	Karachi	1969-70
E.E.Hemmings	International XI v W Indians	Kingston	1982-83
P.Sunderam	Rajasthan v Vidarbha	Jodhpur	1985-86
S.T.Jefferies	Western Province v OFS	Cape Town	1987-88
Imran Adil	Bahawalpur v Faisalabad	Faisalabad	1989-90
G.P.Wickremasinghe	Sinhalese v Kalutara	Colombo	1991-92
R.L.Johnson	Middlesex v Derbyshire	Derby	1994
Naeem Akhtar	Rawalpindi B v Peshawar	Peshawar	1995-96
A.Kumble	India v Pakistan	Delhi	1998-99
D.S.Mohanty	East Zone v South Zone	Agartala	2000-01
O.D.Gibson	Durham v Hampshire	Chester-le-Street	2007
M.W.Olivier	Warriors v Eagles	Bloemfontein	2007-08
Zulfiqar Babar	Multan v Islamabad	Multan	2009-10

MOST WICKETS IN A MATCH

19	J.C.Laker	England v Australia	Manchester	1956

274

MOST WICKETS IN A SEASON

Wkts		Season	Matches	Overs	Mdns	Runs	Avge
304	A.P.Freeman	1928	37	1976.1	423	5489	18.05
298	A.P.Freeman	1933	33	2039	651	4549	15.26

The feat of taking 250 wickets in a season has been achieved on 12 occasions, the last instance being by A.P.Freeman in 1933. 200 or more wickets in a season have been taken on 59 occasions, the last being by G.A.R.Lock (212 wickets, average 12.02) in 1957.

The highest aggregates of wickets taken in a season since the reduction of County Championship matches in 1969 are as follows:

Wkts		Season	Matches	Overs	Mdns	Runs	Avge
134	M.D.Marshall	1982	22	822	225	2108	15.73
131	L.R.Gibbs	1971	23	1024.1	295	2475	18.89
125	F.D.Stephenson	1988	22	819.1	196	2289	18.31
121	R.D.Jackman	1980	23	746.2	220	1864	15.40

Since 1969 there have been 50 instances of bowlers taking 100 wickets in a season.

MOST HAT-TRICKS IN A CAREER

7	D.V.P.Wright
6	T.W.J.Goddard, C.W.L.Parker
5	S.Haigh, V.W.C.Jupp, A.E.G.Rhodes, F.A.Tarrant

ALL-ROUND RECORDS
THE 'DOUBLE'

3000 runs and 100 wickets: J.H.Parks (1937)
2000 runs and 200 wickets: G.H.Hirst (1906)
2000 runs and 100 wickets: F.E.Woolley (4), J.W.Hearne (3), W.G.Grace (2), G.H.Hirst (2), W.Rhodes (2), T.E.Bailey, D.E.Davies, G.L.Jessop, V.W.C.Jupp, J.Langridge, F.A.Tarrant, C.L.Townsend, L.F.Townsend
1000 runs and 200 wickets: M.W.Tate (3), A.E.Trott (2), A.S.Kennedy
Most Doubles: 16 – W.Rhodes; 14 – G.H.Hirst; 10 – V.W.C.Jupp
Double in Debut Season: D.B.Close (1949) – aged 18, the youngest to achieve this feat.

The feat of scoring 1000 runs and taking 100 wickets in a season has been achieved on 305 occasions, R.J.Hadlee (1984) and F.D.Stephenson (1988) being the only players to complete the 'double' since the reduction of County Championship matches in 1969.

WICKET-KEEPING RECORDS
1000 DISMISSALS IN A CAREER

	Career	Dismissals	Ct	St
R.W.Taylor	1960-88	**1649**	1473	176
J.T.Murray	1952-75	**1527**	1270	257
H.Strudwick	1902-27	**1497**	1242	255
A.P.E.Knott	1964-85	**1344**	1211	133
R.C.Russell	1981-2004	**1320**	1192	128
F.H.Huish	1895-1914	**1310**	933	377
B.Taylor	1949-73	**1294**	1083	211
S.J.Rhodes	1981-2004	**1263**	1139	124
D.Hunter	1889-1909	**1253**	906	347
H.R.Butt	1890-1912	**1228**	953	275
J.H.Board	1891-1914/15	**1207**	852	355
H.Elliott	1920-47	**1206**	904	302
J.M.Parks	1949-76	**1181**	1088	93
R.Booth	1951-70	**1126**	948	178
L.E.G.Ames	1926-51	**1121**	703	418
D.L.Bairstow	1970-90	**1099**	961	138
G.Duckworth	1923-47	**1096**	753	343

	Career	*Dismissals*	*Ct*	*St*
H.W.Stephenson	1948-64	**1082**	748	334
J.G.Binks	1955-75	**1071**	895	176
T.G.Evans	1939-69	**1066**	816	250
A.Long	1960-80	**1046**	922	124
G.O.Dawkes	1937-61	**1043**	895	148
R.W.Tolchard	1965-83	**1037**	912	125
W.L.Cornford	1921-47	**1017**	675	342

MOST DISMISSALS IN AN INNINGS

9	(8ct, 1st)	Tahir Rashid	Habib Bank v PACO	Gujranwala	1992-93
9	(7ct, 2st)	W.R.James	Matabeleland v Mashonaland CD	Bulawayo	1995-96
8	(8ct)	A.T.W.Grout	Queensland v W Australia	Brisbane	1959-60
8	(8ct)	D.E.East	Essex v Somerset	Taunton	1985
8	(8ct)	S.A.Marsh	Kent v Middlesex	Lord's	1991
8	(6ct, 2st)	T.J.Zoehrer	Australians v Surrey	The Oval	1993
8	(7ct, 1st)	D.S.Berry	Victoria v South Australia	Melbourne	1996-97
8	(7ct, 1st)	Y.S.S.Mendis	Bloomfield v Kurunegala Youth	Colombo	2000-01
8	(7ct, 1st)	S.Nath	Assam v Tripura (*on debut*)	Gauhati	2001-02
8	(8ct)	J.N.Batty	Surrey v Kent	The Oval	2004
8	(8ct)	Golam Mabud	Sylhet v Dhaka	Dhaka	2005-06
8	(8ct)	D.C.de Boorder	Otago v Wellington	Wellington	2009-10
8	(8ct)	R.S.Second	Free State v North West	Bloemfontein	2011-12
8	(8ct)	T.L.Tsolekile	South Africa A v Sri Lanka A	Durban	2012

MOST DISMISSALS IN A MATCH

14	(11ct, 3st)	I.Khaleel	Hyderabad v Assam	Guwahati	2011-12
13	(11ct, 2st)	W.R.James	Matabeleland v Mashonaland CD	Bulawayo	1995-96
12	(8ct, 4st)	E.Pooley	Surrey v Sussex	The Oval	1868
12	(9ct, 3st)	D.Tallon	Queensland v NSW	Sydney	1938-39
12	(9ct, 3st)	H.B.Taber	NSW v South Australia	Adelaide	1968-69
12	(12ct)	P.D.McGlashan	Northern Districts v Central Districts	Whangarei	2009-10
12	(11ct, 1st)	T.L.Tsolekile	Lions v Dolphins	Johannesburg	2010-11
12	(12ct)	Kashif Mahmood	Lahore Shalimar v Abbottabad	Abbottabad	2010-11
12	(12ct)	R.S.Second	Free State v North West	Bloemfontein	2011-12

MOST DISMISSALS IN A SEASON

128	(79ct, 49st)	L.E.G.Ames			1929

FIELDING RECORDS
750 CATCHES IN A CAREER

1018	F.E.Woolley	1906-38	784	J.G.Langridge	1928-55
887	W.G.Grace	1865-1908	764	W.Rhodes	1898-1930
830	G.A.R.Lock	1946-70/71	758	C.A.Milton	1948-74
819	W.R.Hammond	1920-51	754	E.H.Hendren	1907-38
813	D.B.Close	1949-86			

MOST CATCHES IN AN INNINGS

7	M.J.Stewart	Surrey v Northamptonshire	Northampton	1957
7	A.S.Brown	Gloucestershire v Nottinghamshire	Nottingham	1966
7	R.Clarke	Warwickshire v Lancashire	Liverpool	2011

MOST CATCHES IN A MATCH

10	W.R.Hammond	Gloucestershire v Surrey	Cheltenham	1928
9	R.Clarke	Warwickshire v Lancashire	Liverpool	2011

MOST CATCHES IN A SEASON

78	W.R.Hammond	1928	77	M.J.Stewart	1957

ENGLAND LIMITED-OVERS INTERNATIONALS 2013

INDIA v ENGLAND

LIMITED-OVERS INTERNATIONALS

Saurashtra C.A.Stadium, Rajkot, 11 January. Toss: England. **ENGLAND** won by 9 runs. England 325-4 (50; I.R.Bell 85, A.N.Cook 75). India 316-9 (50; Yuvraj Singh 61, G.Gambhir 52, S.K.Raina 50, J.C.Tredwell 4-44). Award: J.C.Tredwell. England debut: J.E.Root.

Nehru Stadium, Kochi, 15 January. Toss: India. **INDIA** won by 127 runs. India 285-6 (50; M.S.Dhoni 72, R.A.Jadeja 61*, S.K.Raina 55). England 158 (36; B.Kumar 3-29, R.Ashwin 3-39). Award: R.A.Jadeja.

HEC International Cricket Stadium, Ranchi, 19 January. Toss: India. **INDIA** won by seven wickets. England 155 (42.2; R.A.Jadeja 3-19). India 157-3 (28.1; V.Kohli 77*). Award V.Kohli.

Punjab CA Stadium, Mohali, Chandigarh, 23 January. Toss: India. **INDIA** won by five wickets. England 257-7 (50; A.N.Cook 76, K.P.Pietersen 72, J.E.Root 57*, R.A.Jadeja 3-39). India 258-5 (47.3; S.K.Raina 89*, R.G.Sharma 83). Award: S.K.Raina.

Himachal Pradesh CA Stadium, Dharmasala, 27 January. Toss England. **ENGLAND** won by seven wickets. India 226 (49.4; S.K.Raina 83, T.T.Bresnan 4-45). England 227-3 (47.2; I.R.Bell 113*). Award: I.R.Bell. Series award: S.K.Raina.

NEW ZEALAND v ENGLAND

TWENTY20 INTERNATIONALS

Eden Park, Auckland, 9 February. Toss: New Zealand. **ENGLAND** won by 40 runs. England 214-7 (20). New Zealand 174-9 (20; S.C.J.Broad 4-24, S.T.Finn 3-39).

This was England's highest score in all IT20s.

Seddon Park, Hamilton, 12 February. Toss: England. **NEW ZEALAND** won by 55 runs. New Zealand 192-6 (20; B.B.McCullum 74, J.W.Dernbach 3-38). England 137 (19.3; J.C.Buttler 54, J.E.C.Franklin 4-15).

Westpac Stadium, Wellington, 15 February. Toss: England. **ENGLAND** won by ten wickets. New Zealand 139-8 (20; M.J.Guptill 59, S.C.J.Broad 3-15, J.W.Dernbach 3-36). England 143-0 (12.4; A.D.Hales 80*, M.J.Lumb 53*).

LIMITED-OVERS INTERNATIONALS

Seddon Park, Hamilton, 17 February. Toss: New Zealand. **NEW ZEALAND** won by three wickets. England 258 (49.3; I.J.L.Trott 68, I.R.Bell 64, J.E.Root 56, M.J.McClenaghan 4-56, J.E.C.Franklin 3-38). New Zealand 259-7 (48.5; K.S.Williamson 74, B.B.McCullum 69*).

McLean Park, Napier, 20 February. Toss: England. **ENGLAND** won by eight wickets. New Zealand 269 (48.5; L.R.P.L.Taylor 100, B.B.McCullum 74, J.M.Anderson 5-34, C.R.Woakes 3-68). England 270-2 (47.4; J.E.Root 79*, A.N.Cook 78, I.J.L.Trott 65*).

Eden Park, Auckland, 23 February. Toss: England. **ENGLAND** won by five wickets. New Zealand 185 (43.5; B.B.McCullum 79, S.T.Finn 3-27). England 186-5 (37.3; T.G.Southee 3-48).

ENGLAND v NEW ZEALAND

NATWEST LIMITED-OVERS INTERNATIONALS

Lord's, London, 31 May. Toss: New Zealand. **NEW ZEALAND** won by five wickets. England 227-9 (50; T.G.Southee 3-37). New Zealand 231-5 (46.5; M.J.Guptill 103*, L.R.P.L.Taylor 54, J.M.Anderson 3-31). Award: M.J.Guptill.

The Rose Bowl, Southampton, 2 June. Toss: New Zealand. **NEW ZEALAND** won by 86 runs. New Zealand 359-3 (50; M.J.Guptill 189*, L.R.P.L.Taylor 60, K.S.Williamson 55). England 273 (44.1; I.J.L.Trott 109*, M.J.McClenaghan 3-35). Award: M.J.Guptill.

M.J.Guptill's score of 189 was a record for New Zealand and the equal highest LOI innings against England.*

Trent Bridge, Nottingham, 5 June. Toss: New Zealand. **ENGLAND** won by 34 runs. England 287-6 (50; I.R.Bell 82, M.J.McClenaghan 3-54). New Zealand 253 (46.3; L.R.P.L.Taylor 71, J.C.Tredwell 3-51). Award: J.C.Buttler (47* in 16 balls). Series award: M.J.Guptill.

TWENTY20 INTERNATIONALS

The Oval, London, 25 June. Toss: England. **NEW ZEALAND** won by 5 runs. New Zealand 201-4 (20; B.B.McCullum 68, H.D.Rutherford 62). England 196-5 (20; L.J.Wright 52). Award: H.D.Rutherford.

The Oval, London, 27 June. Toss: New Zealand. **NO RESULT**. England 2-1 (0.2).

ICC CHAMPIONS TROPHY 2013

See pages 279-280 for details of these matches.

ENGLAND v AUSTRALIA

TWENTY20 INTERNATIONALS

The Rose Bowl, Southampton, 29 August. Toss: England. **AUSTRALIA** won by 39 runs. Australia 248-6 (20; A.J.Finch 156, J.W.Dernbach 3-34). England 209-6 (20; J.E.Root 90*). Award: A.J.Finch.

A.J.Finch's innings (63b, 11 fours, 14 sixes) was the highest score in all IT20s and the third highest in all T20 cricket.

Riverside Ground, Chester-le-Street, 31 August. Toss: Australia. **ENGLAND** won by 27 runs. England 195-5 (20; A.D.Hales 94, Fawad Ahmed 3-25). Australia 168-9 (20; D.A.Warner 53, J.W.Dernbach 3-23). Award: A.D.Hales.

IRELAND v ENGLAND

RSA CHALLENGE

The Village, Malahide, Dublin, 3 September. Toss: England. **ENGLAND** won by six wickets. Ireland 269-7 (50; W.T.S.Porterfield 112, W.B.Rankin 4-46). England 274-4 (E.J.G.Morgan 124*, R.S.Bopara 101*, T.J.Murtagh 3-33). Award: E.J.G.Morgan. England debuts: G.S.Ballance, M.A.Carberry.

NATWEST LIMITED-OVERS INTERNATIONALS

Headingley, Leeds, 6 September. MATCH ABANDONED.

Old Trafford, Manchester, 8 September. Toss: England. **AUSTRALIA** won by 88 runs. Australia 315-7 (50; M.J.Clarke 105, G.J.Bailey 82). England 227 (44.2; J.C.Buttler 75, K.P.Pietersen 60, E.J.G.Morgan 54, C.J.McKay 3-47). Award: M.J.Clarke.

Edgbaston, Birmingham, 11 September. Toss: Australia. **NO RESULT**. England 59-3 (15.1).

Sophia Gardens, Cardiff, 14 September. Toss: England. **ENGLAND** won by three wickets. Australia 227 (48.2; G.J.Bailey 87, J.C.Tredwell 3-53). England 231-7 (49.3; J.C.Buttler 65*, M.A.Carberry 63, E.J.G.Morgan 53, C.J.McKay 4-39). Award: J.C.Buttler.

The Rose Bowl, Southampton, 16 September. Toss: Australia. **AUSTRALIA** won by 49 runs. Australia 298 (49.1; S.R.Watson 143, M.J.Clarke 75, B.A.Stokes 5-61, C.J.Jordan 3-51). England 249 (48; R.S.Bopara 62, J.P.Faulkner 3-38). Award: S.R.Watson. Series award: M.J.Clarke. England debut: C.J.Jordan.

ENGLAND'S RESULTS IN 2013

	P	W	L	T	NR
Limited Overs	21	10	10	–	1
Twenty20	7	3	3	–	1
Overall	28	13	13	–	2

600 RUNS IN LIMITED-OVERS INTERNATIONALS IN 2013

	M	I	NO	HS	Runs	Avge	100	50	S/Rate
I.R.Bell	16	16	1	113*	645	43.00	1	4	76.87
J.E.Root	20	19	3	79*	626	39.12	–	4	82.15
I.J.L.Trott	14	14	4	109*	611	61.10	1	4	86.05

20 WICKETS IN LIMITED-OVERS INTERNATIONALS IN 2013

	Pl	O	M	R	W	Avge	Best	4wI	Econ
J.C.Tredwell	15	111.2	4	559	25	22.36	4-44	1	5.02
J.M.Anderson	10	82.5	5	351	23	15.26	5-34	1	4.23

ICC CHAMPIONS TROPHY 2013

The seventh ICC Champions Trophy took place in England between 6 and 23 June.

GROUP A	P	W	L	T	A	Pts	Net RR
England	3	2	1	–	–	4	+0.30
Sri Lanka	3	2	1	–	–	4	–0.19
New Zealand	3	1	1	–	1	3	+0.77
Australia	3	–	2	–	1	1	–0.68

Edgbaston, Birmingham, 8 June. Toss: England. **ENGLAND** won by 48 runs. England 269-6 (50; I.R.Bell 91). Australia 221-9 (50; G.J.Bailey 55, J.P.Faulkner 54*, J.M.Anderson 3-30). Award: I.R.Bell.

Sophia Gardens, Cardiff, 9 June. Toss: Sri Lanka. **NEW ZEALAND** won by one wicket. Sri Lanka 138 (37.5; K.C.Sangakkara 68, M.J.McClenaghan 4-43). New Zealand 139-9 (36.3; S.L.Malinga 4-34). Award: N.L.McCullum (New Zealand, 32 and 2-23).

Edgbaston, Birmingham, 12 June. Toss: Australia. **NO RESULT**. Australia 243-8 (50; A.C.Voges 71, G.J.Bailey 55, M.J.McClenaghan 4-65). New Zealand 51-2 (15).

The Oval, London, 13 June. Toss: Sri Lanka. **SRI LANKA** won by seven wickets. England 293-7 (50; I.J.L.Trott 76, J.E.Root 68, A.N.Cook 59). Sri Lanka 297-3 (47.1; K.C.Sangakkara 134*, K.M.D.N.Kulasekara 58*). Award: K.C.Sangakkara.

Sophia Gardens, Cardiff, 16 June. Toss: New Zealand. **ENGLAND** won by 10 runs. England 169 (23.3/24; A.N.Cook 64, K.D.Mills 4-30, M.J.McClenaghan 3-36). New Zealand 159-8 (24/24; K.S.Williamson 67, J.M.Anderson 3-32). Award: A.N.Cook.

The Oval, London, 17 June. Toss: Australia. **SRI LANKA** won by 20 runs. Sri Lanka 253-8 (50; D.P.M.D.Jayawardena 84*, H.D.R.L.Thirimanne 57, M.G.Johnson 3-48). Australia 233 (42.3; K.M.D.N.Kulasekara 3-42). Award: D.P.M.D.Jayawardena.

GROUP B	P	W	L	T	A	Pts	Net RR
India	3	3	–	–	–	6	+0.93
South Africa	3	1	1	1	–	3	+0.32
West Indies	3	1	1	1	–	3	–0.07
Pakistan	3	–	3	–	–	0	–1.03

Sophia Gardens, Cardiff, 6 June. Toss: South Africa. **INDIA** won by 26 runs. India 331-7 (50; S.Dhawan 114, R.G.Sharma 65, R.McLaren 3-70). South Africa 305 (50; R.McLaren 71*, A.B.de Villiers 70, R.J.Peterson 68). Award: S. Dhawan.

The Oval, London, 7 June. Toss: West Indies. **WEST INDIES** won by two wickets. Pakistan 170 (48; Misbah-ul-Haq 96*, Nasir Jamshed 50, K.A.J.Roach 3-28, S.P.Narine 3-34). West Indies 172-8 (40.4; Mohammad Irfan 3-32). Award: K.A.J.Roach.

Edgbaston, Birmingham, 10 June. Toss: South Africa. **SOUTH AFRICA** won by 67 runs. South Africa 234-9 (50; H.M.Amla 81). Pakistan 167 (45; Misbah-ul-Haq 55, R.McLaren 4-19). Award: H.M.Amla.

The Oval, London, 11 June. Toss: India. **INDIA** won by eight wickets. West Indies 233-9 (50; J.Charles 60, D.J.G.Sammy 56*, R.A.Jadeja 5-36). India 236-2 (39.1; S.Dhawan 102*, R.G.Sharma 52, K.D.Karthik 51*). Award: R.A.Jadeja.

Sophia Gardens, Cardiff, 14 June. Toss: West Indies. **MATCH TIED** (D/L method). South Africa 230-6 (31/31; C.A.Ingram 73). West Indies 190-6 (26.1). Award: C.A.Ingram.

Edgbaston, Birmingham, 15 June. Toss: India. **INDIA** won by eight wickets (D/L method). Pakistan 165 (39.4). India 102-2 (19.1/22). Award: B.Kumar (India 2-19).

SEMI-FINALS

The Oval, London, 19 June. Toss: England. **ENGLAND** won by seven wickets. South Africa 175 (38.4; D.A.Miller 56*, J.C.Tredwell 3-19, S.C.J.Broad 3-50). England 179-3 (37.3; I.J.L.Trott 82*). Award: J.C.Tredwell.

Sophia Gardens, Cardiff, 20 June. Toss: India. **INDIA** won by eight wickets. Sri Lanka 181-8 (50; A.D.Mathews 51, I.Sharma 3-33, R.Ashwin 3-48). India 182-2 (35; S.Dhawan 68, V.Kohli 58*). Award: I.Sharma.

FINAL

Edgbaston, Birmingham, 23 June. Toss: England. **INDIA** won by 5 runs. India 129-7 (20/20; R.S.Bopara 3-20). England 124-8 (20/20). Award: R.A.Jadeja (India 33* and 2-24). Series award: S.Dhawan (India).

ICC Champions Trophy winners:

1998-99 in Bangladesh – South Africa
2000-01 in Kenya – New Zealand
2002-03 in Sri Lanka – India/Sri Lanka
2004 in England – West Indies

2006-07 in India – Australia
2009-10 in South Africa – Australia
2013 in England – India

LIMITED-OVERS INTERNATIONALS
CAREER RECORDS

These records, complete to 5 April 2014, include all players registered for county cricket for the 2014 season at the time of going to press, plus those who have appeared in LOI matches for ICC full member countries since 13 November 2012.

ENGLAND – BATTING AND FIELDING

	M	I	NO	HS	Runs	Avge	100	50	Ct/St
K.Ali	14	9	3	39*	93	15.50	–	–	1
M.M.Ali	3	3	–	55	109	36.33	–	1	3
T.R.Ambrose	5	5	1	6	10	2.50	–	–	3
J.M.Anderson	174	69	37	28	237	7.40	–	–	47
J.M.Bairstow	7	6	1	41*	119	23.80	–	–	3
G.S.Ballance	5	5	–	79	132	26.40	–	1	5
G.J.Batty	10	8	2	17	30	5.00	–	–	4
I.R.Bell	140	136	11	126*	4635	37.08	3	29	45
R.S.Bopara	102	94	21	101*	2372	32.49	1	11	30
S.G.Borthwick	2	2	–	15	18	9.00	–	–	–
T.T.Bresnan	84	64	20	80	871	19.79	–	1	20
D.R.Briggs	1	–	–	–	–	–	–	–	–
S.C.J.Broad	108	58	21	45*	470	12.70	–	–	25
J.C.Buttler	27	22	3	99	572	30.10	–	4	41/3
M.A.Carberry	5	5	–	63	108	21.60	–	1	2
G.Chapple	1	1	–	14	14	14.00	–	–	–
R.Clarke	20	13	–	39	144	11.07	–	–	11
P.D.Collingwood	197	181	37	120*	5092	35.36	5	26	108
A.N.Cook	77	77	3	137	2825	38.17	5	18	28
S.M.Davies	8	8	–	87	244	30.50	–	1	8
J.L.Denly	9	9	–	67	268	29.77	–	2	5
J.W.Dernbach	24	8	1	5	19	2.71	–	–	5
S.T.Finn	39	13	6	35	96	13.71	–	–	8
J.S.Foster	11	6	3	13	41	13.66	–	–	13/7
P.J.Franks	1	1	–	4	4	4.00	–	–	1
G.O.Jones	49	41	8	80	815	24.69	–	4	68/4
C.J.Jordan	7	5	3	14	30	15.00	–	–	2
E.C.Joyce †	17	17	–	107	471	27.70	1	3	6
R.W.T.Key	5	5	–	19	54	10.80	–	–	–
C.Kieswetter	46	40	5	107	1054	30.11	1	5	53/12
M.J.Lumb	3	3	–	106	165	55.00	1	–	1
S.I.Mahmood	26	15	4	22*	85	7.72	–	–	1
S.C.Meaker	2	2	–	1	2	1.00	–	–	–
E.J.G.Morgan †	90	84	19	124*	2704	41.60	5	16	34
P.Mustard	10	10	–	83	233	23.30	–	1	9/2
G.Onions	4	1	–	1	1	1.00	–	–	–
M.S.Panesar	26	8	3	13	26	5.20	–	–	3
S.D.Parry	2	–	–	–	–	–	–	–	–
S.R.Patel	36	22	7	70*	482	32.13	–	1	7
K.P.Pietersen	136	125	16	130	4440	40.73	9	25	40
L.E.Plunkett	29	25	10	56	315	21.00	–	1	7
M.J.Prior	68	62	9	87	1282	24.18	–	3	71/8
W.B.Rankin †	7	2	1	4	5	2.50	–	–	–
A.U.Rashid	5	4	1	31*	60	20.00	–	–	2
C.M.W.Read	36	24	7	30*	300	17.64	–	–	41/2
J.E.Root	26	25	3	107	853	38.77	1	5	10
O.A.Shah	71	66	6	107*	1834	30.56	1	12	21
A.Shahzad	11	8	2	9	39	6.50	–	–	4
R.J.Sidebottom	25	18	8	24	133	13.30	–	–	6

	M	I	NO	HS	Runs	Avge	100	50	Ct/St
V.S.Solanki	51	46	5	106	1097	26.75	2	5	16
B.A.Stokes	18	14	–	70	202	14.42	–	1	7
G.P.Swann	79	48	12	34	500	13.88	–	–	29
J.W.A.Taylor	2	2	–	25	26	13.00	–	–	–
J.C.Tredwell	30	15	8	16	59	8.42	–	–	9
C.T.Tremlett	15	11	4	19*	50	7.14	–	–	4
M.E.Trescothick	123	122	6	137	4335	37.37	12	21	49
I.J.L.Trott	68	65	10	137	2819	51.25	4	22	14
J.O.Troughton	6	5	1	20	36	9.00	–	–	1
C.R.Woakes	13	10	4	36	141	23.50	–	–	5
L.J.Wright	50	39	4	52	707	20.20	–	2	18
M.H.Yardy	28	24	8	60*	326	20.37	–	2	10

ENGLAND – BOWLING

	O	M	R	W	Avge	Best	4wI	R/Over
K.Ali	112.1	4	682	20	34.10	4-45	1	6.08
M.M.Ali	10	1	41	3	13.66	1- 5	–	4.10
J.M.Anderson	1434.5	111	7132	245	29.11	5-23	12	4.97
G.J.Batty	73.2	1	366	5	73.20	2-40	–	4.99
I.R.Bell	14.4	0	88	6	14.66	3- 9	–	6.00
R.S.Bopara	257.5	10	1232	34	36.23	4-38	1	4.77
S.G.Borthwick	9	0	72	0	–	–	–	8.00
T.T.Bresnan	697.3	33	3802	108	35.20	5-48	4	5.45
D.R.Briggs	10	0	39	2	19.50	2-39	–	3.90
S.C.J.Broad	912	51	4767	168	28.37	5-23	10	5.22
M.A.Carberry	1	0	12	0	–	–	–	12.00
G.Chapple	4	0	14	0	–	–	–	3.50
R.Clarke	78.1	3	415	11	37.72	2-28	–	5.30
P.D.Collingwood	864.2	14	4294	111	38.68	6-31	4	4.96
J.W.Dernbach	205.4	6	1308	31	42.19	4-45	1	6.35
S.T.Finn	347.2	22	1637	59	27.74	4-34	3	4.71
P.J.Franks	9	0	48	0	–	–	–	5.33
C.J.Jordan	66	2	371	9	41.22	3-51	–	5.62
S.I.Mahmood	199.3	7	1169	30	38.96	4-50	1	5.85
S.C.Meaker	19	1	110	2	55.00	1-45	–	5.78
G.Onions	34	1	185	4	46.25	2-58	–	5.44
M.S.Panesar	218	10	980	24	40.83	3-25	–	4.49
S.D.Parry	19	2	92	4	23.00	3-32	–	4.84
S.R.Patel	197.5	4	1091	24	45.45	5-41	1	5.51
K.P.Pietersen	66.4	0	370	7	52.85	2-22	–	5.55
L.E.Plunkett	227.1	7	1321	39	33.87	3-24	–	5.81
W.B.Rankin	53.1	3	241	10	24.10	4-46	1	4.53
A.U.Rashid	34	0	191	3	63.66	1-16	–	5.61
J.E.Root	79	0	471	10	47.10	2-15	–	5.96
O.A.Shah	32.1	1	184	7	26.28	3-15	–	5.72
A.Shahzad	98	5	490	17	28.82	3-41	–	5.00
R.J.Sidebottom	212.5	12	1039	29	35.82	3-19	–	4.88
V.S.Solanki	18.3	0	105	1	105.00	1-17	–	5.67
B.A.Stokes	87	2	496	16	31.00	5-61	2	5.70
G.P.Swann	634.5	25	2888	104	27.76	5-28	4	4.54
J.C.Tredwell	229.4	11	1092	39	28.00	4-44	2	4.75
C.T.Tremlett	130.4	2	705	15	47.00	4-32	1	5.39
M.E.Trescothick	38.4	0	219	4	54.75	2- 7	–	5.66
I.J.L.Trott	30.3	0	166	2	83.00	2-31	–	5.44
C.R.Woakes	98.2	2	557	15	37.13	6-45	1	5.66

	O	M	R	W	Avge	Best	4wI	R/Over
L.J.Wright	173	2	884	15	58.93	2-34	–	5.10
M.H.Yardy	222	7	1075	21	51.19	3-24	–	4.84

† *E.C.Joyce has also made 23 appearances for Ireland; E.J.G.Morgan has also made 23 appearances for Ireland; and W.B.Rankin has also made 37 appearances for Ireland (see below).*

AUSTRALIA – BATTING AND FIELDING

	M	I	NO	HS	Runs	Avge	100	50	Ct/St
G.J.Bailey	39	37	6	156	1647	53.12	2	12	23
D.E.Bollinger	39	8	2	30	50	8.33	–	–	12
D.T.Christian	19	18	5	39	273	21.00	–	–	10
M.J.Clarke	236	215	43	130	7683	44.66	8	55	100
N.M.Coulter-Nile	7	5	2	16	49	16.33	–	–	1
B.C.J.Cutting	3	1	–	27	27	27.00	–	–	1
X.J.Doherty	54	21	14	15*	100	14.28	–	–	17
J.P.Faulkner	24	16	5	116	506	46.00	1	3	5
Fawad Ahmed	3	1	1	4*	4	–	–	–	–
A.J.Finch	23	22	–	148	772	35.09	3	2	12
B.J.Haddin	105	98	11	110	2753	31.64	2	16	146/10
J.R.Hazlewood	2	–	–	–	–	–	–	–	–
M.C.Henriques	5	5	1	12	32	8.00	–	–	1
P.J.Hughes	20	19	1	138*	660	36.66	2	2	5
D.J.Hussey	69	61	6	111	1796	32.65	1	14	29
P.A.Jaques	6	6	–	94	125	20.83	–	1	3
M.G.Johnson	136	79	27	73*	829	15.94	–	2	29
U.T.Khawaja	3	3	1	8*	14	7.00	–	–	–
C.J.McKay	59	31	10	30	190	9.04	–	–	7
M.R.Marsh	4	4	1	22	39	13.00	–	–	1
S.E.Marsh	45	44	2	151	1667	39.69	3	10	9
G.J.Maxwell	24	23	5	92	621	34.50	–	6	9
J.L.Pattinson	13	7	3	13	40	10.00	–	–	2
K.W.Richardson	1	1	–	0	0	0.00	–	–	–
S.P.D.Smith	34	23	4	46*	399	21.00	–	–	15
M.A.Starc	19	7	4	52*	122	40.66	–	1	4
A.C.Voges	31	28	9	112*	870	45.78	1	4	7
M.S.Wade	42	38	2	75	792	22.00	–	4	43/7
D.A.Warner	42	41	–	163	1287	31.39	2	8	11
S.R.Watson	173	152	24	185*	5256	41.06	9	30	60

AUSTRALIA – BOWLING

	O	M	R	W	Avge	Best	4wI	R/Over
D.E.Bollinger	323.4	28	1482	62	23.90	5-35	5	4.57
D.T.Christian	121.1	0	595	20	29.75	5-31	1	4.91
M.J.Clarke	424.5	7	2130	56	38.03	5-35	2	5.01
N.M.Coulter-Nile	69	0	363	11	33.00	3-34	–	5.26
B.C.J.Cutting	30	1	140	5	28.00	3-45	–	4.66
X.J.Doherty	419.2	16	1987	51	38.96	4-28	3	4.73
J.P.Faulkner	186.4	5	1081	36	30.02	4-48	2	5.79
Fawad Ahmed	24	0	145	3	48.33	1-39	–	6.04
A.J.Finch	6.4	0	26	2	13.00	1- 2	–	3.90
J.R.Hazlewood	9	0	47	1	47.00	1-41	–	5.22
M.C.Henriques	27	1	123	4	30.75	3-32	–	4.55
D.J.Hussey	133.4	1	698	18	38.77	4-21	2	5.22
M.G.Johnson	1107.5	64	5384	208	25.88	6-31	11	4.85

AUSTRALIA – BOWLING (continued)

	O	M	R	W	Avge	Best	4wI	R/Over
C.J.McKay	494.1	38	2364	97	24.37	5-28	6	4.78
M.R.Marsh	8	0	44	1	44.00	1-19	–	5.50
G.J.Maxwell	117.3	3	637	11	57.90	4-63	1	5.42
J.L.Pattinson	106.1	5	572	16	35.75	4-51	1	5.38
K.W.Richardson	6	3	15	0	–	–	–	2.50
S.P.D.Smith	149.5	0	780	22	35.45	3-33	–	5.20
M.A.Starc	145.4	6	737	37	19.91	5-20	6	5.05
A.C.Voges	50.1	1	276	6	46.00	1- 3	–	5.50
D.A.Warner	1	0	8	0	–	–	–	8.00
S.R.Watson	1011.4	35	4933	163	30.26	4-36	3	4.87

SOUTH AFRICA – BATTING AND FIELDING

	M	I	NO	HS	Runs	Avge	100	50	Ct/St
K.J.Abbott	2	1	–	5	5	5.00	–	–	2
H.M.Amla	85	82	6	150	4054	53.34	12	23	40
F.Behardien	11	10	2	58	172	21.50	–	1	4
H.Davids	2	2	–	7	8	4.00	–	–	–
Q.de Kock	16	16	–	135	741	46.31	4	–	25
A.B.de Villiers	154	148	25	146	6181	50.25	16	35	129/3
F.du Plessis	47	45	5	72	1102	27.55	–	7	27
J.P.Duminy	115	106	23	150*	3260	39.27	3	18	46
A.J.Hall	88	56	13	81	905	21.04	–	3	29
Imran Tahir	13	5	3	3	5	2.50	–	–	5
C.A.Ingram	31	29	3	124	843	32.42	3	3	12
J.H.Kallis	320	306	53	139	11545	45.63	17	86	129
R.K.Kleinveldt	10	7	–	43	105	15.00	–	–	4
R.McLaren	40	32	12	71*	410	20.50	–	1	10
D.A.Miller	40	37	11	85*	811	31.19	–	6	12
M.Morkel	70	28	8	23*	148	7.40	–	–	17
C.H.Morris	5	3	1	9*	13	13.00	–	–	–
W.D.Parnell	33	18	5	56	283	21.76	–	1	4
A.N.Petersen	21	19	1	80	504	28.00	–	4	5
R.J.Peterson	77	40	14	68	545	20.96	–	1	27
A.M.Phangiso	5	4	1	18*	27	9.00	–	–	–
V.D.Philander	13	9	4	23	103	20.60	–	–	4
G.C.Smith	196	193	10	141	6989	38.19	10	47	105
D.W.Steyn	77	29	7	35	172	7.81	–	–	21
L.L.Tsotsobe	61	21	13	16*	56	7.00	–	–	9

SOUTH AFRICA – BOWLING

	O	M	R	W	Avge	Best	4wI	R/Over
K.J.Abbott	14.2	0	66	1	66.00	1-35	–	4.60
F.Behardien	25	1	124	6	20.66	3-19	–	4.96
A.B.de Villiers	2	0	22	0	–	–	–	11.00
F.du Plessis	25	0	142	2	71.00	1- 8	–	5.68
J.P.Duminy	295	6	1453	35	41.51	3-31	–	4.92
A.J.Hall	556.5	30	2515	95	26.47	5-18	4	4.51
Imran Tahir	102.3	6	446	26	17.15	4-38	3	4.35
C.A.Ingram	1	0	17	0	–	–	–	17.00
J.H.Kallis	1773	77	8568	269	31.85	5-30	4	4.83
R.K.Kleinveldt	85.3	6	448	12	37.33	4-22	1	5.23
R.McLaren	296.3	13	1519	54	28.12	4-19	4	5.12
M.Morkel	610.3	32	2919	124	23.54	5-38	7	4.78
C.H.Morris	35	1	211	6	35.16	2-25	–	6.02
W.D.Parnell	251.1	13	1389	45	30.86	5-48	3	5.53

SOUTH AFRICA – BOWLING (continued)

	O	M	R	W	Avge	Best	4wI	R/Over
A.N.Petersen	1	0	7	0	–	–	–	7.00
R.J.Peterson	532.1	14	2604	70	37.20	4-12	2	4.89
A.M.Phangiso	46	0	243	4	60.75	1-48	–	5.28
V.D.Philander	85.5	11	354	14	25.28	4-12	1	4.12
G.C.Smith	171	0	951	18	52.83	3-30	–	5.56
D.W.Steyn	644.2	49	3094	121	25.57	6-39	6	4.80
L.L.Tsotsobe	494	44	2347	94	24.96	4-22	7	4.75

WEST INDIES – BATTING AND FIELDING

	M	I	NO	HS	Runs	Avge	100	50	Ct/St
T.L.Best	26	16	8	24	76	9.50	–	–	4
D.J.Bravo	158	135	23	112*	2927	26.13	2	10	72
D.M.Bravo	73	70	9	100*	1893	31.03	1	15	24
S.Chanderpaul	268	251	40	150	8778	41.60	11	59	73
J.Charles	30	39	–	130	869	28.96	2	2	19/1
M.L.Cummins	1	–	–	–	–	–	–	–	–
N.Deonarine	29	27	3	65*	629	26.20	–	4	8
K.A.Edwards	14	14	2	123*	321	26.75	1	1	1
C.H.Gayle	252	247	17	153*	8688	37.77	21	44	107
J.O.Holder	17	8	2	19*	68	11.33	–	–	6
N.O.Miller	45	26	12	51	264	18.85	–	1	17
S.P.Narine	49	32	6	36	272	10.46	–	–	11
B.P.Nash	9	7	3	39*	104	26.00	–	–	1
V.Permaul	6	3	1	10	11	5.50	–	–	–
K.A.Pollard	85	79	4	119	1869	24.92	3	6	45
K.O.A.Powell	28	28	–	83	772	27.57	–	7	8
D.Ramdin	109	81	20	128	1321	21.65	1	3	143/6
R.Rampaul	85	37	9	86*	343	12.25	–	1	14
K.A.J.Roach	61	41	25	34	216	13.50	–	–	14
A.D.Russell	35	28	6	92*	666	30.27	–	3	7
D.J.G.Sammy	111	92	28	84	1550	24.21	–	7	58
M.N.Samuels	159	149	23	126	3951	31.35	5	23	43
R.R.Sarwan	181	169	33	120*	5804	42.67	5	38	45
L.M.P.Simmons	58	57	3	122	1739	32.20	1	15	25
D.R.Smith	91	75	5	68	1195	17.07	–	6	27
D.S.Smith	47	45	2	107	1059	24.62	1	5	13
D.C.Thomas	21	19	2	37	238	14.00	–	–	23/6
C.A.K.Walton	5	4	–	17	17	4.25	–	–	6/1

WEST INDIES – BOWLING

	O	M	R	W	Avge	Best	4wI	R/Over
T.L.Best	216.4	9	1157	34	34.02	4-35	2	5.34
D.J.Bravo	1053.1	37	5680	191	29.73	6-43	6	5.39
S.Chanderpaul	123.2	0	636	14	45.42	3-18	–	5.15
M.L.Cummins	6	1	42	1	42.00	1-42	–	7.00
N.Deonarine	80.3	2	451	6	75.16	2-18	–	5.60
C.H.Gayle	1164.1	38	5498	157	35.01	5-46	4	4.72
J.O.Holder	127.2	11	676	25	27.04	4-13	1	5.30
N.O.Miller	317.4	16	1461	40	36.52	4-43	2	4.59
S.P.Narine	443.4	30	1861	69	26.97	5-27	5	4.19
B.P.Nash	49	3	224	5	44.80	3-56	–	4.57
V.Permaul	51.1	0	240	8	30.00	3-40	–	4.69
K.A.Pollard	298	4	1655	44	37.61	3-27	–	5.55
R.Rampaul	619.3	29	3168	105	30.17	5-49	9	5.11
K.A.J.Roach	511.1	37	2517	94	26.77	6-27	5	4.92

	O	M	R	W	Avge	Best	4wI	R/Over
A.D.Russell	241.5	7	1333	44	30.29	4-35	5	5.51
D.J.G.Sammy	758	40	3459	77	44.92	4-26	1	4.56
M.N.Samuels	752.1	17	3589	80	44.86	3-25	–	4.77
R.R.Sarwan	96.5	3	586	16	36.62	3-31	–	6.05
L.M.P.Simmons	25	0	160	1	160.00	1- 3	–	6.40
D.R.Smith	443.2	18	2190	60	36.50	5-45	4	4.93
D.S.Smith	2.5	0	17	0	–	–	–	6.00
D.C.Thomas	1.1	0	11	2	5.50	2-11	–	9.42

NEW ZEALAND – BATTING AND FIELDING

	M	I	NO	HS	Runs	Avge	100	50	Ct/St
A.R.Adams	42	34	10	45	419	17.45	–	–	8
C.J.Anderson	12	11	3	131*	424	53.00	1	1	1
H.K.Bennett	14	7	5	4*	10	5.00	–	–	2
T.A.Boult	8	4	2	5	8	4.00	–	–	1
D.A.J.Bracewell	7	4	1	8*	14	4.66	–	–	2
A.P.Devcich	6	6	–	46	93	15.50	–	–	2
G.D.Elliott	51	40	6	115	1013	29.79	1	6	8
A.M.Ellis	15	12	1	33	154	14.00	–	–	3
J.E.C.Franklin	110	80	27	98*	1270	23.96	–	4	26
M.J.Guptill	84	82	9	189*	2859	39.16	5	18	36
M.J.Henry	1	–							–
T.W.M.Latham	13	13	2	86	280	25.45	–	1	6/1
M.J.McClenaghan	22	8	6	4	14	7.00	–	–	3
B.B.McCullum	229	199	28	166	5172	30.24	4	26	246/15
N.L.McCullum	67	53	7	65	949	20.63	–	4	34
H.J.H.Marshall	66	62	9	101*	1454	27.43	1	12	18
K.D.Mills	165	98	34	54	1016	15.87	–	2	40
A.F.Milne	7	1	1	12*	12	–	–	–	5
C.Munro	7	6	–	85	167	27.83	–	2	–
J.D.S.Neesham	11	9	3	42*	117	19.50	–	–	5
R.J.Nicol	22	21	2	146	586	30.84	2	2	11
J.S.Patel	39	13	7	34	88	14.66	–	–	12
L.Ronchi	23	19	4	64	339	22.60	–	1	30/3
H.D.Rutherford	4	4	–	11	15	3.75	–	–	–
J.D.Ryder	48	42	1	107	1362	33.21	3	6	15
T.G.Southee	78	45	16	32	313	10.79	–	–	19
L.R.P.L.Taylor	137	125	17	131*	4328	40.07	10	26	91
D.L.Vettori	271	169	49	83	2058	17.15	–	4	76
B.J.Watling	22	20	2	96*	528	29.33	–	5	16
K.S.Williamson	54	49	6	145*	1699	39.51	3	11	18

NEW ZEALAND – BOWLING

	O	M	R	W	Avge	Best	4wI	R/Over
A.R.Adams	314.1	15	1643	53	31.00	5-22	3	5.22
C.J.Anderson	76.2	4	465	19	24.47	5-63	2	6.09
H.K.Bennett	100.2	3	543	23	23.60	4-16	2	5.41
T.A.Boult	58.3	3	286	6	47.66	2-45	–	4.88
D.A.J.Bracewell	64	9	336	8	42.00	3-55	–	5.25
A.P.Devcich	30	1	163	3	54.33	2-33	–	5.43
G.D.Elliott	109.3	7	545	20	27.25	4-31	1	4.97
A.M.Ellis	80	3	425	12	35.41	2-22	–	5.31
J.E.C.Franklin	641.2	34	3354	81	41.40	5-42	1	5.22
M.J.Guptill	13.1	0	68	2	34.00	2- 7	–	5.16
M.J.Henry	10	1	38	4	9.50	4-38	1	3.80

NEW ZEALAND – BOWLING (continued)

	O	M	R	W	Avge	Best	4wI	R/Over
M.J.McClenaghan	188.1	5	1096	48	22.83	5-58	6	5.82
N.L.McCullum	466.2	5	2244	47	47.74	3-24	–	4.81
K.D.Mills	1329.3	122	6284	235	26.74	5-25	9	4.72
A.F.Milne	36.5	0	212	2	106.00	1-17	–	5.75
C.Munro	1	0	10	0	–	–	–	10.00
J.D.S.Neesham	60.5	0	370	14	26.42	4-42	2	6.08
R.J.Nicol	56.3	1	329	10	32.90	4-19	1	5.82
J.S.Patel	300.4	9	1513	42	36.02	3-11	–	5.03
J.D.Ryder	67.5	0	412	12	34.33	3-29	–	6.07
T.G.Southee	636	42	3310	105	31.52	5-33	5	5.20
L.R.P.L.Taylor	7	0	35	0	–	–	–	5.00
D.L.Vettori	2171.3	91	8767	276	31.76	5- 7	8	4.11
K.S.Williamson	129.3	1	711	23	30.91	4-22	1	5.49

INDIA – BATTING AND FIELDING

	M	I	NO	HS	Runs	Avge	100	50	Ct/St
V.R.Aaron	8	3	21	6*	8	8.00	–	–	1
R.Ashwin	79	46	12	65	583	17.14	–	1	22
S.T.R.Binny	2	1	–	0	0	0.00	–	–	–
S.Dhawan	39	38	2	119	1504	41.77	5	7	14
M.S.Dhoni	240	211	62	183*	7872	52.83	8	54	221/77
A.B.Dinda	13	5	–	16	21	4.20	–	–	1
G.Gambhir	147	143	11	150*	5238	39.68	11	34	36
R.A.Jadeja	101	68	22	78	1541	33.50	–	9	36
K.D.Karthik	71	60	13	79	1313	27.93	–	7	49/7
V.Kohli	134	126	18	183	5634	52.16	19	30	62
B.Kumar	35	17	5	31	135	11.25	–	–	12
A.Mishra	23	5	2	9	15	5.00	–	–	4
Mohammed Shami	29	12	6	14*	53	8.83	–	–	8
C.A.Pujara	2	2	–	13	13	6.50	–	–	–
A.M.Rahane	27	27	–	91	687	25.44	–	5	12
S.K.Raina	189	162	32	116*	4596	35.35	3	29	80
A.T.Rayudu	10	8	2	63*	243	40.50	–	2	–
V.Sehwag	241	235	9	219	7995	35.37	15	37	90
I.Sharma	72	27	13	13	72	5.14	–	–	16
M.M.Sharma	5	1	1	0*	0	–	–	–	1
R.G.Sharma	123	117	21	209	3427	35.69	4	22	42
J.D.Unadkat	7	–	–	–	–	–	–	–	–
M.Vijay	14	13	–	33	253	19.46	–	–	8
R.Vinay Kumar	31	13	4	27*	86	9.55	–	–	6
U.T.Yadav	28	10	8	11*	27	13.50	–	–	5
Yuvraj Singh	290	265	38	139	8237	36.28	13	51	92

INDIA – BOWLING

	O	M	R	W	Avge	Best	4wI	R/Over
V.R.Aaron	59.1	2	393	11	35.72	3-24	–	6.64
R.Ashwin	710.4	21	3489	106	32.91	3-24	–	4.90
S.T.R.Binny	5	0	30	0	–	–	–	6.00
M.S.Dhoni	6	0	31	1	31.00	1-14	–	5.16
A.B.Dinda	99	2	612	12	51.00	2-44	–	6.18
G.Gambhir	1	0	13	0	–	–	–	13.00
R.A.Jadeja	828.5	43	3910	120	32.58	5-36	5	4.71
V.Kohli	89.4	1	542	4	135.50	1-15	–	6.04
B.Kumar	291.2	32	1381	37	37.32	4- 8	1	4.74
A.Mishra	204.4	14	911	40	22.77	6-48	3	4.45

INDIA – BOWLING (continued)

	O	M	R	W	Avge	Best	4wI	R/Over
Mohammed Shami	248.3	17	1448	50	28.96	4-50	2	5.82
S.K.Raina	254.2	3	1291	25	51.64	3-34	–	5.07
A.T.Rayudu	7	0	49	0	–	–	–	7.00
V.Sehwag	715	13	3737	94	39.75	4- 6	1	5.22
I.Sharma	560.1	27	3207	102	31.44	4-38	4	5.72
M.M.Sharma	39.3	3	228	4	57.00	2-26	–	5.77
R.G.Sharma	94.5	2	483	8	60.37	2-27	–	5.09
J.D.Unadkat	52	5	209	8	26.12	4-41	1	4.01
R.Vinay Kumar	239.2	19	1423	38	37.44	4-30	1	5.94
U.T.Yadav	215.2	9	1308	30	43.60	3-38	–	6.07
Yuvraj Singh	821.2	18	4171	110	37.91	5-31	3	5.07

PAKISTAN – BATTING AND FIELDING

	M	I	NO	HS	Runs	Avge	100	50	Ct/St
Abdur Rehman	31	23	6	31	142	8.35	–	–	7
Ahmed Shehzad	45	45	1	124	1514	34.40	5	6	17
Anwar Ali	5	5	2	43*	113	37.66	–	–	–
Asad Ali	4	2	–	11	13	6.50	–	–	–
Asad Shafiq	46	45	3	84	1096	26.09	–	8	10
Azhar Ali	14	14	3	96	452	41.09	–	4	2
Bilawal Bhatti	8	5	1	39	80	20.00	–	–	–
Ehsan Adil	2	1	1	5*	5	–	–	–	–
Fawad Alam	29	27	10	114*	791	46.52	1	5	9
Haris Sohail	4	3	–	26	45	15.00	–	–	2
Imran Farhat	58	58	2	107	1719	30.69	1	13	14
Junaid Khan	46	19	10	25	50	5.55	–	–	5
Kamran Akmal	154	135	14	124	3168	26.18	5	10	156/31
Misbah-ul-Haq	146	133	31	96*	4527	44.38	–	37	63
Mohammad Hafeez	146	146	9	140*	4254	31.05	9	20	51
Mohammad Irfan	27	15	10	4*	21	4.20	–	–	5
Mohammad Talha	3	1	–	0	0	0.00	–	–	–
Nasir Jamshed	43	43	3	112	1383	34.57	3	8	12
Saeed Ajmal	110	68	24	33	318	7.22	–	–	25
Sarfraz Ahmed	26	15	4	46*	201	18.27	–	–	19/10
Shahid Afridi	373	345	25	124	7582	23.69	6	36	119
Sharjeel Khan	9	9	–	61	185	20.55	–	1	2
Shoaib Malik	216	193	25	143	5490	32.67	7	31	75
Sohaib Maqsood	14	14	1	73	433	33.30	–	3	6
Sohail Tanvir	58	36	9	59	347	12.85	–	1	13
Umar Akmal	94	83	15	102*	2623	38.57	2	19	59/13
Umar Amin	14	14	1	59	250	19.23	–	1	3
Umar Gul	124	63	17	39	451	9.80	–	–	15
Wahab Riaz	39	29	7	47*	291	13.22	–	–	10
Yasir Arafat	11	8	3	27	74	14.80	–	–	2
Younus Khan	253	243	23	144	7014	31.88	6	48	131

PAKISTAN – BOWLING

	O	M	R	W	Avge	Best	4wI	R/Over
Abdur Rehman	270.4	12	1142	30	38.06	4-48	1	4.21
Ahmed Shehzad	2.3	0	20	0	–	–	–	8.00
Anwar Ali	24.4	1	137	3	45.66	2-24	–	5.55
Asad Ali	30	6	115	2	57.50	1-22	–	3.83
Azhar Ali	8	0	41	0	–	–	–	5.12
Bilawal Bhatti	50.1	4	295	5	59.00	3-37	–	5.88
Ehsan Adil	10	0	49	1	49.00	1-32	–	4.90

PAKISTAN – BOWLING (continued)

	O	M	R	W	Avge	Best	4wI	R/Over
Fawad Alam	62.2	0	344	4	86.00	1- 4	–	5.51
Imran Farhat	360.5	23	1804	74	24.37	4-12	3	4.99
Junaid Khan	119.2	7	567	25	22.68	4-12	2	4.75
Misbah-ul-Haq	4	0	30	0	–	–	–	7.50
Mohammad Hafeez	1034.2	41	4202	118	35.61	3-17	–	4.06
Mohammad Irfan	226.5	14	1058	39	27.12	4-33	1	4.66
Mohammad Talha	20.2	1	146	4	36.50	2-22	–	7.18
Saeed Ajmal	976.5	49	4049	182	22.24	5-24	8	4.14
Shahid Afridi	2756.3	71	12753	376	33.91	7-12	13	4.62
Shoaib Malik	1128	36	5128	141	36.36	4-19	1	4.54
Sohaib Maqsood	3	0	18	0	–	–	–	6.00
Sohail Tanvir	460.3	23	2401	67	35.83	5-48	4	5.21
Umar Amin	5	0	18	0	–	–	–	3.60
Umar Gul	963.4	67	4966	173	28.70	6-42	6	5.15
Wahab Riaz	282.2	12	1562	48	32.54	5-46	1	5.53
Yasir Arafat	69	2	373	4	93.25	1-28	–	5.40
Younus Khan	45.2	1	271	3	90.33	1- 3	–	5.97

SRI LANKA – BATTING AND FIELDING

	M	I	NO	HS	Runs	Avge	100	50	Ct/St
L.D.Chandimal	80	72	12	111	1875	31.25	2	11	28/1
P.C.de Silva	5	5	1	44	78	19.50	–	–	4
L.H.D.Dilhara	9	9	–	29	83	9.22	–	–	3
T.M.Dilshan	277	252	39	160*	8025	37.67	17	34	105/1
R.M.S.Eranga	13	8	5	7*	17	5.66	–	–	5
H.M.R.K.B.Herath	55	24	12	17*	123	10.25	–	–	9
D.P.M.D.Jayawardena	407	380	37	144	11243	32.77	15	69	196
F.D.M.Karunaratne	6	6	1	60	84	16.80	–	1	1
K.M.D.N.Kulasekara	147	95	29	73	1064	16.12	–	3	33
R.A.S.Lakmal	25	11	7	2*	5	1.25	–	–	5
S.L.Malinga	166	80	24	56	424	7.57	–	1	21
A.D.Mathews	121	99	30	80*	2565	37.17	–	19	31
B.A.W.Mendis	70	32	15	15*	135	7.94	–	–	9
B.M.A.J.Mendis	39	29	6	72	468	20.34	–	1	8
J.Mubarak	40	37	6	72	704	22.70	–	4	12
A.K.Perera	3	1	–	1	1	1.00	–	–	1
M.D.K.J.Perera	27	25	3	106	620	28.18	1	3	10
N.L.T.C.Perera	75	55	12	80*	782	18.18	–	3	27
K.T.G.D.Prasad	13	6	3	31*	63	21.00	–	–	1
S.Prasanna	12	10	2	42	101	12.62	–	–	1
S.M.A.Priyanjan	7	7	1	74	200	33.33	–	2	4
K.C.Sangakkara	362	339	36	169	12241	40.39	18	82	358/85
S.M.S.M.Senanayake	28	18	7	42	209	19.00	–	–	12
W.U.Tharanga	171	163	9	174*	5228	33.94	13	28	33
H.D.R.L.Thirimanne	62	47	4	102*	1322	30.74	3	6	24
K.D.K.Vithanage	5	5	1	27	70	17.50	–	–	2

SRI LANKA – BOWLING

	O	M	R	W	Avge	Best	4wI	R/Over
P.C.de Silva	43.4	2	188	5	37.60	2-29	–	4.30
L.H.D.Dilhara	55	3	261	6	43.50	2-30	–	4.74
T.M.Dilshan	751.2	21	3565	76	46.90	4- 4	3	4.74
R.M.S.Eranga	80.2	0	447	16	27.93	3-46	–	5.56
H.M.R.K.B.Herath	408.1	14	1741	54	32.24	4-20	1	4.26
D.P.M.D.Jayawardena	94.4	1	539	7	77.00	2-56	–	5.69

SRI LANKA – BOWLING (continued)

	O	M	R	W	Avge	Best	4wI	R/Over
F.D.M.Karunaratne	1.4	0	11	0	–	–	–	6.60
K.M.D.N.Kulasekara	1131.5	94	5307	161	32.96	5-22	4	4.68
R.A.S.Lakmal	194.2	13	1081	35	30.88	3-22	–	5.56
S.L.Malinga	1333.1	78	6879	256	26.87	6-38	15	5.15
A.D.Mathews	578	36	2602	73	35.64	6-20	2	4.50
B.A.W.Mendis	559.5	30	2481	121	20.50	6-13	9	4.43
B.M.A.J.Mendis	157.5	1	781	23	33.95	3-15	–	4.94
J.Mubarak	21.3	0	95	2	47.50	1-10	–	4.41
A.K.Perera	3	0	17	0	–	–	–	5.66
N.L.T.C.Perera	477.1	21	2605	94	27.71	6-44	5	5.45
K.T.G.D.Prasad	100.1	3	546	21	26.00	3-17	–	5.45
S.Prasanna	99.2	5	496	11	45.09	3-32	–	4.99
S.M.A.Priyanjan	15	0	75	3	25.00	2-11	–	5.00
S.M.S.M.Senanayake	230	7	1079	27	39.96	3-41	–	4.69
H.D.R.L.Thirimanne	8.2	0	41	1	41.00	1-25	–	4.92
K.D.K.Vithanage	1	0	10	0	10.00	–	–	10.00

ZIMBABWE – BATTING AND FIELDING

	M	I	NO	HS	Runs	Avge	100	50	Ct/St
R.W.Chakabva	17	17	1	45	250	15.62	–	–	10
T.L.Chatara	11	6	3	23	27	9.00	–	–	1
C.J.Chibhabha	63	63	1	73	1312	21.16	–	9	24
E.Chigumbura	150	138	16	79	2947	24.15	–	15	46
M.T.Chinouya	2	2	1	6*	6	6.00	–	–	–
C.R.Ervine	25	23	3	85	702	35.10	–	5	3
S.M.Ervine	42	34	7	100	698	25.85	1	2	5
M.W.Goodwin	71	70	3	112*	1818	27.13	2	8	20
A.J.Ireland	26	13	5	8*	30	3.75	–	–	2
K.M.Jarvis	24	15	5	13	52	5.20	–	–	4
T.Maruma	11	10	–	32	83	8.30	–	–	5
H.Masakadza	129	129	4	178*	3429	27.43	3	20	52
S.W.Masakadza	12	8	2	45*	148	24.66	–	–	6
T.M.K.Mawoyo	4	4	–	14	42	10.50	–	–	1
C.B.Mpofu	64	35	19	6	40	2.50	–	–	10
N.Mushangwe	5	5	1	16	38	9.50	–	–	–
C.T.Mutombodzi	3	3	–	13	25	8.33	–	–	2
T.Panyangara	29	24	6	16*	98	5.44	–	–	5
V.Sibanda	109	108	3	116	2626	25.00	2	20	39
Sikandar Raza	8	8	–	82	179	22.37	–	1	3
B.R.M.Taylor	146	145	14	145*	4414	33.69	6	27	86/19
P.Utseya	151	122	46	68*	1319	17.35	–	4	46
B.V.Vitori	13	7	1	17	32	5.33	–	–	1
M.N.Waller	38	35	3	99*	753	23.53	–	4	11
S.C.Williams	58	57	10	78*	1483	31.55	–	14	18

ZIMBABWE – BOWLING

	O	M	R	W	Avge	Best	4wI	R/Over
T.L.Chatara	98.3	9	475	14	33.92	3-48	–	4.82
C.J.Chibhabha	157	2	1099	20	54.95	2-28	–	7.00
E.Chigumbura	630.1	23	3662	89	41.14	4-28	1	5.81
M.T.Chinouya	11	0	50	1	50.00	1-36	–	4.54
S.M.Ervine	274.5	10	1561	41	38.07	3-29	–	5.67
T.N.Garwwe	6	0	50	1	50.00	1-50	–	8.33
M.W.Goodwin	41.2	1	210	4	52.50	1-12	–	5.08
A.J.Ireland	221	13	1115	38	29.34	3-41	–	5.04

ZIMBABWE – BOWLING (continued)

	O	M	R	W	Avge	Best	4wI	R/Over
K.M.Jarvis	202.5	9	1221	27	45.22	3-36	–	6.01
T.Maruma	34.3	1	204	4	51.00	2-50	–	5.91
H.Masakadza	237.3	5	1258	33	38.12	3-39	–	5.29
S.W.Masakadza	99.1	3	704	22	32.00	4-46	3	7.09
C.B.Mpofu	511	36	2689	70	38.41	6-52	3	5.26
N.Mushangwe	46	4	210	1	210.00	1-56	–	4.56
C.T.Mutombodzi	22.5	0	129	2	64.50	2-35	–	5.64
T.Panyangara	228.3	20	12169	27	47.00	3-28	–	5.55
V.Sibanda	15.3	0	88	2	44.00	1-12	–	5.67
B.R.M.Taylor	66	0	406	9	45.11	3-54	–	6.15
P.Utseya	1309.3	60	5691	119	47.82	4-38	2	4.34
B.V.Vitori	111.2	3	600	22	27.27	5-20	2	5.38
M.N.Waller	42	0	254	3	84.66	1-17	–	6.04
S.C.Williams	168.3	2	862	12	71.83	3-23	–	5.11

BANGLADESH – BATTING AND FIELDING

	M	I	NO	HS	Runs	Avge	100	50	Ct/St
Abdur Razzak	150	94	36	53*	758	13.06	–	1	31
Abul Hasan	3	1	–	3	3	3.00	–	–	–
Al-Amin Hossain	3	2	2	2*	2	–	–	–	–
Anamul Haque	16	15	–	120	532	35.46	2	1	8
Arafat Sunny	5	5	3	5	9	4.50	–	–	2
Elias Sunny	4	4	2	1*	2	1.00	–	–	–
Imrul Kayes	49	49	1	101	1374	28.62	1	10	15
Jahurul Islam	14	13	1	53	270	22.50	–	1	7
Mahmudullah	99	84	25	75*	1865	31.61	–	9	26
Mashrafe Mortaza	131	99	18	51*	1244	15.35	–	1	40
Mohammad Ashraful	175	168	13	109	3468	22.37	3	20	35
Mominul Haque	19	17	–	60	449	26.41	–	3	4
Mushfiqur Rahim	129	119	20	117	2780	28.08	2	14	91/34
Naeem Islam	59	51	15	84	975	27.08	–	5	19
Nasir Hossain	35	31	6	100	959	38.36	1	6	14
Robiul Islam	3	1	1	0*	0	–	–	–	–
Rubel Hossain	49	26	13	17	71	5.46	–	–	8
Shafiul Islam	51	28	9	24*	124	6.52	–	–	8
Shahadat Hossain	51	27	17	16*	79	7.90	–	–	5
Shakib Al Hasan	133	128	20	134*	3779	34.99	5	25	36
Shamsur Rahman	8	8	–	96	254	31.75	–	2	3
Sohag Gazi	16	13	4	30	156	17.33	–	–	5
Tamim Iqbal	124	124	1	154	3702	30.09	4	25	33
Ziaur Rahman	11	9	–	41	122	13.55	–	–	3

BANGLADESH – BOWLING

	O	M	R	W	Avge	Best	4wI	R/Over
Abdur Razzak	1302.3	70	5912	206	28.69	5-29	9	4.53
Abul Hasan	14	0	106	0	–	–	–	7.57
Al-Amin Hossain	24.5	3	126	3	42.00	2-42	–	5.07
Arafat Sunny	41	2	207	6	34.50	2-31	–	5.04
Elias Sunny	34	2	161	5	32.20	2-21	–	4.73
Mahmudullah	507.1	12	2566	61	42.06	3- 4	–	5.05
Mashrafe Mortaza	1092.2	92	5114	164	31.18	6-26	6	4.68
Mohammad Ashraful	116.1	4	661	18	36.72	3-26	–	5.69
Mominul Haque	32	1	138	7	19.71	2-13	–	4.31
Naeem Islam	290.3	9	1407	35	40.20	3-32	–	4.84
Nasir Hossain	55.1	2	259	3	86.33	2- 3	–	4.69

	O	M	R	W	Avge	Best	4wI	R/Over
Robiul Islam	22.1	1	117	2	58.50	1-21	–	5.27
Rubel Hossain	375	12	2121	65	32.63	6-26	5	5.65
Shafiul Islam	355.3	24	2089	58	36.01	4-21	4	5.87
Shahadat Hossain	366.2	18	2143	47	45.59	3-34	–	5.84
Shakib Al Hasan	1133.2	67	4884	165	29.60	4-16	4	4.30
Sohag Gazi	124.1	10	559	19	29.42	4-29	1	4.50
Tamim Iqbal	1	0	13	0	–	–	–	13.00
Ziaur Rahman	63	1	290	10	29.00	5-30	1	4.60

ASSOCIATES – BATTING AND FIELDING

	M	I	NO	HS	Runs	Avge	100	50	Ct/St
A.Balbirnie (Ireland)	4	4	–	17	29	7.25	–	–	1
K.J.Coetzer (Scotland)	15	15	1	133	670	47.85	1	5	8
F.R.J.Coleman (Scotland)	8	8	–	40	102	12.75	–	–	3
G.H.Dockrell (Ireland)	38	20	11	19	89	9.88	–	–	16
E.C.Joyce (Ireland)	23	23	3	116*	806	40.30	1	5	5
A.N.Kervezee (Netherlands)	39	36	3	92	924	28.00	–	4	18
C.S.MacLeod (Scotland)	19	18	2	175	477	29.81	1	1	6
M.W.Machan (Scotland)	11	11	–	114	392	35.63	1	1	3
E.J.G.Morgan (Ireland)	23	23	2	115	744	35.42	1	5	9
D.Murphy (Scotland)	8	7	2	20*	58	11.60	–	–	8/3
T.J.Murtagh (Ireland)	9	5	2	23*	50	16.66	–	–	1
N.J.O'Brien (Ireland)	59	59	6	72	1481	27.94	–	11	39/7
W.T.S.Porterfield (Ireland)	68	68	3	112*	2085	32.07	6	10	35
W.B.Rankin (Ireland)	37	16	11	7*	35	7.00	–	–	6
P.R.Stirling (Ireland)	46	46	1	177	1658	36.84	5	6	21
R.M.L.Taylor (Scotland)	8	7	2	46*	109	21.80	–	–	3
R.N.ten Doeschate (Netherlands)	33	32	9	119	1541	67.00	5	9	13
G.C.Wilson (Ireland)	47	46	5	113	1076	26.24	1	7	31/9

ASSOCIATES – BOWLING

	O	M	R	W	Avge	Best	4wI	R/Over
K.J.Coetzer	19	1	125	1	125.00	1-35	–	6.57
G.H.Dockrell	301.1	18	1265	45	28.11	4-24	2	4.20
A.N.Kervezee	4	0	34	0	–	–	–	8.50
C.S.MacLeod	57	2	289	8	36.12	2-26	–	5.07
M.W.Machan	51	2	270	8	33.75	3-31	–	5.29
T.J.Murtagh	63	7	312	7	44.57	3-33	–	4.95
W.B.Rankin	283.2	19	1391	43	32.34	3-32	–	4.90
P.R.Stirling	200.1	4	911	26	35.03	4-11	1	4.55
R.M.L.Taylor	75.5	5	366	13	28.15	3-39	–	4.82
R.N.ten Doeschate	263.2	18	1327	55	24.12	4-31	3	5.03

LIMITED-OVERS INTERNATIONALS RESULTS

1970-71 to 5 April 2014

This chart excludes all matches involving multinational teams.

	Opponents	Matches	Won											Tied	NR
			E	A	SA	WI	NZ	I	P	SL	Z	B	Ass		
England	Australia	127	49	73	–	–	–	–	–	–	–	–	–	2	3
	South Africa	51	22	–	25	–	–	–	–	–	–	–	–	1	3
	West Indies	88	42	–	–	42	–	–	–	–	–	–	–	1	4
	New Zealand	77	33	–	–	–	38	–	–	–	–	–	–	2	4
	India	87	35	–	–	–	–	47	–	–	–	–	–	2	3
	Pakistan	72	42	–	–	–	–	–	28	–	–	–	–	–	2
	Sri Lanka	51	26	–	–	–	–	–	–	25	–	–	–	–	–
	Zimbabwe	30	21	–	–	–	–	–	–	–	8	–	–	–	1
	Bangladesh	15	13	–	–	–	–	–	–	–	–	2	–	–	–
	Associates	18	16	–	–	–	–	–	–	–	–	–	1	–	1
Australia	South Africa	80	–	41	36	–	–	–	–	–	–	–	–	3	–
	West Indies	135	–	70	–	59	–	–	–	–	–	–	–	3	3
	New Zealand	125	–	85	–	–	34	–	–	–	–	–	–	–	6
	India	115	–	66	–	–	–	40	–	–	–	–	–	–	9
	Pakistan	89	–	54	–	–	–	–	31	–	–	–	–	1	3
	Sri Lanka	90	–	55	–	–	–	–	–	31	–	–	–	3	4
	Zimbabwe	28	–	26	–	–	–	–	–	–	1	–	–	–	1
	Bangladesh	19	–	18	–	–	–	–	–	–	–	1	–	–	–
	Associates	19	–	18	–	–	–	–	–	–	–	–	0	–	1
S Africa	West Indies	52	–	–	38	12	–	–	–	–	–	–	–	1	1
	New Zealand	58	–	–	34	–	20	–	–	–	–	–	–	–	4
	India	70	–	–	42	–	–	25	–	–	–	–	–	–	3
	Pakistan	71	–	–	47	–	–	–	23	–	–	–	–	–	1
	Sri Lanka	56	–	–	26	–	–	–	–	28	–	–	–	1	1
	Zimbabwe	32	–	–	29	–	–	–	–	–	2	–	–	–	1
	Bangladesh	14	–	–	13	–	–	–	–	–	–	1	–	–	–
	Associates	20	–	–	20	–	–	–	–	–	–	–	0	–	–
W Indies	New Zealand	60	–	–	–	30	23	–	–	–	–	–	–	–	7
	India	112	–	–	–	59	–	50	–	–	–	–	–	1	2
	Pakistan	126	–	–	–	68	–	–	55	–	–	–	–	3	–
	Sri Lanka	51	–	–	–	27	–	–	–	21	–	–	–	–	3
	Zimbabwe	44	–	–	–	34	–	–	–	–	9	–	–	–	1
	Bangladesh	25	–	–	–	16	–	–	–	–	–	7	–	–	2
	Associates	20	–	–	–	18	–	–	–	–	–	–	1	–	1
N Zealand	India	93	–	–	–	–	41	46	–	–	–	–	–	1	5
	Pakistan	89	–	–	–	–	35	–	51	–	–	–	–	1	2
	Sri Lanka	82	–	–	–	–	37	–	–	38	–	–	–	1	6
	Zimbabwe	35	–	–	–	–	25	–	–	–	8	–	–	1	1
	Bangladesh	24	–	–	–	–	16	–	–	–	–	8	–	–	–
	Associates	13	–	–	–	–	13	–	–	–	–	–	0	–	–
India	Pakistan	126	–	–	–	–	–	50	72	–	–	–	–	–	4
	Sri Lanka	144	–	–	–	–	–	78	–	54	–	–	–	1	11
	Zimbabwe	56	–	–	–	–	–	44	–	–	10	–	–	2	–
	Bangladesh	25	–	–	–	–	–	22	–	–	–	3	–	–	–
	Associates	25	–	–	–	–	–	23	–	–	–	–	2	–	–
Pakistan	Sri Lanka	139	–	–	–	–	–	–	80	54	–	–	–	1	4
	Zimbabwe	47	–	–	–	–	–	–	42	–	3	–	–	1	1
	Bangladesh	32	–	–	–	–	–	–	31	–	–	1	–	–	–
	Associates	26	–	–	–	–	–	–	24	–	–	–	2	–	–
Sri Lanka	Zimbabwe	47	–	–	–	–	–	–	–	39	7	–	–	1	–
	Bangladesh	37	–	–	–	–	–	–	–	32	–	4	–	–	1
	Associates	17	–	–	–	–	–	–	–	16	–	–	1	–	–
Zimbabwe	Bangladesh	59	–	–	–	–	–	–	–	–	28	31	–	–	–
	Associates	43	–	–	–	–	–	–	–	–	34	–	6	1	2
Bangladesh	Associates	33	–	–	–	–	–	–	–	–	–	22	11	–	–
Associates	Associates	147	–	–	–	–	–	–	–	–	–	–	141	1	5
		3466	**299**	**506**	**310**	**365**	**282**	**425**	**437**	**338**	**110**	**80**	**164**	**31**	**119**

293

MERIT TABLE OF ALL L-O INTERNATIONALS

	Matches	Won	Lost	Tied	No Result	% Won (exc NR)
Australia	830	509	282	9	30	63.62
South Africa	504	310	174	6	14	63.26
Pakistan	817	437	355	8	17	54.62
West Indies	713	365	316	8	24	52.97
India	853	425	384	7	37	52.08
England	616	299	289	7	21	50.25
Sri Lanka	714	338	341	4	31	49.48
New Zealand	656	282	333	6	35	45.41
Bangladesh	283	80	200	–	3	28.57
Zimbabwe	421	110	297	5	9	26.69
Associate Members (v Full*)	234	23	204	1	6	10.08

* Results of games between two Associate Members and those involving multi-national sides are excluded from this list; Associate Members have participated in 381 LOIs, 147 LOIs being between Associate Members.

TEAM RECORDS
HIGHEST TOTALS

443-9	(50 overs)	Sri Lanka v Netherlands	Amstelveen	2006
438-9	(49.5 overs)	South Africa v Australia	Johannesburg	2005-06
434-4	(50 overs)	Australia v South Africa	Johannesburg	2005-06
418-5	(50 overs)	South Africa v Zimbabwe	Potchefstroom	2006-07
418-5	(50 overs)	India v West Indies	Indore	2011-12
414-7	(50 overs)	India v Sri Lanka	Rajkot	2009-10
413-5	(50 overs)	India v Bermuda	Port-of-Spain	2006-07
411-8	(50 overs)	Sri Lanka v India	Rajkot	2009-10
402-2	(50 overs)	New Zealand v Ireland	Aberdeen	2008
401-3	(50 overs)	India v South Africa	Gwalior	2009-10
399-6	(50 overs)	South Africa v Zimbabwe	Benoni	2010-11
398-5	(50 overs)	Sri Lanka v Kenya	Kandy	1995-96
397-5	(44 overs)	New Zealand v Zimbabwe	Bulawayo	2005
392-4	(50 overs)	India v New Zealand	Christchurch	2008-09
392-6	(50 overs)	South Africa v Pakistan	Pretoria	2006-07
391-4	(50 overs)	England v Bangladesh	Nottingham	2005
387-5	(50 overs)	India v England	Rajkot	2008-09
385-7	(50 overs)	Pakistan v Bangladesh	Dambulla	2010
383-6	(50 overs)	India v Australia	Bangalore	2013-14
377-6	(50 overs)	Australia v South Africa	Basseterre	2006-07
376-2	(50 overs)	India v New Zealand	Hyderabad, India	1999-00
374-4	(50 overs)	India v Hong Kong	Karachi	2008
373-6	(50 overs)	India v Sri Lanka	Taunton	1999
373-8	(50 overs)	New Zealand v Zimbabwe	Napier	2011-12
372-6	(50 overs)	New Zealand v Zimbabwe	Whangarei	2011-12
371-9	(50 overs)	Pakistan v Sri Lanka	Nairobi	1996-97
370-4	(50 overs)	India v Bangladesh	Dhaka	2010-11
368-5	(50 overs)	Australia v Sri Lanka	Sydney	2005-06
365-2	(50 overs)	South Africa v India	Ahmedabad	2009-10
363-3	(50 overs)	South Africa v Zimbabwe	Bulawayo	2001-02
363-4	(50 overs)	West Indies v New Zealand	Hamilton	2013-14
363-5	(50 overs)	New Zealand v Canada	Gros Islet	2006-07
363-5	(50 overs)	India v Sri Lanka	Colombo (RPS)	2008-09
363-7	(55 overs)	England v Pakistan	Nottingham	1992
362-1	(43.3 overs)	India v Australia	Jaipur	2013-14
362-3	(50 overs)	Australia v Scotland	Edinburgh	2013
361-8	(50 overs)	Australia v Bangladesh	Dhaka	2010-11
360-4	(50 overs)	West Indies v Sri Lanka	Karachi	1987-88
359-2	(50 overs)	Australia v India	Johannesburg	2002-03
359-3	(50 overs)	New Zealand v England	Southampton	2013
359-5	(50 overs)	Australia v India	Sydney	2003-04
359-5	(50 overs)	Australia v India	Jaipur	2013-14

358-4	(50 overs)	South Africa v Bangladesh	Benoni	2008-09
358-4	(50 overs)	South Africa v India	Johannesburg	2013-14
358-5	(50 overs)	Australia v Netherlands	Basseterre	2006-07
358-6	(50 overs)	New Zealand v Canada	Mumbai	2010-11
357-9	(50 overs)	Sri Lanka v Bangladesh	Lahore	2008
356-4	(50 overs)	South Africa v West Indies	St George's	2006-07
356-9	(50 overs)	India v Pakistan	Vishakhapatnam	2004-05
354-3	(50 overs)	South Africa v Kenya	Cape Town	2001-02
354-6	(50 overs)	South Africa v England	Cape Town	2009-10
354-7	(50 overs)	India v Australia	Nagpur	2009-10
353-3	(40 overs)	South Africa v Netherlands	Basseterre	2006-07
353-5	(50 overs)	India v New Zealand	Hyderabad, India	2003-04
353-6	(50 overs)	Pakistan v England	Karachi	2005-06
351-3	(50 overs)	India v Kenya	Paarl	2001-02
351-4	(50 overs)	Pakistan v South Africa	Durban	2006-07
351-4	(49.3 overs)	India v Australia	Nagpur	2013-14
351-5	(50 overs)	South Africa v Netherlands	Mohali	2010-11
351-6	(50 overs)	South Africa v Zimbabwe	Bloemfontein	2010-11
351-7	(50 overs)	Zimbabwe v Kenya	Mombasa	2008-09
350-4	(50 overs)	Australia v India	Hyderabad, India	2009-10
350-6	(50 overs)	India v Sri Lanka	Nagpur	2005-06
350-6	(50 overs)	Australia v India	Nagpur	2013-14
350-9	(49.3 overs)	New Zealand v Australia	Hamilton	2006-07

The highest for Bangladesh is 326-4 (v Pakistan, Dhaka, 2013-14).

HIGHEST TOTALS BATTING SECOND

WINNING:	438-9	(49.5 overs)	South Africa v Australia	Johannesburg	2005-06
LOSING:	411-8	(50.0 overs)	Sri Lanka v India	Rajkot	2009-10

HIGHEST MATCH AGGREGATES

872-13	(99.5 overs)	South Africa v Australia	Johannesburg	2005-06
825-15	(100 overs)	India v Sri Lanka	Rajkot	2009-10

LARGEST RUNS MARGINS OF VICTORY

290 runs	New Zealand beat Ireland	Aberdeen	2008
272 runs	South Africa beat Zimbabwe	Benoni	2010-11
258 runs	South Africa beat Sri Lanka	Paarl	2011-12
257 runs	India beat Bermuda	Port-of-Spain	2006-07
256 runs	Australia beat Namibia	Potschefstroom	2002-03
256 runs	India beat Hong Kong	Karachi	2008
245 runs	Sri Lanka beat India	Sharjah	2000-01
243 runs	Sri Lanka beat Bermuda	Port-of-Spain	2006-07
234 runs	Sri Lanka beat Pakistan	Lahore	2008-09
233 runs	Pakistan beat Bangladesh	Dhaka	1999-00
232 runs	Australia beat Sri Lanka	Adelaide	1984-85
231 runs	South Africa beat Netherlands	Mohali	2010-11
229 runs	Australia beat Netherlands	Basseterre	2006-07
224 runs	Australia beat Pakistan	Nairobi	2002
221 runs	South Africa beat Netherlands	Basseterre	2006-07
217 runs	Pakistan beat Sri Lanka	Sharjah	2001-02
215 runs	Australia beat New Zealand	St George's	2006-07
215 runs	West Indies beat Netherlands	Delhhi	2010-11
212 runs	South Africa beat Zimbabwe	Centurion	2009-10
210 runs	New Zealand beat USA	The Oval	2004
210 runs	Sri Lanka beat Canada	Hambantota	2010-11
209 runs	South Africa beat West Indies	Cape Town	2003-04
208 runs	South Africa beat Kenya	Cape Town	2001-02
208 runs	Australia beat India	Sydney	2003-04
208 runs	West Indies beat Canada	Kingston	2009-10
206 runs	New Zealand beat Australia	Adelaide	1985-86
206 runs	Sri Lanka beat Netherlands	Colombo (RPS)	2002-03

206 runs		South Africa beat Bangladesh	Dhaka	2010-11
205 runs		Pakistan beat Kenya	Hambantota	2010-11
203 runs		Australia beat Scotland	Basseterre	2006-07
203 runs		West Indies beat New Zealand	Hamilton	2013-14
202 runs		England beat India	Lord's	1975
202 runs		South Africa beat Kenya	Nairobi	1996-97
202 runs		Zimbabwe beat Kenya	Dhaka	1998-99
202 runs		New Zealand beat Zimbabwe	Napier	2011-12
200 runs		India beat Bangladesh	Dhaka	2002-03
200 runs		New Zealand beat India	Dambulla	2010
200 runs		Australia beat Scotland	Edinburgh	2013

LOWEST TOTALS (Excluding reduced innings)

35	(18.0 overs)	Zimbabwe v Sri Lanka	Harare	2003-04
36	(18.4 overs)	Canada v Sri Lanka	Paarl	2002-03
38	(15.4 overs)	Zimbabwe v Sri Lanka	Colombo (SSC)	2001-02
43	(19.5 overs)	Pakistan v West Indies	Cape Town	1992-93
43	(20.1 overs)	Sri Lanka v South Africa	Paarl	2011-12
44	(24.5 overs)	Zimbabwe v Bangladesh	Chittagong	2009-10
45	(40.3 overs)	Canada v England	Manchester	1979
45	(14.0 overs)	Namibia v Australia	Potschefstroom	2002-03
54	(26.3 overs)	India v Sri Lanka	Sharjah	2000-01
54	(23.2 overs)	West Indies v South Africa	Cape Town	2003-04
55	(28.3 overs)	Sri Lanka v West Indies	Sharjah	1986-87
58	(18.5 overs)	Bangladesh v West Indies	Dhaka	2010-11
61	(22.0 overs)	West Indies v Bangladesh	Chittagong	2011-12
63	(25.5 overs)	India v Australia	Sydney	1980-81
64	(35.5 overs)	New Zealand v Pakistan	Sharjah	1985-86
65	(24.0 overs)	USA v Australia	Southampton	2004
65	(24.3 overs)	Zimbabwe v India	Harare	2005
67	(31.0 overs)	Zimbabwe v Sri Lanka	Harare	2008-09
67	(24.4 overs)	Canada v Netherlands	King City	2013
68	(31.3 overs)	Scotland v West Indies	Leicester	1999
69	(28.0 overs)	South Africa v Australia	Sydney	1993-94
69	(22.5 overs)	Zimbabwe v Kenya	Harare	2005-06
69	(23.5 overs)	Kenya v New Zealand	Chennai	2010-11
70	(25.2 overs)	Australia v England	Birmingham	1977
70	(26.3 overs)	Australia v New Zealand	Adelaide	1985-86
70	(23.5 overs)	West Indies v Australia	Perth	2012-13

The lowest for England is 86 (v A, Manchester, 2001).

LOWEST MATCH AGGREGATES

73-11	(23.2 overs)	Canada (36) v Sri Lanka (37-1)	Paarl	2002-03
75-11	(27.2 overs)	Zimbabwe (35) v Sri Lanka (40-1)	Harare	2003-04
78-11	(20.0 overs)	Zimbabwe (38) v Sri Lanka (40-1)	Colombo (SSC)	2001-02

BATTING RECORDS

5000 RUNS IN A CAREER

	LOI	I	NO	HS	Runs	Avge	100	50
S.R.Tendulkar	I	463	452	41	200*	18426	44.83	49	96
R.T.Ponting	A/ICC	375	365	39	164	13704	42.03	30	82
S.T.Jayasuriya	SL/Asia	445	433	18	189	13430	32.36	28	68
K.C.Sangakkara	SL/Asia/ICC	369	350	37	169	12500	40.45	18	85
Inzamam-ul-Haq	P/Asia	378	350	53	137*	11739	39.52	10	83
J.H.Kallis	SA/Afr/ICC	325	311	53	139	11574	44.86	17	86
D.P.M.D.Jayawardena	SL/Asia	412	385	38	144	11512	33.17	16	71
S.C.Ganguly	I/Asia	311	300	23	183	11363	41.02	22	72
R.S.Dravid	I/Asia/ICC	344	318	40	153	10889	39.16	12	83
B.C.Lara	WI/ICC	299	289	32	169	10405	40.48	19	63

		LOI	I	NO	HS	Runs	Avge	100	50
Mohammad Yousuf	P/Asia	288	272	40	141*	9720	41.71	15	64
A.C.Gilchrist	A/ICC	287	279	11	172	9619	35.89	16	55
M.Azharuddin	I	334	308	54	153*	9378	36.92	7	58
P.A.de Silva	SL	308	296	30	145	9284	34.90	11	64
Saeed Anwar	P	247	244	19	194	8824	39.21	20	43
S.Chanderpaul	WI	268	251	40	150	8778	41.60	11	59
C.H.Gayle	WI/ICC	255	250	17	153*	8743	37.52	21	45
D.L.Haynes	WI	238	237	28	152*	8648	41.37	17	57
M.S.Atapattu	SL	268	259	32	132*	8529	37.57	11	59
M.E.Waugh	A	244	236	20	173	8500	39.35	18	50
Yuvraj Singh	I/Asia	293	268	39	139	8329	36.37	13	51
V.Sehwag	I/Asia/ICC	251	245	9	219	8273	35.05	15	38
H.H.Gibbs	SA	248	240	16	175	8094	36.13	21	37
M.S.Dhoni	I/Asia	243	214	63	183*	8046	53.28	9	54
S.P.Fleming	NZ/ICC	280	269	21	134*	8037	32.40	8	49
T.M.Dilshan	SL	277	252	39	160*	8025	37.67	17	34
M.J.Clarke	A	236	215	43	130	7683	44.66	8	55
Shahid Afridi	P/Asia/ICC	378	350	25	124	7619	23.44	6	36
S.R.Waugh	A	325	288	58	120*	7569	32.90	3	45
A.Ranatunga	SL	269	255	47	131*	7456	35.84	4	49
Javed Miandad	P	233	218	41	119*	7381	41.70	8	50
Salim Malik	P	283	256	38	102	7170	32.88	5	47
N.J.Astle	NZ	223	217	14	145*	7090	34.92	16	41
Younus Khan	P	253	243	23	144	7014	31.88	6	48
G.C.Smith	SA/Afr	197	194	10	141	6989	37.98	10	45
M.G.Bevan	A	232	196	67	108*	6912	53.58	6	46
G.Kirsten	SA	185	185	19	188*	6798	40.95	13	45
A.Flower	Z	213	208	16	145	6786	35.34	4	55
I.V.A.Richards	WI	187	167	24	189*	6721	47.00	11	45
G.W.Flower	Z	221	214	18	142*	6571	33.52	6	40
Ijaz Ahmed	P	250	232	29	139*	6564	32.33	10	37
A.R.Border	A	273	252	39	127*	6524	30.62	3	39
A.B.de Villiers	SA	159	153	25	146	6331	49.46	16	36
R.B.Richardson	WI	224	217	30	122	6248	33.41	5	44
M.L.Hayden	A/ICC	161	155	15	181*	6133	43.80	10	36
D.M.Jones	A	164	161	25	145	6068	44.61	7	46
D.C.Boon	A	181	177	16	122	5964	37.04	5	37
J.N.Rhodes	SA	245	220	51	121	5935	35.11	2	33
Ramiz Raja	P	198	197	15	119*	5841	32.09	9	31
R.R.Sarwan	WI	181	169	33	120*	5804	42.67	5	38
C.L.Hooper	WI	227	206	43	113*	5761	35.34	7	29
V.Kohli	I	134	126	18	183	5634	52.16	19	30
W.J.Cronje	SA	188	175	31	112	5565	38.64	2	39
Shoaib Malik	P	216	193	25	143	5490	32.67	7	31
M.E.K.Hussey	A	185	157	44	109*	5442	48.15	3	39
A.Jadeja	I	196	179	36	119	5359	37.47	6	30
D.R.Martyn	A	208	182	51	144*	5346	40.80	5	37
S.R.Watson	A	173	152	24	185*	5256	41.06	9	30
G.Gambhir	I	147	143	11	150*	5238	39.68	11	34
W.U.Tharanga	SL/Asia	171	163	9	174*	5228	33.94	13	28
A.D.R.Campbell	Z	188	184	14	131*	5185	30.50	7	30
B.B.McCullum	NZ	229	199	28	166	5172	30.24	4	26
R.S.Mahanama	SL	213	198	23	119*	5162	29.49	4	35
C.G.Greenidge	WI	128	127	13	133*	5134	45.03	11	31
P.D.Collingwood	E	197	181	37	120*	5092	35.36	5	26
A.Symonds	A	198	161	33	156	5088	39.75	6	30
Abdul Razzaq	P/Asia	265	228	57	112	5080	29.70	3	23

The most for Bangladesh 3779 in 128 innings by Shakib Al Hasan.

219	V.Sehwag	India v West Indies	Indore	2011-12
209	R.G.Sharma	India v Australia	Bangalore	2013-14
200*	S.R.Tendulkar	India v South Africa	Gwalior	2009-10
194*	C.K.Coventry	Zimbabwe v Bangladesh	Bulawayo	2009
194	Saeed Anwar	Pakistan v India	Madras	1996-97
189*	I.V.A.Richards	West Indies v England	Manchester	1984
189*	M.J.Guptill	New Zealand v England	Southampton	2013
189	S.T.Jayasuriya	Sri Lanka v India	Sharjah	2000-01
188*	G.Kirsten	South Africa v UAE	Rawalpindi	1995-96
186*	S.R.Tendulkar	India v New Zealand	Hyderabad	1999-00
185*	S.R.Watson	Australia v Bangladesh	Dhaka	2010-11
183*	M.S.Dhoni	India v Sri Lanka	Jaipur	2005-06
183	S.C.Ganguly	India v Sri Lanka	Taunton	1999
183	V.Kohli	India v Pakistan	Dhaka	2011-12
181*	M.L.Hayden	Australia v New Zealand	Hamilton	2006-07
181	I.V.A.Richards	West Indies v Sri Lanka	Karachi	1987-88
178*	H.Masakadza	Zimbabwe v Kenya	Harare	2009-10
177	P.R.Stirling	Ireland v Canada	Toronto	2010
175*	Kapil Dev	India v Zimbabwe	Tunbridge Wells	1983
175	H.H.Gibbs	South Africa v Australia	Johannesburg	2005-06
175	S.R.Tendulkar	India v Australia	Hyderabad, India	2009-10
175	V.Sehwag	India v Bangladesh	Dhaka	2010-11
175	C.S.MacLeod	Scotland v Canada	Christchurch	2013-14
174*	W.U.Tharanga	Sri Lanka v India	Kingston	2013
173	M.E.Waugh	Australia v West Indies	Melbourne	2000-01
172*	C.B.Wishart	Zimbabwe v Namibia	Harare	2002-03
172	A.C.Gilchrist	Australia v Zimbabwe	Hobart	2003-04
172	L.Vincent	New Zealand v Zimbabwe	Bulawayo	2005
171*	G.M.Turner	New Zealand v East Africa	Birmingham	1975
169*	D.J.Callaghan	South Africa v New Zealand	Pretoria	1994-95
169	B.C.Lara	West Indies v Sri Lanka	Sharjah	1995-96
169	K.C.Sangakkara	Sri Lanka v South Africa	Colombo (RPS)	2013
167*	R.A.Smith	England v Australia	Birmingham	1993
166	B.B.McCullum	New Zealand v Ireland	Aberdeen	2008
164	R.T.Ponting	Australia v South Africa	Johannesburg	2005-06
163*	S.R.Tendulkar	India v New Zealand	Christchurch	2008-09
163	D.A.Warner	Australia v Sri Lanka	Brisbane	2011-12
161*	S.R.Watson	Australia v England	Melbourne	2010-11
161	A.C.Hudson	South Africa v Netherlands	Rawalpindi	1995-96
161	J.A.H.Marshall	New Zealand v Ireland	Aberdeen	2008
160*	T.M.Dilshan	Sri Lanka v India	Hobart	2011-12
160	Imran Nazir	Pakistan v Zimbabwe	Kingston	2006-07
160	T.M.Dilshan	Sri Lanka v India	Rajkot	2009-10
159*	D.Mongia	India v Zimbabwe	Gauhati	2001-02
158	D.I.Gower	England v New Zealand	Brisbane	1982-83
158	M.L.Hayden	Australia v West Indies	North Sound	2006-07
158	A.J.Strauss	England v India	Bangalore	2010-11
157*	X.M.Marshall	West Indies v Canada	King City (NW)	2008
157	S.T.Jayasuriya	Sri Lanka v Netherlands	Amstelveen	2006
156	B.C.Lara	West Indies v Pakistan	Adelaide	2004-05
156	A.Symonds	Australia v New Zealand	Wellington	2005-06
156	H.Masakadza	Zimbabwe v Kenya	Harare	2009-10
156	G.J.Bailey	Australia v India	Nagpur	2013-14
154	A.C.Gilchrist	Australia v Sri Lanka	Melbourne	1998-99
154	Tamim Iqbal	Bangladesh v Zimbabwe	Bulawayo	2009
154	A.J.Strauss	England v Bangladesh	Birmingham	2010
153*	I.V.A.Richards	West Indies v Australia	Melbourne	1979-80
153*	M.Azharuddin	India v Zimbabwe	Cuttack	1997-98
153*	S.C.Ganguly	India v New Zealand	Gwalior	1999-00
153*	C.H.Gayle	West Indies v Zimbabwe	Bulawayo	2003-04
153	B.C.Lara	West Indies v Pakistan	Sharjah	1993-94

153	R.S.Dravid	India v New Zealand	Hyderabad	1999-00
153	H.H.Gibbs	South Africa v Bangladesh	Potchefstroom	2002-03
152*	D.L.Haynes	West Indies v India	Georgetown	1988-89
152*	C.H.Gayle	West Indies v South Africa	Johannesburg	2003-04
152	C.H.Gayle	West Indies v Kenya	Nairobi	2001-02
152	S.R.Tendulkar	India v Namibia	Pietermaritzburg	2002-03
152	A.J.Strauss	England v Bangladesh	Nottingham	2005
152	S.T.Jayasuriya	Sri Lanka v England	Leeds	2006
151*	S.T.Jayasuriya	Sri Lanka v India	Bombay	1996-97
151	A.Symonds	Australia v Sri Lanka	Sydney	2005-06
151	S.E.Marsh	Australia v Scotland	Edinburgh	2013
150*	G.Gambhir	India v Sri Lanka	Kolkata	2009-10
150*	J.P.Duminy	South Africa v Netherlands	Amstelveen	2013
150	S.Chanderpaul	West Indies v South Africa	East London	1998-99
150	G.Gambhir	India v Sri Lanka	Colombo (RPS)	2008-09
150	H.M.Amla	South Africa v England	Southampton	2012

HUNDRED ON DEBUT

D.L.Amiss	103	England v Australia	Manchester	1972
D.L.Haynes	148	West Indies v Australia	St John's	1977-78
A.Flower	115*	Zimbabwe v Sri Lanka	New Plymouth	1991-92
Salim Elahi	102*	Pakistan v Sri Lanka	Gujranwala	1995-96
M.J.Guptill	122*	New Zealand v West Indies	Auckland	2008-09
C.A.Ingram	124	South Africa v Zimbabwe	Bloemfontein	2010-11
R.J.Nicol	108*	New Zealand v Zimbabwe	Harare	2011-12
P.J.Hughes	112	Australia v Sri Lanka	Melbourne	2012-13
M.J.Lumb	106	England v West Indies	North Sound	2013-14

Shahid Afridi scored 102 for P v SL, Nairobi, 1996-97, in his second match having not batted in his first.

Fastest 100	36 balls	C.J.Anderson (131*)	NZ v WI	Queenstown	2013-14
Fastest 50	17 balls	S.T.Jayasuriya (76)	SL v P	Singapore	1995-96

15 HUNDREDS

		Inns	100	E	A	SA	WI	NZ	I	P	SL	Z	B	Ass
S.R.Tendulkar	I	452	49	2	9	5	4	5	–	5	8	5	1	5
R.T.Ponting	A	365	30*	5	–	2	2	6	6	1	4	1	1	5
S.T.Jayasuriya	SL	433	28	4	2	–	1	5	7	3	–	1	4	1
S.C.Ganguly	I	300	22	1	1	3	–	3	–	2	4	3	1	4
H.H.Gibbs	SA	240	21	2	3	–	5	2	2	2	1	2	1	1
C.H.Gayle	WI	250	21	2	–	3	–	2	4	3	1	2	1	3
Saeed Anwar	P	244	20	–	1	–	2	4	4	–	7	2	–	–
V.Kohli	I	126	19	2	3	–	2	2	–	1	5	1	3	–
B.C.Lara	WI	289	19	1	3	3	–	2	2	–	5	2	1	1
M.E.Waugh	A	236	18	1	–	2	3	3	3	1	1	3	–	1
K.C.Sangakkara	SL	346	18	1	1	2	–	1	6	2	–	–	4	1
D.L.Haynes	WI	237	17	2	6	–	–	2	2	4	1	–	–	–
T.M.Dilshan	SL	252	17	1	1	2	–	1	4	2	–	2	3	1
J.H.Kallis	SA	311	17	1	1	–	4	3	2	1	3	1	–	1
A.B.de Villiers	SA	153	16	1	–	–	3	1	3	3	1	3	1	–
N.J.Astle	NZ	217	16	2	1	1	1	–	5	2	–	3	–	1
A.C.Gilchrist	A	279	16*	2	–	2	–	2	1	1	6	2	–	–
D.P.M.D.Jayawardena	SL	385	16*	5	–	–	1	2	3	2	–	1	1	1
V.Sehwag	I	245	15	1	–	–	2	6	–	2	2	–	1	1
Mohammad Yousuf	P	273	15	–	1	2	2	1	1	–	2	3	3	–

* = Includes hundred scored against multi-national side. The most for England is 12 by M.E.Trescothick (in 122 innings), for Zimbabwe 7 by A.D.R.Campbell (184), and for Bangladesh 5 by Shakib Al Hasan (128).

HIGHEST PARTNERSHIP FOR EACH WICKET

1st	286	W.U.Tharanga/S.T.Jayasuriya	Sri Lanka v England	Leeds	2006
2nd	331	S.R.Tendulkar/R.S.Dravid	India v New Zealand	Hyderabad (Ind)	1999-00
3rd	238	H.M.Amla/A.B.de Villiers	South Africa v Pakistan	Johannesburg	2012-13
4th	275*	M.Azharuddin/A.Jadeja	India v Zimbabwe	Cuttack	1997-98
5th	226*	E.J.G.Morgan/R.S.Bopara	England v Ireland	Dublin	2013
6th	218	D.P.M.D.Jayawardena/M.S.Dhoni	Asia XI v Africa XI	Chennai	2007
7th	130	A.Flower/H.H.Streak	Zimbabwe v England	Harare	2001-02
8th	138*	J.M.Kemp/A.J.Hall	South Africa v India	Cape Town	2006-07
9th	132	A.D.Mathews/S.L.Malinga	Sri Lanka v Australia	Melbourne	2010-11
10th	106*	I.V.A.Richards/M.A.Holding	West Indies v England	Manchester	1984

BOWLING RECORDS

200 WICKETS IN A CAREER

		LOI	Balls	R	W	Avge	Best	5w	R/Over
M.Muralitharan	SL/Asia/ICC	350	18811	12326	534	23.08	7-30	10	3.93
Wasim Akram	P	356	18186	11812	502	23.52	5-15	6	3.89
Waqar Younis	P	262	12698	9919	416	23.84	7-36	13	4.68
W.P.J.U.C.Vaas	SL/Asia	322	15775	11014	400	27.53	8-19	4	4.18
S.M.Pollock	SA/Afr/ICC	303	15712	9631	393	24.50	6-35	5	3.67
G.D.McGrath	A/ICC	250	12970	8391	381	22.02	7-15	7	3.88
B.Lee	A	221	11185	8877	380	23.36	5-22	9	4.76
Shahid Afridi	P/Asia/ICC	378	16610	12813	378	33.89	7-12	9	4.62
A.Kumble	I/Asia	271	14496	10412	337	30.89	6-12	2	4.30
S.T.Jayasuriya	SL	445	14874	11871	323	36.75	6-29	4	4.78
J.Srinath	I	229	11935	8847	315	28.08	5-23	3	4.44
S.K.Warne	A/ICC	194	10642	7541	293	25.73	5-33	1	4.25
Saqlain Mushtaq	P	169	8770	6275	288	21.78	5-20	6	4.29
A.B.Agarkar	I	191	9484	8021	288	27.85	6-42	2	5.07
D.L.Vettori	NZ/ICC	275	13029	8946	284	31.50	5- 7	2	4.11
Z.Khan	I/Asia	200	10097	8301	282	29.43	5-42	1	4.93
J.H.Kallis	SA/Afr/ICC	325	10750	8680	273	31.79	5-30	2	4.84
A.A.Donald	SA	164	8561	5926	272	21.78	6-23	2	4.15
Abdul Razzaq	P/Asia	265	10941	8564	269	31.83	6-35	3	4.69
M.Ntini	SA/ICC	173	8687	6559	266	24.65	6-22	4	4.53
Harbhajan Singh	I/Asia	229	12059	8651	259	33.40	5-31	3	4.30
S.L.Malinga	SL	166	7999	6879	256	26.87	6-38	7	5.15
Kapil Dev	I	225	11202	6945	253	27.45	5-43	1	3.72
Shoaib Akhtar	P/Asia/ICC	163	7764	6169	247	24.97	6-16	4	4.76
J.M.Anderson	E	174	8609	7132	245	29.11	5-23	2	4.97
H.H.Streak	Z/Afr	189	9468	7129	239	29.82	5-32	1	4.51
D.Gough	E/ICC	159	8470	6209	235	26.42	5-44	2	4.39
K.D.Mills	NZ	165	7977	6284	235	26.74	5-25	1	4.72
C.A.Walsh	WI	205	10822	6918	227	30.47	5- 1	1	3.83
C.E.L.Ambrose	WI	176	9353	5429	225	24.12	5-17	4	3.48
M.G.Johnson	A	136	6647	5384	208	25.88	6-31	3	4.85
Abdur Razzak	B	150	7815	5912	206	28.69	5-29	4	4.53
C.J.McDermott	A	138	7460	5018	203	24.71	5-44	1	4.03
C.Z.Harris	NZ	250	10667	7613	203	37.50	5-42	1	4.28
C.L.Cairns	NZ/ICC	215	8168	6594	201	32.80	5-42	1	4.84

SIX WICKETS IN AN INNINGS

8-19	W.P.J.U.C.Vaas	Sri Lanka v Zimbabwe	Colombo (SSC)	2001-02
7-12	Shahid Afridi	Pakistan v West Indies	Providence	2013
7-15	G.D.McGrath	Australia v Namibia	Potchefstroom	2002-03
7-20	A.J.Bichel	Australia v England	Port Elizabeth	2002-03
7-30	M.Muralitharan	Sri Lanka v India	Sharjah	2000-01
7-36	Waqar Younis	Pakistan v England	Leeds	2001
7-37	Aqib Javed	Pakistan v India	Sharjah	1991-92
7-51	W.W.Davis	West Indies v Australia	Leeds	1983
6-12	A.Kumble	India v West Indies	Calcutta	1993-94

6-13	B.A.W.Mendis	Sri Lanka v India	Karachi	2008
6-14	G.J.Gilmour	Australia v England	Leeds	1975
6-14	Imran Khan	Pakistan v India	Sharjah	1984-85
6-14	M.F.Maharoof	Sri Lanka v West Indies	Mumbai	2006-07
6-15	C.E.H.Croft	West Indies v England	Kingstown	1980-81
6-16	Shoaib Akhtar	Pakistan v New Zealand	Karachi	2001-02
6-18	Azhar Mahmood	Pakistan v West Indies	Sharjah	1999-00
6-19	H.K.Olonga	Zimbabwe v England	Cape Town	1999-00
6-19	S.E.Bond	New Zealand v Zimbabwe	Harare	2005
6-20	B.C.Strang	Zimbabwe v Bangladesh	Nairobi	1997-98
6-20	A.D.Mathews	Sri Lanka v India	Colombo (RPS)	2009-10
6-22	F.H.Edwards	West Indies v Zimbabwe	Harare	2003-04
6-22	M.Ntini	South Africa v Australia	Cape Town	2005-06
6-23	A.A.Donald	South Africa v Kenya	Nairobi	1996-97
6-23	A.Nehra	India v England	Durban	2002-03
6-23	S.E.Bond	New Zealand v Australia	Port Elizabeth	2002-03
6-25	S.B.Styris	New Zealand v West Indies	Port-of-Spain	2002
6-25	W.P.J.U.C.Vaas	Sri Lanka v Bangladesh	Pietermaritzburg	2002-03
6-26	Waqar Younis	Pakistan v Sri Lanka	Sharjah	1989-90
6-26	Mashrafe Mortaza	Bangladesh v Kenya	Nairobi	2006
6-26	Rubel Hossain	Bangladesh v New Zealand	Dhaka	2013-14
6-27	Naved-ul-Hasan	Pakistan v India	Jamshedpur	2004-05
6-27	C.R.D.Fernando	Sri Lanka v England	Colombo (RPS)	2007-08
6-27	M.Kartik	India v Australia	Mumbai	2007-08
6-27	K.A.J.Roach	West Indies v Netherlands	Delhi	2010-11
6-28	H.K.Olonga	Zimbabwe v Kenya	Bulawayo	2002-03
6-29	B.P.Patterson	West Indies v India	Nagpur	1987-88
6-29	S.T.Jayasuriya	Sri Lanka v England	Moratuwa	1992-93
6-29	B.A.W.Mendis	Sri Lanka v Zimbabwe	Harare	2008-09
6-30	Waqar Younis	Pakistan v New Zealand	Auckland	1993-94
6-31	P.D.Collingwood	England v Bangladesh	Nottingham	2005
6-31	M.G.Johnson	Australia v Sri Lanka	Pallekele	2011
6-35	S.M.Pollock	South Africa v West Indies	East London	1998-99
6-35	Abdul Razzaq	Pakistan v Bangladesh	Dhaka	2001-02
6-38	Shahid Afridi	Pakistan v Australia	Dubai	2009
6-38	S.L.Malinga	Sri Lanka v Kenya	Colombo (RPS)	2010-11
6-39	H.H.MacLeay	Australia v India	Nottingham	1983
6-39	D.W.Steyn	South Africa v Pakistan	Port Elizabeth	2013-14
6-41	I.V.A.Richards	West Indies v India	Delhi	1989-90
6-42	A.B.Agarkar	India v Australia	Melbourne	2003-04
6-42	Umar Gul	Pakistan v England	The Oval	2010
6-43	D.J.Bravo	West Indies v Zimbabwe	St George's	2012-13
6-44	Waqar Younis	Pakistan v New Zealand	Sharjah	1996-97
6-44	N.L.T.C.Perera	Sri Lanka v Pakistan	Pallekele	2012
6-45	C.R.Woakes	England v Australia	Brisbane	2010-11
6-46	A.G.Cremer	Zimbabwe v Kenya	Harare	2009-10
6-48	A.Mishra	India v Zimbabwe	Bulawayo	2013
6-49	L.Klusener	South Africa v Sri Lanka	Lahore	1997-98
6-50	A.H.Gray	West Indies v Australia	Port-of-Spain	1990-91
6-52	C.B.Mpofu	Zimbabwe v Kenya	Nairobi (Gym)	2008-09
6-55	S.Sreesanth	India v England	Indore	2005-06
6-59	Waqar Younis	Pakistan v Australia	Nottingham	2001
6-59	A.Nehra	India v Sri Lanka	Colombo (RPS)	2005

HAT-TRICKS

Jalaluddin	Pakistan v Australia	Hyderabad	1982-83
B.A.Reid	Australia v New Zealand	Sydney	1985-86
C.Sharma	India v New Zealand	Nagpur	1987-88
Wasim Akram	Pakistan v West Indies	Sharjah	1989-90
Wasim Akram	Pakistan v Australia	Sharjah	1989-90
Kapil Dev	India v Sri Lanka	Calcutta	1990-91
Aqib Javed	Pakistan v India	Sharjah	1991-92
D.K.Morrison	New Zealand v India	Napier	1993-94

Waqar Younis	Pakistan v New Zealand	East London	1994-95
Saqlain Mushtaq	Pakistan v Zimbabwe	Peshawar	1996-97
E.A.Brandes	Zimbabwe v England	Harare	1996-97
A.M.Stuart	Australia v Pakistan	Melbourne	1996-97
Saqlain Mushtaq	Pakistan v Zimbabwe	The Oval	1999
W.P.J.U.C.Vaas	Sri Lanka v Zimbabwe	Colombo (SSC)	2001-02
Mohammad Sami	Pakistan v West Indies	Sharjah	2001-02
W.P.J.U.C.Vaas[1]	Sri Lanka v Bangladesh	Pietermaritzburg	2002-03
B.Lee	Australia v Kenya	Durban	2002-03
J.M.Anderson	England v Pakistan	The Oval	2003
S.J.Harmison	England v India	Nottingham	2004
C.K.Langeveldt	South Africa v West Indies	Bridgetown	2004-05
Shahadat Hossain	Bangladesh v Zimbabwe	Harare	2006
J.E.Taylor	West Indies v Australia	Mumbai	2006-07
S.E.Bond	New Zealand v Australia	Hobart	2006-07
S.L.Malinga[2]	Sri Lanka v South Africa	Providence	2006-07
A.Flintoff	England v West Indies	St Lucia	2008-09
M.F.Maharoof	Sri Lanka v India	Dambulla	2010
Abdur Razzak	Bangladesh v Zimbabwe	Dhaka	2010-11
K.A.J.Roach	West Indies v Netherlands	Delhi	2010-11
S.L.Malinga	Sri Lanka v Kenya	Colombo (RPS)	2010-11
S.L.Malinga	Sri Lanka v Australia	Colombo (RPS)	2011
D.T.Christian	Australia v Sri Lanka	Melbourne	2011-12
N.L.T.C.Perera	Sri Lanka v Pakistan	Colombo (RPS)	2012
C.J.McKay	Australia v England	Cardiff	2013
Rubel Hossain	Bangladesh v New Zealand	Dhaka	2013-14

[1] The first three balls of the match. Took four wickets in opening over (W W W 4 wide W 0).
[2] Four wickets in four balls.

WICKET-KEEPING RECORDS

100 DISMISSALS IN A CAREER

Total			LOI	Ct	St
472‡	A.C.Gilchrist	Australia/ICC	287	417	55
433†‡	K.C.Sangakkara	Sri Lanka/Asia/ICC	325	346	87
424	M.V.Boucher	South Africa/Africa	295	402	22
304	M.S.Dhoni	India/Asia	243	224	80
287‡	Moin Khan	Pakistan	219	214	73
242†‡	B.B.McCullum	New Zealand	185	227	15
233	I.A.Healy	Australia	168	194	39
220‡	Rashid Latif	Pakistan	166	182	38
206‡	R.S.Kaluwitharana	Sri Lanka	187	131	75
204‡	P.J.L.Dujon	West Indies	169	183	21
189	R.D.Jacobs	West Indies	147	160	29
187	Kamran Akmal	Pakistan	154	156	31
165	D.J.Richardson	South Africa	122	148	17
165†‡	A.Flower	Zimbabwe	213	133	32
163†‡	A.J.Stewart	England	170	148	15
156	B.J.Haddin	Australia	105	146	10
154‡	N.R.Mongia	India	140	110	44
149	D.Ramdin	West Indies	109	143	6
145	T.Taibu	Zimbabwe/Africa	150	112	33
136†‡	A.C.Parore	New Zealand	179	111	25
126	Khaled Masud	Bangladesh	126	91	35
124	R.W.Marsh	Australia	92	120	4
123	Mushfiqur Rahim	Bangladesh	129	89	34
103	Salim Yousuf	Pakistan	86	81	22

† Excluding catches taken in the field. ‡ Excluding matches when not wicket-keeper.

SIX DISMISSALS IN AN INNINGS

6	(6ct)	A.C.Gilchrist	Australia v South Africa	Cape Town	1999-00
6	(6ct)	A.J.Stewart	England v Zimbabwe	Manchester	2000
6	(5ct/1st)	R.D.Jacobs	West Indies v Sri Lanka	Colombo (RPS)	2001-02
6	(5ct/1st)	A.C.Gilchrist	Australia v England	Sydney	2002-03
6	(6ct)	A.C.Gilchrist	Australia v Namibia	Potchefstroom	2002-03
6	(6ct)	A.C.Gilchrist	Australia v Sri Lanka	Colombo (RPS)	2003-04
6	(6ct)	M.V.Boucher	South Africa v Pakistan	Cape Town	2006-07
6	(5ct/1st)	M.S.Dhoni	India v England	Leeds	2007
6	(6ct)	A.C.Gilchrist	Australia v India	Baroda	2007-08
6	(5ct/1st)	A.C.Gilchrist	Australia v India	Sydney	2007-08
6	(6ct)	M.J.Prior	England v South Africa	Nottingham	2008
6	(6ct)	J.C.Buttler	England v South Africa	The Oval	2013
6	(6ct)	M.H.Cross	Scotland v Canada	Christchurch	2013-14

FIELDING RECORDS
100 CATCHES IN A CAREER

Total			LOI
202	D.P.M.D.Jayawardena	Sri Lanka/Asia	412
160	R.T.Ponting	Australia/ICC	375
156	M.Azharuddin	India	334
140	S.R.Tendulkar	India	463
133	S.P.Fleming	New Zealand/ICC	280
130	M.Muralitharan	Sri Lanka/Asia/ICC	350
129	J.H.Kallis	South Africa/Africa/ICC	325
127	A.R.Border	Australia	273
126	Younus Khan	Pakistan	253
124	R.S.Dravid	India/Asia/ICC	344
123	S.T.Jayasuriya	Sri Lanka/Asia	445
120	C.L.Hooper	West Indies	227
120	B.C.Lara	West Indies/ICC	299
119	Shahid Afridi	Pakistan/Asia/ICC	378
113	Inzamam-ul-Haq	Pakistan/Asia	378
111	S.R.Waugh	Australia	325
109	R.S.Mahanama	Sri Lanka	213
108	P.D.Collingwood	England	197
108	M.E.Waugh	Australia	244
108	H.H.Gibbs	South Africa	248
108	C.H.Gayle	West Indies/ICC	255
108	S.M.Pollock	South Africa/Africa/ICC	303
105	M.E.K.Hussey	Australia	185
105	G.C.Smith	South Africa/Africa	197
105	J.N.Rhodes	South Africa	245
100	I.V.A.Richards	West Indies	187
100	M.J.Clarke	Australia	236
100	T.M.Dilshan	Sri Lanka	277
100	S.C.Ganguly	India/Asia	311

The most for Zimbabwe is 86 by G.W.Flower (221), and for Bangladesh 40 by Mashrafe Mortaza (131).

FIVE CATCHES IN AN INNINGS

5	J.N.Rhodes	South Africa v West Indies	Bombay (BS)	1993-94

250 MATCHES

463	S.R.Tendulkar	India	288	Mohammad Yousuf	Pakistan/Asia
445	S.T.Jayasuriya	Sri Lanka/Asia	287	A.C.Gilchrist	Australia/ICC
412	D.P.M.D.Jayawardena	Sri Lanka/Asia	283	Salim Malik	Pakistan
378	Inzamam-ul-Haq	Pakistan/Asia	280	S.P.Fleming	New Zealand/ICC
378	Shahid Afridi	Pakistan/Asia/ICC	277	T.M.Dilshan	Sri Lanka
375	R.T.Ponting	Australia/ICC	275	D.L.Vettori	New Zealand/ICC
369	K.C.Sangakkara	Sri Lanka/Asia/ICC	273	A.R.Border	Australia
356	Wasim Akram	Pakistan	271	A.Kumble	India/Asia
350	M.Muralitharan	Sri Lanka/Asia/ICC	269	A.Ranatunga	Sri Lanka
344	R.S.Dravid	India/Asia/ICC	268	M.S.Atapattu	Sri Lanka
334	M.Azharuddin	India	268	S.Chanderpaul	West Indies
325	J.H.Kallis	South Africa/Africa/ICC	265	Abdul Razzaq	Pakistan/Asia
325	S.R.Waugh	Australia	262	Waqar Younis	Pakistan
322	W.P.J.U.C.Vaas	Sri Lanka/Asia	255	C.H.Gayle	West Indies/ICC
311	S.C.Ganguly	India/Asia	253	Younus Khan	Pakistan
308	P.A.de Silva	Sri Lanka	251	V.Sehwag	India/Asia/ICC
303	S.M.Pollock	South Africa/Africa/ICC	250	C.Z.Harris	New Zealand
299	B.C.Lara	West Indies/ICC	250	Ijaz Ahmed	Pakistan
295	M.V.Boucher	South Africa/Africa	250	G.D.McGrath	Australia/ICC
293	Yuvraj Singh	India/Asia			

The most for England is 197 by P.D.Collingwood, for Zimbabwe 221 by G.W.Flower, and for Bangladesh 175 by Mohammad Ashraful.

The most consecutive appearances is 185 by S.R.Tendulkar for India (Apr 1990-Apr 1998).

100 MATCHES AS CAPTAIN

LOI			W	L	T	NR	% Won (exc NR)
230	R.T.Ponting	Australia/ICC	165	51	2	12	75.68
218	S.P.Fleming	New Zealand	98	106	1	13	47.80
193	A.Ranatunga	Sri Lanka	89	95	1	8	48.10
178	A.R.Border	Australia	107	67	1	3	61.14
174	M.Azharuddin	India	90	76	2	6	53.57
159	M.S.Dhoni	India	88	57	4	10	59.06
150	G.C.Smith	South Africa/Africa	92	51	1	6	63.88
147	S.C.Ganguly	India/Asia	76	66	–	5	53.52
139	Imran Khan	Pakistan	75	59	1	4	55.55
138	W.J.Cronje	South Africa	99	35	1	3	73.33
129	D.P.M.D.Jayawardena	Sri Lanka	71	49	1	8	58.67
125	B.C.Lara	West Indies	59	59	–	7	50.42
118	S.T.Jayasuriya	Sri Lanka	66	47	2	3	57.39
109	Wasim Akram	Pakistan	66	41	2	–	60.55
106	S.R.Waugh	Australia	67	35	3	1	63.80
105	I.V.A.Richards	West Indies	67	36	–	2	65.04

The most for England is 62 by A.J.Strauss, for Zimbabwe 86 by A.D.R.Campbell, and for Bangladesh 69 by Habibul Bashar.

100 LOI UMPIRING APPEARANCES

209	R.E.Koertzen	South Africa	09.12.1992	to	09.06.2010
189	B.F.Bowden	New Zealand	23.03.1995	to	06.03.2014
181	S.A.Bucknor	West Indies	18.03.1989	to	29.03.2009
174	D.J.Harper	Australia	14.01.1994	to	19.03.2011
174	S.J.A.Taufel	Australia	13.01.1999	to	02.09.2012
172	D.R.Shepherd	England	09.06.1983	to	12.07.2005
159	Alim Dar	Pakistan	16.02.2000	to	16.09.2013
139	D.B.Hair	Australia	14.12.1991	to	24.08.2008
130	R.B.Tiffin	Zimbabwe	25.10.1992	to	27.08.2013
122	S.J.Davis	Australia	12.12.1992	to	08.11.2013
122	E.A.R.de Silva	Sri Lanka	22.08.1999	to	13.06.2012
112	B.R.Doctrove	West Indies	04.04.1998	to	20.01.2012
107	D.L.Orchard	South Africa	02.12.1994	to	07.12.2003
100	R.S.Dunne	New Zealand	06.02.1989	to	26.02.2002

INTERNATIONAL TWENTY20 RECORDS

MATCH RESULTS
2004-05 to 8 March 2014

Opponents		Matches	Won											Tied	NR
			E	A	SA	WI	NZ	I	P	SL	Z	B	Ass		
England	Australia	12	4	7	–	–	–	–	–	–	–	–	–	–	1
	South Africa	8	3	–	4	–	–	–	–	–	–	–	–	–	1
	West Indies	9	3	–	–	6	–	–	–	–	–	–	–	–	–
	New Zealand	11	7	–	–	–	3	–	–	–	–	–	–	–	1
	India	7	4	–	–	–	–	3	–	–	–	–	–	–	–
	Pakistan	10	7	–	–	–	–	–	3	–	–	–	–	–	–
	Sri Lanka	4	1	–	–	–	–	–	–	3	–	–	–	–	–
	Zimbabwe	1	1	–	–	–	–	–	–	–	0	–	–	–	–
	Bangladesh	0	0	–	–	–	–	–	–	–	–	0	–	–	–
	Associates	3	1	–	–	–	–	–	–	–	–	–	1	–	1
Australia	South Africa	9	–	5	4	–	–	–	–	–	–	–	–	–	–
	West Indies	10	–	5	–	5	–	–	–	–	–	–	–	–	–
	New Zealand	5	–	4	–	–	0	–	–	–	–	–	–	1	–
	India	8	–	4	–	–	–	4	–	–	–	–	–	–	–
	Pakistan	11	–	4	–	–	–	–	6	–	–	–	–	1	–
	Sri Lanka	8	–	2	–	–	–	–	–	6	–	–	–	–	–
	Zimbabwe	1	–	0	–	–	–	–	–	–	1	–	–	–	–
	Bangladesh	2	–	2	–	–	–	–	–	–	–	0	–	–	–
	Associates	1	–	1	–	–	–	–	–	–	–	–	0	–	–
S Africa	West Indies	6	–	–	5	1	–	–	–	–	–	–	–	–	–
	New Zealand	11	–	–	8	–	3	–	–	–	–	–	–	–	–
	India	7	–	–	2	–	–	5	–	–	–	–	–	–	–
	Pakistan	11	–	–	6	–	–	–	5	–	–	–	–	–	–
	Sri Lanka	4	–	–	3	–	–	–	–	1	–	–	–	–	–
	Zimbabwe	3	–	–	3	–	–	–	–	–	0	–	–	–	–
	Bangladesh	2	–	–	2	–	–	–	–	–	–	0	–	–	–
	Associates	2	–	–	2	–	–	–	–	–	–	–	0	–	–
W Indies	New Zealand	8	–	–	–	2	3	–	–	–	–	–	–	3	–
	India	3	–	–	–	2	–	1	–	–	–	–	–	–	–
	Pakistan	3	–	–	–	1	–	–	2	–	–	–	–	–	–
	Sri Lanka	5	–	–	–	1	–	–	–	4	–	–	–	–	–
	Zimbabwe	3	–	–	–	2	–	–	–	–	1	–	–	–	–
	Bangladesh	4	–	–	–	2	–	–	–	–	–	2	–	–	–
	Associates	2	–	–	–	1	–	–	–	–	–	–	–	–	1
N Zealand	India	4	–	–	–	–	4	0	–	–	–	–	–	–	–
	Pakistan	9	–	–	–	–	3	–	6	–	–	–	–	–	–
	Sri Lanka	12	–	–	–	–	5	–	–	5	–	–	–	1	1
	Zimbabwe	5	–	–	–	–	5	–	–	–	0	–	–	–	–
	Bangladesh	3	–	–	–	–	3	–	–	–	–	0	–	–	–
	Associates	3	–	–	–	–	3	–	–	–	–	–	0	–	–
India	Pakistan	5	–	–	–	–	–	3	1	–	–	–	–	1	–
	Sri Lanka	5	–	–	–	–	–	3	–	2	–	–	–	–	–
	Zimbabwe	2	–	–	–	–	–	2	–	–	0	–	–	–	–
	Bangladesh	1	–	–	–	–	–	1	–	–	–	0	–	–	–
	Associates	4	–	–	–	–	–	3	–	–	–	–	0	–	1
Pakistan	Sri Lanka	12	–	–	–	–	–	–	7	5	–	–	–	–	–
	Zimbabwe	5	–	–	–	–	–	–	5	–	0	–	–	–	–
	Bangladesh	6	–	–	–	–	–	–	6	–	–	0	–	–	–
	Associates	6	–	–	–	–	–	–	6	–	–	–	0	–	–
Sri Lanka	Zimbabwe	3	–	–	–	–	–	–	–	3	0	–	–	–	–
	Bangladesh	4	–	–	–	–	–	–	–	4	–	0	–	–	–
	Associates	3	–	–	–	–	–	–	–	3	–	–	0	–	–
Zimbabwe	Bangladesh	3	–	–	–	–	–	–	–	–	1	2	–	–	–
	Associates	2	–	–	–	–	–	–	–	–	1	–	0	1	–
Bangladesh	Associates	8	–	–	–	–	–	–	–	–	–	5	3	–	–
Associates	Associates	59	–	–	–	–	–	–	–	–	–	–	58	–	1
		360	31	34	39	24	32	25	47	36	4	9	63	8	8

MATCH RESULTS SUMMARY

	Matches	Won	Lost	Tied	NR	Win %
South Africa	63	39	23	0	1	62.90
Sri Lanka	60	36	22	1	1	61.01
Pakistan	78	47	29	2	0	60.25
Ireland	34	18	13	0	3	58.06
Netherlands	22	12	9	0	1	57.14
India	46	25	19	1	1	55.55
Australia	67	34	30	2	1	51.51
England	65	31	30	0	4	50.81
Afghanistan	22	11	11	0	0	50.00
New Zealand	71	32	32	5	2	46.37
West Indies	55	24	27	3	1	44.44
Kenya	29	10	19	0	0	34.48
Scotland	25	8	16	0	1	33.33
Bangladesh	33	9	24	0	0	27.27
Canada	19	4	14	1	0	21.05
Zimbabwe	28	4	23	1	0	14.28
Bermuda	3	0	3	0	0	0.00

INTERNATIONAL TWENTY20 RECORDS

(To 8 March 2014)

TEAM RECORDS

HIGHEST INNINGS TOTALS

† Batting Second

260-6	Sri Lanka v Kenya	Johannesburg	2007-08
248-6	Australia v England	Southampton	2013
241-6	South Africa v England	Centurion	2009-10
225-7	Ireland v Afghanistan	Abu Dhabi	2013-14
221-5	Australia v England	Sydney	2006-07
219-4	South Africa v India	Johannesburg	2011-12
218-4	India v England	Durban	2007-08
215-5	Sri Lanka v India	Nagpur	2009-10
214-5	Australia v New Zealand	Auckland	2004-05
214-6	New Zealand v Australia	Christchurch	2009-10
214-4†	Australia v New Zealand	Christchurch	2009-10
214-7	England v New Zealand	Auckland	2012-13
213-4	Australia v England	Hobart	2013-14
211-5	South Africa v Scotland	The Oval	2009
211-4†	India v Sri Lanka	Mohali	2009-10
211-3	Sri Lanka v Pakistan	Dubai	2013-14
209-3	Australia v South Africa	Brisbane	2005-06
209-2	West Indies v New Zealand	Lauderhill	2012
209-6†	England v Australia	Southampton	2013
208-8	West Indies v England	The Oval	2007
208-2†	South Africa v West Indies	Johannesburg	2007-08
206-7	Sri Lanka v India	Mohali	2009-10
205-6	West Indies v South Africa	Johannesburg	2007-08
205-4	West Indies v Australia	Colombo (RPS)	2012-13
204-5	New Zealand v Bangladesh	Dhaka	2013-14
203-5	Pakistan v Bangladesh	Karachi	2007-08

The highest total for Zimbabwe is 200-2 (v New Zealand, Hamilton, 2011-12) and for Bangladesh is 190-5 (v Ireland, Belfast, 2012).

LOWEST COMPLETED INNINGS TOTALS

† Batting Second

56† (18.4)	Kenya v Afghanistan	Sharjah	2013-14
67 (17.2)	Kenya v Ireland	Belfast	2008
68† (16.4)	Ireland v West Indies	Providence	2009-10
70	Bermuda v Canada	Belfast	2008
71 (19.0)	Kenya v Ireland	Dubai	2011-12
73 (16.5)	Kenya v New Zealand	Durban	2007-08
74 (17.3)	India v Australia	Melbourne	2007-08
74† (19.1)	Pakistan v Australia	Dubai	2012
75† (19.2)	Canada v Zimbabwe	King City (NW)	2008-09
78 (17.3)	Bangladesh v New Zealand	Hamilton	2009-10
78† (18.5)	Kenya v Scotland	Aberdeen	2013
79† (14.3)	Australia v England	Southampton	2005
79-7†	West Indies v Zimbabwe	Port-of-Spain	2009-10
80† (16.0)	Afghanistan v South Africa	Bridgetown	2009-10
80† (15.5)	New Zealand v Pakistan	Christchurch	2010-11
80† (17.2)	Afghanistan v England	Colombo (RPS)	2012-13
80† (14.4)	England v India	Colombo (RPS)	2012-13
81† (15.4)	Scotland v South Africa	The Oval	2009
81 (17.3)	New Zealand v Sri Lanka	Lauderhill	2010
83† (15.5)	Bangladesh v Sri Lanka	Johannesburg	2007-08
84 (15.1)	Zimbabwe v New Zealand	Providence	2009-10
85-9†	Bangladesh v Pakistan	Dhaka	2011-12
85-8†	Ireland v West Indies	Kingston	2013-14
86† (15.3)	Netherlands v Ireland	Dubai	2009-10
86 (18.2)	New Zealand v South Africa	Durban	2012-13
87† (16.2)	Sri Lanka v Australia	Bridgetown	2009-10

The lowest total for South Africa is 100 (v Pakistan, Centurion, 2012-13).

BATTING RECORDS

800 RUNS IN A CAREER

Runs			M	I	NO	HS	Avge	50	R/100B
1959	B.B.McCullum	NZ	64	63	9	123	36.27	14	135.5
1335	D.P.M.D.Jayawardena	SL	49	49	7	100	31.78	9	134.1
1320	T.M.Dilshan	SL	55	54	9	104*	29.33	9	120.8
1311	K.C.Sangakkara	SL	50	48	8	78	32.77	7	120.8
1260	D.A.Warner	A	46	46	2	90*	28.63	10	138.0
1250	Mohammad Hafeez	P	54	52	3	86	25.51	7	118.4
1194	M.J.Guptill	NZ	43	41	6	101*	34.11	6	124.5
1176	K.P.Pietersen	E	37	36	5	79	37.93	7	141.5
1142	J.P.Duminy	SA	48	44	12	96*	35.68	6	122.9
1093	Umar Akmal	P	52	49	9	64	27.32	5	120.2
1044	Shahid Afridi	P	70	65	10	54*	18.98	4	143.0
1030	S.R.Watson	A	39	38	3	81	29.42	10	149.9
1017	C.H.Gayle	WI	35	34	3	117	32.80	11	142.0
982	G.C.Smith	SA	33	33	2	89*	31.67	5	127.5
980	L.R.P.L.Taylor	NZ	55	50	9	63	23.90	4	118.6
942	E.J.G.Morgan	E	41	40	10	85*	31.40	4	132.6
932	G.Gambhir	I	37	36	2	75	27.41	7	119.0
907	Shoaib Malik	P	55	51	12	57*	23.25	3	106.8
886	C.L.White	A	41	38	11	85*	32.81	5	134.6
868	Yuvraj Singh	I	34	32	6	77*	33.38	7	153.0
867	A.B.de Villiers	SA	51	48	8	79*	21.67	4	121.2
859	S.K.Raina	I	37	33	7	101	33.03	4	136.3
849	Kamran Akmal	P	50	45	6	73	21.76	5	123.2

HIGHEST INDIVIDUAL INNINGS

Score	Balls				
156	63	A.J.Finch	A v E	Southampton	2013
123	58	B.B.McCullum	NZ v B	Pallekele	2012-13
117*	51	R.E.Levi	SA v NZ	Hamilton	2011-12
117	57	C.H.Gayle	WI v SA	Johannesburg	2007-08
116*	56	B.B.McCullum	NZ v A	Christchurch	2009-10
104*	57	T.M.Dilshan	SL v A	Pallekele	2011
101*	69	M.J.Guptill	NZ v SA	East London	2012-13
101	60	S.K.Raina	I v SA	Gros Islet	2009-10
100	64	D.P.M.D.Jayawardena	SL v Z	Providence	2009-10
100	58	R.D.Berrington	Sc v B	The Hague	2012
99*	55	L.J.Wright	E v Af	Colombo (RPS)	2012-13
99	68	A.D.Hales	E v WI	Nottingham	2012
98*	55	R.T.Ponting	A v NZ	Auckland	2004-05
98*	56	D.P.M.D.Jayawardena	SL v WI	Bridgetown	2009-10
98*	64	Ahmed Shehzad	P v Z	Harare	2013
98	66	C.H.Gayle	WI v I	Bridgetown	2009-10
96*	57	T.M.Dilshan	SL v WI	The Oval	2009
96*	54	J.P.Duminy	SA v Z	Kimberley	2010-11
96	56	D.R.Martyn	A v SA	Brisbane	2005-06
94	45	L.E.Bosman	SA v E	Centurion	2009-10
94	61	A.D.Hales	E v A	Chester-le-Street	2013
91*	54	M.J.Guptill	NZ v Z	Auckland	2011-12
91	55	B.B.McCullum	NZ v I	Chennai	2012
90*	55	H.H.Gibbs	SA v WI	Johannesburg	2007-08
90*	62	D.A.Warner	A v SL	Sydney	2012-13
90*	49	J.E.Root	E v A	Southampton	2013
89*	58	G.C.Smith	SA v A	Johannesburg	2005-06
89*	56	J.M.Kemp	SA v NZ	Durban	2007-08
89	43	D.A.Warner	A v SA	Melbourne	2008-09
89	55	M.R.Swart	Ne v K	Windhoek	2013
89	52	A.J.Finch	A v I	Rajkot	2013-14
88*	44	D.J.Hussey	A v SA	Johannesburg	2008-09
88*	61	H.Patel	C v Ire	Colombo (SSC)	2009-10
88*	61	Tamim Iqbal	B v WI	Dhaka	2012-13
88	44	S.T.Jayasuriya	SL v K	Johannesburg	2007-08
88	50	C.H.Gayle	WI v A	The Oval	2009
88	44	G.C.Smith	SA v E	Centurion	2009-10

The highest score for Zimbabwe is 79 by H.Masakadza (v Can, King City, 2008-09).

HIGHEST PARTNERSHIP FOR EACH WICKET

1st	170	G.C.Smith/L.E.Bosman	SA v E	Centurion	2009-10
2nd	166	D.P.M.D.Jayawardena/K.C.Sangakkara	SL v WI	Bridgetown	2009-10
3rd	137	M.J.Guptill/K.S.Williamson	NZ v Z	Auckland	2011-12
4th	112*	K.P.Pietersen/E.J.G.Morgan	E v P	Dubai	2009-10
5th	119*	Shoaib Malik/Misbah-ul-Haq	P v A	Johannesburg	2007-08
6th	101*	C.L.White/M.E.K.Hussey	A v SL	Bridgetown	2009-10
7th	91	P.D.Collingwood/M.H.Yardy	E v WI	The Oval	2007
8th	64*	W.D.Parnell/J.Theron	SA v A	Johannesburg	2011-12
9th	63	Sohail Tanvir/Saeed Ajmal	P v SL	Dubai	2013-14
10th	31*	Wahab Riaz/Shoaib Akhtar	P v NZ	Auckland	2010-11

BOWLING RECORDS
35 WICKETS IN A CAREER

Wkts			Matches	Overs	Mdns	Runs	Avge	Best	R/Over
81	Saeed Ajmal	P	59	220.0	2	1379	17.02	4-19	6.26
74	Umar Gul	P	52	175.0	2	1217	16.44	5- 6	6.95
73	Shahid Afridi	P	70	253.2	3	1643	22.50	4-11	6.48
62	B.A.W.Mendis	SL	36	137.0	5	844	13.61	6- 8	6.16
61	S.C.J.Broad	E	51	181.3	2	1363	22.34	4-24	7.50
60	S.L.Malinga	SL	50	175.5	–	1297	21.61	5-31	7.37
51	G.P.Swann	E	39	135.0	4	859	16.84	3-13	6.36
48	N.L.McCullum	NZ	51	145.1	–	995	20.72	4-16	6.85
46	D.W.Steyn	SA	33	117.0	2	726	15.78	4- 9	6.20
44	Mohammad Hafeez	P	54	152.2	1	1008	22.90	4-10	6.61
43	M.Morkel	SA	36	127.4	3	904	21.02	4-17	7.08
40	D.J.G.Sammy	WI	44	123.4	–	842	21.05	5-26	6.80
39	Abdul Razzaq	P	28	106.0	3	739	18.94	4-16	6.97
39	T.G.Southee	NZ	33	117.0	2	991	25.41	5-18	8.47
38	M.G.Johnson	A	30	109.2	2	797	20.97	3-15	7.28
37	D.L.Vettori	NZ	33	128.1	1	720	19.45	4-20	5.61
37	J.Botha	SA	40	129.0	1	823	22.24	3-16	6.37
37	K.M.D.N.Kulasekara	SL	34	120.2	2	880	23.78	3- 4	7.31
36	Shakib Al Hasan	B	28	103.0	1	689	19.13	4-21	6.68
36	S.R.Watson	A	39	109.0	1	810	22.50	4-15	7.43
36	K.D.Mills	NZ	37	130.4	1	1087	30.19	3-33	8.31

BEST FIGURES IN AN INNINGS

6- 8	B.A.W.Mendis	SL v Z	Hambantota	2012-13
6-16	B.A.W.Mendis	SL v A	Pallekele	2011
5- 6	Umar Gul	P v NZ	The Oval	2009
5- 6	Umar Gul	P v SA	Centurion	2012-13
5-13	Elias Sunny	B v Ire	Belfast	2012
5-13	Samiullah Shenwari	Af v K	Sharjah	2013-14
5-18	T.G.Southee	NZ v P	Auckland	2010-11
5-19	R.McLaren	SA v WI	North Sound	2009-10
5-20	N.Odhiambo	K v Sc	Nairobi (Gym)	2009-10
5-26	D.J.G.Sammy	WI v Z	Port-of-Spain	2009-10
5-31	S.L.Malinga	SL v E	Pallekele	2012-13
4- 2	S.O.Tikolo	K v Sc	Dubai	2013-14
4- 6	S.J.Benn	WI v Z	Port-of-Spain	2009-10
4- 7	M.R.Gillespie	NZ v K	Durban	2007-08
4- 8	Umar Gul	P v A	Dubai	2009
4- 9	D.W.Steyn	SA v WI	Port Elizabeth	2007-08
4-10	Mohammad Hafeez	P v Z	Harare	2011
4-10	R.S.Bopara	E v WI	The Oval	2011

HAT-TRICKS

B.Lee	Australia v Bangladesh	Melbourne	2007-08
J.D.P.Oram	New Zealand v Sri Lanka	Colombo (RPS)	2009
T.G.Southee	New Zealand v Pakistan	Auckland	2010-11

WICKET-KEEPING RECORDS
20 DISMISSALS IN A CAREER

Dis			Matches	Ct	St
54	Kamran Akmal	Pakistan	50	24	30
42	K.C.Sangakkara	Sri Lanka	50	23	19
36	D.Ramdin	West Indies	38	28	8

Dis			Matches	Ct	St
32†	B.B.McCullum	New Zealand	64	24	8
30	M.S.Dhoni	India	43	22	8
28	Mushfiqur Rahim	Bangladesh	30	12	16
26†	A.B.de Villiers	South Africa	51	20	6
20	C.Kieswetter	England	25	17	3

† *Excluding catches taken in the field.*

MOST DISMISSALS IN AN INNINGS

4 (4 ct)	A.C.Gilchrist	Australia v Zimbabwe	Cape Town	2007-08
4 (4 ct)	M.J.Prior	England v South Africa	Cape Town	2007-08
4 (4 ct)	A.C.Gilchrist	Australia v New Zealand	Perth	2007-08
4 (4 st)	Kamran Akmal	Pakistan v Netherlands	Lord's	2009
4 (3 ct, 1 st)	N.J.O'Brien	Ireland v Sri Lanka	Lord's	2009
4 (4 ct)	M.S.Dhoni	India v Afghanistan	Gros Islet	2009-10
4 (2 ct, 2 st)	A.B.de Villiers	South Africa v West Indies	North Sound	2009-10
4 (3 ct, 1 st)	G.C.Wilson	Ireland v Kenya	Dubai	2011-12
4 (4 ct)	A.B.de Villiers	South Africa v Zimbabwe	Hambantota	2012-13
4 (4 ct)	M.S.Dhoni	India v Pakistan	Colombo (RPS)	2012-13
4 (2 ct, 2 st)	Q.de Kock	South Africa v Pakistan	Dubai	2013-14
4 (4 ct)	W.Barresi	Netherlands v Kenya	Dubai	2013-14

FIELDING RECORDS

20 CATCHES IN A CAREER

Total			Matches	Total			Matches
36	L.R.P.L.Taylor	New Zealand	55	21	C.L.White	Australia	41
27	D.A.Warner	Australia	46	21	J.P.Duminy	South Africa	48
27	A.B.de Villiers	South Africa	51	21	S.C.J.Broad	England	51
25	Shoaib Malik	Pakistan	55	20	J.M.Bairstow	England	18
24	D.J.Hussey	Australia	39	20	M.E.K.Hussey	Australia	38
23	Umar Akmal	Pakistan	52	20	E.J.G.Morgan	England	41
22	M.J.Guptill	New Zealand	43	20	Shahid Afridi	Pakistan	70
22	T.M.Dilshan	Sri Lanka	55				

MOST CATCHES IN AN INNINGS

4	D.J.G.Sammy	West Indies v Ireland	Providence	2009-10
4	P.W.Borren	Netherlands v Bangladesh	The Hague	2012
4	C.J.Anderson	New Zealand v South Africa	Port Elizabeth	2012-13
4	L.D.Chandimal	Sri Lanka v Bangladesh	Chittagong	2013-14

APPEARANCE RECORDS

50 APPEARANCES

70	Shahid Afridi	Pakistan	52	Umar Gul	Pakistan
64	B.B.McCullum	New Zealand	51	S.C.J.Broad	England
59	Saeed Ajmal	Pakistan	51	A.B.de Villiers	South Africa
55	T.M.Dilshan	Sri Lanka	51	N.L.McCullum	New Zealand
55	Shoaib Malik	Pakistan	50	Kamran Akmal	Pakistan
55	L.R.P.L.Taylor	New Zealand	50	S.L.Malinga	Sri Lanka
54	Mohammad Hafeez	Pakistan	50	K.C.Sangakkara	Sri Lanka
52	Umar Akmal	Pakistan			

UNIVERSITY MATCH RESULTS

Played: 168. Wins: Cambridge 58; Oxford 55. Drawn: 55. Abandoned: 1

In 2001, for the very first time, Cambridge hosted the University Match, cricket's oldest surviving first-class fixture, after the ECB's re-organisation of university cricket around six centres of excellence had removed it from Lord's. Dating from 1827 it has, wartime interruptions apart, been played annually since 1838. With the exception of five matches played in the area of Oxford (1829, 1843, 1846, 1848 and 1850), all the previous fixtures had been staged at Lord's. Since 2001 it has been played over four days rather than three.

In 2003, Oxford (with Brookes), Cambridge (with Anglia) and Durham were joined by Loughborough in playing three first-class matches against counties. In 2012, two other centres – Cardiff (with UWIC and Glamorgan), and Leeds (with Bradford and Leeds Metropolitan) – were also granted first-class status. All six university sides now play two games each against the counties.

1827	Drawn	1878	Cambridge	1925	Drawn	1974	Drawn
1829	Oxford	1879	Cambridge	1926	Cambridge	1975	Drawn
1836	Oxford	1880	Cambridge	1927	Cambridge	1976	Oxford
1838	Oxford	1881	Oxford	1928	Drawn	1977	Drawn
1839	Cambridge	1882	Cambridge	1929	Drawn	1978	Drawn
1840	Cambridge	1883	Cambridge	1930	Cambridge	1979	Cambridge
1841	Cambridge	1884	Oxford	1931	Oxford	1980	Drawn
1842	Cambridge	1885	Cambridge	1932	Drawn	1981	Drawn
1843	Cambridge	1886	Oxford	1933	Drawn	1982	Cambridge
1844	Drawn	1887	Oxford	1934	Drawn	1983	Drawn
1845	Cambridge	1888	Drawn	1935	Cambridge	1984	Oxford
1846	Oxford	1889	Cambridge	1936	Cambridge	1985	Drawn
1847	Cambridge	1890	Cambridge	1937	Oxford	1986	Cambridge
1848	Oxford	1891	Cambridge	1938	Drawn	1987	Drawn
1849	Cambridge	1892	Oxford	1939	Oxford	1988	Abandoned
1850	Oxford	1893	Cambridge	1946	Oxford	1989	Drawn
1851	Cambridge	1894	Oxford	1947	Drawn	1990	Drawn
1852	Oxford	1895	Cambridge	1948	Oxford	1991	Drawn
1853	Oxford	1896	Oxford	1949	Cambridge	1992	Cambridge
1854	Oxford	1897	Cambridge	1950	Drawn	1993	Oxford
1855	Oxford	1898	Oxford	1951	Oxford	1994	Drawn
1856	Cambridge	1899	Drawn	1952	Drawn	1995	Oxford
1857	Oxford	1900	Drawn	1953	Cambridge	1996	Drawn
1858	Oxford	1901	Drawn	1954	Drawn	1997	Drawn
1859	Cambridge	1902	Cambridge	1955	Drawn	1998	Cambridge
1860	Cambridge	1903	Oxford	1956	Drawn	1999	Drawn
1861	Cambridge	1904	Drawn	1957	Cambridge	2000	Drawn
1862	Cambridge	1905	Cambridge	1958	Cambridge	2001	Oxford
1863	Oxford	1906	Cambridge	1959	Oxford	2002	Drawn
1864	Oxford	1907	Cambridge	1960	Drawn	2003	Oxford
1865	Oxford	1908	Oxford	1961	Drawn	2004	Oxford
1866	Oxford	1909	Drawn	1962	Drawn	2005	Oxford
1867	Cambridge	1910	Oxford	1963	Drawn	2006	Oxford
1868	Cambridge	1911	Oxford	1964	Drawn	2007	Drawn
1869	Cambridge	1912	Cambridge	1965	Drawn	2008	Drawn
1870	Cambridge	1913	Cambridge	1966	Oxford	2009	Cambridge
1871	Oxford	1914	Oxford	1967	Drawn	2010	Oxford
1872	Cambridge	1919	Oxford	1968	Drawn	2011	Cambridge
1873	Oxford	1920	Drawn	1969	Drawn	2012	Drawn
1874	Oxford	1921	Cambridge	1970	Drawn	2013	Oxford
1875	Oxford	1922	Cambridge	1971	Drawn		
1876	Cambridge	1923	Oxford	1972	Cambridge		
1877	Oxford	1924	Cambridge	1973	Drawn		

CAMBRIDGE UNIVERSITY RECORDS
ALL FIRST-CLASS MATCHES

Highest Total	For 703-9d		v	Sussex	Hove	1890
	V 730-3		by	W Indians	Cambridge	1950
Lowest Total	For 30		v	Yorkshire	Cambridge	1928
	V 32		by	Oxford U	Lord's	1878
Highest Innings	For 254*	K.S.Duleepsinhji	v	Middlesex	Cambridge	1927
	V 313*	S.S.Agarwal	for	Oxford U	Cambridge	2013
Highest Partnership						
(2nd wicket)	429*	J.G.Dewes/G.H.G.Doggart	v	Essex	Cambridge	1949
Best Innings Bowling	10-69	S.M.J.Woods	v	Thornton's XI	Cambridge	1890
Best Match Bowling	15-88	S.M.J.Woods	v	Thornton's XI	Cambridge	1890
Most Runs – Season	1581	D.S.Sheppard		(av 79.05)		1952
Most Runs – Career	4310	J.M.Brearley		(av 38.48)		1961-68
Most 100s – Season	7	D.S.Sheppard				1952
Most 100s – Career	14	D.S.Sheppard				1950-52
Most Wkts – Season	80	O.S.Wheatley		(av 17.63)		1958
Most Wkts – Career	208	G.Goonesena		(av 21.82)		1954-57

UNIVERSITY MATCH RECORDS

Highest Total	604		Oxford	2002
Lowest Total	39		Lord's	1858
Highest Innings	211	G.Goonesena	Lord's	1957
Best Innings Bowling	8-44	G.E.Jeffery	Lord's	1873
Best Match Bowling	13-73	A.G.Steel	Lord's	1878

Hat-Tricks: F.C.Cobden (1870), A.G.Steel (1879), P.H.Morton (1880), J.F.Ireland (1911), R.G.H.Lowe (1926).

OXFORD UNIVERSITY RECORDS
ALL FIRST-CLASS MATCHES

Highest Total	For 651		v	Sussex	Hove	1895
	V 679-7d		by	Australians	Oxford	1938
Lowest Total	For 12		v	MCC	Oxford	1877
	V 24		by	MCC	Oxford	1846
Highest Innings	For 313*	S.S.Agarwal	v	Cambridge U	Cambridge	2013
	V 338	W.W.Read	for	Surrey	The Oval	1888
Highest Partnership						
(3rd wicket)	408	S.Oberoi/D.R.Fox	v	Cambridge U	Cambridge	2005
Best Innings Bowling	10-38	S.E.Butler	v	Cambridge U	Lord's	1871
Best Match Bowling	15-65	B.J.T.Bosanquet	v	Sussex	Oxford	1900
Most Runs – Season	1307	Nawab of Pataudi sr		(av 93.35)		1931
Most Runs – Career	3319	N.S.Mitchell-Innes		(av 47.41)		1934-37
Most 100s – Season	6	Nawab of Pataudi sr				1931
	6	M.P.Donnelly				1946
Most 100s – Career	9	A.M.Crawley				1927-30
	9	Nawab of Pataudi sr				1928-31
	9	N.S.Mitchell-Innes				1934-37
	9	M.P.Donnelly				1946-47
Most Wkts – Season	70	I.A.R.Peebles		(av 18.15)		1930
Most Wkts – Career	182	R.H.B.Bettington		(av 19.38)		1920-23

UNIVERSITY MATCH RECORDS

Highest Total	611-5d		Oxford	2010
Lowest Total	32		Lord's	1878
Highest Innings	313*	S.S.Agarwal	Cambridge	2013
Best Innings Bowling	10-38	S.E.Butler	Lord's	1871
Best Match Bowling	15-95	S.E.Butler	Lord's	1871

Match Doubles: P.R.le Couteur (160 and 11-66 in 1910); G.J.Toogood (149 and 10-93 in 1985)

INDIAN PREMIER LEAGUE 2013

The sixth IPL tournament was held in India between 3 April and 26 May.

Team	P	W	L	T	NR	Pts	Net RR
1 Chennai Super Kings (4)	16	11	5	–	–	22	+0.53
2 Mumbai Indians (3)	16	11	5	–	–	22	+0.44
3 Rajasthan Royals (7)	16	10	6	–	–	20	+0.32
4 Sunrisers Hyderabad (-)	16	10	6	–	–	20	+0.003
5 Royal Challengers Bangalore (5)	16	9	7	–	–	18	+0.45
6 Kings XI Punjab (6)	16	8	8	–	–	16	+0.22
7 Kolkata Knight Riders (2)	16	6	10	–	–	12	–0.09
8 Pune Warriors (9)	16	4	12	–	–	8	–1.00
9 Delhi Daredevils (1)	16	3	13	–	–	6	–0.84

1st Qualifying Match: At Feroz Shah Kotla, Delhi, 21 May (floodlit). Toss: Chennai Super Kings. **CHENNAI SUPER KINGS** won by 48 runs. Chennai Super Kings 192-1 (20; M.E.K.Hussey 86*, S.K.Raina 82*). Mumbai Indians 144 (18.4; D.R.Smith 68, D.J.Bravo 3-9, R.A.Jadeja 3-31). Award: M.E.K.Hussey.

Elimination Final: At Feroz Shah Kotla, Delhi, 22 May (floodlit). Toss: Sunrisers Hyderabad. **RAJASTHAN ROYALS** won by four wickets. Sunrisers Hyderabad 132-7 (20). Rajasthan Royals 135-6 (19.2; B.J.Hodge 54*). Award: B.J.Hodge.

2nd Qualifying Match: At Eden Gardens, Kolkata, 24 May (floodlit). Toss: Rajasthan Royals. **MUMBAI INDIANS** won by four wickets. Rajasthan Royals 165-6 (20; Harbhajan Singh 3-23). Mumbai Indians 169-6 (19.5; D.R.Smith 62). Award: Harbhajan Singh.

FINAL: At Eden Gardens, Kolkata, 26 May (floodlit). Toss: Mumbai Indians. **MUMBAI INDIANS** won by 23 runs. Mumbai Indians 148-9 (20; K.A.Pollard 60*, D.J.Bravo 4-42). Chennai Super Kings 125-9 (20; M.S.Dhoni 63*). Award: K.A.Pollard. Series award: S.R.Watson (Rajasthan Royals).

IPL winners:	2008	Rajasthan Royals	2009	Deccan Chargers
	2010	Chennai Super Kings	2011	Chennai Super Kings
	2012	Kolkata Knight Riders		

TEAM RECORDS
HIGHEST TOTALS

263-5 (20)	Bangalore v Pune	Bangalore	2013
246-5 (20)	Chennai v Rajasthan	Chennai	2010

LOWEST TOTALS

58 (15.1)	Rajasthan v Bangalore	Cape Town	2009
67 (15.2)	Kolkata v Mumbai	Mumbai	2008

LARGEST MARGINS OF VICTORY

140 runs	Kolkata (222-3) v Bangalore (82)	Bangalore	2008
10 wickets	Mumbai (154-7) v Deccan (155-0)	Mumbai	2008
10 wickets	Rajasthan (92) v Bangalore (93-0)	Bangalore	2010
10 wickets	Mumbai (133-5) v Rajasthan (134-0)	Mumbai	2011
10 wickets	Rajasthan (162-6) v Mumbai (163-0)	Jaipur	2012
10 wickets	Punjab (138) v Chennai (139-0)	Mohali	2013

Delhi beat Punjab by ten wickets in a reduced game in 2009.

BATTING RECORDS
700 RUNS IN A SEASON

Runs			Year	M	I	NO	HS	Ave	100	50	6s	4s	R/100B
733	C.H.Gayle	Bangalore	2012	15	14	2	128*	61.08	1	7	59	46	160.7
733	M.E.K.Hussey	Chennai	2013	17	17	3	95	52.35	–	6	17	81	129.5
708	C.H.Gayle	Bangalore	2013	16	16	4	175*	59.00	1	4	51	57	156.2

HIGHEST SCORES

Score	Balls				
175*	66	C.H.Gayle	Bangalore v Pune	Bangalore	2013
158*	73	B.B.McCullum	Kolkata v Bangalore	Bangalore	2008
128*	62	C.H.Gayle	Bangalore v Delhi	Delhi	2012
127	56	M.Vijay	Chennai v Rajasthan	Chennai	2010
120*	63	P.C.Valthaty	Punjab v Chennai	Mohali	2011

FASTEST HUNDRED

30 balls	C.H.Gayle (175*)	Bangalore v Pune	Bangalore	2013

MOST SIXES IN AN INNINGS

17	C.H.Gayle	Bangalore v Pune	Bangalore	2013

HIGHEST STRIKE RATE IN A SEASON (Qualification: 100 runs or more)

R/100B	Score	Balls			
204.34	188	92	B.B.McCullum	Kolkata	2008

HIGHEST STRIKE RATE IN AN INNINGS (Qualification: 25 runs, 300+ strike rate)

R/100B	Score	Balls			
400.0	28	7	J.A.Morkel	Chennai v Bangalore	Chennai	2012
387.5	31	8	A.B.de Villiers	Bangalore v Pune	Bangalore	2013
385.7	27*	7	B.Akhil	Bangalore v Deccan	Hyderabad	2008
346.1	45*	13	K.A.Pollard	Mumbai v Kochi	Mumbai (BS)	2010
340.0	34	10	L.J.Wright	Pune v Punjab	Mohali	2013
316.6	38	12	C.H.Gayle	Bangalore v Kolkata	Bangalore	2011
306.2	49	16	Yuvraj Singh	Punjab v Rajasthan	Mohali	2008

BOWLING RECORDS
25 WICKETS IN A SEASON

Wkts			Year	P	O	M	Runs	Avge	Best	4w	R/Over
32	D.J.Bravo	Chennai	2013	18	62.3	–	497	15.53	4-42	1	7.95
28	S.L.Malinga	Mumbai	2011	16	63.0	2	375	13.39	5-13	1	5.95
28	J.P.Faulkner	Rajasthan	2013	16	63.1	2	427	15.25	5-16	2	6.75
25	M.Morkel	Delhi	2012	16	63.0	1	453	18.12	4-20	1	7.19

BEST BOWLING FIGURES IN AN INNINGS

6-14	Sohail Tanvir	Rajasthan v Chennai	Jaipur	2008
5- 5	A.Kumble	Bangalore v Rajasthan	Cape Town	2009
5-12	I.Sharma	Deccan v Kochi	Kochi	2011
5-13	S.L.Malinga	Mumbai v Delhi	Delhi	2011

MOST ECONOMICAL BOWLING ANALYSIS

O	M	R	W				
4	1	6	0	F.H.Edwards	Deccan v Kolkata	Cape Town	2009
4	1	6	1	A.Nehra	Delhi v Punjab	Bloemfontein	2009

MOST EXPENSIVE BOWLING ANALYSIS

O	M	R	W				
4	0	66	0	I.Sharma	Hyderabad v Chennai	Hyderabad	2013
4	0	65	0	U.T.Yadav	Delhi v Bangalore	Delhi	2013
4	0	63	2	V.R.Aaron	Delhi v Chennai	Chennai	2012
4	0	63	0	A.B.Dinda	Pune v Mumbai	Mumbai	2013
4	0	62	0	M.G.Neser	Punjab v Bangalore	Mohali	2013
4	0	60	2	R.McLaren	Kolkata v Mumbai	Mumbai	2013

CHAMPIONS LEAGUE TWENTY20 2013

The fifth Champions League Twenty20 tournament took place in India between 17 September and 6 October. Twelve teams took part, having qualified from their domestic Twenty20 competitions: four from India's IPL, two each from Australia and South Africa, and one each from New Zealand, Pakistan, Sri Lanka and West Indies. Faisalabad Wolves and Kandurata Maroons were eliminated in a qualifying round.

GROUP A

	Team	P	W	L	T	NR	Pts	Net RR
1	Rajasthan Royals	4	4	–	–		16	+0.96
2	Mumbai Indians	4	2	1	–	1	10	+1.06
3	Otago	4	2	1	–	1	10	+0.86
4	Lions	4	–	3	–	1	2	–0.72
5	Perth Scorchers	4	–	3	–	1	2	–2.85

GROUP B

	Team	P	W	L	T	NR	Pts	Net RR
1	Trinidad & Tobago	4	3	1	–	–	12	+0.81
2	Chennai Super Kings	4	3	1	–	–	12	+0.27
3	Titans	4	2	2	–	–	8	+0.22
4	Sunrisers Hyderabad	4	1	2	–	1	6	–0.62
5	Brisbane Heat	4	–	3	–	1	2	–1.02

1st Semi-Final: At Sawai Mansingh Stadium, Jaipur, 4 October (floodlit). Toss: Chennai Super Kings. **RAJASTHAN ROYALS** won by 14 runs. Rajasthan Royals 159-8 (20; A.M.Rahane 70, D.J.Bravo 3-26). Chennai Super Kings 145-8 (20; P.V.Tambe 3-10). Award: P.V.Tambe.

2nd Semi-Final: At Feroz Shah Kotla, Delhi, 5 October (floodlit). Toss: Mumbai Indians. **MUMBAI INDIANS** won by four wickets. Trinidad & Tobago 153-5 (20; E.Lewis 62). Mumbai Indians 157-4 (19.1; D.R.Smith 59, S.P.Narine 3-17). Award: D.R.Smith.

FINAL: At Feroz Shah Kotla, Delhi, 6 October (floodlit). Toss: Rajasthan Royals. **MUMBAI INDIANS** won by 33 runs. Mumbai Indians 202-6 (20). Rajasthan Royals 169 (18.5; A.M.Rahane 65, S.V.Samson 60, Harbhajan Singh 4-32, K.A.Pollard 3-31). Award: Harbhajan Singh. Series award: D.R.Smith.

Champions League Winners:	2009	New South Wales	2010	Chennai Super Kings
	2011	Mumbai Indians	2012	Sydney Sixers

TOURNAMENT RECORDS 2009-13

Highest total	242-4		Otago v Perth Scorchers	Jaipur	2013
Lowest total	70		Central Districts v Wayamba	Port Elizabeth	2010
Largest victory	99 runs		KKR (188-5) v Titans (89)	Cape Town	2012
	10 wkts		Sydney (124-0) v Lions (121)	Johannesburg	2012
Highest score	135*	D.A.Warner	New South Wales v Chennai	Chennai	2011
Most runs overall	608	S.K.Raina (ave 33.77)		Chennai	2010-13
Most runs in season	328	D.A.Warner (ave 109.33)	New South Wales		2011
Highest partnership	147	D.J.Jacobs/A.G.Prince	Warriors v CD	Port Elizabeth	2010
Best bowling	5-24	Azhar Mahmood	Auckland v Hampshire	Centurion	2012
Most wickets overall	28	D.J.Bravo (ave 18.28)	Chennai, Mumbai	T&T	2009-13
Most wickets in season	14	M.A.Starc (ave 12.35)	Sydney Sixers		2012
Most economical	4-1-6-2	K.D.Mills	Auckland v Sialkot	Johannesburg	2012
Most expensive	4-0-69-0	S.Aravind	Bangalore v S. Australia	Bangalore	2011
Most catches in field	4	O.A.Shah	Cape Cobras v Mumbai	Bangalore	2011

WOMEN'S LIMITED-OVERS RECORDS

1973 to 1 March 2014

RESULTS SUMMARY

	Matches	Won	Lost	Tied	NR	% Won (exc NR)
Australia	271	208	56	1	6	78.49
England	287	163	112	2	10	58.84
India	209	109	95	1	4	53.17
New Zealand	274	136	130	2	6	50.74
South Africa	115	54	54	1	6	49.54
West Indies	122	58	59	1	4	49.15
Sri Lanka	110	49	57	–	4	46.22
Trinidad & Tobago	6	2	4	–	–	33.33
Ireland	130	38	87	–	5	30.40
Pakistan	106	31	73	–	2	29.80
Jamaica	5	1	4	–	–	20.00
Netherlands	101	19	81	–	1	19.00
Denmark	33	6	27	–	–	18.18
International XI	18	3	14	–	1	17.64
Young England	6	1	5	–	–	16.66
Bangladesh	14	2	11	–	1	15.38
Scotland	8	1	7	–	–	12.50
Japan	5	–	5	–	–	0.00

TEAM RECORDS
HIGHEST INNINGS TOTALS

455-5 (50 overs)	New Zealand v Pakistan	Christchurch	1996-97
412-3 (50 overs)	Australia v Denmark	Mumbai	1997-98
397-4 (50 overs)	Australia v Pakistan	Melbourne	1996-97
376-2 (50 overs)	England v Pakistan	Vijayawada	1997-98

HIGHEST MATCH AGGREGATES

577-12 (96.4 overs)	Australia v New Zealand	Sydney	2012-13
570-14 (98 overs)	New Zealand v Australia	Hamilton	2008-09
563-16 (98.2 overs)	England v New Zealand	Chennai	2006-07

LARGEST RUNS MARGIN OF VICTORY

408 runs	New Zealand beat Pakistan	Christchurch	1996-97
374 runs	Australia beat Pakistan	Melbourne	1996-97

LOWEST INNINGS TOTALS

22 (23.4 overs)	Netherlands v West Indies	Deventer	2008
23 (24.1 overs)	Pakistan v Australia	Melbourne	1996-97
24 (21.3 overs)	Scotland v England	Reading	2001

BATTING RECORDS
2000 RUNS IN A CAREER

Runs		Career	M	I	NO	HS	Avge	100	50
5432	C.M.Edwards (E)	1997-2014	178	167	21	173*	37.20	8	42
4844	B.J.Clark (A)	1991-2005	118	114	12	229*	47.49	5	30
4814	K.L.Rolton (A)	1995-2009	141	132	32	154*	48.14	8	33
4791	M.Raj (I)	1999-2014	148	135	40	114*	50.43	5	36

Runs		Career	M	I	NO	HS	Avge	100	50
4101	S.C.Taylor (E)	1998-2011	126	120	18	156*	40.20	8	23
4064	D.A.Hockley (NZ)	1982-2000	118	115	18	117	41.89	4	34
2919	H.M.Tiffen (NZ)	1999-2009	117	111	16	100	30.72	1	18
2856	S.J.Taylor (E)	2006-2014	88	81	9	129	39.66	5	14
2856	A.Chopra (I)	1995-2012	127	112	21	100	31.38	1	18
2844	E.C.Drumm (NZ)	1992-2006	101	94	13	116	35.11	2	19
2728	L.C.Sthalekar (A)	2001-2013	125	111	22	104*	30.65	2	16
2711	S.R.Taylor (WI)	2008-2014	73	72	9	171	43.03	5	16
2630	L.M.Keightley (A)	1995-2005	82	78	12	156*	39.84	4	21
2505	A.J.Blackwell (A)	2003-2014	106	94	19	106*	33.40	2	18
2354	L.S.Greenway (E)	2003-2014	115	102	25	125*	30.57	1	11
2249	S.J.McGlashan (NZ)	2002-2014	118	112	16	97*	23.42	–	11
2201	R.J.Rolls (NZ)	1997-2007	104	91	3	114	25.01	2	12
2121	J.A.Brittin (E)	1979-1998	63	59	9	138*	42.42	5	8
2091	J.Sharma (I)	2002-2008	77	75	7	138*	30.75	2	14
2047	S.Nitschke (A)	2004-2011	80	69	9	113*	34.11	1	14
2039	S.W.Bates (NZ)	2006-2014	62	60	6	168	37.75	5	10
2002	N.J.Browne (NZ)	2002-2014	125	102	28	63	27.05	–	10

HIGHEST INDIVIDUAL INNINGS

229*	B.J.Clark	Australia v Denmark	Mumbai	1997-98
173*	C.M.Edwards	England v Ireland	Pune	1997-98
171	S.R.Taylor	West Indies v Sri Lanka	Mumbai	2012-13
168	S.W.Bates	New Zealand v Pakistan	Sydney	2008-09
156*	L.M.Keightley	Australia v Pakistan	Melbourne	1996-97
156*	S.C.Taylor	England v India	Lord's	2006
154*	K.L.Rolton	Australia v Sri Lanka	Christchurch	2000-01
153*	J.Logtenberg	South Africa v Netherlands	Deventer	2007
151	K.L.Rolton	Australia v Ireland	Dublin	2005

HIGHEST PARTNERSHIP FOR EACH WICKET

1st	268	S.J.Taylor/C.M.G.Atkins	England v South Africa	Lord's	2008
2nd	262	H.M.Tiffen/S.W.Bates	New Zealand v Pakistan	Sydney	2008-09
3rd	244	K.L.Rolton/L.C.Sthalekar	Australia v Ireland	Dublin	2005
4th	224*	J.Logtenberg//M.du Preez	South Africa v Netherlands	Deventer	2007
5th	188*	S.C.Taylor/J.Cassar	England v Sri Lanka	Lincoln	2000-01
6th	139*	S.J.McGlashan/N.J.Browne	New Zealand v South Africa	Bowral	2008-09
7th	104*	S.J.Tsukigawa/N.J.Browne	New Zealand v England	Chennai	2006-07
8th	85*	S.L.Clarke/N.J.Shaw	England v Scotland	Reading	2001
9th	73	L.R.F.Askew/I.T.Guha	England v New Zealand	Chennai	2006-07
10th	58	A.Sharma/G.Sultana	India v England	Taunton	2012

BOWLING RECORDS
100 WICKETS IN A CAREER

		LOI	Balls	R	W	Avge	Best	4w	R/Over
C.L.Fitzpatrick (A)	1993-2007	109	6017	3023	**180**	16.79	5-14	11	3.01
J.Goswami (I)	2002-2014	133	6342	3388	**157**	21.57	6-31	6	3.20
L.C.Sthalekar (A)	2001-2013	125	5964	3646	**146**	24.97	5-35	2	3.66
N.David .(I)	1995-2008	97	4892	2305	**141**	16.34	5-20	6	2.82
J.L.Gunn (E)	2004-2014	118	4874	3047	**110**	27.70	5-22	4	3.75
C.E.Taylor (E)	1988-2005	105	5140	2443	**102**	23.95	4-13	2	2.85
I.T.Guha (E)	2001-2011	83	3767	2345	**101**	23.21	5-14	4	3.73
N.Al Khadeer (I)	2002-2012	78	4036	2402	**100**	24.02	5-14	5	3.57

SIX OR MORE WICKETS IN AN INNINGS

7- 4	Sajjida Shah	Pakistan v Japan	Amsterdam	2003
7- 8	J.M.Chamberlain	England v Denmark	Haarlem	1991
7-14	A.Mohammed	West Indies v Pakistan	Dhaka	2011-12
7-24	S.Nitschke	Australia v England	Kidderminster	2005
6-10	J.Lord	New Zealand v India	Auckland	1981-82
6-10	M.Maben	India v Sri Lanka	Kandy	2003-04
6-10	S.Ismail	South Africa v Netherlands	Savar	2011-12
6-20	G.L.Page	New Zealand v Trinidad & T	St Albans	1973
6-31	J.Goswami	India v New Zealand	Southgate	2011
6-32	B.H.McNeill	New Zealand v England	Lincoln, NZ	2007-08

WICKET-KEEPING AND FIELDING RECORDS
100 DISMISSALS IN A CAREER

Total			LOI	Ct	St
133	R.J.Rolls	New Zealand	104	89	44
114	J.Smit	England	109	69	45
101	S.J.Taylor	England	88	66	35

SIX DISMISSALS IN AN INNINGS

6 (4ct, 2st)	S.L.Illingworth	New Zealand v Australia	Beckenham	1993
6 (1ct, 5st)	V.Kalpana	India v Denmark	Slough	1993
6 (2ct, 4st)	Batool Fatima	Pakistan v West Indies	Karachi	2003-04
6 (4ct, 2st)	Batool Fatima	Pakistan v Sri Lanka	Colombo (PSS)	2011

45 CATCHES IN THE FIELD IN A CAREER

Total			LOI	Career
50	J.Goswani	India	133	2002-2014
49	L.C.Sthalekar	Australia	125	2001-2013
48	L.S.Greenway	England	115	2003-2014
48	C.M.Edwards	England	178	1997-2014
45	B.J.Clark	Australia	118	1991-2005

FOUR CATCHES IN THE FIELD IN AN INNINGS

4	Z.J.Goss	Australia v New Zealand	Adelaide	1995-96

APPEARANCE RECORDS
120 APPEARANCES

178	C.M.Edwards	England	1997-2014
148	M.Raj	India	1999-2014
141	K.L.Rolton	Australia	1995-2009
133	J.Goswani	India	2002-2014
127	A.Chopra	India	1995-2012
126	S.C.Taylor	England	1998-2011
125	N.J.Browne	New Zealand	2002-2014
125	L.C.Sthalekar	Australia	2001-2013

MOST CONSECUTIVE APPEARANCES

109	M.Raj	India	17.04.2004 to 07.02.2013

75 MATCHES AS CAPTAIN

			Won	Lost	No Result	
104	C.M.Edwards	England	64	33	7	2005-2014
101	B.J.Clark	Australia	83	17	1	1994-2005

WOMEN'S INTERNATIONAL TWENTY20 RECORDS

MATCH RESULTS SUMMARY

	Matches	Won	Lost	Tied	NR	Win %
England	76	53	20	2	1	70.66
West Indies	61	39	19	2	1	65.00
Australia	62	34	26	2	–	54.83
New Zealand	58	29	28	1	–	50.00
Pakistan	42	18	22	1	1	43.90
India	44	19	25	–	–	43.18
South Africa	41	15	25	–	1	37.50
Sri Lanka	39	11	25	–	3	30.55
Ireland	25	7	18	-	–	28.00
Bangladesh	13	3	10	–	–	23.07
Netherlands	11	–	10	–	1	0.00

WOMEN'S INTERNATIONAL TWENTY20 RECORDS
(To 28 February 2014)

TEAM RECORDS
HIGHEST INNINGS TOTALS

205-1	South Africa v Netherlands	Potchefstroom	2010-11
191-4	West Indies v Netherlands	Potchefstroom	2010-11
186-7	New Zealand v South Africa	Taunton	2007
184-4	West Indies v Ireland	Dublin	2008
180-5	England v South Africa	Taunton	2007
180-5	New Zealand v West Indies	Gros Islet	2010

HIGHEST INNINGS TOTAL BATTING SECOND

165-2	England (set 164) v Australia	The Oval	2009

LOWEST COMPLETED INNINGS TOTALS † Batting Second

57†	(19.4)	Sri Lanka v Bangladesh	Guangzhou	2012-13
60†	(16.5)	Pakistan v England	Taunton	2009
62	(18.2)	India v Australia	Billericay	2011
62	(18.0)	Bangladesh v Sri Lanka	Guangzhou	2012-13
62-9		Ireland v Sri Lanka	Dublin	2013
63†	(19.1)	Pakistan v India	Guangzhou	2012-13
64-8		South Africa v Pakistan	Doha	2013-14
65-9		Pakistan v New Zealand	Basseterre	2010
65	(18.5)	Pakistan v West Indies	St Andrew's	2011
65	(19.5)	Ireland v Pakistan	Dublin	2013

The lowest total for England is 96 (v India, Mumbai, 2009-10).

BATTING RECORDS
900 RUNS IN A CAREER

Runs			M	I	NO	HS	Avge	50	R/100B
1921	C.M.Edwards	E	72	70	10	92*	32.01	7	108.1
1505	S.J.Taylor	E	58	56	8	77	31.35	11	111.1
1321	S.R.Taylor	WI	49	48	9	90	33.87	11	100.1†
1202	S.W.Bates	NZ	54	54	2	68	23.11	5	102.2
1120	D.J.S.Dottin	WI	61	60	13	112*	23.82	6	136.1†
1013	L.S.Greenway	E	65	58	17	80*	24.70	2	98.7

Runs			M	I	NO	HS	Avge	50	R/100B
964	M.Raj	I	39	39	10	67	33.24	4	93.2†
929	M.M.Lanning	A	35	35	2	78*	28.15	4	109.9
908	A.J.Blackwell	A	59	53	8	61	20.17	1	93.8

† *No information on balls faced for games at Roseau on 22 and 23 February 2012.*

HIGHEST INDIVIDUAL INNINGS

Score	Balls				
116*	71	S.A.Fritz	SA v Neth	Potchefstroom	2010-11
112*	45	D.J.S.Dottin	WI v SA	Basseterre	2010
96*	53	K.L.Rolton	A v E	Taunton	2005
92*	59	C.M.Edwards	E v A	Hobart	2013-14
90	49	S.R.Taylor	WI v Ire	Dublin	2008
90	61	A.J.Healy	A v I	Visakhapatnam	2011-12

HIGHEST PARTNERSHIP FOR EACH WICKET

1st	170	S.A.Fritz/T.Chetty	SA v Neth	Potchefstroom	2010-11
2nd	118*	S.W.Bates/A.L.Watkins	NZ v A	Taunton	2009
3rd	124	T.D.Smartt/S.A.C.A.King	WI v Neth	Potchefstroom	2010-11
4th	147*	K.L.Rolton/K.A.Blackwell	A v E	Taunton	2005
5th	118	S.F.Daley/D.J.S.Dottin	WI v SA	Basseterre	2010
6th	68	K.L.Rolton/A.J.Blackwell	A v SA	Taunton	2009
7th	51	S.R.Taylor/M.R.Aguilleira	WI v SL	Cayon	2010
8th	32*	M.A.D.D.Surangika/S.S.Weerakkody	SL v WI	Port of Spain	2012
9th	32*	K.J.Martin/M.J.G.Nielsen	NZ v A	Sydney	2011-12
10th	23*	L.N.McCarthy/E.J.Tice	Ire v SL	Dublin	2013

BOWLING RECORDS
45 WICKETS IN A CAREER

Wkts			Matches	Overs	Mdns	Runs	Avge	Best	R/Over
71	A.Mohammed	WI	54	179.4	3	934	13.15	5-10	5.19
63	H.L.Colvin	E	50	186.5	4	971	15.41	4- 9	5.19
61	S.F.Daley	WI	54	181.2	6	852	13.96	5-15	4.69
60	L.C.Sthalekar	A	54	199.2	1	1161	19.35	4-18	5.82
55	D.Hazell	E	48	182.5	4	951	17.29	4-12	5.20
53	S.R.Taylor	WI	49	154.1	4	828	15.62	3-10	5.37
51	L.A.Marsh	E	55	205.1	4	1073	21.03	3-17	5.22
48	E.A.Perry	A	50	173.1	3	1053	21.93	4-20	6.08
46	D.N.Wyatt	E	50	117.3	3	666	14.47	4-11	5.66

FIVE OR MORE WICKETS IN AN INNINGS

6-17	A.E.Satterthwaite	NZ v E	Taunton	2007
5-10	A.Mohammed	WI v SA	Cape Town	2009-10
5-11	A.Shrubsole	E v NZ	Wellington	2011-12
5-11	J.Goswami	I v A	Visakhapatnam	2011-12
5-12	A.Mohammed	WI v NZ	Bridgetown	2013-14
5-15	S.F.Daley	WI v SL	Colombo (RPS)	2012-13
5-16	P.Roy	I v P	Taunton	2009
5-16	S.L.Quintyne	WI v E	Bridgetown	2013-14
5-18	J.L.Gunn	E v NZ	Bridgetown	2013-14
5-22	J.L.Hunter	A v WI	Colombo (RPS)	2012-13

HAT-TRICKS

Asmavia Iqbal	Pakistan v England	Loughborough	2012
Ekta Bisht	Sri Lanka v India	Colombo (NCC)	2012-13
M.Kapp	South Africa v Bangladesh	Potchefstroom	2013-14
N.R.Sciver	England v New Zealand	Bridgetown	2013-14

WICKET-KEEPING RECORDS
25 DISMISSALS IN A CAREER

Dis			Matches	Ct	St
48	S.J.Taylor	England	56	16	32
42	Batool Fatima	Pakistan	37	9	33
40	J.M.Fields	Australia	37	25	15
38	R.H.Priest	New Zealand	35	20	18
33	M.R.Aguilleira	West Indies	52	14	19
31	S.Naik	India	31	10	21
25	T.Chetty	South Africa	39	12	13

FIVE DISMISSALS IN AN INNINGS

5 (1ct, 4st) Kycia A.Knight	West Indies v Sri Lanka	Colombo (RPS)	2012-13
5 (1ct, 4st) Batool Fatima	Pakistan v Ireland	Dublin	2013
5 (1ct, 4st) Batool Fatima	Pakistan v Ireland	Dublin	2013

FIELDING RECORDS
20 CATCHES IN A CAREER

Total			Matches	Total			Matches
47	J.L.Gunn	England	73	22	S.A.C.A.King	West Indies	52
36	L.S.Greenway	England	65	22	A.J.Blackwell	Australia	59
26	J.E.Cameron	Australia	49	20	N.J.Browne	New Zealand	45
24	S.J.McGlashan	New Zealand	51				

FOUR CATCHES IN AN INNINGS

4	L.S.Greenway	England v New Zealand	Chelmsford	2010

APPEARANCE RECORDS
50 APPEARANCES

73	J.L.Gunn	England	54	L.C.Sthalekar	Australia
72	C.M.Edwards	England	52	M.R.Aguilleira	West Indies
65	L.S.Greenway	England	52	S.A.C.A.King	West Indies
61	D.J.S.Dottin	West Indies	52	A.E.Satterthwaite	New Zealand
59	A.J.Blackwell	Australia	51	S.A.Campbelle	West Indies
58	S.J.Taylor	England	51	S.J.McGlashan	New Zealand
55	L.A.Marsh	England	50	H.L.Colvin	England
54	S.W.Bates	New Zealand	50	E.A.Perry	Australia
54	S.F.Daley	West Indies	50	D.N.Wyatt	England
54	A.Mohammed	West Indies			

25 MATCHES AS CAPTAIN

			W	L	T	NR	%age wins
70	C.M.Edwards	England	51	17	1	1	73.91
51	M.R.Aguilleira	West Indies	32	17	1	1	64.00
38	Sana Mir	Pakistan	15	21	1	1	40.54
29	A.L.Watkins	New Zealand	19	10	–	–	65.51
26	J.M.Fields	Australia	16	10	–	–	61.53
25	H.A.S.D.Siriwardene	Sri Lanka	8	15	–	2	34.78

UNICORNS COUNTIES FIXTURES 2014

Sun 27 April
North Devon
Newport
Manor Park
Ipswich School
Woodhall Spa
Jesmond
Colwall
Bicester & North Oxford

KNOCK-OUT TROPHY
Devon v Wiltshire (1)
Wales MC v Cornwall (1)
Norfolk v Cambridgeshire (2)
Suffolk v Hertfordshire (2)
Lincolnshire v Cumberland (3)
Northumberland v Cheshire (3)
Herefordshire v Staffordshire (4)
Oxfordshire v Berkshire (4)

Sun 4 May
Truro
Dean Park
Dunstable
Clare C, Cambridge
Kendal
Shrewsbury
Burnham
Stone

KNOCK-OUT TROPHY
Cornwall v Devon (1)
Dorset v Wales MC (1)
Bedfordshire v Norfolk (2)
Cambridgeshire v Suffolk (2)
Cumberland v Northumberland (3)
Shropshire v Lincolnshire (3)
Buckinghamshire v Herefordshire (4)
Staffordshire v Oxfordshire (4)

Sun 11 May
Sidmouth
Corsham
Radlett
Bury St Edmunds
Neston
Jesmond
Wargrave
Challow & Childrey

KNOCK-OUT TROPHY
Devon v Dorset (1)
Wiltshire v Cornwall (1)
Hertfordshire v Cambridgeshire (2)
Suffolk v Bedfordshire (2)
Cheshire v Cumberland (3)
Northumberland v Shropshire (3)
Berkshire v Staffordshire (4)
Oxfordshire v Buckinghamshire (4)

Sun 18 May
Dean Park
Usk
Cople
Manor Park
Bracebridge Heath
Oswestry
Dinton
Eastnor

KNOCK-OUT TROPHY
Dorset v Wiltshire (1)
Wales MC v Devon (1)
Bedfordshire v Hertfordshire (2)
Norfolk v Suffolk (2)
Lincolnshire v Northumberland (3)
Shropshire v Cheshire (3)
Buckinghamshire v Berkshire (4)
Herefordshire v Oxfordshire (4)

Sun 25 May
Werrington
Warminster
March
Harpenden
Bramhall
Cockermouth
Kidmore End
Himley

KNOCK-OUT TROPHY
Cornwall v Dorset (1)
Wiltshire v Wales MC (1)
Cambridgeshire v Bedfordshire (2)
Hertfordshire v Norfolk (2)
Cheshire v Lincolnshire (3)
Cumberland v Shropshire (3)
Berkshire v Herefordshire (4)
Staffordshire v Buckinghamshire (4)

Sun 8 – Tue 10 June	**CHAMPIONSHIP**
Luton Town & Indians	Bedfordshire v Suffolk
Henley	Berkshire v Cornwall
Barrow	Cumberland v Buckinghamshire
Dean Park	Dorset v Devon
Colwall	Herefordshire v Cheshire
Hertford	Hertfordshire v Cambridgeshire
Sleaford	Lincolnshire v Staffordshire
Tynemouth	Northumberland v Norfolk
Banbury	Oxfordshire v Wiltshire
Pontarddulais	Wales MC v Shropshire
Sun 15 June	**KNOCK-OUT TROPHY Quarter-finals**
Match 1	Winner Gp 2 v Runner-up Gp 1
Match 2	Winner Gp 3 v Runner-up Gp 4
Match 3	Winner Gp 1 v Runner-up Gp 2
Match 4	Winner Gp 4 v Runner-up Gp 3
Sun 22 – Tue 24 June	**CHAMPIONSHIP**
High Wycombe	Buckinghamshire v Cambridgeshire
Alderley Edge	Cheshire v Cornwall
Lord's	MCC v Hertfordshire
S Northumberland	Northumberland v Lincolnshire
Banbury	Oxfordshire v Devon
Shifnal	Shropshire v Herefordshire
Bury St Edmunds	Suffolk v Cumberland
Usk	Wales MC v Berkshire
Corsham	Wiltshire v Dorset
Sun 29 June – Tue 1 July	**CHAMPIONSHIP**
Knypersley	Staffordshire v Hertfordshire
Sun 6 – Tue 8 July	**CHAMPIONSHIP**
Falkland	Berkshire v Wiltshire
Truro	Cornwall v Wales MC
Furness	Cumberland v Bedfordshire
Sidmouth	Devon v Cheshire
Eastnor	Herefordshire v Dorset
Harpenden	Hertfordshire v Norfolk
Bridgnorth	Shropshire v Oxfordshire
West Brom D'mouth	Staffordshire v Northumberland
Ipswich School	Suffolk v Buckinghamshire
Sun 13 July	**KNOCK-OUT TROPHY Semi-finals**
tbc	Winner Match 4 v Winner Match 3
tbc	Winner Match 1 v Winner Match 2
Reserve day Mon 14 July	
Fri 18 July	
S Northumberland	Unicorns v Sri Lanka A

Sun 20 – Tue 22 July	**CHAMPIONSHIP**
Bedford Mod School	Bedfordshire v Cambridgeshire
Finchampstead	Berkshire v Herefordshire
Gerrards Cross	Buckinghamshire v Staffordshire
Bowdon	Cheshire v Wales MC
St Austell	Cornwall v Shropshire
Dean Park	Dorset v Oxfordshire
Cleethorpes	Lincolnshire v Hertfordshire
Manor Park	Norfolk v Cumberland
Jesmond	Northumberland v Suffolk
Devizes	Wiltshire v Devon
Fri 25 July	
Sidmouth	MCC v MCCA Unicorns
Sun 27 – Tue 29 July	**CHAMPIONSHIP**
Wisbech	Cambridgeshire v Lincolnshire
Manor Park	Norfolk v Bedfordshire
Sun 3 – Tue 5 August	**CHAMPIONSHIP**
March	Cambridgeshire v Northumberland
Truro	Cornwall v Herefordshire
Exeter	Devon v Shropshire
Long Marston	Hertfordshire v Cumberland
Grantham	Lincolnshire v Buckinghamshire
Manor Park	Norfolk v Suffolk
Great & Little Tew	Oxfordshire v Berkshire
Longton	Staffordshire v Bedfordshire
Abergavenny	Wales MC v Dorset
South Wilts	Wiltshire v Cheshire
Sun 17 – Tue 19 August	**CHAMPIONSHIP**
Ampthill	Bedfordshire v Lincolnshire
Tring Park	Buckinghamshire v Norfolk
Saffron Walden	Cambridgeshire v Staffordshire
Nantwich	Cheshire v Oxfordshire
Sedbergh School	Cumberland v Northumberland
Exmouth	Devon v Berkshire
Dean Park	Dorset v Cornwall
Brockhampton	Herefordshire v Wales MC
Whitchurch	Shropshire v Wiltshire
Copdock	Suffolk v Hertfordshire
Wed 27 August	**KNOCK-OUT TROPHY Final**
Wormsley	(Reserve day, Thu 28 August)
Sun 7 – Wed 10 September	**CHAMPIONSHIP FINAL**

SECOND XI CHAMPIONSHIP FIXTURES 2014

THREE-DAY MATCHES

APRIL		
Wed 9	Cardiff	Glamorgan v Yorkshire
Tue 15	Notts SC	Notts v Yorkshire
Mon 21	Bristol	Glos v Surrey
Wed 23	Notts SC	Notts v MCC YC
Tue 29	H Wycombe	MCC YC v Warwicks
	Milton Keynes	Northants v Hampshire
Wed 30	Derby	Derbyshire v Worcs
	Taunton Vale	Somerset v Middlesex
MAY		
Tue 6	Leicester	Leics v Notts
Mon 19	Maidstone	Kent v Middlesex
Tue 20	Liverpool	Lancashire v Leics
Mon 26	Eastbourne	Sussex v Hampshire
Tue 27	Bristol	Glos v Essex
	Worcester RGS	Worcs v Notts
JUNE		
Mon 2	Cheam	Surrey v Somerset
	Stamford Br	Yorkshire v Warwicks
Tue 3	Cardiff	Glamorgan v Lancashire
	Shenley	MCC YC v Derbyshire
	Radlett	Middlesex v Essex
Tue 10	Southampton	Hampshire v Surrey
	Crosby	Lancashire v Yorkshire
	Richmond	Middlesex v Glos
	Notts SC	Notts v Derbyshire
	Coventry & NW	Warwicks v Durham
Mon 16	Maidstone	Kent v Glos
Tue 17	tbc	Derbyshire v Durham
	Kidderminster	Worcs v Glamorgan
Wed 18	H Wycombe	MCC YC v Leics
Mon 23	Preston Nom	Sussex v Kent
Tue 24	B Stortford	Essex v Somerset
	Cardiff CC	Glamorgan v Derbyshire
	Southampton	Hampshire v Glos
	Shenley	MCC YC v Durham
	Radlett	Middlesex v Surrey
	Welbeck C	Notts v Lancashire
JULY		
Tue 1	Middlesbrough	Durham v Glamorgan
	Southend	Essex v Sussex
	tbc	Glos v Northants
	Southport	Lancashire v Warwicks
	Taunton Vale	Somerset v Kent
Wed 2	Lutterworth	Leics v Worcs
	Cheam	Surrey v MCC Univs
Mon 7	Oxford	MCC Univs v Sussex
Tue 8	tbc	Derbyshire v Leics
	Cardiff CC	Glamorgan v MCC YC

	Milton Keynes	Northants v Somerset
	Ombersley	Worcs v Lancashire
Tue 15	Southampton	Hampshire v MCC Univs
	Canterbury PF	Kent v Surrey
	Hinckley	Leics v Durham
	Finedon	Northants v Sussex
	Birmingham	Warwicks v Notts
	York	Yorkshire v Worcs
Mon 21	Canterbury	Kent v Hampshire
Tue 22	Coggeshall	Essex v Northants
	Liverpool	Lancashire v Derbyshire
	Hove	Sussex v Middlesex
	Knowle & D	Warwicks v Glamorgan
	Kidderminster	Worcs v MCC YC
Wed 23	Harrogate	Yorkshire v Durham
Mon 28	tbc	Surrey v Essex
Tue 29	Brandon	Durham v Worcs
	Taunton Vale	MCC YC v Somerset
	Notts SC	Notts v Glamorgan
Wed 30	Ashby Hastings	Leics v Warwicks
AUGUST		
Mon 4	Taunton Vale	Somerset v Glos
Tue 5	S N'berland	Durham v Notts
	Newclose IoW	MCC Univs v Kent
	Radlett	Middlesex v Hampshire
	Guildford	Surrey v Northants
	Coventry & NW	Warwicks v Worcs
	York	Yorkshire v Leics
Mon 11	Taunton Vale	Somerset v Hampshire
	Hove	Sussex v Glos
Tue 12	Derby	Derbyshire v Warwicks
	Stockton	Durham v Lancashire
	Halstead	Essex v Kent
	Cardiff CC	Glamorgan v Leics
	Desborough T	MCC Univs v Northants
	Shenley	MCC YC v Yorkshire
Tue 19	Southampton	Hampshire v Essex
	Liverpool	Lancashire v MCC YC
Wed 20	tbc	Glos v MCC Univs
Wed 27	tbc	Derbyshire v Yorkshire
	B Stortford	Essex v MCC Univs
	Desborough T	Northants v Middlesex
	Purley	Surrey v Sussex
SEPTEMBER		
Mon 1	Desborough T	Northants v Kent
	Blackstone	Sussex v Somerset
Tue 2	Shenley	MCC Univs v Middlesex
Tue 16	tbc	FINAL (Four days)

SECOND XI TROPHY FIXTURES 2014

ONE DAY

APRIL		
Tue 8	Cardiff	Glamorgan v Yorkshire
Mon 14	Notts SC	Notts v Yorkshire
Tue 22	Notts SC	Notts v MCC YC
Thu 24	Bristol	Glos v Surrey
	Southampton	Hampshire v Unicorns
Mon 28	H Wycombe	MCC YC v Warwicks
	Milton Keynes	Northants v Hampshire
Tue 29	tbc	Derbyshire v Worcs
	Taunton Vale	Somerset v Middlesex
Wed 30	Horsham	Surrey v Sussex
MAY		
Mon 5	Ivanhoe	Leics v Notts
Tue 6	Arundel	Sussex v Somerset
Thu 15	Dunstable	Northants v Middlesex
Mon 19	Middlewich	Lancashire v Leics
Thu 22	Maidstone	Kent v Middlesex
Mon 26	Bristol	Glos v Ess
	Dunstable	Northants v Kent
Thu 29	Eastbourne	Sussex v Hampshire
Fri 30	Worcester RGS	Worcs v Notts
JUNE		
Mon 2	Shenley	MCC YC v Derbyshire
	Radlett	Middlesex v Essex
	Long Marston	Unicorns v Kent
Thu 5	Cardiff	Glamorgan v Lancashire
Mon 9	Todmorden	Lancashire v Yorkshire
	Notts SC	Notts v Derbyshire
	Kenilworth	Warwicks v Durham
Fri 13	Richmond	Middlesex v Glos
Mon 16	tbc	Derbyshire v Durham
	Radlett	Middlesex v Surrey
	Kidderminster	Worcs v Glamorgan
	Pudsey	Yorkshire v Warwicks
Tue 17	Billericay	Essex v Unicorns
	H Wycombe	MCC YC v Leics
	Taunton Vale	Surrey v Somerset
Wed 18	Saff Walden	Unicorns v Middlesex
Thu 19	Maidstone	Kent v Glos
Mon 23	B Stortford	Essex v Somerset
	Cardiff CC	Glamorgan v Derbyshire
	Southampton	Hampshire v Glos
	Shenley	MCC YC v Durham
	Worsop C	Notts v Lancashire
Thu 26	Preston Nom	Sussex v Kent
Mon 30	Middlesbrough	Durham v Glamorgan
	Southend	Essex v Sussex
	tTc	Glos v Northants
	Westhoughton	Lancashire v Warwicks

	Taunton Vale	Somerset v Kent
JULY		
Tue 1	Leicester	Leics v Worcs
	Reigate Pr	Surrey v Unicorns
Thu 3	tbc	Derbyshire v Yorkshire
Mon 7	tbc	Derbyshire v Leics
	Cardiff CC	Glamorgan v MCC YC
	Milton Keynes	Northants v Somerset
	Ombersley	Worcs v Lancashire
Thu 10	Southampton	Hampshire v Surrey
	Challow & C	Unicorns v Sussex
Fri 11	tbc	Glos v Unicorns
Mon 14	Canterbury PF	Kent v Surrey
	Leicester	Leics v Durham
	Desborough T	Northants v Sussex
	Birmingham	Warwicks v Notts
	Stamford Br	Yorkshire v Worcs
Mon 21	Neston	Lancashire v Derbyshire
	Walmley	Warwicks v Glamorgan
Tue 22	Marske	Yorkshire v Durham
Thu 24	Canterbury	Kent v Hampshire
	Sidmouth	Unicorns v Somerset
Fri 25	Coggeshall	Essex v Northants
	Hove	Sussex v Middlesex
	Bromsgrove	Worcs v MCC YC
Mon 28	Brandon	Durham v Worcs
	Welbeck Coll	Notts v Glamorgan
Tue 29	Leicester	Leics v Warwicks
Thu 31	tbc	Surrey v Essex
AUGUST		
Mon 4	S N'berland	Durham v Notts
	Radlett	Middlesex v Hampshire
	Kenilworth W	Warwicks v Worcs
	Barnsley	Yorkshire v Leics
Thu 7	Taunton Vale	Somerset v Glos
Fri 8	Guildford	Surrey v Northants
Mon 11	Derby	Derbyshire v Warwicks
	Stockton	Durham v Lancashire
	Halstead	Essex v Kent
	Cardiff CC	Glamorgan v Leics
	Shenley	MCC YC v Yorkshire
Thu 14	Taunton Vale	Somerset v Hampshire
	Hove	Sussex v Glos
Mon 18	Southampton	Hampshire v Essex
	Liverpool	Lancashire v MCC YC
Tue 26	tbc	Semi-finals
SEPTEMBER		
Mon 8	tbc	FINAL

SECOND XI TWENTY20 CUP FIXTURES 2014

MAY

Tue 6	York	Yorkshire v Durham
Thu 8	tbc	Glos v Worcs
	Canterbury PF	Kent v Sussex
	Manchester	Lancashire v Derbyshire
Fri 9	Northampton	Northants v Essex
	Taunton Vale	Somerset v Glos
	Worcester	Worcs v Glamorgan
	Sheffield AP	Yorkshire v Lancashire
Mon 12	Chester-le-St	Durham v Lancashire
	Canterbury	Kent v MCC YC
	Northampton	Northants v Leics
	Stirlands	Sussex v Hampshire
Tue 13	Ormskirk	Lancashire v Notts
	Uxbridge	Middlesex v Essex
	Coventry & NW	Warwicks v Glamorgan
Wed 14	Chelmsford	Essex v Unicorns
	Trent C	Notts v Yorkshire
	Taunton	Somerset v Warwicks
	Purley	Surrey v Kent
	Arundel	Sussex v MCC YC
Thu 15	tbc	Derbyshire v Yorkshire
	Chelmsford	Essex v Leics
	Cardiff	Glamorgan v Glos
	Southampton	Hampshire v Kent
	West Brom D	Warwicks v Worcs
Fri 16	Uxbridge	Middlesex v Northants
Mon 19	tbc	Glos v Warwicks
	Southampton	Hampshire v Surrey
	Notts SC	Notts v Durham
Tue 20	Newport	Glamorgan v Somerset
Wed 21	Brandon	Durham v Derbyshire
	Shenley	MCC YC v Hampshire
	Purley	Surrey v Sussex
Thu 22	tbc	Derbyshire v Notts
	Great Tew	Unicorns v Northants
	Kidderminster	Worcs v Somerset
Fri 23	Shenley	MCC YC v Surrey
	Saff Walden	Unicorns v Middlesex
Mon 26	Leicester	Leics v Middlesex
Tue 27	Leicester	Leics v Unicorns

JUNE

Thu 5	Arundel	Semi-finals and FINAL

PRINCIPAL FIXTURES 2014

CC1	LV= County Championship Division 1
CC2	LV= County Championship Division 2
F	Floodlit
FCF	First-Class Friendly
LOI	Royal London Limited-Overs International
50L	Royal London One-Day Cup
T20	NatWest T20 Blast
[T20]	Other Twenty20 match
IT20	NatWest Twenty20 International
TM	Investec Test Match
MCCU	MCC University
Uni	University match

Sun 23 – Wed 26 March
FCF ^F   Abu Dhabi   MCC v Durham

Tue 1 –Thu 3 April
Uni	Cambridge	Cambridge MCCU v Surrey
Uni	Derby	Derbyshire v Durham MCCU
Uni	Cardiff	Glamorgan v Cardiff MCCU
Uni	Oxford	Oxford MCCU v Notts
Uni	Hove	Sussex v Loughboro MCCU
Uni	Leeds	Yorkshire v Leeds/Brad MCCU

Sun 6 – Wed 9 April
CC1	Nottingham	Notts v Lancashire
CC1	Hove	Sussex v Middlesex
CC2	Southampton	Hampshire v Worcs
CC2	Leicester	Leics v Derbyshire
CC2	The Oval	Surrey v Glamorgan

Mon 7 – Wed 9 April
Uni	Cambridge	Cambridge MCCU v Essex
Uni	Chester-le-St	Durham v Durham MCCU
Uni	Bristol	Glos v Cardiff MCCU
Uni	Canterbury	Kent v Loughboro MCCU
Uni	Oxford	Oxford MCCU v Warwicks
Uni	Taunton	Somerset v Leeds/Brad MCCU

Sun 13 – Wed 16 April
CC1	Lord's	Middlesex v Notts
CC1	Northampton	Northants v Durham
CC1	Taunton	Somerset v Yorkshire
CC1	Birmingham	Warwicks v Sussex
CC2	Chelmsford	Essex v Derbyshire
CC2	Bristol	Glos v Hampshire
CC2	Worcester	Worcs v Kent

Sun 20 – Wed 23 April
CC1	Chester-le-St	Durham v Somerset
CC1	Manchester	Lancashire v Warwicks
CC1	Leeds	Yorkshire v Northants
CC2	Derby	Derbyshire v Hampshire
CC2	Cardiff	Glamorgan v Glos
CC2	Canterbury	Kent v Leics
CC2	The Oval	Surrey v Essex

Sun 27 – Wed 30 April
CC1	Lord's	Middlesex v Yorkshire
CC1	Northampton	Northants v Lancashire
CC1	Nottingham	Notts v Warwicks

CC1	Hove	Sussex v Somerset
CC2	Bristol	Glos v Essex
CC2	Southampton	Hampshire v Surrey
CC2	Leicester	Leics v Glamorgan
CC2	Worcester	Worcs v Derbyshire

Sun 4 – Wed 7 May
CC1	Chester-le-St	Durham v Yorkshire
CC1	Manchester	Lancashire v Sussex
CC1	Taunton	Somerset v Notts
CC1	Birmingham	Warwicks v Middlesex
CC2	Chelmsford	Essex v Leics
CC2	Cardiff	Glamorgan v Worcs
CC2	Canterbury	Kent v Surrey

Mon 5 – Wed 7 May
Uni	Durham	Durham MCCU v Northants
Uni	Southampton	Hampshire v Cardiff MCCU

Fri 9 May
LOI   Aberdeen   Scotland v England

Sun 11 – Wed 14 May
CC1	Lord's	Middlesex v Lancashire
CC1	Nottingham	Notts v Northants
CC1	Hove	Sussex v Durham
CC1	Leeds	Yorkshire v Warwicks
CC2	Derby	Derbyshire v Kent
CC2	Southampton	Hampshire v Glamorgan
CC2	The Oval	Surrey v Glos

Mon 12 – Wed 14 May
Uni   Cambridge   Cambridge MCCU v Worcs

Tue 13 May
F   Chelmsford   Essex v Sri Lankans

Fri 16 May
F	Canterbury	Kent v Sri Lankans
T20	Chester-le-St	Durham v Worcs
T20	Bristol	Glos v Somerset
T20 ^F	Southampton	Hampshire v Glamorgan
T20	Leicester	Leics v Derbyshire
T20 ^F	Nottingham	Notts v Lancashire
T20 ^F	Hove	Sussex v Surrey
T20	Leeds	Yorkshire v Northants

Sat 17 May
T20 ^F   Manchester   Lancashire v Worcs

T20	Lord's	Middlesex v Essex
T20	Lord's	Middlesex v Sussex

Sun 18 – Wed 21 May
CC1	Northampton	Northants v Middlesex
CC2	Bristol	Glos v Kent
CC1	Leicester	Leics v Hampshire
CC2	Worcester	Worcs v Essex

Sun 18 May
T20	Taunton	Somerset v Surrey
[T20]	Hove	Sussex v Sri Lankans

Mon 19 – Thu 22 May
CC1	Taunton	Somerset v Durham

Mon 19 – Wed 21 May
Uni	Loughborough	Loughboro MCCU v Lancashire

Tue 20 May
IT20 F	The Oval	**England v Sri Lanka**

Thu 22 May
LOI F	The Oval	**England v Sri Lanka**

Fri 23 May
T20 F	Derby	Derbyshire v Lancashire
T20 F	Chelmsford	Essex v Glamorgan
T20	Bristol	Glos v Middlesex
T20 F	Northampton	Northants v Leics
T20	Nottingham	Notts v Worcs
T20	Taunton	Somerset v Kent
T20 F	Hove	Sussex v Hampshire
T20 F	Birmingham	Warwicks v Yorkshire
[T20]	Oxford	Oxford U v Cambridge U

Sun 25 – Wed 28 May
CC1	Nottingham	Notts v Durham
CC1	Birmingham	Warwicks v Somerset
CC1	Leeds	Yorkshire v Lancashire
CC2	Derby	Derbyshire v Glos
CC2	Chelmsford	Essex v Surrey
CC2	Cardiff	Glamorgan v Leics
CC2	Tunbridge W	Kent v Leics

Sun 25 May
LOI	Chester-le-St	**England v Sri Lanka**
T20	Northwood	Middlesex v Hampshire

Mon 26 – Thu 29 May
CC1	Northwood	Middlesex v Sussex

Wed 28 May
LOI F	Manchester	**England v Sri Lanka**

Thu 29 May
T20 F	Derby	Derbyshire v Northants
T20	Chester-le-St	Durham v Lancashire

Fri 30 May
T20 F	Cardiff	Glamorgan v Sussex
T20 F	Southampton	Hampshire v Essex
T20 F	Canterbury	Kent v Glos
T20 F	Manchester	Lancashire v Warwicks
T20	Nottingham	Notts v Durham
T20 F	The Oval	Surrey v Middlesex
T20	Worcester	Worcs v Northants
T20	Leeds	Yorkshire v Derbyshire

Sat 31 May – Tue 3 June
CC1	Northampton	Northants v Yorkshire

Sat 31 May
LOI	Lord's	**England v Sri Lanka**

Sun 1 – Wed 4 June
CC1	Chester-le-St	Durham v Middlesex
CC1	Manchester	Lancashire v Somerset
CC1	Hove	Sussex v Notts
CC2	Chelmsford	Essex v Glamorgan
CC2	Southampton	Hampshire v Derbyshire
CC2	The Oval	Surrey v Worcs

Sun 1 June
T20	Leicester	Leics v Warwicks

Mon 2 – Thu 5 June
CC2	Leicester	Leics v Glos

Tue 3 June
LOI F	Birmingham	**England v Sri Lanka**

Thu 5 – Sun 8 June
FCF	Northampton	Northants v Sri Lankans

Thu 5 June
T20 F	Southampton	Hampshire v Kent

Fri 6 June
T20 F	Derby	Derbyshire v Notts
T20 F	Canterbury	Kent v Middlesex
T20 F	Manchester	Lancashire v Yorkshire
T20	Leicester	Leics v Worcs
T20	Taunton	Somerset v Glamorgan
T20 F	The Oval	Surrey v Essex
T20 F	Hove	Sussex v Glos
T20 F	Birmingham	Warwicks v Durham

Sat 7 – Tue 10 June
CC2	Canterbury	Kent v Essex

Sat 7 June
T20	Worcester	Worcs v Durham

Sun 8 – Wed 11 June
CC1	Taunton	Somerset v Sussex
CC1	Birmingham	Warwicks v Lancashire
CC1	Leeds	Yorkshire v Notts
CC2	Worcester	Worcs v Hampshire

Sun 8 June
T20   Bristol   Glos v Glamorgan

Mon 9 – Thu 12 June
CC2   Bristol   Glos v Surrey

Mon 9 – Wed 11 June
Uni   Leeds, W'wood Leeds/Brad MCCU v Leics
Uni   Oxford   Oxford MCCU v Middlesex

Wed 11 June
T20^F Canterbury   Kent v Essex

Thu 12 – Mon 16 June
TM1   Lord's   **ENGLAND v SRI LANKA**

Fri 13 June
T20^F Derby   Derbyshire v Worcs
T20^F Chelmsford   Essex v Glos
T20^F Cardiff   Glamorgan v Kent
T20^F Manchester   Lancashire v Leics
T20^F Northampton   Northants v Yorkshire
T20   Nottingham   Notts v Warwicks
T20   Taunton   Somerset v Hampshire
T20^F The Oval   Surrey v Sussex

Sat 14 – Tue 17 June
CC1   Nottingham   Notts v Middlesex

Sun 15 – Wed 18 June
CC1   Chester-le-St   Durham v Lancashire
CC1   Northampton   Northants v Warwicks
CC2   Derby   Derbyshire v Surrey
CC2   Cardiff   Glamorgan v Kent
CC2   Southampton   Hampshire v Essex
CC2   Leicester   Leics v Worcs

Sun 15 June
T20   Arundel   Sussex v Somerset

Mon 16 – Thu 19 June
CC1   Arundel   Sussex v Yorkshire

Wed 18 June
T20   The Oval   Middlesex v Somerset

Thu 19 June
T20   Leicester   Leics v Notts
T20   Birmingham   Warwicks v Northants

Fri 20 – Tue 24 June
TM2   Leeds   **ENGLAND v SRI LANKA**

Fri 20 June
T20   Chester-le-St   Durham v Leics
T20^F Chelmsford   Essex v Middlesex
T20^F Cardiff   Glamorgan v Surrey
T20^F Southampton   Hampshire v Glos
T20^F Canterbury   Kent v Sussex
T20^F Manchester   Lancashire v Northants

T20   Nottingham   Notts v Derbyshire
T20   Worcester   Worcs v Warwicks
          Lord's   Oxford U v Cambridge U

Sat 21 – Tue 24 June
CC2   Bristol   Glos v Glamorgan

Sun 22 – Wed 25 June
CC1   Chester-le-St   Durham v Sussex
CC1   Manchester   Lancashire v Northants
CC1   Nottingham   Notts v Somerset
CC1   Birmingham   Warwicks v Yorkshire
CC2   Canterbury   Kent v Derbyshire
CC2   The Oval   Surrey v Leics

Wed 25 June
T20^F Cardiff   Glamorgan v Hampshire

Thu 26 – Sat 28 June
FCF   Leicester   Leics v Indians

Thu 26 June
T20^F Lord's   Middlesex v Glos

Fri 27 June
T20^F Derby   Derbyshire v Warwicks
T20   Bristol   Glos v Kent
T20^F Northampton   Northants v Durham
T20   Taunton   Somerset v Essex
T20^F The Oval   Surrey v Hampshire
T20^F Hove   Sussex v Middlesex
T20   Worcester   Worcs v Notts
T20   Leeds   Yorkshire v Lancashire

Sat 28 June – Tue 1 July
CC2   The Oval   Surrey v Hampshire

Sat 28 June
T20   Nottingham   Notts v Yorkshire

Sun 29 June – Wed 2 July
CC1   Lord's   Middlesex v Northants
CC1   Taunton   Somerset v Lancashire
CC1   Birmingham   Warwicks v Notts
CC2   Chelmsford   Essex v Glos
CC2   Worcester   Worcs v Glamorgan

Sun 29 June
T20   Chester-le-St   Durham v Derbyshire

Mon 30 June – Thu 3 July
FCF   Oxford   Oxford U v Cambridge U

Tue 1 – Thu 3 July
FCF   Derby   Derbyshire v Indians

Tue 1 July
T20   Leeds   Yorkshire v Leics

Wed 2 July
T20^F The Oval   Surrey v Kent

| T20 | Leeds | Yorkshire v Durham |

Thu 3 July

| T20 | Richmond | Middlesex v Glamorgan |
| T20 F | Northampton | Northants v Warwicks |

Fri 4 July

T20	Chester-le-St	Durham v Notts
T20 F	Chelmsford	Essex v Surrey
T20 F	Cardiff	Glamorgan v Somerset
T20	Bristol	Glos v Sussex
T20 F	Canterbury	Kent v Hampshire
T20	Leicester	Leics v Northants
T20 F	Birmingham	Warwicks v Lancashire
T20	Worcester	Worcs v Yorkshire

Sat 5 July

| | Lord's | MCC v Rest of the World |

Sun 6 – Wed 9 July

| CC1 | Hove | Sussex v Northants |
| CC2 | Colwyn Bay | Glamorgan v Surrey |

Sun 6 July

T20	Chesterfield	Derbyshire v Leics
T20	Southampton	Hampshire v Somerset
T20	Worcester	Worcs v Lancashire

Mon 7 – Thu 10 July

CC1	Uxbridge	Middlesex v Somerset
CC1	Leeds	Yorkshire v Durham
CC2	Chesterfield	Derbyshire v Essex
CC2	Southampton	Hampshire v Glos
CC2	Leicester	Leics v Kent

Tue 8 July

| T20 F | Birmingham | Warwicks v Notts |

Wed 9 – Sun 13 July

| TM1 | Nottingham | ENGLAND v INDIA |

Fri 11 July

T20	Chester-le-St	Durham v Yorkshire
T20 F	Southampton	Hampshire v Middlesex
T20	Leicester	Leics v Lancashire
T20 F	Northampton	Northants v Derbyshire
T20	Taunton	Somerset v Glos
T20 F	The Oval	Surrey v Glamorgan
T20 F	Hove	Sussex v Kent
T20 F	Birmingham	Warwicks v Worcs

Sat 12 – Tue 15 July

| CC1 | Northampton | Northants v Somerset |

Sat 12 July

| T20 | Colchester | Essex v Kent |

Sun 13 – Wed 16 July

| CC1 | Chester-le-St | Durham v Warwicks |
| CC1 | Liverpool | Lancashire v Notts |

| CC2 | Colchester | Essex v Hampshire |
| CC2 | Worcester | Worcs v Leics |

Sun 13 July

| T20 | Chesterfield | Derbyshire v Yorkshire |

Mon 14 – Thu 17 July

| CC2 | Cheltenham | Glos v Derbyshire |

Tue 15 July

| T20 F | Hove | Sussex v Glamorgan |

Wed 16 July

| T20 F | The Oval | Surrey v Somerset |

Thu 17 – Mon 21 July

| TM2 | Lord's | ENGLAND v INDIA |

Fri 18 July

	S North'land	Unicorns v Sri Lanka A
T20 F	Cardiff	Glamorgan v Essex
T20	Cheltenham	Glos v Surrey
T20 F	Southampton	Hampshire v Sussex
T20 F	Canterbury	Kent v Somerset
T20 F	Manchester	Lancashire v Derbyshire
T20	Leicester	Leics v Durham
T20 F	Northampton	Northants v Worcs
T20	Leeds	Yorkshire v Warwicks

Sat 19 – Tue 22 July

| CC1 | Scarborough | Yorkshire v Middlesex |

Sun 20 – Wed 23 July

| CC2 | Derby | Derbyshire v Glamorgan |
| CC2 | Guildford | Surrey v Kent |

Sun 20 July

	Chester-le-St	Durham v Sri Lanka A
T20	Cheltenham	Glos v Essex
T20	Nottingham	Notts v Leics

Mon 21 – Thu 24 July

| CC1 | Horsham | Sussex v Warwicks |
| CC2 | Cheltenham | Glos v Worcs |

Tue 22 July

| T20 F | Chelmsford | Essex v Hampshire |

Wed 23 July

| T20 F | Northampton | Northants v Notts |

Thu 24 July

| T20 F | Manchester | Lancashire v Durham |
| T20 F | Lord's | Middlesex v Surrey |

Fri 25 July

T20	Chester-le-St	Durham v Northants
T20	Chelmsford	Essex v Sussex
T20	Cardiff	Glamorgan v Glos
T20	Canterbury	Kent v Surrey
T20	Taunton	Somerset v Middlesex

T20 Birmingham Warwicks v Leics
T20 Worcester Worcs v Derbyshire
T20 Leeds Yorkshire v Notts

Sat 26 July
50L Derby Derbyshire v Hampshire
50L Cardiff Glamorgan v Middlesex
50L [F] Manchester Lancashire v Yorkshire

Sun 27 – Thu 31 July
TM3 Southampton ENGLAND v INDIA

Sun 27 July
50L Cheltenham Glos v Northants
50L [F] Manchester Lancashire v Hampshire
50L Leicester Leics v Derbyshire
50L Lord's Middlesex v Warwicks
50L Taunton Somerset v Durham
50L Guildford Surrey v Glamorgan
50L Horsham Sussex v Notts
50L Worcester Worcs v Essex

Tue 29 July
50L [F] Canterbury Kent v Durham
50L Milton Keynes Northants v Worcs
50L Nottingham Notts v Somerset
50L [F] Birmingham Warwicks v Sussex
50L Leeds Yorkshire v Glos

Wed 30 July
50L [F] Cardiff Glamorgan v Notts

Thu 31 July
50L Chester-le-St Durham v Warwicks
50L [F] Chelmsford Essex v Leics
50L Bristol Glos v Hampshire
50L Lord's Middlesex v Surrey
50L Taunton Somerset v Kent
50L Worcester Worcs v Derbyshire
     Northampton Northants v New Zealand A
     Leeds Yorkshire v Sri Lanka A

Fri 1 August
T20 tbc Quarter-final 1

Sat 2 August
     Cardiff Glamorgan v Sri Lanka A
     Birmingham Warwicks v New Zealand A
T20 [F] tbc Quarter-finals 2 & 3

Sun 3 August
T20 tbc Quarter-final 4

Tue 5 August
50L Chelmsford Essex v Lancashire
50L Bristol Glos v Leics
50L [F] Northampton Northants v Yorkshire
50L [F] The Oval Surrey v Kent
50L [F] Hove Sussex v Durham

50L [F] Birmingham Warwicks v Somerset
     Somerset Sri Lanka A v New Zealand A

Wed 6 August
50L [F] Southampton Hampshire v Leics
50L [F] Canterbury Kent v Glamorgan
50L [F] The Oval Surrey v Sussex
     Taunton England Lions v Sri Lanka A

Thu 7 – Mon 11 August
TM4 Manchester ENGLAND v INDIA

Thu 7 August
50L [F] Derby Derbyshire v Lancashire
50L Lord's Middlesex v Somerset
50L Leeds Yorkshire v Worcs

Fri 8 August
50L [F] Chelmsford Essex v Glos
50L [F] Cardiff Glamorgan v Durham
50L [F] Southampton Hampshire v Northants
50L Leicester Leics v Yorkshire
50L [F] Nottingham Notts v Kent
50L [F] Hove Sussex v Middlesex
     Bristol England Lions v New Zealand A

Sat 9 August
50L Worcester Worcs v Lancashire
     Bristol Sri Lanka A v New Zealand A

Sun 10 August
50L Derby Derbyshire v Essex
50L Chester-le-St Durham v Middlesex
50L Leicester Leics v Northants
50L Nottingham Notts v Surrey
50L Taunton Somerset v Sussex
50L Rugby S Warwicks v Kent

Mon 11 August
50L [F] Southampton Hampshire v Worcs
50L [F] Northampton Northants v Derbyshire
50L Scarborough Yorkshire v Essex
     Worcester England Lions v Sri Lanka A

Tue 12 August
50L Chester-le-St Durham v Notts
50L Bristol Glos v Lancashire
50L Taunton Somerset v Glamorgan
50L [F] Birmingham Warwicks v Surrey
     Worcester England Lions v New Zealand A

Wed 13 August
50L [F] Chelmsford Essex v Hampshire
50L [F] Canterbury Kent v Sussex
50L Worcester Worcs v Glos
50L Scarborough Yorkshire v Derbyshire

Thu 14 August
50L Chester-le-St Durham v Surrey

50L	Swansea	Glamorgan v Warwicks
50L F	Manchester	Lancashire v Northants
50L	Leicester	Leics v Worcs
50L F	Lord's	Middlesex v Notts
	Southampton	Hampshire v Sri Lanka A

Fri 15 – Tue 19 August
TM5	The Oval	ENGLAND v INDIA

Fri 15 – Mon 18 August
CC1	Manchester	Lancashire v Durham
CC1	Northampton	Northants v Notts
CC1	Taunton	Somerset v Warwicks
CC1	Scarborough	Yorkshire v Sussex
CC2	Swansea	Glamorgan v Essex
CC2	Canterbury	Kent v Hampshire
CC2	Leicester	Leics v Surrey
CC2	Worcester	Worcs v Glos

Wed 20 August
50L F	Canterbury	Kent v Middlesex
50L F	Nottingham	Notts v Warwicks
50L F	The Oval	Surrey v Somerset
50L F	Hove	Sussex v Glamorgan

Thu 21 August
50L F	Derby	Derbyshire v Glos
50L F	Southampton	Hampshire v Yorkshire
50L F	Manchester	Lancashire v Leics
50L F	Northampton	Northants v Essex

Fri 22 August
	Lord's	Middlesex v Indians

Sat 23 August
T20 F	Birmingham	Semi-finals and FINAL

Mon 25 –Wed 27 August
FCF	Canterbury	Kent v New Zealand A

Mon 25 August
LOI	Bristol	England v India

Tue 26 August
50L	tbc	Quarter-final 1

Wed 27 August
LOI	Cardiff	England v India

Thu 28 August
50L	tbc	Quarter-finals 2 & 3

Fri 29 August
50L	tbc	Quarter-final 4

Sat 30 August
LOI	Nottingham	England v India

Sun 31 August – Wed 3 September
CC1	Chester-le-St	Durham v Notts
CC1	Manchester	Lancashire v Yorkshire
CC1	Lord's	Middlesex v Warwicks
CC1	Taunton	Somerset v Northants
CC2	Derby	Derbyshire v Worcs
CC2	Southampton	Hampshire v Leics
CC2	Canterbury	Kent v Glamorgan

Sun 31 August – 2 September
FCF	The Oval	Surrey v New Zealand A

Tue 2 September
LOI	Birmingham	England v India

Thu 4 September
50L	tbc	Semi-final 1

Fri 5 September
LOI	Leeds	England v India

Sat 6 September
50L	tbc	Semi-final 2

Sun 7 September
IT20	Birmingham	England v India

Tue 9 – Fri 12 September
CC1	Lord's	Middlesex v Durham
CC1	Nottingham	Notts v Yorkshire
CC1	Hove	Sussex v Lancashire
CC1	Birmingham	Warwicks v Northants
CC2	Chelmsford	Essex v Kent
CC2	Cardiff	Glamorgan v Derbyshire
CC2	Bristol	Glos v Leics
CC2	Worcester	Worcs v Surrey

Mon 15 – Thu 18 September
CC1	Chester-le-St	Durham v Northants
CC1	Nottingham	Notts v Sussex
CC1	Taunton	Somerset v Middlesex
CC2	Southampton	Hampshire v Kent
CC2	Leicester	Leics v Essex
CC2	The Oval	Surrey v Derbyshire

Sat 20 September
50L	Lord's	FINAL

Tue 23 – Fri 26 September
CC1	Manchester	Lancashire v Middlesex
CC1	Northampton	Northants v Sussex
CC1	Birmingham	Warwicks v Durham
CC1	Leeds	Yorkshire v Somerset
CC2	Derby	Derbyshire v Leics
CC2	Chelmsford	Essex v Worcs
CC2	Cardiff	Glamorgan v Hampshire
CC2	Canterbury	Kent v Glos

TEST MATCH CHAMPIONSHIP SCHEDULE

Months indicate the start of a series. Number of Tests in brackets. All series, especially those involving Pakistan and Zimbabwe, are subject to confirmation.

2014	**May**	**England hosts Sri Lanka (2)**			Zimbabwe hosts West Indies (2)
		West Indies hosts New Zealand (3)			Sri Lanka hosts New Zealand (2)
	June	**England hosts India (5)**		**Oct**	**Pakistan hosts England (3)**
	July	West Indies hosts Bangladesh (2)			Sri Lanka hosts West Indies (2)
		Zimbabwe hosts South Africa (2)			Zimbabwe hosts New Zealand (2)
	Oct	Pakistan hosts Australia (3)			Bangladesh hosts Australia (2)
		Bangladesh hosts Zimbabwe (2)			India hosts South Africa (3)
		India hosts West Indies (3)		**Nov**	Australia hosts New Zealand (3)
	Nov	Pakistan hosts New Zealand (3)		**Dec**	Australia hosts West Indies (3)
	Dec	Australia hosts India (4)			India hosts Sri Lanka (3)
		Pakistan hosts Zimbabwe (2)			New Zealand hosts Pakistan (3)
		South Africa hosts West Indies (3)			**South Africa hosts England (4)**
		New Zealand hosts Sri Lanka (2)			Bangladesh hosts Zimbabwe (2)
2015	**Jan**	Bangladesh hosts Pakistan (2)	**2016**	**Feb**	Sri Lanka hosts Pakistan (3)
	Apr	**West Indies hosts England (3)**			West Indies hosts India (3)
	May	**England hosts New Zealand (2)**			New Zealand hosts Australia (3)
		Sri Lanka hosts South Africa (3)		**May**	**England hosts Sri Lanka (3)**
		West Indies hosts Australia (2)		**July**	**England hosts Pakistan (4)**
	June	Zimbabwe hosts Pakistan (2)			Sri Lanka hosts Australia (3)
		Bangladesh hosts India (2)			West Indies hosts South Africa (2)
		England hosts Australia (5)			Zimbabwe hosts India (2)
	July	Bangladesh hosts South Africa (2)			

FIELDING CHART

(For a right-handed batsman)

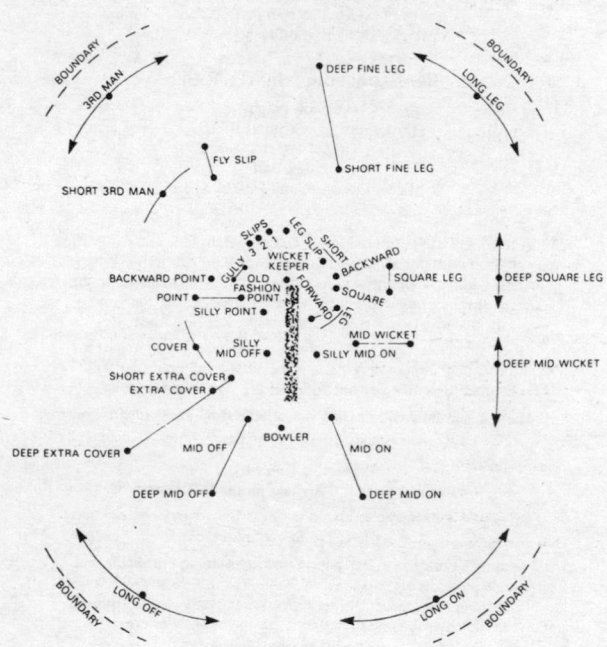

First published in 2014 by
HEADLINE PUBLISHING GROUP

Cover photographs:
(*Front and spine*) Stuart Broad
© Glyn Kirk/AFP/Getty Images
(*Back*) Ian Bell
© Michael Dodge/Getty Images Sport

1

Cataloguing in Publication Data is available from the British Library

ISBN 978 1 4722 1217 7

Typeset in Times by
Letterpart Limited, Caterham on the Hill, Surrey

Printed and bound in Great Britain by
Clays Ltd St Ives plc

Headline's policy is to use papers that are natural, renewable and
recyclable products and made from wood grown in sustainable forests.
The logging and manufacturing processes are expected to conform
to the environmental regulations of the country of origin.

HEADLINE PUBLISHING GROUP
An Hachette UK Company
338 Euston Road
London NW1 3BH

www.headline.co.uk
www.hachette.co.uk